Excavations at Zeugma

VOLUME II

Excavations at Zeugma

Conducted by Oxford Archaeology

Edited by William Aylward

The Packard Humanities Institute

LOS ALTOS, CALIFORNIA
2013

These volumes do not contain a printed index,
but search aids may be available at
zeugma.packhum.org

© 2013 The Packard Humanities Institute, Los Altos, California
United States of America
Book Design: Dean Bornstein
Printed at Meridian Printing, East Greenwich, Rhode Island

ISBN 978-1-938325-29-8

Contents

VOLUME II

CHAPTER ONE
Pottery Other Than Transport Amphorae 1
Philip M. Kenrick

CHAPTER TWO
Petrographic Analysis of Table and Kitchen Wares . . 82
Chris Doherty

CHAPTER THREE
Transport Amphorae of the First to Seventh Centuries: Early Roman to Byzantine Periods 93
Paul Reynolds

CHAPTER FOUR
Petrographic Analysis of Transport Amphorae 162
Chris Doherty

CHAPTER FIVE
Ceramic Oil Lamps 176
Mahmoud Hawari

CHAPTER SIX
Terracotta Figurines 202
Jeffrey Gingras and William Aylward

CHAPTER SEVEN
Bullae 210
Sharon Herbert

CHAPTER EIGHT
Glass 218
R. A. Grossmann

Plates 259

CONTENTS TO VOLUME III

CHAPTER ONE
Coins and Hoards 1
Kevin Butcher

CHAPTER TWO
Copper Alloy Objects 93
Elias Khamis

CHAPTER THREE
Ironwork 167
Ian Scott

CHAPTER FOUR
Gold Objects 279
Ian Scott

CHAPTER FIVE
Worked Bone and Ivory 281
Bethan Charles

CHAPTER SIX
Milling and Weaving Equipment, including Hand-held Stone Tools, Mortars, Querns, and Stone Vessels, Loom Weights, and Spindle Whorls 295
Holly Parton

CHAPTER SEVEN
Textiles 345
Franca Cole

CHAPTER EIGHT
Arms, Armor, and Other Military Objects 353
Ian Scott

CHAPTER NINE
Zeugma's Military History in Light of the Rescue Excavations 375
Hugh Elton

CONTENTS TO VOLUME III (continued)

CHAPTER TEN
*Military Installations at Zeugma:
An Overview of the Swiss Archaeological
Investigations, 2001–2003* 381
M. Hartmann and M. A. Speidel

CHAPTER ELEVEN
Environmental Studies: Overview and Context 393
David Meiggs

CHAPTER TWELVE
Faunal Remains 399
Bethan Charles

CHAPTER THIRTEEN
Charred Plant Remains 411
Dana Challinor and Dominique de Moulins

CHAPTER FOURTEEN
Charcoal 433
Rowena Gale

CONTENTS TO VOLUME I

Foreword · VII
David W. Packard

Preface · IX
William Aylward

CHAPTER ONE
The Rescue Excavations at Zeugma in 2000 1
William Aylward

CHAPTER TWO
Site Conservation during the Rescue Excavations . . . 55
Roberto Nardi and Kristian Schneider

CHAPTER THREE
*The Houses: Domestic Architecture,
Dated Deposits, and Finds in Context* 71
Jennifer Tobin

CHAPTER FOUR
A Monumental Building in Trench 15 119
William Aylward

CHAPTER FIVE
Architectural Elements 124
Sarah Rous and William Aylward

CHAPTER SIX
Mosaics 149
Katherine M. D. Dunbabin

CHAPTER SEVEN
Wall Painting 168
Bettina Bergmann

CHAPTER EIGHT
Graffiti 178
Rebecca Benefiel and Kathleen Coleman

CHAPTER NINE
Inscriptions on Stone 192
Charles Crowther

CHAPTER TEN
*A New Relief of Antiochus I of Commagene and
Other Stone Sculpture from Zeugma* 220
Charles Brian Rose

CHAPTER ELEVEN
Geophysics 232
Jamon Van Den Hoek and William Aylward

CHAPTER TWELVE
*Topographical Survey along the Shoreline of
the Birecik Reservoir in 2001* 247
William Aylward

CHAPTER THIRTEEN
Context Descriptions 251
William Aylward

Plates 281

· CHAPTER ONE ·

Pottery Other Than Transport Amphorae

Philip M. Kenrick

INTRODUCTION

The rescue excavations of 2000 took place alongside parallel investigations at Zeugma by French and Turkish teams. When I was first invited to participate there was also understood to be a possibility of a further long-term research excavation on the site to study the pottery.[1] At the time, it seemed premature to embark upon a comprehensive description of the pottery of Zeugma: It was therefore agreed that I should concentrate on a few contexts that could be reasonably well dated and that might be used to characterize the major chronological phases identified in the trenches for which Oxford Archaeology was responsible: these were Trenches 1, 2, 4, 5, 7, 9, 10, 11, 12, 13, 15, 18, and 19.

The briefest of notes were made upon the entire pottery collection, and these were then used in conjunction with preliminary stratigraphic matrices to select the composition of the chronological groups presented in the report that follows (Groups A–G). The selected contexts were then catalogued in detail. Because of the projected publication schedule, it was not possible to return to Turkey either to verify catalogue descriptions (which would have been desirable, for instance, in the case of "Parthian" glazed ware, which was unfamiliar to me when the catalogue was compiled and which I had therefore failed to distinguish adequately from the Islamic glazed wares) or to make more detailed notes on contexts that had proved to be stratigraphically important since I had made my preliminary selection.

The middle Euphrates region is characterized in archaeological terms by a considerable amount of field survey work, both along the Euphrates itself at points where dams and reservoirs have been constructed, and in the valleys of its tributaries in north Syria, the Balih, and the Habur, but relatively little stratified excavation. It is possible, therefore, to say much more about the geographical distribution of various regional pottery types than about their chronology. I hope that the volume of finds generated by the Zeugma 2000 excavation will prove a useful new anchor point for the latter. The study by Markus Gschwind (2002) of a deposit of the first century A.D. from the Turkish rescue excavations (cf. my Groups B and C) represents an important first step in this direction.

THE POTTERY FABRICS

The pottery is arranged primarily by fabric, in order to distinguish where possible the various sources from which Zeugma was supplied. Since there is also a high degree of correlation between fabrics and the functions for which the vessels were intended, the following conceptual structure was found useful.

- Table wares. Vessels for serving and consuming food: plates, dishes, small bowls, drinking cups, together with lids intended for use with such forms; also some small flagons and jugs intended for use at the table. These are generally made in fine fabrics with smooth surfaces, mostly with a distinctive surface finish such as a slip or glaze.

- Buff wares. A broad category of unslipped vessels made in calcareous clays, which fire to shades of white or gray. They comprise vessels for food preparation, such as large bowls, basins, and mortars, but also storage vessels of all sizes, such as jars, jugs (with a spout), and flagons. They may also overlap to a limited extent with the slipped table wares, providing some small bowls and cups. A specialized form that occurs only in buff ware is the pot stand. There is some overlap with transport amphorae and the border line between amphorae and smaller flagons has been difficult to define.

- Transport amphorae. These are reported on by Paul Reynolds in this volume (chapter 3).

- Cooking wares. Typically made in noncalcareous clays, which fire red to dark gray or black, these are essentially vessels for use over fire: flat pans or deeper casseroles and jars with sagging or rounded bases. There are occasional round-bottomed jugs that belong to this series (traces of lime-scale within show that they were used for boiling water), also lids.

- Storage wares. This category includes large jars in noncalcareous fabrics (i.e., firing red, brown, or gray) not already included under the buff wares. The clay often includes added temper of considerable size (particularly in the largest vessels, described here as pithoi).

Within these categories, the following fabrics were recognized or defined. Fabric descriptions are based on examination with a hand lens; more technical descriptions of those that were subjected to thin-section analysis are given in the petrographic report by Chris Doherty following this chapter. (It is apparent that my use of the term *lime* covers a variety of minerals and should be understood in general to signify white inclusions that are not visibly crystalline.) A fully quantified breakdown of the incidence of each fabric across the dated groups is shown in table 1 on pp. 4–5.

Table Wares

These account for 39.2 percent, by number, of the overall pottery assemblage (excluding transport amphorae and Group G, which was not fully quantified) and 12.6 percent by weight. The proportion of table wares varies markedly between the groups, being highest in Group A (67.3/42.2 percent) and lowest in Group D (6.5/0.8 percent).[2]

BSP

This name has been assigned by Kathleen Slane in her report on the fine wares from Tel Anafa to the *black-slipped predecessor* of Eastern Sigillata A (Slane 1997, 269), implying (reasonably) that it shares a common source with the later red-slipped ware. Vessels from Zeugma attributed to this ware have a fine cream to pale orange clay and a smooth lustrous slip that is chocolate-brown to black.

Local Hellenistic Fine Ware

This was presumed to be local (or at least regional) both because of its predominance amongst the Hellenistic fine wares and because of the resemblance of the clay to that of the principal variety of buff ware. This presumption was broadly confirmed by thin-section analysis. The clay is buff or orange-buff (occasionally greenish-cream) in color and finely granular in texture, sometimes showing very fine white and dark sand and mica; fine white specks are visible at the surface and sparse fine voids are also visible in the break. Vessels are coated with a partial, uneven, dull orange to brown or black slip. The potting is often careless. Initially, an attempt was made to distinguish two qualities, since a small number of pieces displayed a rather harder texture and more careful surface finish (no white specks at the surface), but since this revealed no typological differences it is not sustained here. (Petrographic examination showed that the compositional differences were also minor.[4]) I have retained the term *Hellenistic* throughout for vessels in this ware: Despite the fact that production continues through the first century A.D., the forms produced remain stubbornly in the Hellenistic tradition.[5]

Other Hellenistic Fine Wares

A handful of sherds were identified that did not fall into either of the preceding categories (**PT13, 97–100**).

Eastern Sigillata A (ESA)

It is somewhat surprising in view of the massive distribution (and hence production) of this ware[6] that no specific source has yet been identified, though the possibilities have now been narrowed down to somewhere between Tarsus and Antioch.[7] This is the only imported fine ware of any significance at Zeugma in the late Hellenistic or early Roman period; the earliest forms in this ware were rare, and those of the Hayes' middle Roman series[8] were entirely absent.

Italian and Gaulish Sigillata

Only two tiny fragments of the former were catalogued (**PT144, 324**). There is no Gaulish Sigillata amongst the material presented here, though occasional sherds were noted in other contexts.

Thin-Walled Wares

A small quantity of cups and beakers was recorded, mostly from contexts of the first century A.D. (Groups B and C). They display some variety of fabric and are likely to have come from more than one source.[9]

African Red Slip Ware

The earliest examples of this ware[10] belong to the thin, fine, central Tunisian fabric ("Late A" ware) that appears in the second quarter of the third century A.D. (represented here by one rim of Hayes 1972, form 50, no. **PT327**); the later north Tunisian series is present in slightly greater quantity, particularly in the seventh-century Group F, but this too is rare.

Phocaean Red Slip Ware (formerly Late Roman C)

This ware[11] was a useful chronological indicator for contexts of the fifth to seventh centuries.

Cypriot Red Slip Ware

This ware[12] was present in small quantities in the late levels.

Glazed Fine Wares

As already mentioned, I had assumed at the time of cataloguing in the field that all vessels with a vitreous glaze were of Islamic date; it became clear, however, when seeking parallels, that a small proportion belonged to the glazed ware of Mesopotamia, which has a continuous history from neo-Assyrian/neo-Babylonian times onward.[13] These pieces of "Parthian" glazed ware could readily be identified from their forms (see Group D), but I am not confident of having recognized nondiagnostic body-sherds. The following subclasses were recognized:

1. Finely granular cream or grayish clay with abundant, fine, carbonized plant remains. Thick vitreous glaze, turquoise or bluish-white. Those pieces identified as "Parthian" belong to this subclass.
2. Yellowish-cream clay with abundant very fine angular sand, mostly white and gray; hackly break. Blue-green or green vitreous glaze. Since fragments in this fabric were confined to Groups A, C, and D, they too are presumed to be "Parthian," but from a different source. Petrographic examination showed this fabric NOT to be

similar to any of the buff wares 6, 8, or 10, to which there were superficial similarities.[14]

3   Buff or gray-buff clay with abundant tiny black, white, and red inclusions. Bluish-white, dark green, or blue-green glaze. Exclusive to Group G. Thin-section analysis has shown this subclass to be closely related to the local buff wares 1–3.[15]

4   Very fine fused cream clay, conchoidal break. Thick white or turquoise glaze. Two sherds only (Group G), nondiagnostic.[16]

5   Granular buff to pink clay containing sparse fine to medium white specks and moderate fine mica. Uneven glaze of poor quality and often partial: yellow-green, turquoise, brown. The largest subclass, derived from a typical Euphrates clay:[17] 37 sherds/1.78 kg, all in Group G.

Buff Wares

In the overall assemblage (excluding transport amphorae and Group G), these account for 36.1 percent of the pottery by number and 45.7 percent by weight. The subclasses were numbered as they were encountered; those that related to only one or two individuals have subsequently been suppressed.

Buff 1–4

These are probably all of fairly local origin: The differences between them are not sharply defined and may reflect variations either within the local clay beds or in the process of preparation.[18] They account for 36.7 percent of the buff wares by number and 43.6 percent by weight. Amphorae also occur in these fabrics and are described by Paul Reynolds (this volume, Forms 12–13).[19] Large closed vessels (and occasionally open ones: see **PT156**) not infrequently show string marks around the girth. Such marks have been interpreted as a deliberate form of decoration[20] but testify to a practical means of reinforcing the vessel on the wheel during the process of throwing the upper part. On occasion, the actual fibers of the string are visible in the break, where they have become incorporated in the body.[21]

1   Clay fired orange to buff, hard but not fused; abundant fine angular inclusions up to 0.5 mm, including white, red, gray, and black grits, also sparse to moderate fine mica, mostly muscovite; fine voids.

2   Similar to 1, but the surface is pitted where many white specks of lime have caused the surface to spall.

3   Same inclusions as 1 but finer, up to 0.2 mm; mica barely apparent at the surface.

4   Basically similar to 1 but coarser, with a distinctly abrasive surface; no red particles seen.

Buff 5

Coarse. Rather crumbly buff clay with abundant, ill-sorted, fine to large inclusions of lime (up to 2.5 mm), prominent at surface; also brown and red earthy particles. No mica. This fabric is distinct from the local/regional Euphrates clays.[22] Confined to Group D.

Buff 6

Mortaria. Hard vesicular cream clay, matrix fused and striated in the break; abundant angular white, brown, and gray inclusions up to 0.5 mm (occasionally large, up to 7 mm); very sparse muscovite mica. Thin-section analysis showed that this fabric is related to (but not identical with) Buff 8 and the North Syrian amphora Fabric 13;[23] a Syrian origin is therefore likely. These mortaria do not have added grits on the inner surface, in contrast to their Italian models. Mainly Group D.[24]

Buff 8

This fabric is shared with the North Syrian painted amphorae described by Paul Reynolds in this volume.[25] Listed here are the saucer-lids that appear to belong to these amphorae and a range of other forms, including cups, bowls, basins, jars, and jugs. The clay is greenish-cream to warm buff, and sometimes gray in the core; there are abundant mixed angular inclusions, generally larger than in fabric Buff 1; mica is present but sparse. Surfaces are probably wet-smoothed rather than slipped but are still very rough. The painted decoration, which is confined to flagons and jugs, is dull and may be red, brown, or black. This is effectively the largest subclass of buff ware after Buff 1–4. It is essentially characteristic of the late Groups E–G: the half dozen sherds listed in Groups C and D are surely intrusive.

Buff 10

Finely vesicular buff or cream clay; moderate, fine, angular mixed inclusions (red, white, black, and predominantly gray); very sparse mica.

Buff 12

Pink rather than buff in the core, fired buff in parts at the surface (unless this represents traces of a very thin cream wash). Hard, finely granular fabric with an irregular break; moderate, ill-sorted lime fragments (mainly < 0.5 mm but up to 2 mm), which give the surface a slightly speckled appearance, also sparse ill-sorted darker inclusions (quartz?); very sparse mica. Mainly pot stands, confined to Groups A–C.

Buff 13

Fine buff. Finely granular orange or buff clay with occasional voids. Sparse, very fine specks of lime and mica; very occasional large lumps of lime. Partial slip on some vessels. Thin-section analysis showed that the clay is certainly the same as that of some of the local Hellenistic fine ware, and is also (less closely) related to Buff 1–3.[26] Most common in Groups A–C.

Group:	A		B		C		D		E		F		Total A–F		G	
	No.	Wt.	No.	Wt.	No.	Wt.	No.	Wt.	No.	Wt.	No.	Wt.	No.	Wt.	No.	Wt.
Table wares																
BSP			21	228	3	109	5	31					29	368		
Local Hellenistic	29	1,242	627	14,133	172	4,420	28	616	2	31	14	219	872	20,661		
Other Hellenistic	1	13	7	207			2	36					10	256		
Eastern Sigillata A	2	18	181	2,948	83	1,381	23	187			7	36	296	4,570		
Italian Sigillata			1	3			1	12					2	15		
Thin-walled			7	27	3	20	4	47					14	94		
African Red Slip			1	25			1	17	1	26	11	443	14	511		
Phocaean Red Slip					1	21			5	97	80	2,025	86	2,143		
Cypriot Red Slip							1	50	3	111	1	11	5	172		
Glazed 1			6	37	3	16	4	166					13	219	13	221
Glazed 2	1	23			1	29	3	70					5	122		
Glazed 3															9	305
Glazed 4															2	13
Glazed 5															37	1,775
Other glazed															1	155
Miscellaneous					1	36							1	36		
Total	33	1,296	851	17,608	266	6,011	73	1,253	11	265	113	2,734	1,347	29,167	62	2,469
Buff wares																
Buff 1–4			33	1,713	22	1,284	335	36,241	14	1,396	52	5,552	456	46,186	4	615
Buff 5							5	204					5	204		
Buff 6			1	495			13	6,830	1	850			15	8,175		
Buff 8					1	195	4	173	18	2,952	79	5,947	102	9,267	10	1,430
Buff 10			4	62			3	168			2	212	9	442	10	701
Buff 12	1	75	1	55	7	1,690							9	1,820		
Buff 13	8	309	13	394	15	760	1	28	2	190	5	327	44	2,008		
Buff 14			5	155	5	254	1	455					11	864		
Buff 15							1	55	3	700	19	13,524	23	14,279		
Miscellaneous	4	434	176	3,982	32	1,132	149	10,383	18	511	188	6,206	567	22,648	5	809
Total	13	818	233	6,856	82	5,315	512	54,537	56	6,599	345	31,768	1,241	105,893		

Table 1. *Distribution of pottery fabrics (excluding transport amphorae).*
Group G was not fully listed or quantified. Weights are expressed in grams.
(Continued on following page.)

Group:	A		B		C		D		E		F		Total A–F		G	
	No.	Wt.	No.	Wt.	No.	Wt.	No.	Wt.	No.	Wt.	No.	Wt.	No.	Wt.	No.	Wt.
Cooking wares																
Cooking 1			8	147	3	76	462	15,345	12	240	26	419	511	16,227		
Cooking 2			5	179	15	408	2	45	28	573	126	3,000	176	4,205	10	357
Cooking 6							1	18	1	95	2	65	4	178		
Cooking 7			7	179	7	248			1	140			15	567		
Cooking 8	1	34	3	72	5	54							9	160		
Cooking 9									11	745	6	188	17	933	1	235
Cooking 10															5	227
Miscellaneous			35	644	5	130	23	457					63	1,231		
Total	1	34	58	1,221	35	916	488	15,865	53	1,793	160	3,672	795	23,501		
Storage wares																
Storage 1					1	350	13	65,405			1	180	15	65,935		
Storage 2	1	44			9	358	14	1,821					24	2,223		
Storage 4							2	3,165					2	3,165		
Storage 5			3	112					1	155			4	267		
Miscellaneous	1	880			1	225	2	150			1	420	5	1,675		
Total	2	924	3	112	11	933	31	70,541	1	155	2	600	50	73,265		
Total: all wares	49	3,072	1,145	25,797	394	13,175	1,104	142,196	121	8,812	620	38,774	3,433	231,826		

Table 1. (continued).

Buff 14

Rather soft, granular pale brown clay, porous, with abundant very fine angular gray, brown, or black inclusions and occasional larger grits (chert?); sparse very fine mica. Potting generally very poor. Mainly in Groups B and C.

Buff 15

Hard, finely granular buff clay, slightly vesicular but without obvious inclusions apart from very occasional particles of lime and some very fine mica. Still a Euphrates-region clay, but distinct from any of the preceding.[27] Groups D, E, and F.

Cooking Wares

These include what has often been described as "brittle ware." The term, which appears to have originated in print with Dyson's (1968) report on the common ware from Dura-Europos, seems to me fundamentally unsatisfactory in describing only part of a homogeneous range of cooking wares, while inviting confusion with other wares that have from time to time been described as brittle: thin-walled drinking cups and the like. An important analytical study of cooking wares in northeastern Syria has been published by Bartl et al. (1995), that offers some useful comparisons to the present report.[28] In the overall pottery assemblage (again excluding transport amphorae and Group G), the cooking wares account for 23.2 percent by number and 10.1 percent by weight. The proportion of cooking ware is markedly lower than the mean in Groups A (1.1 percent by weight) and B (4.7 percent by weight). Seven fabrics are represented by more than two sherds each, but only the first two are at all common.

Cooking 1

Principal fabric. Hard clay containing abundant, fine, angular inclusions of light and dark particles, moderate fine mica (muscovite and biotite) and sometimes sparse larger white lumps (lime, feldspar?). The color varies between red and black; the blackening of the outsides of vessels is sometimes a result of use over fire, but a difference between outside and inside is often a result of stacking in the kiln (through which the outsides are affected by the reducing atmosphere at the end of the firing, while the insides, sealed from the change, remain oxidized). Thin-section examination has shown that this is a Euphrates clay, possibly from upstream of Zeugma.[29] An equivalence with Group 3 of Bartl et al. (1995) is possible.[30] Most common in Group D.

Cooking 2

Hard, fine red clay with moderate very fine clear rounded quartz particles and sparse particles of lime up to 1 mm; no mica. A very distinctive fabric whose source remains to be identified.[31] This fabric is surely identical to Group 1 of Bartl et al. (1995).[32] Present in all Groups apart from A, but common only in the late Roman period, Groups E–G.

Cooking 6

Orange-brown clay containing abundant ill-sorted mixed inclusions (black, white, red, and gray), rounded and up to 2 mm across; also sparse large lumps of lime and moderate fine mica. Pink at surface. Four sherds, Groups D–F.

Cooking 7

Hard pink clay containing moderate, medium subrounded gray quartz (?), together with red and black grits (resulting in a black-speckled appearance at the surface) and occasional fragments of lime. Very sparse (and fine) flecks of mica. This seems to be confined to the early Roman period (Groups B and C). A north Syrian coastal source seemed a possibility, but the petrography suggests a region about 100 km upstream of Zeugma as more likely.[33]

Cooking 8

Pink or red clay, sometimes with a paler surface (buff or cream); abundant ill-sorted inclusions, dominated by lime up to 2 mm across, very prominent at surface (spalling); subrounded quartz and other dark inclusions also present.[34] Hackly fracture. Again an early fabric (Groups A–C).

Cooking 9

Hard clay, dark brown in the core and red or pink at the surface. Moderate, medium polycrystalline green inclusions of olivine basalt and occasional rounded specks of lime; very rough surfaces. Possibly from the Karasu Valley north of Antioch.[35] Late Roman contexts, mainly Group E.

Cooking 10

Red-brown to black clay with abundant medium (1 mm) angular quartz and probably limestone, also sparse smaller brown particles (iron ore?). The grits are often very apparent at the surface. Usually darker (often black) on outside. An Islamic production, exclusive to Group G.

Storage Wares

This is a small category, comprising both large pithoi, which are so unwieldy that they must surely have been made more or less locally and which, once installed in a storeroom, would not have been moved, and smaller containers that are more portable but too large to have been used for cooking. Only one complete pithos was catalogued; several others were found in the course of the excavation, but not in the contexts chosen for publication here.

Storage 1

Pink clay, often gray in the core and on the inner surface, with abundant rounded or subrounded inclusions up to 5 mm: limestone, quartz, chert, iron ore? Hackly fracture, surfaces typically abraded. Used for pithoi.

Storage 2

Coarse clay fired brown to black, with abundant angular inclusions up to 2 mm across: white and darker grits, black or dark green glassy fragments (olivine?). Hackly fracture; made on a slow wheel? Used for smaller, ovoid jars. A visual attribution to Ras el-Basit on the Syrian coast to the southwest of Antioch (for which I am indebted to Paul Reynolds) is confirmed by the petrography.[36] Confined to Groups A, C, and D.

Storage 4

Granular clay containing abundant fine angular black and white inclusions and moderate larger rounded pebbles of quartz (up to 4 mm) and angular fragments of lime (up to 2 mm); fired brown to pink, surfaces well smoothed; hackly, somewhat laminar fracture. Paul Reynolds informs me that this fabric occurs at Beirut. Group D.

Storage 5

Pale brown clay, buff at the surface, containing abundant gray-white crystalline grains of calcite spar up to 2 mm across, which give a very sparkly appearance. Very distinctive in the hand and clearly not local, though the petrography alone does not identify its source.[37] Three sherds in Group B and one in Group E.

COMPARATIVE MATERIAL

Zeugma lies a long way from the Mediterranean coast (see fig. 1), and therefore shares relatively little in its pottery assemblage with those sites that provide a basis of reference throughout the eastern Mediterranean. Tarsus and Antioch, the closest of the major coastal cities and the publication of whose pottery has long been a mainstay of ceramic specialists,[38] have little to offer. Certainly, the most prolific fine wares found at those sites penetrate to a small extent into the hinterland, but despite a broad, generic similarity between the Zeugma coarse wares and those of Tarsus, there are almost no specific parallels. The coarse wares of Antioch have, unfortunately, never been published, but there is again no more than a generic similarity between our material and that of, say, Beirut[39] or Pella.[40]

The most fruitful sources for comparison have, rather, proved to be sites along the line of the Euphrates, which clearly constitutes the major axis of communication for the region. Downstream in Syria and on the Tigris in Iraq, parallels have been established for the Hellenistic and early to mid-Roman periods at Dibsi Faraj,[41] Rusafa,[42] Dura-Europos,[43] Ain Sinu,[44] Tell Halaf,[45] Seh Qubba,[46] Nimrud,[47] and

Samarra;[48] for the late Roman and Early Islamic periods, Déhès,[49] Dibsi Faraj,[50] Rusafa,[51] Qusair as-Saila,[52] Qasr al-Hayr East,[53] and Raqqa[54] are relevant. The surveys of the river valleys of the Quwaiq,[55] Balih,[56] and Habur[57] provide further evidence of distribution. Upstream, published material is less easy to come by. From Arsameia-on-the-Nymphaios[58] virtually only fine wares have been published, but surveys carried out around Lidar Höyük[59] and Kurban Höyük[60] in the area now flooded by the Atatürk Dam have reported much that is similar to Zeugma. Further upstream, there are no close parallels at Aşvan Kale,[61] which presumably therefore lies beyond the area of pottery production and exchange with which we are concerned.

THE DATED GROUPS

The presentation of the groups on the pages that follow begins with a discussion of the character and date of each group. A quantified table of the content is provided: Sherds were counted after any joins had been made, except where the joins were between different contexts. (Nonjoining fragments that could confidently be ascribed to a single vessel were also counted as a single item.)

The first line of each catalogue entry contains the inventory number, which is written on the sherd (generally of the form "P.nnn"; sometimes there is additionally a number allocated at the time of discovery, prefixed by "SF"), followed by the excavation context in which it was found. Types are generally illustrated only in the earliest group in which they were recorded. Subsequent occurrences are, however, cross-referenced throughout.)

The following abbreviations are used:

L.	Length	max.	maximum
D.	Diameter	pres.	preserved
H.	Height	est.	estimated
W.	Width	int.	internal

Diameters are indicated with such precision as could be determined, thus:

"D. 25.0 cm"   signifies a diameter between 24.8 and 25.2 cm;
"D. 25 cm"   signifies a diameter between 24 and 26 cm;
"D. ca. 25 cm" represents a best guess.

Uninventoried items worthy of note appear in the catalogue with a bullet, where appropriate.

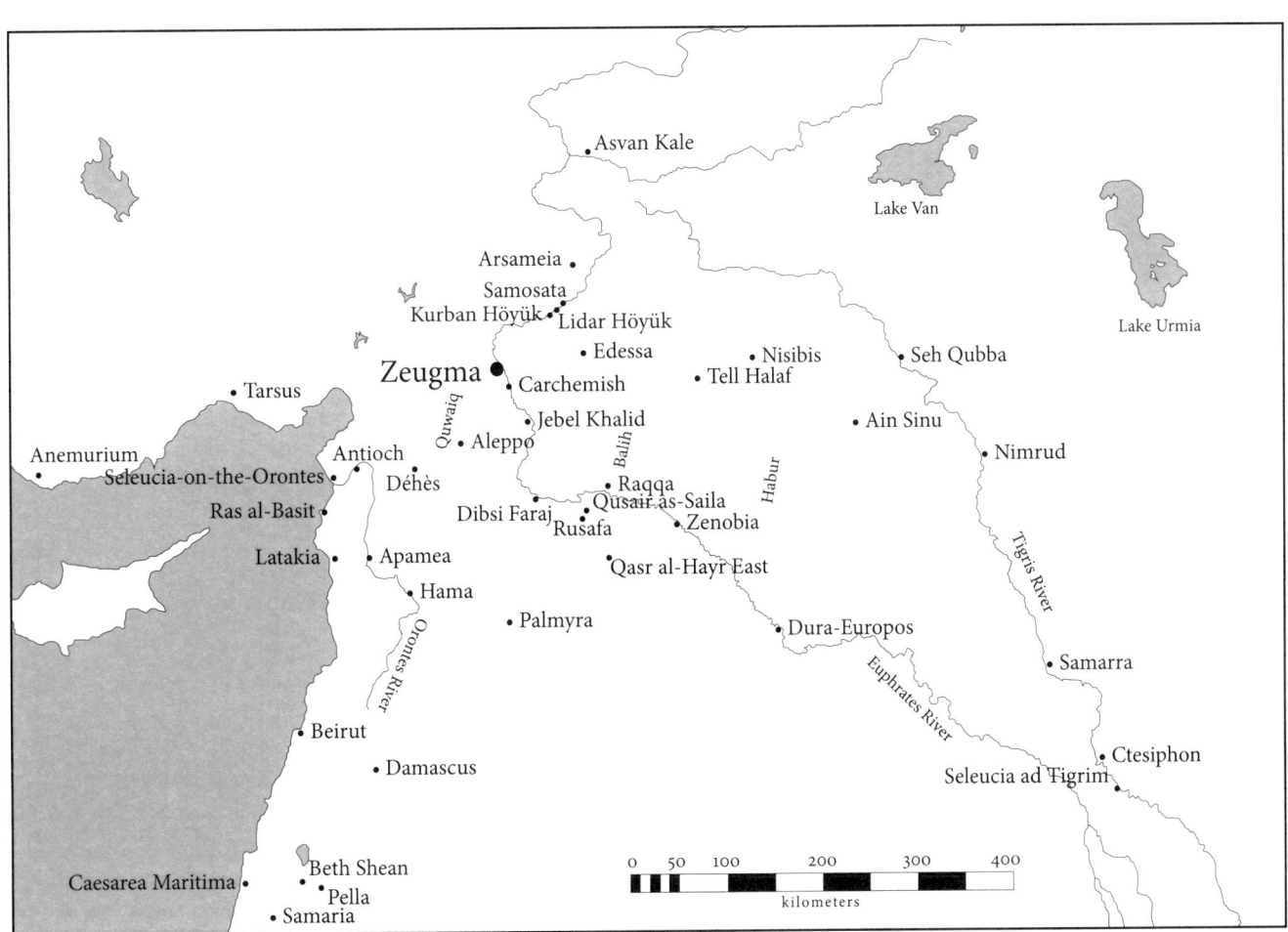

Figure 1. Map with sites mentioned in the text.

Group A:
Hellenistic, Second Half of Second Century B.C.

No contexts were found that could definitely be associated with the earliest occupation of the site. The earliest deposit that yielded enough material to give some idea of the pottery in use in the Hellenistic period was a make-up level (context 19005) in the small Trench 19, sealed beneath a white, mortar-rich surface (context 19002), which may have been a bedding for a stone floor.[62] The breakdown of the pottery from this context is as follows.

	No. of pieces	% of total no.	Weight (gm)	% of total weight
Hellenistic fine ware	30	61.2	1,255	40.9
Eastern Sigillata A	2	4.1	18	0.6
Glazed ware	1	2.0	23	0.7
Total table wares	33	67.3	1,296	42.2
Buff wares	13	26.5	818	26.6
Cooking wares	1	2.0	34	1.1
Storage wares	2	4.1	924	30.1
TOTAL	49		3,072	

It is notable that there is a very high proportion of table ware compared to other contexts and only a single sherd of cooking ware. The table ware is almost entirely "local," with one sherd of an imported fine gray ware (**PT13**), two of Eastern Sigillata A, and one fragment of a jar with a dark blue glaze that is presumably "Parthian." The local fine ware shows shapes that are typical of anywhere in the eastern Mediterranean in the second and first centuries B.C.; the presence of Eastern Sigillata A shows that the deposit cannot have been sealed before the middle of the second century, but the two fragments recorded are not necessarily later than the end of the century.

Table Wares
LOCAL HELLENISTIC FINE WARE

PT1 (P.302, context 19005)
Plate with convex rim
D. 19.5 cm. PL. 1

Buff clay; uneven dull red to brown slip all over; rather rough surfaces.
Similar: 2 rims in Group B (p. 11), D. 13.5, ? cm
Cf. Gerber 1996, fig.1.5, 7 (Lidar Höyük survey).

PT2 (P.303, context 19005)
Plate with thickened rim
D. ca. 32 cm PL. 1

Gray-buff clay; traces of brown slip on inside.
Cf. Gerber 1996, fig. 1.6 (Lidar Höyük survey).

PT3 (P.304, context 19005)
Plate with hooked convex rim and central recess
D. 14.6 cm, H. 3.5 cm. Two nonjoining sherds. PL. 1

Finely granular buff clay with moderate very fine lime and red specks, also occasional subrounded black grits up to 1.5 mm (not glassy: iron ore?), causing drag-marks in an otherwise smooth exterior surface. Blotchy, semilustrous red slip all over, including inside foot. This ware?

PT4 (P.311, context 19005)
Ring-foot of dish with central recess
D.foot 4.7 cm PL. 1

Orange-buff clay; dull red slip on inside only.
Similar: 2 bases in this group; 30 bases in Group B (p. 11).

PT5 (P.305, context 19005)
Mastos with chamfered rim
D. 19.4 cm, H. 6.9 cm PL. 1

Two shallow grooves on inside. Orange-buff clay; dull orange slip all over (brown over rim: stacking).

PT6 (P.306, context 19005)
Bowl with incurved rim
D.max. 16 cm PL. 1

Pale orange clay, dull slip all over: red on inside and lower part of outside, brown on upper part of outside (stacking).

PT7 (P.307, context 19005)
Bowl with incurved rim
D.max. 14.5 cm PL. 1

Orange-buff clay; partial dull red slip.
Similar: 14 rims in Group B (p. 12), D.max. 12–ca. 30 cm; 10 rims in Group C (p. 26), D.max. 10.5–ca. 26 cm; 1 rim in Group D (p. 38).

PT8 (P.308, context 19005)
Bowl with incurved rim
D.max. 11.5 cm PL. 1

Slightly greenish-buff clay with thin brown slip, burnt off on outside of rim (stacking).
Similar: 2 rims in this group, D.max. 10.5, ca. 16 cm; 22 rims in Group B (p. 12), D.max. 11–24 cm.

PT9 (P.309, context 19005)
Bowl with thickened vertical rim and slight lip
D. ca. 17 cm PL. 1

Buff clay; partial dull brown slip.
Similar: 1 rim fragment in Group B (p. 12).
Cf. Oates 1958, pl. 23.12 in local ware (Nimrud).

PT10 (P.313, context 19005)
Part of bowl with ring-foot
D.foot 5.3 cm   PL. 1

Buff clay; partial dull red slip.
Similar: 8 bases.

PT11 (P.312, context 19005)
Bowl with (incurved rim and) ring-foot
D.foot 4.3 cm (distorted)   PL. 1

Hard greenish-yellow clay (overfired) with the usual inclusions; drip only of brown slip on outside (the rest lost, presumably as a result of overfiring).

PT12 (P.310, context 19005)
Deep bowl with flaring hooked rim
D. ca. 31 cm (rim deformed). Three nonjoining fragments.
                                                                              PL. 1

Finely granular orange to pink clay (inclusions very fine), with dull red slip on inside and over rim. The potting is careless but all surfaces appear to be wet-smoothed. This ware?
Similar: 1 rim in Group B (p. 13), D. ca. 37 cm.

- Battered fragment of collar, part of a pedestal-base or perhaps a lid. Fine buff clay; dull red slip: this ware?
- 2 rims of handled cups, very fragmentary but perhaps as **PT51/52** in Group B.
- 2 unclassified body-sherds.

HELLENISTIC FINE GRAY WARE

PT13 (P.314, context 19005)
Bowl with everted rim
D. 14 cm   PL. 1

Fine gray clay containing moderate very fine muscovite mica; surfaces slightly darker and carefully burnished, but not obviously slipped. Clearly an import.

EASTERN SIGILLATA A

PT14 (P.315, context 19005)
Part of hemispherical cup with molded foot
D.foot 7.5 cm   PL. 1

Similar: 2 bases in Group B (p. 16), D.foot 7.8, 8.0 cm. Hayes 1985, form 22A; Slane 1997, Type TA 25a or b as, e.g., FW 189 (pl. 18): from mid-second century B.C. onwards.

- Small body-sherd of dish, probably Hayes 1985, form 3 (cf. **PT102–104**), fairly thin-walled. From mid-second century B.C. onwards.

GLAZED FINE WARE

- Rim-fragment of a jar with dark blue glaze. Presumably "Parthian."

Buff Wares
BUFF WARE 13

PT15 (P.316, context 19005)
Rolled rim of bowl
D.max. 34 cm   PL. 2

PT16 (P.317, context 19005)
Rolled rim of bowl
D.max. 31 cm   PL. 2

Very fine mica (muscovite *and* biotite) very noticeable.

PT17 (P.318, context 19005)
Bowl with convex triangular rim
D.max. 27 cm   PL. 2

Mica prominent at surface, as in **PT16**. A blob of red paint on the rim could be either accidental or decorative.

PT18 (P.319, context 19005)
Rim of flagon or amphora
D. 15 cm   PL. 2

PT19 (P.321, context 19005)
Rim of flagon or jar   PL. 2

Rim-sherd, badly distorted by heat: angle and diameter difficult to ascertain. Yellow to gray clay with moderate fine inclusions, difficult to identify.

- 3 sherds of closed vessels.

BUFF WARE 12

PT20 (P.320, context 19005)
Closed vessel with recessed base
Int. D. of recess 5.7 cm   PL. 2

Finely granular pinkish-buff clay with moderate very fine white specks (and one large lump of lime 4 mm across).

Cooking Wares

PT21 (P.322, context 19005)
Cooking ware 8, part of jar or bowl with rolled rim
D. ca. 23 cm   PL. 2

Hard pink clay with abundant ill-sorted inclusions up to 1 mm: lime prominent, quartz, brown and black particles also present, with moderate fine muscovite mica. This fabric?

Storage Wares

- Sherd of pithos, inclusions fairly fine (mostly up to 1 mm).
- Storage 2, sherd of large closed vessel.

PT22–30 *vacant*

Group B: Late Augustan or Tiberian

This group is made up of pottery from three contexts. The majority of the material derives from the backfilling behind a major terrace wall in Trench 15 (contexts 15009 and 15095).[63] To this I have added the pottery from a make-up level (context 7118) beneath floor 7117 in Trench 7A, which seems to be essentially similar in character.[64] There are substantial quantities of Eastern Sigillata A in these levels. The latest of the four sherds from context 7118 is the center of a plate with a stepped underside (**PT130**) which can be no earlier than Augustan; the very much larger body of material in the other two levels includes a number of chalice fragments (**PT119–122**), which are likely to be late Augustan or later, together with typical forms of the early first century A.D. (**PT123–131, 136–142**: Hayes 1985, Forms 28, 30, 42, 46, 47). There is also a tiny fragment (**PT144**) of late or post-Augustan Italian Sigillata. It is difficult to place a very clear terminal date on this deposit, as there are a few individual later pieces (**PT132–135, 143**: Hayes 1985, Forms 34, 35, 51); but the very marked difference in character between this group and the Flavian/Trajanic Group C suggests that this is basically considerably earlier. The fact that there is a small amount of intrusive material is demonstrated by the presence of a seventh-century rim of African Red Slip Ware (**PT149**). A terminal date in the second quarter of the first century A.D. seems to me reasonable.

The breakdown of the pottery in this group is as follows.

	No. of pieces	% of total no.	Weight (gm)	% of total weight
Hellenistic fine ware	655	57.2	14,568	56.5
Eastern Sigillata A	181	15.8	2,948	11.4
Italian Sigillata	1	0.1	3	0.0
Thin-walled ware	7	0.6	27	0.1
African Red Slip Ware	1	0.1	25	0.1
Glazed wares	6	0.5	37	0.1
Total table wares	**851**	**74.3**	**17,608**	**68.2**
Buff wares	233	20.3	6,856	26.6
Cooking wares	58	5.1	1,221	4.7
Storage wares	3	0.3	112	0.4
TOTAL	**1,145**		**25,797**	

The proportion of table ware is again very high in this group and that of cooking ware is still low, but slightly higher than before. Amongst the table wares, the local Hellenistic fine ware still predominates, showing that it is surely still in production. The forms have evolved somewhat from the previous group: Small dishes/bowls with everted rims are now common (**PT43–46**), and the bowls with incurved rims are increasingly angular (**PT54–63**). There is also a substantial range of larger bowls with a variety of different rim profiles (**PT64–80**) and a number of fragments of closed vessels (**PT89–96**). The body shapes of these last are unclear; it may well be that their lower parts are unslipped and catalogued amongst the buff wares. The buff wares show a bewildering variety of fabrics, very difficult to classify, also a very high proportion of profiles that are attested once only. The cooking wares are also very varied in fabric, including both varieties that are confined to the early period (Cooking 7 and 8) and the first appearance of the main categories that will dominate in mid- and late Roman contexts (Cooking 1 and 2). One body-sherd in each of these last two fabrics shows the corrugations that are typical of the later periods, but in view of the presence of occasional intrusions, it is not possible to assert that corrugated ("brittle") cookpots begin at Zeugma as early as the Tiberian period.

Table Wares
BSP

PT31 (P.424, context 15009)
Plate with down-turned rim
D. ca. 19 cm
PL. 3

Fine cream clay; semilustrous, slightly metallic, gray-brown slip, red-brown towards center of floor (stacking). Probably a fish plate, though smaller and less elegant in its proportions than those found at Tel Anafa (Slane 1997, type TA 1). Second century B.C.?

PT32 (P.323, context 15095)
Bowl with incurved rim
D.max. 18 cm
PL. 3

Fine buff clay; smooth surface with barely lustrous slip, black on outside and red on inside.
Similar: another rim fragment with two-tone slip (black and purplish-gray — stacking).
Related to Slane 1997, type TA 4, though rather more rounded. Presumably late third (?) or second century B.C.

PT33 (P.324, context 15095)
Small cup with incurved rim
D.max. 9 cm
PL. 3

Fine pale gray clay, well smoothed, with barely lustrous black slip.
Cf. the preceding.

PT34 (P.325, context 15095)
Rim of mastos with internal moldings
D. ?
PL. 3

Fine buff clay, excellently smoothed; semilustrous slip, black on outside, dark brown below molding on inside. Slane 1997, type TA 6, but with a band of raised dots on the lowest molding as in no. FW 218 in Eastern Sigillata A. Second century B.C.?

PT35 (P.425, context 15009)
Rim of shallow thin-walled bowl
D. 17 cm
PL. 3

Figure 2. **PT36**, **PT37**, **PT213**, *fragments of Hellenistic relief bowls in BSP from Groups B and C.*

Fine cream clay; worn but lustrous black slip with double-dipping streak.
Cf. Crowfoot et al. 1957, 259, fig. 53.1 from Samaria ("red ware, reddish glaze, blackish at rim outside").

PT36 (P.326, context 15095)
Rim of relief bowl
D. ?   FIG. 2, PL. 3

Ovolo with bead-and-reel below. Fine buff clay, lustrous black slip. Cornell (1997) gives a brief account of the BSP and Eastern Sigillata A molded bowls from Tel Anafa; the BSP examples certainly begin before 125 B.C. (Cornell 1997, 409). For the ovolo and beaded cordons cf. Christensen and Johansen 1971, 29 and figs. 13, 14, nos. 121–3 (Hama), attributed to Antioch (p. 25).

PT37 (P.327, context 15095)
Sherd of relief bowl
Guilloche band.   FIG. 2, PL. 3

Fine buff clay; barely lustrous black slip.
Cf. Jones 1950, fig. 130.G (Tarsus).

- Small fragment of a relief bowl.
- Fragment of a ring-foot of a bowl as **PT211** in Group C.
- 11 unclassified sherds; one is a small fragment of a cup with an incised scroll-band on the outside.

LOCAL HELLENISTIC FINE WARE

PT38 (P.331, context 15095)
Plate with down-turned rim
D. ca. 35 cm   PL. 3

Fine orange-brown clay with few inclusions and fairly smooth surfaces; dull gray to brown slip all over.
Similar: 3 rims, D. 21–ca. 32 cm.

- 2 convex rims of plates as **PT1** in Group A.

PT39 (P.287, context 7118)
Base of dish or bowl with grooves on floor
D.foot 9.6 cm   PL. 3

Orange-buff clay; partial dull red slip.

PT40 (P.288, context 7118)
Base of dish with low ring-foot
D.foot 11 cm   PL. 3

Granular pale brown clay that appears to have the usual inclusions, with worn, dull red slip all over. Inside surface is particularly abraded and somewhat laminar.

PT41 (P.328, context 15095)
Small dish with thickened rim and central recess
D. 11.8 cm, H. 3.7 cm   PL. 3

Crudely formed and soft-fired. Orange-buff clay with thin, dull red slip, more or less all over.
Similar: 17 rims in this group, D. 11–14 cm; 1 rim in Group C (p. 26), D. 12.2 cm.

PT42 (P.173, context 2283)
Ring-foot of plate with central recess bounded by a raised edge
D.foot 5.6 cm   PL. 3

Orange-buff clay, casual potting; partial dull red to black slip. The illustrated example was found in Group C.
Similar: 2 bases in this group; a fourth example in Group C (p. 26).

- 30 bases with simple central recess as **PT4** in Group A.

PT43 (P.332, context 15095)
Dish/bowl with sharply down-turned rim
D. 22 cm   PL. 3

Soft orange-buff clay; poor red slip.

PT44 (P.329, context 15095)
Small bowl with convex rim
D. ca. 19 cm   PL. 3

Fine buff clay with very sparse inclusions; surface smoother than usual; worn but slightly lustrous red slip
Similar: 5 rims, D. 13 cm (3 exx.).

PT45 (P.330, context 15095)
Dish with flaring triangular rim
D. 18 cm   PL. 3

Soft orange-buff clay; poor red slip.

PT46 (P.279, context 7118)
Small hemispherical bowl with flat rim
D. 14 cm (uneven), H. 4.3 cm   PL. 3

Carelessly formed. Light groove on floor. Buff clay; partial red/dark brown slip (stacking).
Similar: 1 ex., D. 14 cm, H. 4.6 cm.

PT47 (P.336, context 15095)
Hemispherical bowl with everted lip
D. ca. 13 cm   PL. 3

Orange-buff clay, poor surface finish; poor red slip. Probably an imitation of a footless relief bowl; for another example from Zeugma, cf. Gschwind 2002, 336, no. 50.

PT48 (P.337, context 15095)
Rim of hemispherical bowl
D. 17 cm   PL. 3

Buff clay, poor surface finish; partial poor orange-red slip.
Similar: 27 rims in this group, D. 11–28 cm; 1 rim in Group C (p. 26), D 11.5 cm.

PT49 (P.275, context 7118)
Bowl with incurving rim and groove at lip.
D. ca. 15 cm, angle uncertain   PL. 3

Pinkish-buff clay; poor red slip.

PT50 (P.357, context 15095)
Ring-foot of bowl
D.foot 5.8 cm   PL. 3

Buff clay; poor, partial red to brown slip.
Similar: 55 bases.

- 14 incurving rims of bowls as **PT7** in Group A.

PT51 (P.338, context 15095)
Cup with incurved rim and vertical handle
D.rim 13 cm   PL. 4

One handle preserved: presence of second uncertain. Orange-buff clay, poor surface; dull red to brown slip.
Similar: 5 rims, D. ca. 12–20 cm in this group; 12 handle-fragments. 4 rims in Group C (p. 26), D. 12–14 cm.

PT52 (P.427, context 15009)
Carinated bowl with ring-handle
D. ca. 15 cm   PL. 4

Very hard-fired greenish-cream clay, messy potting; thin brown slip all over.
Similar: 1 handle fragment in this group in gray clay with poor black slip (this ware?); 2 rim/handle fragments in Group A (p. 9); 2 rims, 5 handles in Group C (p. 27); 1 rim with handle in Group D (p. 38).

PT53 (P.255, context 7007)
Rim of carinated bowl
D. 17 cm   PL. 4

Buff clay, white specks prominent at surface; dull orange slip, darker over rim. The illustrated example was found in Group C.
Similar: 3 rims in this group, D. 13–15 cm.

- 22 incurved rims of bowls as **PT8** in Group A.
- Rim fragment of bowl with thickened vertical rim and slight lip as **PT9** in Group A.

PT54 (P.254, context 7007)
Large bowl with sharply incurved rim
D.max. 27 cm, D.foot 9.5 cm   PL. 4

Nonjoining rim and base, surely of the same vessel. Buff clay, dull partial slip: orange on inside, brown on outside. The illustrated example was found in Group C.
Similar: 2 rims and 22 bases in this group; 6 further rims in Group C (p. 27), D. 21–27 cm.

PT55 (P.276, context 7118)
Bowl with incurved rim
D.max. 16 cm   PL. 4

Buff clay; partial dull brown slip.
Similar: 31 rims in this group, D. 16–27 cm; 4 rims in Group C (p. 27), D. 14–22 cm.

PT56 (P.286, context 7118)
Base of bowl with groove on floor
D.foot 5.2 cm   PL. 4

Cream clay; partial thin brown slip. Surfaces very rough.
Similar: 5 bases.

PT57 (P.339, context 15095)
Bowl with sharply incurved rim
D.max. 19 cm	PL. 4

Buff clay, poor surfaces; poor red to brown slip.
Similar: 4 rims, D. 13–22 cm.

PT58 (P.278, context 7118)
Shallow bowl with short incurved rim
D.max. 19 cm	PL. 4

Buff clay, dull red slip all over. Carelessly finished.
Similar: 2 rims, D. 18, 22 cm.

PT59 (P.340, context 15095)
Bowl with sharply incurved rim
D.max. 22 cm	PL. 5

Buff clay, poor surfaces; partial poor red slip.
Similar: 8 rims, D. 17–25 cm.

PT60 (P.256, context 7007)
Dish with short inturned rim
D.max. 16.5 cm, H. 4.1 cm	PL. 5

Hard-fired buff clay, abrasive surface; partial dull yellow-brown slip. The illustrated example was found in Group C.
Similar: 3 rims in this group, D. 25, 28 cm.

PT61 (P.341, context 15095)
Bowl with short, tapering vertical rim
D.max. 20.5 cm	PL. 5

Orange clay, poor surfaces; poor red slip.
Similar: 5 rims in this group, D. 13–22 cm; 4 rims in Group C (p. 27), D. 21–26 cm.

PT62 (P.277, context 7118)
Conical bowl with short vertical rim
D. 20 cm	PL. 5

Buff clay; thin, dull red to brown slip all over. Rough surfaces, carelessly finished.

PT63 (P.342, context 15095)
Conical bowl with short, tapering vertical rim
D.max. ca. 29 cm	PL. 5

Buff clay, poor surfaces with prominent turning marks on outside; poor black slip on inside only.
Similar: 3 rims, D. 29, 30 cm.

- Deep bowl with flaring hooked rim as **PT12** in Group A.

PT64 (P.343, context 15095)
Large bowl with hammer-head rim
D. ca. 28 cm	PL. 5

Buff clay, poor surfaces; poor red slip on inside only.

PT65 (P.428, context 15009)
Bowl with grooved triangular rim
D. ?	PL. 5

Pinkish-buff clay; dull red slip on inside and over rim.

PT66 (P.344, context 15095)
Large bowl with short flat rim
D. ca. 27 cm	PL. 5

Buff clay, poor surfaces; partial poor brown to black slip.
Cf. Gschwind 2002, no. 64 (Zeugma, deposit of first century A.D.) and an unslipped example, **PT186** in Buff ware 14.

PT67 (P.345, context 15095)
Bowl with short flat rim
D. 22 cm	PL. 5

Buff clay, poor surfaces; partial, poor orange to red slip.

PT68 (P.353, context 15095)
Hemispherical cup with down-turned rim
D. 16 cm	PL. 5

Orange-buff clay, poor surfaces; poor red slip.

PT69 (P.334, context 15095)
Bowl with short flat rim
D. 20 cm	PL. 5

Soft orange-buff clay; poor red slip.
Similar: 1 rim fragment, thicker than the drawn example and certainly larger.

PT70 (P.346, context 15095)
Large bowl with molded rim
D. ca. 33 cm	PL. 6

Pink clay; purplish-brown slip on inside and over rim.
Similar: 2 rims, D. ca. 33, ca. 38 cm.

PT71 (P.350, context 15095)
Large bowl with molded rim
D. 33 cm	PL. 6

Buff clay; poor red to brown slip on inside only.

PT72 (P.351, context 15095)
Large bowl with molded rim
D. 32 cm	PL. 6

Buff clay; possibly traces of thin red slip on inside.
Similar: 5 rims, D. 26–37 cm.

PT73 (P.280, context 7118)
Bowl with broad sloping rim
D. ca. 28 cm   PL. 6

Buff clay; dull, uneven brown slip all over.

PT74 (P.281, context 7118)
Large bowl with broad hooked rim
D. ca. 27 cm   PL. 6

Buff clay; dull, even red slip all over.
Similar: 1 rim fragment in this group; 1 rim in Group C (p. 27).
D. 30 cm.

PT75 (P.349, context 15095)
Large bowl with molded rim
D. 35 cm   PL. 6

Buff clay, good surface finish; dull red-brown slip on inside and over rim.

PT76 (P.283, context 7118)
Part of bowl with thickened offset rim
D. 25 cm   PL. 6

Buff clay; dull red slip all over.

PT77 (P.352, context 15095)
Part of dish or bowl with flaring rim
D. 19 cm   PL. 6

Buff clay, poor surfaces; poor black slip.

PT78 (P.347, context 15095)
Large bowl with molded rim
D. 29 cm   PL. 6

Stump of horizontal handle on wall. Pink clay; poor red slip on inside and over rim.
Similar: 1 rim, D. 28 cm.

PT79 (P.348, context 15095)
Part of large bowl with horizontal handle, pressed in against the wall   PL. 6

Buff clay, fired cream on outer face and with dull red slip on inside.
Presumably related to the preceding.

PT80 (P.282, context 7118)
Bowl with hanging lip
D. 19 cm   PL. 6

Inscribed wavy line on the outer face. Finely granular buff clay; usual inclusions present but extremely fine; dull red slip all over, surfaces well smoothed.

PT81 (P.335, context 15095)
Bowl with steep flaring rim
D. 18 cm   PL. 7

Orange-buff clay with dull but even slip: black on outside and over rim, red on inside (stacking).
Presumably a bowl rather than a jar.

PT82 (P.176, context 2283)
Ring-foot of bowl
D.foot 5.9 cm   PL. 7

Buff clay, careless potting; partial poor orange-red slip. The illustrated example is from Group C.
Similar: 18 bases in this group; 44 bases in Group C (p. 27).

PT83 (P.358, context 15095)
Ring-foot of bowl
D.foot 6.8 cm   PL. 7

Orange clay, rough surfaces; poor red to brown slip all over.
Similar: 61 bases.

PT84 (P.359, context 15095)
Part of dish or bowl with narrow ring-foot
D.foot 8.2 cm   PL. 7

Hard cream clay, surface smoother on outside than on inside; partial dull brown slip.
Similar: 4 bases.

PT85 (P.171, context 2283)
Square-cut ring-foot of heavy bowl
D.foot 8.5 cm   PL. 7

Buff clay, fine scratches at surface; traces of thin brown slip on inside only. The illustrated example is from Group C.
Similar: 8 bases in this group; 3 further bases in Group C (p. 27).

PT86 (P.432, context 15009)
Base of large bowl with ring-foot
D.foot 9.5 cm   PL. 7

Pinkish-buff clay, buff at surface; dull pink slip on inside only.

PT87 (P.356, context 15095)
Base of bowl with raised lip to central recess
D.foot 6.5 cm   PL. 7

Buff clay, inside surface fairly smooth, outside rough; traces (?) of thin orange slip on inside.

The steep wall clearly indicates that the use of the central recess was not confined to plates/dishes.
Similar: 4 bases.

PT88 (P.433, context 15009)
Part of bowl with flat base
D.base 4.0 cm   PL. 7

Orange-buff clay; poor red slip on inside only.

- 13 miscellaneous bases of dishes or bowls, two of which approximate to **PT226** in Group C.

PT89 (P.284, context 7118)
Rim of flagon
D. 8.2 cm   PL. 7

Buff clay; dull red-brown slip that probably ends on inside close to break.
Similar: 1 rim in cream clay with poor black slip, D. 12 cm.

PT90 (P.355, context 15095)
Rim of flagon
D. 8.5 cm   PL. 7

Buff clay, poor surface; dull red slip on outside and over top of rim.
Similar: 3 rims, D. 8.5–15 cm.

PT91 (P.431, context 15009)
Part of flagon with triangular rim
D.rim 11.5 cm   PL. 7

Rather gritty buff clay as Buff 1, with poor, uneven red to black slip (possibly all over but so worn on the inside that it is impossible to tell).

PT92 (P.430, context 15009)
Part of flagon with everted rim
D.rim ca. 12 cm   PL. 7

Buff clay; dull black slip on outside and a little way into neck.

PT93 (P.285, context 7118)
Part of flagon   PL. 7

Bulbous body, fairly wide neck with groove on outside at junction with body; one handle preserved. Pale buff clay with typical fine inclusions (close to Buff 1) and dull brown to black slip on outside and just into neck.

PT94 (P.354, context 15095)
Twisted handle of a closed vessel
P.L. 8.5 cm   PL. 7

Orange-buff clay; poor red slip.

Similar: 1 handle fragment in buff clay with poor black slip. Perhaps part of a West Slope–type amphora. Cf. Rotroff 1997, nos. 407–59.

PT95 (P.429, context 15009)
Stem of fusiform unguentarium
D.base 2.4 cm   PL. 7

Pinkish-buff clay; dull red slip on all except underside.
Similar: 2 feet and a stem fragment.

PT96 (P.360, context 15095)
Part of small closed vessel with flat base
D.base 2.8 cm   PL. 7

Buff clay; worn but slightly lustrous red slip on outside. Possibly the base of a piriform unguentarium.

- 3 sherds with external fluting, two from bowls (mastoi?), one perhaps from a closed vessel.
- 6 handle fragments, mostly from closed vessels, one from a cup with applied astragal.
- 147 unclassified body-sherds.

HELLENISTIC FINE GRAY WARE

PT97 (P.333, context 15095)
Small dish with internally rolled rim
D. 14.5 cm   PL. 7

Hard gray clay with occasional voids, sparse very fine white specks and moderate very fine muscovite mica. Surfaces show line-burnishing and traces of thin black slip (?).

PT98 (P.426, context 15009)
Ring-foot of bowl
D.foot 6.5 cm   PL. 7

Fine, hard, gray clay containing moderate very fine muscovite mica and sparse very fine rounded quartz(?); smoothly burnished on inside, possibly with thin black slip (but this may be just the effect of burnishing).

- Sherd of large dish 8–12 mm thick, fabric probably the same as **PT97/98** but mica barely apparent; black slip, highly lustrous line-burnish inside and out.
- Tiny fragment of bowl with flaring molded rim in very fine gray clay, finely smoothed, with traces of black slip.

MISCELLANEOUS HELLENISTIC FINE WARE

PT99 (P.434, context 15009)
Dish with ring-foot and central recess
D.foot 6.9 cm   PL. 7

Hard, fine red clay containing moderate very fine specks of lime and sparse darker inclusions (larger, but also very fine); metallic blue-black slip all over.

PT100 (P.300, context 7118)
Part of curving bowl with hollow base
D.base 2.7 cm
PL. 7

Granular grayish-cream clay containing many fine black specks or voids which have the appearance of black smudges, perhaps tiny carbonized seeds. Dull, dark gray slip on inside. Open or closed vessel?

- Stem of fusiform unguentarium. Hard red clay (brown on outside) with moderate very fine white and dark inclusions.

EASTERN SIGILLATA A

PT101 (P.367, context 15095)
Part of dish with simple upcurving rim
D. ca. 30 cm
PL. 8

Similar: 2 rims in this group, D. ca. 28, 30 cm; 1 rim in Group F (p. 57), D. 29 cm.
Hayes 1985, Form 2B; Slane 1997, Type TA 13a (as FW55): second half of second century B.C.

PT102 (P.259, context 7007)
Part of dish with tapering and upcurving rim
D. 21 cm
PL. 8

The illustrated example is from Group C.
Similar: 1 rim fragment in this group.
Hayes 1985, Form 3; Slane 1997, Type TA 13b: from mid-second century B.C.

PT103 (P.258, context 7007)
Part of dish as the preceding, thicker rim
D. ca. 29 cm
PL. 8

The illustrated example is from Group C.
Similar: 1 rim fragment in this group.
Hayes 1985, Form 3 or 4; Slane 1997, Type TA 13b or c: late second century B.C. to 10/1 B.C.

PT104 (P.370, context 15095)
Base of large dish with low, broad ring-foot
D.foot 12 cm
PL. 8

Similar: 1 base, D.foot 17 cm.
Hayes 1985, Form 3; Slane 1997, Type TA 13b: second half of second or first half of first century B.C.

PT105 (P.371, context 15095)
Base of dish with low, broad ring-foot
D.foot 13 cm
PL. 8

Similar: 2 bases, D.foot ca. 16, 17 cm.
Cf. the preceding, probably somewhat later.

PT106 (P.289, context 7118)
Base of dish, similar to the preceding
D.foot 13 cm
PL. 8

PT107 (P.440, context 15009)
Base of large dish, similar to the preceding
D.foot 21 cm
PL. 8
Two pairs of narrow grooves/rouletting on floor.
Hayes 1985, Form 4; Slane 1997, Type TA 13c: first century B.C.

PT108 (P.438, context 15009)
Part of (flat-based) dish with bead rim
D. ca. 31 cm
PL. 8

Hayes 1985, Form 12; Slane 1997, Type TA 19: from ca. 40 B.C. (Hayes), but essentially Augustan.

PT109 (P.377, context 15095)
Part of hemispherical cup with tiny ledge-foot
D.foot 3.4 cm
PL. 8

Similar: a second base, rather larger.
Hayes 1985, Form 19A (probably first half of first century B.C.); Slane 1997, Type TA 27c (predominantly first century B.C.).

PT110 (P.368, context 15095)
Part of bowl with curving wall and plain rim
D. 24 cm
PL. 8

Not enough is preserved to show whether this piece belongs to the (carinated) bowl Hayes 1985, Form 5A, or to an exceptionally large hemispherical cup, Hayes 1985, Form 22. Presumably first century B.C.

PT111 (P.369, context 15095)
Base of bowl with molded ring-foot
D.foot 8.0 cm
PL. 8

Similar: 2 bases, D.foot 7.7, 8.0 cm. None of these three pieces clearly belongs to the preceding rim, but they must belong to similar large hemispherical cups.
Hayes 1985, Form 22; Slane 1997, Type TA 25: presumably first century B.C.

- 2 rims of similar profile to **PT110** but smaller in diameter: D. 14, 16 cm. These surely belong to Hayes 1985, Form 22/Slane 1997, Type TA 25 (as FW 205, 212 on pl. 20).
- 2 bases of hemispherical cups as **PT14** in Group A.

PT112 (P.365, context 15095)
Sherd of relief bowl
FIG. 3, PL. 8

Figure 3. **PT112–118**, *fragments of relief bowls in Eastern Sigillata A from Group B.*

Frieze of running horses (?); winged figure with lyre.
Hayes 1985, Form 24: first century B.C. to first century A.D. The figures are perhaps leaping goats, tipped meaninglessly forwards to fit the space available: cf. Christensen and Johansen 1971, fig. 48.11 (Hama) and Waagé 1948, fig. 17.7 (Antioch).

PT113 (P.436, context 15009)
Sherd of relief bowl FIG. 3, PL. 8

Radiating leaf.
Cf. Cox 1949, no. 73, pl. 4 (Dura-Europos).

PT114 (P.291, context 7118)
Sherd of relief bowl FIG. 3, PL. 8

Long palm-frond.

PT115 (P.435, context 15009)
Sherd of relief bowl FIG. 3, PL. 8

Radiating leaves. Cf. Christensen and Johansen 1971, 132 and figs. 46, 50, no. 31a (Hama).

PT116 (P.437, context 15009)
Sherd of relief bowl FIG. 3, PL. 8

Radiating leaf. Same leaf as on **PT113**?

PT117 (P.361, context 15095)
Rim of relief bowl with vine scroll
D. 12.5 cm FIG. 3, PL. 8

The slightly angular lower profile suggests the later version of the relief bowl, Hayes 1985, Form 25: its occurrence in this deposit provides useful evidence of date.

PT118 (P.362, context 15095)
Sherd of relief bowl FIG. 3, PL. 8

Radiating palm branches.
Cf. the preceding. Christensen and Johansen 1971, 132 and fig. 50, no. 38a and b, shows a similar composition, but with two different, alternating, types of palm branch (Hama).

- 5 unclassified fragments of relief bowls.

PT119 (P.443, context 15009)
Rim of chalice with hanging lip
D. 16 cm PL. 8

Hayes 1985, Form 26A: derived from Italian prototypes and therefore unlikely to be earlier than 10 B.C. Cf. Christensen and Johansen 1971, figs. 74–77, for fragments of decorated chalices from Hama.

Figure 4. **PT120–122**, *fragments of decorated chalices in Eastern Sigillata A.*

PT120 (P.363, context 15095)
Rim of decorated chalice
D. 18 cm
FIG. 4, PL. 8

Ivy scroll with fruits, dancing winged figures. Three nonjoining fragments. Hayes 1985, Form 26B: date as the preceding.
Hayes 1976, no. 76, is part of a chalice with similar figures, perhaps kalathiskos dancers.

PT121 (P.364, context 15095)
Rim of decorated chalice
D. 22 cm
FIG. 4, PL. 8

Similar: 1 rim (only), D. 17 cm. Cf. the preceding.

PT122 (P.366, context 15095)
Sherd of decorated chalice
FIG. 4, PL. 8

Ivy-band, seated figure.

• Unclassified fragment of decorated chalice.

PT123 (P.378, context 15095)
Rim of plate with internal moldings
D. ? cm
PL. 9

Tripartite internal moldings, following Italian prototypes (Ettlinger 1990, 12).
Similar: 2 rims, D. 28, 37 cm, 1 body-sherd.
Hayes 1985, Form 28/Slane 1997, Type TA 22, imitating Ettlinger 1990, 12, in Italian Sigillata: probably no earlier than 5 B.C.

PT124 (P.439, context 15009)
Plate with internal moldings
D. 23 cm   PL. 9

A simpler variant of the preceding.

PT125 (P.381, context 15095)
Dish with sloping rouletted wall and slightly offset lip
D. 29 cm   PL. 9

Similar: 2 rims, D. 23, 25 cm.
Hayes 1985, Form 30 (ca. A.D. 10–50); Slane 1997, Type TA 21.

PT126 (P.380, context 15095)
Dish with rouletted wall and offset lip
D. ca. 15 cm (very uncertain)   PL. 9

A smaller version of the preceding.

PT127 (P.372, context 15095)
Base of small dish with low foot
D.foot 8.8 cm   PL. 9

Similar: 3 bases, D.foot 9, 11, 13 cm.
Related to the preceding. Note the lightly stepped underside of the floor, a characteristic that is not seen before the Augustan period.

PT128 (P.441, context 15009)
Plate with concave vertical rim
D. 24.5, H. 3.4 cm   PL. 9

Rouletting on outside of wall; a broad groove on inside of lip.
Close to Hayes 1985, Form 33, but a more faithful reproduction of an Italian prototype (Ettlinger 1990, 20.3) that is late Augustan/Tiberian. Waagé 1948, Shape 410.

PT129 (P.373, context 15095)
Base of dish with stepped underside
D.foot ca. 18 cm   PL. 9

A band of rouletting on the floor.
Similar: 3 bases, D.foot 11, 13, 17 cm.

PT130 (P.290, context 7118)
Plate with stepped underside and graffito

Center of floor only, three crosses on underside.

PT131 (P.374, context 15095)
Base of dish with square-cut ring-foot
D.foot 16 cm   PL. 9

Similar: 1 base, D.foot 9.5 cm.

PT132 (P.379, context 15095)
Dish with short vertical rim bounded above and below by projecting moldings
D. ca. 40 cm   PL. 9

Hayes 1985, Form 34 (second quarter of first century A.D.); Slane 1997, Type TA 23 (essentially Claudian–Neronian).

PT133 (P.376, context 15095)
High ring-foot of dish
D.foot 17 cm   PL. 9

Possibly related to the preceding.

PT134 (P.382, context 15095)
Base of dish with vertical wall and low tapering foot
D.max. 15 cm   PL. 9

Similar: 2 base fragments.
Hayes 1985, Form 34 or 35?

PT135 (P.375, context 15095)
Base of dish with tapering foot
D.foot 17.5 cm   PL. 9

Similar: 4 base fragments.
Probably Hayes 1985, Form 35: ca. A.D. 40–70.

PT136 (P.386, context 15095)
Conical cup with plain flaring rim
D. ? cm   PL. 9

Hayes 1985, Form 42; Slane 1997, Type TA 32: 10 B.C.–A.D. 25/30.

PT137 (P.387, context 15095)
Conical cup with sharply everted rim
D. ca. 12 cm   PL. 9

This may be another example of the same form as the preceding, or a residual rim of a much earlier cup, Hayes 1985, Form 23/Slane 1997, Type TA 29.

PT138 (P.385, context 15095)
Conical cup with concave rouletted rim and a broad band of rouletting on the wall immediately beneath the rim
D. 17 cm   PL. 9

Similar: nonjoining rim and body-sherd, D. ca. 16 cm.
Hayes 1985, Form 46; Slane 1997, Type TA 34c: early first century A.D.

PT139 (P.389, context 15095)
Part of conical cup with curving floor and flaring ring-foot
D.foot 6.5 cm   PL. 9

Cf. the preceding.

PT140 (P.384, context 15095)
Conical cup with vertical molded rim
D. ca. 14 cm   PL. 9

Similar: 2 body-sherds.
Hayes 1985, Form 47; Slane 1997, Type TA 34a. Hayes suggests ca. A.D. 10–60/70, though the evidence from Tel Anafa favors a slightly earlier first appearance, before 5 B.C. (though it cannot be earlier than 10 B.C., the date of first appearance of the Italian *Conspectus*, 22, which it copies: see Ettlinger et al. 1990, 90–91).

Figure 5. **PT141**, *stamped base in Eastern Sigillata A from Group B. Scale 2:1*

PT141 (P.442, context 15009)
Part of conical cup with flat floor and oblique ring-foot; stepped underside
D.foot 4.0 cm   FIG. 5, PL. 9

Central stamp, KEP[ΔOC]. Same form as the preceding. Cf. Christensen and Johansen 1971, 176 and figs. 42, 67, no. 11 for a similar base and stamp from Hama.

PT142 (P.388, context 15095)
Base of conical cup as the preceding; tapering foot
D.foot 6.1 cm   PL. 9

Similar: 2 bases, D.foot 6.0, 7.1 cm.

PT143 (P.390, context 15095)
Part of hemispherical cup with high, oblique foot
D.foot 3.7 cm   PL. 9

Hayes 1985, Form 51: ca. A.D. 70–120. Surely intrusive. (Cf. **PT262–263** in Group C.)

- 92 unclassified sherds of open vessels, 4 sherds of closed vessels.

ITALIAN SIGILLATA

PT144 (P.383, context 15095)
Part of plate with tapering ring-foot
D. ? cm   PL. 9

Conspectus 1990, B2.5 (Ettlinger et al. 1990, 157): late Augustan/Tiberian.

THIN-WALLED WARE

PT145 (P.391, context 15095)
Part of beaker or bowl with grooved rim
D. 10 cm   PL. 10

Fine, hard, orange-brown clay containing moderate very fine black and white specks. Smoothed but unslipped.

PT146 (P.392, context 15095)
Base of (hemispherical?) cup with tiny ledge-foot
D.base 4.2 cm   PL. 10

Fine, hard brown clay as the preceding, unslipped. Outside more carefully finished than inside.
Similar: 2 bases, one with a slightly simpler profile.
For the shape, cf. Hayes 1973, nos. 187, 189 (Neronian/Flavian deposit at Corinth, but not in this fabric).

PT147 (P.393, context 15095)
Part of (hemispherical?) cup with horizontally ribbed body and flat base
D.base 4.5 cm   PL. 10

Hard orange-brown clay as **PT145**; outside carefully finished, inside with turning marks.
Hayes 1973, no. 188 (see under the preceding) shows similar ribbing.

- Fragment of small flagon or jug? Fabric as **PT145**.

PT148 (P.444, context 15009)
Base of hemispherical cup
D.base 3.8 cm   PL. 10

Very fine, hard, red-brown clay; unslipped but very carefully smoothed on the outside.

AFRICAN RED SLIP WARE

PT149 (P.394, context 15095)
Knobbed rim of dish
D. ca. 32 cm   PL. 10

Hayes 1972, Form 105: A.D. 600–660+ (Pröttel 1996, 65: 600 / 610–700). Intrusive.

GLAZED WARE 1

- 6 body-sherds in yellowish-cream clay with turquoise glaze. "Parthian."

Buff Wares
BUFF WARES 1–4

PT150 (P.294, context 7118)
Bowl with incurved rim
D.max. 17 cm   PL. 10

Buff 3, fired buff to cream; two nonjoining sherds.

PT151 (P.402, context 15095)
Large bowl with incurved rim
D.max. ca. 34 cm
PL. 10

Buff 3: buff body, cream at surface.

PT152 (P.401, context 15095)
Incurved rim of bowl
D. 26 cm
PL. 10

Buff 1: orange-buff, paler at surface; no mica visible.

PT153 (P.447, context 15009)
Part of basin with tapering horizontal rim
D. ca. 34 cm
PL. 10

Buff 1.

PT154 (P.449, context 15009)
Large bowl with flat rim
D. 37 cm
PL. 10

Buff 1: brownish-buff.

PT155 (P.403, context 15095)
Large bowl with convex rim and internal bead
D. ca. 35 cm
PL. 10

Rim somewhat uneven. Buff 1.

PT156 (P.395, context 15095)
Deep basin with short everted rim
D. 44 cm
PL. 10

Roughly finished; string mark on wall just beneath rim. Hard buff clay, pink at the surface; abundant fine quartz (plus darker grits?), occasional larger grains up to 1 mm, very sparse fine muscovite mica. Buff 1?

PT157 (P.445, context 15009)
Wide-mouthed jar with bifurcated rim
D.rim 19 cm
PL. 10

Buff 3, cream on outside surface.

PT158 (P.473, context 7118)
Flagon with cylindrical neck and grooved triangular rim
D.rim 12.8 cm
PL. 10

Traces of handle attachment immediately beneath rim at edge of sherd. Buff 3 with moderate very fine mixed inclusions, fired cream at the surface. Mica not apparent.

PT159 (P.405, context 15095)
Flagon with grooved rim
D.rim 8.5 cm
PL. 10

Buff 3: pink clay, fired cream on outside. Narrow band of dull red slip on top of rim and just inside.

PT160 (P.408, context 15095)
Flagon with simple triangular rim
D.rim 10.5 cm
PL. 10

Buff 3: orange-buff clay, paler on outside surface.
Similar: 1 rim, D. 8.0 cm, possibly Buff 14.

PT161 (P.410, context 15095)
Part of flagon with barely thickened rim
D.rim 9 cm
PL. 10

Buff 1: orange-buff clay, cream at surface.

PT162 (P.297, context 7118)
Part of flagon with collar-rim
D.rim 12 cm
PL. 10

Buff 1: buff clay, cream at surface.
Cf. Gschwind 2002, nos. 85–89.

PT163 (P.411, context 15095)
Part of flagon with hooked rim
D.rim 14 cm
PL. 10

Buff 1: orange-buff clay, cream on outside.
Similar: 2 rims, D. 9.8, 11.5 cm, unclassified buff wares.

• Buff 1, handle of flagon.

PT164 (P.413, context 15095)
Rim of small flagon or unguentarium
D.rim 3.8 cm
PL. 10

Buff 3: pinkish-buff clay. Cf. **PT183** in Buff 13.

PT165 (P.446, context 15009)
Part of (bowl or) wide-mouthed jar with everted rim
D.rim 21 cm
PL. 10

Buff 1: orange-buff clay, paler on outside surface.

PT166 (P.448, context 15009)
Part of (bowl or) wide-mouthed jar with thickened everted rim
D. ca. 26 cm
PL. 10

Buff 3: orange clay, cream surface.

PT167 (P.397, context 15095)
Rim of jar or pot stand with frilled band
D.rim 35 cm
PL. 10

Inscribed wavy lines and horizontal grooves on wall. Buff 2: buff clay, paler on outside surface.
Similar: 4 rim fragments in unclassified buff fabrics, one of which is rather more everted.

In cases such as the present, it is impossible to be certain whether the rim belongs to a pot stand, open at both ends, or to a wide-mouthed jar. No complete profile of such a pot stand was recorded in the present excavations, whereas **PT388** in Group D is unquestionably a jar. But note the pot stands from Tell Halaf: Hrouda 1962, 89, 106 and PL. 73, 80, nos. 97–100 (plus PL. 70 no. 7). No. 97 (PL. 73) is low and plain, with sharply hooked rims; no. 98 has more elaborate rims with three or four projecting moldings, one of which is a typical frilled band as on the rim of the present example. (The frill is formed by drawing out a projecting cordon and then pushing it against the wall at intervals with a finger.) For a further example from Nimrud, see Oates 1958, PL. 25.9 and 29.d, a short pot stand in dark buff gritty clay with frilled decoration ("Hellenistic"). The technique seems to be particularly characteristic of Mesopotamian pottery and will be seen again later on the amphora lids in Group F (**PT540–542**). It is also found on amphorae of Islamic date at Raqqa (Miglus et al. 1999, PL. 42, 43). Compare also a pot stand of Hellenistic date from Maresha in central Israel (Kloner et al. 2003, 183, Form 97) that is frilled on the upper and lower rims (rather than on a band adjacent to the rim).

- Buff 1, part of jar/pot stand with frilled band below rim: close in character to **PT182** in Buff 13.
- Buff 1, rim fragment of pot stand as **PT280** in Group C.

PT168 (P.416, context 15095)
Part of closed vessel with recessed base
D.recess 5.7 cm   PL. 10

Buff 3: hard buff clay; two drips of dull red slip on outside.
Similar: 1 base, Buff 1. Cf. **PT20** in Group A.

PT169 (P.417, context 15095)
Ring-foot of closed vessel
D.foot 8.5 cm   PL. 10

Buff 1: buff clay, cream at surface.
Similar: 4 bases, mostly this fabric.

PT170 (P.272, context 7007)
Ring-foot of closed vessel
D.foot 10 cm   PL. 10

Buff 1: buff clay, moderate fine angular quartz, very sparse mica; lime not apparent. The illustrated example is from Group C.
Similar: 4 bases in this group in various buff fabrics including Buff 13; 3 further bases in Group C.

PT171 (P.418, context 15095)
Ring-foot of closed vessel
D.foot 9.5 cm   PL. 10

Buff 3: pink clay, cream on outside surface.

- Buff 2, sherd of large storage vessel 15 mm thick, with red slip/paint on outside down to base of neck.

BUFF WARE 6

PT172 (P.450, context 15009)
Mortarium with short flaring rim
D. 46 cm   PL. 11

Slight raised cordon on inside of rim. Hard-fired cream clay. The grits of the regular inclusions are more prominent inside the bowl than elsewhere, probably through attrition of the surface rather than additional gritting. Cf. Gschwind 2002, 341, nos. 75–77.

BUFF WARE 10

PT173 (P.404, context 15095)
Large bowl with short flat rim
D. ca. 25 cm   PL. 11

Cream clay.

PT174 (P.412, context 15095)
Part of beaker with steep rim
D.rim 7.2 cm   PL. 11

Cream clay.

PT175 (P.409, context 15095)
Rim of flagon
D.rim 6.8 cm   PL. 11

Greenish-cream clay; occasional lime-specks at surface.

PT176 (P.415, context 15095)
Pointed base of closed vessel
P.H. 6.0 cm   PL. 11

Hard cream clay, very fine multicolored inclusions.

BUFF WARE 13

PT177 (P.398, context 15095)
Deep basin with hooked rim
D. ? cm   PL. 11

Finely granular buff clay without obvious inclusions, paler at surface.

- Base of closed vessel as **PT170** above.

PT178 (P.295, context 7118)
Rim of handled beaker or jar
D.rim ca. 10 cm   PL. 11

Simple everted rim; handle stump. Finely granular orange-buff clay with very fine mixed inclusions.

PT179 (P.407, context 15095)
Rim of small flagon or beaker
D.rim ca. 11 cm   PL. 11

Buff clay; traces of thin brown slip over all (?).
Similar: 1 rim in this group, D. 8 cm, usual inclusions but no mica — this fabric? 2 rims in Group F (pp. 62, 63), fabrics Buff 8 (D. 10 cm) and Buff 13 (D. ca. 12 cm).

PT180 (P.298, context 7118)
Everted, stepped rim of flagon
D. 13 cm   PL. 11

Fine pale orange clay, cream at surface.

PT181 (P.451, context 15009)
Part of narrow-necked flagon with bead rim
D.rim 5.0 cm   PL. 11

Probably only one handle. Buff clay, paler on outside.
Similar: 1 neck/handle fragment.

PT182 (P.292, context 7118)
Pot stand or wide-mouthed jar with frilled rim
D. ca. 22 cm   PL. 11

Lower rim molding crudely frilled; two grooves on neck. Finely granular orange-buff clay with a little very fine lime and mica. Cf. **PT167** and references; also Hrouda 1962, 86, 102 and pl. 70, no. 7, a pot stand from Tell Halaf with a very similar rim ("Hellenistic").

- Rim of pot stand as **PT280** in Group C.

PT183 (P.203, context 2283)
Jar with everted almond rim
D.rim ca. 11 cm   PL. 11

Part of one handle preserved. Pinkish-buff. The illustrated example was found in Group C.
Similar: 1 rim in this group, D. ca. 11 cm.

PT184 (P.293, context 7118)
Part of closed vessel with angular ring-foot
D.foot 8.5 cm   PL. 11

Finely granular buff clay with moderate very fine inclusions; surfaces finely smoothed.

PT185 (P.452, context 15009)
Part of closed vessel with high ring-foot
D.foot 8.0 cm   PL. 11

Fine pale pink clay without visible inclusions, fired buff on outside.
Similar: 1 base.

OTHER BUFF WARES

PT186 (P.399, context 15095)
Large bowl with short sloping rim
D. ca. 34 cm   PL. 11

Buff 14: granular pale brown clay with abundant fine-to-medium angular inclusions, mostly dark; a little fine biotite mica.
Cf. **PT66** in local slipped ware.

PT187 (P.396, context 15095)
Base of large bowl or basin
D.base 16 cm   PL. 11

Hard pink clay with abundant fine angular inclusions, mostly dark in color; mica virtually absent. Very rough potting.

PT188 (P.400, context 15095)
Deep bowl with everted rim
D. ? cm   PL. 11

Hard, granular brown clay with hackly break; very occasional fine to medium specks of lime; buff at surface.

- Rim of flagon as **PT160**: Buff 14?

PT189 (P.296, context 7118)
Part of flagon with everted rim and raised inner edge to lip
D. 7.5 cm   PL. 11

Greenish-cream clay with abundant fine quartz but no mica.

PT190 (P.406, context 15095)
Part of narrow-necked flagon with simple everted rim
D.rim 4.7 cm   PL. 11

One handle only (neck complete). Buff 12: pink clay, cream in patches on outside.

PT191 (P.420, context 15095)
Part of flagon or jug with handle on shoulder   PL. 11

Rather soft buff clay with fine red, white, and black inclusions but barely any mica. Could be Buff 1; but, if so, the technique is very poor.

PT192 (P.414, context 15095)
Hollow knob base
D.knob 3.0 cm   PL. 11

Granular brown clay containing moderate fine quartz: Buff 14?
Similar: a second as the drawn example and a third, slightly smaller (D.knob 2.3 cm); all in the same fabric.

- 19 handles and 146 unclassified body-sherds of buff wares.

Cooking Wares

COOKING WARE 1

PT193 (P.457, context 15009)
Casserole with short rim and pinched ring-handle
D.rim ca. 23 cm   PL. 12

Two handles assumed. Brown clay, fired gray outside and red inside, containing abundant very fine inclusions, mostly white, also sparse very fine mica. This fabric?
Similar: rim fragment of a second example.

The following four shapes (which occur in both of the major cooking-ware fabrics) are particularly enigmatic: they are well attested in this group, and can hardly all be intrusive. Yet they are virtually absent from the Flavian and third-century Groups C and D, reappearing in significant numbers in the sixth- and seventh-century Groups E and F (see **PT495–497**). Such parallels as I have found from datable contexts also seem to belong exclusively to the later period.

PT194 (P.453, context 15009)
Globular cookpot with inset bead rim
D.rim 10.0 cm   PL. 12

Red clay, fired gray on outside surface; lime specks prominent on outside.
Similar: 1 rim in Group F (p. 64), D. 14 cm.
Cf. Konrad 2001a, pl. 84.3 (Qusair as-Saila), possibly this ware but attributed to the fifth–seventh centuries A.D.

PT195 (P.454, context 15009)
Globular cookpot with inset rolled rim
D.rim 13 cm   PL. 12

Fired red throughout.
Similar: 1 rim in this group, D. 13.5 cm; 2 rims in Group D (p. 48), D. 12, 13 cm; 1 rim in Group F (p. 64), D. 12 cm.
Cf. Konrad 2001a, pl. 84.4 (Qusair as-Saila), attributed to the sixth century. Could be this fabric.

- 3 sherds of globular cookpots, one with typical corrugations.

COOKING WARE 2

PT196 (P.456, context 15009)
Globular cookpot with inset everted rim
D.rim 13.2 cm   PL. 12

Fired red throughout, partly brown on outside surface.

For this, **PT197** and **PT497**, cf. Konrad 2001a, pl. 84.5, 6 (Qusair as-Saila), possibly this fabric, attributed to the sixth century; also Harper 1980, fig. C, no. 58 (Dibsi Faraj: "later Roman"). Konrad 1992, fig. 8.9–14 (from Rusafa) fully encompasses this type with unribbed exterior. The Rusafa examples appear to belong to the second half of the fourth or to the fifth century.

PT197 (P.455, context 15009)
Part of globular cookpot with inset everted rim
D.rim 13 cm   PL. 12

Red clay, with clear quartz the only visible inclusion, fired gray on outside. Cf. the preceding.

PT198 (P.423, context 15095)
Neckless jar with thickened rim and handle(s)
D.rim ca. 21 cm   PL. 12

One handle preserved. Hard, dark brown clay, apparently containing only quartz.

- 2 sherds of thin-walled cookpots, one with tentative grooves/corrugations, the other a flat center of a base.

COOKING WARE 7

PT199 (P.301, context 7118)
Wide-mouthed jar with short vertical rim
D.rim 16 cm   PL. 12

Rough surfaces with projecting grits.
Similar: 3 rims, D. ca. 14, 16, ca. 20 cm; one has a handle attachment at the rim.
This form is represented by numerous examples in the deposit of the middle years of the first century A.D. published by Gschwind (2002, 343, nos. 99–127), albeit in what seems to be Cooking ware 1.

- Rim of jar as **PT200** below, this fabric?
- 2 sherds of closed vessels, this fabric?

COOKING WARE 8

PT200 (P.419, context 15095)
Wide-mouthed jar with short vertical rim
D.rim ca. 15 cm   PL. 12

Red clay, lime prominent at surface; very rough.
Similar: 1 rim in Cooking 7(?), D. 16.
Cf. Aubert 2002, figs. 7, 11 (Beirut), Hellenistic.

PT201 (P.458, context 15009)
Part of large jar(?) with incurving rim and handle
D. ca. 25 cm (very uncertain)   PL. 12

Two handles assumed. Hard gray clay, brown at surface; moderate ill-sorted mixed inclusions up to 1 mm, lime specks prominent at surface. Rough, uneven potting.

- Sherd of bulbous jar with stump of handle.

MISCELLANEOUS COOKING WARES

PT202 (P.422, context 15095)
Jar with everted rim
D. 18 cm   PL. 12

Greenish-gray clay with abundant, fine, angular dark inclusions, possibly quartz but certainly not lime; dark gray surfaces.
Cf. Aubert 2002, fig. 8 (Beirut, with ribbed body), Hellenistic.

- 34 unclassified sherds of closed cooking or storage vessels in gritty pink to brown wares.

Storage Wares
STORAGE WARE 5

PT203 (P.421, context 15095)
Jar with almond rim
D. 23 cm   PL. 12

- Sherd of large globular jar with stump of vertical strap handle.
- Sherd of closed vessel.

PT204–210 *vacant*

Group C: Flavian(/Trajanic)

Four contexts have been combined to compose this group, as follows.

2283 Trench 2, House of the Helmets, Room 2I, make-up beneath floor 2195;[65]
2300 Trench 2, House of the Peopled Plaster, Room 2D, make-up layer beneath floor 2178;[66]
7007 Trench 7A, Room 7A, occupation level;[67]
7023 Trench 7A, Room 7B, make-up level beneath floor 7021.[68] A number of joins within the pottery suggest that this material, while surely redeposited, is less mixed and rather more coherent than in other make-up levels.

The defining characteristic of the pottery that has been used to distinguish these contexts from those in Group B is the occurrence in all of them of Hayes (1985) Form 37 in Eastern Sigillata A (**PT254–256**), accompanied in some by cups of Hayes (1985) Forms 49–51 (**PT260–263**). Slane has argued for a Claudian–Neronian date for Hayes Forms 34–37 on the basis of the material from Tel Anafa,[69] but Tel Anafa does not in fact seem to have yielded examples definitely attributable to Hayes Forms 36 and 37; this may itself favor a later date for them. Hayes ascribes a Flavian date to his Forms 37, 50, and 51 on the basis of their frequency at Pompeii, and this seems a good reason for regarding the contexts in this group as Flavian. The stratigraphy at Zeugma and the other finds from these and associated contexts offer little other firm guidance as to date; context 2300 is associated with the construction of the House of the Peopled Plaster in Trench 2, which is perhaps more accurately dated by two Trajanic coins (**C131** and **C129**; see Tobin, volume 1, p. 76). It seems nonetheless reasonable to use this group to demonstrate the evolution of the regional pottery in use at Zeugma in the later first century A.D.

The breakdown of the pottery in this group is as follows.

	No. of pieces	% of total no.	Weight (gm)	% of total weight
Hellenistic fine ware	175	44.4	4,529	34.4
Eastern Sigillata A	83	21.1	1,381	10.5
Thin-walled ware	3	0.8	20	0.2
Misc. fine ware	1	0.3	36	0.3
Glazed ware	4	1.0	45	0.3
Total table wares	**266**	**67.6**	**6,011**	**45.7**
Buff wares	82	20.8	5,315	40.3
Cooking wares	35	8.9	916	7.0
Storage wares	11	2.8	933	7.1
TOTAL	394		13,175	

The "Hellenistic" fine ware (predominantly "local") is still the largest class of table ware and is presumably, therefore, still current. It continues unimaginatively to reproduce the same basic shapes and shows no obvious influence from the higher-quality Eastern Sigillata A. The latter ware is, however, considerably more common than in Group B. The glazed fine ware is again "Parthian."

The buff wares appear rather scrappy, though pot stands now clearly comprise a significant part of the assemblage (**PT280, 281**). Amongst the cooking wares, the thin-walled corrugated cookpot with everted rim, which pervades the third-century destruction levels of Group D, makes its first appearance (**PT294, 295**). Storage ware 2, never common, is represented here by nine sherds, which at 2.3 percent of the assemblage by number is the highest level that it reaches.

Table Wares
BSP

PT211 (P.151, context 2283)
Base of bowl with rouletting and palmette stamp
D.foot 12.5 cm   FIG. 6, PL. 13

One tiny palmette stamp preserved. Very fine orange-buff clay, well-smoothed surfaces, semilustrous black slip with finger marks around foot-ring.
Similar: ring-foot without stamp in Group B (p. 11). Partial dull black slip but the fineness of the clay clearly indicates this ware.
Not in Slane 1997: the profile suggests an earlier date than that of the material from Tel Anafa reported by her (ca. 160 B.C. onwards). The origin of this piece is uncertain, and while it is unlikely to be Attic, Rotroff 1997, no. 893 (ca. 225–175 B.C.) provides an approximate parallel for both profile and stamp.

Figure 6. **PT211**, *base of bowl with palmette stamp in BSP from Group B.*

PT212 (P.152, context 2283)
Base of large dish
D.foot 12 cm   PL. 13

Very fine pale orange clay containing very occasional specks of lime and a little very fine mica. Surfaces excellently smoothed; lustrous blue-black slip, uneven inside foot.
Slane 1997, 286, type TA 2 or 3a/b (Tel Anafa): second half of second century B.C.

PT213 (P.212, context 2300)
Rim of relief bowl
D. ca. 15 cm   FIG. 2, PL. 13

Two grooves on lip; ovolo between bands of dots. Fine orange-buff clay; black slip of medium luster, pock marked on inside. Cf. **PT36**.

LOCAL HELLENISTIC FINE WARE

PT214 (P.162, context 2283)
Plate with down-turned rim
D. 17 cm   PL. 13

Pink clay; poor, uneven red slip all over.
Similar: 1 rim-fragment.

PT215 (P.215, context 2300)
Plate with down-turned rim
D. 19 cm   PL. 13

Soft buff clay, poor brown slip all over.
Similar: 6 rims, D. 12–19 cm.

PT216 (P.163, context 2283)
Plate with sharply down-turned rim
D. ca. 35 cm (very uncertain)   PL. 13

Buff clay, buff to cream at the surface; poor brown slip on inside and over rim.

PT217 (P.213, context 2300)
Plate with hooked rim, grooved on top
D. 22 cm   PL. 13

Cream clay, hard-fired, with dull, adherent red to black slip all over.

• Thickened rim of small dish as **PT41** in Group B.

PT218 (P.216, context 2300)
Small plate with barely articulated rim
D. 12.5 cm (somewhat uneven)   PL. 13

Soft orange-buff clay, poor, partial red slip.

PT219 (P.214, context 2300)
Small plate with hooked rim
D. 12.4 cm   PL. 13

Buff clay, partial poor red slip.

PT42
Ring-foot of plate with central recess bounded by a raised edge   PL. 3

See under Group B. Similar: 1 base.

PT220 (P.233, context 7023)
Ring-foot of dish with central recess, raised lip
D.foot 6.2 cm   PL. 13

Gray-buff clay; dull, uneven brown to black slip over all except inside of foot. Potting careless.
Similar: 1 base, very sandy, rough internal surface: D.foot 6.2 cm.

PT221 (P.174, context 2283)
Ring-foot with simple central recess
D.foot 5.7 cm   PL. 13

Buff clay, partial poor red slip.
Similar: 13 bases, D.foot 4.0–6.6 cm.

PT222 (P.175, context 2283)
Ring-foot with simple central recess
D.foot 4.1 cm   PL. 13

Generally careless potting: asymmetrical foot. Buff clay; dull slip, brown on inside, orange-brown and patchy on outside.
Similar: this kind of foot with central recess, but possibly a closed form. Unslipped: see under fabric Buff 13.

• Rim of hemispherical bowl as **PT48** in Group B.
• 10 rims of hemispherical bowls as **PT7** in Group A.
• 4 incurved rims of cups as **PT51** in Group B.

- 2 rims and 5 handles of (carinated?) bowls as **PT52** in Group B.

PT53
Rim of carinated bowl PL. 4

See under Group B.

PT54
Large bowl with sharply incurved rim PL. 4

See under Group B. Similar: 6 rims.

- 4 incurved rims of bowls as **PT55** in Group B.

PT60
Dish with short inturned rim PL. 5

See under Group B.

- 4 rims of bowls with short, tapering vertical rim as **PT61** in Group B.

PT223 (P.164, context 2283)
Bowl with horizontal grooved rim
D. 16 cm PL. 13

Buff clay, fired cream at surface, well-smoothed; poor brown to black slip, possibly originally over all.

PT224 (P.161, context 2283)
Bowl with everted hanging rim
D. very uncertain, perhaps ca. 35–40 cm PL. 13

Finely granular buff clay with moderate very fine mixed sand and sparse biotite mica. Surfaces fired cream and well smoothed; thin but adherent dull brown slip on inside and over top of rim.

- Part of bowl with broad hooked rim as **PT74** in Group B.

PT225 (P.257, context 7007)
Plate with broad sloping rim
D. ca. 30 cm PL. 13

Hard, granular buff clay containing sparse medium white, brown, and gray inclusions and a little muscovite mica. Dull dark red slip all over. Cf. **PT73** in Group B.

PT82
Ring-foot of bowl PL. 7

See under Group B.
Similar: 44 bases.

Figure 7. **PT226**, *base with palmette stamp in local Hellenistic fine ware from Group C.*

PT85
Square-cut ring-foot of heavy bowl PL. 7

See under Group B.
Similar: 3 bases.

PT226 (P.168, context 2283)
Base of dish/bowl with stamped decoration
D.foot ca. 15 cm FIG. 7, PL. 13

Groove on floor, possibly a second at outer edge of sherd; one palmette stamp preserved; square-cut ring-foot. Hard, finely granular brown clay, almost devoid of visible inclusions (sparse specks of lime, some very fine mica); surfaces well-smoothed, fired buff on outside; dull, even, red-brown slip on inside only.
Similar: 2 bases in Group B (p. 15), D.foot 10, 13 cm, grooves only preserved.
The palmette stamp is typical of the late Hellenistic period elsewhere (second–first centuries B.C.).

PT227 (P.169, context 2283)
Ring-foot of large bowl
D.foot 15 cm PL. 13

Buff clay; inside surface well-smoothed, outside less so; dull, uneven but generally adherent dark red-brown slip all over.

PT228 (P.234, context 7023)
Base of plate
D.foot 9 cm PL. 13

Very flat floor and relatively square-cut foot-ring: influenced by sigillata? Buff clay; dull orange-red slip all over. Potting moderate.

PT229 (P.218, context 2300)
Ring-foot of large bowl
D.foot 10.4 cm   PL. 13

Pinkish-buff clay, potting mediocre, traces of dull orange-red slip on inside.
Similar: 2 bases, D.foot 8.5, 11 cm; also a third, D.foot 9 cm, more or less Buff 1 with a possible trace of brown slip on the inside; hardly fine ware.

PT230 (P.178, context 2283)
Ring-foot of bowl
D.foot 7.8 cm   PL. 13

Buff clay, careless potting; dull orange slip on inside only.

PT231 (P.170, context 2283)
Ring-foot of bowl
D.foot 9.0 cm   PL. 13

Buff to gray clay; surface well smoothed and profile carefully formed; dull brown/black slip on inside, with drips on outside.

PT232 (P.177, context 2283)
Ring-foot of bowl
D.foot 6.4 cm   PL. 13

Thin-walled and well-shaped, though surface finish is rough with scratches. Greenish-cream clay, hard-fired; dull brown slip on inside only.
Similar: 4 bases, D.foot 5.8–6.5 cm.

PT233 (P.179, context 2283)
Ring-foot of bowl (?)
D.foot 7.4 cm   PL. 13

The inside has prominent turning marks: is this part of a closed form? Hard grayish-cream clay with abundant very fine mixed sand but no mica; dull black slip, irregular on inside, drips only on outside.

PT234 (P.172, context 2283)
Base of cup with high, narrow foot
D.foot 6.5 cm   PL. 13

Hard greenish-cream clay, surfaces finished with moderate care; dull brown to black slip, even on inside, irregular on outside, absent beneath foot.
This looks like a copy of a conical cup in Eastern Sigillata A, such as **PT261**.

PT235 (P.247, context 7023)
Everted rim of small flagon
D. 5.2 cm   PL. 14

Buff clay; dull red-brown slip inside and out.

PT236 (P.236, context 7023)
Part of globular flagon or beaker
D.max. 11.2 cm   PL. 14

Hard finely granular buff clay without obvious inclusions apart from an occasional speck of mica. Carefully smoothed on outside. External semilustrous black slip down to maximum diameter. Unslipped lower part fired cream down to a point that suggests that the rim diameter of the next vessel beneath was ca. 7 cm (implying that the vessel was a beaker rather than a closed form). This fabric?

PT237 (P.235, context 7023)
Flagon with everted triangular rim
D.rim 13 cm   PL. 14

Buff clay; thin, crazed black slip on outside so far as preserved and part way down inside of neck.

PT238 (P.181, context 2283)
Fragment of fluted amphora (?)
D.max. ca. 20 cm   PL. 14

Inscribed vertical flutes on wall beneath an angular shoulder. Cream clay, soft-fired; traces of dull brown to black slip on outside.
Similar: fragment in granular clay, close to Buff 1, with dull brown slip on the outside.
For amphorae in the West Slope style with fluting/ribbing on the body, see J. Schäfer, "Hellenistische Keramik aus Pergamon" (*Pergamenische Forschungen*, Bd. 2 [Berlin 1968: De Gruyter]), Abb. 3.1, 2, 4; also Jones 1950, fig. 125 no. 115 (Tarsus).

PT239 (P.180, context 2283)
Pedestal base
D.base 4.6 cm   PL. 14

Buff clay, fired cream at surface; a single drip of dull red slip on the outside of the wall.
Cf. Oates 1959, pl. 56.39 (Ain Sinu, buff ware).

PT240 (P.182, context 2283)
Part of fusiform unguentarium   PL. 14

Buff clay, moderately well smoothed; poor black slip on outside.
Similar: 2 further fragments.

- 2 fragments of bowls with a deep conical center (and huge — missing — ring-foot?).
- 17 unclassified sherds.

EASTERN SIGILLATA A

PT102
Part of dish with tapering and upcurving rim   PL. 8

See under Group B.

Figure 8. **PT247**, *fragments of relief bowls in Eastern Sigillata A from Group C.*

PT241 (P.153, context 2283)
Dish with upcurving rim
D.rim 29.5 cm, D.foot 8.5 cm   PL. 14

Nonjoining rim and base, surely the same vessel. Cream clay, excellent surface, lustrous red slip.
Hayes 1985, Form 3, early; Slane 1997, Type TA 13a/b (the rim is tending towards vertical but the resting-surface of the foot is still hollowed): second half of second century B.C.
Similar: rim, D. 29 cm but not the same vessel.

PT103
Part of dish as the preceding, thicker rim   PL. 8

See under Group B.

PT242 (P.260, context 7007)
Dish with stepped underside
D.foot 10.5 cm   PL. 14

Broad angular foot, slightly sloping resting surface.
Hayes 1985, Form 4A; Slane 1997, Type TA 13c. The stepped underside shows this piece to be no earlier than Augustan (Hayes 1985, 10).

- One body-sherd and one base fragment, generally as the preceding (Hayes 1985, Form 3 or 4).

PT243 (P.261, context 7007)
Part of dish with sloping wall and plain rim
D. ca. 24 cm   PL. 14

Hayes 1985, Form 5B; Slane 1997, Type TA 14b: probably Augustan.

- Fragment of large dish with short flat rim (not illustrated). Hayes 1985, Form 7; Slane 1997, Type TA 18: Augustan (Slane).

PT244 (P.238, context 7023)
Part of flat-based dish with bead rim
D. 30 cm   PL. 14

Similar: rim, D. 33 cm. Cf. **PT108**.

PT245 (P.239, context 7023)
Small flat-based dish, similar to the preceding
D. 18 cm, H. 2.4 cm   PL. 14

Buff clay, semilustrous slip. Surface finish generally careless. This seems a very degenerate example of this form.

- Handle fragment from a chalice (not illustrated). Hayes 1985, Form 15; Slane 1997, Type TA 30: from the late second century B.C.
- Base fragment of a footless bowl with gouged fluting on the wall (not illustrated). Hayes 1985, Form 19B; Slane 1997, Type TA 27a: perhaps first three quarters of first century B.C.
- Rim fragment of hemispherical cup (not illustrated). Perhaps Hayes 1985, Form 22/Slane 1997, Type TA 25.

Figure 9. **PT248**, *fragment of relief bowl in Eastern Sigillata A from Group C.*

PT246 (P.262, context 7007)
Part of hemispherical cup with molded foot
D.foot 5.1 cm   PL. 14

Hayes 1985, Form 22A/Slane 1997, Type TA 25a or b: cf. **PT14** in Group A.

PT247 (P.237, context 7023)
Fragments of relief bowls
D.rim 10.8 cm   FIG. 8, PL. 14

Eleven fragments of very thin footless bowls, with rounded carination. At least two bowls are represented, maybe more. Simple patterns of leaves or narrow ribs are visible, also fragments of large letters. Buff clay, semilustrous red slip; brush marks on inside.
Hayes 1985, Form 25: first century A.D., possibly continuing into the second. Christensen and Johansen 1971, 146 and figs. 56, no. 20.95 (Hama) has sparse narrow ribs; Waagé 1948, figs. 15.19–21 (Antioch) have net patterns of ribs, nos. 21 and 27 appear also to have lettering.

PT248 (P.154, context 2283)
Fragment of relief bowl   FIG. 9, PL. 14

Poppy-head scroll on body. Orange-buff clay, barely lustrous red slip with double-dipping streak.
Jones 1950, no. 326 (Tarsus) has a similar style of decoration, but with ivy leaves and berries rather than poppy heads; Waagé 1948, fig. 16.27 (Antioch) is a small fragment that may have the same decoration as our piece.

PT249 (P.264, context 7007)
Dish with curving wall and hanging lip
D. ca. 30 cm   PL. 14

Cream clay, lustrous chocolate-brown slip.
Hayes 1985, Form 28/Slane 1997, Type TA 22: cf. **PT123**.

- Rim fragment of dish (not illustrated). Hayes 1985, Form 33: first half of first century A.D.

PT250 (P.265, context 7007)
Part of dish with vertical rim bounded by small moldings above and below
D. ca. 28 cm   PL. 14

Concave molding at internal junction of wall and floor, demarcated by offsets.
Hayes 1985, Form 34: cf. **PT132**.

PT251 (P.157, context 2283)
Fragment of dish as the preceding
D.max. very uncertain, possibly ca. 35 cm   PL. 14

Similar: another body-sherd, D.max. ca. 22 cm.

- Rim fragment of dish (not illustrated) Hayes 1985, Form 35: ca. A.D. 40–70.

PT252 (P.267, context 7007)
Base of dish with stamp and graffito
D.foot 5.6 cm   FIGS. 10, 11, PL. 14

Flat floor, low foot. Part of central stamp, XA/PI[C]; graffito on underside, ?BΔX[ ].
XAPIC stamps of this type are typical of the years around the middle of the first century A.D. (Hayes 1985, 11); the profile of the present piece suggests Hayes 1985, Forms 33–35. The graffito does not lend itself to easy interpretation, but is probably a mark of ownership.

PT253 (P.266, context 7007)
Base of small dish with vertical rim, flat floor, and low ring-foot
D. (outer edge of foot) 13 cm   PL. 15

Hayes 1985, Form 36: ca. A.D. 60–100.

PT254 (P.240, context 7023)
Rim of large dish with vertical rim, flat floor, and high ring-foot
D. ca. 28 cm   PL. 15

Similar: 2 rim fragments of a single vessel.
Hayes 1985, Form 37A: ca. A.D. 60–100.

PT255 (P.211, context 2300)
High foot of large dish/plate
D.foot 14.5 cm   PL. 15

Similar: base, D.foot 13 cm.
Same form as the preceding.

PT256 (P.158, context 2283)
High foot of dish
D.foot 11 cm   PL. 15

Similar: foot and body-sherd of something similar.
This too must belong to Hayes 1985, Form 37.

Figure 10. **PT252**, *stamped base in Eastern Sigillata A from Group C.*

Figure 11. **PT252**, *graffito on underside.*

PT257 (P.241, context 7023)
Base of dish with flaring wall and low ring-foot
D.foot 7.9 cm   PL. 15

No stamp or grooves.
Hayes 1985, Form 40: ca. A.D. 80–120.

PT258 (P.155, context 2283)
Conical cup with vertical molded rim; rouletting on upper and lower moldings
D.rim ca. 11.5 cm   PL. 15

Similar: 2 rims in this group, D. ca. 11, 16 cm, 3 body-sherds; 1 rim in Group D (p. 38), D. ca. 10 cm.
Hayes 1985, Form 47; Slane 1997, Type TA 34a. Hayes suggests ca. A.D. 10–60/70, though the evidence from Tel Anafa favors a slightly earlier first appearance, before 5 B.C. (though it cannot be earlier than 10 B.C., the date of first appearance of the Italian *Conspectus* 22, which it copies: see Ettlinger et al. 1990, 90–91))

PT259 (P.156, context 2283)
Base of conical cup corresponding to the preceding
D.foot 5.6 cm   PL. 15

Similar: 2 bases, D.foot 4.5, 4.6 cm.
See **PT258**.

- Body-sherd of a large hemispherical cup with flanged rim, D. 20+ cm (not illustrated). Hayes 1985, Form 48: ca. A.D. 40–70 and beyond.

PT260 (P.268, context 7007)
Part of cup with shallow curving body and inset vertical rim
D.max. 7.5 cm   PL. 15

Hayes 1985, Form 49? Date probably as the preceding.

PT261 (P.242, context 7023)
Conical cup with vertical rim; simple moldings above and below
D.max. 8.6 cm, H. 4.6 cm   PL. 15

Similar: 2 rims, D. 7.2, 11 cm.
Hayes 1985, Form 50: ca. A.D. 60/70–100.

PT262 (P.269, context 7007)
Part of thin-walled hemispherical cup with plain rim
D.rim ca. 13 cm   PL. 15

Hayes 1985, Form 51: ca. A.D. 70–120.

PT263 (P.243, context 7023)
Thin-walled hemispherical cup with high foot
D.max. 7.6 cm, H. 4.2 cm   PL. 15

Similar: 4 rims, D.max. 9–14 cm; 5 body-sherds.

Cf. the preceding.

PT264 (P.263, context 7007)
Ring-handle (of cup?)   PL. 15

Buff clay, lustrous slip. Apparently this ware (cf. Hayes 1985, Form 61, "Trajanic?"), but possibly the handle of a lamp.

PT265 (P.159, context 2283)
Part of large closed vessel with broad ring-foot
D.foot 21 cm   PL. 15

Fine orange-buff clay with sparse fine voids. Surfaces on outside carefully smoothed, turning marks on inside. Barely lustrous brown slip on outside only.
The profile suggests a lagynos as Hayes 1985, Form 101: first century B.C.?

- Sherd of a thin-walled closed vessel: cream clay, excellent lustrous red slip.
- 11 unclassified sherds of open vessels.

THIN-WALLED WARES

PT266 (P.183, context 2283)
Base of hemispherical cup
D.base 3.2 cm   PL. 15

Buff clay; thin, dull pinkish-brown slip all over (as **PT325** in Group D).

PT267 (P.184, context 2283)
Rim of beaker with fine groove at lip
D.rim 9.5 cm   PL. 15

Hard buff clay containing moderate very fine lime, some darker specks and a little biotite mica; thin, dull slip over all, adherent and red-brown on inside, evanescent and brown to black on outside.
Possibly local or regional. Cf. Hayes 1973, 461 and pl. 89, no. 181 for an Italian example of this shape at Corinth; also Ricci 1985, type 2/231, pl. 91.11, produced throughout the first century A.D. in northern Italy.

PT268 (P.244, context 7023)
Globular sanded beaker
D.rim 6.5 cm, D.max. ca. 8 cm   PL. 15

Nonjoining rim and body-sherds of the same vessel. Hard brown clay containing moderate very fine white specks and some darker ones. Sanded on the outside with fine white and dark (greenish?) grits. Dull maroon slip on outside; lustrous, blue-black, and crazed on inside. Cf. Marabini Moevs 1973, no. 304 (Cosa) in "Metallic Glaze ware" with external sanding: Tiberian/early Claudian.

GLAZED FINE WARES

- 3 small sherds in sandy cream clay with dark green, turquoise, and royal blue glaze, respectively. Glazed 1: "Parthian."
- Sherd of thick heavy bowl with thick blue-green glaze. Glazed 2: "Parthian."

MISCELLANEOUS FINE WARE

PT269 (P.186, context 2283)
Closed vessel with flaring base
D.base 8.7 cm   PL. 15

Prominent turning marks on inside, carefully smoothed on outside. Very fine, hard red clay, fired gray in the core in thicker parts and brown on the outside. Moderate very fine specks of lime, sparse rounded dark specks (iron ore?), no mica; unslipped. Clean break.

Buff Wares
BUFF WARES 1–4

PT270 (P.194, context 2283)
Part of shallow bowl with hammer-head rim
D. ?   PL. 15

Buff 1: clay gray to pink in the core, buff at the surface (grayer on inside). Reddish on top of rim, but this is not obviously a paint or slip.

- Base of bowl as **PT229** in local Hellenistic fine ware but apparently in Buff 1.

PT271 (P.193, context 2283)
Part of basin with broad grooved rim
D. 42 cm   PL. 15

(Coarse) Buff 4: buff core, paler at surface.
Cf. Gschwind 2002, 341, nos. 65–72.

PT272 (P.191, context 2283)
Part of bucket(?) with short flat rim
D. ca. 21 cm   PL. 15

Buff 3: pink clay, buff at surface.
Cf. **PT343** in Group D. This rim could possibly also belong to a pot stand as **PT359** (also in Group D).

PT273 (P.190, context 2283)
Part of jar with rolled rim
D. 18 cm   PL. 15

Buff 4: pink on inside, buff on outside.

PT274 (P.249, context 7023)
Wide-mouthed jar(?) with flat rim
D. 24 cm   PL. 15

Buff 1? Hard, vesicular pale brown clay with moderate fine white, brown, and gray inclusions and very fine biotite mica. Same color throughout.

PT275 (P.201, context 2283)
Flagon with everted rim
D.rim 7.6 cm   PL. 16

One handle preserved. Buff 1: orange-pink clay, buff at surface.

PT276 (P.199, context 2283)
Part of flagon or jar with ring-handle on shoulder   PL. 16

Buff 1: buff clay, rather rough potting, fired cream on outside.
Cf. **PT368** in Group D.

PT277 (P.220, context 2300)
Small closed vessel with recessed base
D.recess 5.6 cm   PL. 16

Buff 3: buff clay, fired cream on outside. Outside quite carefully finished.
Cf. **PT20** in Buff 12.

PT278 (P.202, context 2283)
Part of large flagon with molded rim
D.rim 11 cm   PL. 16

Buff 4: fired buff throughout.
Similar: fragmentary rim in Buff 2, D. 10.5 cm, perhaps this type.

PT279 (P.271, context 7007)
Closed vessel with ring-foot
D.foot 10.2 cm   PL. 16

Buff 1: fired buff in the core, cream at the surface.

Similar: 3 bases in Buff 1, D.foot 7.8–9.6 cm; base in Buff 13, D.foot 9.0, with a drip of black slip on the outside (= local Hellenistic fine?).

PT170
Ring-foot of closed vessel PL. 10

See under Group B. Similar: 3 bases, Buff 1 or similar.

- Buff 1: base of closed vessel as **PT293** (below).
- Buff 1: 3 bases of closed vessels as **PT385** in Group D.
- Buff 2: heavy strap-handle of large jar; also a body-sherd of a large jar with traces of dull brown/black paint on outside.

BUFF WARE 12

PT280 (P.188, context 2283)
Pot stand with double moldings above and below
D.rim 21.8 cm, D.base 22.3 cm, H. 20.1 cm PL. 16

Wear suggests that the end with the larger diameter rested on the ground. Pink clay with few of the dark inclusions. Cream to buff film over part of surface.
Similar: 5 rims/bases in this group as this or the following, D. 21–25 cm; 2 rims in Group B (pp. 22, 23), D. uncertain (Buff 1), 22 cm (Buff 13). Cf. Hrouda 1962, 89, 106 and pl. 80, no. 99 from Tell Halaf (triple moldings at rims, two openings in wall).

PT281 (P.189, context 2283)
Pot stand with double moldings above and below
D.rim 19.0, D.base 21.2, H. 17.6 cm PL. 16

Fabric as defined; dark specks visible at surface in parts. Cf. the preceding, also Oates 1958, pl. 28.1 from Nimrud, with simple moldings above and below (Hellenistic).

BUFF WARE 13

PT282 (P.195, context 2283)
Part of bowl with flaring, knobbed rim
D. 33 cm PL. 16

Buff clay, cream surface.

- Ring-foot with central recess as **PT222**, possibly from a closed form. Soft-fired, surface almost flaked off on inside.

PT183
Jar with everted almond rim PL. 11

See under Group B.

PT283 (P.251, context 7023)
Part of jar with bead rim
D.rim 13 cm PL. 16

Buff clay, surfaces well-smoothed.

PT284 (P.198, context 2283)
Fragment of closed vessel with incised lattice
8.0 × 5.8 cm PL. 16

Finely granular pale orange clay, buff towards outside and fired cream at surface. Rather rough finish with scratches. Lattice cut in the form of rounded grooves.

PT285 (P.200, context 2283)
Part of jar with horizontal loop-handle PL. 16

Buff clay, fired cream on outside.

- Base of closed vessel as **PT279**: see above.

PT286 (P.196, context 2283)
Base of closed vessel with high, flaring foot
D.foot 16 cm PL. 16

Foot battered but profile is probably complete. Fine orange-buff clay, cream at surface and finely smoothed on outside; trace of dark brown slip on outside at upper edge of sherd. Also: base of something similar but with the foot-ring completely broken away—perhaps reused as a lid.

- 3 bases of closed vessels as **PT293** (below).
- Base of closed vessel as **PT385** in Group D.
- 2 sherds of closed vessels with traces of red-painted decoration.

BUFF WARE 14

PT287 (P.192, context 2283)
Part of basin with horizontal rolled rim
D. ca. 24 cm PL. 16

Rather soft, porous brown clay with moderate very fine quartz; pale brown surface.
Similar: slightly narrower rim, D. 22 cm.

PT288 (P.248, context 7023)
Curving bowl with short flat rim
D. 25 cm PL. 16

Soft, vesicular pale brown clay containing sparse fine white (lime), brown (chert?), and gray (quartz?) inclusions.
Similar: rim-fragment, this fabric or Buff 1.
Profile reproduced very approximately at Tarsus: Jones 1950, fig. 200.C.

PT289 (P.219, context 2300)
Part of bowl with squashed ring-foot
D.foot 6.3 cm PL. 16

Open or closed vessel? Rather soft, granular brown clay, somewhat vesicular, with occasional very fine black specks and moderate very fine mica. Buff on outside (trace of a drip of red slip?), a sooty black on inside (= closed vessel?). Very careless potting.

OTHER BUFF WARES

PT290 (P.270, context 7007)
Bowl with knobbed rim
D. 24 cm
PL. 16

Granular buff clay containing abundant fine angular quartz and other dark particles (chert?) but no lime. A little fine mica.

PT291 (P.273, context 7007)
Ring-foot of small bowl
D.foot 8 cm
PL. 16

Finely granular clay, gray in the core, brown at the surface; vesicular, with moderate very fine, glassy black specks and a little very fine mica. Related to Storage 2?

PT292 (P.250, context 7023)
Small globular flagon with painted decoration
D.max. 17 cm
PL. 16

Buff 8: hard, vesicular pink clay with moderate fine white inclusions, also sparse gray and black and very sparse mica. Fired cream on the outside (or with a thin wash?); traces of painted spiral on shoulder: The paint is lost but the pattern is shown by the absence of the cream surface, with the pink showing through.
This is a typical example of the painted jugs found in the Byzantine levels (cf. **PT572, 573** in Group F): unquestionably intrusive here.

PT293 (P.197, context 2283)
Part of closed vessel with ring-foot
D.foot 10.4 cm
PL. 16

Rather soft brown clay with moderate, fine, subrounded inclusions: some white but mostly dark; sporadic lumps of lime up to 8 mm. Careless potting; prominent turning marks on inside.
Similar: 5 bases in various buff fabrics, including Buff 1 and Buff 13, D.foot 5.7–9 cm.

- 2 bases of closed vessels as **PT385** in Group D.
- 23 unclassified body-sherds.

Cooking Wares
COOKING WARE 1

PT294 (P.185, context 2283)
Everted rim of corrugated cookpot
D.rim 19.5 cm
PL. 17

Corrugations rather more prominent than in mid-Roman types, body perhaps less bulbous. Trace of handle at edge of sherd. Typical fabric, fired red throughout.
Cf. Orssaud 1980, fig. 307, type 3b (Déhès), attributed to the fifth–sixth centuries, which can hardly be right.

PT295 (P.187, context 2283)
Corrugated cookpot with everted rim
D.rim 22 cm
PL. 17

Dark gray throughout.
Similar: rim, D. 15 cm (context 2300).

COOKING WARE 2

PT296 (P.245, context 7023)
Corrugated cookpot with folded triangular rim
D.rim (outer edge) 15.5 cm
PL. 17

One handle preserved, two assumed. Hard-fired red clay with abundant very fine colorless quartz and no other inclusions apart from rare specks of lime up to 1 mm. Internal surface red, outside dark gray.
Similar: 3 rims, D.rim (outer edge) 13–15 cm.
Cf. Harper 1980, fig. C, no. 57 (Dibsi Faraj: "later Roman"); Oates 1959, pl. 58.76 (Ain Sinu). This form is well attested in this group, and I see no reason to regard it as intrusive.

PT297 (P.246, context 7023)
Folded base of corrugated vessel
D.base ca. 18 cm
PL. 17

Hard, granular red clay containing abundant very fine quartz, very occasional specks of lime and at least one green glassy particle (olivine?).
Cf. Dyson 1968, nos. 428, 449 (Dura-Europos): casseroles.

- 10 unclassified body-sherds of closed (corrugated) vessels.

COOKING WARE 7

PT298 (P.204, context 2283)
Jar with chamfered, everted rim
D.rim 11 cm
PL. 17

PT299 (P.205, context 2283)
Jar with everted rim, thickened internally
D.rim ca. 16 cm (very uncertain)
PL. 17

One handle preserved, two assumed.
Similar: rim fragment with handle, D. ca. 13 cm (very approximate), same inclusions, but abundant and occasionally up to 2 mm; the gray quartz is particularly prominent, resulting in a decidedly rough surface. Also another rim fragment, perhaps this form but with a smaller handle, oval in section, and a body-sherd with handle scar.

- Part of a broad strap-handle, this ware or similar: hard, fused pink clay with abundant medium subrounded quartz sand, also some blacker grits. A second handle is slightly narrower: gray core, pink at surface, same inclusions.

COOKING WARE 8

PT300 (P.274, context 7007)
Part of jar with simple everted rim
D.rim ca. 13 cm   PL. 17

Granular red-brown clay; buff film on inside surface, outside darker.

PT301 (P.253, context 7023)
Small jar or cookpot with thickened rim
D.rim ca. 15 cm (very uncertain)   PL. 17

Red clay, pink at surface with a creamy film on outside.

- 2 sherds of corrugated cookpot, grossly overfired (largely fused). Hard dark gray clay throughout; lime is the only obvious inclusion, sparse, 0.5–2 mm, creating a distinctly spotty appearance on the outside where the surface has spalled. This fabric?
- Handle of small closed vessel.
- 5 sherds of unclassified coarse red or gray cooking vessels.

Storage Wares
STORAGE WARE 2

PT302 (P.206, context 2283)
Small everted rim of jar
D. ca. 10 cm   PL. 17

Top of fragment uneven: angle difficult to judge. Conceivably the same vessel as **PT304**. Orange-brown clay, black on outside, dark brown on inside.

PT303 (P.208, context 2283)
Jar with short everted rim
D.rim ca. 14 cm   PL. 17

Virtually black clay with medium subrounded inclusions that are very difficult to distinguish. Fired partly dark brown at the surface: this fabric?

PT304 (P.207, context 2283)
Part of jar with vertical strap-handle(s)   PL. 17

Part of handmade jar with very uneven surfaces: angle very uncertain. Conceivably the same vessel as **PT302**. Dark brown.
Similar: 2 handles in Group D (p. 52).

- 6 sherds of closed vessels, this ware or similar.

OTHER STORAGE WARES

PT305 (P.209, context 2283)
Rim of pithos
D.rim ca. 40 cm   PL. 17

Angle uncertain. Gray core, buff closer to surface, pink at surface. Granular clay containing moderate very fine and sparse larger gray particles (up to 1 mm) that do not look quite like quartz. The general effect does not suggest added temper (possibly Storage ware 1 without additions?).

- Very heavy angular handle (of pithos?). Storage ware 1: red clay, fired dark brown at surface, containing abundant medium angular quartz and rounded dark red grits (iron ore?); also some whiter quartzite (?).

PT306–310 *vacant*

Group D: A.D. 253

This is the largest group of the seven defined in this report, by weight, though not by number, in which it is exceeded by Group B. The difference in character from the earlier groups is very striking: the proportion of table wares (by number) has diminished from between 67 and 74 percent in the earlier groups to less than 7 percent (almost entirely residual) here. The far greater weight of material in this group is accounted for by the fact that it is composed almost wholly of utility vessels (not counting a single complete pithos, which adds 45 kg to the total).

The group is composed of material from 15 different contexts, all but one in Trench 2, where the evidence of destruction in the Sasanian sack was most compelling and extensive. The date of the sack is established by historical evidence and by coins from associated contexts, which fix it firmly in A.D. 252/253.[70] The contexts of burnt destruction and collapse from which this group is composed are the following:

2010	2039	2160	2376
2012	2080	2260	18108
2023	2139	2278	

To these are added contexts 2191 and 2130 from Room 2F of the House of the Helmets in Trench 2, which were interpreted as a make-up layer and a beaten floor immediately beneath the destruction levels;[71] in ceramic terms they cannot be differentiated in date and may represent refurbishment immediately prior to the sack. Context 2130 yielded three coins, the latest of which is dated to A.D. 244–249.

Context 2016 was allocated to a complete pithos (**PT452**) found in Room 2H of the House of the Helmets:[72] it may be of somewhat earlier date, but was presumably still in use at the time of the sack. It was found to contain amphora **AM148**.[73]

Context 2176 was allocated to a group of ten vessels and a quern stone (context 2171) found on floor 2195 in Room 2I of the House of the Helmets.[74] Some, but not all of them, were complete, and traces of organic remains were recorded in the two dishes, **PT311** and **PT312**. Their character hardly accords with the dignity of the building within which they were found, but they had presumably been in use in that position immediately before the sack. They are listed together at the head of the group as **PT311–320**.

The breakdown of the pottery in this group is as follows.

	No. of pieces	% of total no.	Weight (gm)	% of total weight
Hellenistic fine ware	35	3.2	683	0.5
Eastern Sigillata A	23	2.1	187	0.1
Italian Sigillata	1	0.1	12	0.0
Thin-walled ware	4	0.4	47	0.0
African R.S. Ware	1	0.1	17	0.0
Phocaean R.S. Ware	1	0.1	21	0.0
Cypriot R.S. Ware	1	0.1	50	0.0
Glazed ware	7	0.6	236	0.2
Total table wares	**73**	**6.7**	**1,253**	**0.8**
Buff wares	512	46.4	54,537	38.4
Cooking wares	488	44.2	15,865	11.2
Storage wares	31	2.8	70,541	49.6
TOTAL	**1,104**		**142,196**	

It is clear from the fine wares and the amphorae that there are a few late intrusions in the upper contexts 2012, 2039, and 2080; since there was no later reoccupation of the structures in Trench 2, these presumably represent only casual scatter, and perhaps some recovery of building materials in the Late Imperial period. They introduce an element of uncertainty into previously undated forms that are attested either in these three contexts alone, or only in these and later contexts, but on the whole Group D offers a broad picture of the pottery in use at Zeugma in the first half of the third century A.D.

I have already mentioned the striking diminution in the occurrence of table wares. This cannot be purely a matter of nonavailability. Zeugma was an extremely prosperous city in the third century A.D., and at Antioch, between it and the Mediterranean coast, African Red Slip Ware was plentiful.[75] It was less so at Tarsus,[76] but still well represented. It is also present at Dura-Europos.[77] Only a single sherd (**PT327**) is present in Group D, and very little was noted from the excavation as a whole. Neither is its role fulfilled by any other production;[78] table ware as a class of functional goods seems to have gone wholly out of fashion at Zeugma! It is difficult to pinpoint the moment at which this occurred. Second-century forms in Eastern Sigillata A[79] are also absent; this may be because no substantial second-century deposits were identified, but if that were the reason, one would still expect them to occur residually in Group D amongst the 23 listed fragments of that ware.

Other sites in the region seem to participate in the same phenomenon, and Dura-Europos begins to look like an exception. A gap in the fine-ware sequence during the same period has been reported both at Dibsi Faraj[80] and in the material from the River Quwaiq survey.[81] In a large body of second-century material from Beirut published by Paul Reynolds, the fine wares account for only 3.6 percent of the pottery by number, contrasting with substantially higher figures in first- and fourth-century deposits.[82]

If the reason for the lack of table wares is not because they were not available (and Antioch seems to demonstrate that they were), should we consider some kind of cultural change? Materials for serving food and drink were surely still required: either these took forms that have become invisible to us (e.g., wood), or perhaps the use of individual dishes was replaced by communal eating from large basins such as those now attested in plain buff wares (**PT345–351**). While it is entirely speculative, I wonder whether the frequency of pot stands at Zeugma, and particularly in this group (**PT355–359**), is connected with this phenomenon. In the Late Imperial period there occur round-bottomed amphorae[83] for which such stands would be eminently suited. But the stands do not appear to be current in that period (or that fabric), and the regional amphorae of the third century have ring-bases and do not require stands![84] The stands show no evidence of burning, and they are clearly not braziers: were they in fact used to support a communal bowl of food in the midst of a circle of diners.

The buff and cooking wares in use in the third century show greater uniformity than in other periods. Buff wares 1–4 account for 343 out of a total of 521 catalogued sherds of buff wares, and only 29 sherds were attributed to other specific fabrics. Likewise, Cooking ware 1 accounts for 462 of the 488 sherds of cooking wares. These were surely being made somewhere not very far away.[85] Transport amphorae were being made in the same buff wares at this time,[86] and the separation, for purposes of study, of these from wide-mouthed jars and other smaller containers is necessarily artificial. In general, body- and base-sherds of closed vessels that could not be identified specifically as amphorae have remained with the bulk of the pottery. A form of decoration that is first attested on closed vessels in buff ware in this period is composed of bands of multiple grooves, applied with a comb while the vessel is on the wheel.[87] In one instance (**PT387**), this is combined with wavy combed lines and with black paint. Wide-mouthed jars with a frilled band beneath the rim and with more exotic inscribed decoration on the body also feature strongly in these deposits, having first appeared in Group B (see **PT167** and **PT182**); these vessels seem quite alien to the Mediterranean ceramic tradition and perhaps derive their inspiration from Mesopotamian sources.

Mortaria have hitherto been represented by a single example in Group B (**PT172**);[88] they are notably common in Group D (**PT396–402**), mainly in Buff ware 6, and disappear from the scene again thereafter. (If the disappearance of the table wares seems an un-Roman trait in this group, the occurrence of mortaria would usually be taken as a sign of increasing Romanization!)

The cooking wares are basically restricted to three shapes: a flat-based pan with an incurving rim, presumably related to the *patinae* in Pompeian Red Ware that are common throughout the Mediterranean (**PT311, 312, 414–**

417); a two-handled carinated casserole with a corrugated underside and rounded bottom (PT313, 314, 422–426); and an ovoid or globular cookpot, again with corrugations on the wall and a rounded bottom (PT316–319, 429–437). The casserole has a narrow, inward-sloping rim and two small vertical handles, attached at the rim and carination. It is quite unlike those with variously bifurcated, stepped, or seated rims that are common in the Mediterranean world. (To take but two examples, those of Benghazi in Libya and Tel Anafa in Israel have more in common with each other than either does with Zeugma.)[89] The globular shape of the cookpot is familiar enough elsewhere,[90] but the flaring rim with slight internal seating of most examples seems to be a regional peculiarity. The very thin walls of the casseroles and cookpots have given rise to the denomination "brittle ware": the lightness in the hand of a complete vessel is remarkable,[91] and they display the very highest level of technical skill in the potter. The cultural milieu of this pottery is clearly Mesopotamia and the Euphrates Valley, with parallels to be found in the Lidar Höyük and Kürban Höyük survey areas, at Dibsi Faraj, Ain Sinu, Seh Qubba, and Dura-Europos. There are related casseroles and cookpots at Tarsus, but they display thicker walls and other differences of detail that suggest a different source. (Those in second-century deposits at Beirut are also quite different: see Reynolds 1997–1998.)

In addition to the three basic shapes, there exist also in Cooking ware 1 a round-bottomed bowl with a simple incurving rim (PT419–21), occasional lids (PT427, 428), and a lantern, represented by PT320 and fragments of four others.

Storage ware 2, from Ras el-Basit on the Syrian coast, is numerically best represented in this group (see PT458, 459), though it has already made an appearance in Groups A and C.

Pottery from Context 2176

The vessels in this group were identified by individual context numbers (rather than Small Find numbers) as listed below. All are in Cooking ware 1.

PT311 (P.7, 'context' 2175)
Flat-based cookpan with incurving rim and offset at edge of floor
D.max. 21.8 cm, H. 3.8 cm   PL. 18

Red clay, fired brown at the surface; wet-smoothed but dull inside and out, sooted beneath. Complete; found containing wheat and other carbonized material (context 2180, sample 2026).
Similar: 2 profiles, 1 base, 2 body-sherds from other contexts in Group D, D. 19, 21 cm.
Cf. Dyson 1968, fig. 19, types III A 1–3 (Dura-Europos) for this and the following.

PT312 (P.6, 'context' 2174)
Larger example of the preceding, sagging floor
D.max. 28.6 cm, H. 4.9 cm   PL. 18

Complete; remains of *Pinus* and other carbonized matter found within (context 2179, sample 2025; cf. Vol. 3: Challinor & DeMoulin, pp. 420, 422; Gale, p. 435). Red clay, fired brown at the surface; wet-smoothed but dull inside and out, sooted beneath.
Similar: 3 profiles, 9 rims, 1 base fragment from other contexts in Group D, D. 20–30 cm.

PT313 (P.4, 'context' 2173)
Casserole
D.rim 23.0 cm, H. 10.1 cm   PL. 18

Carinated casserole with sagging floor, corrugated beneath towards the outer edge, and inset vertical rim; lip marked off by an external groove; small vertical handles on wall. About one-third preserved (including one handle). Fired gray throughout.
Similar: 10 rims from other contexts in Group D, D. 19–25 cm.
For this general type, cf. Dyson 1968, no. 42 (Dura-Europos), "good quality gray clay with white flecks in it," also fig. 19, types III B 2, 3; Campbell 1989, nos. 60, 61 (Seh Qubba); Harper 1980, fig. C, no. 55 (Dibsi Faraj); Wilkinson 1990, fig. B.25.11 (Kürban Höyük survey, site 8, multiperiod); also (less close) Jones 1950, fig. 191.362 (Tarsus).

PT314 (P.1, 'context' 2166)
Casserole as the preceding, thicker rim
D.rim 26.5 cm, H (pres.) 10.0 cm   PL. 18

About one-quarter preserved (including one handle). Fired red; blackened beneath.
Similar: 4 rims, 1 body-sherd from other contexts in Group D, D. 20–25 cm.

PT315 ('context' 2169)
Another example as PT314
D.rim 20.2 cm, H. 8.0 cm

About one third preserved.

PT316 (P.3, 'context' 2170)
Globular corrugated cookpot
D.rim 15.8 cm, D.max. 18.6 cm, H. 16.8 cm   PL. 18

Short vertical neck with a slight internal seating, everted rim, vertical handles from rim to body. About half preserved, including one handle. Orange-red clay, fired dark brown on outside. Sooty on lower part.
Similar: 15 rims from other contexts in Group D, D.rim 13.5–19 cm.

Globular cookpots with ribbing on the body first occur at Tarsus in the Hellenistic period, developing further in the Hellenistic-Roman Unit (Jones 1950, 179 with figs. 187.c and 191.363, 364). They have everted rims, but these are not close to the examples from Zeugma. Wilkinson 1990, fig. B.15.6 (Kürban Höyük survey: site 12) is closer.

PT317 ('context' 2168)
Another example as PT316
D.rim 17 cm, H. 18.2 cm

About one-third preserved.

PT318 ('context' 2172, sherd unrelated to the next item)
Body-sherd of a globular corrugated cookpot

PT319 (P.5, 'context' 2172)
Globular vessel with recessed base
D.base 4.5 cm   PL. 18

Red-brown clay, fired darker on the outside; signs of burning beneath.
Similar: 5 bases from other contexts in Group D
Cf. Oates 1959, pl. 58.80, 85 (Ain Sinu); 85 is a spouted jug. Dyson 1968, fig. 13, no. 440 (Dura-Europos) is a piriform cookpot or jug with a recessed base and rim as **PT439**.

PT320 (P.2, 'context' 2167)
Lantern
D.base 13.2 cm   PL. 18

Several nonjoining fragments of a cylindrical lantern with frontal opening (which should probably be about twice the width shown in the drawing) and various circular air holes (on all parts of the lower body but only on the front of the shoulder). About one-fifth preserved. Very flaky, uniformly dark red-brown clay. No signs of burning except for a small darkened area at the front of the shoulder.
Similar: 2 bases and 2 body-sherds from other contexts in Group D, D.base 15, 18 cm.
The fragments have been reconstructed on the basis of three intact examples on display in Gaziantep Museum; other fragments were found in the Turkish excavations at Zeugma in 2000 and such lanterns were clearly not uncommon in the city. They would readily have accommodated oil lamps, and both the holes in the front of the shoulder and the darkening in that area suggest a flame towards the front, rather than centrally within. Cf. Dyson 1968, nos. 193–6 (Dura-Europos), generally in the same fabric as the "brittle ware." Bailey 1988, 291 and pl. 62, no. Q2357 in the British Museum from "Anatolia," is very similar in shape, but in an "orange-brown" micaceous clay.

Other Pottery from Group D: Table wares
BSP (RESIDUAL)

PT321 (P.36, context 2160)
Ring-foot of bowl
D.foot ca. 12 cm   PL. 18

Curving body, high ring-foot; two narrow bands of rouletting on floor. Fine cream clay with smooth, slightly metallic slip, mostly chocolate-brown but grayer on outside.
Not directly paralleled in Slane 1997, though the pale fabric is surely Levantine. The profile of the foot is closer to Attic examples of the first half of the third century B.C. such as Rotroff 1997, nos. 870–881 or 970.

PT322 (P.221, context 2191)
Incurved rim of bowl
D.max. ca. 17 cm   PL. 18

Very fine buff clay, moderately well finished surfaces; semi-lustrous dark red-brown slip on inside, black and worn on outside. Slane 1997, type TA 4: present at Tel Anafa before 125 B.C.

- 2 sherds of dishes and a fragment of a mastos (? – cf. **PT34**).

LOCAL HELLENISTIC FINE WARE (RESIDUAL)

- Incurved rim of bowl as **PT7** in Group A.
- Part of hemispherical bowl with ring-handle as **PT52** in Group B.

PT323 (P.45, context 2130)
Ring-foot of bowl
D.foot 7.0 cm   PL. 18

Buff clay; partial, uneven, dull orange-brown slip.
Similar: 2 bases.
Cf. **PT54** in Group B: the present examples are clearly residual, but more carefully formed.

- 23 unclassified sherds.

MISCELLANEOUS HELLENISTIC FINE WARES

- 2 sherds of closed vessels with external brown or black slip.

EASTERN SIGILLATA A (RESIDUAL)

- Part of conical cup with vertical molded rim as **PT258** in Group C.
- 22 unclassified sherds.

ITALIAN SIGILLATA (RESIDUAL)

PT324 (P.50, context 2039)
Part of platter with vertical rim
D. ca. 40 cm   PL. 18

Fine pink clay; highly lustrous red-brown slip. *Conspectus* 1990, 20.4: ca. A.D. 30–70 (see Ettlinger et al. 1990, 86–87).

THIN-WALLED WARES

PT325 (P.97, context 2278)
Thin-walled cup with disc-base
D.base 4.4 cm   PL. 18

Finely granular buff clay without mica; thin, dull and uneven (but adherent) pink slip (as **PT266**). Presumably residual (first century A.D.?).

PT326 (P.52, context 2039)
Rim of folded beaker
D.rim 9.2 cm   PL. 18

Part of beaker with folded body (only one, fairly narrow indentation preserved), two steps on shoulder, restricted neck and plain flaring rim. Somewhat flaky orange-brown clay with abundant very fine muscovite mica and sparse larger dark inclusions. Carefully smoothed but unslipped. No convincing parallels found.

- 2 small sherds of closed vessels, ware as the preceding.

AFRICAN RED SLIP WARE

PT327 (P.51, context 2039)
Part of flat-based dish with sloping wall and plain tapering rim
D. ca. 20, H. 3.4 cm   PL. 18

Fine hard ware, entirely burnt brown to black.
Hayes 1972, Form 50A (Pröttel 1996, 32): ca. A.D. 230–325.

PHOCAEAN RED SLIP WARE

- Base of dish (context 2080). Fifth century A.D. or later: intrusive.

CYPRIOT RED SLIP WARE

- Base of dish (context 2012), probably this ware. Late fifth century A.D. or later: intrusive.

Glazed Wares

PT328 (P.53, joining sherds from contexts 2039 and 2080)
Carinated footless bowl with upcurving rim
D. 24 cm   PL. 18

Profile of floor restored from a body-sherd of another vessel. Glazed 1: gray-buff clay; pale blue-green glaze.
Similar: body-sherd (context 2039).
Despite the fact that this form was recorded only from contexts that suffered from late intrusions, parallels from other sites clearly indicate that it belongs to the "Parthian" series. Cf. Oates 1959, pl. 56.5, 6, 11–13 (Ain Sinu, destroyed in A.D. 237, common); Toll 1943, fig. 29 no. 1938.4860 etc., type XI-H-1 (Dura-Europos, destroyed in A.D. 256). All of the Dura bowls have disc-bases and are considered probably to

Figure 12. **PT330**, *cylindrical ointment-jar in "Parthian" glazed ware from Group D.*

belong to the second or third century A.D. For similar fragments from Tell Seh Hamad in the lower Habur Valley, see Römer 1996, 20, fig. 2a–c, found in levels dated between the second half of the first century B.C. and the first half of the first century A.D. (generally in the same levels as Eastern Sigillata A).

PT329 (P.54, context 2039)
Heavy ring-foot of bowl
D.foot 11 cm   PL. 18

Glazed 2: gray-buff clay (burnt?); blue-green glaze. "Parthian."
Cf. Toll 1943, fig. 28 (Dura-Europos): a few of the bowls have developed ring-feet, but this is much less common than a barely articulated disc base. Hrouda 1962, 91, 109, and pl. 73, no. 16 (Tell Halaf) is a bowl with incurved rim and this foot profile ("gelbgrünlicher, feinkörniger Ton. Außen und innen grünbräunliche Glasur"). See also Oates 1958, pl. 24.6 (Nimrud), very like the Tell Halaf example — "Hellenistic."

- 2 sherds of Glazed 2 (contexts 2012, 2039).

PT330 (P.662, SF 2133, context 2039)
Cylindrical ointment jar
D. 4.4, H. 8.9 cm   FIG. 12

Small cylindrical jar with short concave neck and everted rim; high disc-base. Glazed 1: very sandy cream clay with turquoise glaze on outside and over rim. Described from

notes made in 2000: missing in 2002 (in Gaziantep Museum?).
"Parthian." Cf. Toll 1943, 54 with fig. 26 and pl. 18 (Dura-Europos); close to no. 1935.547, rigidly cylindrical, with sharp angles at top and bottom of body. Numerous at Dura-Europos from the first century A.D. onwards.

Buff Wares

BUFF WARES 1–4

• Ring-foot of bowl, possibly Hellenistic.

PT331 (P.74, context 2039)
Small bowl with plain rim
D. 13.2, H. 4.0 cm   PL. 19

Buff 1: grayish-cream throughout; very roughly formed. Possibly Late Imperial and intrusive.

PT332 (P.76, context 2039)
Conical cup with vertical molded rim
D. 11 cm   PL. 19

Buff 1: orange-buff clay, carefully smoothed and fired buff on the outside.
Similar: rim, D. 13 cm (context 2012).
Perhaps a copy of the conical cups of the first century A.D. in Eastern Sigillata A (cf. **PT258/259**).

PT333 (P.75, context 2039)
Conical cup with concave vertical rim
D.rim 10.4, H. 7.0 cm   PL. 19

Buff 1: fired pale orange to gray (burnt?); carelessly wet-smoothed. Cf. the preceding.

PT334 (P.79, context 2039)
Conical bowl with vertical rim
D.max. 18 cm   PL. 19

Buff 3? Hard buff clay containing sparse fine sand with barely any visible mica. Surfaces reasonably smooth.
Similar: 5 nonjoining rim fragments of the same vessel in Buff 1, D. 25 cm (context 18108).

PT335 (P.120, context 2023)
Curving bowl with plain vertical rim
D. 21 cm   PL. 19

Buff 1: buff clay, cream at surface.
Similar: 3 rims in Group F (pp. 59, 64: 2 in Buff 15, one in Buff 1), D. 18–24 cm. This is a very simple form, found in the fine wares of the Hellenistic period, but very possibly recurring subsequently without the necessity of any direct connection.

PT336 (P.587, context 2012)
Ribbed bowl with down-turned rim
D. 21 cm   PL. 19

Buff 1: pinkish-buff throughout.
Cf. **PT531** in Group F: possibly intrusive here.

PT337 (P.585, context 2012)
Part of handled bowl with everted rim, concave on top
D. 34 cm   PL. 19

Two nonjoining fragments; one handle preserved, two assumed. Buff 1: buff throughout.
Cf. **PT405, 406** in other buff wares.

PT338 (P.48, context 2130)
Dish or bowl with triangular rim
D. ?   PL. 19

Angle and diameter uncertain. Buff 1: pale pink, fired buff on outside.
Possibly related to **PT270** in Group C.

PT339 (P.586, context 2012)
Deep bowl with folded rim
D. 36 cm   PL. 19

Buff 1: buff throughout; badly flaked and affected by burning. Three nonjoining fragments.

PT340 (P.107, context 18108)
Large bowl with incurved molded rim
D. ?   PL. 19

Buff 1? The clay appears to be typical, fired buff, but there appears to be a thin dull brown slip over all.

PT341 (P.22, context 2010)
Miniature spouted cup
D. 4.2, H. 3.9 cm   PL. 19

About one third of a small cup with flat base, steep straight wall, and plain rim. Scar on wall of an applied tubular spout. Buff 1: buff with cream surface.

PT342 (P.588, context 2012)
Knobbed rim of bowl or bucket
D. 21 cm   PL. 19

Buff 1: buff clay, paler at surface.
Possibly a bowl (cf. **PT290** in Group C), or part of a bucket as the following.

PT343 (P.11, context 2010)
Rim of bucket
D. 22 cm   PL. 19

Part of a large vessel with steep wall and short sloping rim; tiny trace of handle scar just beneath rim. Buff 1: gray in the core, buff at surface.
Similar: rim, D. 27 cm.
This could conceivably be the mouth of a very large jar, but a flat-based bucket seems more likely. Cf. Gerber 1996, fig. 2.19 (Lidar Höyük area: rim fragment, possibly this form). Jones 1950, no. 784 (figs. 161, 204), from Tarsus is a bucket with a single vertical handle in buff ware, D. 31.2, H. 33.7 (unstratified). Note also **PT272** in Group C.

PT344 (P.10, SF 2098, context 2010)
Base of cylindrical bucket (?)
D.base 15.5 cm   PL. 19

Part of large vessel with flat base and steep, slightly flaring wall. Buff 1: pinkish in the core, buff at surface.

PT345–351, which follow, mark the first significant appearance of a basic form of basin (with a flat base and steep conical sides) that persists hereafter into the Islamic period. The Middle Imperial type appears to be characterized by a fairly broad rim with a concave upper surface. In the Late Imperial period, this is replaced by a rounded convex rim (see nos. **PT478, 479, 483, 493, 494** in Group E and **PT535** in Group F, also the intrusive **PT352** here); the Islamic version is characterized by a short knobbed or square-cut rim (see **PT620, 627, 643–645** in Group G).

For comparable basins from Beirut, see Reynolds 1998, 55 with figs. 107–9 (with red grits on the underside, context first half of second century), and 193, fig. 211 (context late second century), thought to be from Cilicia or the Antioch region).

PT345 (P.106, context 18108)
Basin with short, angular, sloping rim
D. ca. 32 cm   PL. 19

Buff 1: buff core, pink at surface.
Similar: 1 rim in Group F (p. 59), D. ca. 36 cm.

PT346 (P.56, context 2039)
Basin with sloping rim, concave on top
D. 41 cm   PL. 19

Buff 1: orange-buff in the core, buff on the inside, browner on the outside. Outside surface more carefully smoothed than inside. Partly burnt. The marks of burning confirm that this is a third-century piece.
Similar: 1 rim, D. 39 cm (context 2012).

PT347 (P.39, context 2160)
Part of basin with steep wall and flat base
D.base ca. 22 cm   PL. 19

Buff 1: fired pink throughout but appears otherwise to be this fabric. Wet-smoothed inside and out but very rough (no turning marks) beneath, from resting on sand.
Similar: 3 base-sherds.

PT348 (P.47, context 2130)
Basin with short rim, concave on top
D. ca. 40 cm   PL. 20

Buff 1: buff, wet-smoothed.
Similar: 2 rims, D. ca. 26, ca. 45 cm.

PT349 (P.55, context 2039)
Basin with sloping rim, concave on top
D. 37.5 cm   PL. 20

Slightly sagging floor, very rough beneath. Buff 1, burnt.
Similar: 1 profile (D. 35 cm, H. 10.8 cm), 2 rims, D. 34–38 cm (distorted), uncertain.

PT350 (P.131, context 2080)
Conical basin with flat base and everted rim, concave on top
D. 39, H. 11.9 cm   PL. 20

Buff 1: mostly fired pale pink, buff on outside of wall.

PT351 (P.57, context 2039)
Basin with broad sloping rim, concave on top
D. 39 cm   PL. 20

Buff 1: buff in the core, cream at surface.
Similar: 6 rims, D. 40–48 cm (contexts 2012, 2039, 2080).

PT352 (P.132, context 2080)
Conical basin with flat base and sloping rim
D. 39, H. 12.1 cm   PL. 20

Buff 1, fired buff.
Similar: 3 rims in Group E (pp. 53, 55), Buff 1 and Buff 13, D. 34, 37 cm; 9 rims in Group F (pp. 59, 64), Buff 1 and Buff 15, D. 37–48 cm.
Konrad 1992, fig. 14.7 (Rusafa: context, 475–518) has a similar simple profile. Cf. **PT535** in Group F. Certainly intrusive here.

PT353 (P.133, context 2080)
Conical basin with flat tapering rim
D. ca. 39 cm   PL. 20

Buff 1, fired pinkish-buff.
Similar: 1 rim in Group E (p. 53), D. ca. 30 cm. This seems likely to be a Late Imperial intrusion.

PT354 (P.584, context 2012)
Basin with short flat rim
D. 38 cm   PL. 20

Buff 1, fired buff throughout. Date uncertain, but in view of the context this may well also be intrusive here.

- 5 unclassified base-sherds of conical basins.

Pot stands have made their first definite appearance in Group C (**PT280, 281**, but see also **PT167, 182** in Group B), but characterize the Middle Imperial destruction levels *par excellence*. The rim has changed from a solid double molding in the earlier examples to a simpler out-turned flange.

Pot stands are not uncommon in the Mediterranean region, but they are generally unlike those from Zeugma, which are distinguished by greater overall size and height. Cf. Jones 1950, nos. 719, 720 (fig. 201: Tarsus); Williams 1989, nos. 598–603 (Anemurium); Reynolds 1998, figs. 184–8 (Beirut); Riley 1979, 353, MR Plain 9 (Berenice). Oates 1959, plates 55.5, 10; 59.104 illustrates two stands from Ain Sinu that are rather closer to the Zeugma Middle Imperial types. Note also Kloner et al. 2003, 183, Forms 96 and 97, from Maresha in central Israel.

PT355 (P.105, context 18108)
Pot stand with simple out-turned flanges
D.rim 20.6, D.foot 19.8, H. 11.2 cm   PL. 20

Buff 1, fired gray-buff throughout.
Similar: 5 rims, D. 21–22 cm. (Note: since this form does not have a distinguishable base, the number of rims should theoretically be divided by two when comparing frequencies with other types of vessel.)

PT356 (P.9, context 2010)
Pot stand with sloping lower flange which curves gently into body
D.base 21.5 cm   PL. 20

Buff 1, fired buff throughout.
Similar: 9 rims, Buff 1–4, D. 20–24.

PT357 (P.8, context 2010)
Pot stand with simple flanges, turned sharply outwards at a right angle
D.top 21.4, D.base 24, H. 8.9 cm   PL. 20

Buff 1: orange in core, buff towards surface.
Similar: 5 rims, Buff 1 and Buff 3, D. 19–23 cm.

PT358 (P.135, context 2080)
Part of pot stand with short rolled flange
D. 23.5 cm   PL. 20

Buff 1, fired buff throughout.
Similar: 1 rim, D. 22 cm (context 2012). In view of the contexts, it is possible that this short rim is a later development, but the evidence is lacking for certainty.

PT359 (P.121, context 2023)
Pot-stand with short square flange
D.base 24.8 cm   PL. 21

Buff 1: buff clay, grayish-cream at surface.
Cf. **PT272**.

PT360 (P.20, context 2010)
Conical lid with plain rim
D. 29 cm   PL. 21

Buff 1, fired buff throughout. Outside is slightly more carefully smoothed than inside, suggesting a lid.

PT361 (P.38, context 2160)
Conical lid with plain rim
D. 31 cm   PL. 21

Buff 1: typical fabric, wet-smoothed inside and out.

PT362 (P.21, context 2010)
Part of lid (?) with shallow curving body and squat central knob
D.knob 6.1 cm   PL. 21

(Coarse) Buff 4: pale gray-brown. Very rough knife-cut finish on outside; inside wet-smoothed.

PT363 (P.145, context 2080)
Small conical lid with plain rim
D. 12.5 cm   PL. 21

Buff 1: fired brownish-buff.

PT364 (P.141, context 2080)
Flagon with narrow tapering neck and triangular rim
D.rim 5.4 cm   PL. 21

A single handle from neck to shoulder. Buff 1? Rather soft gray-buff clay with the usual inclusions.
Similar: rim, D. 6.6 cm, body-sherd with handle (both from context 2080). In view of the contexts, it is possible that this type is Late Imperial.

PT365 (P.82, context 2039)
Part of narrow-necked ovoid flagon
D.max. 15 cm   PL. 21

There is definitely only one handle. Buff 2: buff throughout, well-smoothed on the outside, rather flaky on the inside. Possibly a Late Imperial intrusion: cf. the preceding.

PT366 (P.83, context 2039)
Small flagon with thickened rim
D.top of rim 7.0 cm   PL. 21

Buff 3: buff clay, pinkish at the surface.
Similar: 2 rims in Buff 1, D. 5.2, 7.5 cm.

PT367 (P.122, context 2023)
Rim of one-handled flagon
D.rim 10.4 cm   PL. 21

Thickened rim, short neck; seven-eighths of rim preserved, with one handle scar only. Buff 1: seems to be this fabric, but rather soft and fired pale gray with a creamier surface.

PT368 (P.16, context 2010)
Small ring-handled jar
D.rim 9.8 cm, D.max. 14.6 cm, H. (est.) 15.5 cm   PL. 21
Small jar with ovoid body, short curving neck, thickened rim (flat on top), and ring-foot. A single groove on body, just above mid height, with a small vertical ring-handle just above that. Nonjoining rim and base; two handles assumed. Buff 1: fired buff throughout.
Similar: 3 rims (Buff 1 and 4), D. 10 cm; 4 bases, generally this size. A handle of this type may belong to the rim **PT371**.
Cf. also **PT411** in miscellaneous buff ware. This kind of small jar may exist already in the Flavian period: cf. **PT276** in Group C.

PT369 (P.81, context 2039)
Small ovoid jar with combed-band decoration
D.rim 9.5 cm, D.max. 15.5 cm   PL. 21

Handle scar on upper body; two rather light and careless combed bands. Buff 1: mostly orange-buff, but affected by burning.

PT370 (P.99, context 2278)
Small jar with triangular flaring rim
D. 9.5 cm   PL. 21

Top of rim is curiously uneven, as if something else had been luted on. Buff 3: buff clay, possibly this fabric, with irregular traces of surface discoloration in brown-black, which may be casual but may conceivably be paint.

PT371 (P.224, context 2191)
Flaring rim of small jar
D.rim 10.4 cm   PL. 21

A ring-handle as **PT368** from the same context may be part of this vessel. Buff 1: buff clay, cream at surface.

PT372 (P.77, context 2039)
Globular corrugated jar with flaring rim
D.rim 10.8 cm   PL. 21

Buff 1: rather soft, but apparently this fabric, fired warm buff throughout.
Similar: rim, D. ca. 11 cm (context 2039).

PT373 (P.149, context 2260)
Small globular jar with everted rim
D.rim 11 cm   PL. 21

Buff 3: buff clay, fired cream on the outside.

PT374 (P.78, context 2039)
Small jar with grooved vertical rim
D.rim 10 cm   PL. 21

Buff 1: probably this fabric, originally fired gray-buff, but extensively burnt.

PT375 (P.18, context 2010)
Spout of jar
D. at level of groove ca. 15 cm   PL. 21

Part of globular vessel with a groove around the upper body (as **PT368**?) and projecting tubular spout. Buff 3: well smoothed on outside; irregular patches of black which may be paint.
Similar: fragment of closed vessel with short tubular spout (Buff 1).

PT376 (P.37, context 2160)
Ring-foot of small closed vessel?
D.foot 7.0 cm   PL. 21

Prominent turning marks on inside suggest a closed shape. Buff 1: buff clay, tending towards cream at surface.
Cf. **PT408** in Buff ware 10.

PT377 (P.104, context 18108)
Part of narrow closed vessel with ring-foot
D.base 6.8 cm   PL. 21

Buff 1: buff clay, paler at surface.
Similar: 2 bases.

PT378 (P.17, context 2010)
Base of small closed vessel
D.base 8.0 cm   PL. 21

Part of steep-walled, almost cylindrical vessel with false ring-base; prominent turning marks on inside. Buff 1: mainly gray-buff but with a pinkish tinge on outside.

PT379 (P.144, context 2080)
Closed vessel with broad flat base
D.base 9 cm   PL. 21

Buff 3: fired buff with pink patches at the surface. Possibly a Late Imperial intrusion.

PT380 (P.143, context 2080)
Part of small closed vessel with restricted base
D.base 3.8 cm
PL. 21

(Coarse) Buff 4: buff clay, rather rough surfaces.
Similar: base (context 2080).
Cf. similar small "bottles" from Ain Sinu: Oates 1959, pl. 56.30–38.

PT381 (P.142, context 2080)
Small closed vessel with flat base
D.base 2.8 cm
PL. 21

Buff 1: rather granular clay with worn surfaces, but apparently this fabric.

- Buff 1: base of small handleless jar as **PT582** in Group F (context 2039): surely intrusive.
- Buff 1: 2 heavy bases of small closed vessels as **PT580** in Group F (context 2012): intrusive?

PT382 (P.12, context 2010)
Upper part of two-handled flagon with combed-band decoration
D.rim 9.8 cm, D.max 24.8 cm
PL. 22

Part of flagon or amphora with cylindrical neck, very slightly thickened rim and ovoid body. Vertical handles from neck to shoulder. Combed bands beneath lip, two at shoulder, one on upper body. Buff 2: fired buff throughout.

PT383 (P.102, context 18108)
Rim of flagon with combed band
D.rim 10.0 cm
PL. 22

Molded collar-rim; combed band between the handles. Buff 1: pale orange core, cream surface.

PT384 (P.589, context 2012)
Square-cut rim of flagon (?)
D.rim 17 cm
PL. 22

Buff 3: buff throughout.
Similar: 2 rims, same context, D. 21 cm.
Though the fabric appears to be local, the profile resembles that of the Late Imperial Syrian amphora Form 17F (Reynolds, this volume). Probably intrusive.

PT385 (P.15, context 2010)
Ring-foot of closed vessel
D.foot 11 cm
PL. 22

Buff 1: fired buff throughout. Traces on outside and beneath foot of thin white slip.
Similar bases, ranging in size between that of **PT368** and the present example: 6 in Group C (pp. 33, 34: one in Buff 13); 50 in Group D (one in Buff 5, p. 45); 1 in Group E (p. 54); 1 in Group F (p. 61).
Many of these may belong to amphorae such as Form 13D (Reynolds, this volume, pp. 97, 111–112).

PT386 (P.150, context 2260)
Large jar with wide, straight neck and bead rim
D.rim ca. 15 cm
PL. 22

One handle preserved, also two massive nonjoining sherds from lower body, 16 mm thick. Buff 3: orange-pink clay, fired buff towards the outside and with a finely-smoothed cream surface, perhaps a refined self-slip.
Similar: sherd of another large jar, same context.

PT387 (P.32, joining sherds from contexts 2139 and 2160)
Wide-mouthed jar with combed and painted decoration
D.rim 21.5 cm, D.max. 33.8 cm
PL. 22

Bulbous body; wide, tall cylindrical neck; and projecting, square-cut rim. One handle preserved. Decorated with alternate straight and wavy combed bands, also swirls of dull dark brown paint. Buff 1: fired buff, well smoothed on outside.
Similar: 2 rims, D. 20 cm, and 2 body-sherds.

PT388 (P.583, context 2012)
Wide-mouthed jar with frilled rim
D.rim 19.5 cm, D.max. 32.1 cm
PL. 23

Thickened rim, slightly concave on top and with a frilled band immediately beneath; tall tapering neck and bulbous biconical body; inscribed decoration on body, composed of wavy lines and stab-marks. Handles not preserved, but presence assured by other examples. Buff 1: pink clay, buff at surface (black encrustations on inside).
Similar: body-sherd with wavy line and pricked decoration (Buff 3, context 2376).

PT389 (P.46, context 2130)
Rim of wide-mouthed jar with frilled band
D. 28 cm
PL. 23

Zigzag decoration of prick marks, probably made with comb for combed bands. Buff 3: buff clay, wet-smoothed; very fine mixed inclusions, mica very sparse.
Similar: 2 rims, D. 21, 29 cm, no decoration other than the frilled band preserved on neck; trace of handle attachment immediately beneath the rim on one.

PT390 (P.73, context 2039)
Rim of wide-mouthed jar with frilled band
D. 27 cm   PL. 23

Buff 3: cream clay. In instances such as this example, one cannot be certain that this type of rim was not applied to pot-stands (as **PT355–359**) as well as to wide-mouthed jars. Cf. **PT167** and **PT182** in Group B.

PT391 (P.91, context 2039)
Neckless ovoid jar with wavy combed band
D.rim 21 cm, D.max. 35 cm   PL. 23

One handle preserved, two assumed. Wavy combed band between two straight ones. Buff 1: gray to brown.
Similar: 2 body-sherds, one with handle (context 2039). Cf. **PT459** in Storage ware 2.

PT392 (P.92, context 2039)
Neckless ovoid jar with horizontal combed bands
D.rim 24 cm   PL. 23

Buff 1: buff throughout. Similar to the preceding.

- 45 sherds of closed vessels with combed-band decoration; 2 sherds of closed vessels with wavy combed bands.

PT393 (P.95, context 2039)
Rim of large ovoid jar/small pithos
D.rim 28 cm   PL. 24

Buff 1: fired buff throughout; surfaces smoothed as well as on smaller vessels. Impossible to judge whether this is Middle or Late Imperial.

PT394 (P.595, context 2012)
Disc-lid with impressed decoration
D. 14 cm, thickness 1.4 cm   PL. 24

Decorated with circular impressions made with a tubular tool. Probably fitted with a strap-handle across the center (not preserved). Buff 1: fired pinkish-buff throughout. Rough surfaces.
Cf. Orssaud 1980, fig. 309, type 1a, a fragment of a very similar lid from the Late Imperial/Early Islamic settlement at Déhès in Syria. Clearly intrusive here.

PT395 (P.594, context 2012)
Disc-lid of pithos?
D. ca. 25 cm, thickness 2.8 cm   PL. 24

Crudely formed circular disc. Buff 1: fired buff throughout. This may have served as a lid for a large storage vessel, or it may be simply a circular building brick or *pila* (though, so far as I know, no *pilae* were recorded from the excavations). Intrusive?

- Buff 1: base of large round-bottomed vessel.
- Buff 1: base of knobbed amphora lid (cf. **PT538** in Group F). Intrusive.
- 21 handles and 105 body-sherds of unclassified closed vessels.

(COARSE) BUFF WARE 5

This rare fabric was recorded only in this group: petrographic examination suggests that it is an import from outside the Euphrates region.

- Ring-foot of closed vessel as **PT385**.
- One handle and 3 body-sherds of closed vessels.

BUFF WARE 6 (MORTARIA)

PT396 (P.59, context 2039)
Mortarium with broad convex rim and spout
D. 34.5 cm, H. 11.0 cm   PL. 24

Molded spout on top of rim; slightly raised inner lip. Affected by intense fire, but appears to be typical. No added grits. Similar: 2 rims, D. 31, 43 cm, one base.

PT397 (P.129, joining sherds from contexts 2039 + 2080)
Mortarium with broad convex rim and spout
D. 44 cm   PL. 24

Raised boss on (either) side of spout.
Similar: rim, D. 44 cm, burnt. Cf. the preceding.

PT398 (P.223, context 2191)
Mortarium with broad convex rim
D. 33 cm   PL. 24

Hard, fused cream clay with abundant fine quartz and darker grits; sparse flakes of mica. A large lump of quartz at least 6 mm across seen through a break in the outer surface.
A variant of the preceding, with a more sharply downturned rim, but the inner lip is still demarcated.

PT399 (P.30, context 2139)
Mortarium with broad convex rim
D. 47 cm   PL. 25

No demarcation of inner lip; broad turning marks on outside.

PT400 (P.60, context 2039)
Small mortarium with convex rim
D. 29 cm, H. 8.0 cm   PL. 25

- Base and body-sherd of mortaria.
- Fragment of a large closed vessel, showing a string mark around the girth (cf. **PT156**): this fabric?

BUFF WARE 8 (INTRUSIVE)

- Rim of amphora lid as **PT561** in Group F (context 2012).
- Base of small closed vessel as **PT568** in Group F (context 2012).
- 2 sherds of closed vessels with painted decoration (context 2080).

OTHER BUFF WARES

PT401
Mortarium with heavy, sharply down turned rim
(P.210, context 2012) D. 51 cm   PL. 25

Hard pale pink clay, cream at surface, containing mixed glassy grits: green (olivine?), black, orange, red, clear (quartz), also some biotite mica. Gritted on the inside with the same minerals.
Surely Campanian: see Hartley 1973 with fig. 2, type 2.

PT402 (P.130, context 2080)
Mortarium with broad convex rim
D. 55 cm, H. 16.6 cm   PL. 25

Raised internal lip. Hard greenish-gray clay with abundant very fine dark inclusions and very occasional lumps of lime (up to 8 mm). Gritted internally with dark rounded basaltic grits about 2 mm across. See the petrographic report by Doherty, this volume, p. 88 (question 14).
Jones 1950, no. 706 (Tarsus: unstratified but classed as early imperial) is approximately this shape but probably not in this fabric ("clay red-buff, coarse; mica, sand, lime"); also ibid., fig. 204.A.

PT403 (P.138, context 2080)
Base of dish with flat floor and ledge-foot
D.foot ca. 18 cm   PL. 25

Pale brown clay with abundant very fine dark sand and occasional specks of mica. Carefully turned; traces on underside only of a smooth burnish or slip, also brown. Possibly an imitation of a third-century dish in African Red Slip Ware: cf. **PT327**.

PT404 (P.100, context 2278)
Part of thick-walled vessel with ring-foot
D.foot 8 cm   PL. 25

Pale pink clay containing abundant very fine mixed inclusions and very occasional mica; rough, worn surfaces.
Similar: 2 bases, D.foot 5.2, 6.4 cm.
Open or closed vessels?

PT405 (P.140, context 2080)
Bowl with curving body and everted rim with internal seating
D. 31 cm   PL. 25

Buff 10: hard orange-buff clay.
Possibly a handled bowl or skyphos as the following; cf. also **PT337** in Buff ware 1.

PT406 (P.123, context 2023)
Large two-handled skyphos
D.rim 18.5 cm, D.max. 19.8 cm, H.est. 15.2 cm   PL. 25

Four nonjoining pieces. Buff 14: fired pale gray on the inside, pale brown on the outside. Heavy, rough, irregular potting.
Cf. the preceding.

PT407 (P.139, context 2080)
Curving bowl with bead rim and raised inner lip
D. ca. 25 cm   PL. 25

Angle of rest uncertain. Buff 10: buff clay, fired cream at surface.

PT408 (P.226, context 2191)
Ring-foot of small closed vessel
D.foot 6.4 cm   PL. 26

Encrusted on inside, due to contents (?). Buff 10: hard cream clay. Cf. **PT376** in Buff ware 1.

PT409 (P.84, context 2039)
Ring-foot of small closed vessel
D.foot 5.0 cm   PL. 26

Prominent turning marks on inside suggest a closed form. Fired mainly buff, but yellowish-cream on outside, which is fairly well smoothed; abundant fine angular lime, sparse fine rounded quartz, no mica.

PT410 (P.134, context 2080)
Rim of large jar (or pot stand?)
D. 25 cm   PL. 26

Tall neck and flaring, square-cut rim. A band of stabbed decoration around the neck. Worn and rounded at lower edge of sherd as if it has been cut back to make a pot stand (or was it a pot stand anyway?). Flaky pink to gray clay containing abundant, very fine dark sand; mica detectable but very sparse.
Cf. **PT355–359** (pot stands) and **PT388–390** (jars).

PT411 (P.80, context 2039)
Small ovoid jar with triangular rim
D.rim 11 cm   PL. 26

One handle preserved, two assumed. Granular gray-buff clay with moderate medium inclusions, mostly black (iron ore?). Very rough surfaces, no mica. Cf. **PT368–370** in Buff wares 1 and 3.

PT412 (P.88, context 2039)
Part of flagon or jar with flat rim
D.rim 17 cm   PL. 26

One handle preserved; at least two grooves on neck (not combed). Hard brown clay with mixed, ill-sorted inclusions, mostly dark and including some large lumps of iron ore, fired gray towards the surface but warm buff at the surface. Partly burnt.

PT413 (P.137, context 2080)
Handle of large vessel
L.pres. 10.0 cm, W. 5.5 cm   PL. 26

Broad strap-handle with two deep grooves at one edge. Dense orange to buff clay containing abundant very fine mica, moderate to sparse fine subrounded quartz grains and earthy red particles (looks superficially like Buff ware 1, but it isn't!).

- Buff 13: part of closed vessel with recessed base as **PT572** in Group F (context 2012). Surely intrusive.
- Buff 15: rim fragment of basin with short convex rim as **PT493** in Group E (context 2012). Surely intrusive.
- Miscellaneous buff wares: 108 unclassified sherds, mostly closed vessels.

Cooking Wares
COOKING WARE 1

PT414 (P.113, context 18108)
Flat-based cookpan with incurved rim
D.max. 40 cm, H. 6.1 cm   PL. 26

Bulge in floor towards edge, with two narrow grooves (but not multiple grooves). Orange-brown clay containing abundant fine black and white inclusions (not obviously volcanic) and a little fine muscovite mica. Burnished cherry-red slip on inside and over rim.
This seems to be a faithful copy of an Italian *patina* in the local cooking ware fabric. Cf. Kenrick 1985, Form B479 and references, extending from the Augustan period into the second century A.D.

PT415 (P.61, context 2039)
Flat-based cookpan with incurving rim
D.max. ca. 70 cm, H. 6.9 cm   PL. 26

Typical fabric, fired red through the core and on the inner surface, dark brown on the outside. Wet-smoothed but unslipped.
Similar: 2 small rim fragments of one vessel, even larger (context 2039).

PT416 (P.40, joining sherds in contexts 2139 and 2160)
Flat-based cookpan with incurving rim
D.max. 26 cm, H. 3.2 cm   PL. 26

Typical clay, fired gray in the core and red-brown towards the surface. The whole surface inside and out (but not beneath) is carefully burnished to a low lustre, producing a dark brown stripy effect, but is not slipped.

PT417 (P.110, context 18108)
Cookpan with incurved rim and offset floor
D.max. 29 cm, H. 4.3 cm   PL. 26

Offset at edge of floor on inside only. Fired gray throughout; wet-smoothed but not slipped or burnished.
This vessel seems to represent a transition between the preceding examples, which are close to their Italian models, and the version with an offset floor, which appears to be standard in this group, represented by **PT311, 312**.

- Base fragment of cookpan, unclassified.

PT418 (P.126, context 2080)
Dish with broad sloping rim
D. 28 cm   PL. 26

Dark brown clay, patchy brown to black at surface.
In view of the context, one cannot be sure that this piece belongs here. Cf. Wilkinson 1990, fig. B.25.13 (Kürban Höyük survey: site 8, multiperiod), a small fragment of a flat rim.

PT419 (P.111, context 18108)
(Round-bottomed) bowl with incurving rim
D.max. 27 cm   PL. 26

Rounded lip, groove on outside. Lime more prominent at the surface than mica; fired gray throughout, with some surface patches of maroon.
Similar: rim in this group, D.max. 26 cm; rim fragment in Group F (p. 64).
I have found no close parallel for this very pleasing and simple shape, which was presumably used for cooking. Apart from **PT419** and a second rim from the same context, which belongs securely to Group D, the remaining examples (**PT420, 421**, and parallels) are from contexts that are either contaminated or late. It must be borne in mind, therefore, that this may be a Late Imperial form and hence intrusive in this group.

PT420 (P.62, joining sherds from contexts 2039 and 2080)
(Round-bottomed) bowl with incurving rim
D.max. 21 cm   PL. 26

Fired dark red; black on upper part of outside (stacking).

Similar: rim in Group E (p. 55), D.max. ca. 22 cm.
See under the preceding.

PT421 (P.63, nonjoining sherds from contexts 2039 and 2080)
(Round-bottomed) bowl with incurving, square-cut rim
D.rim 25 cm   PL. 26

Fired gray in the core, brown towards the surface and black at the surface.
Similar: rim fragment, possibly this form, in Group F (p. 64). See under **PT419**.

PT422 (P.109, context 18108)
Carinated casserole
D.rim 19.0 cm, D.max. 20.5 cm   PL. 26

Similar to **PT313** but with a very sharp carination. One handle preserved, two assumed. Dark gray throughout.
Similar: 7 rims, D. 18–ca. 28 cm; 1 body-sherd.
Cf. Oates 1959, pl. 58.77, also 78, 79, less close (Ain Sinu, very common).

PT423 (P.225, context 2191)
Carinated casserole
D.rim 19.6 cm, D.max. 22.0 cm   PL. 26

Sharply incurved at lip. One handle preserved, two assumed. Red core and inner surface, slightly browner on outside.

PT424 (P.33, context 2139)
Rim of carinated casserole
D. 21 cm   PL. 26

Sloping floor (corrugated beneath), short inward-sloping wall, and tapered almond rim. Typical fabric, rather flaky, fired black on outside and maroon on inside.
Similar: rim fragment (context 2039).

PT425 (P.591, context 2012)
Part of casserole with concave vertical rim
D. 22 cm   PL. 26

Fired red throughout.
Possibly a late intrusion, but note **PT193** in Group B. Cf. Gerber 1996, fig. 2.1 (Lidar Höyük survey).

PT426 (P.590, context 2012)
Part of casserole with concave vertical rim
D. 19 cm   PL. 26

Red clay, fired black on outside.
Similar: rim fragment (context 2012).
Possibly intrusive: cf. the preceding.

- 12 unclassified body-sherds of casseroles.

Figure 13. **PT429**, *globular corrugated cookpot in Cooking ware 1 from Group D.*

PT427 (P.112, context 18108)
Corrugated conical lid with square-cut rim
D. 19 cm   PL. 26

Fired dark brown to gray.
Lids such as this and the following presumably served for both casseroles and cookpots, despite the absence of lid seatings on the former at Zeugma; the corrugated underside would have assisted them to remain in position.
Cf. Dyson 1968, fig. 19, types III A 4, 5 (Dura-Europos).

PT428 (P.592, context 2012)
Rim of shallow conical lid
D. 23 cm   PL. 26

Dark brown throughout. Cf. the preceding.

- 2 rims of globular cookpots with inset rolled rim as **PT195** in Group B.

PT429 (P.598, SF 3453, context 18108)
Globular corrugated cookpot with everted rim
D.rim 11.5 cm, D.max. 12.3 cm, H. 13.2 cm   FIG. 13, PL. 27

Slight internal lid seating. Intact; two handles. Black on lower part, inside and out; red-brown over rim.
Similar: 4 rims, D.rim 10.4–17 cm.
Cf. Oates 1959, pl. 58.83 (Ain Sinu: rim only).

PT430 (P.24, context 2010)
Rim of globular corrugated cookpot
D.rim 14.5 cm   PL. 27

Pronounced convex curve to neck on both inner and outer surfaces. Fired brown on inside and black on outside.
Similar: 20 rims in this group, D.rim 14–20 cm; 2 rims in Group F (p. 64), D. 15, 16 cm.
Cf. Oates 1959, pl. 55.1 and 58.81 (complete: Ain Sinu, very common); Dorna-Metzger 1996, fig. 24 (Upper Khabur survey: less common than rims as **PT444**); Dyson 1968, fig. 19, type III D 4 (Dura-Europos, as **PT429–431**).

PT431 (P.64, context 2039)
Rim of globular corrugated cookpot
D.rim 24 cm   PL. 27

Similar to **PT429**, but with barely articulated lid seating. Dark red at core and on inside, black outside.
Similar: 16 rims, D. 15–23.5 cm.
Cf. Gerber 1996, fig. 1.18 (Lidar Höyük survey); Campbell 1989, no. 59 (Seh Qubba); also **PT295** in Group C.

PT432 (P.146, context 2260)
Rim of corrugated cookpot
D.rim 15 cm   PL. 27

Sharply everted rim, slightly concave on upper surface, square-cut at lip. Outer surface brown, otherwise red.
Similar: rim, D. 18 cm.

PT433 (P.34, context 2139)
Rim of corrugated cookpot
D.rim 13 cm   PL. 27

Similar to the preceding. Red core and inner surface, brown on outside.

PT434 (P.25, context 2010)
Rim of corrugated cookpot
D.rim 14 cm   PL. 27

Sharply everted rim, straight and plain. One handle preserved. Mainly fired red but with some dark gray on part of outside.
Similar: rim, D. ca. 14 cm.
Cf. Harper 1980, fig. C, no. 54 (Dibsi Faraj).

PT435 (P.118, context 2023)
Small corrugated cookpot
D.rim 11.0 cm, D.max. 12.7 cm, H.est. 12.0 cm   PL. 27

Simple flaring rim without lid seating. One handle preserved. Red core and inside surface; patchy red to gray on outside.
Similar: 6 rims, D. 9–12 cm.

Cf. Dyson 1968, nos. 429–36 (Dura-Europos: white particles frequently noted; rim profiles not well drawn, but probably this generally simple type); Orssaud 1980, fig. 307, type 3a (Dèhes), attributed to the fifth–sixth centuries (hardly!).

PT436 (P.35, context 2139)
Cookpot with incurved, rolled rim
D. ca. 16 cm   PL. 27

Part of (globular, corrugated?) cookpot with no neck and with incurved rolled rim. Maroon throughout.

PT437 (P.119, context 2023)
Corrugated cookpot with inturned rim
D.rim (max.) 15.5 cm, D.max. 23.7 cm   PL. 27

Sharply incurved rim, angular on outside. Both handles preserved. Red core and inside surface; gray to brown on outside.
Possibly similar is Dyson 1968, fig. 19, type III D 3 (Dura-Europos: drawing not clear). Cf. also Northedge 1981, fig. 245.1 (River Quwaiq survey: Hammamat tomb group, together with types as **PT495**, **PT588** in Groups E and F); Gerber 1996, fig. 8.15 (Lidar Höyük survey), with Byzantine/Islamic material; Aubert 2002, figs. 5, 6, 12 (Beirut), Hellenistic. Williams 1989, no. 407 (Anemurium) is very like this in profile, though not in fabric (considered Cypriot, sixth–seventh centuries). The parallels quoted suggest that, although the context of the present piece should be sound for the third century A.D., something very similar recurs in the Late Imperial period. A complete cookpot, very similar in profile to **PT437**, was recovered from a seventh-century context in a cave on Cyprus (Catling and Dikigoropoulos 1970, fig. 3 no. 14), but with the handles attached below the rim. The Zeugma material suggests that there is a recognizable change of practice from handles between rim and shoulder in the Middle Imperial period, to handles placed wholly on the body in the Late Imperial period. (See groups E and F.)

- 208 unclassified body-sherds of globular corrugated cookpots.
- 8 body-sherds of corrugated cookpots, rather thicker-walled (up to 6 mm) and with broader corrugations (contexts 2039 and 2080): probably Late Imperial intrusions.

PT438 (P.26, context 2010)
Long-necked cookpot with wavy-line decoration

D.rim ca. 10 cm, D.max. ca. 18.5 cm   PL. 27

Part of globular (?) vessel with tall tapering neck (undifferentiated) and vertical bead rim. Vertical handle from rim to body; inscribed decoration of wavy lines from neck

down to maximum diameter. Fired gray throughout.
Similar: rim fragment with handle in Group F (p. 64).

PT439 (P.67, context 2039)
Long-necked cookpot with bead rim
D.rim 12.8 cm   PL. 27

Red core, red inner surface, dark brown on outside.
Similar: 2 rims, D. 9.5 cm (both), contexts 2039 and 2260. Possibly to be reconstructed as Dyson 1968, no. 440 (Dura-Europos), which is smoothly pear-shaped and without ribbing, with a recessed base as **PT319**. See also ibid., fig. 19, type III C 6. One handle only is indicated at Dura-Europos.

PT440 (P.68, context 2039)
Long-necked cookpot with bead rim
D.rim 7.5 cm   PL. 27

Smaller example of the preceding. Red core, red inner surface, gray on outside.
Similar: rim, D. 7 cm.

PT441 (P.125, context 2080)
Long-necked cookpot with vertical rim
D.rim 9.0 cm   PL. 27

Barely thickened lip; trace of handle attachment at rim; external corrugations begin at lower edge of sherd. Dark brown clay, fired dark gray on outside.

PT442 (P.49, context 2130)
Long-necked cookpot with bead rim.
D.rim 12 cm   PL. 27

Slightly incurving neck. Mainly red but fired gray-brown on the outside.
Similar: rim in this group (context 2012), D. ca. 12 cm; rim in Group F (p. 64), D. 10 cm.

PT443 (P.65, context 2039)
Globular cookpot with sharply down-turned rim
D.rim 17 cm   PL. 27

Red throughout, brown on outside surface.
Similar: rim, D. 20 cm (context 2012).
The contexts at Zeugma make this form slightly suspect for the third century, but Oates 1959, pl. 58.84 from Ain Sinu is part way between this and **PT430** and may indicate that it belongs here.

PT444 (P.72, context 2039)
Wide-mouthed jar or cookpot with almond rim
D.max. 15 cm   PL. 27

Red clay, fired black on outside.
Cf. Dorna-Metzger 1996, fig. 23 (Upper Khabur survey), citing Venco Ricciardi 1982, 67, fig. 47 (Tell Barri), "late Parthian-Roman period."

PT445 (P.66, context 2039)
Small globular jar or cookpot with plain everted rim
D.rim 10 cm   PL. 27

One handle preserved, on body; no corrugations on preserved part. Probably this fabric, hard and fired dark gray throughout. Intrusive?

PT446 (P.69, context 2039)
Thickened, bifurcated rim of jar
D.max. 8 cm   PL. 27

Trace of handle scar at rim on edge of sherd. Possibly belongs with **PT447**. Probably this fabric: fired dark gray throughout, only fine angular quartz sand visible.
Intrusive? Cf. Konrad 2001a, pl. 84.35 (Qusair as-Saila); Orssaud 1980, fig. 307, type 2 (Déhès); also **PT500** in Group E.

PT447 (P.70, context 2039)
Closed vessel with false ring-foot
D.base 5.5 cm   PL. 27

Possibly belongs with **PT446**. Dark gray throughout.

- 3 fragments of closed vessels with pinched spouts.
- 58 unclassified body-sherds.

COOKING WARE 2

PT448 (P.124, context 2080)
Part of cookpot with folded inturned rim
D.rim 21 cm   PL. 28

One handle preserved. Dark brown clay, fired dark gray on outside.
Cf. **PT296** in Group C.

- Small tubular spout: cf. **PT591** in Group F.

OTHER COOKING WARES

PT449 (P.147, context 2260)
Wide-mouthed jar or cookpot with lid seating
D.rim ca. 18 cm   PL. 28

Hooked rim; pronounced concave lid seating. Cooking 6: orange-brown clay, pink at surface.
Cf. Gerber 1996, fig. 5.8 (Lidar Höyük survey). This type of rim (related examples: figs. 1.20, 21; 10.5) is better represented around Lidar Höyük than at Zeugma. See also Wilkinson 1990, fig. B.19.12, 13 (Kürban Höyük survey: site 2, multi-period); fig. B.25.10 (site 8, ditto).

PT450 (P.128, context 2080)
Part of biconical cookpot (?)
D.max. 25 cm   PL. 28

Very uneven surfaces: made on a slow wheel. Granular brown clay with abundant fine rounded sand (feldspar) and abundant fine biotite mica, very noticeable at the surface. A dull red slip on the upper part of the inside, outside entirely black (firing or use?). This is a very distinctive non-Euphrates fabric, but its source cannot readily be identified petrographically. If it is to be identified with Group 2 of Bartl et al. (1995), it may have been made in the Habur Valley. (See the petrographic report by Doherty, this volume, pp. 89 and 90, questions 19 and 23).

PT451 (P.127, context 2080)
Rim of casserole
D. 22 cm   PL. 28

Slightly inflected vertical rim. Dense orange-brown clay containing moderate fine angular quartz and quartzite together with fine streaky black inclusions and moderate fine biotite mica. Fired brown at the surface, with a thin, mottled maroon coloring on the outside that may be a slip. Cf. **PT426**.

- 21 unclassified body-sherds of closed vessels, including 5 handles.

Storage Wares
STORAGE WARE 1

PT452 (P.252, SF 2067, context 2016)
Small globular two-handled pithos
D.rim 49.5 cm, D.max. 67.5 cm, H. 62 cm   FIG. 14, PL. 28

Reconstructed from fragments but largely complete. Found in situ in Room 2H of the House of the Helmets in Trench 2; the amphora **AM148** was found within it (see Tobin, volume 1, p. 80 and Plate 24). Made in two sections, the lower part having been allowed to dry and to gain strength before the upper part was added: It has separated extensively along the join, which shows regular finger indentations (clearly visible just above mid height in fig. 14). The simple rim is decorated on the outside with a band of circular finger impressions. Ring-foot. Pale gray clay, fired pink towards the outside, containing moderate inclusions up to 3 mm across of lime, quartz, and red earthy particles. Hackly break, very crumbly.

PT453 (P.116, context 2376)
Rim of decorated pithos
D.rim ca. 35 cm   PL. 28

Squat rolled rim with a narrow band of circular finger impressions on outer face; two lightly inscribed wavy lines on body. Trace of a handle attachment at left-hand edge of sherd. Coarse gray clay with various large subrounded or rounded inclusions: probably this fabric.

Figure 14. **PT452**, *reconstructed pithos from Room 2H of the House of the Helmets in Trench 2 (Group D).*

PT454 (P.101, SF 2329, context 2278)
Base of pithos
D.base 17 cm   PL. 28

Square-cut disc-base, very thin in the center. Pinkish-brown clay with abundant, ill-sorted angular inclusions of all sorts, up to 3 mm.
Similar: base, D. 20 cm.

PT455 (P.93, context 2039)
Disc-base of pithos
D.base 15.0 cm   PL. 28

Mainly pink; gray on inner surface.

PT456 (P.28, context 2010)
Knob-base of pithos
D.knob 16.2 cm   PL. 28

Pink clay, fired pale gray on inside; surfaces abraded.

PT457 (P.222, context 2191)
Knob-base of pithos
D.knob 11.9 cm   PL. 28

Granular gray clay, fired pink at surface, with abundant ill-sorted inclusions: lime, quartz, also gray and dark brown.
Similar: base.

- 5 body-sherds of pithoi in this ware.

STORAGE WARE 2

PT458 (P.94, joining sherds from contexts 2039 and 2012)
Ovoid wide-mouthed jar with hooked rim and horizontal loop-handles
D.rim 32 cm   PL. 29

Parts of two handles present. Fired a fairly uniform reddish-brown; surfaces wet-smoothed but very uneven.
Similar: 3 rims, D. 25–32 cm (all context 2012).

PT459 (P.596, context 2012)
Part of ovoid wide-mouthed jar with short almond rim
D.rim 28 cm   PL. 29

Typical hackly fabric, red to brown in the core, brown on the outside.
Similar: 4 rims, D. 20–28 cm (contexts 2010, 2012, 2039).

- 2 handles as **PT304** in Group C; 2 unclassified body-sherds (all context 2012).

STORAGE WARE 4

PT460 (P.148, context 2260)
Part of wide-mouthed pithos with heavy triangular rim
D.rim 72 cm   PL. 29

Raised facet on top of rim.

PT461 (P.593, context 2012)
Part of ovoid pithos with squat rolled rim
D.rim 33 cm   PL. 29

Brown core, pink towards surface, buff at surface. Appears to be this fabric but contains in addition some large red fragments of grog up to 12 mm.

UNCLASSIFIED STORAGE WARE

- 2 sherds of large cooking or storage vessel 7–8 mm thick, burnished and brown but rough on outside, black and extremely rough on inside. Brown to gray clay ("Storage 3"), extremely friable and rough to the touch; abundant angular or subrounded quartz, mostly about 1 mm, abundant fine muscovite mica, occasional other large dark grits.
- These two sherds were the only representatives of this distinctive fabric, which seemed possibly related to that of **PT450**; thin-section analysis showed, however, that this was illusory. (See the petrographic report by Doherty, this volume, p. 91, question 25.)

PT462–470 *vacant*

Group E: Early Sixth Century A.D.

The trenches yielded no contexts that could be securely dated between the mid-third century and the second half of the fifth. The very small quantity of residual pottery in later levels that could be dated to this period, together with a few coins, imply that occupation did continue, but on a significantly reduced scale.[92] The contexts assembled here offer a small, but reasonably coherent, sample of the pottery that was in use when the settlement began to expand once again around the beginning of the sixth century.

This group is composed of material from five contexts in two different trenches. Trench 4 was a very small excavation in the edge of the modern road (Tobin, volume 1, pp. 85–86) which revealed part of a limestone structure, possibly a stoa. It was covered by several layers of colluvium containing building debris and possible traces of burning, presumably related to its destruction or abandonment. Three of these layers (contexts 4004, 4008, and 4011) yielded pottery. The latest datable item was part of a dish in Cypriot Red Slip Ware from context 4004 (**PT477**), attributable to the late fifth or early sixth century. There were joins between sherds in 4008 and 4011.

In Trench 5 (Tobin, volume 1, pp. 91–93) were found traces of a Hellenistic or early Roman structure, followed after a long interval by renewed building activity in the Late Imperial period. The latest phase was built over, and cut into, the colluvial layers 5048 and 5078. The latest item in context 5048 was a rim of a dish in Phocaean Red Slip Ware (**PT472**) of the third quarter of the fifth century, but both layers are surely contemporary, and their terminal date must be placed in the early sixth century through the presence of a later rim in Phocaean Red Slip Ware (**PT473**) and of two fragments of Cypriot Red Slip Ware (**PT475, 476**).

The breakdown of the pottery in this group is as follows.

	No. of pieces	% of total no.	Weight (gm)	% of total weight
Hellenistic fine ware	2	1.7	31	0.4
African R.S. Ware	1	0.8	26	0.3
Phocaean R.S. Ware	5	4.1	97	1.1
Cypriot R.S. Ware	3	2.5	111	1.3
Total table wares	**11**	**9.1**	**265**	**3.1**
Buff wares	56	46.3	6,599	74.9
Cooking wares	53	43.8	1,793	20.3
Storage wares	1	0.8	155	1.8
TOTAL	121		8,812	

The most obvious development is the reemergence of table wares, represented essentially by imports of Phocaean and Cypriot Red Slip Ware. Large basins in buff ware are still present in this group (it was suggested, in regard to Group D, that in the Middle Imperial period these had perhaps replaced the use of individual dishes for communal eating) but there seems to have been some reversion towards earlier practices. Pot stands, on the other hand, were not recorded.

The buff wares are marked by the appearance on the scene of Buff 8, a hard-fired fabric used for amphorae,[93] smaller closed vessels, and the saucer-shaped amphora lids that are so characteristic of the Euphrates region in the Late Imperial period.[94] The amphorae regularly bear painted decoration, which also occurs on jugs with pinched spouts (see **PT572, 573** in Group F). These appear to be imports from northern Syria;[95] I have regarded the few pieces attested in Groups C and D as intrusive, though Catherine Abadie-Reynal informs me that they are present in a fourth-century context in Trench 14 (pers. comm., context 14075: see now Abadie-Reynal et al. 2007).

There are also unpainted narrow-necked flagons in the same (or a very similar) ware with combed decoration on the body in the form of arcs and patterns of prick marks. These are distinguished by the high quality of their potting (fine detailing of moldings, smooth surface finish). A body-sherd from Group E (**PT491**) may demonstrate that these vessels were already being made in the early sixth century, unless it is intrusive. They are much more common in Group F (see **PT562–566**) and the largest single fragment is listed in Group G (**PT628**); parallels from elsewhere are generally Islamic in date (see under **PT628**).

The cooking wares are more diverse in fabric than in Group D: Cooking 1 (12 sherds) is now outnumbered by more than 2:1 by Cooking 2 (28 sherds), and Cooking 9 (11 sherds) makes its first (and most prolific) appearance. The shapes, however, are more limited: The pans and casseroles have entirely disappeared and the only cooking vessels attested are cookpots. While these are still globular, and mostly thin-walled and corrugated, the flaring rims of the earlier period have been replaced by more or less cylindrical necks and molded rims; the handles are placed entirely on the body instead of being attached to the rim.

Table Wares

LOCAL HELLENISTIC FINE WARE

- 2 bases of bowls.

AFRICAN RED SLIP WARE

- Fragment of dish or bowl with flat rim, fourth–seventh century fabric.

PHOCAEAN RED SLIP WARE

PT471 (P.488, context 5078)
Part of dish with vertical flanged rim
D. (top of rim) 32 cm   PL. 30

Hayes 1972 ('Late Roman C') Form 3C: third quarter of fifth century; Pröttel 1996, 90: ca. 450–500.

PT472 (P.474, context 5048)
Rim of dish, similar to the preceding
D. ca. 28 cm   PL. 30

PT473 (P.489, context 5078)
Part of dish with short flanged rim
D. (top of rim) 22 cm   PL. 30

Similar: 2 rims in Group F (p. 58), D. 29, 31 cm. Hayes 1972 (Late Roman C) Form 3F: first half of sixth century.

PT474 (P.475, context 5048)
Base of small dish
D.foot 7.0 cm   PL. 30

Similar: base.

CYPRIOT RED SLIP WARE

PT475 (P.490, context 5078)
Part of dish with multiple rouletting on wall and grooved rim
D. 27 cm   PL. 30

Pinkish-brown clay, barely lustrous slip.
Hayes 1972, Form 2: late fifth/early sixth century.

PT476 (P.491, context 5078)
Base of dish corresponding to the preceding
D.foot 17 cm   PL. 30

Fine orange clay, dull red slip.

PT477 (P.459, context 4004)
Rim of dish, smaller example of the preceding
D. 14.5 cm   PL. 30

Fine, hard brown clay without visible inclusions; barely lustrous pinkish-brown slip.

Buff Wares

The buff-ware basins that occur in this group (in several fabrics) show a distinct evolution from those that characterize Group D (**PT346–351**): The slightly concave upper surface to the rim has disappeared, and the rim has a simpler convex profile.

BUFF WARE 1–3

- Buff 1: sloping rim of basin as **PT352** (intrusive in Group D).
- Buff 1: tapering rim of basin as **PT353** (intrusive in Group D?).

PT478 (P.460, context 4004)
Conical basin with flaring, down-turned rim
D. ca. 48 cm   PL. 30

Buff 1: pinkish-buff throughout.
Similar: rim fragment in Group F (p. 59). Cf. Wilkinson 1990, fig. B.22.38 (Kürban Höyük survey: site 7, multi-period).

PT479 (P.478, context 5048)
Basin with short convex rim
D. ca. 42 cm   PL. 30

Buff 1: pinkish-buff clay, paler at surface; wet-smoothed.
Similar: rim fragment in this group, more sharply down turned; rim in Group F (p. 59), D. 49 cm.
See also **PT493** in Buff 15. Cf. Konrad 1992, fig. 15.3 (Rusafa: context of 475–518).

- Buff 1: part of conical basin with flat base.

Amphora lids, which make their first appearance in this group, are found in a variety of buff wares, but predominantly in Buff 8. It is logical to associate their introduction with that of the painted amphorae in the same ware (Reynolds, this volume, Forms 15–17), though the local potters clearly incorporated the form into their own repertoire very quickly. They display considerable variety in detail, which almost defies classification. The rims vary from very simple (as **PT480**) to highly decorative, with grooves, oblique slashes, or frilled edges (see **PT540–542**, **PT579** in Group F). It has been suggested by others that the more elaborate lids are later: All that one can point to in the present material is the absence of frilled rims with finger impressions from Group E. The lids seem to occur equally with and without central knobs. The knob identifies the type unequivocally as a lid, though those examples without them could clearly have served other purposes as well.

Like so many of the other forms at Zeugma, these lids seem to be largely specific to sites within reach of the Euphrates. Fragmentary knobbed amphora lids are attested at Tarsus (Jones 1950, fig. 210.D–K, illustrated but not described), but they do not appear to have been accompanied by the corresponding amphorae. At Raqqa, on the other hand, there are knobbed lids, many of them up to 25 cm in diameter, continuing well into the Islamic period (Miglus et al. 1999, groups AX/AY).

PT480 (P.495, context 5078)
Rim of amphora lid
D. 14.5 cm   PL. 30

Simple flaring rim, flat on top. Buff 1: buff throughout, some blackening on underside of rim. Rather rough surfaces.
Similar: rim in Group F (p. 59), D. 13 cm (red clay, possibly Buff 2).
Cf. Konrad 2001a, pl. 99.7 (Qusair as-Saila).

PT481 (P.481, context 5048)
Central knob of amphora lid, recessed top   PL. 30

Buff 1: fairly soft-fired orange-pink clay, inclusions sparse.
Similar: 3 bases with knobs, Buff 1 or 2.

- Buff 1: base of knobbed amphora lid as **PT538** in Group F (i.e., with domed knob).
- Buff 1: knob fragment, unclassified.
- Buff 1? Rim/handle of flagon as **PT490** in Buff 8.

PT482 (P.482, context 5048)
Small flagon or jar with inset vertical rim
D.rim 12 cm, D.max. 17 cm   PL. 30

Buff 3: buff clay, not fused; fired cream on outside; perhaps a thin brown wash on inside and top of rim. It is possible that this is a section of water pipe, but it does seem to be curving inwards at the lower edge.

- Buff 3: base of closed vessel as **PT385** in Group D.
- Buff 3: sherd of globular vessel as **PT572** in Group F, with brown-painted swirls on shoulder. Buff clay, much finer than Buff 8; the usual mixed inclusions, but sparse and very fine. Fired cream on outside.

BUFF WARE 6

PT483 (P.477, context 5048)
Basin with short convex rim and flat base
D. 37.5, H. 12.6 cm   PL. 30

Hard cream clay. Cf. **PT479**.

BUFF WARE 8

PT484 (P.466, context 4008)
Amphora lid with grooved rim
D. 12.0 cm   PL. 31

Rather fine, hard, gray-buff clay with few inclusions: presumably this fabric.
Cf. Bartl 1996, fig. 2.7 (Balih Valley survey); Miglus et al. 1999, group J as pl. 7j and 22e–o (Raqqa). Not very common at Raqqa, almost exclusively in Horizon III (last quarter of eighth century), regularly distinguished by concentric grooves on rim crossed by oblique slashes.

PT485 (P.480, context 5048)
Knobless amphora lid
D. 13.3 cm, H. 4.0 cm   PL. 31

Hard cream clay.
Similar: 2 rims in Group F (p. 62), D. 12, 14 cm.
Cf. Gerber 1996, fig. 4.18 (Lidar Höyük survey); Konrad 2001a, pl. 106.4 (Qusair as-Saila: light finger-depressions around rim).

PT486 (P.493, context 5078)
Knobless amphora-lid
D. 12.0 cm, H. 4.0 cm   PL. 31

Hard cream clay.
Similar: intact example, 13.0 × 4.7 cm, and a further rim in Group F (p. 62), D. 14 cm.

PT487 (P.494, context 5078)
Rim of amphora lid
D. 13.5 cm
PL. 31

Hard cream clay.
Similar: 3 rims in Group F (p. 62), D. 12.8–13.8 cm.
Cf. Bartl 1996, fig. 2.9 (Balih Valley survey).

- 3 centers of knobbed amphora lids, knob as **PT538** in Group F.

PT488 (P.461, context 4008)
Narrow-necked flagon with painted decoration
D.neck 3.7 cm
PL. 31

Mouth badly abraded: rim probably missing. Traces of dark brown painted crescents on shoulder. Hard pink to buff clay, fired cream on outside; rough finish.

PT489 (P.463, joining sherds from contexts 4008 and 4011)
Globular one-handled flagon
D.rim 9.4 cm, D.max. 22.3 cm
PL. 31

Slight horizontal ribs on neck, multiple grooves on shoulder. Pink clay, fired cream on most of outside.
Similar: rim in Group F (p. 63), D. 7.4 cm.

PT490 (P.462, context 4008)
Flagon with stepped, flaring rim
D.rim 10.5 cm
PL. 31

Presence of second handle uncertain. Hard brown clay, buff on outside; no mica visible.
Similar: rim/handle, D. ca. 13, Buff 1?

PT491 (P.483, context 5048)
Part of globular vessel with combed and pricked decoration
D. at lower edge of sherd ca. 20 cm
PL. 31

Decoration (but not horizontal grooves above) executed with a 4-pronged comb. Orange-pink clay with fused matrix and typical inclusions, patches fired buff on outside. Cf. **PT628** in Group G. See also the general discussion at the head of this group.

PT492 (P.464, context 4008)
Part of closed vessel with false ring-foot
D.base 8.7 cm
PL. 31

Pinkish-buff clay, fired cream on outside.
Similar: base in Group F (p. 61), D. 8.5 cm.

- 2 bases of closed vessels as **PT573** in Group F.
- Body-sherd of closed vessel and 2 handles of small jugs or flagons.

BUFF WARE 13

- 2 rims of conical basins as **PT352** (intrusive in Group D).

BUFF WARE 15

PT493 (P.479, context 5048)
Part of basin with convex rim
D. 47 cm
PL. 31

Buff clay, inclusions sparse, cream at surface.
Similar: rim fragment in Group D (p. 47, intrusive); 5 rims in Group F (pp. 59, 64), D. ca. 35–54 cm, Buff 3 (1) and 15 (4).
Cf. **PT479** in Buff 1.

PT494 (P.492, context 5078)
Part of basin with short convex rim
D. ca. 40 cm
PL. 31

Buff clay, wet-smoothed.
Similar: 5 rims in Group F (pp. 59, 64), D. 34–44 cm.

- Flat base-sherd of basin.

MISCELLANEOUS BUFF WARES

- 15 unclassified body-sherds.

Cooking Wares
COOKING WARE 1

- Part of bowl with incurving rim as **PT420** in Group D.

PT495 (P.484, context 5048)
Part of globular cookpot with inset rolled rim
D.rim 14 cm
PL. 32

Red clay, gray on outside surface.
Similar: 2 rims, D. 12, 13 cm, this fabric; rim, D. 13 cm, Cooking 2.
Cf. Northedge 1981, fig. 245.2 (River Quwaiq survey). For the difficulty in reconciling the related rims **PT194–197**, well-attested in the first century A.D. in Group B, with **PT495–497**, equally well-attested in Late Imperial levels, see above, p. 24 (**PT194**).

PT496 (P.485, context 5048)
Corrugated cookpot with short everted rim
D.rim ca. 18 cm
PL. 32

Red clay, fired brownish-buff on outside. Inclusions normal.
Cf. **PT194**; **PT496** is the only rim of this type to show definite evidence of corrugations on the body.

- 6 body-sherds of corrugated cookpots, one handle fragment.

COOKING WARE 2

- Rim of globular cookpot as **PT495** above.

PT497 (P.486, context 5048)
Small cookpot with everted rim
D.rim 10.5 cm   PL. 32

Rather clean, hard red clay, but the only visible inclusions are probably quartz; fired dark gray at surface.

PT498 (P.487, context 5048)
Cookpot with short tapering neck and bead rim
D.rim ca. 12 cm   PL. 32

Small fragment, angle uncertain. Red clay, black on outside.

PT499 (P.496, context 5078)
Part of globular corrugated cookpot with handle on shoulder   PL. 32

Fine red clay, fired purplish-brown on outside.
Cf. Orssaud 1980, fig. 307, type 5b (Déhès: "apparaît au cours du VIe s.").

PT500 (P.470, context 4011)
Cookpot with tall neck and inset rim
D.rim (max.) 10.8 cm   PL. 32

Red core, dark gray at surface, with occasional specks of lime.
Similar: 2 rims in Group F (p. 65), D. 12 cm.
Cf. Konrad 2001a, pl. 84.23, 34 (Qusair as-Saila), possibly this fabric, Islamic?

- 5 handle fragments and 18 body-sherds of (corrugated) cookpots.

OTHER COOKING WARES

PT501 (P.469, context 4008)
Body with handle of globular cookpot
D.max. ca. 19 cm   PL. 32

Vertical handle on shoulder (two assumed); broad tentative corrugations begin at mid-height. Cooking 6.

PT502 (P.476, SF 752, context 4011)
Large pedestal base (?)
D.base 6.5 cm   PL. 32

Cooking 7: gray core, buff at surface with black specks. Appears to be this fabric. This is presumably a base: it seems rather too large for a handle.

PT503 (P.468, context 4008)
Cookpot with cylindrical neck and everted lip
D.rim 11.5 cm   PL. 32

Cooking 9.
Similar: rim in this group, D. 13 cm; Rim in Group F (p. 66), more or less this type (plainer), D. 9 cm.

PT504 (P.471, context 4011)
Globular cookpot with cylindrical neck and bead rim
D.rim 13 cm   PL. 32

Three nonjoining fragments. Cooking 9: gray on inside, pinkish-red on outside; some darkening on lower part of outside (cooking?).
Similar: rim, D. 12.5 cm; handle fragment and body-sherd with handle in Group F (p. 66).
Cf. Konrad 2001a, pl. 84.29 (Qusair as-Saila: white and black inclusions), late Roman–Islamic.

- Cooking 9: 7 sherds of globular cookpots, thick-walled (ca. 7 mm) and not corrugated.

STORAGE WARES

PT505 (P.472, context 4011)
Handle of large jar   PL. 32
Angle uncertain; diameter unknown but large. Storage 5: gray core, pink inner surface, pale gray outer surface.

PT506–510 *vacant*

Group F: Early Seventh Century A.D.

Pottery from two trenches has been conflated to create this group. The dating evidence from both is broadly similar, and I have no hesitation in regarding them as contemporary (at least in ceramic terms).

In Trench 7B a Late Imperial house of perhaps the early fifth century A.D. was overlaid by extensive layers of burnt destruction and collapse.[96] The pottery in the latest "occupation" levels was identical to that contained in the overlying layers, and both contained an unusual number of largely complete vessels. It seems that, at the time of abandonment/destruction, these vessels must have remained in the building: Those in the upper destruction debris had presumably fallen from an upper floor. (There were no examples of well-preserved items of fine ware: were these removed because they were of higher value?) The relevant contexts were the following:

Occupation:	7036	7076
	7062	7203
	7065	7214
	7066	
Destruction:	7005	7026

The pottery was broadly similar to that already encountered in Group E, but there is a clear change in the Phocaean Red Slip Ware. Hayes 1972 ('Late Roman C') Form 3F was the latest form attested in Group E; the fine ware of the present group is dominated by Hayes Form 10, including the latest variant, 10C (see **PT527**). This is placed by Hayes in the early to mid-seventh century, while Pröttel suggests a slightly earlier introduction, ca. 580.[97]

The second body of material included in this group comes from Trench 12.[98] This was a small trench, whose structures and chronology were difficult to interpret. The latest levels were composed of several layers of colluvium, of which 12012, 12011, and 12002 yielded pottery; they also yielded several sixth-century coins, possibly a dispersed hoard.[99] The majority of the datable pottery is attributable to the first half of the sixth century (typically Hayes Form 3F in Phocaean Red Slip Ware), but there are again rims of Hayes Form 10C in Phocaean Red Slip Ware, together with pieces of African Red Slip Ware (almost the only significant concentration of this ware) of the later sixth and early seventh centuries (**PT513–515**). It might be argued that occupation in this trench came to an end in the mid-sixth century, but if so, there is certainly an element of later activity.

The breakdown of the pottery in this group is as follows:

	No. of pieces	% of total no.	Weight (gm)	% of total weight
Hellenistic fine ware	14	2.3	219	0.6
Eastern Sigillata A	7	1.1	36	0.1
African R.S. Ware	11	1.8	443	1.1
Phocaean R.S. Ware	80	12.9	2,025	5.2
Cypriot R.S. Ware	1	0.2	11	0.0
Total table wares	113	18.3	2,734	7.0
Buff wares	345	55.6	31,768	81.9
Cooking wares	160	25.8	3,672	9.5
Storage wares	2	0.3	600	1.5
TOTAL	620		38,774	

The table ware in use at this time is mainly Phocaean Red Slip Ware, with a minor presence of the latest African products; the Cypriot Red Slip that was present in the previous group makes no impact here. Amongst the buff wares, there is naturally rather more variety than in the smaller Group E, though their character is much the same. The large conical basins continue, alongside some smaller, thinner-walled bowls. There are also in this group some small handle-less jars, heavily and crudely made (**PT550, 581, 582**), indeed so solid that they tend to be preserved intact. The amphora lids first encountered in Group E are prolific, and there are several largely complete examples of small jugs with painted decoration in North Syrian fabric (Buff ware 8: nos. **PT572, 573**). The same type is also represented in the local buff ware (**PT547**). A narrow-necked flagon in Buff ware 8 was recorded in Group E (**PT488**): Now we see a number of variously inflected narrow flagon mouths in the same ware.

The two principal cooking wares are still both represented, but Cooking 1 (26 sherds) is now heavily outnumbered by Cooking 2 (126 sherds). Much of the former is probably residual, but the fact that it is still in production is indicated by the shape of **PT584**, with the handles placed on the body of the vessel rather than descending from the rim (as seen already in **PT499, 504** in Group E).

Table Wares

LOCAL HELLENISTIC FINE WARE

- 14 sherds, unclassified.

EASTERN SIGILLATA A

- Part of dish with simple upcurving rim as **PT101** in Group B.
- 6 sherds, unclassified.

AFRICAN RED SLIP WARE

PT511 (P.549, context 12011)
Part of (flat-based) dish with offset vertical rim
D. ca. 42 cm   PL. 33

Burnished semilustrous slip on inside and over rim.
Similar: rim fragment of approximately similar form, but in a fine orange-buff clay as Buff ware 13, with a thin red slip that is dull on the outside but burnished on the inside.
Hayes 1972, Form 61B: from ca. 360/370 (Pröttel 1996, 56).

- 2 sherds of flanged bowls, Hayes 1972, Form 91A or B (context 12002): ca. 400–500+ (Pröttel 1996, 50).

PT512 (P.517, context 7214)
Small bowl with hooked rim
D. 17 cm   PL. 33

Hard, finely granular red clay with barely lustrous slip on inside and over rim.
Hayes 1972, Form 80B/99; Mackensen 1993, Form 28.1 (Period 4a: first half of sixth century).

- Ring-foot of bowl, probably Hayes 1972, Form 99, entirely gray (burnt?) (context 12011): ca. 480/490–650 (Pröttel 1996, 55).

PT513 (P.550, context 12011)
Knobbed rim of dish
D. ca. 33 cm   PL. 33

Barely lustrous burnished slip on inside and over rim.
Similar: rim, probably part of the same vessel (context 12002).
Hayes 1972, Form 104C: ca. 580–640 (Pröttel 1996, 53).

PT514 (P.552, context 12011)
Base of dish with low triangular foot
D. foot 11.5 cm   PL. 33

Traces only of a large stamped motif in center (very poorly impressed). Semilustrous slip on inside only.
Hayes 1972, Form 104B? From ca. 500 (Pröttel 1996, 53).

PT515 (P.551, context 12011)
Part of bowl with flat rim, rolled beneath
D. ca. 30 cm   PL. 33

Barely lustrous slip on inside and over rim.
Hayes 1972, Form 107: ca. 600–650.

- 1 unclassified body-sherd.

PHOCAEAN RED SLIP WARE

PT516 (P.528, context 12012)
Part of dish with flanged rim, rolled beneath; three light bands of rouletting on outer face
D. 28 cm   PL. 33

Similar: 3 rims, D. 23, 24, 28, (two in 12011, one in 12012) one of them perhaps part of the illustrated vessel.
Hayes 1972 ('Late Roman C') Form 3D: second half of fifth century (Pröttel 1996, 90).

PT517 (P.529, context 12012)
Part of dish with short flanged rim
D. 23 cm   PL. 33

Unusually ribbed underside.
Hayes 1972 ('Late Roman C') Form 3F: first half of sixth century.

PT518 (P.530, context 12012)
Part of dish with short flanged rim
D. 24 cm   PL. 33

Similar: 8 rims, D. 22–26 cm (6 in 12011, 2 in 12012).
Hayes Form 3F, as the preceding.

PT519 (P.531, context 12012)
Part of dish with short flanged rim
D. 22 cm   PL. 33

Similar: rim, D. 24 cm (12011).
Hayes Form 3F, as the preceding.

- 2 rims of dishes, Hayes Form 3F, as **PT473** in Group E (context 12002).

PT520 (P.554, context 12011)
Part of dish with inturned, square-cut rim
D.max. 26 cm   PL. 33

Hayes Form 3G: dated ca. 500–560 by Pröttel (1996, 90) and apparently common in the mid-sixth century at Butrint (Reynolds, pers. comm.: see also Reynolds 2002, 224, fig. 22.16).

PT521 (P.553, context 12011)
Part of dish with faceted, knobbed rim
D. 21 cm   PL. 33

Hayes 1972 ('Late Roman C') Form 6: early sixth century.

PT522 (P.555, context 12011)
Part of dish with knobbed rim
D. 26.5 cm   PL. 33

Similar: 5 rims, D. 19, 27–30 cm (12011). Hayes 1972 ('Late Roman C') Form 10A: ca. 550 to early seventh century (Pröttel 1996, 92).

PT523 (P.512, context 7066)
Part of dish with knobbed rim
D. ca. 24 cm   PL. 33

Hayes Form 10A, as the preceding.

PT524 (P.518, context 7214)
Part of dish with knobbed rim
D. 25 cm   PL. 33

Similar: 2 rim-fragments (7036, 12002).
Hayes Form 10A, as the preceding.

PT525 (P.497, 3 nonjoining sherds from context 7005)
Dish with elongated knobbed rim
D. 28 cm   PL. 33

Hayes 1972 ('Late Roman C') Form 10B: ca. 550 to early seventh century (Pröttel 1996, 92).

PT526 (P.578, context 12002)
Dish with elongated knobbed rim
D. 28 cm   PL. 33

Similar: rim D. 28 cm (12002).
Hayes Form 10B, as the preceding.

PT527 (P.499, context 7026)
Dish with elongated knobbed rim, slightly concave on top
D. 20.4 cm   PL. 33

Similar: 5 rims, D. 25, ? cm (2 in 7066, 3 in 7214).
Hayes 1972 ('Late Roman C') Form 10C: ca. 580–660+ (Pröttel 1996, 92).

PT528 (P.532, context 12012)
Dish with elongated knobbed rim
D. 23.5 cm   PL. 33

Similar: 4 rims, D. 21, 27 cm (1 in 12002, 3 in 12011).
Hayes Form 10C, as the preceding.

- 36 sherds, unclassified.

CYPRIOT RED SLIP WARE

- Sherd of dish with rouletting on wall.

Buff Wares
BUFF WARES 1–4

PT529 (P.537, context 12012)
Part of dish with hooked triangular rim
D.max. 29 cm   PL. 34

Buff 1: orange-buff throughout.
Cf. Orssaud 1980, fig.306.2 (Déhès: no fabric described or date suggested).

- Buff 1: rim of curving bowl as **PT335** in Group D (context 12012).

PT530 (P.560, context 12011)
Bowl with plain vertical rim
D. 21 cm   PL. 34

Buff 1: fired orange-buff.
Similar: rim fragment (12012).

PT531 (P.557, context 12011)
Bowl with molded rim
D. ca. 21 cm   PL. 34

Buff 1: orange-buff clay, buff at surface.
Similar: rim, D. 18 cm (12011).
Cf. Konrad 2001a, pl. 98.7 (Qusair as-Saila: third century through to Umayyad); Gerber 1996, fig. 6.12 (Lidar Höyük survey: more angular), with Byzantine/Islamic material; Konrad 1992, fig. 18.4–6 (Rusafa: context, 475–518). See also **PT336** in Group D.

PT532 (P.561, context 12011)
Part of bowl with concave vertical rim
D. 25 cm   PL. 34

Buff 1: orange-buff clay, paler at surface.
Cf. Konrad 2001a, pl. 96.10 (Qusair as-Saila: fifth–sixth century); Konrad 1992, fig. 17.8 (Rusafa: context, 475–518).

- Buff 1: part of basin with short, angular, sloping rim as **PT345** in Group D (context 12012).

PT533 (P.559, context 12011)
Steep conical basin with short everted rim
D. 31 cm   PL. 34

Two nonjoining fragments. Buff 3: buff clay, well-smoothed inside and out.

PT534 (P.558, context 12011)
Part of conical basin with bead rim
D. 37 cm   PL. 34

Buff 3: buff clay, paler at surface.

- Buff 1: 3 rims of conical basin with sloping rim as **PT352** (intrusive in Group D) (context 12011).
- Buff 4: rim of basin with flaring down-turned rim as **PT478** in Group E (context 12011).
- Buff 1: rim of basin with short convex rim as **PT479** in Group E (context 12012).
- Buff 3: rim of basin with convex rim as **PT493** in Group E (context 12011).
- Buff 1: 2 rims of basin with short convex rim as **PT494** in Group E (context 12012).

PT535 (P.535, context 12012)
Basin with broad convex rim
D. 52 cm   PL. 33

Buff 1: pink clay, fired cream at surface in parts.
Cf. Konrad 2001a, pl. 92.6 (Qusair as-Saila: contexts of early to mid-sixth century).

PT536 (P.536, context 12012)
Part of basin or mortarium with flaring rim and finger-impressed decoration
D. ca. 42 cm   PL. 34

Applied strip of clay on top of rim with finger impressions; this appears to turn outwards (to form a spout?) at edge of sherd. Buff 1: fired buff throughout.
Cf. Gerber 1996, figs. 6.13, 8.18 (Lidar Höyük survey), with Byzantine/Islamic material.

PT537 (P.556, context 12011)
Part of basin with convex down-turned rim
D. 44 cm   PL. 34

Buff 3: fired orange-buff.

- Buff 2? Rim of amphora lid in red clay as **PT480** in Group E (context 12011).

PT538 (P.523, SF 649b, context 7065)
Knobbed amphora lid
D. 13.2 cm, H. 4.3 cm   PL. 34

Flat rim, slightly concave on top. Intact. Buff 1: pink core, buff surface.
Similar: 4 bases with domed knob in Group E (pp. 54, 55), Buff 1 and 8; 20 bases with domed knobs in this group, mainly Buff 8 (4 in 12002, 9 in 12011, 7 in 12012).
Cf. Konrad 2001a, pl. 99.1 (rim); 106.6 (with knob) (Qusair as-Saila); Orssaud 1980, fig. 309.2 (Déhès); Harper 1980, fig. E, no. 72 (Dibsi Faraj); Gerber 1996, fig. 3.1 (Lidar Höyük

Figure 15. PT544, *perforated conical lid in Buff ware 3 from Group F.*

survey). Wilkinson 1990, fig. B.16.1 (Kürban Höyük survey: site 3) is a rim with combed band and oblique slashes; fig. B.28.54 (field scatter) is a fragment with a central knob.

- Buff 1: knob of amphora lid, cut down to a smaller size (SF 644, context 7062).

PT539 (P.505, SF 660, context 7062)
Knobless amphora lid
D. 13.0 cm, H. 5.2 cm   PL. 34

Uneven base, rim similar to the preceding. Nearly complete. Buff 1: pinkish-buff clay, fairly soft-fired.
Similar: 4 rims in Buff 1 and 8, D. 12.5–18.5 cm (1 in 7065, 2 in 12011, 1 in 12012).
Konrad 1992, fig. 19 shows a wide variety of knobless amphora lids from Rusafa.

PT540 (P.564, context 12011)
Part of amphora lid with decorated rim
D. 13.8 cm   PL. 34

Finger impressions around outer edge of rim. Buff 1: orange-buff clay, paler at surface.
Similar: 2 rims in Buff 1 and 8, D. 14, 16 cm (12011).
Qusair as-Saila: Konrad 2001a, pl. 106.7. Lidar Höyük area: Gerber 1996, figs. 3.5, 10.3. Kürban Höyük survey: Wilkinson 1990, fig. B.25.11 (site 8, multiperiod).

PT541 (P.534, context 12012)
Part of amphora lid with decorated rim
D. 15 cm, H. 4.3 cm   PL. 34

Finger impressions around outer edge of rim; high inner lip. Presumably without knob. Buff 3: pink clay, buff at surface.

Cf. Konrad 1992, fig. 19.4 (Rusafa: context, 475–518); Konrad 2001a, pl. 98.18; 113.15 (Qusair as-Saila: context, late sixth/early seventh century); 114.C4 (context, second half of sixth century).

PT542 (P.562, context 12011)
Part of amphora lid with decorated rim
D.max. 15 cm   PL. 34

Tapered and sharply inturned rim with finger impressions around outer edge. Buff 1: buff clay, cream at surface.
Cf. Konrad 2001a, pl. 78.8 and 114.B4, the only example from Qusair as-Saila that is sharply inturned on the inside (context, first half of seventh century); Gerber 1996, fig. 5.5 (Lidar Höyük survey: similar profile, but plain).

PT543 (P.565, context 12011)
Rim of shallow conical lid
D. 17 cm   PL. 34

Buff 1: pinkish-buff clay.

PT544 (P.521, SF 500, context 7036)
Perforated conical lid
D. 19.4 cm, H. 12.3 cm   FIG. 15, PL. 34

Four holes around circumference, central vent through knob. Complete. Buff 3: hard, granular buff clay. Typical inclusions but very sparse.

PT545 (P.543, context 12012)
Part of flagon with everted rim
D. 12 cm   PL. 34

Buff 1: orange-red clay, pink at surface. Carefully smoothed.

PT546 (P.570, context 12011)
Part of long-necked flagon with plain rim
D.rim 10 cm   PL. 34

Buff 1: brown clay, grayish-buff at surface.

PT547 (P.599, SF 655b, context 7076)
Biconical jug with pinched spout
D.max. 12.6 cm, H. 16.6 cm   FIG. 16, PL. 34

Light ridges on neck; broad groove between shoulder and body, thick, heavy base. Almost intact.
Buff 1: buff throughout.
Similar: handle, Buff 2 (7076).

PT548 (P.544, context 12012)
Rim of small jar
D.rim 10 cm   PL. 34

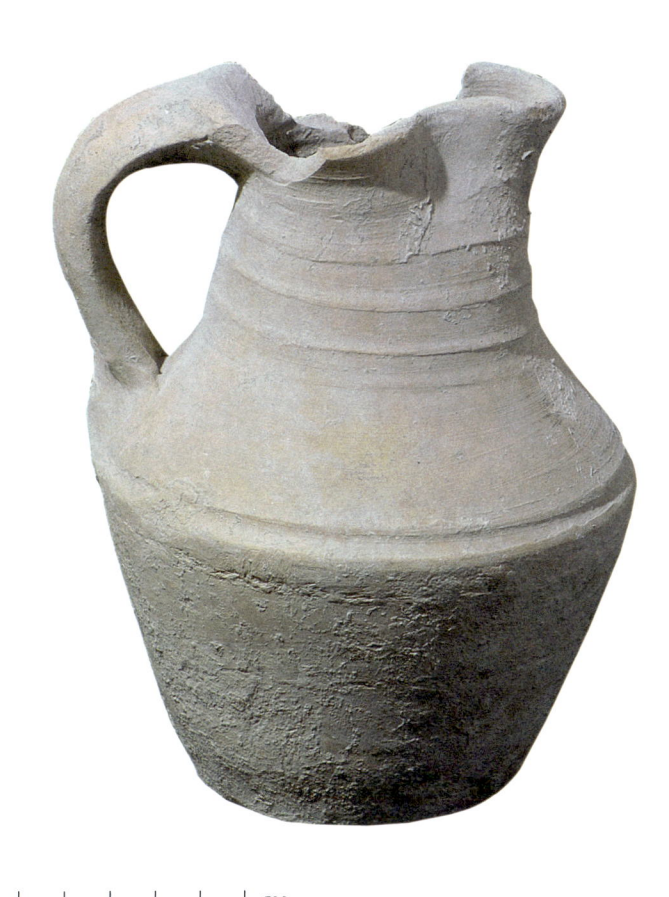

Figure 16. **PT547**, *jug with pinched spout in Buff ware 1 from Group F.*

One handle preserved. Buff 3? Gray-buff clay, sparse mixed inclusions, no mica visible.

PT549 (P.545, context 12012)
Rim of small jar
D.rim ca. 5.5 cm   PL. 34

Surely only one handle. Buff 4: very gritty buff clay, worn abrasive surfaces.

PT550 (P.507, SF 647, context 7062)
Small handle-less jar
D. 10.2 cm, H. 8.7 cm   PL. 34

Everted rim, thick string-cut base. Almost complete. Buff 1: fired buff throughout.
Similar: rim D. 9 cm, Buff 13 (12011).
Cf. **PT581, 582**; Miglus et al. 1999, group L as pl. 23p, u (Raqqa: very rare).

PT551 (P.566, context 12011)
Part of jar with angular shoulder and inset rim
D.rim 14 cm   PL. 34

Stabbed decoration at angle. Buff 3: fired buff.

- Buff 1: base of closed vessel as **PT385** in Group D (context 12002).
- Buff 1: base of closed vessel as **PT492** in Group E (context 12011).

PT552 (P.541, context 12012)
Part of closed vessel with flat base
D.base 3.8 cm   PL. 34

Buff 1: buff clay, rough finish.
Similar: 2 bases, Buff 8 (12011).

- Buff 1: 3 heavy bases of closed vessels as **PT580** (1 in context 12002, 2 in 12012).

PT553 (P.574, context 12011)
Flanged base of closed vessel (?)
D.base 8.8 cm   PL. 34

Buff 1: pinkish-buff clay, paler on outside.
Possibly residual: cf. **PT239** in local Hellenistic fine ware (Group C) and Oates 1959, pl. 56.39 (Ain Sinu, buff ware).

PT554 (P.573, context 12011)
Tall pedestal base
D.base 5.3 cm   PL. 35

Clearly opens out into some sort of turned vessel above (not a pan handle). Buff 3: orange clay; occasional specks of lime up to 2 mm prominent at surface. Crude potting. Cf. **PT577**.

PT555 (P.547, context 12012)
Part of zoomorphic vessel (?)
D. of closed end 6 cm   PL. 35

Turned as a closed vessel, but two attached projections near the base seem only intelligible as legs. Buff 1: buff to pink clay, fired buff on outside.
This vessel is closely paralleled by two complete examples of one-handled jugs in el-Aouja ware of the mid-third century from central Tunisia, interpreted as imitating animal skins. See J. W. Salomonson, "Kännchen in der Form eines Tierbalgs-askos," *BABesch* 50 (1975): 37f.; P. La Baume and J. W. Salomonson, *Römische Kleinkunst: Sammlung Karl Löffler* (Köln 1976: Römisch-Germanisches Museum), no. 592.

PT556 (P.546, context 12012)
Part of colander (?)
D.max. 15 cm   PL. 35

Two rows of holes punched through roughly from the outside before firing. Buff 1: buff clay, cream at surface.
Cf. Dyson 1968, nos. 315, 316 (Dura-Europos: flaring rim).

BUFF WARE 8

PT557 (P.538, context 12012)
Rim of small hemisperical cup
D. 9 cm   PL. 35

Orange clay, cream at surface.

- 2 rims of amphora lids as **PT485** in Group E (contexts 12011, 12012).

PT558 (P.502, context 7036)
Knobbed amphora lid
D. 12.4 cm, H. 4.4 cm   PL. 35

Sloping rim, slightly concave on top. Largely intact. Gray-green clay but surely this fabric (overfired?); poorly shaped. Similar: complete example in Buff 8, 14.2 × 4.9 cm (SF 741, context 7076); rim in Buff 13, D. 12.5 cm (12002).

- 20 knobbed bases of amphora lids as **PT538**, mostly this fabric (4 in context 12002, 9 in 12011, 7 in 12012).
- Rim of amphora lid as **PT539** (context 12012).
- Rim of amphora lid as **PT540** (context 12011).

PT559 (P.506, context 7062)
Stepped rim of amphora lid
D. 14 cm   PL. 35

Hard orange-buff clay, cream in parts.

- Intact amphora lid as **PT486** in Group E (SF 654, context 7076); also another rim (context 12012).
- 3 rims of amphora lids as **PT487** in Group E (contexts 7203, 12011, 12012).

PT560 (P.563, context 12011)
Square-cut rim of amphora lid
D.max. 12.4 cm   PL. 35

Cream clay.
Similar: 2 rims, D. 13, 14 cm (12002, 12011).
Cf. Gerber 1996, figs. 3.2 (with central knob), 10.9 (Lidar Höyük survey).

PT561 (P.533, context 12012)
Hooked rim of amphora lid
D. 13.5 cm   PL. 35

Toothed notches around outer edge of top. Cream clay.
Similar: rim in Group D (p. 46, intrusive), D. 13 cm.
Cf. Wilkinson 1990, fig. B.25.29 (Kürban Höyük survey: site 8, multiperiod).

- Rim of amphora lid as **PT574** below (context 7203).
- Rim of amphora lid as **PT579** below (context 12011).

- Rim of small flagon or beaker as **PT179** in Group B (context 12011).

PT562 (P.580, context 12002)
Part of flagon with square-cut rim
D.rim 8.2 cm   PL. 35

Orange-buff core, cream at surface.

PT563 (P.569, context 12011)
Flagon with flanged neck
D.rim 6.2 cm   PL. 35

Buff clay, carefully smoothed.

PT564 (P.581, context 12002)
Flagon with ribbed neck
D.rim 6.2 cm   PL. 35

Greenish-cream clay.
Cf. Gerber 1996, fig. 3.11 (Lidar Höyük survey): not close, but a narrow, tapering neck, early Islamic?

PT565 (P.542, context 12012)
Narrow-mouthed flagon with flanged neck
D.rim (max.) 4.8 cm   PL. 35

Scar of handle on rim. Pale brown clay, pink to cream at surface.
Similar: rim, D. 7.2 cm (12011).
Konrad 1992, fig. 12.13, 14, are narrow flagon necks from Rusafa with various moldings, dated approximately A.D. 475+. Cf. also Miglus et al. 1999, group AO as pl. 51d (Raqqa: rim and neck of pilgrim flask?).

PT566 (P.582, context 12002)
Narrow-necked flagon with everted rim
D. 6.5 cm   PL. 35

Buff clay, cream at surface.
Cf. Konrad (1992) fig. 12.6 with one handle attached at lip (Rusafa: A.D. 425+).

- 3 body-sherds of flagons with incised decoration as **PT628** in Group G (2 in context 12011, 1 in 12012) (cf. also **PT491** in Group E).

PT567 (P.540, context 12012)
Part of small closed vessel with disc-base
D.base 3.1 cm   PL. 35

Cream clay.

Figure 17. **PT572, PT573**, *painted jugs in Buff ware 8 from Group F.*

PT568 (P.571, context 12011)
Part of closed vessel with restricted disc-base
D.base 4.8 cm   PL. 35

Buff clay.
Similar: base in Group D (p. 46, intrusive?), D. 2.6 cm; base in this group, D. 5.0 cm (12011).

- 2 bases of closed vessels as **PT552** (context 12011).
- Rim of flagon as **PT489** in Group E (context 7203).

PT569 (P.579, context 12002)
Flagon with straight neck and everted rim
D.rim 7.8 cm   PL. 35

Second handle uncertain. Orange clay, orange-buff at surface.

PT570 (P.663, context 12011)
Part of flagon with steep thickened rim
D. 10.5 cm   PL. 35

PT571 (P.526, context 7065)
Rim of painted flagon
D.rim 11.0 cm   PL. 35

Bands of thin brown paint on rim and neck. Cream clay.

PT572 (P.501, SF 503, context 7036)
Jug with painted decoration
D.max. 17.4 cm, H.pres. 18.7 cm   FIG. 17, PL. 35

Decoration on shoulder in brown paint; scar of single handle. The mouth presumably had a pinched spout as the following. Three-quarters preserved. Fired variously cream to pink.
Similar: **PT292** in Group C (intrusive); base in Group D (p. 47, intrusive), Buff 13; body-sherd in Group E (p. 54), Buff 3; shoulder and 6 bases in this group (7036, 7065, 7076, 7203, 3 in 12011).

PT573 (P.516, context 7203)
Jug with pinched spout and painted decoration
D.max. 17.0 cm, H. 23.0 cm   FIG. 17, PL. 35

Almost complete. Hard, fused cream clay. Decoration in brown paint.
Similar: 2 bases in Group E (p. 55); rim/handle fragment in this group (7036).

- 2 handles, 6 sherds of closed vessels with painted decoration, 3 other unclassified sherds.

BUFF WARE 10

PT574 (P.513, context 7066)
Knobless amphora lid
D.max. 13.3 cm, H. 4.1 cm   PL. 36

Prominently raised inner lip. More than half preserved. Hard greenish-buff clay with barely perceptible mixed inclusions. Roughly shaped on outside.
Similar: rim, Buff 8, D. 13.0 cm (7203).
Konrad (1992) fig. 19.5–7 (Rusafa) show a similarly accentuated inner lip.

PT575 (P.567, context 12011)
Jar with thickened vertical rim
D.rim 22 cm   PL. 36

Buff clay, cream at surface.
Cf. Bartl 1994, pl. 14.11, Form F I.8 (Balih Valley survey).

BUFF WARE 13

PT576 (P.525, SF 651, context 7065)
Three-handled conical cup
D.max. 10.3 cm, H. 7.4 cm   PL. 36

Handles formed from long strips of clay pressed against wall. Complete. Buff clay with sparse very fine mixed inclusions, including muscovite mica. Rough, heavy potting.
Harper (1980) fig. E, no. 78, from Dibsi Faraj is a bowl (D. 28 cm.) with similar handles, described as "early Islamic."

- Rim of amphora lid as **PT558** above (context 12002).
- Rim of small jar as **PT550** above (context 12011).
- Rim of flagon as **PT179** in Group B (context 12011).

PT577 (P.572, context 12011)
Large pedestal base
D.base 6.6 cm   PL. 36

Fine orange-brown clay.
Cf. Konrad 2001a, pl. 90.29 (Qusair as-Saila), described as an amphora stopper; Gerber 1996, fig. 11.21 (Lidar Höyük survey), clearly a pedestal foot. Cf. also **PT554**.

BUFF WARE 15

- 2 rims of bowls with plain vertical rim as **PT335** in Group D (context 12011).
- 6 sloping rims of conical basins as **PT352** in Group D (context 12011).
- 4 convex rims of conical basins as **PT493** in Group E (3 in context 12002, 1 in 12011).
- 3 short convex rims of basins as **PT494** in Group E (1 in context 7214, 2 in 12011).

PT578 (P.514, context 7066)
Deep three-handled basin with hooked rim
D. 50.8 cm, H. 30.5 cm   FIG. 18, PL. 36

Largely complete. Hard, finely granular buff clay, slightly vesicular but without obvious inclusions; fired buff at surface.
Similar: rim, D. 53 cm (12011).
Cf. Konrad 2001a, pl. 115.D (Qusair as-Saila: slightly broader rim, no handles reported, string marks on wall).

PT579 (P.524, SF 650, context 7065)
Knobless amphora lid with wavy-line decoration
D. 12.4 cm, H. 4.7 cm   PL. 36

Inscribed wavy line on top of rim. Complete. Vesicular greenish-buff clay with very occasional lumps of lime up to 2 mm.
Similar: rim, D. 12 cm, Buff 8 (12011).
Cf. Gerber 1996, fig. 2.8 (Lidar Höyük survey: more rounded profile, but with wavy line on top).

PT580 (P.539, context 12012)
Closed vessel with heavy flat base
D.base 4.5 cm   PL. 36

Finely granular buff clay, no obvious inclusions.
Similar: base in Group D (intrusive?); 3 bases in Group F, Buff 1 (1 in 12002, 2 in 12012).

OTHER BUFF WARES

PT581 (P.520, SF 495, context 7036)
Small handle-less jar
D.rim 7.7 cm, D.max. 9.3 cm, H. 9.8 cm   FIG. 19, PL. 36

Intact. Finely granular buff clay with large lumps of lime breaking through the surface; surface pink with cream patches. Cf. **PT550**.

PT582 (P.522, SF 656, context 7065)
Small handle-less jar
D.rim 8.1 cm, D.max. 9.7 cm, H. 9.9 cm   FIG. 19, PL. 36

Intact. Almost identical to the preceding, with occasional very large lumps of lime up to 8 mm that have disrupted or burst through the surface; fired cream on outside.

Figure 18. **PT578**, *three-handled basin in Buff ware 15 from Group F. Scale 10 cm.*

Similar: base in Group D (p. 44, surely intrusive), Buff 1.
Cf. **PT550, 581**; also Konrad (1992) fig. 20.11 (Rusafa), similar rim in greenish-yellow clay with white inclusions up to 1 mm and thick slip (context date 475–518).

PT583 (P.568, context 12011)
Part of small jar with inward-sloping rim
D.rim 9.0 cm   PL. 36

Hard greenish-buff clay with occasional irregular grayish inclusions up to 2 mm, which appear to be fossiliferous.

- 185 body-sherds, unclassified.

Cooking Wares
COOKING WARE 1

- Rim fragment of (round-bottomed) bowl with incurving rim as **PT419** in Group D (context 7214).
- Rim fragment of bowl, possibly as **PT421** in Group D (context 12012).
- Part of globular cookpot with inset bead rim as **PT194** in Group B (context 12011).
- Part of globular cookpot with inset rolled rim as **PT195** in Group B (context 12002).
- 2 rims of globular corrugated cookpots as **PT430** in Group D (context 12011).
- Rim/handle fragment of long-necked cookpot as **PT438** in Group D (context 12011).
- Rim of long-necked cookpot as **PT442** in Group D (context 7026).

PT584 (P.503, context 7036)
Cookpot with plain rim, tapering neck, and handle on shoulder
D.rim 14 cm   PL. 36

Red clay, dark brown on outside. A similar rim/shoulder profile is attested at Dura-Europos (Dyson 1968 no. 453 [illus. 454]), but with handles from rim to shoulder (i.e., typical of the Middle Imperial period).

Figure 19. **PT581**, **PT582**, *small handle-less jars in buff ware in Group F.*

PT585 (P.498, context 7005)
Narrow-necked jug with pinched spout   PL. 36

Red clay, fired gray to brown on outside.
Cf. Dyson 1968, no. 455 (illus. 456: Dura-Europos), jug with pinched spout. Residual?

- 2 rim/handle-fragments of Middle Imperial cookpots.
- 3 handles and 11 body-sherds of corrugated cookpots.

COOKING WARE 2

PT586 (P.576, context 12011)
Cookpot with handle attached to everted rim
D.rim ca. 10 cm   PL. 37

Two handles assumed. Red clay, maroon at surface.
This seems to be an Early to Middle Imperial shape: cf. **PT299** in Group C (Cooking 7) and **PT434** in Group D (Cooking 1).

PT587 (P.548, context 12012)
Corrugated cookpot with cylindrical neck and bifurcated rim
D.rim 12 cm   PL. 37

Handle(s) set on shoulder. Brown clay, fired gray at surface.
Similar: 1 rim, D. 11.5 cm (12011), 13 body-sherds, more or less this form (12012).
Cf. Orssaud 1980, fig. 307.1 (Déhès: rim only); Harper 1980, fig. D, no. 63 (Dibsi Faraj: very close, "early Byzantine").

- 2 rims of cookpots as **PT500** in Group E (context 12011).

PT588 (P.515, context 7066)
Cookpot with corrugated neck and small triangular rim
D.rim 13 cm   PL. 37

Dark maroon clay, fired black at surface in parts.
Similar: 6 rims, D. 10–13 cm (4 in 12002, 2 in 12011).

Cf. Konrad 2001a, pl. 105.12 (Qusair as-Saila); Orssaud 1980, fig. 307.4 (Déhès: plain neck but similar lip); ibid., fig. 308.6 is a ribbed neck of a flagon of similar profile; Bavant and Orssaud 2001, fig. 2.7 (Déhès, dated 560+, flat-topped rim); Northedge 1981, fig. 245.3 (River Quwaiq survey).

PT589 (P.500, context 7026)
Cookpot with corrugated neck and molded rim
D.rim ca. 13 cm   PL. 37

Red clay, purplish-brown on outside.
Similar: rim, D. 12 cm (12002).
Dyson 1968, no. 457 (illus. 458) is a ribbed cylindrical neck with handle (rim missing), generally this form, from Dura-Europos. See also fig. 19, type III C 10, certainly this form (but with handle from neck to shoulder). Cf. Konrad 1992, fig. 8.4 (Rusafa: "second half of fifth century"); Konrad 2001a, pl. 84.24, late fifth–sixth century (Qusair as-Saila: fabric 1?); Harper 1980, fig. D, no. 62 (Dibsi Faraj: "early Byzantine," handle set wholly on body); Wilkinson 1990, fig. B.15.30 (Kürban Höyük survey: site 14).

PT590 (P.575, context 12011)
Cookpot with cylindrical neck and flanged rim
D.rim (max.) 13 cm   PL. 37

Dark brown core, black at surface.
Similar: 3 rims, D. 11–13 cm (12011).
Cf. Mackensen 1984, pl. 11.13, 14 (Rusafa), two similar rims, unstratified; Konrad 1992, fig. 8.6 (Rusafa), "second half of fifth century"; Konrad 2001, pl. 84. 25, 27, 28 (Qusair as-Saila), possibly all this fabric, sixth–seventh century (p. 74); Orssaud 1980, fig. 307.5a–b (Déhès), "appears during the sixth century" (handles on shoulder, one example ribbed, one plain); Harper 1980, fig. D, no. 64 (Dibsi Faraj), "early Byzantine" (handles on shoulder).

PT591 (P.527, SF 655, context 7076)
Globular corrugated kettle
D.rim 6.8 cm, D.max. 19.2 cm, H. 25.3 cm   PL. 37

Small tubular spout on shoulder, corrugated neck, flanged rim; handle from neck to shoulder. Red clay, dark brown on outside. Lime-scale on inside; more than half preserved.
Similar: spout in Group D (p. 50, intrusive?).
Cf. Konrad 2001a, pl. 84.26 (Qusair as-Saila), rim, wider but similar, "sehr fein"; Bavant and Orssaud 2001, figs. 4.20, 6.27 (Déhès: deposits of 560+, 600+); Harper 1980, fig. C, no. 59 (Dibsi Faraj: body unribbed).

PT592 (P.519, context 7214)
Center of conical lid (?)
D.knob 5.0 cm   PL. 37

Fired maroon throughout.

- 16 handles and 77 body-sherds of cookpots. Where it can be determined, the handles are all attached at the shoulder.

COOKING WARE 6

PT593 (P.577, context 12011)
Wide-mouthed jar with short tubular spout
D.rim ca. 18 cm (very approximate)　　　　　PL. 37

Hard brown clay with abundant, ill-sorted mixed inclusions and very rough surfaces: this fabric?

- Body-sherd of globular cookpot.

COOKING WARE 9

- Rim of cookpot more or less as **PT503** in Group E (plainer) (context 12011).
- Handle fragment and body-sherd with handle of cookpot as **PT504** in Group E (contexts 12002, 12011).
- Handle (context 7203) and two body-sherds (context 12011) of cookpots.

STORAGE WARES

PT594 (P.504, SF 739, context 7036)
Heavy cylindrical knob
D. 8.4 cm, H. 5.9 cm　　　　　PL. 37

Worn knob, perhaps originally the base of a large storage vessel. It seems to have been deliberately ground to its present shape (as a weight?) but the surface coloration suggests an original body flaring outwards. Pink clay containing moderate ill-sorted lime, quartz, red/brown, and black inclusions; fired slightly paler at surface.

- Storage 1: fragment of pithos (context 7203).

PT595–600 *vacant*

Group G: Islamic

This group is composed entirely of material from Trench 1, which was distinguished from the other areas precisely by the amount of Islamic material that it yielded. This was only a small trench, and there are considerable difficulties in interpreting the stratigraphic data.[100] For this reason, and partly also for lack of time, the pottery from it was not fully quantified; rather, I chose to list as far as possible informative profiles of vessels not encountered in earlier contexts. These give some idea of the pottery in use at Zeugma during the Islamic period.

How late does this material go, and how far does it reflect the (ceramic) culture of Zeugma in its declining years? The city still possessed a bishop in 1048[101] but had presumably disappeared at the time of the First Crusade in 1098: when Baldwin of Boulogne established himself at Edessa (Urfa), Birecik/Birtha some 15 km downstream is mentioned as a strategic crossing point on the Euphrates,[102] and the castle of Birecik must have been constructed at this time. With regard to the pottery, there is little firmly dated material to guide us. Parallels with Madinat al-Far[103] and Qasr al-Hayr East (founded ca. 730)[104] take us into the eighth century. The most important publication is that of the Islamic pottery dumps in the potters' quarter at Raqqa.[105] The various strata of the Tall Aswad dump can be dated only approximately, but the tremendous flowering of pottery production there in Horizon II has been reasonably associated with the establishment of a palace at Raqqa by the caliph Harun al-Rashid in 796. There are extensive parallels to the Zeugma Group G pottery at Raqqa, and the Zeugma material therefore surely extends at least into the ninth century. The absence of sgraffito wares may preclude the tenth.[106] The only Islamic coin (**C234**) was also found in Trench 1. It is a dirhem of Harun, dated 786–809; it is worn, and pierced for suspension, suggesting that at the time of its loss it was of some age and was no longer serving as currency.

The table wares of this period are now essentially glazed, often with polychrome decoration ("Splash Glaze," "Yellow Glaze").[107] Several fabrics were differentiated, presumably indicating a multiplicity of sources (amongst which Raqqa is likely to have been an important one). The colors used are plain blue/green, also decorative patterns in dark green and brown on a pale yellow background.

In the buff wares, the flat-based conical basins continue, now with (mainly square-cut) knobbed rims (**PT620, 627, 633, 643–5**). Amongst the closed forms, a wide variety of incised or even cut-glass ("Kerbschnitt") patterns are applied to the walls of storage vessels (**PT640–642**), though the small fragments recovered give little clue to the motifs or overall composition. A couple of fragments belong to smaller, mold-made flagons with highly decorated surfaces (**PT629, 630**).

The cooking wares include distinctive "hole-mouth" cookpots with incurved rims. Handles take the form either of sharply angular vertical loops on the shoulder or of horizontal lugs (**PT655, 656**). Corrugations on the body disappear, but there is sometimes a kind of zigzag or "chattered" decoration on the shoulder, executed with a comb or "rocker stamp" (see **PT652**). The only (questionable) examples of casseroles were **PT648** and **PT660**; the type with a distinctive inset rim,[108] well attested elsewhere, was not found.

Table Wares
GLAZED WARE 1

This ware has been encountered in earlier contexts, as "Parthian" glazed ware. The three items listed here as sharing (more or less) the same clay are somewhat diverse, and I am not confident that they are related to one another.

PT601 (P.602, context 1010)
Part of dish with sloping wall and flaring rim
D. ca. 32 cm　　　　　PL. 38

Fine granular clay, vesicular, no visible inclusions. Smooth, brilliant white glaze.

Figure 20. A selection of Islamic glazed sherds from Group G.

PT602 (P.613, context 1010)
Cup (or flagon?) with grooved vertical rim
D. 11 cm PL. 38

Yellow-green glaze inside and out; possible brown stripe on outside.

PT603 (P.614, context 1010)
Mug with plain vertical rim
D. 12 cm FIG. 20, PL. 38

Hard, finely mottled pinkish-buff clay with thin, brilliant glaze (less smooth on inside). Pale brown ground inside and out; dark greenish-brown patches on outside. Looks comparatively recent.
Harper 1980, fig. C, no. 83, a small cylindrical bowl from Dibsi Faraj, may be similar: "medium ware, paste 7.5 YR 7/4 pink, glazed on interior and exterior in dark green and light yellow and green." See also Bartl 1996, fig. 5.2 (Balih Valley survey): "interior: green-yellow splash glaze, exterior: buff clay." (The drawing suggests that these descriptions may be transposed.) This piece is dated "early Abbasid" on the basis of similarities to Madinat al-Far and Raqqa.

Grabar et al. 1978, illus. H, no. 3a (Qasr al-Hayr East), yellow glaze, dense green splashes. See also **PT608**.

GLAZED WARE 3

PT604 (P.597, context 1010)
Base of bowl with low foot
D.foot 13.5 cm PL. 38

Gray-buff clay, abundant tiny black and red specks; thin, even, bluish-white glaze, smooth and brilliant on inside, dull on outside.
Similar: another base: smooth, brilliant white glaze on inside; thin, dull, and rough on outside.

PT605 (P.600, context 1010)
Base of bowl with low foot
D.foot 12 cm PL. 38

Buff clay, moderate very fine dark inclusions, rough but brilliant dark green glaze on inside only.
Cf. Bartl 1996, fig. 5.3 (Balih Valley survey), with green-brown splash glaze, dated "early Abbasid" on the basis of similarities to Madinat al-Far and Raqqa.

PT606 (P.601, context 1010)
Base of closed vessel
D.base 7.5 cm   PL. 38

Cream clay with moderate very fine black, white, and red inclusions. Patchy, uneven turquoise glaze on outside; drips only on underside.

GLAZED WARE 4

- 2 sherds of bowls with patchy white to turquoise glaze.

GLAZED WARE 5

PT607 (P.612, context 1010)
Plate with sloping rim and flat base
D. 31 cm, H. 4.0 cm   PL. 38

Thin, decayed, bluish-white glaze all over. Rough turning marks beneath base.
Similar: profile, 28 × 4.0 cm, coloring as drawn example; 2 rims, bluish-white, D. ca. 22, 24 cm; 1 rim, yellow-brown.
Cf. Miglus et al. 1999, group H as pl. 210–t (Raqqa: very rare); also a plate found at al-Zubayr (old Basra) and possibly made there: Mason and Keall 1991, fig. 2.6, opaque white glaze splashed turquoise. Fig. 5.975 in the same article is in the same fabric and is from Siraf. Dating possibly 9th–10th century but could be earlier.

PT608 (P.606, context 1010)
Deep bowl with plain vertical rim
D. 18 cm   PL. 38

Internal surface completely lost; worn dark greenish-brown glaze on outside.
Similar: rim fragment with external brown stripes over yellow-green (fig. 20).
Cf. **PT603**; also Miglus et al. 1999, group F as pl. 21b (Raqqa); Bartl 1994, pl. 37.8, Form A8 (Balih Valley survey), with yellow-green splash on outside only.

PT609 (P.603, context 1010)
Shallow bowl with plain tapering rim
D. 25 cm   PL. 38

Glaze bluish-white on inside, yellow to green on outside; no pattern visible. Very worn.
Cf. Miglus et al. 1999, group C as pl. 19c (Raqqa).

PT610 (P.605, context 1010)
Bowl with incurved rim
D.max. 19 cm   PL. 38

Chocolate-brown glaze on inside and over rim.
Cf. Bartl 1996, fig. 5.4 (Balih Valley survey) with yellow-blue splash glaze; Miglus et al. 1999, group C as pl. 18a (Raqqa: but with diameter 30 cm).

PT611 (P.607, context 1010)
Bowl with incurved rim
D.max. 28 cm   PL. 38

Glaze almost wholly lost: diagonal green stripes on inside.

PT612 (P.604, context 1010)
Curving bowl with plain rim
D. 28 cm   FIG. 20, PL. 39

Glazed on inside only. Stripes of turquoise over thin yellow-green.
Similar: 5 rims, D. 27–28 cm. Stripes of green and brown over bluish-white; two with partial glaze on outside.
Cf. Wilkinson 1990, fig. B.17.1–3 (Kürban Höyük survey: site 6, late Roman continuing to 9th/10th century). Grabar et al. 1978, illus. H, no. 13 (Qasr al-Hayr East) is this type, with a low, broad ring-foot as **PT615, 616**; no. 10 is a smaller example. Illus. H-1, no. 14, has chamfered rim as **PT613** with internal stripes of green and brown beneath yellow. For Raqqa, see Miglus et al. 1999, group C as pl. 19a; "sparse decorated ware" as pl. 96a, in which the yellow glaze is almost transparent or indeed absent.

PT613 (P.608, context 1010)
Curving bowl with chamfered rim
D. ca. 28 cm   FIG. 20, PL. 39

Glaze largely lost, but on inside only; green stripes.
Similar: 3 rim fragments, brown and turquoise stripes inside and out over yellow-green.
Cf. Lugar 1992, fig. 13.3 (Rusafa), decorated in green and brown "Laufglasur" on a yellow background; Miglus et al. 1999, group C as pl. 19h (Raqqa).

PT614 (P.611, context 1010)
Base of bowl with low ring-foot
D.foot 16 cm   FIG. 20, PL. 39

Glazed over all except inside of foot (drips). Yellow-green ground inside and out; brown solid and dotted lines on inside alternating with turquoise stripes. Decoration on outside was probably similar.
For similar decoration cf. Grabar et al. 1978, illus. H-1, no. 9 (Qasr al-Hayr East); Miglus et al. 1999, pl. 96f, in "sparse decorated ware" (Raqqa).

PT615 (P.609, context 1010)
Base of bowl with ring-foot
D.foot 17 cm   PL. 39

Glaze on inside only: turquoise blobs and brown line over pale yellow-green ground.
Similar: 8 bases, D.foot 12–18 cm.
For **PT615–617**, see Grabar et al. 1978, illus. H-1, nos. 15a–g (Qasr al-Hayr East), base fragments of bowls with similar

geometric or floral designs in brown and green on yellow glaze; Miglus et al. 1999, "Yellow glazed ware with painted decoration," as PL. 94f–i, 95 (Raqqa).

PT616 (P.650, context 1007)
Base of bowl with low foot
D.foot 17 cm   FIG. 20, PL. 40

Good glaze on inside only: yellow-green ground, pattern in green and brown. Cf. the preceding.

PT617 (P.610, context 1010)
Base of bowl with low foot
D.foot 9.2 cm   FIG. 20, PL. 40

Very rough potting on outside, which shows only drips and splashes of glaze. Inside has pale yellow ground with flower pattern outlined in brown with pale blue petals.
Similar profile: 2 bases.
Cf. **PT615, 616** and refs., especially Miglus et al. 1999, pl. 94i (profile, pl. 91f).

- Base and 2 sherds of closed vessels, brown patterns.

OTHER GLAZED WARE

PT618 (P.615, context 1010)
Part of cylindrical handled bucket (?)
D. ca. 22 cm   PL. 40

Granular red clay, hackly break, with abundant ill-sorted fine to medium angular quartz and moderate fine brown or black particles (iron ore?). Fired brown on the outside with blotches only of green to brown glaze; even, dark bluish-green glaze on inside.

Buff Wares
BUFF WARES 1–3

PT619 (P.621, context 1010)
Small basin with sloping rim
D. 26.5 cm   PL. 40

Buff 1: buff throughout.

PT620 (P.619, context 1010)
Basin with triangular rim
D. ca. 40 cm   PL. 40

Buff 3: orange-buff core, buff towards surface, cream at surface.
Cf. Miglus et al. 1999, group A as pl. 14f (Raqqa), more common in Horizon III than in the upper horizons (i.e., in circulation before A.D. 796).

PT621 (P.628, context 1010)
Part of jar (?) with sloping rim
D. 21 cm   PL. 40

Buff 1: buff throughout.

PT622 (P.637, context 1010)
Part of closed vessel with flat base
D.base 8.3 cm   PL. 40

Buff 3: orange-buff clay, buff on outside.

BUFF WARE 8

PT623 (P.624, context 1010)
Bowl with vertical hooked rim
D. 20.5 cm   PL. 41

Cream throughout.
Cf. Gerber 1996, fig. 7.6 (Lidar Höyük survey).

PT624 (P.623, context 1010)
Carinated bowl (or wide-mouthed jar?) with flat rim
D. 22.5 cm   PL. 41

Fired cream. Grayish patina on inside surface rather suggests a closed vessel.

PT625 (P.625, context 1010)
Handled bowl with everted triangular rim
D. ca. 20 cm   PL. 41

Two handles assumed. Buff core, cream at surface.

PT626 (P.651, context 1007)
Deep bowl or wide-mouthed jar with triangular rim
D. 32 cm   PL. 41

Buff throughout.
Cf. Wilkinson 1990, fig. B.17.30 (Kürban Höyük survey, site 6: late Roman, continuing to 9th/10th century).

PT627 (P.657, context 1024)
Basin with knobbed rim and raised inner lip
D. 55 cm   PL. 41

Buff clay, cream at surface.
Cf. Northedge 1981, figs. 246–7, 16–18 (River Quwaiq survey), Early Islamic? Bartl 1994, pl. 3.4, Form A2 (Balih Valley survey); Bartl 1996, fig. 4.1, 2 (ditto), "early Islamic"; Mackensen 1984, pl. 12.16, 14.1 (Rusafa); Konrad 2001a, pl. 91.8, 9 (Qusair as-Saila: uppermost layers), Umayyad or even Abbasid; Grabar et al. 1978, illus. A-3, no. 5 (Qasr al-Hayr East); Miglus et al. 1999, group A as pl. 12b, c (Raqqa), more common in Horizon III than in upper horizons. See also **PT644**.

PT628 (P.631, context 1010)
Flagon with radial incised decoration
D.rim 6.9 cm, D.max. 17.0 cm   PL. 41

Decoration composed of combed and "chattered" lines and arcs. One handle. Cream throughout.

Figure 21. **PT629**, **PT630**, *fragments of mold-made decorated flagons in Buff ware 8 from Group G.*

Similar: **PT491** in Group E; 3 body-sherds in Group F (p. 62).
Cf. Konrad 2001a, pl. 76.5 = 109.A16 (Qusair as-Saila), fragment with similar decoration (Umayyad context); Orssaud 1980, fig. 304.4a is a rim only, wider (D. 14 cm) but shaped with similar delicacy (Déhès: seventh century); Gerber 1996, fig. 3.13–5 (Lidar Höyük survey), body-sherds of this form and decoration, on a late site with a distinctively different assemblage from most others: Early Islamic. Also ibid., figs. 4.15, 6.16. At Tarsus, fragments of buff ware with combed decoration (Jones 1950, fig. 168) appear to be distantly related in style.

PT629 (P.654, context 1018)
Fragment of relief-decorated flagon
6.1 × 4.3 cm   FIG. 21, PL. 41

Part of closed vessel with ribbed finger marks on inside where the clay has been pressed into the mold. Grayish-cream throughout.
This and the following are fragments of flagons with a globular body made in a two-part mold, tall cylindrical neck, single vertical handle, and pedestal-foot: see *The Arts of Islam, Hayward Gallery 8 April–4 July 1976* (London: Arts Council of Great Britain), no. 251. Konrad 2001a, pl. 101.9 (Qusair as-Saila) "mit modelverzierte Barbotineauflage" (p. 85 with refs., n. 368) looks rather like this and is described as Early Islamic of the seventh–ninth centuries. Harper 1980, fig. E, no. 90 (Dibsi Faraj) is part of a globular vessel with a cylindrical neck showing finger marks on the inside, surely of similar origin: "early Islamic." Cf. also Bartl 1994, pl. 27.3–12 (Balih Valley survey); ibid., pl. MF11.13–8 (Madinat al-Far). Sarre 1925, 12 ff., nos. 48–52 at Samarra seem to be of this type. No. 52 is dated tentatively 11th–12th century. Lugar (1992, fig. 10) illustrates various pieces of relief ware from Rusafa described as having barbotine decoration, but this seems unlikely for some of them, at least. Dating could be seventh–eighth century. Grabar et al. (1978, illus. A-4, A-8) show numerous examples from Qasr al-Hayr East, several with oblique hatched lozenges, teardrops and circles within circles (A-8 no. 9 is particularly close to **PT630**), 10th–13th centuries? Considered Abbasid at Raqqa (Miglus et al. 1999, 57): the finds include 16 fragments of molds. Predominantly Horizons III and II; globular flagons with vegetal ornament predominantly III (early Abbasid?).

PT630 (P.655, context 1024)
Fragment of closed vessel with relief decoration
4.7 × 4.4 cm   FIG. 21, PL. 41

Shoulder and base of neck. Greenish-cream throughout. Cf. the preceding. Miglus et al. 1999, pl. 86c (no. 196) from Raqqa shows the medallion of circles.

PT631 (P.633, context 1010)
Tall grooved rim of flagon
D. 15 cm   PL. 41

Cream clay, surfaces well smoothed. Cf. Guérin 1996, fig. 2.4 (Nisibis), "eighth–ninth century"; Bartl 1994, pl. 23.1, Form F III.16 (Balih Valley survey); Miglus et al. 1999, group AH as pl. 44d (approx.) (Raqqa), ninth century or later.

Figure 22. **PT632**, *rim of large decorated jar in Buff ware 8 from Group G.*

PT632 (P.652, context 1007)
Rim of large decorated jar
D. 35 cm   FIG. 22, PL. 41

Incised decoration with applied boss. Cream throughout. Grabar et al. 1978, illus. A-5, nos. 7 and 8 (Qasr al-Hayr East) show similar decoration on rim (7) and wall (8): considered earlier (Umayyad?) rather than later. Cf. also Miglus et al. 1999, group AC as pl. 38a for profile, 73e, 76f for decoration (Raqqa); Bartl 1994, pl. 19.1, Form F III.1 (Balih Valley survey) for form and decoration; ibid., pl. MF 5.5 (Madinat al-Far).

BUFF WARE 10

PT633 (P.656, context 1024)
Part of basin with rolled rim
D. 38 cm   PL. 41

Fine, hard, greenish-cream clay with very fine, barely perceptible inclusions.
Cf. Miglus et al. 1999, group A as pl. 110 (Raqqa), more common in III than in upper horizons.

PT634 (P.635, context 1010)
Part of flagon with grooved vertical rim
D. 8 cm   PL. 41

Hard and greenish-yellow throughout (overfired).

PT635 (P.634, context 1010)
Flagon with collar rim
D. 14 cm   PL. 41

Trace of handle scar immediately beneath lip. Buff clay, grayish-cream at surface.

Miglus et al. 1999, group AM as pl. 49b (Raqqa) is approximately similar. Cf. also Bartl 1994, pl. 22.15, Form F III.11 (Balih Valley survey).

PT636 (P.626, context 1010)
Jar with inset rim
D.rim 10.8 cm   PL. 41

Hard, vesicular, finely granular buff clay with sparse fine mixed inclusions; greenish-cream at surface.
Cf. Guérin 1996, fig. 6.28 (Nisibis), "ninth–tenth century."

PT637 (P.636, context 1010)
Base of closed vessel with false ring-foot
D.base 7.8 cm   PL. 41

Fired cream throughout. Cf. Grabar et al. 1978, illus. A-1, nos. 4a–c (Qasr al-Hayr East).

PT638 (P.632, context 1010)
Large flagon with wavy-line decoration
D.rim (max.) 19 cm   PL. 41

Handle scar on lower edge of sherd. Hard, finely granular yellowish-cream clay with no perceptible inclusions; smooth finish.
Guérin 1996, fig. 5.24–26 (Nisibis) are lips of more rectangular profile but with similar wavy-line decoration, dated 9th–10th century. Bartl 1994, pl. 4.8, Form A1 (Balih Valley survey) is approximately this form, but with the highest point at the outer edge.

PT639 (P.627, context 1010)
Jar or bucket with external decoration
D. 31 cm   PL. 41

Stabbed frilling on cordon, traces of wavy-line decoration below. Pinkish-buff clay, fired cream towards outside; moderate very fine red, white, and black inclusions, a little very fine mica.
Cf. Guérin 1996, fig. 2.2 (Nisibis), "eighth–ninth century"; Miglus et al. 1999, group AC as pl. 38a for profile, 74j for decoration (Raqqa). This seems to be a bulbous wide-mouthed jar with vertical handles between middle and base of neck. Predominantly Horizons II and I at Raqqa (ninth century onwards). Cf. **PT632**.

PT640 (P.653, context 1007)
Fragment of jar with incised decoration   FIG. 23, PL. 42

Turning marks suggest that this is from the shoulder of a large closed vessel. Other sherds in fig. 23 are all from context 1010. Greenish-buff.
Cf. Konrad 2001a, pl. 77.3 = 101.3 (Qusair as-Saila), possibly this ware (Byzantine–Early Islamic); Orssaud 1980, figs. 334, 341 (Déhès: sherds with incised lines). Harper 1980, fig.

Figure 23. **PT640** *and other fragments of large closed vessels with incised decoration in Buff ware 10 from Group G.*

E, nos. 81, 82 (Dibsi Faraj), similar sherds with Kerbschnitt and crude incised scenes, "early Islamic"; Bartl 1994, pl. 26 (Balih Valley survey), several examples; Miglus et al. 1999, pl. 75 (Raqqa), sherds with incised lattice and abstract decoration.

PT641 (P.629, context 1010)
Sherd of jar with incised decoration   PL. 42

Orange core, cream surfaces. Cf. the preceding.

PT642 (P.630, context 1010)
Sherd of large vessel with incised decoration
D.int. ca. 35 cm   PL. 42

Fine grooves, stabbed dots, and deep cut-glass incisions ("Kerbschnitt"). Buff with cream surfaces.
Cf. Orssaud 1980, figs. 342–5 (Déhès), sherds with Kerbschnittmuster (considered Umayyad, found in association with a coin of 750 to early ninth century); Miglus et al. 1999, pl. 76a–e, g (Raqqa), varied examples of Kerbschnitt (some of high quality).

OTHER BUFF WARES

PT643 (P.618, context 1010)
Shallow basin with square-cut rim
D. 29.5 cm, H. 11.1 cm   PL. 42

Granular yellowish-cream clay with sparse very fine white inclusions (lime?) and darker specks (as **PT645**).
Cf. Konrad 2001a, pl. 93.8 (Qusair as-Saila: late Roman or early Islamic?); Bartl 1994, pl. 4.3, Form A3 (Balih Valley survey); Miglus et al. 1999, group A as pl. 14j (Raqqa), more common in Horizon III than in upper horizons.

PT644 (P.622, context 1010)
Basin with square-cut rim and internal lip
D. ca. 60 cm (very approximate)   PL. 42

Buff clay fired cream at surface; moderate rounded red pebbles up to 1 mm, also soft white inclusions (chalk? shell?) of similar size. Possibly the same clay as **PT647**.
Cf. Konrad 2001a, pl. 91.8, 9 (Qusair as-Saila: latest levels); Miglus et al. 1999, group A as pl. 13L (Raqqa), more common in Horizon III than in upper horizons. See also **PT627**.

PT645 (P.620, context 1010)
Basin with thickened, rounded rim
D. 50 cm   PL. 42

Granular greenish-cream clay as **PT643**; no perceptible inclusions.

PT646 (P.617, context 1010)
Rim of amphora lid (?)
D. 14 cm   PL. 42

Incurved rim with pronounced external flange. Brown clay, fired orange-brown at surface; sparse fine black inclusions (0.2 mm), larger, soft, grayish-white ones (1 mm: chalk?), sparse lumps of quartz up to 2 mm.

PT647 (P.616, context 1010)
Steep-sided amphora lid (?)
D.base 5.5 cm   PL. 42

Pink to buff clay (alternating layers in break), fine in texture but vesicular, with sparse mixed inclusions up to 2 mm: lime, rounded red pebbles, possibly a little quartz. Outside surface fired cream. Possibly the same clay as **PT644**. Konrad 1992, fig. 20.9 (Rusafa) is a knobbed base with similarly steep sides, interpreted as a lid (context date ca. 425–475).

Cooking Wares
COOKING WARE 2

PT648 (P.660, context 1024)
Rim of carinated bowl or casserole
D.rim ca. 28 cm   PL. 42

Red clay, brown on outside. Cf. **PT424, 451** in Group D (neither of them in this fabric): residual?

PT649 (P.642, context 1010)
Cookpot with ribbed cylindrical neck and thickened rim
D.rim 13 cm   PL. 42

Red clay, black on outside.
Cf. Konrad 2001a, pl. 84.31 (Qusair as-Saila), probably this fabric; Wilkinson 1990, fig. B.17.24 (Kürban Höyük survey: site 6), with medium-coarse white sand inclusions.

PT650 (P.639, context 1010)
Cookpot with thickened incurved rim
D.rim ca. 20 cm   PL. 42

Dark brown clay, black on outside.
Cf. Konrad 2001a, pl. 84.10 (Qusair as-Saila), "Ton kompakt, verbrannt"; Bartl 1994, pl. 283, Form A I.1 (Balih Valley survey); Bartl 1996, fig. 4.4 (ditto), dated "early Abbasid" on the basis of similarities to Madinat al-Far and Raqqa; Wilkinson 1990, fig. B.17.32-6 (Kürban Höyük survey: site 6, varying in detail). Cf. **PT656** and references for the lug-handles which belong with this shape.

PT651 (P.640, context 1010)
Cookpot with thickened incurved rim
D.rim 16 cm   PL. 42

Very fine red clay, but certainly still this fabric. Dark brown on outside.
Cf. Bartl 1994, pl. 29.3, Form A I.2 (Balih Valley survey).

PT652 (P.661, context 1047)
Cookpot with thickened incurved rim and "rocker-stamp" decoration
D.rim 13 cm   PL. 42

Very hard (but not particularly smooth) maroon clay, black on outside.
Cf. Orssaud 1980, fig. 307.7 (Déhès) for this type of decoration (second half of eighth century); Bavant and Orssaud 2001, fig. 10.44 (ditto) rim (not before the Umayyad period); Harper 1980, fig. D, no. 66 (Dibsi Faraj), "early Abbasid"; Bartl 1996, fig. 4.5 (Balih Valley survey), "early Abbasid"; Bartl 1994, pl. MF8 (Madinat al-Far), several examples; Sarre 1925, 21 no. 82 (Samarra: with decoration and lug-handles).

PT653 (P.638, context 1010)
Cookpot with square-cut incurved rim
D.rim 12 cm   PL. 42

Red core and inside surface, maroon on outside. Cf. Orssaud 1980, fig. 307.6 (Déhès), with horizontal lug-handle.

PT654 (P.641, context 1010)
Cookpot with convex vertical rim
D.rim 17 cm   PL. 42

Dark brown clay, black on outside.

PT655 (P.649, context 1004)
Part of cookpot with arched handle   PL. 42

Diameter large but undeterminable. Fine red clay, red at surface.
Cf. Orssaud 1980, fig. 307, type 5 (Déhès) for this kind of handle: "appears during the sixth century"; Northedge 1981, fig. 245.4 (River Quwaiq survey); Harper 1980, fig. D, no. 61 (Dibsi Faraj), "Umayyad?"

PT656 (P.658, context 1024)
Horizontal lug-handle of cookpot
D.int. at lug ca. 20 cm   PL. 42

Fine, hard red clay, reddish-brown on outside.
Cf. Konrad (1992) fig. 9.2–5 (Rusafa) with characteristic decoration and (9.4) lug-handles, some associated with a building phase attributed to A.D. 518 (?); Orssaud 1980, fig. 307.6 (Déhès), cookpot with rim as **PT650-2**, "second half of eighth century"; Bavant and Orssaud 2001, fig. 10.43 (ditto), "not before the Umayyad period"; Northedge 1981, fig. 245.8-11 (River Quwaiq survey: rims as **PT650-652**),

widespread in the survey area and in northern Syria, not found in the southern Levant; Harper 1980, fig. D, no. 65 (Dibsi Faraj), "early Abbasid"; Gerber 1996, fig. 2.4 (Lidar Höyük survey); Bartl 1996, fig. 4.5 (Balih Valley survey); Grabar et al. 1978, illus. B, no. 11 (Qasr al-Hayr East) with broad horizontal fluting on body, mainly early; Miglus et al. 1999, group U as pl. 31a–i, esp. a, b (Raqqa): essentially Horizons III and II, i.e. eighth–ninth century? Cookpots found at Tarsus, in this fabric and with this kind of lug-handle, were kindly shown to me in 2002 by Çiğdem Toskay Evrin.

PT657 (P.643, context 1010)
Sherd of cookpot with incised lattice   PL. 42

Red clay, dark brown at surface.

COOKING WARE 9

PT658 (P.648, context 1010)
Part of heavy jar with plain vertical rim
D.rim ca. 13 cm, angle uncertain   PL. 42

Two handles assumed. Dark brown clay, black at surface. Very heavy and rough.

COOKING WARE 10

PT659 (P.646, context 1010)
Shallow bowl (?) with thickened rim
D. 23 cm   PL. 42

Edge of sherd at break is very thin: what happens next is quite unclear! Brown throughout.

PT660 (P.647, context 1010)
Corrugated casserole or bowl with flat inturned rim
D.max. 26 cm   PL. 42

Black core, gray-brown at surface.
Cf. Konrad 2001a, pl. 84.16 (Qusair as-Saila) "Magerung dicht; weiss (bis 0.5 mm)," possibly Islamic.

PT661 (P.659, context 1024)
Cookpot with ribbed neck and chamfered rim
D.rim 11 cm   PL. 42

Gritty orange-brown clay, inclusions prominent on inside; outside fired maroon to black.

PT662 (P.644, context 1010)
Cookpot with thickened incurved rim
D.rim 14 cm   PL. 42

Two handles assumed. Pinkish-brown clay with abundant medium (1 mm) angular quartz and probably limestone, also sparse smaller brown particles (iron ore?). The grits are often very apparent at the surface. Black on outside. Cf. **PT650–652**, here with vertical loop-handles.

PT663 (P.645, context 1010)
Cookpot with incurved grooved rim
D.rim 13 cm   PL. 42

Pinkish-red clay, brown on outside. Cf. the preceding.

CONCLUSIONS

The pottery described in the foregoing report is only a small part of that recovered from the rescue excavations in trenches supervised by Oxford Archaeology at Zeugma in 2000, which in turn constitute only part of the overall (and closely connected) excavations that have taken place on the site. Any conclusions drawn from it are therefore necessarily partial and subject to revision as more of the finds are published. Nonetheless, I believe that the evidence presented here has a threefold value. In the first place, it constitutes of course the principal source for the chronology of the excavated sequences. Secondly, the dated groups, sometimes containing substantial quantities of material, offer new anchor points for the dating of the ceramics of the middle Euphrates region. Thirdly, the evolving character of the ceramics in use at Zeugma gives us some indication of the cultural leanings of the inhabitants and of their trade relations at different times.

Chronology

Little needs to be added on this score to the discussion that precedes each of the dated groups and to the use made of the pottery evidence in the stratigraphic reports in volume 1. The earliest context that could be clearly dated by its pottery (Group A) has a terminal date after the middle of the second century B.C.; residual pieces that may be attributable to the period between the foundation of the settlement in 300 B.C. and this date are exiguous in the extreme.[109] The initial settlement will naturally have been modest, and it presumably did not lie close to any of the trenches discussed here.

There is also a significant gap in the pottery record following the Sasanian sack. It was not possible to identify from the first review of the material any contexts of the later third, fourth, or fifth centuries A.D.; in the later groups there was very little datable pottery that could be considered as residual from this interval.[110] The coin sequence shows a general paucity of coins postdating the mid-third century apart from a group of Justinianic pieces in Trench 12 that may represent a dispersed hoard.[111] However, the French excavations in zone 3 and zone 5 did yield both coins and fine ware (African Red Slip) of the fourth and fifth centuries,[112] showing that occupation of the area after the sack did continue, but in the form of patches of habitation amongst abandoned ruins.

Those parts of the excavated area that have yielded evidence of occupation in the Late Imperial period seem to have been abandoned again either at the time when the region was lost to the Arabs (A.D. 636) or already before then. The evidence from Group F is somewhat mixed: Trench 12 yielded the Justinianic coins mentioned above (and none later) and most of the pottery could be contemporary with these; there are, however, undeniably some pieces of the late sixth or early seventh century. The pottery associated with the final destruction of the building in Trench 7B points rather more consistently towards the latter date. I suspect that we must beware of placing too much reliance for the end date of occupation on the absence of specific Mediterranean fine wares, or indeed of Byzantine coins: Zeugma must have been increasingly isolated from the Byzantine/Mediterranean world at this time and may not have had the same access to imports as it had enjoyed previously.

Of the Islamic material in Trench 1, there is little to add to the discussion at the beginning of Group G. In retrospect, it is a pity that there was not more extensive excavation in that part of the site, but this was hardly obvious at the time. The French Chantier 10, close to Trench 1, also yielded stratified Islamic material, as did the superficial levels of Trench 6 in zone 9 (where it had perhaps washed down from somewhere higher up the slope).[113]

The Pottery of the Middle Euphrates

While the fine wares imported from the Mediterranean world are now relatively well known and well dated, the study of the majority of the pottery encountered at Zeugma still has some way to go in this respect. Over the past generation, the construction of numerous dams and reservoirs along the Euphrates has given rise to a wide variety of archaeological investigations and reports. These have already been enumerated above (pp. 6–7) and have been extensively drawn upon for parallels to the Zeugma finds. The various surface surveys are useful in terms of the geographical distribution of different wares and types, but are rarely helpful in terms of chronology. For chronological data we are dependent on older excavations of sites with known dates of destruction or abandonment (e.g., Dura-Europos, Ain Sinu) or more recent work with well-defined and published stratigraphic groups, such as Rusafa and Qusair as-Saila. With regard to Zeugma itself, Markus Gschwind has already published an important group of the first century A.D., and further studies of the material excavated by the French and Turkish teams are to be expected.

Into this scene, the dated groups presented here introduce a substantial sequence of stratified material that is comparatively well dated, that extends over at least a thousand years, and in the description of which careful attention has been paid to the identification of fabrics. The visual descriptions are backed up by petrographic examination, which has often proved illuminating despite the broad uniformity of the alluvial deposits over vast tracts of the middle and lower Euphrates. It can almost never be claimed that a stratified context is free from contamination: Even if the context was well defined in the ground, there is always the possibility on a large excavation of pieces being misplaced or mislabeled in the course of finds processing. Where, therefore, the chronological evidence from Zeugma appears to conflict with that from other sites, I cannot claim that it is always right; but the total sum of evidence available is certainly fuller and clearer than before. We may expect some refinement as further material from Zeugma is published.

The value of petrographic studies in clarifying our understanding of pottery distribution is today unquestioned. The terms in which fabrics are reported are not always uniform in style, and it is sometimes difficult to make comparisons between different studies; however, in the present instance I have profited from the published work of Bartl, Schneider, and Bohme,[114] as well as from the extensive geological knowledge displayed by Chris Doherty in the petrographic report following this chapter. It has thus been possible to define various categories of buff, cooking, and storage wares, and to differentiate those that are either local or, at least, regional from those that have come from further afield. In the case of the minor fabrics of which only a few examples were recognized, this is a stepping-stone on which it may be hoped that future studies in the region may build.

The Ceramic Culture of Zeugma

The twin towns of Apamea and Seleucia were founded in 300 B.C. by Seleucus I Nikator. They will have represented settlements of alien Greeks in a territory that was culturally associated with Mesopotamia rather than the Mediterranean. It is not surprising, therefore, that the table wares of the period should be entirely Hellenistic in character, even when locally produced. Imported fine wares (the black-slipped BSP and its successor, Eastern Sigillata A) show contact with the Mediterranean coastal region around Antioch. The typology of Eastern Sigillata A changes substantially in the first century A.D. under the influence of Italian Sigillata, and the presence of these new forms helps to establish the terminal dates of Groups B and C. There are also at Zeugma (though they barely figure in the groups presented here) actual imports of Italian, and even Gaulish, Sigillata. Curiously, however, the local table-ware production ignores these developments completely and persists in the Hellenistic tradition into the late first or early second century A.D.; Gschwind has already drawn attention to this.[115]

In the second and third centuries A.D. an even more curious phenomenon occurs, with an almost total disappearance of table wares of any description, whether locally made or imported. This is a widespread phenomenon in the eastern Mediterranean, by no means exclusive to Zeugma: I have discussed it in the introduction to Group D[116] and have suggested that there may have been some sort of cultural change in eating habits. John Lund has demonstrated the occurrence of this phenomenon both at Hama in Syria[117] and at a range of sites in southwestern and southern Asia Minor.[118] He has discussed various possible causes, such as the cessation of many of the major fine-ware workshops (surely a consequence of the change, rather than a cause of it), generalized economic decline, and the substitution of other materials (metal, glass) for ceramic table ware. None of these alone seems to offer a satisfactory explanation; on the other hand, the very extent of the phenomenon does not altogether favor my suggestion of a change in eating habits. I can add to the debate only the fact that it occurs at Zeugma at a time when the settlement is clearly prosperous and when contemporary fine wares are still being imported to Antioch. Economic decline therefore does not provide a plausible explanation here. (Apart from the evident prosperity of the houses destroyed in the Sasanian sack, economic decline would in any case have initially favored cheap local production over imports, rather than seeing the disappearance of both.)

The buff and cooking wares are too poorly represented in Groups A and B for any cogent conclusions to be drawn from their character, but when the cooking wares become prolific in Group D, there are some notable absences from the repertoire. There are, for instance, no examples of the frying pan with tubular handle that is so common around the shores of the eastern Mediterranean,[119] and the Pompeian-Red *patina* is represented by local versions that are mostly far smaller than their Italian prototypes.[120] The pottery seems to suggest that in culinary practice, no less than in geographical terms, the inhabitants of Zeugma were on the very confines between the Mediterranean world and Mesopotamia.

In the Late Imperial period, imported table wares reappear, presumably through a reversal of whatever had brought about their disappearance in the second century. This is documented in the groups presented here only in the second half of the fifth century, though a little African Red Slip ware of the fourth and earlier fifth century was recovered in other parts of the Oxford Archaeology excavations, and in some of the French trenches.[121] The table ware comes from Africa, Cyprus, and western Asia Minor (Phocaea), while the cooking and storage wares belong very specifically to their own region, the middle Euphrates. After the Arab conquest, contact with the Mediterranean comes definitively to an end: Glazed fine wares and other high-quality ceramics are made within the region, but in a tradition that was developed in Mesopotamia and that owes nothing to the earlier fine wares of the Mediterranean world.

Finally, what of the position of Zeugma in regard to the so-called Silk Route between the Mediterranean and the Orient? Can we see at any point, in the ceramic record presented here, evidence of trade between the Mediterranean and the Far East? The answer to this is unequivocally 'No': while textiles might readily have been traded along this route, Chinese pottery would hardly have survived the rigors of such long journeys on carts or pack animals over hundreds of miles of mountainous terrain, and it is not surprising that it is absent.

INDEX TO OCCURRENCE OF FABRICS

Numbers shown in parentheses indicate parallels to the illustrated items.

Table Wares

BSP, PT31–37, 211–3, 321, 322
Local Hellenistic fine, PT1–12, 38–96, 214–240, 323
Hellenistic fine gray, PT13, 97, 98
Miscellaneous Hellenistic fine, PT99, 100
Eastern Sigillata A, PT14, 101–143, 241–265
Italian Sigillata, PT144, 324
Thin-walled wares, PT145–148, 266–268, 325, 326
African Red Slip, PT149, 327, Group E (before PT471), PT511–515
Phocaean Red Slip, Group D (after PT327), PT471–474, 516–528
Cypriot Red Slip, Group D (after PT327), PT475–477, Group F (after PT528),
Glazed 1, Group B (after PT149), Group C (after PT268), PT328, 330, 601–603
Glazed 2, Group C (after PT268), PT329
Glazed 3, PT604–606
Glazed 4, Group G (after PT606)
Glazed 5, PT607–617
Miscellaneous glazed, Group A (after PT14), PT618
Miscellaneous fine, PT269

Buff Wares

Buff 1–4, PT150–171, (229,) 270–279, (280, 293,) 331–395, 478–482, (490, 493,) 529–556, (572, 580, 582,) 619–622
Buff 5, (PT385,) Group D (after PT395)
Buff 6, PT172, 396–400, 483
Buff 8, (PT179,) 292, Group D (after PT400), PT484–492, (538–540,) 557–573, (574, 579,) 623–632
Buff 10, PT173–176, 405, 407, 408, 574, 575, 633–642
Buff 12, PT20, 190, 280, 281
Buff 13, PT15–18, (170,) 177–185, (222, 279, 280,) 282–286, (293, 352, 511, 550, 558, 572) 576, 577
Buff 14, (PT160,) 186, 192, 287–289, 406
Buff 15, (PT335, 352,) 493, 494, 578–580
Miscellaneous buff, PT19, 187–189, 191, 290, 291, 293, 401–404, 409–413, 581–553, 583, 643–647

Cooking Wares

Cooking 1, PT193–195, 294, 295, 311–320, 414–447, 495, 496, 584, 585

Cooking 2, PT196–198, 296, 297, 448, (495,) 497–500, 586–592, 648–657

Cooking 6, PT449, 501, 593

Cooking 7, PT199, 298, 299, 502

Cooking 8, PT21, 200, 201, 300, 301

Cooking 9, PT503, 504, Group F (after PT593), PT658

Cooking 10, PT659–663

Miscellaneous cooking, PT202, 450, 451

Storage Wares

Storage 1, Group C (after PT305), PT452–457, Group F (after PT594)

Storage 2, Group A (after PT21), PT302–304, 458, 459

Storage 4, PT460, 461

Storage 5, PT203, 505

Miscellaneous storage, Group A (after PT21), PT305, Group D (after PT461), PT594

INDEX OF CONTEXTS INCLUDED IN THE DATED GROUPS

1004	G	4008	E
1007	G	4011	E
1010	G	5048	E
1018	G	5078	E
1024	G	7005	F
1047	G	7007	C
2010	D	7023	C
2012	D	7026	F
2016	D	7036	F
2023	D	7062	F
2039	D	7065	F
2080	D	7066	F
2130	D	7076	F
2139	D	7118	B
2160	D	7203	F
2176	D	7214	F
2191	D	12002	F
2260	D	12011	F
2278	D	12012	F
2283	C	15009	B
2300	C	15095	B
2376	D	18108	D
4004	E	19005	A

NOTES

1. The study of the material in Turkey was carried out by myself during two weeks of August 2000, while the excavation was in progress, and over three periods amounting to 10 further weeks during the study season of 2002. During these periods, my comfort was greatly enhanced by the residential and working facilities provided at Birecik by GAP and by the day-to-day administrative support of the staff of Oxford Archaeology (OA). Amongst the latter, it is a pleasure to record that Adam Brossler, Andy Miller, and Philippa Walton were constantly and sympathetically supportive of my needs. Sait Yilmaz, the Turkish government representative, was unfailingly cooperative and proved himself to have a keen eye and steady hand for both the sorting and mending of pottery!

    Pencil drawings were made for me in the field by Luke Adams, with the assistance of Sara Lucas and Laura Fyles, and were worked up for publication in Oxford by the staff of OA. I am grateful to Luke, Sara, and Laura for their competence, companionship, and constant good humor. My thanks go to Bruce Sampson for the photographs.

    In the course of studying the pottery, I have benefited from discussions with William Aylward, Jennifer Tobin, and various other specialists involved in the production of the report: I record here my appreciation of the close liaison it has been possible to achieve between contributors. Discussion with Paul Reynolds (transport amphorae) has been particularly necessary and fruitful, not least for his extensive firsthand knowledge of Levantine pottery of all kinds. I am also indebted to Chris Doherty of the Research Laboratory for Archaeology and the History of Art (University of Oxford) for his petrographic report and for the input of his very considerable geological expertise.

    Finally, I am also grateful to Catherine Abadie-Reynal, director of the French team at Zeugma, for her willingness to discuss with me in June 2004 her preliminary impressions of the pottery found in the course of her excavations.

2. The dating and composition of the chronological groups is discussed on p. 10 ff. The periods assigned to them are as follows:
    A: Hellenistic, second half of second century B.C.
    B: Late Augustan or Tiberian
    C: Flavian (possibly Trajanic)
    D: Destruction levels associated with the Sasanian sack in A.D. 253
    E: Early sixth century A.D.
    F: Early seventh century A.D.
    G: Islamic, possible extending to the ninth or tenth century A.D.
3. See Doherty, question 1, this volume p. 85 (question 1).
4. See Doherty, question 1, this volume p. 85 (question 1).
5. See also Gschwind 2002, passim, for the same point.
6. See primarily Hayes 1985, 9–48, and Slane 1997, 269–346.
7. Schneider 2000, 531, 532; Malfitana et al. 2005.
8. Hayes 1985, forms 52–61, generally second century A.D.
9. See also Gschwind 2002, 336, nos. 57–63.
10. See Hayes 1972 and 1980; also the important reevaluation of dating in Pröttel 1996, 8–88, and the recent study by M. Bonifay, *Études sur la céramique romaine tardive d'Afrique*, BAR-IS 1301 (Oxford: 2004).
11. See Hayes 1972 and 1980; Pröttel 1996, 89–96.
12. See Hayes 1972 and 1980.
13. See particularly Toll 1943 on the material from Dura-Europos; a few sherds reached as far west as Antioch, but apparently only in the Hellenistic period: Waagé 1948, 80.
14. See Doherty, question 4 (this volume).
15. See Doherty, question 3 (this volume).
16. See Doherty, question 5 (this volume).

17. See Doherty, this volume, p. 86 (question 5).
18. See Doherty, this volume, pp. 86–87 (questions 6 and 8).
19. See Doherty, this volume, p. 87 (question 9).
20. Konrad 2001b, 164 and fig. 2.1: "a very traditional pattern on ceramics of the Euphrates region since Babylonian times."
21. I have seen the technique in use in a present-day potter's workshop near Aydın in western Turkey.
22. See the petrographic report by Doherty, this volume, p. 87 (question 9).
23. See Doherty, this volume, page 87 (questions 10–12).
24. Note one example in Group B (**PT172**) and three in the first-century deposit published by Gschwind (2002, 341; nos. 75–7).
25. See Doherty, this volume, p. 87 (question 12).
26. See Doherty, this volume, p. 85 (question 1).
27. See Doherty, this volume, p. 88 (question 16).
28. See Doherty, this volume, p. 90 (question 23).
29. See Doherty, this volume, p. 88 (question 17).
30. This constituted the second largest group in their study. The sherds were "mainly dated to the late Roman/early Byzantine periods" (p. 172).
31. See by Doherty, this volume, p. 88 (question 18).
32. Group 1 was the largest in their study, accounting for nearly half of the sherds examined, occurring in all areas and at all periods (p. 172). It predominates in the Balih Valley. The relative incidence of Cooking 1/Bartl Group 3 and Cooking 2/Bartl Group 1 at Zeugma vis-à-vis the survey area rather suggests that the former was produced upstream of Zeugma, and the latter somewhere downstream.
33. See Doherty, this volume, p. 89 (question 20).
34. See Doherty, this volume, p. 89 (question 21).
35. See Doherty, this volume, p. 90 (question 22). A single sherd from the study of Bartl et al. (1995: Group 4, found in the Balih Valley) may correspond to this fabric.
36. See Doherty, this volume, p. 91 (question 24). One sherd studied by Bartl et al. (1995: Group 5, from Tell Sheikh Hasan upstream of Dibsi Faraj) may correspond to this fabric.
37. See Doherty, this volume, p. 91 (question 26).
38. Jones 1950; Waagé 1948.
39. Aubert 2002.
40. McNicoll et al. 1982; 1992.
41. Harper 1980.
42. Konrad 1992.
43. Toll 1943; Cox 1949; Dyson 1968.
44. Oates 1959.
45. Hrouda 1962.
46. Campbell 1989.
47. Oates 1958.
48. Sarre 1925.
49. Orssaud 1980; Bavant and Orssaud 2001.
50. Harper 1980.
51. Mackensen 1984; Lugar 1992.
52. Konrad 2001a.
53. Grabar et al. 1978.
54. Miglus et al. 1999.
55. Kenrick 1981; Northedge 1981.
56. Bartl 1994, 1996.
57. Dorna-Metzger 1996.
58. Dörner and Goell 1963; Hoepfner 1983.
59. Gerber 1996.
60. Wilkinson 1990.
61. Mitchell 1980.
62. See Tobin, volume 1, p. 97.
63. See Aylward, volume 1, p. 122 n.16.
64. See Tobin, volume 1, p. 99.
65. Tobin, volume 1, p 78.
66. Tobin, volume 1, p 76.
67. Tobin, volume 1, p. 99.
68. Tobin, volume 1, p. 100.
69. Slane 1997, 307–8, Type TA 23.
70. See chapter by Aylward in volume 1, pp 8–9, 12.
71. Tobin, volume 1, p. 79.
72. Tobin, volume 1, p. 80.
73. See Reynolds, this volume, pp. 97–98, 109–110, context 2017.
74. Tobin, volume 1, p. 80, plate 30c.
75. Waagé 1948, Late A and B wares.
76. Jones 1950, 203–6.
77. Cox 1949, 14–6.
78. **PT331–340** and **PT403–407** in the buff wares hardly fill the gap.
79. Hayes 1985, Forms 52 ff., PL. 6–7.
80. Harper 1980, 331.
81. Kenrick 1981, 439.
82. Reynolds 1997–98, esp. 56 f.
83. Reynolds, this volume, pp. 112–17, Forms 14–9.
84. See Reynolds, this volume, p. 112, Form 13.
85. See Doherty, this volume, pp. 86, 88 (questions 6 and 17).
86. Reynolds, this volume, p. 111.
87. Cf. Reynolds, this volume, pp. 111–12, Forms 12–3.
88. Note also those in the first-century deposit published by Gschwind (2002, 341, nos. 75–7).
89. See Riley 1979, fig. 98, 100–2 and Berlin 1997, pl. 28–33.
90. E.g. Riley 1979, fig. 104.
91. **PT429**, which is intact, weighs only 370 g.
92. Catherine Abadie-Reynal informed me in 2004 that there was stratified material of the fourth and fifth centuries in Trench 14. See now Abadie-Reynal et al. 2007.
93. See Reynolds, this volume, pp. 90–91.
94. Knobbed lids of a broadly similar (though shallower) type occur at Dura-Europos before A.D. 256 (Dyson 1968, nos. 264–8).
95. See the petrographic report by Doherty, this volume, p. 87 (question 12) and the amphora report by Reynolds, this volume, pp. 112–17.
96. See Tobin, volume 1, pp. 101–02.
97. Pröttel 1996, 92.
98. See Tobin, volume 1, pp. 97–99.
99. See Butcher, volume 3, p. 4.
100. Tobin, volume 1, pp. 108–9.
101. Kennedy 1998, 161 no. 113.
102. See Runciman 1954, 210, 211.
103. Bartl 1994, 121–49.
104. Grabar et al. 1978, 157.
105. Miglus et al. 1999.
106. See Northedge 2001, 212.
107. For a useful summary of the state of research on Islamic glazed wares up to 1994, see Northedge 2001.
108. E.g. Miglus et al. 1999, Group Y.
109. See **PT32, 211, 321**.
110. Note three sherds of African Red Slip Ware of the fourth or fifth centuries in Group F: **PT511** and the two sherds listed after it.
111. See Butcher, volume 3, p. 4.
112. To be published by Catherine Abadie-Reynal, to whom I am grateful for this information. See provisionally Abadie-Reynal et al. 2007.
113. Information kindly provided by Catherine Abadie-Reynal.
114. Bartl et al. 1995.
115. Gschwind 2002, 349–50.
116. See p. 36.
117. Lund 1995.
118. Lund 1996.
119. See Riley 1979, 253–5 (Benghazi), "imported frying pan" and references.
120. See **PT311, 312, 414–417**.
121. Information from Catherine Abadie-Reynal.

BIBLIOGRAPHY

Abadie-Reynal, C., A.-S. Martz and A. Cador 2007. "Late Roman and Byzantine Pottery at Zeugma. Groups of the beginning of the 5th century." In *Çanak. Late Antique and Medieval Pottery and Tiles in Mediterranean Archaeological Contexts*, edited by B. Bohlendorf-Arslan, A. Osman Uysal and J. Witte-Orr, 181–194. Byzas 7. Istanbul: DAI Abteilung Istanbul.

Abadie-Reynal, C. and A.-S. Martz 2010. "La céramique commune de Zeugma et les problèmes de provenance (Ve–VIIe s.)." In *LRCW3—Late Roman Coarse Wares, Cooking Wares and Amphorae in the Mediterranean: Archaeology and Archaeometry. Comparison between western and eastern Mediterranean*, edited by S. Menchelli, S. Santoro, M. Pasquinucci, G. Guiducci, 839–845. BAR IS-2185. Oxford: British Archaeological Reports.

Aubert, C. 2002. "Les céramiques hellénistiques de Beyrouth: Caractéristiques des productions locales." In *Céramiques hellénistiques et romaines: Productions et diffusion en Méditerranée orientale (Chypre, Égypte et côte syro-palestinienne)*, edited by F. Blondé, P. Ballet, and J.-F. Salles, 73–84. Lyon: Maison de l'Orient Méditerranéen–Jean Pouilloux.

Bailey, D.M. 1988. *A Catalogue of the Lamps in the British Museum*. Vol. 3, *Roman Provincial Lamps*. London: British Museum Press.

Bartl, K. 1994. *Frühislamische Besiedlung im Balih-Tal/Nordsyrien*. Berlin: Reimer.

———. 1996. "Balih Valley Survey: Settlements of the Late Roman/Early Byzantine and Islamic Period." In *Continuity and Change in Northern Mesopotamia from the Hellenistic to the Early Islamic Period. Proceedings of a Colloquium Held at the Seminar für Vorderasiatische Altertumskunde, Freie Universität Berlin, 6–9 April 1994*, edited by K. Bartl and S.R. Hauser, 333–48. Berliner Beiträge zum Vorderen Orient 17. Berlin: Reimer.

Bartl, K., G. Schneider, and S. Bohme. 1995. "Notes on 'Brittle Wares' in North-Eastern Syria." *Levant* 27:165–77.

Bavant, B., and D. Orssaud. 2001. "Stratigraphie et typologie: Problèmes posés par l'utilisation de la céramique comme critère de datation: L'exemple de la fouille de Déhès." In *La céramique Byzantine et proto-islamique en Syrie-Jordanie (IVe–VIIIe siècles apr. J.-C.). Actes du colloque tenu à Amman les 3, 4 et 5 Décembre 1994*, edited by E. Villeneuve and P.M. Watson, 33–48. BAHBeyrouth 159. Beirut: Institut français d'archéologie du Proche-Orient.

Berlin, A. 1997. "The Plain Wares." In *Tel Anafa*. Vol. 2, pt. 1, *The Hellenistic and Roman Pottery*, edited by S.C. Herbert, ix–244. JRA Suppl. 10. Ann Arbor: Kelsey Museum of the University of Michigan.

Campbell, B. 1989. "The Roman Pottery from Seh Qubba, North Iraq." In *The Eastern Frontier of the Roman Empire: Proceedings of a Colloquium Held at Ankara in September 1988*, edited by D.H. French and C.S. Lightfoot, 53–65. BAR-IS 553. Oxford: British Archaeological Reports.

Catling, H.W., and A.I. Dikigoropoulos. 1970. "The Kornos Cave: An Early Byzantine Site in Cyprus." *Levant* 2:37–62.

Christensen, A.P., and C.F. Johansen. 1971. *Hama: Fouilles et recherches 1931–1938*. Vol. 3, pt. 2, *Les poteries hellénistiques et les terres sigillées orientales*. Copenhagen: Nationalmuseet.

Cornell, L. 1997. "A Note on the Molded Bowls." In *Tel Anafa*. Vol. 2, pt. 1, *The Hellenistic and Roman Pottery*, edited by S.C. Herbert, 407–16. JRA Suppl. 10. Ann Arbor: Kelsey Museum of the University of Michigan.

Cox, D.H. 1949. *The Excavations at Dura-Europos, Final Report*. Vol. 4, pt. 1, fasc. 2, *The Greek and Roman Pottery*. New Haven: Yale University Press.

Crowfoot, J.W., G.M. Crowfoot, and K.M. Kenyon. 1957. *The Objects from Samaria*. London: Palestine Exploration Fund.

Dorna-Metzger, F. 1996. "Hellenistic and Parthian-Roman Pottery from the Upper Khabur Survey: A Preliminary Study." In *Continuity and Change in Northern Mesopotamia from the Hellenistic to the Early Islamic Period. Proceedings of a Colloquium Held at the Seminar für Vorderasiatische Altertumskunde, Freie Universität Berlin, 6–9 April 1994*, edited by K. Bartl and S.R. Hauser, 363–75. Berliner Beiträge zum Vorderen Orient 17. Berlin: Reimer.

Dörner, F.K., and T. Goell. 1963. *Arsameia am Nymphaios: Die Ausgrabungen im Hierothesion des Mithridates Kallinikos von 1953–1956*. Berlin: Gebr. Mann.

Dyson, S. 1968. *The Excavations at Dura-Europos, Final Report*. Vol. 4, pt.1, fasc.3, *The Commonware Pottery: The Brittle Ware*. Locust Valley: J.J. Augustin for Dura-Europos Publications.

Ettlinger, E., et al. 1990. *Conspectus formarum terrae sigillatae italico modo confectae*. Materialien zur römisch-germanischen Keramik 10. Bonn: Rudolf Habelt.

Gerber, C. 1996. "Die Umgebung des Lidar Höyük von hellenistischer bis frühislamischer Zeit." In *Continuity and Change in Northern Mesopotamia from the Hellenistic to the Early Islamic Period. Proceedings of a Colloquium Held at the Seminar für Vorderasiatische Altertumskunde, Freie Universität Berlin, 6–9 April 1994*, edited by K. Bartl and S.R. Hauser, 303–22. Berliner Beiträge zum Vorderen Orient 17. Berlin: Reimer.

Grabar, O., et al. 1978. *City in the Desert: Qasr al-Hayr East*. Cambridge: Harvard University Press.

Gschwind, M. 2002. "Hellenistische Tradition contra italische Mode: Ein frühkaiserzeitliche Keramikkomplex aus den türkischen Rettungsgrabungen in Zeugma am mittleren Euphrat." *DM* 13:321–59.

Guérin, A. 1996."L'occupation abbasside de Nasibin: Typologie et chronologie préliminaires de la céramique prospectée en surface." In *Continuity and Change in Northern Mesopotamia from the Hellenistic to the Early Islamic Period. Proceedings of a Colloquium Held at the Seminar für Vorderasiatische Altertumskunde, Freie Universität Berlin, 6–9 April 1994*, edited by K. Bartl and S.R. Hauser, 377–400. Berliner Beiträge zum Vorderen Orient 17. Berlin: Reimer.

Harper, R.P. 1980. "Athis—Neocaesareia—Qasrin—Dibsi Faraj." In *Le moyen Euphrate, zone de contacts et d'échanges. Actes du colloque de Strasbourg 10–12 mars 1977*, edited by J.C. Margueron, 327–48. Leiden: Brill.

Hartley, K.F. 1973. "La diffusion des mortiers, tuiles et autres produits en provenance des fabriques italiennes." *Cahiers d'archéologie subaquatique* 2:49–60.

Hayes, J.W. 1967. "North Syrian Mortaria." *Hesperia* 36:337–47.

———. 1972. *Late Roman Pottery*. London: The British School at Rome.

———. 1973. "Roman Pottery from the South Stoa at Corinth." *Hesperia* 42:416–70.

———. 1976. *Roman Pottery in the Royal Ontario Museum: A Catalogue*. Toronto: Royal Ontario Museum.

———. 1980. *A Supplement to Late Roman Pottery*. London: The British School at Rome.

———. 1985. "Sigillate orientali." In *EAA Atlante delle forme ceramiche ii: Ceramica fine romana nel bacino mediterraneo (tardo ellenismo e primo impero)*, 1–96. Rome: Istituto della Enciclopedia Italiana.

Hoepfner, W. 1983. *Arsameia am Nymphaios*. Vol. 2, *Das Hirothesion des Königs Mithridates I. Kallinikos von Kommagene nach den Ausgrabungen von 1963 bis 1967*. Tübingen: Wasmuth.

Hrouda, B. 1962. *Tell Halaf*. Vol. 4, *Die Kleinfunde aus historischer Zeit*. Berlin: De Gruyter.

Jones, F.F. 1950. "The Pottery." In *Excavations at Gözlü Kule, Tarsus*. Vol. 1, edited by H. Goldman, 149–296. Princeton: Princeton University Press.

Kennedy, D.L., et al. 1998. *The Twin Towns of Zeugma on the Euphrates: Rescue Work and Historical Studies.* JRA Suppl. 27. Portsmouth: Journal of Roman Archaeology.

Kenrick, P.M. 1981. "Fine Wares of the Hellenistic and Roman Periods." In *The River Qoueiq, Northern Syria, and Its Catchment*, edited by J. Matthers, 439–58. BAR-IS 98. Oxford: British Archaeological Reports.

———. 1985. *Excavations at Sidi Khrebish, Benghazi (Berenice).* Vol. 3, pt. 1, *The Fine Pottery: Supplements to Libya Antiqua* 5.3.1. Tripoli: Department of Antiquities, and London: Society for Libyan Studies.

Kloner, A., et al. 2003. *Maresha Excavations Final Report I: Subterranean Complexes 21, 44, 70.* IAA Reports 17. Jerusalem: Israel Antiquities Authority.

Konrad, M. 1992. "Flavische und spätantike Bebauung unter der Basilika B von Resafa." *DM* 6:313–402.

———. 2001a. *Resafa.* Vol. 5, *Der spätrömische Limes in Syrien: Archäologische Untersuchungen an den Grenzkastellen von Sura, Tetrapyrgium, Cholle und in Resafa.* Mainz am Rhein: Philipp von Zabern.

———. 2001b. "Umayyad Pottery from Tetrapyrgium (Qseir es-Seileh), North Syria. Traditions and Innovations." In *La céramique Byzantine et proto-islamique en Syrie-Jordanie (IVe–VIIIe siècles apr. J.-C.). Actes du colloque tenu à Amman les 3, 4 et 5 décembre 1994*, edited by E. Villeneuve and P.M. Watson, 163–91. BAHBeyrouth 159. Beirut: Institut français d'archéologie du Proche-Orient.

Lugar, N. 1992. "Die Kleinfunde aus dem Westhofbereich der großen Basilika von Resafa." *DM* 6:417–78.

Lund, J. 1995. "A Fresh Look at the Roman and Late Roman Fine Wares from the Danish Excavations at Hama, Syria." In *Hellenistc and Roman Pottery in the Eastern Mediterranean—Advances in Scientific Studies. Acts of the II Nieborów Pottery Workshop*, edited by H. Meyza and J. Młynarczyk, 135–61. Warsaw: Research Centre for Mediterranean Archaeology, Polish Academy of Sciences.

———. 1996. "From Archaeology to History? Reflections on the Chronological Distribution of Ceramic Finewares in South Western and Southern Asia Minor from the 1st to the 7th c. A.D." In *Hellenistischer und kaiserzeitliche Keramik des östlichen Mittelmeergebietes. Kolloquium Frankfurt 24–25 April 1995*, edited by M. Herfort-Koch, U. Mandel, and U. Schädler, 105–25. Frankfurt am Mainz: Arbeitskreis Frankfurt und die Antike.

Mackensen, M. 1984. *Resafa.* Vol. 1, *Eine befestigte spätantike Anlage vor den Stadtmauern von Resafa.* Mainz am Rhein: Philipp von Zabern.

———. 1993. *Die spätantiken Sigillata- und Lampentöpfereien von El Mahrine (Nordtunesien).* Munich: Beck.

Malfitana, D., J. Poblome, and J. Lund. 2005. "Eastern Sigillata A in Italy: A Socio-economic Evaluation." *BABesch* 80:190–212.

Marabini Moevs, M.T. 1973. *The Roman Thin-Walled Pottery from Cosa.* MAAR 32.

Martz, A.-S., 2007. "Les vases a cuire de Zeugma du IIIe au VIIe s.", *LRCW2—Late Roman Coarse Wares, Cooking Wares and Amphorae in the Mediterranean: Archaeology and Archaeometry*, edited by M. Bonifay and J.-C. Treglia, 739–743. BAR IS-1662. Oxford: British Archaeological Reports.

Mason, R.B., and E.J. Keall. 1991. "The Abbasid Glazed Wares of Siraf and the Basra Connection: Petrographic Analysis." *Iran* 29:51–66.

McNicoll, A., R. H. Smith, and B. Hennessy. 1982. *Pella in Jordan.* Vol. 1, *An Interim Report on the Joint University of Sydney and The College of Wooster Excavations at Pella 1979–1981.* Canberra: The Australian National Gallery.

McNicoll, A.W., et al. 1992. *Pella in Jordan.* Vol. 2, *The Second Interim Report of the Joint University of Sydney and College of Wooster Excavations at Pella 1982–1985.* Mediterranean Archaeology Suppl. 2. Sydney: MeditArch.

Miglus, P.A., et al. 1999. *Ar-Raqqa.* Vol. 1, *Die frühislamischeKeramik von Tall Aswad.* Mainz am Rhein: Philipp von Zabern.

Mitchell, S. 1980. *Aşvan Kale, Keban Rescue Excavations, Eastern Anatolia.* Vol. 1, *The Hellenistic, Roman and Islamic Sites.* BAR-IS 80. Oxford: British Archaeological Reports.

Northedge, A. 1981."Selected Late Roman and Islamic Coarse Wares." In *The River Qoueiq, Northern Syria, and Its Catchment*, edited by J. Matthers, 459–71. BAR-IS 98. Oxford: British Archaeological Reports.

———. 2001 "Thoughts on the Introduction of Polychrome Glazed Pottery in the Middle East." In *La céramique Byzantine et proto-islamique en Syrie-Jordanie (IVe–VIIIe siècles apr. J.-C.). Actes du colloque tenu à Amman les 3, 4 et 5 décembre 1994*, edited by E. Villeneuve and P.M. Watson, 207–14. BAHBeyrouth 159. Beirut: Institut français d'archéologie du Proche-Orient.

Oates, D., and J. Oates. 1958. "Nimrud 1957: The Hellenistic Settlement." *Iraq* 20:114–57.

———. 1959. "Ain Sinu: A Roman Frontier Post in Northern Iraq." *Iraq* 21:207–42.

Orssaud, D. 1980. "La céramique." In "Déhès (Syrie du Nord), Campagnes I–III (1976–1978). Recherches sur l'habitat rural," edited by J.-P. Sodini et al., 234–66. *Syria* 57:1–304.

Pröttel, P.M. 1996. *Mediterrane Feinkeramik des 2.–7. Jahrhunderts n. Chr. im oberen Adriaraum und in Slowenien.* Kölner Studien zur Archäologie der römischen. Provinzen 2. Espelkamp: Verlag Marie Leidorf.

Reynolds, P. 1997–1998. "Pottery Production and Economic Exchange in Second Century Berytus: Some Preliminary Observations of Ceramic Trends from Quantified Ceramic Deposits from the AUB-Leverhulme Excavations in Beirut." *Berytus* 43:35–110.

———. 2002. "The Pottery." In "Roman and Late-Antique Butrint: Excavations and Survey 2000–2001," edited by W. Bowdon, R. Hodges, and K. Lako, 221–7. *JRA* 15:199–229.

Ricci, A. 1985. "Ceramica a pareti sottili." In *EAA Atlante delle forme ceramiche ii: Ceramica fine romana nel bacino mediterraneo (tardo ellenismo e primo impero)*, 231–357. Rome: Istituto della Enciclopedia Italiana.

Riley, J.A. 1979. "The Coarse Pottery from Berenice." In *Excavations at Sidi Khrebish, Benghazi (Berenice)*, Vol. 2, edited by J.A. Lloyd, 91–467. Supplements to Libya Antiqua 5.2. Tripoli: Department of Antiquities.

Römer, C. 1996. "A First Glimpse at Glazed Pottery from Tell Seh Hamad." In *Continuity and Change in Northern Mesopotamia from the Hellenistic to the Early Islamic Period. Proceedings of a Colloquium Held at the Seminar für Vorderasiatische Altertumskunde, Freie Universität Berlin, 6–9 April 1994*, edited by K. Bartl and S.R. Hauser, 13–21. Berliner Beiträge zum Vorderen Orient 17. Berlin: Reimer.

Rotroff, S.I. 1997. *The Athenian Agora.* Vol. 29, *Hellenistic Pottery: Athenian and Imported Wheelmade Tableware and Related Material.* Princeton: The American School of Classical Studies at Athens.

Runciman, S. 1954. *A History of the Crusades.* Vol. 1, *The First Crusade.* Cambridge: Cambridge University Press.

Sarre, F. 1925. *Die Ausgrabungen von Samarra.* Vol. 2, *Die Keramik von Samarra.* Berlin: Reimer.

Schneider, G. 2000. "Chemical and Mineralogical Studies of Late Hellenistic to Byzantine Pottery Production in the Eastern Mediterranean." *Rei Cretariae Romanae Fautorum Acta* 36:525–36. Abingdon: R.C.R.F.

Schneider, G. et al. 2007. "Some new results of archaeometric analysis of brittle wares." In *LRCW2—Late Roman Coarse Wares, Cooking Wares and Amphorae in the Mediterranean: Archaeology and*

Archaeometry, edited by M. Bonifay and J.-C. Treglia, 715–729. BAR IS-1662. Oxford: British Archaeological Reports.

Slane, K.W. 1997. "The Fine Wares." In *Tel Anafa*. Vol. 2, pt. 1, *The Hellenistic and Roman Pottery*, edited by S.C. Herbert, 247–418. *JRA* Suppl. 10. Ann Arbor: Kelsey Museum of the University of Michigan.

Toll, N. 1943. *The Excavations at Dura-Europos, Final Report.* Vol. 4, pt. 1, fasc. 3, *The Green Glazed Pottery.* New Haven: Yale University Press.

Venco Ricciardi, R. 1982. "La ceramica partica." In *Tell Barri/Khahat, relazione preliminare sulle campagne 1980 e 1981 a Tell Barri/Khahat nel bacino del Habur*, edited by P.E. Pecorella and M. Salvini, 55–76. Rome: CNR Istituto per gli Studi Micenei ed Egeo-Anatolici.

Vokaer, A. 2010. "Cooking in a perfect pot. Shapes, fabrics and function of cooking ware in Late Antique Syria." In *LRCW3—Late Roman Coarse Wares, Cooking Wares and Amphorae in the Mediterranean: Archaeology and Archaeometry. Comparison between western and eastern Mediterranean*, edited by S. Menchelli, S. Santoro, M. Pasquinucci, G. Guiducci, 115–119. BAR IS-2185. Oxford: British Archaeological Reports.

———. 2011. *La Brittle Ware en Syrie. Production et diffusion d'une céramique culinaire de l'époque hellénistique à l'époque omeyyade.* Fouilles d'Apamée de Syrie, 2, Mémoires de la Classe des Lettres in 4°, tome III. Brussels: Académie royale de Belgique.

Waagé, F.O. 1948. "Hellenistic and Roman Tableware of North Syria." In *Antioch-on-the-Orontes*. Vol. 4, pt. 1, *Ceramics and Islamic Coins*, edited by F.O. Waagé, 1–60. Princeton: Princeton University Press.

Wilkinson, T.J. 1990. *Town and Country in Southeastern Anatolia.* Vol. 1, *Settlement and Land Use at Kürban Höyük and Other Sites in the Lower Karababa Basin.* OIP 109. Chicago: Oriental Institute of the University of Chicago.

Williams, C. 1989. *Anemurium: The Roman and Early Byzantine Pottery.* Subsidia Mediaevalia 16. Toronto: Pontifical Institute of Mediaeval Studies.

POSTSCRIPT (August 2012)

The foregoing report was submitted for publication in 2004. In the intervening years, much has been published on the pottery of the region, not least by the French team that has worked at Zeugma. Regrettably, it has not been possible to revise the text to take account of those studies. The reader is directed in particular to Abadie-Reynal et al. (2007), Abadie-Reynal and Martz (2010), Martz (2007), Schneider et al. (2007), Vokaer (2010) and Vokaer (2011) which entries have at least been added to the bibliography.

· CHAPTER TWO ·

Petrographic Analysis of Table and Kitchen Wares

Chris Doherty

TERMS OF REFERENCE

This report presents a petrographic study of table and kitchen ware pottery samples from the rescue excavations at Zeugma. Petrographic analysis of pottery employs the concept of the pottery fabric, which is defined by the sum of the constituent minerals and tempers, etc., and the overall micro structure. The fabric is the common descriptive unit, and a series of fabrics may be interpreted to provide the following information:

- The existence of fabric groups, i.e., classification of the total sherds into groups based on similar fabric elements. This provides a very valuable method of comparison, independent from that based on external characteristics (i.e., pottery form and style).

- Technological aspects such as evidence for raw material processing (e.g., the addition of temper), surface decoration, and firing conditions.

- The source of the raw materials (i.e., their provenance). This involves a comparison with the known or predicted characteristics of usable clays in the site area, or from other areas from where pottery might have been traded or imported.

Lab ref.	Fabric group	Sample ref.	Visual characteristics
ZG1	"Local" Hellenistic fine ware	Sample A	very fine — orange — oxidized
ZG1a	"Local" Hellenistic fine ware	Sample B	very fine — orange — oxidized
ZG2	Glazed fine ware	Fabric 1	very fine — greenish — oxidized — low Fe
ZG3	Glazed fine ware	Fabric 2	greenish — abundant fine sand — low Fe
ZG4	Glazed fine ware	Fabric 3	very fine — greenish — oxidized — low Fe
ZG5	Glazed fine ware	Fabric 4	very fine — greenish — not fully oxidized — low Fe
ZG6	Glazed fine ware	Fabric 5	very fine — orange — oxidized
ZG7	Buff ware	Fabric 1	orange — fine sand
ZG8	Buff ware	Fabric 2	orange — fine sand — underoxidized inner
ZG9	Buff ware	Fabric 3	fine sand — orange — oxidized throughout
ZG10	Buff ware	Fabric 4	brown — fine sand — underoxidized
ZG11	Buff ware	Fabric 5	orange — fine sand — with coarser carbonate
ZG12	Buff ware	Fabric 6	buff — fine sand (with ferruginous grains)
ZG13	Buff ware	Fabric 8	buff — fine sand (with ferruginous grains)
ZG14	Buff ware	Fabric 10	buff outer but orange core — fine sand
ZG15	Buff ware	Fabric 11 (**PT402**)	brown — fine sand — underoxidized
ZG16	Buff ware	Fabric 13	buff-orange — very fine sand
ZG17	Buff ware	Fabric 15	buff — very fine sand/silt
ZG18	Cooking ware	Fabric 1	red — fine sand — high Fe/low Ca
ZG19	Cooking ware	Fabric 2	red — fine sand — high Fe/low Ca
ZG20	Cooking ware	Fabric 4 (**PT450**)	light brown/buff — fine sand — underoxidized core
ZG21	Cooking ware	Fabric 7	orange/buff — medium sand
ZG22	Cooking ware	Fabric 8	orange — medium sand
ZG23	Cooking ware	Fabric 9	coarse sand — red outer but underoxidized core/inner
ZG24	Storage ware	Fabric 2	coarse mixed sand and carbonate–red with brown core
ZG25	Storage ware	Fabric 3	coarse mixed sand and carbonate–red with brown core
ZG26	Storage ware	Fabric 5	buff — coarse angular sand
ZG27	Reference only	Euphrates sand	Birecik: locally extracted building sand

Table 1. Zeugma table and kitchen ware sherds submitted for fabric analysis

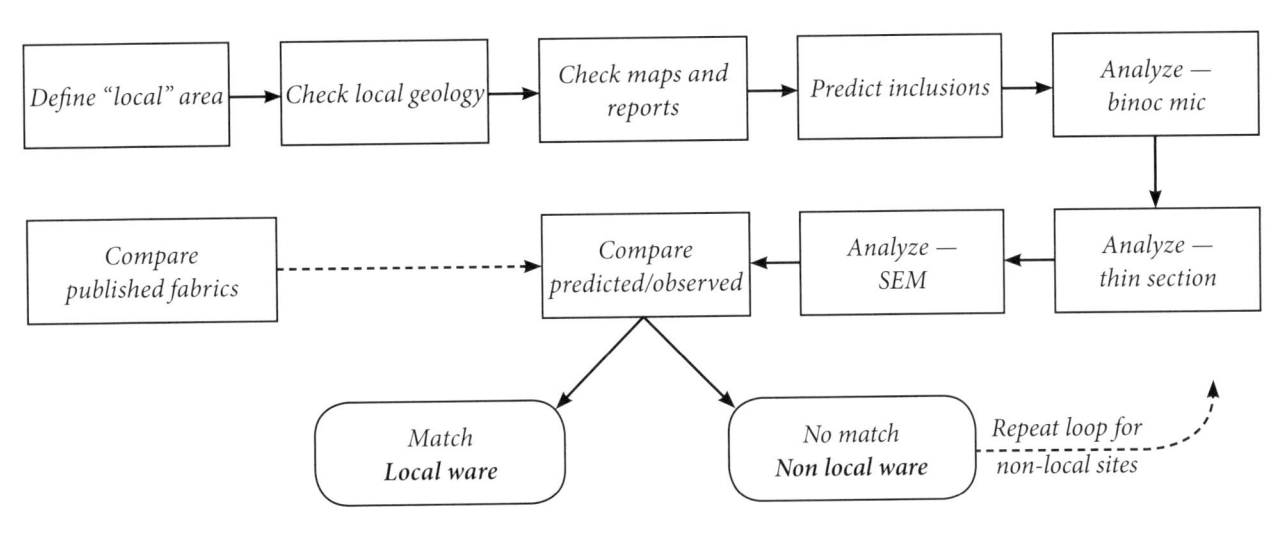

Figure 1. Outline of petrographic provenancing method.

These general aspects are reported in this chapter, in addition to answers to a series of more specific questions posed by the pottery specialist, Dr. Philip Kenrick, when the samples were submitted.

THE SAMPLES

A total of 28 samples were submitted for analysis, including a reference sample of graded building sand from a plant at Birecik that dredges its material from the Euphrates. Table 1 lists the sample details.

METHODS

All samples were initially observed using low-magnification stereo binocular microscopy in the as-received state, to record those macro-characteristics often less evident in thin section (e.g., overall color and color distribution, presence of mica at surfaces, etc.). Next, sherds were prepared as standard petrographic thin sections following impregnation with epoxy resin.

Thin sections were examined using a standard polarizing microscope (a Nikon Optiphot-2 model) to record the nature of the inclusions and clay matrix, i.e., the fabric of the sherd.

Compositionally these fabrics are complex, containing a relatively large suite of mineral and other inclusions. This is consistent with the highly varied geology of southeast Turkey, the catchment of the Euphrates headwaters. The petrography is further complicated due to

- natural weathering of many of the minerals, obscuring some of their diagnostic optical properties;
- transformation of many minerals due to firing;
- the very fine grain size.

Clearly, discriminating between locally produced pottery and that which may have been traded demands a comprehensive understanding of the compositional characteristics of the local clay. Towards this end, thin-section analysis of the Birecik sand reference sample was supplemented by scanning electron microscopy (SEM). This technique combines very high magnification with the ability to perform discrete quantitative chemical analysis on individual minerals, to assist the identification of problematic inclusions. The instrument used in this study was a Cameca SU30 Semprobe fitted with a PGT energy dispersive analyzer (EDA). Typical operating conditions for quantitative EDA were 15 kV, 10 nA, 100 second count time.

THE NATURE OF THE LOCAL POTTERY CLAYS AT ZEUGMA

Ideally, pottery provenance studies should involve the sampling of potential clay deposits at the site, for petrographic characterization and to determine the degree of stratigraphic and lateral variation. Unfortunately, there was no opportunity for such fieldwork in this case, and the expected nature of the locally available clay had to be modeled indirectly. This is commonly the case for many provenance studies, as sites are often not accessible (or even known). In these cases, the success of indirect modeling is very dependant on the quality of the available geological and soil maps and reports of the area. For Zeugma the degree of geological coverage is moderately good.

Figure 1 shows the general scheme adopted for identifying the possible provenance for these wares. A review of the local geology of Zeugma and of the Euphrates headwaters allows a prediction to be made of the types of inclusions likely to be present in Zeugma clays. The predicted mineralogy is then tested against the observations made on the reference sand samples and the inclusion list is

	Sedimentary	Igneous	Metamorphic
Rock type	Conglomerates, sandstones, siltstones, mudstones, marl (including gypsum-bearing), carbonates, chert.	Acid, intermediate, basic, and ultra-basic intrusives (granite, granodiorite, diorite, gabbro, etc.), extrusives (rhyolite, dacite, andesite, basalt, etc.), and volcanoclastics (tuff, tuffite).	Medium- and low-grade regional metamorphic rocks of amphibolite and greenschist facies. Dynamometamorphic rocks (i.e., crushed, sheared fabrics) with abundant vein quartz.
Main minerals and rock debris	Quartz, potassium feldspar, plagioclase feldspar, muscovite, chert, calcite, fossil fragments, Foraminifera, etc.	Quartz, potassium feldspar, plagioclase, feldspar, muscovite, biotite, amphiboles, clinopyroxene, olivine, volcanic glass, groundmass.	Quartz, epidote, albite, chlorite, biotite, muscovite, amphibole (Ca+Mg), serpentine, zeolites.
Minor minerals	Amphibole, pyroxene, olivine, rutile, zircon.	Chromite, magnetite, ilmenite, sphene, zircon, tourmaline, rutile, anatase.	Kyanite, garnet, stauralite, chloritoid, talc.

Table 2. The geology of the Euphrates headwaters.

modified accordingly. A final modification may be made to accommodate clay/inclusion details published in archaeological site or pottery reports for the region, particularly those employing a similar or overlapping methodology. However, a main difficulty when comparing fabrics against those previously published is the petrographic detail in the latter. Where this is comprehensive, then a useful comparison can be made. More commonly, however, published petrographic descriptions are brief, often designed to summarize rather than fully characterize the pottery. Here it is often very difficult to make comparisons with the fabrics being studied.

At the end of this procedure we have a good working list of inclusions that can be considered to be characteristic of the local clay and, from our review of the sedimentology and climate of the region, an understanding of how much variation might be expected on a local and regional scale.

Predicted Euphrates Clay Mineralogy at Zeugma

There are two sources for predicting the expected clay characteristics: geological maps and published reports. In this study we are interested in a relatively large area upstream of Zeugma. This is because sediments being deposited at Zeugma are mainly derived from the headwaters of the Euphrates and closely reflect the geology of southeast Turkey. These inherited sediment characteristics persist the full length of the Euphrates but become increasingly modified by sediment coming in from local tributaries and the eroding river banks. At Zeugma the local geology is dominated by limestones, with lesser interbedded sandstones. These variably dilute the main Euphrates sediment by adding mainly limestone (including fossil debris) and sand grains. The magnitude of this local modification increases away from the main Euphrates channel, being most marked at the floodplain margins.[1]

By any standard, the geology of southeast Turkey is very complex, with a wide range of rock types occurring in a relatively small geographical area. Further, many of the rock units have an overall east-west trend, and as the Euphrates flows north-south over a large part of its upper course it erodes a relatively large range of rock types. The result is a mineralogically complex sediment load. Table 2 summarizes the main rock types within the Euphrates catchment and predicts the minerals likely to be liberated by their erosion.

Observed Euphrates (Clay) Mineralogy at Zeugma

The typical inclusions that might be expected in clay made from Zeugma can be approximated by analysis of a sand fraction taken from the active channel at Birecik. While there will be some differences, most of the sand inclusions will also be those found in near-channel clays. Table 3 identifies the inclusions found in this reference sand.

A comparison of table 2 with table 3 shows that there is a relatively good agreement between the predicted and observed inclusion types. The main differences result from the fact that the predicted inclusion list is based mainly on material being eroded in the Euphrates headwaters and does not account for sediment from local tributaries and wadis. This latter input is volumetrically less significant in the center of the floodplain but becomes more important towards the margins. The local geology at Zeugma is dominated by limestones with interbedded sandstones. These would be expected to contribute mainly carbonate, fossil debris, and sand grains, all of which are observed in the Birecik sand.

Having verified the predicted characteristics of the local clay at Zeugma, we can now confidently recognize non-local fabrics on the basis of their anomalous inclusions.

Aegerine-augite	Colorless amphibole	Phrenite	Serpentine
Allanite	Clinopyroxene	Plagioclase	Sphene
Apatite	Dacite	Polycrystalline quartz	Titanaugite
Basalt	Epidote	Phyllite	Titanomagnetite
Basaltic glass	Fe-alteration	Magnetite	Tourmaline
Biosparite	Foraminifera	Micrite	Trachyte
Bioclasts	Garnet	Monocrystalline quartz	Tremolite
Biotite	Granite	Muscovite	Vein quartz
Calcite	Granodiorite	Myrmekite	Zircon
Chert	Hornblende	Orthoclase	
Chlorite	Ilmenite	Rutile	
Chromite	Potassium feldspar	Rhyolite	

Table 3. Inclusions observed in Euphrates sand from Birecik.

RESULTS

This program of petrographic analysis addresses several queries relating to fabric groups for the Zeugma table and kitchen wares, these groups having been established in the field by the pottery specialist. Accordingly, the findings of this analysis are presented here as replies to these specific questions.

"Local" Hellenistic Fine Ware

Question 1: This is presumed to be local (or at least regional) because of its frequency and because of the resemblance of the clay to that of the most common buff ware fabric. Is this justified? Two samples are submitted: Sample A has no visible inclusions; B contains some very fine white specks and mica. Are these merely variants of the same clay, or are there significant differences? **Responses:** Sample A: a comparison of the following list of mineral inclusions with table 2 verifies that this is a local fabric. These are chert, basalt, zoned plagioclase, monocrystalline quartz, polycrystalline quartz, carbonate, microgranite, orthoclase, muscovite, biotite, altered basalt (ferruginous alteration products), serpentine, augite, and epidote. Inclusions are typically angular in shape, are of very fine grain size (estimated mean 0.15 mm, max. 0.75 mm), and represent 10–15 percent of the total sherd volume.

Sample B: this sample has a very similar suite of inclusions to sample A, but there are some small differences, i.e.:

- B has a significant amount of Ca-amphiboles; these are absent/very rare in A.
- B has a much higher proportion of total inclusions (estimated at 25–30 percent of total sherd volume). The inclusion size and shape characteristics are the same as in sample A.
- B has more fine-grained carbonate in the matrix (although the latter is likely to be less conspicuous in the higher fired sample A).

Clearly, these samples are closely related, as both contain the typical Euphrates mineralogy. Both are micaceous but this is more obvious with sample B, which is more inclusionrich. The lighter color of sample B is mainly due to dilution by a high proportion of light-colored carbonate. However, the presence of significant amounts of amphibole in sample B does suggest the use of slightly different clays. The shape of these amphibole grains (euhedral) suggests that they are derived from volcanic material, either (andesitic) lava flows or ash. The interpretation suggested here is that these clays are derived from different floodplain terraces, one of which (B) was forming at a time when volcanic activity was introducing ash or flows into the Euphrates catchment. Unfortunately the existing geological literature does not record compositional differences between the Euphrates terraces at this resolution. Table 4 summarizes the similarities and differences between the relevant fabrics.

Glazed Fine Wares

Question 2: Are fabrics 1 ("Parthian") and 3 related or distinct?* **Response:** These are quite different. Fabric 1 is very fine-grained, has no sand, and has abundant carbonized plant remains. Fabric 3 is higher-fired but originally would have contained a significant amount of rhombic (soil) carbonate plus small amounts of granitic sand. These fabrics could be lateral floodplain equivalents, with fabric 1 clays being derived from near the main Euphrates channel, fabric 3 at the flood plain margin.

Question 3: Is fabric 3 related to Buff fabrics 1–3? **Response:** Yes. Fabric 3 is characterized by a fairly typical Euphrates mineral/clastic assemblage including quartz, potassium feldspar, plagioclase feldspar, chert, basalt, micaschist, quartz-epidote, carbonates, and ferruginous weath-

---

*The samples were chosen and the questions formulated before it was appreciated that not all of the glazed wares are Islamic in date. — PMK

	Local Hellenistic fine (A)	Local Hellenistic fine (B)
Buff 1	Similar inclusions but Buff 1 is a much coarser fabric (mean grain size 0.5 mm compared to 0.15 mm for sample A).	Differs in grain size, as with sample A. Also sample B has significant amphibole content (absent from Buff 1).
Buff 2	Different fabrics. Both have local Euphrates clay inclusions but differ significantly in relative proportions, total amount of all inclusions (Buff 2 > sample A), and grain size (Buff 2 > sample A).	Different fabrics (as for sample A).
Buff 3	Essentially the same inclusions but Buff 3 is coarser (mean 0.5 mm; sample A mean 0.15 mm) and has a higher overall total of inclusions (estimated at 40% of sherd volume). Also carbonate-rich.	Different fabrics. Same as for sample A, but Buff 3 also lacks the euhedral amphibole (hornblende) that is a feature of sample B.
Buff 13	Near-identical fabrics.	Differs only by the amphibole content of sample B.

Table 4. Comparison of "local" Hellenistic fine ware and plain buff fabrics.

ering products (mainly after basic igneous rocks). Buff 1 is similar but has noticeably more quartz and feldspars, suggesting a greater input from acid igneous rocks (granite, etc.) Buff 2 has similar inclusions but these are present in different proportions. It is also more micaceous and has rounded carbonate grains. Buff 3 is similar to Islamic glazed fabric 3.

Question 4: Is fabric 2 ("Parthian") related to buff fabrics 6, 8, or 10? **Response:** No. Fabric 2 is tempered with tectonized[2] quartz and quartzite, chert, schist, and basalt; it has no limestone. Buff 6 has a very different clay matrix that is rich in foraminifera and has a lower sand content with little or no basaltic or secondary ferruginous aggregates. Buff 8 is different, again having a foraminifera-rich matrix, significant soil carbonate, and a lower siliclastic input. Buff 10 differs by having a high-calcareous matrix and fewer inclusions, which are also finer-grained.

Question 5: What are the characteristics/possible sources of fabrics 4 and 5? **Response:** Fabric 4 is a very fine-grained calcareous fabric with a pale green fired body color. Inclusions are estimated at 15 percent of the total volume and have a maximum grain size of 0.6 mm. Inclusions are mainly (>80 percent) carbonate, being a mix of micrite, foraminifera, and thin-walled shells. Most carbonate grains have thermally decomposed during the high firing. Other inclusions comprise small amounts of quartz with rare potassium and plagioclase feldspars. This is a naturally fine-grained clay.

Fabric 5 is an orange-brown fabric with abundant natural inclusions (mean grain size 0.6 mm). Inclusions are typical of those expected from the Euphrates sediments and include: quartz (mono- and polycrystalline), potassium feldspar, plagioclase feldspar, clinopyroxene, hornblende, biotite, trachytic basalt, basalt, epidote, rhyolite, muscovite schist, serpentine, and chromite (rare).

Plain Buff Wares

Question 6: Buff 1–3 are presumed to be local. Are they distinct or merely gradational? **Response:** Gradational. Essentially these share the same suite of mineral and rock inclusions, which is consistent with a Euphrates source at Zeugma. Buff 1 and 3 are similar, having a reddish-firing clay suggesting proximity either to the main river channel or an abandoned cut-off. Buff 2 is not red-firing, suggesting a higher Ca:Fe ratio, further born out by its more frequent (degraded) carbonate grains. Buff 2 could represent clay from the floodplain margin, being diluted by carbonate from groundwater and a clastic input from adjacent limestone formations.

Question 7: Buff 1 and 2 should correspond to the (local?) amphora fabrics 1 and 2: Is this so? **Response:** To answer this it is necessary to compare them with individual members of amphora fabric groups 1 and 2, as both were found to show considerable variations (summarized in tables 5 and 6, respectively). The results of this comparison are shown in table 7.

Lab ref.	I.D.	Initial fabric group	Revised fabric group
ZG28	2010.7	AM93 fabric 1	fabric 1
ZG29	2012.2	AM125 fabric 1	fabric 1 fine
ZG30	2012.2	AM125 fabric 1	fabric 1 fine
ZG31	2012.3	AM126 fabric 1	fabric 1
ZG32	2039.8	PT387 fabric 1	fabric 1

Table 5. Amphora fabric 1 members.

Lab ref.	I.D.	Initial fabric group	Revised fabric group
ZG41	2039.25	AM171 fabric 2	fabric 2: redder with abundant carbonate
ZG42	2260.60	AM219 fabric 2	fabric 1
ZG43	2080.16	AM183 fabric 2	separate fabric: dacite + schist with abundant carbonate
ZG44	2080.1	AM197 fabric 2	fabric 1

Table 6. Amphora fabric 2 members.

Amphora fabric Fabric 1	Plain buff ware Buff 1
ZG28	Similar except that Buff 1 has a lower total inclusion content and fewer fossil fragments/foraminifera
ZG29	Not similar: Buff 1 lacks a significant silt content, has coarser sand, and has more basalt-derived inclusions
ZG30	As for ZG29
ZG31	Similar except amphora has more silt/fine sand and more fine-grained carbonate in the matrix
ZG32	As for ZG31

Fabric 2	Buff 2
ZG41	Not similar: Buff 2 has more acid igneous inclusions (granite/dacite), has less basalt, and has more carbonate grains including rounded foraminifera/gastropod infills
ZG42	(Reassigned to fabric 1)
ZG43	Very similar fabrics
ZG44	(Reassigned to fabric 1)

Table 7. Comparison of plain buff fabrics with local amphora fabrics 1 and 2.

Buff 1 may therefore be said to be similar to the coarser subgroup of amphora fabric 1, whereas Buff 2 corresponds to only one member of amphora fabric 2 (as visually defined).

Question 8: Buff 4 is coarser (more sandy) in appearance than Buff 1–3. Is this a different clay? **Response:** No. Although more gritty, this is essentially the same clay as the Buff 1–3 series. It has slightly more limestone and chert but shares most of its inclusion types with Buff 1–3.

Question 9: What are the characteristics of Buff 5?

Response: Buff 5 has a pale brown fabric with conspicuous inclusions of up to 2.5 mm maximum grain size (mean 0.5 mm). Inclusions are mainly (>95 percent) those derived from the erosion of a recent fossiliferous limestone and comprise micrite, foraminifera, and thin-walled shells. Other inclusions are mainly basalt (ophitic) and corresponding clinopyroxene and plagioclase feldspar. Quartz is present as a minor component. This fabric is derived from a clay formed in a limestone-dominated area but with basaltic outcrops in the catchment. There are none of the typical Euphrates-channel-type inclusions.

Question 10: Buff 6 (mortaria) is not far removed in appearance from Buff 8. Are they the same? **Response:** No. There are some similarities, mainly that both are made from very fine-grained calcareous clay with conspicuous foraminifera, but there are important differences in their inclusions. Buff 6 inclusions are mainly derived from acid to intermediate igneous rocks (dacite, granodiorite) and chert with little or no basic igneous material. Buff 8 has acid, igneous-derived, and chert, but also basic igneous types, degraded limestone, and a higher content of ferruginous alteration products (from weathered basalt/gabbro).

Question 11: How does Buff 6 relate to the Syrian amphora fabric 13? **Response:** First, amphora fabric 13 shows sufficient variation to warrant subdivision into two separate subfabrics as shown in table 8. Buff 6 and amphora 13 fabrics are compared in table 9.

Question 12: Is Buff 8 the same as the Syrian amphora 13? **Response:** Confirmed. All the amphora fabric 13 members are very similar to Buff 8, allowing for differences in firing, proportions of inclusions, etc. Overall, Buff 8 is more closely matched to the amphora fabric 13 sherds than Buff 6. The latter lacks the colorless amphibole that characterizes Buff 8 and amphora fabric 13.

Question 13: Buff 10 looks like a finer version of Buff 8: Is this so? **Response:** No. The inclusions are similar but the clay bodies are different. Buff 8 has abundant foraminifera whereas these are rare in Buff 10 (allowing for loss with the higher firing of Buff 10). Buff 10 also has a more developed red color, due to a relatively high concentration of very fine reddish ferruginous material (from weathered basalt/gabbro).

Lab ref.	I.D.	Initial fabric group	Revised fabric group
ZG51	2010.6	AM110 fabric 13	fabric 13
ZG52	2080.4	AM194 fabric 13	fabric 13
ZG53	2154.1	—— fabric 13	fabric 13, coarser variety
ZG54	5034.1	AM264 fabric 13	fabric 13
ZG55	7026.1	AM295 fabric 13	separate fabric, schistose
ZG56	7036.1	AM296 fabric 13	separate fabric, granodioritic
ZG57	12012.59	—— fabric 13	fabric 13

Table 8. Amphora fabric 13 members.

Amphora fabric 13	Plain buff fabric 6
ZG51	Similar fabrics; Syrian 13 also has a very calcareous matrix that is rich in foraminifera. Notably there is very little in the way of fine siliclastic material but a relatively well sorted medium sand. Arguably this could represent tempering, but natural sand incursion into a lagoonal environment is not ruled out.
ZG52	Similar fabrics although Syrian 13 fabric has no/little tuff and has more altered ferruginous material (laterite — basalt derived?).
ZG53	Similar in terms of inclusions and the calcareous nature of the clay. This Syrian 13 fabric has intraclasts of laminated calcareous clay.
ZG54	Less similar on account of the much higher proportion of ferruginous material (altered basalt) shown by Syrian 13. Also has no tuff.
ZG55	Same fabrics.
ZG56	Very similar fabrics but Syrian 13 has significantly more carbonate grains and foraminifera.
ZG57	Similar fabrics (Syrian 13 higher fired).

Table 9. Comparison of plain buff fabric 6 with Syrian amphora fabric 13.

Question 14: PT402 (Buff 11) is an isolated example of a mortarium with distinctive black grits: any comments? **Response:** Most of the inclusions in this fabric have been derived from a highly weathered basalt/gabbro. Here, iron released on weathering has reprecipitated to form a black colored cement or coating on grains. This results in the dark color of the matrix. A variety of basaltic textures are observed, including serpentinized and vesicular types. Other typical Euphrates minerals are present but do not significantly dilute the altered basaltic signature. This implies use of a clay either from a Euphrates tributary draining a basalt area, or immediately downstream of where the Euphrates incises a basaltic outcrop.

Question 15: Buff 13 is a fine buff ware. Is it related to Buff 1–3 or to "local" Hellenistic fine ware? **Response:** Although they have similar inclusions, Buff 1 and Buff 13 are different, as the latter has a significantly higher proportion of angular fine material. Buff 13 and Buff 2 also differ, with Buff 2 having much more mica and epidote (derived from micaschist). Buff 13 differs from Buff 3 in having significantly less limestone — although it shares most of the other inclusions and is probably related laterally on the flood plain. Finally, Buff 13 is almost identical to the Hellenistic fine A sample (see question 1); it has some similarities to Hellenistic fine B, which, however, has much more fine-grained limestone/carbonate.

Question 16: Is Buff 15 related to any of the preceding? **Response:** This fabric has a very high proportion of fines as well as the typical Euphrates mineralogy represented in the coarser fraction. This could possibly be a finer (distal[3]) variant of Buff 11 (PT402). There may be a reworked tuff component.

Augite	Micrite
Basalt	Microdirite
Biotite	Monocrystalline quartz
Caliche	Muscovite
Chromite	Plagioclase
Colorless Amphibole	Polycrystalline quartz
Epidote	Potassium feldspar
Fe-alteration	Serpentine
Hornblende	Titanaugite
Mica Schist	Trachy-basalt

Table 10. Inclusions observed in Cooking 1.

Characterization of Cooking Wares

Cooking 1

Question 17: This is a red fabric with an extensive suite of inclusions (table 10). A comparison with table 3 suggests a strong similarity with the Euphrates sediment samples at Zeugma. However, Cooking 1 shows some subtle but significant differences, i.e.:

- Cooking 1 grains are very angular;
- plagioclase feldspar are not conspicuously zoned;
- muscovite laths are commonly kinked (suggesting a metamorphic/tectonized history);
- there is a relatively high concentration of basalt and derived minerals.

Pinpointing a possible provenance for this material is difficult. The overlap with many of the Euphrates sand minerals suggests it could be derived from the same catchment, i.e., southeastern Turkey. The listed differences could be consistent with Euphrates clay upstream from Zeugma, nearer to the major east-west faults and outcrops of volcanics. One problem here is that basalts from this area tend to contain the distinctive titanaugite clinopyroxene. Only a single occurrence of titanaugite was noted for Cooking 1, despite other indicators that the clay must have been formed relatively close to a basaltic outcrop.[4]

Cooking 2

Question 18: This fabric is based on a red clay that has been tempered with a very pure quartz sand. An estimated 98 percent of all sand grains are mono-crystalline and are essentially strain-free (with extinction complete in under five degrees of rotation). The sand grains are moderately well sorted with a subangular to subrounded morphology. Many are subhedral (i.e., showing partial crystal faces), which, with the mono-crystalline and strain-free characteristics, suggests derivation either as quartz phenocrysts from acid volcanics (e.g. rhyolite/rhyolitic tuff) or from vein quartz.

Of these two possibilities vein quartz is favored as, unlike a rhyolitic source, this would not introduce other siliceous material. This is a compositionally very mature sand temper and is undiluted by alluvial material or carbonate, suggesting a short transport history, possibly a residual material.

The deep red color of the clay indicates that this is iron-rich. Possible sources here are residual clays developed on limestone (terra rossa) or those derived from the weathering of basalt. In the latter case this weathering would have to be very complete and the clay subsequently redeposited to remove all coarser material and give the observed very clean fabric. The use of a residual terra rossa clay, being free from coarse impurities, presents a simpler scenario and is favored in this interpretation.

Accepting the above, Cooking 2 could have been made at a site where limestone, possibly with quartz veining, has undergone extensive weathering. Existing geological reports and maps do not have sufficient resolution to identify possible sites from within the extensive outcrops of Mesozoic limestone in the area. Archaeological input is required at this stage to narrow down possible locations.

Cooking 4

Question 19: This is an obviously non-Euphrates alluvium fabric dominated by andesitic volcanic material including ash and pumice. This fabric exhibits a simple mineralogy of plagioclase feldspar (andesine), hornblende, biotite, and very rare quartz. The quartz shows an embayed texture and is associated with a glassy matrix, indicating that it is also derived from a volcanic source.

All of these inclusions reconstruct to give an intermediate volcanic rock type, andesite. There are no mineral inclusions that are foreign to andesite and that would imply some degree of sediment mixing. This single rock parentage, and the very angular shape of the inclusions, indicates that this clay has not been transported by an alluvial system but has formed as a residual deposit on the andesitic parent. The clay matrix has derived from the chemical weathering of the andesite and has become naturally mixed with volcanic ash (andesitic) during down-slope movement. Such an environment would be found on the lower slopes of a recent volcanic cone. The lack of chemical alteration of the hornblende and plagioclase suggests a relatively young age for the parent andesitic ash.

Numerous small andesitic cones and flows occur within the limestone country within 30 km east and west of Zeugma and also downstream in the Euphrates Valley to the Syria-Iraq border at Deir-az-Za. All of these are young (Neogene) volcanic features that petrographically are likely to be very similar. Outside of the Euphrates Valley, similar andesitic outcrops are found westward to the Syrian-Turkish coastline and are common across much of the eastern Mediterranean. It is not possible to present a unique provenance for this fabric unless archaeological criteria can be invoked to reduce the field.

Cooking 7

Question 20: This fabric appears initially to have many of the Euphrates alluvium minerals/lithologies sampled at Birecik, but is now seen to have some significant differences. Inclusions of fine-grained limestone, chert, basalt, quartz (mono- and polycrystalline), orthoclase, plagioclase, hornblende, augite, and serpentine are similar to those found in Euphrates alluvium (see table 3). However, there is an additional suite of inclusions not noted in the reference Euphrates sand or the local fabrics. These include epidiorite, psammite, quartz-epidote, zoisite, mica-schist, tectonized granite, anthophyllite, and tectonized/sheared quartz vein material. Together, these inclusions indicate the incorporation of a significant amount of metamorphic material. This includes regionally metamorphosed material of greenschist and amphibolite facies, as well as dynamo-metamorphic material associated with shear zones and major faults. This amount of metamorphic material is not seen in local Euphrates sediments but a close match is seen with the one fabric 8 amphora (ZW50). Two possible sources are considered that should have metamorphic components:

THE COASTAL STRIP ALONG THE TURKISH-SYRIAN BORDER: Here the Baer-Bassit ophiolite and associated metamorphic sole could furnish the observed inclusions. Material moving southwards from this outcrop mixes with north-moving Nile sediment, which could introduce the other observed inclusions. However, there are several difficulties with this source, such as:

- the amount of metamorphic rocks is volumetrically small;
- serpentine and ultrabasic igneous inclusions should be more abundant;
- these metamorphics are of a higher grade than observed in Cooking 7 and include exotics such as skarns;
- crushed fabrics should be limited.

THE METAMORPHIC BELT EXTENDING SOUTHEAST FROM MALATYA, TURKEY: This extensive metamorphic zone is intersected by the Euphrates headwaters about 100 km upstream of Zeugma. Clays immediately south of this area should show significant amounts of metamorphic materials of the types observed, in addition to the typical Euphrates mineralogy. From a purely compositional viewpoint, this is the better of the two sources for this fabric.[5]

Cooking 8

Question 21: This fabric is characterized by abundant rounded limestone, and more angular quartz, orthoclase, euhedral plagioclase, quartzite, quartz-epidote, chert, granodiorite, volcanic tuff (minor), schist, and various tectonized materials suggesting a significant input from a faulted metamorphic basement. Many of these inclusions are typical of Euphrates sediments but there are some notable absences. Compared to the reference sand sampled at Birecik, Cooking 8 has almost no basalt or andesite/dacite-derived material and has no serpentine.

Cooking 9

Question 22: The inclusions in this fabric are dominated by olivine basalt and gabbroic temper, accounting for an estimated 95 percent of the total inclusion population. Others comprise rounded grains of soil carbonate (caliche), angular mono-crystalline quartz, and fine-grained ferruginous material derived from basalt weathering. These inclusions indicate a clay source very near to a basalt/gabbro outcrop as there is minimal dilution by nonbasaltic material.

In terms of a possible source of olivine basalt, there are several contenders (i.e., from a strictly geological viewpoint).[6] Outcrops of olivine basalt occur in several regions near Zeugma. These are:

1. Turkish outcrops in the Euphrates headwaters, e.g., the Elazığ area (Malatya) and the Bitlis massif and its westward continuation
2. Turkish outcrops in the Karasu Valley north of Antioch
3. Turkish outcrops along a major fault running northeast-southwest just to the north of Adana
4. Along the Golan Heights of Israel and Syria
5. Along the central valley of Lebanon
6. The Badia platform of Jordan

As stated previously, a robust provenance identification would really require a geochemical comparison between the pottery temper of Cooking 9 and these sources. However we can evaluate each of these on the basis of their petrography and their geological settings. Olivine basalts occur in the Euphrates headwaters between Malatya and the Bitlis massif.[7] The Malatya olivine basalts are described as containing the mineral titanaugite, a distinctive pyroxene showing a purplish color in thin section. Small amounts of this mineral are recorded in the Zeugma reference sand and some local fabrics, which is to be expected given that the Euphrates headwater tributaries traverse this region. Titanaugite, however, is not seen in Cooking 9. Further, the Malatya olivine basalts are recorded as being closely associated with other volcanic rocks (andesites and dacites): again, these occur in the Zeugma sand but are absent from Cooking 9.

Olivine basalts of the Bitlis massif are also characterized by titanaugite.[8] This area has also been subjected to metamorphism and fracturing associated with major faulting. However no metamorphic or crushed material is seen associated with the olivine basalt fragments in Cooking 9. Turkish sources north of Zeugma are not considered to be likely candidates.

Olivine basalts outcrop in the Karasu Valley north of Antioch (Hatay).[9] Here they are associated with two other related volcanic rocks, quartz tholeiite and olivine tholeiite. These are recorded as showing a variable replacement of olivine by iddingsite, a feature seen in Cooking 9. Similarly titanaugite is not recorded (calcic augite is the characteristic clinopyroxene), making the Karasu Valley a possible source of Cooking 9–type fabrics.

In the Iskenderun Gulf region (east Ceyhan) two olivine-bearing volcanic rock types are represented, alkali olivine basalts and basanites.[10] However, although these have the essential mineralogy seen in Cooking 9 (i.e., olivine, augite, and plagioclase) they are not a good match when compared texturally (even allowing for variations expected from different cooling histories within the basalt flow). These volcanics are described in the field as being highly vesicular, with olivine phenocrysts often showing signs of partial re-absorption and Cr-spinel and titanomagnetite inclusions in olivines. As these features are absent from Cooking 9, this region is not considered to be a likely source.

Syrian outcrops of olivine basalt are seen in the Tartous area (Dahr-Safra plateau) as localized outcrops of olivine-bearing high-aluminous basalt.[11] However, again there are significant petrographic differences between these and the Cooking 9 basalt inclusions. Here the olivine crystals have been derived from earlier volcanics and as such are extensively corroded or replaced by secondary minerals including serpentine. These basalts (and similar outcrops east of Damascus) are not considered as likely sources of the Cooking 9 clay.

The Golan Heights have Pleistocene volcanics consisting of volcanic flows of olivine-bearing basalts.[12] Like the Cooking 9 fabric, these basalts are relatively fresh and do not contain distinctive minerals such as titanaugite. Geologically these would be capable of yielding clays similar to those comprising Cooking 9, but it is questionable whether residual clays would develop sufficiently, given the elevated and arid location.

Finally, central Lebanon has significant deposits of olivine basalt, with flows ranging from 5 to 20 m thick.[13] A wide variety of textures are present, but olivine is usually fresh and clinopyroxenes are colorless in thin section. On these Cooking 9 could be derived from these basalts; again, field sampling and geochemistry would be required to further test this.

To conclude, on geological and locational grounds the Karasu Valley north of Antioch is the best regional contender for the provenance for Cooking 9. This match is made on fairly simple petrographic criteria and would require further geochemistry and field sampling to verify it.

Comparison of Zeugma Cooking Ware Fabrics with Syrian "Brittle Wares"

Question 23: How do these compare? **Response:** A brief comparison is made between these Zeugma cooking wares and published "brittle ware" fabrics from Syria. This comparison is based on a single source, Bartl et al. 1995. More recent fabric work on Syrian "brittle wares" is nearing completion but is as yet unpublished (Agnès Vokaer, personal communication).

Following a geochemical and thin-section study of 54 North Syrian brittle wares, Bartl, Schneider, and Bohme identified three major groups plus the suggestion of two further groups. These are clearly defined by both chemical and petrographic criteria, although the petrographic summaries given are very brief.

GROUP 1: Pottery is made of "a non-calcareous clay with a high amount of equally-sized fine-grained rounded to subrounded quartz" — a perfect match to Zeugma Cooking 2.

GROUP 2: These fabrics are characterized by the use of a calcareous clay and inclusions of "medium to coarse grained fragments of a volcanic rock, possibly from a trachytic tuff." This description is perhaps rather general, but from the figure it can be estimated that tuff represents more than 75 percent of the total temper. Group 2 sherds seemed to occur only in the later periods and were distributed mainly in the Habur valley. The one Zeugma sherd with this amount of tuff is **PT450**, but here the temper is 100 percent andesitic tuff (ash) and shows a very different size range.

GROUP 3: Fabrics have "a high amount of fine to very fine grained inclusions of various minerals and rock fragments such as quartz, feldspars, micas, serpentine, volcanic rock, chert, limestone, marble and the remains of fossils."

These minerals are clearly similar to those observed in the Birecik reference sand (table 3) and the majority of the Zeugma buff wares. This mineral assemblage identifies the clays as being derived from the same general catchment area as the Euphrates sediments (i.e., southeastern Turkey) but without further detail on the specific minerals/rock inclusions it is not possible to restrict the provenance to the Euphrates Valley.

GROUP 4: This is represented by a single member whose coarse inclusions are described as being from a "crushed coarse-grained basaltic rock." This is unfortunately far too general a description to be diagnostic. If the basaltic rock is an olivine basalt then there are obvious close similarities with Zeugma Cooking 9, if not then there is no match with the Zeugma cooking wares.

GROUP 5: Again represented by only a single member, here briefly described as being from "an altered gabbro as is typical for ophiolitic rocks from a greenstone belt." A possible match here would be with Zeugma Storage 2 which is tempered with altered gabbro and associated basic rocks. Again more petrographic detail for the Group 5 fabric would be required to verify this match.

Characterization of Storage Wares
Storage 2
Question 24: This fabric contains inclusions derived from basic igneous rock, many of which have been extensively converted to secondary minerals. Olivine, augite, and plagioclase composite grains identify olivine gabbro as one of the parent rock types. Olivine grains are heavily altered to iddingsite and serpentine, and augite is largely replaced by green fibrous amphibole. Amphiboles are also represented by euhedral (i.e., displaying good crystal faces) hornblende and lenses of colorless tremolite/anthophyllite. The hornblende identifies andesite/diorite as a second parent to this clay. The colorless amphibole (tremolite/anthophyllite) is associated with the alteration/low-grade metamorphism of the olivine gabbro.

In the hand specimen this fabric appears similar to that described by Hayes (1967) for the north Syrian mortaria of Ras el-Basit (which have not been found in the British excavations). Both have a "deep chocolate brown color" (this is common feature of basalt/gabbro derived clays), are "generally free from mica" and are "liberally tempered with white and black grits." The white grits in Storage 2 correspond to plagioclase grains and colorless amphibole (which is soft and superficially resembles lime — otherwise absent in this fabric), and the black grits correspond to all the colored ferromagnesian minerals in this section (in particular augite and hornblende). Hayes also describes "particles of what appears to be crushed glass" and something resembling this description is seen on the surface of the sherd where the angular, dark-green colored ferromagenesian minerals protrude.

This provenance is now confirmed following a review of the local geology. Ras el-Basit is a headland formed by hard basic igneous rocks including the same types of gabbros and associated rocks seen in storage 2. These comprise a late Cretaceous ophiolite.[14] Furthermore, the rocks have been extensively altered to secondary minerals such as serpentine, fibrous amphibole (including anthophyllite), iddingsite, etc., which again closely match the Storage 2 fabric.

Storage 3: Two Sherds from Context 2080, Listed after PT461

Question 25: This is an iron-rich fabric that is characterized by a very high proportion of tectonized material. This is predominantly acid igneous-derived (granite–diorite) and schist, but there is some basaltic material. Limestone is absent, and the lack of dilution by other material may argue for a residual clay developed in a fault/crush zone. There are some complex mineral associations seen here (e.g., quartz–epidote–sphene–hornblende–olivine). This fabric is different from that of **PT450** (above, question 19) which appeared superficially to be similar.

Storage 5

Question 26: The fabric is tempered by calcite spar (vein calcite), which appears as white-gray rhombic grains. This represents very select tempering, the vein material having to be removed from the host limestone, none of which is included in the fabric. Minor soil carbonate. No quartz, basalt, or Euphrates-type minerals. Vein calcite can be sourced from almost any limestone country: No specific provenance is indicated.

NOTES

1. Where, additionally, carbonates are also introduced via groundwater precipitation.
2. Tectonized material has been crushed and deformed as a result of intense faulting and folding (i.e., tectonic activity). Major active fault systems capable of producing tectonized microstructures occur to the north and west of Zeugma.
3. I.e., from the margin of the channel flood-plain.
4. Cooking 1 contains several composite grains of angular basalt (or iron-rich clays produced by basalt weathering) cemented together by soil carbonate (caliche). These are mechanically very weak grains and would not survive alluvial transport beyond short distances.
5. Again it must be stated that there are no direct descriptions of clays from these two regions: Field sampling would be necessary to verify these predictions.
6. It should be noted that provenancing basalts is usually approached by a combination of thin-section analysis and geochemistry. One reason for this is that any given lava flow will show a range of textures, for example depending on whether cooling was rapid (such as for the upper surface of the flow), or slow (e.g., in the center). What this means is that most published references to basalt outcrops emphasize geochemical rather than petrographic characteristics. Further, the bulk chemical analysis of basalts is based on large samples (> 0.5 kg), as this is an analytical requirement to ensure that the sample is fully representative. SEM analysis of the basalt inclusions from pottery cannot give reliable data for comparison, as many of these are small grains, often with a mass of less than 0.1 gm.
7. Arger et al. 2000.
8. Beyarslan and Bingol 2000.
9. Alici et al. 2001.
10. Yurtmen et al. 2000.
11. Mahfoud and Beck 1993.
12. Weinstein et al. 1994.
13. Abdel-Rahman 2002.
14. An ophiolite is a rock unit representing a fragment of former ocean crust that has been thrust-faulted to lie with continental crust. These occur at several locations in the eastern Mediterranean, the largest example being Cyprus. Ophiolites comprise basic igneous rocks (gabbros, basalts, etc.) that have been heavily crushed and altered to new minerals (e.g., serpentine) as a result of thrust-faulting.

BIBLIOGRAPHY

Abdel-Rahman, A.F.M. 2002. "Mesozoic Volcanism in the Middle East: Geochemical Isotopic and Petrogenetic Evolution of Extension-Related Alkali Basalts from Central Lebanon." *Geological Magazine* 139:621–40.

Alici, P., A. Temel, A. Gourgaud, P. Vidal, and M.N. Gundogdu. 2001. "Quarternary Tholeiitic to Alkaline Volcanism in the Karasu Valley, Dead Sea Rift Zone, Southeast Turkey: Sr-Nd-Pb-O Isotopic and Trace Element Approaches to Crust-Mantle Interaction." *International Geology Review* 43:120–38.

Arger, J., J. Mitchell, and R.W.C. Westaway. 2000. "Neogene and Quarternary Volcanism of Southeastern Turkey." *Geology Society Special Publication* 173:459–87.

Bartl, K., G. Schneider, and S. Bohme. 1995. "Notes on 'Brittle Wares' in Northeast Syria." *Levant* 27:165–77.

Beyarslan, M., and A.F. Bingol. 2000. "Petrology of a Supra-Subduction Zone Ophiolite (Elazig, Turkey)." *Canadian Journal of Earth Sciences* 37:1411–24.

Hayes, J.W. 1967. "North Syrian Mortaria." *Hesperia* 36:337–47.

Mahfoud, R.F., and J.N. Beck. 1993. "Petrographic Study of, and Trace Element Distribution in, High-MgO, Transitional and High-Al 'SUB 2' O 'SUB 3' Basalts from the Coastal Region and SW-Central Syria: A Comparative Study with Similar Basalts from the Aleutian Island Arc." *Journal of Geodynamics* 17:57–76.

Weinstein, Y., O. Navon, and B. Lang. 1994. "Fractionation of Pleistocene Alkali-Basalts from the Northern Golan Heights, Israel." *Israel Journal of Earth Science* 43:63–79.

Yurtmen, S., G. Rowbotham, F. Isler, and P.A. Floyd. 2000. "Petrogenesis of Basalts from Southern Turkey: The Plio-Quarternary Volcanism to the North of Iskenderun Gulf." *Geological Society Special Publication* 173:489–512.

· CHAPTER THREE ·

Transport Amphorae of the First to Seventh Centuries: Early Roman to Byzantine Periods

Paul Reynolds

INTRODUCTION

Philip Kenrick, in the introduction to his chapter on the fine and coarse wares, has outlined the strategy adopted for study of the ceramics from the rescue excavations at Zeugma in 2000.[1] During my short, one-month trip to Turkey the task of the selection of amphora assemblages for study was thus both assisted and streamlined by his assessment of the composition of ceramic assemblages and selection of significant groups for full classification (Groups A–G), ranging from the Hellenistic to Islamic periods.

Transport amphorae of the Hellenistic to Byzantine periods were allocated to me for study. These were easy to select in the case of forms imported from overseas (e.g., Spanish and Italian amphorae). The functional interpretation and division of the closed forms into "jugs" and "transport amphorae" in the case of the remaining local and close regional products at first proved difficult until it was decided that all two-handled flagon-like vessels, of large, medium, and small module sizes were to be classified as amphorae. That this principle is probably on the right lines is supported by the fact that all of the painted two-handled flagons encountered in seventh-century levels were regional imports from Syria and were imported for the contents they were carrying (Forms 14–19). It is possible that this also applies to the smallest one-handled jug forms from the same regional sources. As will be discussed shortly, amphorae of the Roman and Byzantine periods in this region of the Levant, as in Cilicia and parts of northwestern Syria, were typically freestanding flagon-like two-handled table amphorae.[2]

Other local amphorae encountered, namely in the first- and third-century deposits, were bag-shaped, again relatively small, amphorae, in this case with a vertical "collar" rim (Form 3), similar in style to Palestinian bag-shaped amphorae of the first century A.D. onward (Late Roman Amphora 5 and its antecedents). Another class found in first-century deposits is quite distinct, having a long, rather cylindrical body (Form 1 and Form 2) and demonstrates the hazards of trying to predict the shape of amphorae based on rim type alone. Indeed some of the typological problems discussed below, in particular the possible development of Form 1 into Form 2, and the suggested attribution of first-century A.D. ring-foot bases to the bag-shaped type Form 3 are hampered by the absence of complete examples, whether from Zeugma or published elsewhere.

Quite another typological problem was classification of the enormous range of rim types of painted Syrian amphorae that were contemporary finds in sometimes very large deposits of seventh-century date (see Amphora Typology). Once the observation was made that the same rim types occurred in large, medium, and small sizes, it was possible to break the series down into six main groups, with further subdivision in some cases according to significant details of rim type. This has to be regarded as a working model and aid to the classification, which needs to be confirmed by the study of production sites so far not located. Nevertheless, the principle does seem to be sound, as variants defined here can be spotted in other publications (see Typology for parallels). Other variants not present in the Zeugma assemblage can also be picked out, notably in the report on the pottery of Qusair as-Saila.[3] Overall, this is an indication of both the complexity of production of the painted Syrian amphora class, and also of its conformity to workshop styles (a phenomenon paralleled in the case of the Beirut amphora: Reynolds 1999; 2000) and the specific marketing and distribution of products of individual workshops.

Once the guidelines were established for the division of the buff wares into amphorae and one-handled jugs (studied by Philip Kenrick), all Roman-Byzantine period deposits selected for study by Philip Kenrick were scanned for possible amphorae and catalogued by myself (see below, Catalogue of Transport Amphorae, hereafter "Catalogue"). Only one Hellenistic deposit was securely identified (19005) and two possible amphorae in the group are included in Philip Kenrick's chapter (**PT18–19**). Other Roman-Byzantine deposits not fully recorded by Philip Kenrick, though summarized in his initial scanning of the material, were found to contain amphorae of note. These amphorae are either fully classified in the Catalogue or, in a few cases, only the significant imported sherds are mentioned (indicated as "not on PK list" in the Catalogue). A few other imported sherds, for example Dressel 20 Baetican amphorae or sherds of Late Roman Amphora 1, were noted by Philip Kenrick in his initial assessment in deposits that were not selected for final publication and were not included in my Catalogue. For the sake of completeness the deposits, where they occur, are noted below in the text at points where the relevant products are discussed.

The study of the Islamic material from Trench I was undertaken entirely by Philip Kenrick, including any possible transport amphorae within them: these, in imported Buff ware 8 and 10, are classified as flagons. Arab transport

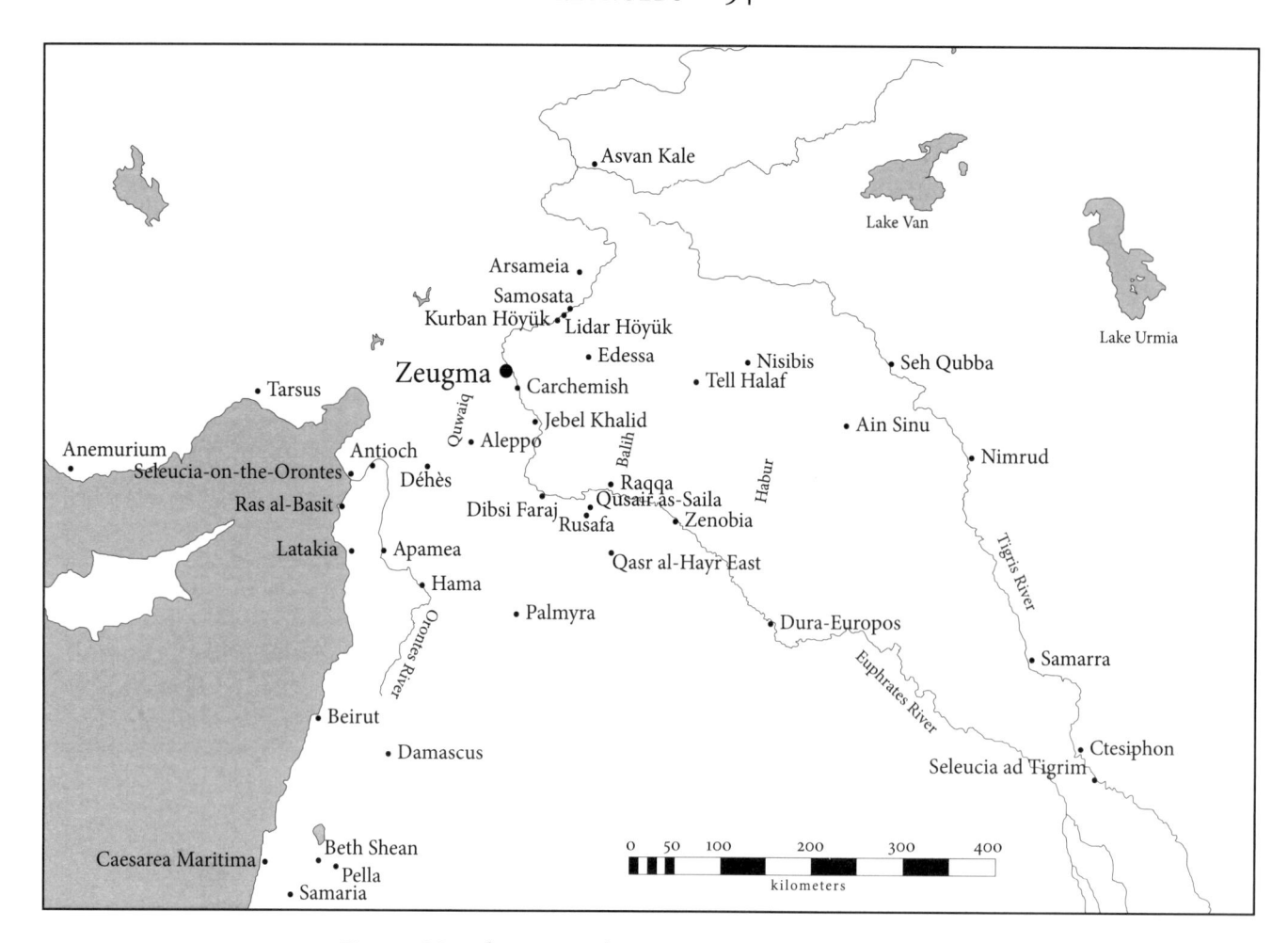

Figure 1. Map of eastern Mediterranean sites mentioned in the text.

amphorae were generally relatively small, two-handled flagons with cylindrical necks and freestanding bases, for example the ninth-century complete example from Raqqa.[4] Because of the rather late date of the Islamic material, from the ninth century onward, there has been no opportunity to examine the question of the Byzantine to Omayyad and Abbasid continuity of production of Byzantine Syrian amphora forms (i.e., those presented in the Typology), as is proposed for Tetrapyrgium / Qusair as-Saila.[5] Our examples of painted amphorae, as the example published from Déhès,[6] and most of the examples from Qusair as-Saila, are definitely Byzantine, and no later than the first half of the seventh century in date.

This chapter comprises three parts, an evaluation and discussion of the material, a typology with a summary of forms (Plates 43–48: drawings at 1:4; parallels illustrated on Plates 49–51, also at 1:4, with the exception of Plate 51c, not to scale), and a catalogue arranged, in numerical order of deposits, according to the ceramic periods defined by Philip Kenrick (Plates 52–74, drawings at 1:3). The stratigraphic location and character of the deposits have also been outlined and discussed by Philip Kenrick, with his commentary on each of the ceramic periods. It should be noted that his Group E, dating to the early sixth century, unfortunately did not comprise any amphorae and is there-

fore not represented in my section. Numbers in bold with the prefix **AM** refer to items in the Catalogue; these often appear with four- or five-digit context numbers assigned by the excavators (e.g., 7118) or context numbers with database extensions assigned for individual items by the author and marked in ink on the object (e.g., 7118.2). Numbers in bold with the prefix **PT** refer to items catalogued in the chapter by Philip Kenrick; numbers with the prefix **ZG** refer to items in the following chapter, by Chris Doherty.

Though in the case of the fine and coarse wares the sheer volume of the material, and other reasons outlined by Philip Kenrick in the introduction to his chapter, made the undertaking of a complete typology for these products an unreasonable proposition, this was not so in the case of the amphorae. The lesser numbers and somewhat repetitive range of forms of amphorae have made it possible to offer a comprehensive typology and catalogue of forms encountered in the selected deposits.

It should be stressed that by focusing on the fabrics and allowing these to define wares and hence the shared origins of local products and close regional imports common to all the ceramics classes (notably in the case of the Buff Ware category), it has been possible to discover, or at least suggest, major trends and links in the close regional trade of specific regional products and functional classes (e.g., imported Syrian buff mortars, jugs, and amphorae; imported Syrian "brittle" cooking wares). This was achieved, furthermore, through regular dialogue and the joint examination of the ceramic material by the two parties concerned. I am most grateful to Philip Kenrick for his knowledge and fruitful collaboration in this respect, as well as for his comments on the text.[7]

In the following outline and discussion of the amphora finds at Zeugma an attempt has been made to place observed trends of supply of imported amphorae within the wider context of general patterns of trade and shipments of goods in the Roman-Byzantine Mediterranean. There is also regular reference to trends observed elsewhere in the Levant, particularly those gained through my work on the classification of contemporary assemblages from Beirut. The latter provide a means with which to compare and gauge the circulation of amphorae along coastal cities of the Levant with the supply encountered at Zeugma, in inland Roman Syria, and illuminate both shared features and major, important differences between the two regions.

For ease of reference, where illustrated, the **AM** catalogue entry number is quoted in bold (e.g., **AM1**). Non-illustrated sherds referred to in the text appear unhighlighted.

The Late Augustan / Tiberian Phase (Group B): Typology Plates 43–44, 49 Catalogue Plates 52–53

The most common forms in this phase are Form 1 and Form 3. The former is a large amphora with a grooved rim face and sloping collar rim. It is well paralleled by complete examples discovered in the Necropolis excavated at Dura-Europos that show the form to have a long, almost cylindrical body and long, narrowing hollow toe (as Base 3?; Base 4).[8] Though some examples occur at Hammam-et-Turkman (see Typology), most examples, including those at Dura-Europos, bear no handles. The absence of handles on a transport amphora is quite unusual, as this would have made the handling of the vessel difficult.

Form 1, and its likely successor the Flavian type Form 2A, have a markedly Phoenician appearance, recalling second-century B.C. Hellenistic local amphorae of Beirut, Sidon, and northern Palestine. The latter differ in that they have vertical strap handles attached to the upper wall.[9] Ring-strap handles are indeed a Palestinian characteristic that continued through the Roman, Byzantine, and post-Byzantine-Arab periods (see below, Typology, Palestinian amphorae LRA 4 and LRA 5).

Form 1 has been found reused to cover or mark early Roman-period inhumation burials in sites in the Tabqa Dam section of the Euphrates, at Shams ed-Din, at Tell Kannâs, and apparently at Dibsi Faraj (fig. 1).[10]

The Dura-Europos tombs with Form 1 contained coins of 58–38 B.C. and a coin of Domitian that give some indication of a late first-century B.C. to late first-century A.D. date for their use, which is supported by the date of examples at Zeugma.[11] The Shams ed-Din vessels are undated and were not associated with any occupation. However, a burial (of this type?) in the same cemetery at Tell Kannâs contained a worn coin of Nero(?), and a Flavian date is possible.[12] It should be noted that both Form 1A with a narrow rim diameter (as **AM25**) and a version with a similar rim with a much wider diameter (cf. Form 2C) were found together in the same grave at Tell Kannâs.[13] Both Form 1 and Form 2 are particularly common on sites in the Balih Valley, including Hammam-et-Turkman, associated with early Roman, first-century A.D. fine wares.

It seems, however, that this burial practice and the amphora type itself have a much earlier origin. A similar cemetery of inhumations marked by rows of amphorae was excavated in 1926 and 1927 at Neirab, near Aleppo, but this cemetery is clearly datable to no later than the fourth century B.C.[14] Though at first sight the amphorae appear to be Form 1 (they are even the same size at about 80–85 cm and have similar small-diameter bulbous rims and a cylindrical body), the drawings indicate that they have solid toes or simply tapered pointed bases. The rims are apparently not grooved.[15] A unique amphora at the site is clearly Phoenician Levantine in shape, with two ring-handles on the upper body, and is drawn with a solid toe.[16] Another, with a single twisted(?) ring-handle (cf. Tyrian products), has a wide inverted cone base and no foot.[17] The excavators also state that some are not fired (soft "dried clay"), quite distinct to the hard-fired characteristics of Form 1.

To return to Form 1, though the fabric, rather finer than that of local amphorae of the mid-Roman period, need not rule out its local manufacture, the finds to the immediate south and southeast in the Tabqa-Dam section of the Euphrates and in the Balih Valley, as well as in distant Dura-Europos, could indicate that the type was not local to Zeugma.

It is possible that the Balih Valley, or at least the most western sector of the Syrian Euphrates, was the source of Forms 1–2 and the produce they contained. In the Balih Valley they have been termed "Roman / Parthian" amphorae.[18] The Roman or Parthian origin of the recipients and producers of these traded goods is an interesting question. All of the small necropolises in the Tabqa Dam stretch of the Euphrates we have noted were interpreted as being associated with Roman garrisons of small outposts on the early Roman frontier that in the first century A.D. was still restricted to the Euphrates. The Balih Valley, however, lay within Parthian territory during this period until the Roman expansion of the eastern territories in the course of the second century A.D. A major, central, and well-planned system of irrigation works was established in the northern Balih Valley in the later Hellenistic period and seems to be associated with an expansion of rural and urban settlement that continued into a second phase in the early Roman period, contemporary with the finds of Forms 1–2.[19] There is documentary evidence, furthermore, that sites along the

Balih Valley were well-known road stations on the major trade route that ran from Zeugma to Iran and India, via Mesopotamia, during the late Hellenistic period. Hammam-et-Turkman is almost certainly one of the towns mentioned in Isidore's *Itinerary*, as was Raqqa / Nicephorium.[20] Indeed it was this route that Crassus took during the disastrous campaign that ended at Carrhae in 53 B.C. (see also Hartmann and Speidel in volume 3 for the military role of Zeugma). Zeugma continued to provide the vital river crossing between the Roman and Parthian sectors of this route when Roman territory was extended east to include the new province of Mesopotamia under Severus and following Julian's disastrous campaign, from the late fourth century onward, when the Habur Valley was finally set as Rome's most eastern frontier.

In the Typology it is argued that the dominance of ring-foot bases (Base 1A–E) in this early phase suggests that they were the bases of the collared amphora with triangular band rim (Form 3A–B) that also occurs in these contexts. If so, Form 3, presumably bag-shaped and small, as the later, mid-third-century versions (Form 3D–G) lost its ring base by that date. Only one rounded base was found and in a Flavian context (Base 2A). Given that the form seems to continue into the third century, it is possible that Form 3A–B, and possibly C, all in Fabric 1, are local products. The possible absence of this form on Balih Valley sites (in contrast to Forms 1–2) could also be taken as supporting evidence for its more local (Zeugma) origin.

Long-distance imports from overseas are relative rare, the most common being Rhodian amphorae (Contexts 15095 × 3; 15009 × 2). That some of these are residual Hellenistic finds cannot be ruled out. A wide oval handle may also be Rhodian but is not a typical Rhodian form (7118.1). Two sherds of either Cádiz or Dressel 6 Istrian amphorae were found and are contemporary (15095; 15009) (both regional sources have a similar fabric). There was a single possibly Koan amphora handle (context 15095.2).

Given the rich supply of southern Spanish (fish-sauce-garum and wine) amphorae in contemporary late Augustan-Tiberian and mid-first-century contexts in Beirut, the rarity or absence of Baetican imports at Zeugma is quite striking.[21] Istrian Dressel 6 amphorae, an alternative identification for the few Zeugma wall fragments, are occasionally found in Beirut contexts of this period. The absence of Campanian "black sand" wine amphorae in this period of occupation at Zeugma is notable, given that they are a major feature of the supply in the third century (see below). In Beirut Campanian amphorae do occur, but are surprisingly rare, in contemporary late Augustan-Tiberian and mid-first-century contexts, even though Italian fine wares are common in the first half of the first century A.D. These Italian imports cease after A.D. 50 in Beirut.[22]

The Flavian (/ Trajanic) Phase (Group C): Typology Plates 43–44, 49 Catalogue Plate 53

The most striking feature of this period, and an indication of a change in the ceramic repertoire to some degree, is the dominance of a new style of "collar neck" form, Form 2A, with a pronounced concave band rim, rather wide in diameter, and a cylindrical neck. It is likely that this is, nevertheless, a development of the early form Form 1 (or perhaps Form 2C–D that also occur in Augustan / Tiberian contexts), but one cannot be sure until complete examples of Form 2A–D are published. The most common bases in Flavian contexts are the hollow-toe bases already mentioned, Base 4. They may belong to Form 2A and would strengthen the suggestion that Form 2A is a similar shape to Form 1. It is assumed that a ring handle in one of these Flavian contexts (**AM79**: 7007.10) belongs to another amphora type.

The ring-foot base Base 1, here slightly different, with a thin, sagging floor (Type 1F), is a rare occurrence in this Flavian phase. Examples of Form 3A–B, probably associated with these bases, continue to occur in Flavian contexts, there being also a single example of another variant Form 3C (Plate 43; **AM83**: 7007.4).

We may just note here that there are occasional, often single examples of local fabric amphorae / flagons with vertical, cylindrical necks in this period (Forms 4–6, 7A, Plate 44). These may equally have had ring-foot bases.

Imports are rare and largely restricted to Rhodian amphora fragments (**AM72**, 2283.1; **AM75–76**, 2300 × 2). A large hollow base seems to be in Fabric 1 (for the thick-walled Form 2C–D?) (**AM88**, Base 5: 7007.1). Alternatively it may be a late Rhodian base type (similar occur in Beirut) or even a Cádiz fish-sauce amphora toe. The hollow Base 6 (**AM24**: 15009.8) is possibly Cretan. One could say that Zeugma's isolation from long-distance supply networks was even more marked in this period.

Figure 2. Form 3D AM148.

A.D. 253 (Group D):
Typology Plates 43–45
Catalogue Plates 54–61

The destruction levels associated with the Sasanian sack of A.D. 252/253 have yielded a rich assemblage of amphora finds, including a number of complete or semicomplete amphorae. A very clear picture of the general range of amphora supply to the city in this period can be gauged from these deposits.

The absence of second-century levels, however, does prevent us from tracing the direct development of forms and supply patterns from the Flavian period to the third century. This is unfortunate, as there are some marked shifts in the supply of imports and in the appearance of a new series of local amphora forms by the third century that, at present, appear as isolated phenomena.

This phase is notable for the appearance of a new class of amphora with a ring-foot base and short oval body, in a well-fired, probably local fabric (Fabric 1; occasionally in Fabric 2, with more lime). Two groups have been isolated on the basis of both size and rim type. Form 12 and Form 13D (fig. 3: a complete example) are larger modules than Form 13A–C. These vessels are characteristically decorated with sparsely located, finely combed, horizontal bands (on the neck and shoulder). There is no evidence that the forms were painted. The ware, rim forms, and decoration are shared by some of the nonamphora forms, for example the jar **PT387**. This shares the rim type of Form 12A, but notably was additionally decorated with combed wavy line bands, never encountered on the amphora series (for the fabric analysis of one of these jars, included so as to compare it with the amphorae, see ZG32).

Another product, Form 11, clearly less common than Forms 12–13, shares the ring-foot base type (Base 1H), hence general shape, but is a separate form and from a different close regional source. It has a distinctive band rim, lightly concave on top, and long, rather square sectioned handles that are placed at an angle on the (similarly sloping) shoulder. The handles and rim are decorated with a painted band. The fabric is paler and coarser than that of Forms 12–13 (Fabric 8), perhaps containing organic temper, and it is clear that this is a close-regional import. If it is Syrian it is not from the same source as the later painted amphora series (Forms 14–19), a point also borne out by more detailed fabric analysis.[23] Form 10 shares the handle type and fabric but has a different rim type. This ware is absent in earlier phases and does not occur in sixth- to seventh-century levels.

The general shape of local (Forms 12–13) and close-regional (Forms 10–11) forms, that is small, freestanding "table amphorae" can perhaps be seen in the context of other similar forms of first- to third-century date that are characteristic of the Roman province of Rough Cilicia (the Pompeii 5 class, e.g., here Plate 50a and later, larger versions of it.)[24] Sites immediately to the south on the Syrian coast (Ras al Basit and environs) within the Roman province of Syria also engaged in the production of similar shapes during the second to fourth centuries (Plate 50b–f).[25] One might extend the distribution of Roman "table" transport amphorae further west in Turkey to Sagalassos, where globular/piriform-bodied amphorae occur in the Roman period.[26] In Roman Phoenicia, in contrast, the local amphorae of the Roman colony of Beirut clearly followed Graeco-Roman models in the production of its amphorae.[27] The same can be said for Akko, located in southern Phoenicia.[28]

In conclusion, we may make the suggestion that Zeugma or a city nearby engaged in the production of "table" amphorae, rather than amphorae more typical of the Graeco-Roman tradition. Given that amphorae with ring-foot bases were also a feature of the first-century phases of Zeugma, some continuity in this practice can be observed. The hollow-toe amphorae (in theory, Forms 1 and 2) followed a distinct, perhaps Phoenician tradition, which, notably had ended by the third century. There are no possible successors to Form 1 in third-century levels.

What does continue and is another major feature of local amphora production is the globular amphora with a collar neck, band rim, and strap-handles attached from the rim to the shoulder (Form 3). Examples of third-century date, best illustrated by the complete example AM148 (2017.1: fig.

Figure 3. Form 13D. AM202.

Figure 4. Form 16A. **AM270**.

2), have a rounded base. Two principal variants of Form 3 are found in third-century levels, one is thin walled and well fired (Form 3D–E), the other is thicker walled with a wider band rim (Form 3F). The variant Form 3G is related to the latter.

Syrian, pale greenish-white-fabric, painted amphorae are characteristic close regional imports in seventh-century contexts in Zeugma, as we shall see (Plates 46–48). It is not clear whether the three examples of one of the amphora classes within that production found in mid-third-century levels are contemporary or intrusive later pieces. The amphorae in question are examples of Form 14A (**AM110**: 2010.6) and 14B (**AM194**: 2080.4; and a handle: **AM195**, 2080.5). There is certainly some intrusive seventh-century material in some of the Sasanian sack deposits. What is clear is that such central Syrian imports are either absent or rare in the mid-third century. They are certainly absent in first-century levels.

Imported amphorae from long-distance sources overseas, however, are a characteristic and constant feature of the supply of third-century Zeugma. Though quantities are not great, the range of forms is consistent throughout the contexts and is also confirmed by observations of finds in the excavations at Zeugma and Apamea-on-the-Euphrates by the University of Nantes.

Occasional finds of Campanian wine, carried in Dressel 2–4 imitations of Koan amphorae (with long, double-barreled handles) are important evidence not only for the contact between the twin cities (through the port of Seleucia-on-the-Orontes, presumably) and Campania-Naples, but also for the evidence this provides for the continuity of not only production but also long-distance exports of Campanian wine to the East.[29] The latter had been clearly severely curtailed following the devastation caused by the eruption of Vesuvius in A.D. 79. Paul Arthur and David Williams have provided evidence for the eventual recovery of the Campanian wine industry, on the basis of second- and third-century finds of amphorae still modeled on the Koan shape.[30] These later exports are rarely found outside Italy, being targeted at military sites in Germany (e.g., Neuss) and Britain.[31] Third-century papyri from Egypt referring to Aminean wine may document similar Campanian wine imports.[32] Campanian amphorae, though present in the first half of the second century in Beirut, are notably absent in numerous contexts of the early to mid-third century. This, and the military character of the markets supplied in Britain and Germany, makes the finds in Zeugma all the more interesting.

These imports of Campanian amphora at Zeugma and Apamea were, furthermore, accompanied by the occasional imported example of Pompeian Red Ware baking dishes in the third century (see Kenrick, this volume). Similar Pompeian Red Ware dishes and other Campanian region products were regularly exported to Beirut, but earlier, in the first half of the second century. In the case of these earlier imports to Beirut, they were probably transported alongside the wide range of Baetican and Portuguese garum amphorae that are found in the same contexts.[33]

Other significant imports at Zeugma are Dressel 20 oil amphorae from production sites along the Guadalquivir Valley.[34] We may also note the likely Baetican/Guadalquivir source of a Dressel 2–4 amphora (**AM116**, 2011.1). These Spanish amphorae are particularly interesting because of the rarity of Baetican oil exports to sites in the eastern Mediterranean in the third century.[35] Dressel 20 amphorae are notably rare in Beirut, for example, even though there are massive early third-century contexts that contain a large percentage of western Mediterranean amphora imports from Baetica, Lusitania, and Forlimpopuli.[36]

As Beirut did not receive Campanian wine with these western imports, the supply of both Dressel 20 and Campanian amphorae to Zeugma, even if in small quantities, is evidence for not only a distinct pattern of western exports to the two regions, but also that it is possible, though by no means necessarily the case, that Baetican oil and Campanian wine traveled in the same shipments. The exclusively military character of the distribution of Campanian third-century amphorae in the West outside Italy and the well-known established links between the distribution of Spanish oil and the *annona civica* and *militaris* strongly suggest, together with the known distribution of these amphorae in the East, that the supply to Zeugma was exceptional and primarily due to its military status.[37]

The absence of Tunisian amphorae at Zeugma, Tunisian cooking wares, and the rarity of African Red Slip Ware (see Kenrick, this volume) are other examples of its distinct supply with respect to Beirut, which has yielded examples of all these products: generally central Tunisian fish amphorae, associated with Tunisian cooking wares and African Red Slip Ware, the latter being notably common only in the mid-third century (central Tunisian ARS C).

Another western import that should be mentioned is a large fragment of a Mauretanian Keay 1A wine amphora, such as those that are particularly common imports at Rome in this period.[38] I have only come across a few examples of its companion type with a wide band rim, Keay 1B in Beirut, the variant that is perhaps more common on the east coast of Spain and was also exported to Rome.[39] Finally, there are two possibly southern Portuguese examples of the Keay 23 fish sauce amphora, though their fragmentary condition and unusual fabric make this identification tentative.[40] Similar amphorae are regular finds in early third-century contexts in Beirut but were not encountered in mid-third-century contexts (Portuguese imports reappear in the early/mid-fourth century). Baetican–southern Lusitanian Keay 16 amphorae and other Iberian products, on the other hand, continued to be imported to Beirut into the mid-third century but did not occur in the Zeugma assemblage.

True Koan amphorae with double-barreled handles, from Kos, are also regular finds at Zeugma in this phase (**AM142**: 2012.18; **AM114**: 2010.3; **AM174**: 2039.1; **AM217**: 2158.1). They do not occur in Beirut third-century contexts. Another so far unprovenanced but probably Aegean import is one of the more common imported amphora classes at Zeugma: the Kapitän II/Peacock and Williams Class 47/Riley MRA 7 (**AM113**: 2010.2; **AM152**: 2031.1; **AM146**–**147**: 2014 × 2; **AM218**: 2241.1; **AM220**: 2269.1; not in the Catalogue is a large neck fragment from Trench 8 (context 8000), and others observed by Philip Kenrick: a rim in 2332 and single wall fragments in 7066, 11034, 18000, and possibly 18015). These also reach Beirut in quantity during the early to mid-third century. Though rare, it may be significant that the amphora also reached the eastern Euphrates Roman fort of Ain Sinu (Iraq) in the third century.[41] Other rarer finds at Zeugma, from southern Asia Minor and the Ephesos region, are early versions of the late Roman Amphora 3 micaceous amphora type, here the type of the first to third centuries that had one handle and a large domed foot (**AM221**: 2278.3; **AM117**: 2011.3; **AM260**: 18108).[42] The well-fired fabric of **AM221** suggests an origin other than Ephesos (which is typically rather soapy and red brown).

A single handle fragment of a Gazan amphora and a wall of a bag-shaped Palestinian amphora found in mid-third-century contexts are not necessarily intrusive, given that they were certainly traded in the Levant from the early second century onward.[43]

Figure 5. Form 16A. **AM332**.

What is surprising in this respect is Zeugma's lack of or poor connection with Syria Libanensis and Syria Palaestina (i.e., Lebanon and Palestine) throughout the early to mid Roman period, a trend that will change by the seventh century, as we shall see. Perhaps more revealing is the scarcity, or again possible absence, of products of Ras al Basit (a possible wall fragment was noted in 2039). The large globular amphorae of Basit and environs, already alluded to, are a major component of several mid-third-century assemblages in Beirut (e.g., Plate 50c; Plate 50d for a fourth-century example). The absence of these and East Cilician early to mid-third-century precursors to the LRA 1 type also found in early to mid-third-century levels in Beirut (the latter mid-third-century deposits being accompanied by abundant ARS C) is important evidence for major differences in the supply of coastal close-regional provincial amphorae in this sector of the Levant. In contrast to the long-distance imports of Spain and Italy, they appear not to have penetrated into inland Syria.

The Ras al Basit large stamped mortars and dolia that were also widely traded, as were the dolia of the region of Tartus/Antaradus and Amrit/Marathus, are not found at Zeugma (see Kenrick, this volume). Several complete Ras al Basit dolia are on display in the Archaeological Museum at Antakya/Antioch. Their absence, at Zeugma, however, is surely due to the difficulties of transporting such objects long distances inland, in contrast to the ease of shipping them from these coastal cities to others further south, such as Beirut.

The Early Seventh-Century Phase (Group F):
Typology Plates 46–48, 51
Catalogue Plates 62–74

Undoubtedly the most significant observable phenomenon during this, the latest period of pre-Islamic occupation on the site, is the shift toward central Syria for the supply of amphora-borne commodities and the total absence of what could be considered local amphorae (in Fabric 1) during this period. Quite when this trend occurred cannot be answered at this stage, due to the gap in the ceramic, or at least, amphora record from the Sasanian sack till the early seventh century.

These excavations at Zeugma, as also those carried out by the University of Nantes, provide evidence for the major and overwhelming importation of painted north Syrian amphorae to the twin cities of Zeugma and Apamea in the later Roman period (fifth to seventh centuries).[44] Though this amphora class is now well known and very common on sites such as Tetrapyrgium/Qusair as-Saila and Resafa/Sergiopolis, in the Syrian sector of the Middle Euphrates, the assemblages presented here demonstrate their similar importance to sites further upstream. The strategic location of Zeugma and Apamea on the only crossing point of the upper Euphrates and on the major east-west trade

	R	B	H	S	
Sinope	1	1	2	3	Includes a complete example
Syrian forms 14–19	6	9	8	54	–
LRA 1	–	–	–	3	–
LRA 4	–	–	–	3	–
LRA 5	–	–	–	5	–

a. Contexts 7060, 7036 (early seventh century).

	R	B	H	S	
Sinope	–	–	1	–	–
Syrian forms 14–19	20	5	28	27	–
LRA 1	1	1	2	*	AM348
LRA 4	1	–	1	–	–
LRA 5	2	2	4	–	Two complete examples
Ung.	–	1	–	–	–

b. Contexts 7003, 7004, 7005, 7006, 7026, 7061, 7062, 7064, 7065, 7214, 7306. Early seventh century. Combined figures.

	R	B	H	S	
Sinope	–	–	1	7	–
Ephesos unguentarium	–	2	–	1	–
Syrian forms 14–19	3	5	8	48	–
LRA 1	–	–	3	7	–
LRA 5	–	–	2	5	–

c. Context 12002 (early seventh century).

	R	B	H	S	
Local?	–	–	–	2	–
Sinope	1	4	6	23	–
Sinope var.	–	–	2	–	–
FAM202?	–	1	–	–	AM455
AM486	–	–	–	1	Black Sea?
Ephesos unguentarium	–	2	–	3	–
Samos	–	–	–	1	–
Samos var.	–	–	1	–	–
Syrian forms 14–19	26	11	41	142	–
Regional	–	–	–	1	–
LRA 1	3	–	3	25	–
LRA 5	–	2	1	10	–
Agora M 334?	–	–	–	1	AM496
Palestinian?	–	–	–	1	Aqaba? AM497
LRA 4	–	–	–	1	–
Egyptian Nile silt	–	1	–	1	–
Unclassified Import	–	–	–	1	AM501

d. Context 12011 (A.D. 550–600?).

	R	B	H	S
Sinope	2		5	24
Ephesos unguentarium		1		
Syrian forms 14–19	18	4	31	23
Regional				3
LRA 1		1	3	13
LRA 5		2		
LRA 4		1		

e. Context 12012 (A.D. 525–550 and early seventh-century fine wares).

Table 1. Summary by count of rim (R), base (B), handle (H), and wall sherds (S) of amphorae in period F contexts. Note that rim, base, and handles have been counted separately, even if they comprised one sherd (i.e., R/N/H = rim × 1, H × 1).

Figure 6. Large Form 17A. AM296/303.

route linking the Mediterranean (Seleucia-on-the-Orontes and Antioch) to Mesopotamia, Iran, and India beyond must surely account for such a focus of Syrian-Euphrates imports in this period.

The deposits studied here provide us with the opportunity to attempt a typology for this painted amphora class (see Typology). Given the absence of anything but rounded bases in the Syrian fabrics (Fabric 13), it is likely that all vessels in this series (Forms 14–19) followed the same general typological format: a somewhat bag-shaped amphora with cylindrical body and sagging, rounded base, a cylindrical neck with oval-section handles springing from the mid or upper neck.

What would seem to be a key observation for the understanding of the complex typology of this class is that in addition to having a number of identifiable rim types and subtypes of the latter (Forms 14–19 and variants within each), each variant was produced in several sizes, large, medium, and small. One-handled jugs represent the smallest versions of these individual products (for these, see Kenrick, this volume, buff ware forms). The interrelationship of particular variants within the entire class suggests that production was prolific and to be ascribed to many workshops. Fabrics, painted decoration schemes or their rarity in some cases, and typological links between some designated variants but not others suggest that there were two major production areas for the class (see Typology, with respect to Forms 14–16 and Form 17). This remains a theoretical model until production sites are located and studied.

Vessels of Form 17, though also comprising a wide range of variants, seem to be more closely knit in typological details and fabric (almost invariably the well-fired, fine matrix version of Fabric 13B). Their rim types are not found in Forms 14–16, which, as stated, do not generally have the same fine matrix fabric as Form 17. In other words, there are possibly two sources of production.

Given that rims of Forms 15 and 16 were noted in the Jabbul Plain sites near Aleppo (Plate 49a–b) and amphorae of the more granular pale green fabric were present on sites of the limestone massif to the West, it is possible that Forms 14, 15, and possibly 16 were products of workshops (on the Euphrates) closer to Aleppo. Form 17, found at Resafa and environs (see Typology for the numerous examples) may have been produced on the Euphrates further to the east. Though Form 14 appears to be rare at Qusair as-Saila, and could thus support this argument or at least the separate marketing of the two groups of forms, Form 15 was, in contra, present. Form 16, with its grooved rim, is the most common variant at Resafa and is also common at Qusair as-Saila. It occurs in the Jabbul Plain, as we have noted. The variant Form 17F, with its unusual ribbed neck, rare at Zeugma, is not uncommon at Qusair as-Saila and occurs at Resafa.

The decorative motifs and schemes found on Forms 15, 16, and in particular on Form 17 are described and discussed in the Typology (see under Form 17). The principal motif employed in the decoration of the shoulder is what seems to be a leaf with a spiral attachment to the left (e.g., Plates 63, 65, 66, and 68; figs. 6–9). It could be argued that the careful repetition of this motif by the numerous potters producing the plethora of regional variants is an indication that the motif represented something well known to the potter-painter. Perhaps, though not necessarily, it is an indication of the amphora's contents. It is not the traditional representation of an acanthus leaf, palmette or palm frond, or vine leaf.

These amphorae apart, the only other amphorae present in seventh-century contexts are also imports, but from long-distance sources. The two largest deposits, 12011 and 12012, as well as the smaller deposit 12002, were fully quantified (rims, bases, handles, sherds counted and weighed) in order to determine the relative roles of Syrian and other regional imports in the supply of Zeugma in the early seventh century (table 1c–e). These figures can also be eventually compared with other seventh-century or earlier deposits in the Levant (notably Beirut, Caesarea, and Alexandria, once these massive urban excavations are published).

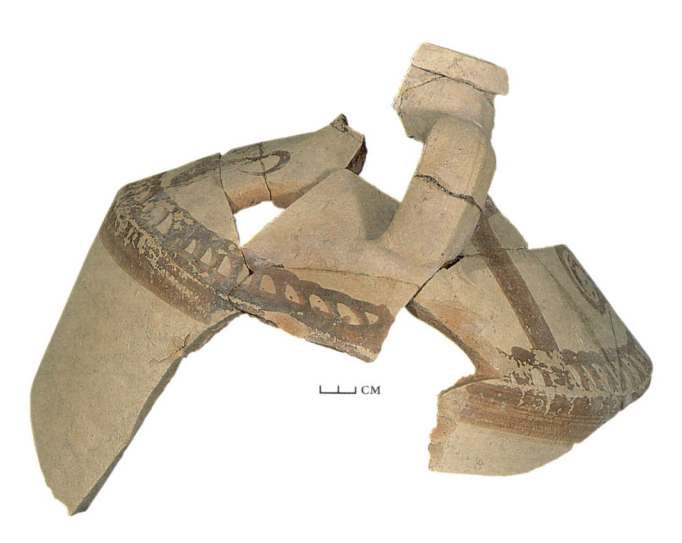

Figure 7. Small Form 17A **AM310**.

The most common long-distance imports are amphorae from Sinope, on the Black Sea (e.g., **AM324**, figs. 10–11: 7060.14, almost complete; **AM440, 441,** and **449**: 12011). During the late fifth to seventh centuries these were fired to a pale greenish-white color,[45] and sherds and even handles are sometimes difficult to distinguish from those of the equally common form "Late Roman Amphora 1" / Peacock and Williams Class 44.[46]

Examples of the third to early / mid-fifth centuries were fired to a redder color. A well-known shape with a carrot body and tall cylindrical neck in the red fabric is a typical find in Beirut contexts of the early fifth century.[47] The pale late-Sinope amphorae are very common in Beirut assemblages of the late fifth to mid-sixth century, but probably become scarcer after the A.D. 551 earthquake.[48] The form was also exported to Jordan.[49] Significant with respect to the supply mechanisms that brought Sinope amphorae (and perhaps all non-Syrian imports) to Zeugma is the presence of abundant examples of Sinope amphorae (and LRA 1 amphorae) at Seleucia-on-the-Orontes, the port of Antioch. Though interpreted as evidence for the manufacture of this class at Seleucia-on-the-Orontes,[50] it is more likely that the abundant examples indicate the location of a warehouse for Sinope amphorae alongside the docks of the port.[51]

It would also seem likely that it was fish sauce that was carried in these amphorae, as Sinope was famous for its garum exports, from Hellenistic times.[52] It may be no coincidence that the narrow-necked shape of Early Imperial small modules[53] is close to that of the Pompeian form chosen to package the garum of A. Umbricius Scaurus, illustrated on the mosaic floor of his home.[54] Beirutis, furthermore, appear to have had a penchant for consuming fish sauce, whether from Spain, Portugal, Tunisia, or Sinope. With the drop in Baetican exports to Levantine sites that may have resulted from the geopolitical changes and shifts in focus of western exports following the Vandal and Visigothic conquests of North Africa and Spain, respectively, it is possible that Sinope during the fifth century may have replaced Baetica-Portugal as the principal supplier of fish sauce to the Levant.[55] This in turn is reflected in the supply to Zeugma.

The other principal import, Late Roman Amphora 1 (LRA 1), though mostly represented by body sherds and few diagnostics, derived from sources closer to Zeugma, in Cyprus and eastern Cilicia, where kilns of LRA 1 have been located (see Plates 67 and 73: **AM327, AM462–465**; Table 1).[56] An important find is a complete narrow-bodied version of LRA 1, typical of the seventh century, from the seventh-century context 7062 (**AM336***bis*; fig. 12).

Though Empereur and Picon "identified" production sites of LRA 1 at Arsuz and Seleucia-on-the-Orontes (the former on the border of Roman Syria and Cilicia, but by this period probably within Syria, the latter lying in Syria), the production of LRA 1 at these two coastal sites remains highly contested. The only definite production of LRA 1 is that in Cilicia, and production within Syria still needs confirmation, even though Antioch clearly would have played a major role both in the export of LRA 1 (notably to western Mediterranean sites)[57] and in the supply of LRA 1 to sites in inland Syria.

Cyprus, later, from the early sixth century, was also a major exporter of goods contained in the LRA 1 form produced on the island (kiln sites are known at Zygi and Paphos, for example; Salamis and Kition are as yet unproven, but likely exporters of LRA 1). One major fabric of LRA 1 that supplied Beirut in the late sixth century is also very common in Salamis (perhaps its source), but is not present at Zeugma. This is just one example of how the marketing of LRA 1 can vary from region to region. Southern Britain, for example, was supplied by very specific LRA 1 sources, as were Butrint (southern Albania) and Leptis Magna (Libya).[58]

Just as contested is the nature of the goods carried in LRA 1. There is much debate as to whether this was wine or oil or both.[59] This problem may eventually be solved if attention is focused on the sites that were truly connected with its production and purpose, probably the numerous villages with presses that populate Cilicia, rather than the similar sites that are more well known in the limestone massif east of Antioch. On the latter press sites, it is only the pale green central Syrian amphorae that are found and not LRA 1.[60]

The only other notable imports in the late phase at Zeugma are Palestinian amphorae. Large, globular variants of the Palestinian Late Roman 5 amphora are not uncommon—there are several complete examples.[61] Of these, one was completely restored (Plate 62 and fig. 13: **AM263**: 5001.1). Of two complete examples in context 7065, one only was drawn, and without restoration (Plate 62: **AM349**: 7065.11; **AM348**). There were numerous finds of diagnostics and walls in seventh-century contexts: **AM199** (2080.20); **AM330–331** (7060); **AM380–384** (12002); **AM488–495** (12011); **AM554–555** (12012); see table 1. Whereas some are probably imports from Caesarea, others, such as **AM263**, have a fabric close to that of Gazan amphorae.

These very globular variants were typical exports to Beirut during the sixth and seventh centuries, to Butrint in the sixth century, as well as to sites in the western Mediterranean, notably to Marseille and Carthage.[62]

Gazan amphorae, in contrast, are quite rare at Zeugma (**AM293**: 7006.12; single wall fragments in 7060, 12011, and 12012). By the late sixth century Gazan amphorae were also notably rare in Beirut, in contrast to the supply of LRA 5, which continued unabated. The Gazan supply certainly represents a major drop with respect to the large numbers imported throughout the fourth to mid-sixth centuries in Beirut. It is possible that Zeugma is here following the same trends in Gazan and LRA 5 imports, but this, of course, cannot be demonstrated until contexts of fifth- to sixth-century date are excavated. What is interesting with respect to both sites in the seventh century and the general direction of Gazan exports in the Mediterranean is that Marseille, Carthage, and to some extent Naples were, in contrast, major importers of Gazan amphorae during the late sixth and seventh centuries.[63] Again one can detect major marketing trends for regional products if the general distribution is observed.

Also of note, though only attested as a single wall sherd, is a possible example of the carrot-bodied north Palestinian Agora M 334 type (**AM496**). This is not necessarily a residual fourth- or fifth-century piece. Late, small-module versions of Agora M 334, current from the late fifth century onward, some originating in the territory of Akko/Acre, are common finds in a large early seventh-century deposit in Beirut (BEY 006 5503) and continued to be exported to Rome as late as the second half of the seventh century.[64] Another sherd may be another example or possibly from an Aqaba amphora, another carrot-bodied type (**AM497**).[65] A ship carrying at least one Aqaba amphora together with example(s?) of Beirut amphorae, small Egyptian LRA 5, globular Pieri 3/LRA 5, and Gazan amphorae was wrecked off Iskandil Burnu, near Bodrum in the first half of the seventh century.[66] The presence of an Aqaba amphora this far north, presumably offloaded at Seleucia-on-the-Orontes, is thus not impossible.

A final note needs to be made on the regular presence of small and larger size micaceous unguentaria with roughly pinched bases, in contexts 12002, 12011, and 12012 (**AM369–370, AM456, AM458, AM557**; the larger variant/module Base 9B: **AM459**). These, in a soapy, highly micaceous fabric, are almost certainly products of the region of Ephesos (the fabric identical to that of the amphora LRA 3/Peacock and Williams Class 45). One could go further and suggest that their distribution in the eastern Mediterranean in particular (e.g., Butrint, Beirut, and sites in Lebanon) is connected with the cult of St. John at Ephesos, these unguentaria carrying holy oil brought back home as souvenirs by pilgrims.[67] A similar interpretation might be given for another type of unguentarium in a hard fabric, sometimes stamped and slipped, that is extremely common in Constantinople and Tocra (Libya) and sites in the western Mediterranean, but not in Zeugma, Beirut, or Butrint.[68] This, given its distribution in Lycia (at Limyra, for example), may be connected with the cult of St. Nicholas at Myra.[69] Yet another unguentarium, also a very common find in late fifth-century deposits in Beirut, can be clearly associated with the martyrion excavated at Hierapolis.[70]

Perhaps associated with the imports of Ephesian unguentaria, at least in terms of the proximity of the regional sources, are two amphora fragments in the distinctive sparkly micaceous red-brown fabric that appears to be typical of the island of Samos. One is a shoulder, almost certainly of the well-known sixth- to seventh-century Samos Cistern Amphora type (**AM460**: 12011). This was a major import at Butrint, where there were long-standing connections with Samos and neighboring islands, and is a regular,[71] if relatively rare, find in late sixth- to seventh-century levels in Naples, Marseille, and Tarragona.[72] Another fragment, also in context 12011, is a thick handle that is part of a larger module of the Samos amphora (**AM461**), a variant that also occurs in Butrint in mid- to late sixth-century contexts.[73]

Conclusions

The comparison of the supply of imported amphorae to Zeugma on the Euphrates and Beirut on the coast of Syria Libanensis highlights major differences in the supplies of the first and third centuries, as it does the notable similarities between them in the seventh century. Long-distance amphorae from Baetica and Campania that were an important feature of Beiruti assemblages in the first century are not encountered in Zeugma, even though both sites share imports of Italian fine wares and cooking wares.[74] Amphorae in early first-century deposits at Zeugma are

Figure 8. Small Form 17A. **AM335**.

Figure 9. Small Form 17A. AM335.

predominantly either local (Form 3) or from close regional, probably Syrian sources (western Euphrates, or in the Balih Valley?) (Form 1; Form 2C–D). Form 1 and Form 2 may well be Parthian transport amphorae — they are certainly found in Parthian territories from the Balih Valley to as far east as Dura-Europos. The flow of these amphorae to Zeugma may partly be due to the major caravan trade route in exotic goods that connected Hellenistic and, later, Roman Antioch and the Mediterranean to Mesopotamia and the Far East as it breached the Euphrates at Zeugma. The city thus acted as a bridge between Rome and Parthia and a high-earning customs point for Roman Syria, in the same way that Palmyra controlled eastern trade further to the south. This trade did not result in large-scale amphora-borne imports from the west, however. The isolation of Zeugma may even have increased in the Flavian / Trajanic period, imports being almost entirely solely from the same close regional source as earlier in the century (Form 1 and Form 2).

The deposits of A.D. 253 offer an extremely valuable, well-dated key to the nature of local and imported amphorae in the city. One is struck primarily by Zeugma's supply of Campanian wine amphorae and cooking wares and Baetican oil amphorae carried in Dressel 20 amphorae, all of which do not reach Beirut, even though the port commanded a rich range of imported western, Aegean–Asia minor, and Black Sea amphora-borne produce in the early third century.[75] Dressel 20s are rare indeed in the Levant, being perhaps regularly supplied only to major provincial capitals such as Caesarea and Alexandria. Though Zeugma received these particular western imports, the products of nearby, eastern Cilicia, amphorae of the Pompeii 5 class and its successors, all precursors to the LRA 1, as well as the amphorae of Ras al Basit, are absent. Though the presence of these Cilician and coastal Syrian amphorae in Beirut is partly explained by the coastal location of Beirut, for some reason amphorae penetrated inland Syria to Zeugma from much more distant sources, namely those carrying Campanian wine and Baetican oil, whereas the amphorae of Cilicia and Ras al Basit did not reach Zeugma.

Some explanation for this phenomenon is needed. It is possible that Zeugma's peculiar supply of Spanish oil, Campanian wine, and perhaps also that of the Aegean wine amphora Kapitän II (encountered at the third-century fort of Ain Sinu), was connected with the *annona militaris* and thus was related to the supply directed toward the Roman troops on the eastern limes and to the legionary base of Zeugma in particular (see Hartmann and Speidel, volume 3). Though Tunisian fine wares were imported to Zeugma in the mid-third century they are rare (see Kenrick, this volume), rarer than at Dura-Europos.[76] It is probably significant that amphorae from the same source are absent at Zeugma, even though they were regularly, if sparsely, supplied to Beirut in the early to mid-third century, together with Tunisian ARS and cooking wares (we have no details for Dura-Europos). In the case of Beirut's western supply one is reminded of the mixed Tunisian, Baetican, and Portuguese amphora cargo of the Cabrera III wreck, located off Mallorca,[77] a ship that was probably en route for Rome. The notable and important difference is the major presence of Baetican oil amphorae on that ship, products that did not reach Beirut, but which were supplied to Alexandria, as we have noted. Could the find in Zeugma of a Mauretanian amphora type regularly imported to Rome but rarely encountered elsewhere[78] be a further hint that the shipments of western amphorae reaching Seleucia-on-the-Orontes, and then Zeugma, were redistributed from Rome or perhaps more likely Pozzuoli in the Bay of Naples, the source of the Campanian wine imports?

This was a period, furthermore, in which Zeugma became otherwise largely self-sufficient in local wine(?) production (carried in Forms 12–13; see fig. 3). Amphorae imported from Syria in the first century (i.e., as Forms 1–2) are now absent in the third. Though in the third century Syrian mortars (e.g., Kenrick, this volume, PT396–402) were imported in a fabric close to that of some of the Syrian amphorae later encountered in seventh-century deposits, very few, and possibly intrusive examples, of this class of amphora reached Zeugma in the third century. Amphorae of Forms 10–11 (Fabric 8), relatively rare, represent the only definite close regional, presumably Syrian, imports.

The seventh century could not be more of a contrast. In this period Zeugma was swamped with imports of Euphrates-region amphorae containing an unknown content, possibly wine (or oil) (Forms 14–19). These pale colored amphorae are a feature of military sites on the eastern frontier, and appear to be more rarely encountered on sites in western Syria (the impression is that the painted amphorae such as Form 17 are not common at Déhès). That said, Syrian amphorae of this class, but in the more granular fabric of some examples of Forms 14 and 16, were regular, if relatively rare, finds on two of the highland village sites of the limestone massif east of Antioch, where they comprise the only amphorae on these sites (mostly handle fragments), and were similarly a feature of sites surveyed by Hans Curvers to the east of Aleppo, in the Jabbul Plain (cf. Plate 49a–b).

One would expect such a shift in local provincial supply to have occurred in the fourth and fifth centuries, when the structure of the provinces in the Levant was altered and the supply networks to the frontier garrison towns and forts seem to reflect a strongly centralized, well-organized system, essentially under the control of the Praetorian Prefect of the East, based at Antioch.[79] One can also detect a trend of increased regionalization and self-sufficiency in production from the fourth century onward within Syria, evident in the case of its brittle cooking ware production and distribution and the distribution of its pale amphorae, found throughout northern Syria, but never in the Roman provinces to the south (e.g., Lebanon and Palestine).

In addition to these close regional Syrian imports, from a wide range of middle Euphrates sources, Zeugma in the seventh century also benefited from a regular and somewhat plentiful supply of long-distance imports from the Black Sea (Sinope fish sauce amphorae) and LRA 1 amphorae from Cilicia and possibly Cyprus, with rarer Palestinian imports.

As such, the supply of imports was very similar to that of Beirut in the early to mid-sixth century. What Zeugma regularly imported in the seventh century that was by that period a much rarer find in Beirut were amphorae from Sinope. This is probably significant and may be directly related to the primary role of Seleucia-on-the-Orontes as the most northern Syrian distribution point of Sinope amphorae. For some reason these rarely traveled further south by the late sixth century, even though Beirut was a major importer of LRA 1 amphorae. If it were to be found that Beirut shifted its supply of LRA 1 from Cilicia to primarily Cyprus by the late sixth century, then we might find there a partial explanation for the differences in the distribution of Sinope amphorae.

Here one is reminded of another major regional difference in the supply of fine wares to the two regions. Beirut from the late fourth to seventh centuries was in major contact with Cyprus, as well as Asia Minor, from about A.D. 450 onward, with respect to its fine wares (Cypriot Late Roman D and Phocean Late Roman C, respectively). In contrast, Cypriot table wares were rarely imported into northern Syria, an exception to some extent being Antioch. Even in Antioch and on coastal sites of Roman Syria (personal observation of surface finds at Arzuz, Ras al Basit, Ras Ibn Hani, and Amrit) it was LRC that dominated the fine ware market, penetrating into inland Syria, to sites on the limestone massif and on the Jabbul Plain (personal observation), to Zeugma (see Kenrick, this volume), Resafa, and Qusair as-Saila, sites where LRC is truly abundant, with rarer African Red Slip Ware and even scarcer Cypriot LRD.[80]

Though the supply of LRC to Zeugma followed the pattern for inland Syrian sites it could nevertheless be said that quantities are far lower than those encountered at Resafa and Qusair as-Saila (there were only two contemporary examples of LRC 10 recovered in the seventh-century deposits and only eight examples of LRC from The Packard Humanities Institute excavations). A further and certainly significant difference in the supply of imports is that whereas Zeugma received a major quantity of Sinopean and LRA 1 amphorae, neither are present at Resafa and Qusair as-Saila, despite what does appear to be a fully comprehensive catalogue of the amphora finds. Though the sites on the Jabbul Plain sites, east of Aleppo, did import LRA 1 (Sinope amphorae so far being not noted), they appear not to have traveled further east by that land route.

The distribution of imports and Syrian amphorae in inland Syria is surely in part explained by the location and continued links of sites with the provisioning of the Byzantine limes, with Seleucia-on-the-Orontes and Antioch acting as the initial focal point for the redistribution of imported amphorae and fine wares, and sources along the Euphrates supplying their local regional amphora-borne products more directly to sites on the Euphrates. The range

Figure 10. Sinope amphora. AM324.

of forms, sources, and quantities of redistributed goods, including Syrian amphorae, were, however, not homogeneous throughout the region and reflect complex, diverse mechanisms of supply.

AMPHORA TYPOLOGY: LOCAL AND REGIONAL AMPHORA FORMS

The following offers a comprehensive typology of the local and close regional (probably north Syrian) imported transport amphorae encountered in the deposits selected for study. A full list of all the amphora finds in each of these deposits is given in the Catalogue. This includes all long-distance imports from overseas, which are of well-known types and are thus not described in this Typology.[81] Additional references to such imports are also given where necessary in the Catalogue and in the text. A few of the latter long-distance imports are also listed in the Catalogue from deposits that were otherwise not fully catalogued. Figures illustrate the amphorae found in each context and are presented in chronological group order, by context (Plates 52–74: Late Augustan/Tiberian deposits; Flavian (to Trajanic) deposits; Sasanian sack deposits of A.D. 252/253; deposits of the first half of the seventh century). See also the photographs, figs. 2–13. An additional series of figures provide a summary of the local–close regional imported amphorae (Amphora Typology Plates 43–51). In the Typology the distribution and number of examples per context of each form and variant is given. Fragments noted that are not illustrated are simply referred to by context and number of sherds (e.g., 2010; 2010 × 3: where 2010 = 1 example not illustrated). Drawings are at 1:3, except for those in the Typology, presented at 1:4.

Amphora Fabrics

The principal local–close regional (Syrian) amphora fabrics are paralleled in the buff and coarse ware fabric series and were followed up to a point. However, during classification there were intermittent additions of fabrics by myself, notably (amphora) Fabric 13 to distinguish the more common painted amphorae (e.g., Form 17) from the more granular Buff ware 6 (that of granular Syrian mortars). I also assigned (Amphora) Fabric 8 (originally Philip Kenrick's definition for all painted amphorae) to a separate group or source of painted amphorae (Forms 10–11). These changes have led to some confusion between us (of my doing). In order to not add to the confusion, it seems best to establish the appropriate correlations between the buff ware and amphora fabrics where they exist. Hence:

Buff ware 1 and 2 equal (Amphora) Fabric 1 and Fabric 2. In other words, no change. Buff ware 2/Amphora Fabric 2 was established to distinguish the more lime-rich examples of (local) Buff ware 1/(Amphora) Fabric 1. Chris Doherty, on the other hand, has reasonably demolished this tenta-

Figure 11. Sinope amphora. AM324.

tive distinction and would see all products as being from the same source (probably Zeugma).[82]

Buff ware 6 (e.g., pale granular fabric Syrian mortars) equals (Amphora) Fabric 13A, the more granular fabric that is more typical of Syrian amphorae forms 14, 15, and 16.

Buff ware 8 (cf. painted jugs, referred to in Philip Kenrick's chapter as the Syrian painted amphorae) equals Fabric 13B. Essentially, the more well-fired, compact fabric that is typical of small modules of Form 17.

(Amphora) Fabric 8 is not paralleled in the buff ware fabric series and seems to be solely encountered in two similar forms of painted amphorae of third-century A.D. date (Forms 10–11). Thus Buff ware 8 is not equivalent to (Amphora) Fabric 8.[83]

Chris Doherty at a later stage analyzed a larger and more representative group of Fabric 13 samples, comprising a much larger number of Fabric 13 Syrian painted amphora variants.[84] Here he recognized that there was a more granular group of vessels and suggested that this was due to the firing conditions whence the lime was burnt out, more so than the compact examples of Fabric 13 (here Fabric 13B). He nevertheless concluded that the range of inclusions in my Fabric 13A and 13B (granular and compact painted Syrian amphorae, respectively) were the same and that variants and production centers could not be separated on the basis of fabric inclusions. I would nevertheless still argue that the production and distribution of variants within the Syrian painted amphora series is not homogeneous and that the firing factor, coupled with associated rim variants, may eventually help to separate production regions within this amphora class.

Amphorae with "Collar" Neck, Long Body, and Hollow Toe (Forms 1 and 2)

Form 1 (West Syrian Euphrates?) (Group B)

Sloping, collar neck, and thick, rounded rim face bearing a groove. Three rim variants are distinguished (Form 1A–C). This form, with the grooved rim clearly distinguishable, is well paralleled in photographs of the numerous examples found in the necropolis excavated at Dura-Europos (Toll 1946). Complete examples (e.g., Plate 49a, from Tomb 54) show the form to be without handles, between 78 and 88 cm in height, with a collar rim and long semicylindrical body that widens toward the base, the foot being a hollow, long tronco-conical cylinder (as here Base 4, though these bases occur at Zeugma in later, Flavian contexts). Numerous examples found in the Balih Valley, including the site of Hammam-et-Turkman, are also handle-less (Lázaro 1988, pls. 165–6, nos. 80–105, and pl. 167.115–7; Gerritsen unpublished, 30, figs. 18–9). However, occasionally the type bears a single handle, attached from the rim to the shoulder (e.g., Plate 49b; Lázaro 1988, pl. 167.106–8, from Hammam-et-Turkman; for a similar, earlier one-handled form with an oval body and pointed base from the early Hellenistic necropolis excavated at Neirab: Abel and Barrois 1927, fig. 1, J18).

The Dura-Europos examples appear to date from 51–38 B.C. to the late first century, though the dating of the tombs is by no means precise.[85] In a presumably late Hellenistic or first-century phase of burials cut into Bronze Age levels at the site of Shams ed-Din, excavated during the construction of the Tabqa Dam, five examples of the same amphora type were laid side by side to cover or mark a grave. There were fragments of others reused in a similar fashion in four other burials (al-Radi and Seeden 1980, figs. 33 and 52, Sector A4). This type of amphora burial was commonly encountered on other sites that were surveyed and excavated in the Tabqa Dam / Lake Assad section of the Euphrates, for example at Tell Kannâs and Dibsi Faraj (fig. 1) (e.g., Finet 1979, 81, 83, fig. 6; Helga Seeden, pers. comm.). One of the graves at Tell Kannâs contained a worn coin of Nero(?) and a Flavian date is possible for the amphorae. These notably comprised both the small-diameter grooved-rim variant Form 1A and a much larger diameter vessel with a grooved or narrow concave rim (perhaps Form 2C or a larger version of Form 1A). It has the same body and base shape as its Form 1 companions (Finet 1979, fig. 6). As discussed above, the necropolis at Neirab, with a similar amphora burial practice comprising long cylindrical amphorae of similar type, but distinct in certain typological details, is dated to the early Hellenistic period (Abel and Barrois 1927; 1928). This cemetery and its amphorae would seem to provide antecedents for both Form 1 and the burial practices encountered in late first-century B.C. and first-century A.D. Syria.

The fabric of Form 1 is quite different to that of the painted Syrian amphora of the late Roman period (see below, Forms 14–19). That the amphora was local to Zeugma is nevertheless not assured, given the distribution and the somewhat finer and cleaner fabric of examples in comparison to what is more likely to be the local fabric, that of Form 3 and the third-century amphorae Forms 12–13 (Fabric 1).

The distribution of Form 1 covers a wide area comprising the Balih Valley, the most western section of the Eu-

Figure 12. Narrow-bodied LRA 1. AM336*bis.*

phrates (Lake Assad to Zeugma). The finds well to the east at Dura-Europos, though numerous, are so far somewhat isolated. The predominantly western Euphrates / Balih Valley distribution could be an indication that its production and the agricultural products it transported were located in that general region rather than further to the east or west.

FORM 1A

Pronounced, thick convex band with marked groove on outer face. Relatively tall collar. Usually a small diameter, but note the wide-diameter vessel, not necessarily Form 2C, that accompanies Form 1 in a burial at Tell Kannâs (the rim face is difficult to discern from the photograph: Finet 1979, fig. 6).

Frequency and date: Single example (**AM25**: 15095). Late Augustan / Tiberian.

FORM 1B

Small rim face. Tall tronco-conical collar, marked off from the shoulder.

Frequency and date: Single example (**AM14**: 15009). Late Augustan / Tiberian.

FORM 1C

Thick rim, but only lightly grooved.

Frequency and date: Single example (**AM26**: 15095). Late Augustan / Tiberian.

Form 1 in general, other sites: could date as late as the Flavian period at Dura-Europos and Tell Kannâs; possibly late Hellenistic at Hammam-et-Turkman. Form 1 (A–C) in general, distribution and dating: Dura-Europos necropolis: late first century B.C. to Flavian (Toll 1946: all of the amphorae photographed are of this type, e.g., Plate 49a); Balih Valley surveyed sites, associated with late Hellenistic to first-century A.D. material (Gerritsen unpublished: figs. 185–6; fig. 19.1: wide rim; fig. 19.4–5; fig. 19.6, small-diameter rim); Hammam-et-Turkman: late Hellenistic to first century A.D. (Lázaro 1988); Shams ed-Din: no dating evidence (al-Radi and Seeden 1980); Tell Kannâs: Flavian? (Finet 1979, 81, 83); Dibsi Faraj: Roman (Finet 1979, 61). Possible fourth-century B.C. predecessors of Form 1 at the Neirab necropolis have also been noted (Abel and Barrois 1927; 1928).

Form 2 (Western Syrian Euphrates? Balih Valley?) (Groups B and C)

Within the four variants classified under this form, there are two basic shapes distinguished. One has a cylindrical collar neck and a concave band-rim face and is Flavian in date (Form 2A). Two other variants (Form 2C–D; Plate 49c) have a sloping neck, similar to that of Form 1, but differ from Form 1 in having a wide concave band rim and a rather wide rim diameter, as well as thicker walls. The thick-walled, hollow-foot Base 5 (Plate 43) is possibly its base type, though the latter may also be a Cadiz or even Rhodian amphora. Form 2C–D should perhaps be considered a separate form within this general class, particularly given that they were contemporary late Augustan / Tiberian finds with the quite distinct rims of Form 1. Form 2C–D finds are especially common in the Balih Valley at Hammam-et-Turkman and other sites, where they seem to be associated with late first-century B.C. to early first-century A.D. material (so similar to Zeugma). Form 2B, Flavian, with its markedly beveled rim face, has a profile more in line with Form 1 and Form 2A. The hollow-toe bases found in Flavian contexts (Base 4) could equally belong to Form 2 and indicate that all variants of Form 1 and Form 2 (late Augustan to Flavian) were similar in body and toe shape. It is assumed here that a ring handle that occurred in a Flavian context does not belong to Form 2 (**AM79**, 7007.10).

Figure 13. Palestinian LRA 5. **AM263**.

FORM 2A

Distinctive, with a vertical neck and step marking off the neck from the shoulder. The rim diameter is wider than that of Form 1.

Frequency and date: Rare (**AM77**: 7007 × 2). Flavian. This form is present at Hammam-et-Turkman (Lázaro 1988, 157, plate 1565.80) and sites in the Balih Valley (Gerritsen unpublished: fig. 18.4). It is considered later in date than Form 1 (so follows the pattern established for Zeugma).

FORM 2B

Beveled rim band, neck slightly flared troncoconical. A small rim diameter, as examples of Form 1.

Frequency and date: single example in 2283 (Flavian: **AM65**) and likely residual example in mid-third-century 2012 (if this form: **AM122**). Other sites: Balih Valley (Gerritsen fig. 18.3; fig. 20.5–7, 9: though classified as late Roman).

FORM 2C

Narrow, thick, beveled rim band. Sloping neck/shoulder without the vertical collar that typifies Form 2A. This variant has a wide rim diameter, as Form 2A. Probably thick-walled, as Form 2D (see Plate 49c).

Frequency and date: Single example (**AM1**: 7118). Late Augustan or Tiberian. Other sites: Hammam-et-Turkman, Form 2C/D (Lázaro 1988, fig. 166.93–100, Type AA); Balih Valley (Gerritsen unpublished, fig. 18.1; fig. 19.2).

FORM 2D

Wide, concave band, with the top of the rim well rounded. Only rim preserved, but may be of similar sloping neck shape to Form 2C. It shares a similar wide rim diameter of that variant. Examples at Hammam-et-Turkman have rather thick walls (e.g., here Plate 49c).

Frequency and date: Single example (**AM2**: 7118). Late Augustan or Tiberian. Other sites: Hammam-et-Turkman (Lázaro 1988, fig. 166.93–100, Type AA; Balih Valley (Gerritsen unpublished, fig. 19.2).

Small "Table Amphorae" with Collar Rim, Strap-Handles, and Ring-Foot or Rounded-Sagging Base (Local? Fabric 1)

Form 3 (Groups B–D)

Collar neck with thin band rim. Strap-handles attached to the top of the rim. The form is long-lived, if, as is possible, there is a straight development from the late Augustan and Tiberian variants Form 3A to the mid-third-century variants Form 3D–E. A complete example of the latter (**AM148**; fig. 2) shows the mid-third-century version to have a bag-shaped body and rounded base, slightly indented at the center. Rounded bases are rare in first-century contexts, however (e.g., Form Base 2A, a single example, in the Flavian context 7023: **AM89**), in comparison to the bases with ring-foot, Base 1A–F. Given that the base type for Form 1 was the hollow-toe type as Bases 3–4, the ring-foot bases could correspond to either Form 2 or, perhaps more likely, to Form 3, which in its early phase may thus have had a ring-foot (see below). Note that whereas Forms 1–2 (imported to Zeugma) are well represented at Hammam-et-Turkman and other sites in the Balih Valley, and at Dura-Europos, Form 3 (local to Zeugma?) may be absent in both regions or sites. Beyond Zeugma, it seems, Form 3 was not distributed by the same mechanisms as Form 1 (and Form 2). This may be further evidence (apart from its fabric, as that of Forms 12–13) for a source lying at or close to Zeugma. The same can be said for the distribution pattern of (local) Forms 12–13. Seven variant rim types were noted, Types A–C dating to the first century, Types 3D–G to the mid-third century.

FORM 3A

Thicker, pronounced but narrow band rim.

Frequency and date: One example in 15095 (**AM27**: late Augustan/Tiberian), two examples in 7007 (**AM80–81**: Flavian) and a single example in 2158 (**AM205**: mid-third century).

FORM 3B

Small thin triangular band rim. The rim type and method of manufacture (clay blobs on the inside) close to those of the mid-third-century variants Form 3D–E.

Frequency and date: Common in late Augustan/Tiberian contexts 7118 (× 2: **AM3**) and 15095 (× 5: **AM29, AM32, AM33**). Rims classified as Form 3A or B occur in Augustan/Tiberian contexts (15009; 15095 × 2) and in a Flavian context (7007). Residual in 7003 (seventh century). Probably replaced by, or evolves into, Form 3D by the third century.

Form 3B is the most common variant of this form in late Augustan/Tiberian and Flavian contexts. The most common amphora type in late Augustan/Tiberian contexts.

FORM 3C

Rounded, more pronounced rim, pinched rim face.

Frequency and date: Rare. Single example in a Flavian context (**AM83**: 7007). A residual example in 7061 (seventh century).

FORM 3D

The only complete vessels of this class are of this variant. Thin-walled, bag-shaped amphora with rounded base, center indented slightly. Strap-handles attached to the rim and shoulder. Some examples (as **AM148**: 2017.1) have the rim bent inward, others have a more vertical rim with an indent on the inner face marking the transition from rim to neck. No further subdivision has been made on this basis. It is possible that some broad painted bands(?) decorate the mid wall and neck of **AM148**.

Frequency and date: Typical of mid third-century contexts (**AM148**, fig. 2: 2017; **AM155–156**: 2039 × 2; **AM238–239**: 18108 × 2). Two vessels classified as Form 3D/E and 3D/F, respectively, occurred in the mid-third-century context 2158.

FORM 3E

As Type D, but with a plain inner face and vertical rim. The only example of this variant has a relatively tall neck.

Frequency and date: Rare. A single example in a mid-third-century context (**AM181**: 2080).

FORM 3F

Thicker-walled, with a wide band rim. Handles attached from the top of the rim. Collar well offset from the shoulder.

Frequency and date: Common in mid-third-century contexts (**AM118–119**: 2012 × 2; **AM157**: 2039; **AM182–183**: 2080 × 2; **AM203**: 2139; **AM219**: 2260, but here in a coarse fabric and possibly painted, cf. Fabric 8/Forms 10–11; 18108). Two examples were found in the late Augustan/Tiberian context 15095 (**AM52**) and are perhaps intrusive. Absent in Flavian contexts. So probably a third-century variant.

FORM 3G

A pronounced thick band rim, similar to Form 3F, but thicker and flat on top (2080.18 is the type piece: **AM184**). The vessel **AM120** (2012.14), with half of its upper body preserved, is classified under this variant. Both examples have a relatively small rim diameter.

Frequency and date: Rare. Two examples of mid-third-century date (**AM120**: 2012; **AM184**: 2080).

Bases of First-Century Date

BASE 1A–F

A deep, curved lower body, with a ring-foot base. The outer walls, foot, and underside are usually "turned" smooth. The differences in the designated variants are due to the type of foot, beveled and flaring or rounded (less common), or due to the slope of the floor (horizontal or dipping). One would have thought these bases belonged with Form 3, as it is equally common in late Augustan/Tiberian contexts (as stated, the base type of Form 1 and possibly Form 2 is a hollowed-toe type, equal Bases 3–4). Base 1 is absent in Flavian contexts. Form 2 is exclusively Flavian. It is thus possible that Form 3 in the early Roman period had a ring-foot base and not the rounded base of the mid-Roman period (i.e., not as Base 2B: see Base 2A for the sole rounded base found in early Roman contexts, in this case Flavian).

Frequency and date: The general base type is common in late Augustan/Tiberian contexts (**AM10**, Type F: 7118; **AM17**, Type E: 15009; **AM35, 39–41**, Types A to D: 15095 × 7) but absent in Flavian contexts. It is absent in third-century contexts.

Other First-Century Bases (Close Regional Imports?) (Groups B–C)

Bases 3–4 are hollow-toe forms. Similar bases are typical finds on Form 1 and could equally correspond to Form 2.

BASE 3

A small flared cone, hollow foot. As Base 4, this may be a base for Form 1.

Rare. In late Augustan/Tiberian (**AM18**: 15009) and Flavian (**AM74**: 2300) contexts. Another example with a somewhat micaceous fabric was residual (7006, seventh century).

BASE 4

This is a base with a long hollow toe. As stated (Form 1) it should be the base type for the late Augustan/Tiberian form Form 1, as in examples found at Dura-Europos (Plate 49a) and Shams ed-Din. That the base occurs in Flavian and not earlier contexts is thus surprising. The typological similarity of collared band-rim amphora Form 2 of the Flavian period to Form 1 lends the possibility that Flavian examples of Base 4 belong to Form 2, rather than 1.

Three variants were distinguished (Base 4A–C), all three occurring in a Flavian context (**AM66–68**: 2283).

First-Century Amphorae with a Vertical Neck (as Flagons) (Groups B–C)

Form 4

Short projecting rim with a flat top. Two examples in late Augustan/Tiberian contexts (**AM16**: 15009; **AM43**: 15095).

Form 5

Thin-walled, with a rounded rim top.

Frequency and date: Single example (**AM44**: 15095). Late Augustan/Tiberian.

Form 6

Slightly bell-shaped rim, with a groove on the outer face.

Frequency and date: Single example (**AM45**: 15095). Late Augustan/Tiberian.

Form 7

Two triangular band-rim types (Form 7A and B), as Form 3B and Form 3D, respectively, but probably not amphorae with a collar neck. Form 7B has the trace of a handle attachment on the upper neck, not on the rim face.

Frequency and date: Rare. Single examples of Form 7A (**AM46**: 15095), late Augustan/Tiberian; Form 7B (**AM84**: 7007), Flavian.

Form 8

Small rounded band rim. Handle attached to the upper neck. Light groove-lid seat on rim top.

Frequency and date: Rare. Single example in a Flavian context (**AM85**: 7007).

Third-Century "Table Amphora" Forms (Group D)

Form 9 (Separate Fabric: Same Ware as 7003.4)

Flat band rim, well marked off from a vertical neck. Beveled-angled rim top. Any connection with Koan style, Dressel 2–4 amphorae? For the fabric analysis of this piece, see ZG35. Chris Doherty thought this to be a separate fabric, close to that of the **PT387** jar fragment that was analyzed as ZG40 (combed wavy band decoration). Not Fabric 1 or related to Fabric 8 (see below Forms 10–11).

Frequency and date: A single example in a mid-third-century context (**AM123**: 2012).

Form 10 (Fabric 8) (Plate 44)

Thin-walled, flaring, curved neck with a small convex rim. Handles slanted, as those of Form 11. Similar coarse, probably regionally imported fabric to that typical of Form 11 (Fabric 8).

Frequency and date: A single example of Form 10 and two handles probably of Form 10 rather than Form 11 in a mid-third-century context (**AM158 and 160**: 2039). Though the fabric and handle type link the shape with the production of Form 11, this is, in contrast, a rarer form in the repertoire of the workshops of Fabric 8 and related coarse fabrics, that supply only Form 11 in relative quantity to Zeugma. A close regional import.

Form 11 (Fabric 8) (Plate 44)

FORM 11A AND B

There are two variants, one with the handle attached to the rim top (Form 11A), the other with the handle attached below the rim (Form 11B). The rim form and handles are the same in both cases: a pronounced band rim with a concave top, similar to Fabric 1 contemporary forms 3F and 3G (Plate 43). Handles slanted, indicating perhaps that the neck was wide and tronco-conical. It is likely that the ring-foot base Base 1H belongs to Form 11 (Plate 44). There are no complete specimens so it is impossible to determine whether the amphora body was globular (as Form 3) or as the local forms 12 and 13 (see below). Bands of dark red-brown paint are typical on the rim top and face and along the outer face of the handles.

Frequency and date: Moderate numbers in mid-third-century contexts. Clearly far rarer than the local fabric forms 12 and especially 13. This and the distinct fabric of Forms 10–11 mark them out as close regional imports.

Form 11A: Single examples in mid-third-century contexts 2039 (**AM161**) and 2080 (**AM185**).

Form 11B: Single examples in mid-third-century contexts 2039 (**AM162**) and 2080 (**AM186**); intrusive in late Augustian / Tiberian context 15009 (**AM20**), though handle tye and fabric are not typical.

Handle of Form 11: 2039.

Handle of Form 10 or 11: 2010 × 2 (mid-third century).

BASE 1H (FABRIC 8 LIKELY)

Ring-foot base. One example, notably from the same mid-third-century context as other finds of Form 11 (**AM173**: 2039). The base has organics in the fabric.

Local Amphorae (Fabric 1): Forms 12–13

Form 12

The general shape of Form 12 is that of the more common Form 13, in the same fabric, and should be considered part of the same repertoire of the same production center. Though no complete examples of Form 12 survive, both forms would have had a ring-foot base (Base 1G), as the complete example of Form 13D (**AM202**, Fig. 3: 2086.1). Both Form 12 and 13 are typical of the mid-third-century Sasanian sack in-situ floor deposits of A.D. 252/253.

Form 12 has a thicker, often squarer rim profile than Form 13. Form 12A is clearly related to the jar form **PT387** (with a much wider diameter and bearing combed wavy-line band decoration). Form 12, as Form 13, is decorated with sparse horizontally combed narrow bands, just below the rim and on the upper shoulder (two bands in the case of Form 12D). The rim diameters of Form 12 are wider than those of Form 13A–C, but equivalent to those of Form 13D–E, the larger modules of Form 13 that share the convex rim type that is characteristic of the smaller-module Form 13A. The variant Form 12B, in fact, could be classified within Form 13D–E, but for the fact that its rim top is flat. It is interesting that there are more unique variant types of Form 12 than those encountered for Form 13. The latter, in contrast, are essentially variations on a convex-rim theme. Six variants of Form 12 have been classified.

FORM 12A

With a concave rim top and more triangular rim face, paralleled by the jar form **PT387**.

Frequency and date: The most common variant. Mid-third-century contexts (**AM124**: 2012; **AM145/150**: 2014.3/2031.2; **AM151**: 2031.3).

FORM 12B

Rim as Form 13D, but with a flat top and squarer profile.

Frequency and date: Mid-third-century contexts (**AM125**: 2012 × 2; 18108: **AM244** probably this, rather than Form 13D).

FORM 12C

A thick, square rim bent upwards and with a concave lid seat on the rim top (as Form 12A).

Frequency and date: Rare. Mid-third-century context (**AM92**: 2010).

FORM 12D

A thick, square rim.

Frequency and date: Rare. Mid-third-century context (**AM245**: 18108).

FORM 12E

A squarish rim but the top is convex and the rim is bent upwards. The neck may be more convex, recalling that of the jar form **PT387**.

Frequency and date: Rare. Mid-third-century context (**AM93**: 2010).

FORM 12F

A thick band rim with flat top and convex inner face. This rim variant is atypical of the Form 12 and 13 series.

Frequency and date: Rare. Mid-third-century context (**AM153**: 2032).

Other Form 12 fragments: 2010 × 3 (all shoulder fragments).

Form 13

The type piece for the shape is the complete example of the larger module of this form, 2086.1 (Form 13D: **AM202**; fig. 3). Both the small (Form 13A–C) and larger modules have a tall slightly tronco-conical neck, with a convex, projecting rim. Form 13C differs slightly in being more obviously a folded, projecting rim with thinner walls and more delicate features. Form 13 has an ovoid body, with the transitions from shoulder to lower body being fairly marked. The amphora was freestanding and relatively small, like a "table amphora." That the painted, coarser-fabric products Forms 10 and 11 would have been similar in body and base shape has already been noted. Unlike the latter, the Form 12–13 series appear not to have been painted (though see **AM140**, classified under Fabric 1). The more complete examples of Form 13 show the form to share the comb band under the rim, and one or two bands on the upper shoulder and one on the lower shoulder.

These forms thus appear to continue the tradition of "table amphora" shapes that feature also in the first century A.D. (i.e., Form 3A–C, if these were provided with the numerous ring-foot bases that are found in the same contexts: Base 1A–F). For a discussion of this type of small transport amphora as a characteristic north-Levantine class, see above (with reference to the Early Imperial Pompeii 5 type and the amphorae of Ras al Basit: Plate 50).

The variants of Form 13 that have been distinguished do not differ markedly from each other, but could nevertheless represent the activities of different workshops. This may account for the variation in fabric that is also encountered, basically there being a finer and a coarser grade of clay matrix. Occasionally vessels are fired to a buff color, rather than the more typical red, with reduced grayish surfaces.

FORM 13A (SMALLER MODULE)

With a small, convex, well projecting rim. **AM127** (2012.7) may have paint on its handle.

Frequency and date: The most common variant, typical of mid-third-century contexts (**AM127**: 2012 × 2; **AM164**: 2039, fired buff, coarser fabric; **AM189**: 2080 × 2; **AM224**: 2295 × 2). Residual in the Byzantine context 7006 (**AM289**).

FORM 13B (SMALLER MODULE)

A small convex rim, not well projecting. Some examples fired buff.

Frequency and date: Almost as common in mid-third-century contexts as Form 13A (**AM99–100**: 2010 × 2; **AM129**: 2012 × 2; **AM165**: 2039; **AM208**: 2158). Intrusive in the late Augustan / Tiberian context 15095 (**AM54**).

FORM 13C (SMALLER MODULE)

Thin-walled, with a folded, projecting small rim. A light molding on the top of the rim, perhaps serving as a lid seat.

Frequency and date: A single example only (**AM190**: 2080), mid-third century.

FORM 13D (LARGER MODULE)

Could be classified under Form 12, but has the convex, projecting rim of the common variant Form 13A, and not the squarer rim more typical of Form 12. Hence, a large module of Form 13A.

Frequency and date: Relatively rare. A complete example of Form 13D was found on a floor, in situ, in the mid-third-century context 2086 (**AM202**; fig. 3); Other mid-third-century contexts: 2012 (**AM131**), 2032 (**AM154**), 2158 (**AM209**). Intrusive in Flavian context 2283 (**AM71**).

FORM 13E (LARGER MODULE)

A more pronounced, well-projecting, wider, convex rim.

Frequency and date: Relatively rare and solely in mid-third-century contexts (**AM190**: 2080; **AM226**: 2295).

BASE 1G

The ring-foot base type of Forms 12 and 13 is very common in contexts of the Sasanian sack (2010 × 8; 2012 × 4: **AM133**; 2039 × 3: **AM170–171**; 2158; 2295: **AM228**; 2376; 18108 × 6).

There are numerous handles and body sherds of Forms 12–13 in third-century levels (2010: 3 shoulders; 2012: shoulder; 2039: shoulder; 2158: handle; 2295: 2 handles; 18108: handle).

Pale-Fabric Painted Amphora Series: Syrian Euphrates Region Imports (Forms 14–19) (Group F)

The following amphorae, Forms 14–19, are closely related in terms of fabric (the granular Fabric 13A; more compact Fabric 13B), hence source, and form. They all share a pale greenish-white fabric, evidence for its derivation from lime-rich clays. No production centers have been located, but this general fabric can be said to be typical of sites in northern Syria and, as the additional inclusions indicate, the general regional source(s) should lie close to the River Euphrates.[86]

Amphorae in this type of fabric have been found to the West, in the limestone massif east of Antioch (notably at Déhès, though rare?) and on sites on the Jabbul Plain east of Aleppo (personal observation of Hans Curver's survey material), and more commonly on sites on the eastern limes, at Resafa, Qusair as-Saila/Tetrapyrgium, and other military sites on the Strata Diocletiana (see below, under each variant for these parallels), and further to the east at Halabiyya-Zenobia (Orssaud 1991). Painted fragments of this class and rims of jugs (and possibly amphorae?) of Form 16 also occur, though sparsely, on some Byzantine sites of the upper Habur Valley (north of Hassake) on the furthest limits of the eastern limes (Lyonnet 2001, 26–27, figs. 5 and 6, with map of Byzantine forts on fig. 3: the amphorae are distributed mostly in the far western corner of the survey area, and along the River Habur).

The majority of these amphorae have a compact, well-fired version of this clay with visibly prominent multicolored inclusions and lime (especially the small modules of Form 17) (Fabric 13B). Others, notably some examples of Forms 14 and 16, occur in a fabric with a markedly more granular break, less prominent colored inclusions, and, in some cases, more evident gray inclusions (Fabric 13A). Both fabric groups are paralleled in the range of plain-ware mortars and jars that were also, clearly, imported as special functional items, from the same regional, Syrian sources as these amphorae (see Kenrick, this volume, Fabric 6, for the granular fabric and Fabric 8 for the more compact, plastic clay). The more granular fabric is due to the abundance of calcareous material in the clay. Where the calcareous inclusions are smaller or have been lost through firing to a higher temperature the clay appears to be more plastic.[87]

The classification of vessels within these amphora forms, and variants within each, has not been a simple matter and, if the classification is sound, probably is a reflection of the production of these vessels by a multitude of workshops, perhaps over a relatively wide region.

The amphorae in this group, furthermore, would appear to comprise a range of products in large and small modules that can be differentiated according to six basic rim types (Forms 14–19) and variants within each of these classes (e.g., Form 14A and Small 14A; Form 15B and Small 15B). Here Form 14, Form 15, etc., refer to the large module, the smaller module being so indicated. In a few cases, only the large module of a subtype was present (e.g., Form 17B and Form 17C).

The complete profiles of an example of Form 16A (**AM332**; fig. 5), of two large modules, probably of Form 17A (**AM264**: 5034.1; **AM296/303**; fig. 6: 7036.1/7060.15), and a complete profile (**AM344**) and several almost complete profiles of Small 17A (**AM310**, fig. 7; **AM335**, figs. 8–9), as well as several well-known previously published examples from Resafa, Déhès (Plate 51c), and Halabiyya-Zenobia (see Small Form 17A for all three), provide an indication of the general shape that is common to this series: a painted amphora with a sagging round base, cylindrical body, and cylindrical neck, with two "well-sprung" handles attached from the upper or mid neck to the shoulder.

There are nevertheless details in the form, decoration, and fabric, and the possible distinct regional marketing of certain variants (see above for some observations), that suggest that there are at least two major regional products within Forms 14–17, notably Forms 14–16 and Form 17. The rims of Form 14 show more typological links with the group Form 15 than Form 17. Some examples, furthermore, occur in a more granular fabric that never occurs within Form 17 (Fabric 13A). Thus a separate production region for both forms is possible. A few examples of Form 14 have the ends of paint brush strokes over the handle attachment (e.g., Form 14A, 2010.6: **AM110**), and occasionally on the rim top (not a typical feature of Form 17), but most are undecorated (though few portions of neck survive to be sure of this: most are rim or handle fragments). This could be a further indication, with the noted differences in fabric, to a distinct regional source for Form 14. Form 14, common at Zeugma, is notably rare at Resafa and Qusair as-Saila. The large and small modules of Form 17 also differ from the rest in the more detailed and more carefully executed decorative schemes on their necks and shoulders. The decoration on Form 15 (**AM338**) and Form 16 (**AM332**; fig. 5), when it occurs (perhaps, as with Form 14, they were not usually painted?), seems rather crude. The rim types of Forms 14–16 have features in common and that do not occur in Form 17. The rather plain, simple rim types of Forms 18–19 sit apart, though Form 18 is closest to Form 17, and Form 19 to Form 14.

Some of these amphora variants also occur in small one-handled jug form (e.g., **PT562** with a plain rim related to Form 15A; the grooved-rim jug **PT570** similar to Form 15C or Form 16; a jug with a beveled/pinched rim top similar to Form 14A or 16. Note that some vessels classified as small-module amphorae could equally be one-handled jugs: e.g., **AM409**, **AM411**, **AM413**, and **AM420**). The range of sizes and shared rim variants suggests that the production centers involved had a repertoire of similar vessels in a range of sizes, from very large amphorae to small one-handled jugs. Whether the latter were also imported for their contents is possible, but cannot be proven at this stage. There are certainly modern and ancient north Levantine parallels for the similar production of a range of modules for traded, presumably liquid, commodities. (cf. modern oil jars at Rashaiya, southern Lebanon; north Lebanese Roman amphorae and small flagons; Hellenistic and Roman Tyrian containers).

The decorative motifs and schemes found on these amphorae, notably on Forms 15–17, are described under the section on Form 17, below. The handle widths are generally noted in the Catalogue, so that they may be an aid to the identification of large, medium, and small modules. Large- and small-module sagging bases are identified where possible in the Catalogue as, respectively, Base 8A and Base 8B. Shoulder fragments bearing painted decoration in the style of Form 17 are classified as large or small variants where possible. They are loosely classified as Forms 15–17 (i.e., large), and Small Form 17 (though other small modules may be represented).

Form 14

As argued above, it is likely that Form 14 is a similar shape to Forms 15–17. Some of the variants and their typological link to variants within Forms 15–17 and jug forms have also been mentioned. It may be significant that, in contrast to Forms 15, 16, 17, and 18, there would appear to be no definite examples of Form 14A in the numerous vessels of this painted Syrian amphora class studied by Konrad (2001: i.e., at Tetrapyrgium and other sites nearby). Some possible examples of Form 14B, however, were noted. All examples in granular Fabric 13A.

FORM 14A

A rather triangular rim, with a narrow band rim face, its top lightly concave or pinched and its inner face convex. A similar band rim is also a feature of Form 15B. Large and small modules. Some examples are painted (**AM20**; **AM110**). Common.

Frequency and date: Intrusive in late Augustan/Tiberian (15009: **AM20**). Intrusive in mid-third century? (Large-module Form 14A: 2010 [**AM110**].) Seventh century (large-module Form 14A: 7060 [**AM300**]; 12011 × 3 [**AM385 and 387**]; 12012 [**AM502**]; Medium/Small module Form 14A: 12011 [**AM388**]; Small module Form 14A: 12011 × 3 [**AM408–409**]).

FORM 14B

Similar, with a more pronouncedly concave or beveled rim top.

Frequency and date: Intrusive in mid-third century? (Large-module Form 14B: 2080 [**AM194**; handles **AM195–196**?]. Seventh century (Large module Form 14B: 7003 [**AM266**]; 7064 [**AM337**]; handle 7006.6? [**AM281**]). Further parallels: Qusair as-Saila (Konrad 2001, Tafel 110D.1, from the vicus, Fdnr. 94/60).

Form 15

As noted, some variants (Form 15B and C) have a similar rim to Form 14A. Large, medium(?) (Form 15B), and small modules have been identified. Only one example of Form 15 is preserved to its shoulder, the latter bearing painted decoration that is typical on Form 15 and Form 17 (**AM338**). There are three subtypes based on rim type.

FORM 15A

A rather bell-shaped neck may be characteristic. It has a plain band rim, projecting a little, with a plain convex top. Of the two known examples, one, the largest, has the typical painted scheme found on Forms 16 and 17. Unlike Form 17 and Form 16B, the neck of the latter piece seems to be unpainted. Large and small modules.

Frequency and date: seventh century (large-module Form 15A: 7064.1 [**AM338**]; Medium(?) Form 15A (or Form 17A): 12011.67 [**AM395**]; Small module Form 15A: 7026.2 [**AM294**]).

FORM 15B

A band rim with a concave top and beveled inner face. Similar in style to Form 14A. Note the "well-sprung" handles with multi-ribbing of **AM354** (7306.1), and its relatively short neck. Medium (rather than large) and small modules.

Frequency and date: Seventh century (large-module Form 15B: 7060.24 [**AM301**]; 7306.1 [**AM354**]; Small module Form 15B: 12012.23a [**AM521**]). Further parallels: Qusair as-Saila (Konrad 2001, Tafel 112.8: from the vicus Fdnr. 94/61 level: illustrated with an early sixth-century example of LRC 3F: Tafel 112.2).

FORM 15C

As Form 15B, but the inner face of the rim is double facetted. The rim top is slanted. Large, medium(?), and small variants. The small variant **AM522** is also similar in rim type to **AM502**, classified under Form 14A.

Frequency and date: Seventh century (Large Form 15C: 12011 [**AM389**], 12012 × 2 [**AM503–504**]; Medium(?) Form 15C: 12012 [**AM505**]; Small Form 15C: 12012 [**AM522**]). Further parallels: Jabbul Plain site survey (Aleppo): several examples, e.g., Plate 51b (personal observation: this example published here with thanks to Hans Curvers); Qusair as-Saila (Konrad 2001a, Tafel 112.5: large module, from the vicus Fdnr. 94/61 level: illustrated with an early sixth-century example of LRC 3F, Tafel 112.2).

Form 16

A grooved rim top is the distinguishing feature of this type. A whole range of sizes of Form 16 type, from large- to small-module amphorae and small jugs (e.g., Kenrick, this volume, **PT570**) are documented. An almost complete example of Type 16A (7061.1: **AM332**; fig. 5) gives an idea of the size, shape, and painted decoration of the large module of this amphora. Many examples of Form 16 are decorated with a horizontal painted band on the neck (as typical for Form 17 also). There are a number of examples of this form published from Resafa, where it is perhaps the most common type, and Qusair as-Saila (see below), and jugs and possibly amphorae of this type occur on Byzantine sites on and east of the Bahour Valley (Lyonnet 2001, 26–27, fig. 5). Coarser fabric with gray inclusions (Fabric 13A) the norm, as Form 14?

FORM 16A

A distinctive variant, with a grooved rim top. Vessels classified under Form 16C are very close in shape. Only the lower part of the painted decoration of the shoulder of 7061.1 (AM332; fig. 5) survives, being a parallel hatched motif (notably not an interlaced continuous loop design, as that on Form 17. Large and small modules.

Frequency and date: Seventh-century contexts (large module: 7004.1 [AM270, fig. 4: granular Fabric 13A]; 7006 [AM282]; 7061 [AM332, fig. 5: almost complete profile; granular Fabric 13A]; Small Form 16A: 12011.81 [AM411]; 12012.26 [AM523]; Small Form 16A or C: 12002.2 [AM361]). Further parallels: Jabbul Plain site survey (Aleppo): several examples with granular fabric, e.g., Plate 51a (personal observation: this example published here with thanks to Hans Curvers); Resafa (Mackensen 1984, Tafel 13.1: small module; Tafel 25.23: large module). Qusair as-Saila (Konrad 2001a, Tafel 85.9 and 11).

FORM 16B

Rim thickened inside, lightly pinched top, rather than a groove, and slight rim projection. Plain outer face. Rather large, long handles. Large and small modules.

Frequency and date: Rare. Seventh century (Large Form 16B: 12002 [AM356]; 12011 × 2 [AM390]; Small Form 16B: 12011 [AM412]). Further parallels: Resafa (Mackensen 1984, Tafel 14.19); Qusair as-Saila (Konrad 2001a, Tafel 85.10, 12, 13, 19, and 26).

FORM 16C

Thicker rim, with less marked convex inner face. A deep groove on the rim top. Larger and small modules. Note the band of paint on the lower neck of the small module AM524.

Frequency and date: Seventh-century contexts (Large Form 16C: 12012.33 [AM506]; Small Form 16C: 12011.90? [AM413: could be a jug]; 12012.60 [AM524]). Further parallels: Resafa (Mackensen 1984, Tafel 13.20); Qusair as-Saila (Konrad 2001a, Tafel 85.8: or is Form 14B); similarly the small modules Tafel 85.7; more clearly Form 16C, with a plain rim face and no band, is a small-module vessel from the vicus, Fdnr. 94/12 level: Tafel 113.5; another is the small-module Tafel 112.6, from the vicus, Fdnr. 94/61 level: illustrated with an early sixth-century example of LRC 3F, Tafel 112.2).

Form 17

Both large and small modules have been classified under this type, which bears a variety of rather square or triangular band or Small Form 17 rim types. The small-module Form 17 is particularly common in late sixth/seventh-century contexts at Zeugma and on sites in northern Syria. Several almost complete small modules of Form 14 were found in seventh-century contexts: 7065.1/7006.1 (AM283/344: complete profile); 7060 (AM310, fig. 7: rim to base fragment); 7004 (AM271: upper half); 7062 (AM335, figs. 8–9: base missing). The two largely complete large-module vessels AM264 (Plate 63) and AM296/303 (Plate 66, fig. 6) could be examples of Form 17A, rather than, say, Form 16. The decoration on these two vessels is as that typically found on the many examples of the smaller module Form 17, being complex and well executed. In this respect their decoration differs from the known decorated examples of Forms 14–16. Small-module Form 17 amphorae are carefully made, some with crisp features, helped by the very "plastic" nature of the clay.

FORM 17A

A plain band rim, square or more typically triangular: considerable variation on this theme. Both examples classified as large modules of this variant have a wide brushed band of paint on the neck, typical on small modules of Form 17A. AM343 (7065.3) is unusual in being painted both inside and all over the rim and neck. The small modules of 17A are the most common variants of Form 17 and of the painted amphora series in general, only matched in numbers by Form 14. The small-module AM295 (7026.1) is unusual both for its pronounced triangular rim and the presence of a stepped band on the upper shoulder, at the junction with the neck, with a corresponding indent on the inside. The fabric of this vessel (sample ZG55), with schist, is notably set apart from others in this series by Doherty, and we may conclude that is the product of a particular, distinct workshop to the others that usually supplied Form 17 to Zeugma.[88]

Frequency and date: Seventh century (Large Form 14A: 7065 [AM343]; 12011 × 2 [AM393]; Small Form 17A, very common in seventh-century contexts: 7006 × 3 [AM283–284]; 7026.1 variant with ridge on upper shoulder [AM295]; 7060 [AM310, fig. 7: almost complete]; 7060.18 [AM311]; 7062.1 [AM334]; 7062.3 [AM335, figs. 8–9: almost complete]; 7065.1/7006.1 [AM283/344: complete]; 7065.2 [AM345]; 12002 [AM360]; 12011.72 [AM414]; 12011.68 (AM415: could be also Form 18]; 12011.84? [AM416]). A complete small module Form 17 housed in the Gaziantep Museum (7006.2: AM285) was noted by Philip Kenrick, but I was unable to examine it.

Other parallels: the well-known complete example published from Déhès is a small-module Form 14A (Plate 51c; Orssaud 1992, 221, 224, fig. B/2.14, found in situ from the latest Byzantine abandonment phase, associated with a complete profile of LRC 10C, dated to the first half of the seventh century; also published by Bavand and Orssaud 2001, 37, fig. 5.25); another well-known vessel is a small-module Form 14A, with a typical painted band on the neck, spiral/"palmette" and horizontal band of interlaced loops on the shoulder published from Qusair as-Saila by Mackensen: 1984, Tafel 28.1, also reproduced by Sodini and Villeneuve (1992, fig. 3.3); a complete example of Small 17A with the usual spiral/"palmette" and looped band on the shoulder is published from Halabiyya-Zenobia (Orssaud 1991, 267, fig. 123.35, with reference to a similar example at Tas'as on the Euphrates); other examples are published from the Fortress of Qusair as-Saila by Konrad (2001a, Tafel 85.-6.5 and 7; Tafel 87.1, 3 [as our **AM334**], 8, and 13).

LARGE MODULE FORM 17(A)?

Mostly complete examples, but for rim, with large body and large sagging base (Base 8A):

Frequency and date: Seventh-century contexts: 7036.1/7060.15 (**AM296/303**, Fig. 6); 5034.1 (**AM264**); Large/Medium: 5001.2 (top soil: **AM262**, not illustrated).

FORM 17B

Unique, large module. A square rim, markedly stepped underside. Streak of paint on handle.

Frequency and date: Unique. Seventh-century context (12011.58: **AM396**). Further parallels: Though not stepped, a similar profile is published from Qusair as-Saila, from the Fortress (Konrad 2001, Tafel 87.10, also a large module).

FORM 17C

Unique, large module. A very thick rim band with a projecting molding at its lowest edge. It has a particularly wide rim diameter.

Frequency and date: Unique. Seventh-century context (7060.23: **AM302**). Further parallels: Qusair as-Saila (Konrad 2001a, from the Fortress, Tafel 85.25 and 27); Resafa (Mackensen 1984, Tafel 12.19).

SMALL MODULE FORM 17D

Only a small module of this variant was encountered. As Form 17A, but with a more pronounced, hooked, triangular rim with a concave rim top.

Frequency and date: Unique example. Seventh century: 7003.1/7004.2 (**AM268/271**: upper half of vessel).

SMALL MODULE FORM 17E

Only a small module of this variant was encountered. Rim bent back, outer face flat, rim undercut.

Frequency and date: Unique example. Seventh-century context (7066.22: **AM312**). Further parallels: Qusair as-Saila (Konrad 2001a, Tafel 87.14).

SMALL MODULE FORM 17F

Small rounded rim, neck is ribbed outside and inside. Painted on the neck (not illustrated). Perhaps a little more common at Tetrapyrgium.

Frequency and date: Unique. Seventh-century context (7065.4: **AM346**). Further parallels: Three vessels from Qusair as-Saila have the same combination of rather thick, rounded rim and ribbed neck, two of them bearing a painted band on the neck (Konrad 2001a, Tafel 86.9, 10 and 12). Another example has the same rim or is an example of Form 17A, with narrow ribs present on the lower neck only, and bearing the usual spiral/"palmette" motif on the shoulder (Konrad 2001a, Tafel 86.11); Resafa (Mackensen 1984, Tafel 15.7).

The Decorative Schemes of Forms 15–17

Several almost complete examples of Form 17 survive that demonstrate the similarity of the painted decoration motifs for this form. A brushed horizontal across the neck is a common feature. This, on the complete examples **AM335** (7062.3: figs. 8–9) and **AM283/344** (7006.1/7065.1), is on both sides of the neck, between the handles. The shoulder is decorated with the same motifs that occur on the large-module vessels **AM264** (5034.1) and **AM296/303** (7036.1/7060.15: fig. 6), probably also to be ascribed to Form 17: a vegetal motif, a leaf with a spiral attached to the left, occurs singly, on each side of small-module Form 17A (e.g., **AM335**, figs. 8–9: 7062.3), whereas there is space for several to be painted on the larger module. This motif is more stylized and small in the case of Small Form 17D **AM271** (7003.1/7004.2) and Small Form 17A **AM310** (7060.19: fig. 7), and is, as the larger motif on small Form 17A **AM335** (7062.3: Figs. 8–9), only present twice on the shoulder. Below this motif, in a band running above the shoulder/wall carination, is usually the same motif encountered on the large module (i.e., as **AM296/303**, fig. 6), an interlaced spiral (e.g., **AM295**: 7026.1) or more commonly a series of parallel convex strokes, as **AM271** (7003.1/7004.2). This same pattern also occurs on the large module (e.g., **AM264**: 5034.1). Some examples of Form 17A have dots in the center of each half-circle (e.g., **AM283/344**: 7065.1). The spiral arch motif that occurs on the large module **AM264** (5034.1) is never found on small modules of Form 17, probably due to lack of space. It is interesting that the only example of Form 15 with its painted shoulder extant (**AM338**: 7064.1) betrays a little less finesse in its execution than the large modules **AM264** (5034.1) and certainly **AM296/303** (7036.1/7060.15: fig. 6).

Below the carination, on the upper wall is generally found a plain, horizontal band of paint, a feature that is also found on both large and small modules of Form 17. In some cases, e.g., **AM344**, the painting was applied in two stages (in this case the band on the neck was painted twice). The effect is to render the second layer a darker shade of red-brown. Where the border motif on the lower shoulder is formed by an overlapping brush stroke, this also led to darker sections where the lines overlapped. The large-module Form 17A **AM343** is unusual, as its entire neck surface was painted and then the horizontal band was added. In the case of the large modules **AM264** (Plate 63) and **AM296/303** (Plate 66 and fig. 6) and some of the small-module Form 17 (**AM310**, fig. 7; **AM335**, figs. 8–9) the surfaces were given a cream undercoat prior to painting.

The identification of the leaf with spiral motif with a particular plant is quite possible, given that its exact repetition is so frequent. One would think this represents a specific plant and may be a clue as to the contents. The identification by some authors of this motif with a palm leaf is not convincing, nor is it a traditional depiction of an acanthus leaf. A vine tendril would have been represented with accompanying grapes and vine leaves.

Form 18

With a plain rim, beveled flat on its outer face, and no rim projection. Large and small modules. **AM507**, a medium module, has a horizontal band of paint on its neck, as examples of Form 17. The small-module **AM419** is decorated with a band of paint on one side of the handle that is preserved.

Frequency and date: All contexts are seventh century (Medium Form 18: 12012 [**AM507**]; Small Form 18: 12011.70 [**AM419**]; 12011.71? [**AM420**]). Other parallels: The upper half of a vessel of Form 18 with part of the shoulder decoration preserved is published from Qusair as-Saila (Konrad 2001a, Tafel 86.2, and Tafel 87.21, both from the Fortress; a small module from the vicus, Fdnr. 94/1, may also be a variant of this form: Tafel 108.7).

Form 19

Plain outer face, rim not marked off from the neck. Plain, rounded rim top, convex on the inside. Small modules are quite common. There is one possible large module with similar features.

Frequency and date: Relatively common. Seventh-century contexts (Large Form 19: 12012 × 2 [**AM508–509**]; small modules are more common: 7005.1? [**AM278**]; 12011 × 2 [**AM421–422**]; 12012.28, 31, 32, 41? [**AM527–529**]). There were a fair number of small handles in 12011 and 12012 that might belong to this variant.

Handles and Painted Shoulders of Forms 14–19

Handles and painted shoulder fragments of small modules as Form 17 are very common in seventh-century contexts, particularly the large deposits 12011 and 12012: 7005; 7006; 7060 × 10; 7065; 7214 x 2; 12011 × 85; 12012 × 17; 12002 × 7. Large handles and painted shoulders of large modules of Forms 14–19 (Forms 15–17 in the Catalogue) are less common: 7003; 7060.3 (**AM304**); 7060 × 3; 7214; 12002 × 3; 12011 × 8; 12012 × 8.

LARGE MODULE BASE 8A

Large sagging bases, as on the largely complete vessel **AM264** (5034.1).

Frequency and date: All seventh-century contexts: 7036 × 3; 7060; 12011 × 2; 12012 × 2.

SMALL MODULE BASE 8B

The rounded base type for small-module amphorae such as those of the complete vessel of Form 17A (**AM283/344**: Plate 70; 7065.1/7006.1) was far rarer than one would expect. This may be due to their being missed during collection (even though many body sherds were collected in the large deposits such as 12011 and 12012): 7004; 12002 × 5; 12011 × 4; 12012 × 2.

CATALOGUE OF TRANSPORT AMPHORAE

The following abbreviations are used in the catalogue (list arranged by column heading):

Cat: sequential numbering of catalogued items for this catalogue

Dbase: my original Dbase catalogue numbering. This number is marked on the vessel in ink

NS: number of sherds

Wt: weight in grams

S: sherd type (wherein R = rim; B = base; H = handle; W = wall; Ft = foot; fr = fragment; frs = fragments; N = neck; st = handle stump; Sm = handle smear; Sh = shoulder)

Form: form according to the above Typology, or other well-known types (e.g., LRA 1; Keay 23)

No: number of vessels represented

%: percentage of rim or base survival

Dia: rim or base diameter in cm

De: decoration (wherein CB = combed band(s); P = painted; G = groove; Di = dipinto)

Ill: where illustrated (figures appear within the text; plates appear at the end)

Note on painted decoration: The "border band motif" is the looped or, in some cases, parallel curved strokes in a band on the lower shoulder of amphorae of the Syrian painted series (Form 15–17), usually with a plain band beneath. In some cases "looped arches" constructed in this manner occur on the shoulder. "Spiral": the "spiral" / "palm frond", snail-like painted motif that often decorates the shoulder section.

Note on fabrics: Samples analyzed by Chris Doherty are assigned ZG numbers.[89] In some cases in the Fabrics column my original fabric classification is included in parentheses, corrected or, in contrast, supported by the thin-section sample results. Palestinian is abbreviated "Pal."

Groups: Contexts marked * are contexts not included in Philip Kenrick's plain and cooking ware deposits: primarily amphorae or single vessels. Joins between contexts are also indicated. A summary of contexts with amphorae presented is as follows:

- Group B (Late Augustan to Tiberian)
  7118; 15009; 15095

- Group C (Flavian)
  2283; 2300; 7007; 7023

- Group D (A.D. 253)
  2010; 2011*; 2012 (joins 2080); 2014* (joins 2031); 2017* (single vessel); 2023; 2031* (joins 2014); 2032*; 2039; 2080 (joins 2012); 2086*(single vessel); 2139; 2158; 2241*; 2260; 2269*; 2278; 2295*; 2376; 18108

- Group F (first half of seventh century, except where indicated)

5001; 5034*; 7003* (joins 7004; 7060?); 7004* (joins 7003); 7005; 7006* (joins 7065); 7026; 7036 (joins 7060); 7060* (joins 7036; 7003?); 7061*; 7062; 7064; 7065 (joins 7006); 7214; 7306 (above 7064); 12002 (A.D. 525/550 to seventh; ARS 104C FW join with 12011?); 12011 (A.D. mid-sixth to 600 at most, with at least one early seventh; ARS 104C join with 12002? And LRC 3F join with 12012?); 12012 (7 × A.D. 525–550 and 1 × early seventh century; LRC 3F FW join with 12011?).

Cat	Dbase	Fabric	NS	Wt	S	Form	No	%	Dia	De	Ill	Comments
\multicolumn{13}{c}{**Late Augustan or Tiberian (Group B)**}												
\multicolumn{13}{c}{*Context 7118 (Plate 52)*}												
AM1	7118.2	Fabric 1	1	24	R/N fr	Form 2C	1	14	13 out	–	PL. 52	Type piece. Pronounced concave band. Similar form and fabric to Flavian piece 7007.2 (AM77), here with a wider rim band and angled neck.
AM2	7118.3	Fabric 1	1	21	R	Form 2D	1	12	12 out	–	PL. 52	Type piece. Similar to AM1 (7118.2), but rounded rim top.
AM3	7118.4	Fabric 1	1	18	R/N/Shfr	Form 3B	1	17	9 in	–	PL. 52	Thin walled collared rim, thin triangular band, as examples in 15095. Pale yellow ochre surfaces.
AM4	7118.6	Fabric 1	1	15	R/N	Form 3B	1	20	8 in	–	–	Identical to 7118.4 (AM3). Fired green. Light weight.
AM5	7118.5	Fabric 2	2	59	R/N/spur	Unclassified	1	50	7.5 in	–	PL. 52	Seems to have a projecting spur on the neck, not a handle. Triangular rim band bent inward. Flagon likely. Lime eruptions but not as coarse as Fabric 2.
AM6	7118.7	Fabric 1	1	18	R/N fr	Unclassified	1	15	9 top	–	–	Unique. Rounded rim, bulbous neck. Buff.
AM7	7118.10	Fabric 1	1	55	H	–	1	–	–	–	–	Jug or flagon. Handle width 3 cm.
AM8	7118.11	Fabric 1	1	41	Hfr/N	–	1	–	–	–	–	Handle attached to neck, not rim top. Yellow ochre surfaces. Handle width 4 cm.
AM9	7118.12	Fabric 1	2	55	Hfr	–	2	–	–	–	–	–
AM10	7118.13	–	1	177	B/W	Base 1F	1	50	4 in	–	PL. 52	Splayed, beveled foot. Closed form. Well turned, smoothed, out-burnished. Buff surfaces and pale orange fabric.
AM11	7118.14	Fabric 1	1	51	B	As Base 1G	1	22	11 out	–	PL.52	Shape as that of mid-third-century Forms 12–13. Perhaps intrusive.
AM12	7118.15	Fabric 1	1	35	B/Wfr	Base 1	1	12	12 out	–	–	–
AM13	7118.1	Rhodian?	1	147	Hfr	Unclassified	1	–	–	–	–	Hard fine pale red fabric with pale orange brown-salmon, smooth surfaces. Oval section, as that of "mushroom rim"/"Graeco-Italic" amphorae. Fabric as Cretan or Rhodian. Not a Koan fabric. Handle shape should be Hellenistic.

TRANSPORT AMPHORAE OF THE FIRST TO SEVENTH CENTURIES · 119

Cat	Dbase	Fabric	NS	Wt	S	Form	No	%	Dia	De	Ill	Comments
	*Context 15009 (with intrusive mid-third century) (Plate 52)*
AM14	15009.1	Fabric 1	1	54	R/N	Form 1B	1	25	10.5 top	–	PL. 52	Groove on rim face.
AM15	15009.2	Coarse Fabric 1	1	19	R/N fr	Form 3A or 3B	1	20	10 top	–	PL. 52	–
AM16	15009.3	Probably Fabric 1	1	24	R/N	Form 4	1	20	8 in	–	PL. 52	Form as 15095.6 (AM43). Fired green with abundant fine-.5 mm black inclusions and lime.
AM17	15009.7	Fabric 1	1	76	Ftfr/W	Base 1E	1	20	–	–	PL. 52	Turned outer wall. Beveled foot.
AM18	15009.4	Fabric 1?	1	25	B	Base 3	1	–	–	–	PL. 52	As 7006.14 (AM287) and 2300.1 (AM74). Hollow conical toe.
AM19	15009.12	Local	68	1,662	W	–	68	–	–	–	–	–
AM20	15009.5	Fabric 13B	1	59	R/N/Hfr	Form 14A?	1	–	–	–	PL. 52	Painted band on rim top. Should be an intrusive piece. Handle type and fabric are not typical for Form 11; cf. Form 14A (AM110), also painted.
AM21	15009.10	Rhodian	1	12	Rfr/Nfr	Rhodian	1	–	–	–	–	–
AM22	15009.11	Rhodian	2	40	Sh/W	–	2	–	–	–	–	–
AM23	15009.6	Dressel 6?	1	160	W	Dressel 6?	1	–	–	–	–	Dressel 6 (Dalmatian coast) wine amphora or a Cádiz fish sauce amphora. Moderate .5–1 mm red-brown inclusions (iron oxide).
AM24	15009.8	Import	1	23	Bfr	Base 6	1	50	4.5	–	PL. 52	Type piece. Unique. Cream out, with deep orange salmon fabric. Marine shell present. Compact fabric, with scattered fine rounded quartz. Hollow foot, but flaring immediately. Cretan?
	*Context 15095 (with some intrusive mid-third century) (Plates 52 and 53)*
AM25	15095.4	Fabric 1? ZG61 = Fabric 1	1	25	R/N	Form 1A	1	23	8 in	–	PL. 52	Type piece. Collared tall neck. Rim face folded into two convex sections. Neck is tronco-conical. Greenish buff surfaces. Yellow-pale orange fabric. Well fired. ZG60 = More chert than AM77 (7007.2), but is still Fabric 1.
AM26	15095.5	Coarse Fabric 1?	1	14	R/N	Form 1C	1	15	7.5 in	–	PL. 52	Type piece. Same rim type, but light groove only and shorter neck. Fabric more pimply, cf. 2039.16 (AM155). Orange-yellow buff surfaces.
AM27	15095.14	Fabric 1	1	16	R/N	Form 3A	1	18	9 in	–	PL. 52	Type piece. Thick. wide, rim band. Lime eruptions.
AM28	15095.42	–	1	45	R/H fr	Form 3A or B	1	–	–	–	–	Handle width 3 cm.
AM29	15095.9	Fabric 1 = ZG61	2	66	R/N/Shfr	Form 3B	1	23	9	–	PL. 52	Type piece. Collar neck, triangular rim band. Buff to pale orange brown mottled. Clay blob on inner neck. ZG61: Fine Fabric 1.
AM30	15095.10	Fabric 1	1	10	R/N	Form 3B	1	10	–	–	–	More pimply with common fine lime.
AM31	15095.12	Fabric 1	1	13	R/N fr	Form 3B	1	18	9	–	–	–

Cat	Dbase	Fabric	NS	Wt	S	Form	No	%	Dia	De	Ill	Comments
AM32	15095.13	Coarse Fabric 1	1	13	R/N	Form 3B	1	10	9 in	–	PL. 52	–
AM33	15095.16	Fabric 1	1	50	Hst/Sh/N	Form 3B	1	–	–	–	PL. 52	Should be this.
AM34	15095.41	–	4	144	Hfr	Form 3A or B	4	–	–	–	–	Strap-handles, cf. Form 3.
AM35	15095.28	Fabric 1	2	166	B/W	Base 1A	1	50	10	–	PL. 52	Type piece. Lower wall well preserved. Foot not beveled (as is that of 15095. 34 and 33: AM39 and AM40).
AM36	15095.29	Fabric 1	1	55	B/W	Base 1A	1	20	10	P	–	Similar, but with a white cream coat and trace of red paint outside near the foot and under part of the base.
AM37	15095.30	Fabric 1	1	20	Ft/W	Base 1	1	5	–	–	–	–
AM38	15095.31	Fabric 1	1	52	Ft/W	Base 1	1	5	–	–	–	–
AM39	15095.34	Fabric 1	1	98	B/W	Base 1B	1	35	11 out	–	PL. 52	Foot beveled outside. Scattered white material, with some black. Pale red fabric and buff surfaces. So probably Fabric 1. Floor is horizontal, not sagging.
AM40	15095.33	Coarse Fabric 1?	1	96	B/W	Base 1C	1	30	10 out	–	PL. 52	Volcanic fragments more visible on surface than in the fabric. Sagging base. Beveled foot, concave inner face.
AM41	15095.35	Coarse Fabric 1	1	46	B/W	Base 1D	1	15	12 out	–	PL. 52	Sloping floor, as 15095.33 (AM40). But foot not beveled.
AM42	15095.15	Fabric 1	1	16	R/N fr	Unclassified Related to Form 2?	1	18	11 in	–	PL. 52	Type piece. Unique. Thin, band rim, bell shaped. Not necessarily related to Form 2. Pimply coarse Fabric 1. Whitish buff.
AM43	15095.6	Coarse Fabric 1	1	22	R/N	Form 4	1	15	8.3 in	–	PL. 53	Type piece. Cylindrical neck and short flat projecting rim, like a flagon. Fired yellowish buff.
AM44	15095.7	Coarse Fabric 1	1	27	R/N	Form 5	1	20	8 in	–	PL. 53	Type piece. Similar simple rounded rim to third-century Form 13, but thinner and smaller rim. Buff.
AM45	15095.8	Fabric 1?	1	21	R/N	Form 6	1	17	8 in	G	PL. 53	Type piece. Groove marking off rounded rim. Pale orange clay and orange-brown surfaces. Not pimply. A little mica dust.
AM46	15095.11	Fabric 1? ZG62 = similar to Fabric 1	1	17	R/N	Form 7A	1	20	8 in	–	PL. 53	Type piece. Neck probably vertical, not collar type. Triangular rim band. Pale greenish yellow fabric, softer. ZG62: Similar to Fabric 1, finer sand.
AM47	15095.36	–	44	1,821	W	–	44	–	–	–	–	Local-regional plain ware, probably an amphora.
AM48	15095.37	–	60	1,809	W	–	60	–	–	–	–	–
AM49	15095.38	–	28	648	W	–	28	–	–	–	–	–
AM50	15095.24	Fabric 13B?	2	22	W	–	1	–	–	–	–	Near base. More uneven and finer matrix than Fabric 13B but similar elements. Well fired, pale green. Base area scraped smooth.
AM51	15095.27	–	1	46	Sh/W	–	1	–	–	P	–	Rounded shoulder, so probably a painted jug. Horizontal band with two filled circles below. Band on wall.

Cat	Dbase	Fabric	NS	Wt	S	Form	No	%	Dia	De	Ill	Comments
AM52	15095.19	Fabric 1	1	113	R/H/N/Sh	Form 3F rather than Form 3A?	1	–	–	–	PL.53	The large rim could indicate that it is the mid-third-century variant Form 3F. Handle with central flat rib. Stepped shoulder, with offset at base of neck.
AM53	15095.25	Fabric 2	1	16	R	Form 3F	1	10	10	–	–	Intrusive? Lime-rich fabric. Probably this third-century variant.
AM54	15095.18	Fabric 13B?	1	37	R/N	Form 13B?	1	10	–	P	PL. 53	An intrusive mid-third-century piece? But fabric seems to be closer to Fabric 13. Pale pink core, pale green surfaces. Usual black and hard semiclear material. Granular break. Horizontal stroke of paint across lower neck (not illustrated) is however not a feature of third-century pieces. Note presence of a likely third-century piece in this deposit (**AM53**, Form 3F).
AM55	15095.20	Coarse Fabric 1	1	47	Hfr/N	–	1	–	–	–	–	Could be mid Roman. Yellow ochre.
AM56	15095.26	Fabric 13B	1	92	W	Cf. Large Forms 15–17	1	–	–	P	–	Vertical wide bands. Thick-walled, wide shoulder as the sixth- to seventh-century form. Still, as this decoration is not encountered, could be early Roman?
AM57	15095.1	Rhodian	1	68	Hst/Sh	Rhodian	1	–	–	–	–	–
AM58	15095.39	Rhodian?	1	28	Sh/W		1	–	–	–	–	–
AM59	15095.21	Rhodian	1	83	Wfr	Rhodian	1	–	–	–	–	Possibly Rhodian, near base area. But has lime reactions. Abundant fine lime and dust in break. Some clay fragments? Well fired. Not Koan.
AM60	15095.3	Buff import	1	45	Hfr	Rhodian imitation	1	–	–	–	–	Round section. Rather powdery for Rhodian.
AM61	15095.2	Koan?	1	25	Hfr/Shfr	Dressel 2–4	1	–	–	–	PL. 53	Import. Fired yellowish buff. Half of double rod handle: narrow rod. Fabric has superficial similar appearance to Sinope with lime reactions but with no volcanics. Smooth, matt surfaces. Well fired. Moderate + .5–1 mm red-brown haematite. Several .5 mm gold flakes. Perhaps Koan. If not, east Cilician, related to LRA 1 fabrics.
AM62	15095.22	Import Cádiz?	1	179	W	–	1	–	–	–	–	Thick-walled amphora. Fine fabric. Perhaps not enough oxide for Cádiz. Not enough mica for Dressel 6?
AM63	15095.23	Tunisian?	1	248	W	–	1	–	–	–	–	Rounded quartz fabric. Buff outer surfaces. Pale salmon-orange fabric and inner surface. Granular. Pimply surface inside. Has some voids, cf. north Tunisian spatheia/Keay 26. Could well be Tunisian.
AM64	15095.40	Buff import	1	28	N	–	1	–	–	–	–	–

Flavian (Group C)

Context 2283 (Flavian with intrusive mid-third century) (Plate 53)

Cat	Dbase	Fabric	NS	Wt	S	Form	No	%	Dia	De	Ill	Comments
AM65	2283.2	Fabric 1	1	25	R/N fr	Form 2B	1	23	9 in	–	PL. 53	Type piece. Smooth surfaces. Should be Fabric 1. Pale orange-salmon fabric and buff surfaces. Well fired. Fine shell?
AM66	2283.3	–	1	29	Ft	Base 4A	1	100	–	–	PL. 53	Type piece. Unique. Quite micaceous, brown–dark buff fabric. Similar fabric to AM67 (2283.4). Should be base for Form 1 or Form 2.
AM67	2283.4	Fabric 1?	1	35	Ft	Base 4B	1	100	–	–	PL. 53	Type piece. Unique. Fine matrix. Base for Form 1 likely.
AM68	2283.5	Fabric 1?	1	25	Ft	Base 4C	1	100	–	–	PL. 53	Type piece. Unique. Similar base to 2283.4 (AM66). Base for Form 1 likely.
AM69	2283.7	Fabric 1?	1	62	N/Shfr	Unclassified	1	25	9 in	–	PL. 53	Fairly vertical neck, right angle at start of shoulder. Yellow buff outer surface, pale red-brown inside. Some gold mica flakes. Could be Fabric 1.
AM70	2283.8	Fabric 1	1	54	Sh	–	1	–	–	–	–	Thick-walled, rounded shoulder fragment.
AM71	2283.6	Fabric 1	1	33	R/N/Hst	Form 13D	1	17	9 in	CB	PL. 53	Should be an intrusive third-century piece? If not, earliest example of this shape. Grooving under rim. Similar rim to 2086.1 (AM202), similar rather wide diameter.
AM72	2283.1	Rhodian	1	98	Hfr	Rhodian	1	–	96	–	–	Handle width 3 cm.

Context 2300 (Plate 53)

Cat	Dbase	Fabric	NS	Wt	S	Form	No	%	Dia	De	Ill	Comments
AM73	2300.3	Fabric 1	1	90	Hst/Sh	–	1	–	–	–	–	Double grooved band on outer shoulder. Fired pale salmon orange, with a cream coat. Smoother inside.
AM74	2300.4	Local	1	25	Bfr	Base 3	1	100	–	–	PL. 53	Type piece. Like a Cretan amphora base. Same form and fabric is 7006.14 (AM287). Fabric has some gold mica and common fine-.5 mm lime. Fired dark brown-orange with brown-buff surface. Another base variant for Form 1 or Form 2A–B? Form 2C–D are too thick-walled?
AM75	2300.1	Rhodian	1	165	N	Rhodian	1	–	–	–	–	–
AM76	2300.2	Rhodian	1	73	Hfr	Rhodian	1	–	–	–	–	–

Context 7007 (Plate 53)

Cat	Dbase	Fabric	NS	Wt	S	Form	No	%	Dia	De	Ill	Comments
AM77	7007.2	Fabric 1 ZG59	1	38	R/N	Form 2A	1	25	11 in	–	PL. 53	Type piece. Collar neck, with band rim, pronounced concave face. Cf. Hellenistic/early Roman Palestinian amphorae. Fired yellowish buff. Common fine to .5 mm lime. Granular break. Well fired. Could be a coarse Fabric 1, with common fine gray inclusions and common lime. ZG59: classified as Fabric 1.
AM78	7007.3	Coarse Fabric 1?	1	10	R/N fr	Form 2A	1	16	9 in	–	–	Same fabric as AM77.

Cat	Dbase	Fabric	NS	Wt	S	Form	No	%	Dia	De	Ill	Comments
AM79	7007.10	Fabric 1?	1	35	Hfr/Sh	Ring handle	1	–	–	–	PL. 53	Ring handle attached to shoulder. Cream-white outer surface. Well fired. Orange brown fabric. It was classified as the same fabric as 2011.2 (AM115), which I thought to be related to Fabric 13. In the latter case (ZG34) the fabric analysis suggested it belonged to Fabric 1.
AM80	7007.5	Coarse Fabric 1?	1	16	R/N	Form 3A	1	12	10 out	–	PL. 53	Type piece. Rather coarse fabric with fine–.5 mm gray and lime.
AM81	7007.8	Coarse Fabric 1	1	36	R/N/Hfr	Form 3A	1	13	9 in	–	PL. 53	Collared rim type with handle from rim top. Rim obscured but has a hooked band.
AM82	7007.9	Coarse Fabric 1	1	26	R/N/Hfr	Form 3A or 3B	1	15	–	–	–	Similar to 7007.8 (AM81). Rim obscured. Greenish granular porous fabric. Handle width 3 cm.
AM83	7007.4	Fine Fabric 1?	1	29	R/N	Form 3C	1	28	11 out	–	PL. 53	Type piece. Smooth greenish buff surfaces and pale red core, with common fine silver mica. Like a Rhodian fabric. Folded band rim, short collar.
AM84	7007.6	Fabric 1	1	12	R/N/Hst	Form 7B	1	15	8 in	–	PL. 53	Type piece. Thin neck, thin band rim, thin neck, rim bent inward, as the third-century variant Form 3D. Buff.
AM85	7007.7	Fabric 1	1	14	R/N/Hsm	Form 8	1	15	8 in	–	PL. 53	Thin walled. Small rounded band rim, groove-lid seat on rim top. Thin neck. Buff.
AM86	7007.11	Fabric 1	1	32	Hfr	Jug or flagon	1	–	–	–	–	Smooth, buff surfaces. Quite micaceous. Handle width 4 cm.
AM87	7007.12	Fabric 1	1	98	Hst/Sh	–	1	–	–	G	–	Rather heavy-dense fabric. Fired brown with orange brown surfaces. Wide groove at lower edge of shoulder. Probably Fabric 1, not Fabric 13 group. Fine rounded quartz and dark gray inclusions present. Even break.
AM88	7007.1	Fabric 1 ZG66	1	78	Ftfr	Base 5/ (Form 2C–D?)	1	100	–	–	PL. 53	Type piece. Unique. Large hollow foot with molding at end. Close to Fabric 1 (confirmed by Chris Doherty: ZG66). Finely sandy texture. Pale orange brown fabric with a porous break. Buff-brownish surface. Could be a base for the thick-walled amphora Form 2C–D (see Plate 49c).

Context 7023 (Plate 53)

Cat	Dbase	Fabric	NS	Wt	S	Form	No	%	Dia	De	Ill	Comments
AM89	7023.1	–	1	30	B/Wfr	Base 2A	1	20	–	–	PL. 53	Small jug or amphora/flagon base, rounded, sagging base. Rather porous, almost white, greenish fabric. Has occasional+ white material that is in the Syrian fabric, but fabric is finely granular-even, not as Syrian painted amphorae. Not enough gray (lime or iron oxide) inclusions for coarse Fabric 1. No mica either. There is Hellenistic to Flavian material in this context.

A.D. 253 Assemblages (Group D)
Context 2010 (Plate 54)

Cat	Dbase	Fabric	NS	Wt	S	Form	No	%	Dia	De	Ill	Comments
AM90	2010.12	Fabric 8	1	67	Hfr/N	Form 10 (or Form 11)	1	20	8	–	–	Finger indent at top of handle near neck. Thin neck. Rather coarse with 1–2 mm black inclusions. Green tint. Narrow neck and coarse fabric, cf. 2039.22 (**AM160**).
AM91	2010.13	Fabric 8	1	50	Hfr/N	Form 10 (or Form 11)	1	–	–	–	–	Same handle form and fabric. Concave rim face, rather square profile.
AM92	2010.5	Fabric 1	1	64	R/N	Form 12C	1	22	9 in	CB	PL. 54	Type piece. Thick square rim. Lightly concave lid set. Combed band on neck.
AM93	2010.7	Fabric 1 ZG28	1	119	R/N/Hfr	Form 12E	1	10	10 in	CB	PL. 54	Type piece. Well convex inner neck and square rim. Band of horizontal grooves below rim. Form close to the Fabric 1 jar with wavy line decoration (**PT387**). Diameter too small for this. Gray brown surfaces and pale red core.
AM94	2010.9	Fabric 1	1	173	Sh/Nfr	Form 12	1	–	–	CB	–	–
AM95	2010.10	Fabric 1	4	572	Sh/W	Form 12	1	–	–	CB	–	Four fragments of the same or similar vessel. Broad curved shoulder with combed band at top and bottom. Fired yellow buff surfaces, pale orange brown fabric. Large jar or amphora.
AM96	2010.11	Fabric 1	1	50	Sh	Form 12	1	–	–	CB	–	Two narrow bands of combing on upper shoulder.
AM97	2010.14	Fabric 1	2	88	Sh	Forms 12–13	2	–	–	CB	–	–
AM98	2010.15	Fabric 1	1	79	Sh/Nfr	Forms 12–13	1	–	–	CB	–	Cream surface. Single band of combing upper shoulder.
AM99	2010.4	Fabric 1	1	131	R/N/Hfr	Form 13B	1	25	8 in	CB	PL. 54	Type piece. Fired buff. Probably normal Fabric 1. Same variant as 2012.4 (**AM129**).
AM100	2010.8	Coarse Fabric 1	2	166	R/N/Hfr/Sh/Hfr	Form 13B	1	10	9 in	CB	PL. 54	The tronco-conical, slanted neck is atypical. The neck/shoulder fragment may belong to this. Has a double set of combed bands on the upper shoulder. Fired yellow buff. Should be coarse Fabric 1, as quite granular. But no different to 2012.3 (**AM126**).
AM101	2010.18	Coarse Fabric 1	1	116	B/W	Base 1G/Forms 12–13	1	25	9	–	–	Ring-foot base for Forms 12–13. Gray brown.
AM102	2010.19	Coarse Fabric 1	1	70	B/W	Base 1G	1	45	9.5	–	–	Buff.
AM103	2010.20	Fabric 1	1	29	B/W	Base 1G	1	12	10	–	–	–
AM104	2010.21	Fabric 1	1	39	B/W	Base 1G	1	25	?	–	–	–
AM105	2010.22	Fabric 1	1	20	B/W	Base 1G	1	15	11	–	–	–
AM106	2010.23	Fabric 1	1	37	B/W	Base 1G	1	50	6	–	–	–
AM107	2010.24	Fabric 1	1	23	B/W	Base 1G	1	25	9	–	–	Too small for an amphora.
AM108	2010.25	Fabric 1	1	19	B/W	Base 1G	1	15	7	–	–	Too small for an amphora.

Cat	Dbase	Fabric	NS	Wt	S	Form	No	%	Dia	De	Ill	Comments
AM109	2010.27	Fabric 1	1	69	Hfr/N	–	1	–	–	–	–	Handle width 3 cm. Fired salmon-orange. Well fired. Small vertical amphora handle type. Occasional rounded red, occasional gray fossil shell? Rather fine matrix, probably Fabric 1, rather than Fabric 13B.
AM110	2010.6	Fabric 13A ZG51	1	108	R/N/Hfr	Form 14A	1	17	9 in	P	PL. 54	Could be contemporary and evidence for mid-Roman date of the "Syrian" series in Fabric 13A. Probably same form as **AM194** (2080.4), of same date. Fabric fired pale green-yellow, with yellow-buff surfaces.
AM111	2010.16	Fabric 13	1	39	Sh/Nfr	–	1	–	–	CB	–	Cream-yellow surface out. Double set of combed bands. This fabric? Not Fabric 1.
AM112	2010.1	Campania	16	3,611	B/W	Dressel 2–4	1	100	–	–	PL. 54	Large part of vessel. Compact fabric with abundant fine to .5 mm black sand. Given the base type, should be a Dressel 2–4.
AM113	2010.2	Kap 2	1	206	Hfr/N	Kapitän 2	1	–	–	–	PL. 54	For Kapitän 2 / Peacock and Williams 1986, Class 47, see text.
AM114	2010.3	Kap 2	1	57	Nfr	Kapitän 2	1	–	–	–	–	–

Context 2011 (not on PK list) (Plate 55)

Cat	Dbase	Fabric	NS	Wt	S	Form	No	%	Dia	De	Ill	Comments
AM115	2011.2	Fine Fabric 1 ZG34	1	250	Hfr/Sh/Nfr	Unclassified	1	–	–	CB	PL. 55	Two combed bands on upper shoulder. Cream-yellow outer surface coat and edge. Pale orange-brown fabric, with common fine to .5 mm lime visible on inner surface. Some .5 mm hard fine white material (limestone?); occasional white marine shell? Occasional red stone. The ring handle **AM79** (7007.10) was classified as the same fabric variant. The sample taken of **AM115**, ZG34, was nevertheless classified as a "Fine Fabric 1."
AM116	2011.1	Baetica-Guadal Quivir ZG65	3	1,487	R/N/Hfr/B	Dressel 2–4	1	20	11 top in	–	PL. 55	Type piece. Large bulbous rim. Double-barreled wide handle. A solid, thick base belongs to this vessel, as it has same fabric. No wall sherds were collected. Coarse laminar fabric, pale red to gray-brown. 1–1.5 mm angular moderate semiclear quartz, and rounded white-yellow soft lime lumps. Moderate rounded plates of mudstone, in a hackly break. One piece may be calcite. Baetican Guadalquivir Dressel 20 fabric likely. ZG65: south Spanish origin possible.
AM117	2011.3	LRA 3	1	18	W	Early "LRA 3"	1	–	–	–	–	I.e., as Agora P 65–66 (Robinson 1959). See text.

Context 2012 (joins 2080) "with later intrusions" (Plate 55)

Cat	Dbase	Fabric	NS	Wt	S	Form	No	%	Dia	De	Ill	Comments
AM118	2012.13	Coarse Fabric 1 ZG36	1	159	R/N/H/Sh	Form 3F	1	25	11 in	–	PL. 55	Type piece. Well fired.
AM119	2012.10	Fabric 1	1	88	R/N/Hfr/Shfr	Form 3F	1	23	11 in	–	PL. 55	Handle width 4 cm.

Cat	Dbase	Fabric	NS	Wt	S	Form	No	%	Dia	De	Ill	Comments
AM120	2012.14	Coarse Fabric 1 ZG37	1	229	R/W	Form 3G	1	12	8 in	–	PL. 55	Type piece. Short collar with band, plain wall. Smaller diameter than usual, cf. 2080.18 (**AM184**)? Close in rim type to Form 3F. The body shape is not that of Form 3D. Buff outside, pale red inside, with common fine gray/black inclusions. Common lime is dominant. Red stone present (cf. Cilician fabrics). Moderate gold mica flakes.
AM121	2012.16	Fabric 1	1	51	Hfr	Form 3	1	–	–	–	–	–
AM122	2012.12	Coarse Fabric 1	1	9	R	Form 2B?	1	8	9 in	–	PL. 55	Residual? As 2283.2 (**AM65**)? Band with concave face. Neck flaring as collar. Buff.
AM123	2012.11	ZG35: New fabric but related to Fabric 1	1	57	R/N	Form 9	1	50	8 in	–	PL. 55	Type piece. Pronounced rim band with concave lid seat on top. Buff fabric with hackly break. Has perhaps more dominant fine to .5 mm gray inclusions than usual for Fabric 1. ZG35: Not coarse Fabric 1, as I thought. A separate fabric. It is compared with 7003.4, a shoulder of a jug or flagon with combed wavy line and combed horizontal band decoration (a third-century intrusive piece in Context 7000).
AM124	2012.1	Fabric 1	1	52	R/N	Form 12A	1	35	10 in	CB	PL. 55	Joins R/N/Hfr **AM188** (2080.7). Combed band below rim. Greenish-buff surface with yellowish fabric.
AM125	2012.2	Fabric 1 ZG29 and ZG30	2	146	R/N/Hfr	Form 12B	1	60	9 in	CB	PL. 55	Type piece. Rim top flattened with a squarer profile. Combed band below rim. Buff surface with pale red fabric. Plain oval handle. ZG29 and ZG30: Fine Fabric 1.
AM126	2012.3	Fabric 1 ZG31	1	154	R/N/Hfr	Form 12B/ Handle 2	1	23	9 in	CB	–	As 2012.2. (**AM125**). Combed band below rim. Handle width 4 cm.
AM127	2012.7	Fabric 1	1	56	R/N/Hfr	Form 13A	1	12	8 in	P? CB	PL. 55	Small convex rim, hooked, as 2039.11 (**AM164**), but smaller. Plain oval handle. Combed band below rim. There may be paint on handle. Cream-buff. Very pale orange fabric.
AM128	2012.8	Fabric 1	1	22	R/N	Form 13A	1	17	9 in	CB	–	Cf. 2080.8 (**AM189**).
AM129	2012.4	Fabric 1	3	116	R/N/Hfr	Form 13B/ Handle 2	1	45	8 in	CB	PL. 55	Rounded rim top with sharp edge.
AM130	2012.5	Fabric 1	1	26	R/N	Form 13B	1	18	8 in	CB	–	Grooved band is low on neck.
AM131	2012.6	Fabric 1	1	24	R/N	Form 13D	1	22	9 in	CB	–	Thick convex rim. Groove 1 cm down on neck. Beveled under rim. Greenish tint
AM132	2012.9	Fabric 1	1	83	H/Nfr	Handle 2/ Form 13	1	–	–	–	–	Probably a handle for Form 13 (4 cm width). Buff.
AM133	2012.20	Fabric 1 ZG38	1	66	B/Wfr	Base 1G/ Forms 12–13	1	15	10	–	PL. 55	Base type for Forms 12–13. ZG38: Fabric 1. Finest of Fabric 1 samples.
AM134	2012.21	Fabric 1	1	30	B/Wfr	Base 1G	1	15	11	–	–	–
AM135	2012.22	Fabric 1	1	24	B/Wfr	Base 1G	1	12	12	–	–	–
AM136	2012.23	Fabric 1	1	48	B/Wfr	Base 1G	1	30	9	–	–	Here fired pale salmon-orange.

Cat	Dbase	Fabric	NS	Wt	S	Form	No	%	Dia	De	Ill	Comments
AM137	2012.24	Fabric 1?	1	47	Bfr	Base 2B	1	25	–	–	PL. 55	Type piece. Flat base section of sagging base type Form 3, cf. 2017.1 (**AM148**: Form 3D). Fabric described as "micaceous" (perhaps not a problem, as Fabric 1 does contain mica: e.g., **AM155**, also Form 3D).
AM138	2012.26	Fabric 1	1	72	Hfr / Nfr	Handle 2 / Forms 12–13	1	–	–	–	–	Small handle (3 cm).
AM139	2012.27	Fabric 1	2	165	Sh	Cf. Forms 12–13	1	–	–	CB	–	Fine gray inclusions common. Fired buff. Combed band at edge and start of shoulder.
AM140	2012.15	Fabric 1	1	58	Sh / Wfr	Painted amphora	1	15	–	P	PL. 55	Note that this painted vessel was classified by me as Fabric 1 and not in the "Syrian" Fabric 13 group. Narrow horizontal band of paint below shoulder and complex design on shoulder: large filled circle.
AM141	2012.28	Coarse Fabric 1?	1	85	W	Painted amphora	0	–	–	P	–	Probably Fabric 1. But could be a fine Fabric 13B or a coarse Fabric 1.
AM142	2012.18	Koan?	1	152	Hfr / Nfr	Koan?	1	–	–	–	PL. 55	Type piece. Wide double-barreled handle. Pale red core and buff surfaces. Could be Koan, but not as obvious as the rim 2039.1 (**AM174**).
AM143	2012.17	LRA 1D ZG70	1	49	Hfr / Nfr	LRA 1	1	–	–	–	PL. 55	Type piece. Narrow handle, as late fifth-century examples of LRA 1 in Butrint and Beirut. Fired yellow-buff, almost white. Burnt out lime pin holes. Some red stone. Gray. Intrusive.
AM144	2012.19	Gaza	1	54	Hfr	LRA 4	1	–	–	–	–	Concave central molding (4 cm wide). Not necessarily intrusive?

Context 2014 (not on PK list) (joins 2031) (Plate 56)

Cat	Dbase	Fabric	NS	Wt	S	Form	No	%	Dia	De	Ill	Comments
AM145	2014.3	Fabric 1	1	27	R / N	Form 12A	1	20	10 in	CB	PL. 56	Joins R / N / Hfr 2031.2 (**AM150**).
AM146	2014.1	Kap 2	1	128	Hfr / Sh	Kapitän 2	1	–	–	–	–	–
AM147	2014.2	Kap 2	1	191	Hfr / Sh	Kapitän 2	1	–	–	–	–	–

Context 2017 (not on PK list: single find) (Plate 56)

Cat	Dbase	Fabric	NS	Wt	S	Form	No	%	Dia	De	Ill	Comments
AM148	2017.1	Fabric 1	1	?	R / 2H / Sh / W / B	Form 3D / Base 2B	1	80	8.9 in	P?	PL. 56 FIG. 2	SF2068. Type piece. Complete but for a few sherds. Has broad painted band(?) on mid wall and probably on neck (not illustrated). Fired gray-brown dark buff out with pale red fabric. Thin strap-handles. Bag-shaped base. Same hard-fired compact ware as 18108.2 (**AM238**).

Cat	Dbase	Fabric	NS	Wt	S	Form	No	%	Dia	De	Ill	Comments
\multicolumn{13}{c}{*Context 2023*}
AM149	2023.1	Coarse Fabric 1 or Fabric 13A	2	362	Hst / Sh / W	Unclassified	1	–	–	CB Di	–	Two combed bands on upper and lower shoulder, wall carinated. Dipinto "C" on upper wall.
\multicolumn{13}{c}{*Context 2031 (not on PK list) (joins 2014) (Plate 56)*}
AM150	2031.2	Fabric 1	5	353	R / N / Hfr / Hfr / Sh / W	Form 12A	1	30	8 in	CB	PL 56	Form and Fabric Type Piece. Rim joins rim in 2014 (**AM145**). Combed horizontal grooved bands on neck and shoulder. Pimply surfaces greenish gray, with moderate .5 mm gold mica flakes. Coarse break, porous, with occasional rose quartz. Well fired.
AM151	2031.3	Fabric 1	2	296	Hst / Nfr / Sh	Form 12	1	–	–	CB	PL. 56	Same fabric as 2031.2 (**AM150**), but fired pale orange-red, so inclusions are easier to see. Grooved band at base of neck. Same rather narrow handle base. Not clear if there is mortar, rather than a clay spread, cf. Gazan amphorae, over shoulder of one fragment; latter would indicate clay support of vessel during manufacture). Granular fabric, well fired, with common rounded quartz and occasional red-brown, as some LRA 1 fabrics.
AM152	2031.1	Kap 2	1	502	R / N / Hfr	Kapitän 2	1	100	5.1	–	PL. 56	Narrow rim. Handle width 7 cm.
\multicolumn{13}{c}{*Context 2032 (not on PK list) (Plate 56)*}
AM153	2032.2	Fabric 1	2	223	R / N / H	Form 12F	1	40	9 in	CB	PL. 56	Type piece. Unique. One fragment is burnt the other not. Rim has a flat band. Combed horizontal band under rim. Plain oval handle, classic for Forms 12–13. Fired buff with yellowish fabric. Hard fired, rather compact with scatter of red and calcite? / white-semi-clear angular fragments.
AM154	2032.1	Fabric 1	1	421	R / N / H / Sh	Form 13D	1	32	10 in	CB	PL. 56	Type piece. Same rim as complete vessel 2086.1 (**AM202**). Rather thick rim, rounded top. Combed band under rim. Plain handle.
\multicolumn{13}{c}{*Context 2039 "with later intrusions" (Plate 57)*}
AM155	2039.16	Coarse Fabric 1 ZG33	1	24	R / N	Form 3D	1	20	9 in	–	PL. 57	Typical compact Fabric 1 pimply surface, gold mica. Pale red edges and dark buff-brown core and pale grayish brown surfaces.
AM156	2039.17	Fabric 1	1	15	R / N fr	Form 3D variant	1	18	8 in	G	PL. 57	Type piece. Double groove under a band rim. Should be a collared rim as Form 3.
AM157	2039.15	Fabric 1	1	31	R / N	Form 3F variant	1	18	9 in	–	PL. 57	Type piece. Wet clay runs on inside (made upside down: Philip Kenrick's observation). Classic Fabric 1, compact. Fired pale orangey and yellow buff.

Cat	Dbase	Fabric	NS	Wt	S	Form	No	%	Dia	De	Ill	Comments
AM158	2039.20	Fabric 8 ZG45	3	207	R/N/ 2Hfr	Form 10	1	55	8 in	–	PL. 57	Fabric and Form Type piece. With large 1–1.5 mm lumps of lime and rounded hard fine pale gray material, possibly also lime? Fabric 8. Pronounced convex rim and flaring handle with indent at top of handle, which is then spread across neck. Here with granular pale red core and pale gray surfaces. Burnt. ZG45: Probably Fabric 8.
AM159	2039.12	Fabric 8	2	248	Rfr/H/ N	Form 10?/ Handle 1	1	–	–	P	–	Too granular for Fabric 1. Trace of paint on handle and upper neck below rim. So likely to be connected with Form 11 (e.g., AM161). Fired buff throughout. Plain neck, rim missing. Thin oval plain handle, rather sloping shoulder.
AM160	2039.22	Fabric 8	3	163	2Hfr/N	Form 10?	1	–	–	–	PL. 57	Unusual, with a square handle section. Handle below rim, as Form 10 (AM158). Fabric as Form 11. Neck probably the same vessel. Fired greenish buff-cream. Granular, with moderate .5 mm and occasional 1 mm dark gray inclusions.
AM161	2039.21	Fabric 8 var = ZG46	1	68	R/N/ Hfr	Form 11A	1	25	7 in	P	PL. 57	Type piece. Dark brownish-red paint over rim top and down top left side of handle. Fired creamy orange-buff. Granular fabric with evident fine dark gray inclusions, usual red-brown angular red quartz of Fabric 1 and Fabric 8. Not the usual large lime of Fabric 8, but occasional 1 mm lime. Handle attached over rim top. ZG46: lateritic sub-fabric of Fabric 8.
AM162	2039.24	Fabric 8	1	29	R/N/ Hsm	Form 11B	1	17	9.5	P	PL. 57	Wider rim than 2039.21 (AM161). Handle not attached over rim top, so must be Form 11B. Painted band over top and outer face of rim band. Here is dark gray. The fabric is coarse with prominent lime. Coarser than AM161 with more lime.
AM163	2039.31	Fabric 8	1	73	Hfr/Sh	Form 11	1	–	–	P	–	Fabric type piece. Coarse with large lime and white quartz(?) and brown-black inclusions.
AM164	2039.11	Coarse Fabric 1 ZG39	1	28	R/N	Form 13A variant	1	21	9 in	CB	PL. 57	Fabric and form type piece. Small rounded-convex rim, here with ridge on top inner face (unique example with this feature). Fired buff throughout, distinct to the usual firing of Forms 12–13. Moderate gray inclusions, granular porous break. Has round marine shell likely. Occasional semitransparent material found in Syrian Euphrates Fabric 13. ZG39: Coarse Fabric 1, with garnet.
AM165	2039.29	Fabric 1	1	29	R/N	Form 13B?	1	23	9 in	–	PL. 57	Narrow grooved band below rim. Inner face rounded. Could also be a jug, given the angle of the neck.
AM166	2039.13	Fabric 1	2	207	H/ Nfr/ Sh	Handle 2/ Forms 12–13	1	15	9 in	CB	–	Handle width 4 cm. Cf. handle of form 13D 2086. 1 (AM202). Narrow combed band on upper shoulder near neck. Thin neck, relatively wide.

Cat	Dbase	Fabric	NS	Wt	S	Form	No	%	Dia	De	Ill	Comments
AM167	2039.14	Coarse Fabric 1	1	121	H/Nfr	Handle 2/ Forms 12–13	1	–	–	–	–	Handle narrows toward base (4 cm wide). Fired buff throughout. Has more fine gray than usual, but shows how this fabric (2039.11: **AM164**) is related to Fabric 1.
AM168	2039.18	Fabric 1	1	57	Hsm/N	Forms 12–13	1	20	11	–	PL. 57	Could be a new variant, as the neck/shoulder seems to be fairly right angled. String-cut join at base of neck. Grooved band at base of neck.
AM169	2039.23	Fabric 13A	1	45	Sh	Painted amphora	1	–	–	P	PL. 57	Linked "arches" painted in band around shoulder. Coarse fabric with the gray material dominant. Fired almost white. Not as hard-fired as Fabric 13B, so closer to 2080.4–5 (**AM194–195**). Unclear if intrusive.
AM170	2039.27	Fabric 1	1	90	B	Base 1G	1	50	10	–	PL. 57	–
AM171	2039.25	Fabric 2 ZG41	1	205	B/Wfr	Base 1G variant	1	100	9.2	–	PL. 57	Type piece. Rather large version. Here with common-abundant fine lime dots and moderate .5–1 mm dark gray material and occasional rounded dark brown pellet.
AM172	2039.26	Fabric 8	1	43	B	Base 1G	1	35	9	–	–	–
AM173	2039.28	Fabric 8 with organics	2	93	B/Wfr	Base 1H/ Form 11 base?	1	40	9	–	PL. 57	Form and Fabric Type piece. Fired very pale pinkish-salmon. Abundant .5–1 mm voids on inner surface due to lime and organics. 1.5 mm rounded gray lime lump. Perhaps the base for Form 11.
AM174	2039.1	Koan	2	147	R/N/ 2H sm	Koan Dressel 2–4	1	37	12 top in	–	PL. 57	As Koan amphorae in Beirut, a true Koan import. Well fired. White skin and fine to .5 mm lime and black inclusions. Convex band rim, convex top. Pale red core.
AM175	2039.2	Baetica/ Lusit?	1	104	R/N/ Hfr	Keay 23	1	50	10 out	–	PL. 57	Fine brown-orange fabric, with common air holes, smooth surfaces, inside of neck turned-scraped. Shape as the small fish sauce amphora Keay 23 (Keay 1984: 172–178). Fabric is micaceous, like a fine Egyptian Nile silt fabric. However, SW Baetican or S Lusitanian likely.
AM176	2039.5	Baetica/ Lusit?	1	36	Hfr/N	Unclassified	1	–	–	–	–	Narrow neck, oval handle likely. Smooth. Fabric may be the same as 2039.2 (**AM175**), but handle type not for Keay 23 (Keay 1984, 172–178). A few 1 mm organics. As **AM175**, it looks like a fine Egyptian Nile silt fabric. SW Baetican or S Lusitanian likely.
AM177	2039.3	Dressel 20	1	1012	Hfr/Sh	Dressel 20	1	20	–	–	–	Sawn off at the start of the neck. Baetican Guadalquivir fabric.
AM178	2039.4	Rhodian?	1	244	N/ Shfr	Late Rhodian?	1	40	–	G	PL. 57	Fine yellow-buff fabric, well fired. Turned smooth outside. Groove at base of neck. Late Rhodian amphora? Could be Cádiz, but not necessarily. Only inclusions comprise rare red-brown material that may be too hard for hematite.

Cat	Dbase	Fabric	NS	Wt	S	Form	No	%	Dia	De	Ill	Comments
AM179	2039.6	Ras al-Basit?	1	116	W	–	1	–	–	–	–	Imported, cf. fabric of imperial period Ras al-Basit amphorae (Reynolds 1999, Cat. 150–151). Dark brown fabric. Outside scraped-smoothed, inside pimply due to quartz. Gold mica flakes, with quartz.
AM180	2039.7	NW Syrian?	1	136	W	–	1	–	–	–	–	Either south Spanish Dressel 20 or a storage-jar import, coastal Syrian. Layered break. Smoothing inside at different angle to outside. Syrian more likely.

Context 2080 "with later intrusions" (joins 2012) (Plate 58)

Cat	Dbase	Fabric	NS	Wt	S	Form	No	%	Dia	De	Ill	Comments
AM181	2080.17	Fabric 1	1	44	R/N/Shfr	Form 3E	1	25	11 in	–	PL. 58	Type piece. As Form 3D, but inner rim plain. Unique. Thin walled. Compact Fabric 1, but does have common fine gray material.
AM182	2080.15	Fabric 2	1	38	R/N/Hfr	Form 3F	1	16	12 in	–	PL. 58	Pitted surfaces, with fine lime, more gold mica than usual? Ware as the base 2039.25 (AM171). Rim obscured but has a wide plain band.
AM183	2080.16	Not Fabric 2 ZG43	1	47	R/N	Form 3F	1	25	10 in	–	PL. 58	"Same fabric and form as 2080.15 (AM182)." Classified as Fabric 2, i.e., more lime rich, coarser version of Fabric 1, but not supported by the thin-section analysis. ZG43: Not Fabric 2. A separate fabric: dacite, schist, and abundant carbonate.
AM184	2080.18	Fabric 1	1	18	R/N fr	Form 3G	1	10	8 in	–	PL. 58	Type piece. Diameter smaller than usual and rim band pronounced. Clearly close to Form 3F. Have linked to 2012.14 (AM120). Compact with fine gray present. Still Fabric 1. Fired grayish buff.
AM185	2080.14	Fabric 8 ZG49	1	138	R/H	Form 11A	1	15	7 in	P	PL. 58	Type piece. Rim face obscured. Groove rim top. Handle springing from top of rim, as 2039.21 (AM161). Not as coarse as Fabric 8. Band of paint down center of handle face.
AM186	2080.12	Fabric 8 ZG47	1	112	R/N/Hfr	Form 11B	1	10	8 in	P	PL. 58	Band rim with concave top. Red-brown paint on rim and outer face. Coarse but not with the coarse lime of Fabric 8. Gray common. Gold mica flakes and occasional organic. Fired cream-yellow.
AM187	2080.13	Fabric 8 ZG48	2	79	W	Form 11	0	–	–	P	–	Band of paint with linked motif below. Same vessel as above likely. Same fabric.
AM188	2080.7	Fabric 1	1	146	R/N/Hfr	Form 13A	1	35	10 in	CB	PL. 55	Joins AM124 (2012.1). Same variant as 2014.3 / 2031.2 (AM145/150). Grooved band under rim. Pale orange-brown fabric and yellowish-buff surfaces. Common fine gray present. Handle has concave central molding as that of the Fabric 1 jar PT387.
AM189	2080.8	Fabric 1	1	130	R/N/Hfr	Form 13A	1	25	9 in	CB	PL. 58	Type piece. Form with small rounded rim. Wide oval handle is unusual.

Cat	Dbase	Fabric	NS	Wt	S	Form	No	%	Dia	De	Ill	Comments
AM190	2080.6	Fabric 1	1	317	R/N/H/Sh	Form 13C	1	38	8 in	CB	PL. 58	Type piece. Unique. Thin-walled neck. Folded rim with a light groove-molding on rim top. Rounded oval, plain handle. Fine gray inclusions present. Even surfaces.
AM191	2080.9	Fabric 1	1	20	R/N fr	Form 13E	1	14	10 in	CB	PL. 58	Type piece. Pronounced wide convex rim. Grooved band below rim. A large module of Form 13A (e.g., AM224)? Fired pale green. Fine fabric as Fabric 1, but has moderate fine gray inclusions.
AM192	2080.11	Fabric 1	1	127	H/Nfr	Handle 2	1	–	–	–	–	Handle width 4 cm.
AM193	2080.19	Fabric 2	1	42	Sh	–	1	–	–	P	–	Vertical, parallel lines on shoulder? Lime-rich fabric.
AM194	2080.4	Fabric 13A ZG52	1	102	R/N/Hfr	Form 14B	1	10	c.c.14 out	–	PL. 58	Pinched rim top. This variant occurs in seventh-century contexts. Unclear if similar shape could be contemporary (cf. 2010.6: AM110). Fired greenish white. Here again with dominant .5 mm black material, perhaps volcanic. ZG52 = "usual Fabric 13A," though more lateritic basalt weathering material.
AM195	2080.5	Fabric 13A	1	102	Hfr/N	Form 14(B)	1	–	–	–	PL. 58	Handle juts out as 2080.4 (AM194). This has 1–2mm rounded dark gray material.
AM196	2080.3	Fabric 13A	1	138	Hfr	Handle 4	1	–	–	–	PL. 58	Type piece. Wide handle with 3 concave ribs and beveled sides. Fired pale greenish white with common fine to .5 mm dark gray to black inclusions, some red stone, as usual. Coarse break.
AM197	2080.1	Dressel 20	1	387	H/Nfr	Dressel 20	1	–	–	–	PL. 58	Handle short and vertical.
AM198	2080.2	Sinope "argile claire"	1	103	Hfr/Sh	Sinope	1	–	–	–	PL. 58	Type piece. The fabric suggests fifth century or later. Abundant well-sorted angular black volcanics in a pale yellowish-buff fabric with cream-buff surfaces. Pimply surfaces except underside of shoulder that has additional lime-reaction rims. Intrusive.
AM199	2080.20	Pal	1	19	Sh	LRA 5	1	–	–	–	–	Well-cut deep ribs. Should be LRA 5, but not in a fabric I recognize. Cf. some of the Gazan amphorae in non-Gazan fabric with cream coat present in Beirut. Cream coat with pale pink-red streak out and matt pale red inside. Common lime and shell(?). Intrusive.
AM200	2080.21	Import	1	92	W	Unclassified	1	–	–	–	–	Fired gray-black surface with pale orange-brown inner surface. Abundant fine rounded quartz, but not Palestinian. Plain surface, not ribbed. Related to nonlocal brittle ware?
AM201	2080.22	LRA 1C	1	25	W	LRA 1	1	–	–	–	–	Could be LRA 1, but fabric is pretty close to Fabric 1. Fired yellow-buff out. Wide stepped clapper-board ribs. Presumably intrusive.

TRANSPORT AMPHORAE OF THE FIRST TO SEVENTH CENTURIES · 133

Cat	Dbase	Fabric	NS	Wt	S	Form	No	%	Dia	De	Ill	Comments
					Context 2086 (not on PK list = single find) (Plate 59; fig. 3)							
AM202	2086.1	Fabric 2 ZG44: same as Fabric 1	1	8000	R/H/ Hst/ Sh/W/B	Form 13D/H2/ Base 1G	1	80	9 in	CB	PL 59 FIG. 3	Type piece. Classified as Fabric 2, in fact the type piece for this fabric, because has common lime, with some eruptions. Could also call it "coarse Fabric 1." Thick rim. Grooved band under rim. Double combed band on upper shoulder, one on lower shoulder. Perhaps the type piece for the double grooved band body-shoulder fragments. However, a sample of this vessel, ZG44, demonstrates it to be the same as Fabric 1. Of the Fabric 2 vessels sampled only 2039.25 (AM171, ZG41) and 2080.16 (AM183, ZG43) had more lime inclusions than a normal Fabric 1.
					Context 2139 (Plate 59)							
AM203	2139.1	Fabric 1	1	119	R/H/N/ Sh	Form 3F	1	18	9 in	–	PL. 59	Wide band rim. Rather plain handle. Thick, collared band rim. Clay blobs inside shoulder.
AM204	2139.2	Fabric 1	5	227	W	–	3	–	–	–	–	–
					Context 2158 (Plate 59)							
AM205	2158.15	Fine Fabric 1	1	22	R/N fr	Form 3A	1	24	8 in	–	PL. 59	Early Roman, cf. 15095 examples.
AM206	2158.2	Fabric 1	1	110	R/Hfr/ N/Sh	Form 3D–E	1	23	11 in	–	–	–
AM207	2158.11	Fabric 1	1	62	Hfr/Sh	Form 3D–F	1	–	–	–	–	–
AM208	2158.4	Coarse Fabric 1	1	29	R/N	Form 13B	1	18	7 in	CB	PL. 59	Cf. 2010.4 (AM99), small rolled rim. Combed band below rim. Common fine gray inclusions visible. Pale brown.
AM209	2158.3	Fabric 1	1	98	R/N/Hfr	Form 13D	1	15	8 in		PL. 59	Handle width 4 cm.
AM210	2158.6	Fabric 1	1	89	Hst/Sh/ Nfr	Form 13	1	–	–	CB	–	Combed band on upper shoulder.
AM211	2158.8	Coarse Fabric 1	1	77	B	Base 1G	1	–	100	–	–	–
AM212	2158.9	Fabric 1	1	112	B/W	Ring-foot base	1	25	–	–	–	Pale orange-buff fabric and buff outer surface.
AM213	2158.10	Fabric 1	1	84	Hfr/Sh	Forms 12–13	1	–	–	CB	–	Fired red-brown. Wide handle base (4 cm) placed over combed horizontal band. Not a typical handle.
AM214	2158.5	Fabric 1	1	86	H/N	–	1	–	–	–	–	Could be a jug.
AM215	2158.13	Fabric 1	3	313	W	–	3	–	–	–	–	–
AM216	2158.12	Fabric 13B	1	138	Sh	Painted amphora	1	–	–	P	PL. 59	Broad curved stroke as "spiral." Seems to be curved wall-shoulder, not a carinated shape. Intrusive seventh century likely.

Cat	Dbase	Fabric	NS	Wt	S	Form	No	%	Dia	De	Ill	Comments
AM217	2158.1	Koan ZG64	1	358	Hfr/Sh	Koan Dressel 2–4	1	–	–	–	PL. 59	Thick double rod handle (6 cm) placed at edge of carinated shoulder. Finger indents at base of handle. Fine, hard, dark orange fabric, with greenish-cream wash. Should be Koan. Has common lime and occasional glassy irregular quartz(?). Some rounded black–dark brown material.

Context 2241 (not on PK list)

Cat	Dbase	Fabric	NS	Wt	S	Form	No	%	Dia	De	Ill	Comments
AM218	2241.1	Kap 2	1	95	W	Kapitän 2	1	–	–	–	–	–

Context 2260

Cat	Dbase	Fabric	NS	Wt	S	Form	No	%	Dia	De	Ill	Comments
AM219	2260.1	Fabric 2 ZG42: same as Fabric 1	1	63	R/N/ Hfr/ Shfr	Form 3F	1	25	10 in	P?	–	Form as 2080.15 (AM182). Handle width 3 cm. Fabric is quite coarse and granular. Hard. Pale brown wash paint all over? Fired pale brown-fawn. Surfaces smoothed over, but gray and volcanic(?) present with common fine lime (as AM182). "Perhaps a coarse version of Fabric 1." ZG42: same as Fabric 1 (no real difference in lime content).

Context 2269 (not on PK list)

Cat	Dbase	Fabric	NS	Wt	S	Form	No	%	Dia	De	Ill	Comments
AM220	2269.1	Kap 2	1	?	B	Kapitän 2	1	75	–	–	–	Other amphorae in the bag were not catalogued.

Context 2278 (Plate 60)

Cat	Dbase	Fabric	NS	Wt	S	Form	No	%	Dia	De	Ill	Comments
AM221	2278.3	Asia minor LRA 3 var	2	82	Ftfr/B/ W/Sh	Agora P 65–66	1	–	–	–	PL. 60	Small ring-foot. Variant product with a well-fired fabric, fired dark brown to gray surfaces. Very micaceous, but harder fired and not soapy as Ephesos LRA 3 products. For contemporary examples from southern France see Lemaître (1997).
AM222	2278.2	Import	1	239	W	–	1	–	–	–	–	Unique. Well-cut flat band ribbing is distinctive, as are mudstone plate inclusions. Moderate fine gold mica flakes. Well fired, with a rather hackly break. Scattered irregular white quartz. Pimply inside, with lime common; 1 mm reaction rims.
AM223	2278.1	Mauretanian? ZG63	3	592	R/N/H	Keay IA?	1	100	9.8 top in	–	PL. 60	Well-fired, fine pale red fabric with a buff surface, occasional lime burnt out, occasional hematite. Could be a south Gaulish import, but more likely a Mauretanian Keay 1A (Keay 1984, 95–99). See comments on ZG63, bearing in mind I thought the vessel to be Gallic. Some Algerian clays are also micaceous.

Cat	Dbase	Fabric	NS	Wt	S	Form	No	%	Dia	De	Ill	Comments
					Context 2295 (not on PK list) (Plate 60)							
AM224	2295.1	Fabric 1	1	650	R/N/ 2H/Sh	Form 13A	1	100	7.7 in	CB	PL. 60	Type piece. Large fragment of vessel, upper half. All burnt. Burning across break. Grooved band below rim, one on lower neck and one on the lower shoulder.
AM225	2295.3	Fabric 1	1	100	R/H fr	Form 13A	1	5	–	–	–	The handle has marked concave moldings (width 4 cm). Top of neck obscured.
AM226	2295.4	Fabric 1	1	19	R/N fr	Form 13E	1	25	8 in	CB	PL. 60	Band under pronounced, convex rim. Thin-walled neck.
AM227	2295.2	Fabric 1	1	285	H/Sh	Form 13	1	–	–	CB	PL. 60	All fresh breaks, except handle stump that has old break. Double horizontal bands on upper shoulder. Narrow handle.
AM228	2295.9	Fabric 1	1	74	B/Wfr	Base 1G	1	50	4.7		PL. 60	Note the central dip.
AM229	2295.5	Fabric 1	1	110	Hfr/Sh	Cf. Form 13	1	–	–	CB	–	Double band of grooves on upper shoulder.
AM230	2295.6	Fabric 1	1	68	Hst/Sh	Forms 12–13	1	–	–	CB	–	Double band of grooves on upper shoulder.
AM231	2295.7	Fabric 1	6	743	Sh/W	–	6	–	–	–	–	–
AM232	2295.8	Fabric 1	4	464	W	–	4	–	–	–	–	–
AM230	2295.6	Fabric 1	1	68	Hst/Sh	Forms 12–13	1	–	–	CB		Double band of grooves on upper shoulder.
AM231	2295.7	Fabric 1	6	743	Sh/W	–	6	–	–	–	–	–
AM232	2295.8	Fabric 1	4	464	W	–	4	–	–	–	–	–
					Context 2376							
AM233	2376.1	Fabric 1	2	439	Sh/W	–	1	–	–	–	–	Well-smoothed outer surface, with cream coat. Fine, pale orange fabric. Rounded shoulder.
AM234	2376.2	Fabric 1	1	42	B/W	Base 1G	1	30	9 out	–	–	–
AM235	2376.3	Fine Fabric 1	4	71	W	–	4	–	–	–	–	Combed horizontal band.
AM236	2376.4	Fabric 1	1	39	W	–	1	–	–	–	–	–
AM237	2376.5	Local-regional	1	87	Sh/W	–	1	–	–	–	–	Thick-walled shoulder. Fabric looks regional.
					Context 18108 (Plate 61)							
AM238	18108.2	Fabric 1	7	581	R/N/Sh/ H/2Hfr	Form 3D	1	10	10.5 in	–	PL. 61	Type piece. Collared rim. For complete example of form see 2017.1 (**AM148**). Narrow band. Rim bent inward. Step on shoulder/neck. Thin walled. Thin strap-handle, with concave central band. Typical Fabric 1. Good scatter of gold mica. Compact and pimply surfaces. Fired very pale brown–yellowish buff.

Cat	Dbase	Fabric	NS	Wt	S	Form	No	%	Dia	De	Ill	Comments
AM239	18108.8	Fabric 2	1	20	R/N	Form 3D	1	12	8 in	–	PL. 61	Coarse fabric with common .5 mm lime eruptions.
AM240	18108.9	Fabric 2	4	86	R/2H	Form 3F	1	15	–	CB	–	Common lime, surface pitted and erupting. Rim obscured, but a short handle. Combed band on upper shoulder. Rim type as 2080.15–16 (AM182–183). Handle width 3 cm.
AM241	18108.10	Fabric 2	1	25	Hfr	Form 3D	1	–	–	–	–	Handle of 18108.8 (AM239)? Handle width 3 cm.
AM242	18108.12	Fabric 1	1	44	Bfr	Base 2B	1	25	–	–	PL. 61	Rounded base, cf. Form 3D (2017.1, AM148).
AM243	18108.23	Fabric 1	1	66	Bfr/W	Base 2B	1	15	–	–	–	–
AM244	18108.4–5	Fabric 1	15	1912	R/N/H/Hfr/W	Form 12B	1	55	8 in	CB	PL. 61	Type piece. Rather flat rim top. Wide body, identical to size of 2086.1 (AM202). The latter, however, has a taller neck. Form 12B, rather than Form 13D. Rounded shoulder with combed horizontal band on the lower section and near neck.
AM245	18108.6	Fabric 1	4	349	R/N/Hfr/Hst	Form 12D	1	40	9 in	CB	PL. 61	Type piece. Double set of combed horizontal bands on upper shoulder, as 18108.3 (AM246). Rim here is present: flat top, rather thick, so another variation. Combed band under rim.
AM246	18108.3	Fabric 1	24	1,765	Hfr2/Nfr/Sh/W	Large module Form 12 or 13D–E	1	–	–	CB	PL. 61	SF3459. Largely complete but for base and R/N/2H. Buff outer surface. Very pale orange fabric. Pale red-maroon inner surface. Two narrow combed bands on the upper shoulder and one lower down. Narrow handle base, narrower than usual for amphorae. Coarse fabric 1? Or normal Fabric 1.
AM247	18108.11	Fabric 1	1	122	Hfr/N	Forms 12–13	1	–	–	–	–	Classic Fabric 1. Handle width 4 cm.
AM248	18108.7	Fabric 1	1	58	Hfr/N	–	1	–	–	–	–	Handle width 4 cm.
AM249	18108.13	Fabric 2	1	94	B/Wfr	Base 1G/Forms 12–13	1	100	7.5	–	–	Ring foot, cf. Forms 12–13.
AM250	18108.14	Coarse Fabric 1	1	40	B/Wfr	Base 1G	1	65	7.5	–	–	Fired buff throughout.
AM251	18108.15	Fabric 1	1	20	Bfr/Wfr	Base 1G	1	15	9 out	–	–	Buff.
AM252	18108.16	Fabric 2	2	54	B/Wfr	Base 1G	1	50	7.5 out	–	–	–
AM253	18108.17	Fabric 1	1	39	B/Wfr	Base 1G	1	75	7.3 out	–	–	–
AM254	18108.18	Fabric 1	1	37	B/Wfr	Base 1G	1	18	8 out	–	–	–
AM255	18108.20	Fabric 1	2	35	B/Wfr	–	1	–	8 out	–	–	–
AM256	18108.21	Fabric 1	18	785	W	–	18	–	–	–	–	–
AM257	18108.22	Local-regional	7	199	W	–	7	–	–	–	–	May include PL sherds.
AM258	18108.24	Fabric 2	3	137	W	–	2	–	–	–	–	–
AM259	18108.25	Coarse Fabric 1	2	100	W	–	1	–	–	–	–	–

Cat	Dbase	Fabric	NS	Wt	S	Form	No	%	Dia	De	Ill	Comments
AM260	18108.1	LRA 3	1	38	W	LRA 3 Ceramic disc	1	–	–	–	–	Trimmed to make a disc/lid?
AM261	vacant											

Mostly Late Sixth to Seventh Century (Group F)

Context 5001 (Plate 62; fig. 13)

Cat	Dbase	Fabric	NS	Wt	S	Form	No	%	Dia	De	Ill	Comments
AM262	5001.2	Fabric 13B	?	8,200	2Hst/Sh/W/B	Medium Form 17(A?) (or Forms 15–16)/Base 8A	1	–	–	P	–	SF67. × 134. Not assembled. Same decoration on shoulder as 5034.1 (AM264), i.e., looped arches. With roughly drawn spirals. One size smaller than AM264.
AM263	5001.1	Pal	74	7,300	R/2H/Sh/W/B	LRA 5 / Pieri 3	1	100	–	–	PL. 62 FIG. 13	SF68. Reconstructed. Almost complete. Fabric similar to that of Gazan amphorae.

Context 5034 (not on PK list) (Plate 63)

Cat	Dbase	Fabric	NS	Wt	S	Form	No	%	Dia	De	Ill	Comments
AM264	5034.1	Fabric 13B ZG54	1	?	N/H/Sh/W/B	Form 17A? (or Forms 15–16)/Base 8A	1	–	–	P	PL. 63	SF85. Not recovered complete? Thick-walled yellow-buff. Rim missing. Perhaps large module Form 17(A)? Round-based. Arches on shoulder and stylized "spirals," with the typical border motif.

Context 7003 (joins 7004; 7060?) (not on PK list) (Plate 64)

Cat	Dbase	Fabric	NS	Wt	S	Form	No	%	Dia	De	Ill	Comments
AM265	7003.6	Fabric 1	1	12	R/N/Shfr	Form 3A or B	1	7	9 in	–	PL. 64	Residual early Roman, fired brown, with common gold mica flakes. Small band rim, thin walled, short collar.
AM266	7003.2	Fabric 13A ZG Subfabric	1	153	R/N/Hfr	Form 14B	1	10	8 in	–	PL. 64	Pronounced beveled-pinched rim top. Large handle (5 cm). Here fired with yellow-cream-buff surface, with pale red core and yellow-ochre edges. Same fabric as 7004.1 (AM270). Well fired, compact, but more hackly than 7003.1 (AM268).
AM267	7003.3	Fabric 13A	1	87	Hfr	Cf. Large Forms 14–17	0	–	–	–	PL. 64	Could be same vessel as 7003.2 (AM266).
AM268	7003.1	Fabric 1 3B	2	138	R/N/Hfr	Small Form 17D	1	50	8 in	P	PL. 64	See joining sherds of 7004.2 (AM271).
AM269	7003.5	Fabric 13B Melted	1	155	W	Painted amphora	1	–	–	P	–	Splash of paint on wall. Well-smoothed cream surface. Same ware as 7060.4 (AM306): same vessel? Even, "melted" break.

Context 7004 (not on PK list) (joins 7003) (Plate 64; Fig. 4)

Cat	Dbase	Fabric	NS	Wt	S	Form	No	%	Dia	De	Ill	Comments
AM270	7004.1	Fabric 13A	1	686	R/N/2Hfr/Shfr	Form 16A	1	100	10.6 in	P	PL. 64 FIG. 4	Well-grooved rim top. Same source as 7061.1 (AM332). Fired greenish buff. Granular fabric with common fine to 5 mm gray material. Mortar coat over large area. Painted horizontal stroke on the neck, as indicated in the photograph (omitted from drawing).

Cat	Dbase	Fabric	NS	Wt	S	Form	No	%	Dia	De	Ill	Comments
AM271	7004.2	Fabric 13B Melted	3	375	R/Hst/ N/ Sh/W	Small Form 17D	1	25	8 in	P	PL. 64	Type piece. Joins of rim 7003.1 (**AM268**). Decorative scheme as on 7061.1 (**AM332**) and 7064.1 (**AM338**). Groove on lower neck. "Melted" fine version of fabric. Pale pink core and yellow-green edges and surface. Surface brushed cream. Painting: pale brown under painting and dark brown shading. Good evidence for care taken when painting some of these amphorae. Often only the lower coat survives. Part of "spiral" on shoulder, with border motif band below.
AM272	7004.9	Fabric 13B	1	175	B/W	Base 8B	1	25	c. 17	–	–	Same ware and treatment as 7036.1 (**AM296**). Brushed cream coat, but smaller size.
AM273	7004.4	Fabric 13B	1	84	Hfr	Small Form 17	1	–	–	–	PL. 64	Handle narrows toward base. Same sandwich fabric as type piece 7064.7 (**AM339**), same rather short profile. Compact but hackly break. Not the fine "melted" fabric.
AM274	7004.6	Fabric 13B	1	35	Sh	–	1	–	–	–	–	Pale yellow. Compact Fabric 13B. Brushed cream-yellow surface, even. Rough, finely pitted underside.
AM275	7004.5	Fabric 1	1	61	B/Wfr	Base 1G	1	22	11.8	–	–	Moderate mica. Ring-foot base more typical of third century. Residual.
AM276	7004.3	Sinope argile claire	1	103	Hfr/Sh	Sinope	1	–	–	–	–	Common fine to .5 mm lime reactions. Occasional black rounded volcanic (cf. ones typical at Seleucia-on-the-Orontes, with few volcanics).

Context 7005 (Plate 64)

Cat	Dbase	Fabric	NS	Wt	S	Form	No	%	Dia	De	Ill	Comments
AM277	7005.3	Fabric 13B	1	40	Sh/N	Small Form 17?	1	–	–	–	P	–	Cream orange slip with pale rusty orange paint. Arches. Neck is thin, so could be a jug or small amphora.
AM278	7005.1	Fabric 13B	1	104	R/N/ Hfr	Small Form 19 (or small Form 14A)	1	15	c. 8 in	–	PL. 64	Handle is narrow. Slightly pinched rim top. Rim obscured but probably plain. Fired pale yellow-buff.
AM279	7005.2	Fabric 1	1	49	B/Wfr	Base 1G	1	25	12	–	–	Fired dark brown. Residual mid-third-century piece likely.
AM280	7005.4	Coarse Fabric 1?	1	28	Sh	–	1	–	–	G	–	Three grooves, 1 cm band. Not combed. Pale green outer coat and gray-brown inside.

Context 7006 (joins 7065) (not on PK list) (some residual third century A.D.) (Plates 64 and 70)

Cat	Dbase	Fabric	NS	Wt	S	Form	No	%	Dia	De	Ill	Comments
AM281	7006.6	Fabric 13A?	1	91	Hfr	Form 14?	1	–	–	–	PL. 64	Pinkish surface. Coarser fabric but well fired. Does not have the usual fracture of Fabric 13B. Pink-orange. Rounded inclusions common.

Cat	Dbase	Fabric	NS	Wt	S	Form	No	%	Dia	De	Ill	Comments
AM282	7006.7	Fabric 13B ZG	1	78	R/N	Form 16A	1	28	14 out	P	PL. 64	Rim is more bell-shaped than type piece 7061.1 (**AM332**). Cf. smaller module examples **AM412** and 12012.27 (**AM522**: latter classified as a small 15C). End of narrow paintbrush stroke on lower neck (not illustrated), rest is unpainted. Well-fired yellow-buff with pale pink-salmon core.
AM283	7006.1	Fabric 13B	1	?	Hfr/Sh	Small Form 17A	0	–	–	–	PL. 70	Joins largely complete 7065.1 (**AM344**).
AM284	7006.4	Fabric 13B	1	?	R/N/Hfr	Small Form 17A	1	28	10 out	P	PL. 64	A little mortar. Convex ribs on inner neck. Pale red core and yellow-buff surfaces. Horizontal thin paint stroke on side of handle (not illustrated).
AM285	7006.2	–	1	?	R/2H/B	Small Form 17(A?)	1	–	–	P	–	SF494. Complete painted amphora. In Gaziantep Museum. Not seen.
AM286	7006.5	Fabric 13B	1	107	Hfr/N	Small Form 17	1	–	–	P	–	Five concave ribs on handle.
AM287	7006.14	ZG58	1	48	B	Base 3	0	–	–	–	–	Type piece. As 2300.1 (**AM74**). Early Roman residual piece likely. Fabric is orange-brown, quite micaceous and finely sandy. ZG58: Not Fabric 1.
AM288	7006.8	Fabric 1	1	35	B/W	Base 1G	1	10	9	–	–	Should be residual-disturbed, note burning.
AM289	7006.9	Coarse Fabric 1	1	32	R/N	Form 13A?	1	22	9 in	–	PL. 64	Should be residual third-century piece, given the fabric, but the rim looks more like Form 17. Cannot be latter if it is in coarse Fabric 1.
AM290	7006.10	Coarse Fabric 1	1	54	R/N/Hfr	Form 3	1	25	10 in	–	–	Again a residual piece.
AM291	7006.11	Fabric 1?	1	40	Sh/N	Forms 12–13 likely	1	–	–	CB	–	Cream-buff out with a pale orange (brown) fabric. Probably the same ware as amphora rim 2012.3 (**AM126**: ZG31). Double set of combed grooves on shoulder. Could be as shoulder fragment **AM115** (2011.2) that also has two sets of grooves. So probably residual.
AM292	7006.13	LRA 1A ZG71	1	188	W	LRA 1 Ceramic disc	1	–	15	–	–	Large piece of wall cut down to make a large circular lid. Well-fired, rather dense-heavy dark orange-brown fabric. Hard, fine, even, very compact break with scattered inclusions, some gray fossil shell? Narrow stepped band ribs. Near base.
AM293	7006.12	Fine Gazan	2	339	R/H/W	LRA 4	1	23	10 top in	–	PL. 64	Small ring-handle, lightly ribbed. Steep short late rim. Type fabric seems to be fine variety and walls are quite thin in places.

Context 7026 (Plate 65)

Cat	Dbase	Fabric	NS	Wt	S	Form	No	%	Dia	De	Ill	Comments
AM294	7026.2	Fabric 13B ZG	1	110	R/N/Hfr	Small Form 15A	1	18	9 in	–	PL. 65	Type piece. Small version of form as 7064.1 (**AM338**). Narrow handle. Small squared rim band.

Cat	Dbase	Fabric	NS	Wt	S	Form	No	%	Dia	De	Ill	Comments
AM295	7026.1	Fabric 13B (variant) ZG55	1	1,018	R/N/ 2H/ Sh/Wfr	Small Form 17A variant	1	100	9 in	P	PL. 65	Originally in one piece. 75% of rim, but presumably 100%. Fired cream almost throughout. Note the step at the base of the neck. It is the only variant with this feature. Spiral on upper shoulder, with arches below. Band on upper body as usual. Thin mortar present inside neck? ZG55: Very high carbonate context (matrix) and a low siliclastic content. The latter includes schistose/tectonized material.

Context 7036 (joins 7060) (Plate 66; Fig. 6)

Cat	Dbase	Fabric	NS	Wt	S	Form	No	%	Dia	De	Ill	Comments
AM296	7036.1	Fabric 13B ZG56	19	5,601	H/ Sh/W/ Bfr	Form 17 (A)? (or Forms 15–16)/ Base 8A	1	–	–	P	PL. 66 FIG. 6	Joins fragments 7060.15 (AM303). Almost complete profile of large painted amphora, but missing essential R/N and center of base. Presumably rounded based. Seven sherds of this vessel are in 7060 (AM303). Outer surfaces brushed with cream slip, then painted. Inside is rough and pitted. Dark orange-brown-fawn painted decoration, spirals and border band motif. Three "spirals," with looped band below. Handle narrows toward base. Wide handle section. ZG56: Distinct to granular Fabric 13A. Abundant granodiorite and a very high concentration of carbonates.
AM297	7036.7	Fabric 13B	1	159	Bfr/W	Base 8A	1	15	–	–	–	–
AM298	7036.2	Fabric 13B	1	241	B	Base 8A	1	45	–	G	–	Type piece but was not drawn. Rounded-sagging base. Base set off from lower wall by double groove. Fired green, with inner surface flaking off inside. Fabric 13B.
AM299	7036.6	Fabric 13 variant?	2	2,038	Bfr/W	Base 8A?	1	75	–	–	–	Large part of wall. Large amphora. Rather smooth matt surfaces. Surfaces fired greenish buff with a yellowish dark buff. Even break, granular, but apparently not Fabric 13A. Has scatter of fine rounded red inclusions (as Cilician fabrics).

Context 7060 (not on PK list) (joins 7036) (Plates 65–68; Figs. 6–7, 10–11)

Cat	Dbase	Fabric	NS	Wt	S	Form	No	%	Dia	De	Ill	Comments
AM300	7060.2	Fabric 13A ZG	1	197	R/N/ Hfr	Form 14A	1	15	8 in	–	PL. 67	Handle is large, so probably large module. Fired greenish white. Granular break with common but fine to .5 mm gray inclusions.
AM301	7060.24	Fabric 13B	1	65	R/N	Form 15B	1	30	11 in	–	PL. 67	For very similar profile see 7306.1 (AM354).
AM302	7060.23	Fabric 13B	1	35	R/N	Form 17C	1	13	12 in	–	PL. 67	Type piece. Unique. Base of rim projecting. Unusually thick rim. Wide diameter.
AM303	7060.15	Fabric 13B	7	1,166	Shfr/ W/Bfr	Form 17(A)? (or Forms 15–16)/ Base 8A	1	–	–	P	PL. 66 FIG. 6	Joins larger part of vessel 7036.1 (AM296).

Cat	Dbase	Fabric	NS	Wt	S	Form	No	%	Dia	De	Ill	Comments
AM304	7060.3	Fabric 13A? ZG sub fabric	2	1,252	Sh/W	Forms 15–17	1	40	–	P	PL. 65	Large module. Compact, but hackly break. Gray inclusions (of Fabric 13A) not dominant. Common fine lime. Pimply surface with lime visible. Outer surfaces have been turned smooth prior to painting. Painted spiral and looped border motif below. Would link with the mortar fabric, i.e., Fabric 13A. Some red stone as usual and there are .5 mm gray inclusions. ZG: Fired redder, less carbonate; volcanic ash and silt. More northern source. Same variant fabric as 7003.2 (**AM266**; Form 14B).
AM305	7060.30	Fabric 13B	1	193	Sh/Nfr	Forms 15–17	1	20	–	P	–	Surface unusually smooth. Double groove at base of neck also odd. Festoon strip runs across the shoulder, rather than lower down. Fabric looks like normal Fabric 13B, but for firing to a pale salmony orange.
AM306	7060.4	Fabric 13B	4	325	Hst/Sh/W	Forms 15–17	1	20	–	P	–	Thinner walled, with smaller band of painted festoon on outer edge of shoulder.
AM307	7060.5	Fabric 13B	1	67	Sh/W	Forms 15–17	1	10	–	P	–	Painted horizontal bands 1 cm below carination and on outer shoulder. Fired green-white. Fine gray inclusions common.
AM308	7060.34	Fabric 13B	1	148	Bfr/W	Base 8A	1	15	–	–	–	Large module. Same ware as 7036.1 (**AM296**).
AM309	7060.26	Fabric 13B	1	125	H	Forms 15–17	1	–	–	–	–	Large module.
AM310	7060.19–20	Fabric 13B	7	2,145	R/N/H/Sh/W/Bfr	Small Form 17A/Base 8B	1	15	8 in	P	PL. 67 FIG. 7	Type piece. Almost complete profile with base missing. Cream-yellow surface brushed, with dark red-brown paint. Border motif and rather stylized "spirals." Pale red core. Walls weighed 521g; diagnostics, 1624g.
AM311	7060.18	Fabric 13B	2	617	R/N/H/Sh	Small Form 17A	1	55	8 in	–	PL. 67	Typical example of a Small Form 17A rim type, with concave rim top. Usual horizontal painted band on neck and lower frieze above shoulder line. But central shoulder decoration too worn to make out. Fired pale cream. Well-fired, rather sandy, but compact texture.
AM312	7060.22	Fabric 13	1	28	R/N	Small Form 17E	1	25	8	–	PL. 67	Distinctive variant related to Small 17A and 17D. With well-hooked underside and rim bent back.
AM313	7060.21	Fabric 13B	1	236	Sh/W	Small Form 17	1	30	–	P	–	Large front section of "spiral." Identical to 7062.3 (**AM335**). Located directly on the shoulder band: no border band motif below.
AM314	7060.25	Fabric 13B	1	229	H/N/Sh	Small Form 17	1	–	–	–	–	–
AM315	7060.27	Fabric 13B	1	57	Hfr	Small Form 17	1	–	–	–	–	–
AM316	7060.28	Fabric 13B	1	58	Hfr/N	Small Form 17	1	–	–	–	–	–
AM317	7060.32	Fabric 13B	2	72	Shfr/W	Small Form 17	2	–	–	P	–	Two other vessels.

Cat	Dbase	Fabric	NS	Wt	S	Form	No	%	Dia	De	Ill	Comments
AM318	7060.36	Fabric 13B	3	42	Sh/W	Small Form 17	3	–	–	P	–	–
AM319	7060.35	Fabric 13B	1	107	Bfr/W	Base 8B	1	25	–	–	–	Rounded base, almost white.
AM320	7060.31	Fabric 13B	14	858	W	–	14	–	–	–	–	–
AM321	7060.6	Fabric 1	1	188	Sh	–	1	–	–	–	–	No paint or grooving. Buff.
AM322	7060.7	Fabric 1	1	15	Sh	–	1	–	–	CB	–	Surface smoothed, not turned. Combed horizontal band.
AM323	7060.13	Sinope argile claire	1	54	W	Sinope	1	–	–	–	–	Fabric has scatter of .5–1 mm volcanic glass. Lime reactions. Cf. examples typical at Seleucia-on-the-Orontes (see text, though here not buff but fired pale salmon-orange-fawn.
AM324	7060.14	Sinope argile claire	1	3,000	R/2H/Sh/Bfr	Sinope	1	–	–	Di	PL. 68 FIGS. 10–11	SF662. Complete. Dipinto on neck and shoulder. Fired pale green. Only a rough weight was possible due to limitations of scales. End of base is missing. Part of handle missing is fresh break. Not clear if base originally there. Ribbing is spiral.
AM325	7060.16	Sinope argile claire	1	57	W	Sinope	1	–	–	–	–	–
AM326	7060.17	Sinope argile claire	1	76	Sh/W	Sinope	1	–	–	–	–	–
AM327	7060.8	LRA 1A ZG72 and ZG73	2	381	Sh/W	LRA 1	1	–	20	–	PL. 67	Same fabric as 7006.13 disc (AM292), also thin sectioned (ZG71). Sample of each 7060.8 fragment taken (ZG72 and ZG73). Fired salmon-orange. Red stone only moderate. Gray material common. Inclusions a little multicolored.
AM328	7060.9	LRA 1B ZG74	1	68	W	LRA 1	1	–	–	–	–	Not in Beirut? Surfaces fired almost cream but fabric is pale yellow-orange. Red stone common. Sharp concave bands.
AM329	7060.10	Fine Gazan	3	145	W	LRA 4	1	–	–	CB	–	Very thin walled with a 3 cm combed band. Could be same vessel as 7006.12 (AM293).
AM330	7060.11	N Pal	4	164	W	LRA 5	1	–	–	P	–	Trace of circular motif painted on wall. Fired pale orange. Akko or fine Caesarea. Size suggests a large variant, as Pieri Type 3 (cf. 5001.1: AM263)
AM331	7060.12	N Pal	1	18	Shfr	LRA 5/Pieri 3	1	–	–	–	–	Not a normal fabric for LRA 5. Common .5 mm lime, occasional 1–2 mm. Even, matt surfaces. Sharp fine-cut combed ribs. Could be a Caesarea product, but not the coarsest. Quartz range is uneven, not even as AM330.

TRANSPORT AMPHORAE OF THE FIRST TO SEVENTH CENTURIES · 143

Cat	Dbase	Fabric	NS	Wt	S	Form	No	%	Dia	De	Ill	Comments
Context 7061 (not on PK list) (Plate 69; fig. 5)											
AM332	7061.1	Fabric 13A	9	?	R/N/ H/ Sh/Bfr	Form 16A/ Base 8A	1	60	10 in	P	PL. 69, FIG. 5	Rim to lower wall and start of base area. Gives size of amphora. Groove on rim top. Painted parallel curved lined border on outer edge of shoulder. Narrow horizontal band of paint on upper wall below carination. Fired pale green-white. Fine to .5 mm gray inclusions. So as examples in 7060 and in 2060. Unfortunately there was no fabric taken of this important piece. It was classified as a fine version of Fabric 13A: i.e., that of 2080.4 (**AM194**: Form 14B) and 7060.2 (**AM300**: Form 14A).
AM333	7061.2	Fabric 1	1	?	R/N	Form 3C	1	17	11 out	–	–	Pronounced band rim. Flaring neck. Amphora, rather than pot-stand. Same form as 7007.4 (**AM83**). Should be residual early Roman.
Context 7062 (Plate 68; figs. 8–9 and 12)											
AM334	7062.1	Fabric 13B Melted	1	26	R/N	Small Form 17A	1	20	7	P	PL. 68	Pronounced band rim, here bent inward. Fabric is compact, fine matrix scattered inclusions. Cream surface, pale orange edges and pale grayish core. "Melted" break with white, red, and volcanic black inclusions.
AM335	7062.3	Fabric 13B	1	?	R/2H/ N/ Sh/W	Small Form 17A variant	1	100	8 in	P	PL. 68 FIGS. 8–9	Type piece. All fresh breaks. Almost complete profile, large percentage of vessel present, but missing base. Rim type close to 7062.1 (**AM334**), but more bulbous, with a beveled face. Pale pink to buff surfaces. Abundant lime.
AM336	7062.2	Fabric 13B	1	24	Sh	–	1	–	–	–	–	–

Cat	Dbase	Fabric	NS	Wt	S	Form	No	%	Dia	De	Ill	Comments
AM336 bis	7062.5	–	–	870	R/2H/W/B	Narrow-bodied LRA 1	1	100	5.3	–	PL. 68 FIG. 12	SF643. Philip Kenrick catalogue **PT508**. Body width 10.8 cm, height 31.3 cm. It was described as Fabric 13 (North Syrian). "Hard yellowish-cream clay with the usual inclusions. The potting is extremely rough and messy. There is also a small hole near the base which appears to be the result of organic material (a large seed?) in the clay at the time of manufacture." Clearly a narrow-bodied LRA 1, typical of seventh-century contexts (e.g., Salamis: Diederichs 1980, 55, pl. 19.211–2, with reference to John Hayes's comments on similar finds at Kourion in the seventh century; Benghazi: Riley 1979, 216, fig. 91.346–7, LRA 1a, Deposit 153; Peacock and Williams 1986, fig. 104B, Class 44B, notably the photograph on the right, an example from the Dardanelles on display in the British Museum, originally noted by Riley). Our example, with its very narrow cylindrical body, is very close in shape to the Dardanelles piece. Though an eastern Syrian version of the variant would be novel, it is perhaps more likely to be a normal buff ware LRA 1 product, of either Cilician or Cypriot manufacture.

Context 7064 (Plate 69)

Cat	Dbase	Fabric	NS	Wt	S	Form	No	%	Dia	De	Ill	Comments
AM337	7064.2	Fabric 13A	1	37	R/N fr/H fr	Form 14B	1	–	7	–	PL. 69	Thick rim, but here the handle is quite narrow. Some mortar present? Buff.

TRANSPORT AMPHORAE OF THE FIRST TO SEVENTH CENTURIES · 145

Cat	Dbase	Fabric	NS	Wt	S	Form	No	%	Dia	De	Ill	Comments
AM338	7064.1	Fabric 13A? (or 13B) Melted ZG	8	?	R/2H N/Sh	Form 15A	1	75	10 in	P	PL. 69	Type piece. So far unique, but a smaller version would seem to be 7026.2 (AM294). Thick square rim, wide handles, with five concave ribs. Painted decoration: inside is dark red-brown to dark yellow-ochre with edging and shading in dark brown paint. Just remnants of color in some areas, especially on right side. Hole pierced through the shoulder. This was originally described as a "coarse pale green fabric, like a coarse version of 2080.14 (AM185) (i.e., fabric 8). Cf. mortars in Philip Kenrick Fabric 6 and that of Form 14A. Granular surfaces." When fabric sample taken the break was hackly, but very hard, with a fine matrix with inclusions melted into it. Red stone, hard white limestone(?). Conclusion was that it was probably a harder fired version of Fabric 13A, that of 2080.4–5 (AM194–195) (both Form 14) than a Fabric 13B, despite the melted appearance. The rough surfaces did differ from those of the "classic" Small Form 17 amphorae. The rather simple decoration is also distinct to that found on large modules of Form 17. However the small module of this variant was classified as Fabric 13B (AM294).
AM339	7064.7	Fabric 13?	1	85	Hfr	Handle 5	1	–	–	–	PL. 69	Type piece. Well-fired, buff-cream surface with yellow-ochre edges and pale red fabric and ochre core. Sandwich. Not clear if fine Fabric 13 or a coarse Fabric 1. Does have some rectangular, white inclusions and same material in the impressed jug likely (so closer to Fabric 13).
AM340	7064.5	(Fabric 13B)	1	20	Sh/Wfr	Painted amphora	1	–	–	P	–	Brown paint, ware as 7036.1 (AM296).
AM341	7064.6	–	4	99	Shfr	Painted amphora	4	–	–	P	–	–
AM342	7064.8	Mica Asia Minor	1	11	Bfr	Ung	1	–	–	–	PL. 69	Narrow hollow base, as unguentaria. Rather wet clay, uneven end, but not the Ephesos fabric. Very pale orange-yellow-ochre surfaces with fine gold mica glitter. Fine pale orange fabric.

Context 7065 (joins 7006) (Plates 62 and 70)

| AM343 | 7065.3 | Fabric 13B | 1 | ? | R/N | Form 17A | 1 | 25 | 9 in | P | PL. 70 | A larger amphora rim than 7065.1 (AM344). Square band rim. Painted inside and outside, with another band of paint across the neck. Greenish buff-cream. |

Cat	Dbase	Fabric	NS	Wt	S	Form	No	%	Dia	De	Ill	Comments
AM344	7065.1	Fabric 13B	?	2800	R/N/ 2H/Sh/ W/B	Small Form 17A/Base 8B	1	100	9.5 out	P	PL. 70	Type piece. Complete profile. From 7065 and 7006 = Hfr/Sh/W (**AM283**). Would have been complete, but partially recovered. Old breaks present. Pronounced band rim. Plain inner rim face. Similar size and shape to 7062.3 (**AM335**). Overlapping rather than looped border band motif, with dots in spaces between. Double band of paint across the neck. Carefully painted.
AM345	7065.2	Fabric 13B	1	40	R/N	Small Form 17A	1	28	8 in	P	PL. 70	Buff with dark red-brown paint below rim. Pronounced concave rim top.
AM346	7065.4	Fabric 13B	1	32	R/N	Small Form 17F	1	25	9 top	P	PL. 70	Type piece. Unique. Fine groove-convex moldings on neck. Rounded rim is atypical and the surfaces are smoother. Fabric is pale yellow-buff throughout, without the pale red core of the others.
AM347	7065.10	Fabric 13B	1	78	Sh/W	Small Form 17	1	–	–	P	–	Band of paint.
AM348	7065.9	LRA 1	?	?	W	LRA 1	1	–	–	–	–	SF649. Walls of LRA 1. Part of a single vessel?
AM349	7065.11	Gaza?	1	1,319	R/N 2H/Sh/ W/B	LRA 5/ Pieri 3	1	80	9 in	–	PL. 62	SF4249. Deep-cut grooves. Clay spread on rim and part of shoulder, as Gazan. Vessel has a very laminar break. No time to reassemble and would be difficult due to fragmentary condition. Fabric again reminiscent of Gazan: scattered quartz, a little micaceous, pale orange-salmon, with pale orange-salmon surface. Fine fabric.
AM350	7065.8	Pal	?	?	R/2H/ W/B	LRA 5/ Pieri 3	1	–	–	–	–	SF4249. Complete LRA 5. Not drawn unfortunately. Same variant as **AM349**.

Context 7214

Cat	Dbase	Fabric	NS	Wt	S	Form	No	%	Dia	De	Ill	Comments
AM351	7214.3	Fabric 13B	1	40	Shfr/ Wfr	Cf. Forms 15–17	1	–	–	P	–	Painted border band motif on the shoulder/wall as on 7036.1 (**AM296**).
AM352	7214.1	Fabric 13B	1	33	Hfr	Cf. Small Form 17	1	–	–	–	–	–
AM353	7214.2	Fabric 13B	1	20	Sh	Cf. Small Form 17	1	–	–	P	–	Thick curved band of paint, cf. "spiral."

Context 7306 (above 7064) (Plate 70)

Cat	Dbase	Fabric	NS	Wt	S	Form	No	%	Dia	De	Ill	Comments
AM354	7306.1	Fabric 13B ZG	1	375	R/N/ H/Sh	Form 15B	1	25	9.5 in	P	PL. 70	Type piece. Fired yellow-buff out with a pale red core. A bit of paint on shoulder by the handle. A relatively wide shoulder.
AM355	7306.2	Fabric 13B	1	168	H/Nfr/ Shfr	Small Forms 15–17	1	–	–	–	–	Narrow handle. Handle arched.

Cat	Dbase	Fabric	NS	Wt	S	Form	No	%	Dia	De	Ill	Comments
		Context 12002 (Plate 71) (mid-sixth to early seventh century FW: one join with 12011?)											
AM356	12002.1	Fabric 13B	1	75	R/N	Form 16B	1	22	14 out	P	PL. 71	Large rim, similar to 12011.55 (AM390). Horizontal band of paint on neck.
AM357	12002.4	Fabric 13B	1	135	Hfr/N	Forms 15–17	1	–	–	–	–	–
AM358	12002.7	Fabric 13B	4	295	Sh/W	Forms 15–17	4	–	–	P	–	–
AM359	12002.8	Fabric 13B	1	154	Sh/W	Forms 15–17	1	–	–	P	–	–
AM360	12002.3	Fabric 13B	1	21	R/N fr	Small Form 17A	1	22	7 in	–	PL. 71	–
AM361	12002.2	Fabric 13B	1	75	R/N/ Hfr	Small Form 16A or C	1	20	8 in	–	PL. 71	Grooved rim variant, as 12011.90 (AM413).
AM362	12002.5	Fabric 13B	7	429	Hfr	Small Form 17	7	–	–	P	–	–
AM363	12002.6	Fabric 13B	42	1,914	W	Small Form 17	42	–	–	–	–	Shoulder/wall fragments, some with neck fragments.
AM364	12002.22	–	5	304	Bfr/W	Base 8B	5	–	–	–	–	–
AM365	12002.28	Fabric 13	1	55	W	–	1	–	–	–	–	–
AM366	12002.9	Sinope argile claire	1	81	Hst/Sh	Sinope	1	–	–	–	–	–
AM367	12002.10	Sinope argile claire	2	201	Sh/W	Sinope	1	–	–	–	–	–
AM368	12002.11	Sinope argile claire	5	284	W	Sinope	5	–	–	–	–	–
AM369	12002.15	LRA 3	1	39	Ft	Ung/ Base 9A	1	–	–	–	–	Unguentarium. Ephesos region.
AM370	12002.16	LRA 3	1	74	Bfr/Wfr	Ung/ Base 9A	1	–	–	–	–	Ephesos region.
AM371	12002.17	LRA 3	1	32	Sh	Ung	1	–	–	–	–	Ephesos region.
AM372	12002.18	LRA 3	1	19	Ft	Agora P 65–66/Base 7	1	30	6	–	–	Agora P 65–66, early to mid-Roman one-handled version of LRA 3 (Robinson 1959). Ephesos region. Shape as 2278.3 (AM221). Residual third-century piece.
AM373	12002.12	LRA 1	1	75	Hfr/Sh	LRA 1	1	–	–	–	–	Pale salmon-red.
AM374	12002.13	LRA 1 ZG75	1	69	Hfr	LRA 1	1	–	–	–	–	Yellow buff. Groove down the center, rather narrow. Pin holes due to burnt lime.
AM375	12002.14	LRA 1	1	81	Hst/Sh	LRA 1	1	–	–	–	–	Cream white surface and very pale orange fabric.
AM376	12002.19	LRA 1	4	274	W	LRA 1	1	–	–	–	–	–
AM377	12002.20	LRA 1	1	37	W	LRA 1	1	–	–	–	–	–
AM378	12002.21	LRA 1	1	50	Sh	LRA 1	1	–	–	–	–	–
AM379	12002.23	LRA 1	1	31	W	LRA 1	1	–	–	–	–	–

Cat	Dbase	Fabric	NS	Wt	S	Form	No	%	Dia	De	Ill	Comments
AM380	12002.24	Pal	1	172	H/Sh	LRA 5	1	–	–	–	–	–
AM381	12002.25	Pal	1	199	H/Sh	LRA 5	1	–	–	–	–	Dense fine fabric, quite clean. Fired pale orange. Like a fine Gazan fabric. Rather square handle section with two shallow concave moldings.
AM382	12002.26	Pal	1	268	W	LRA 5	1	–	–	–	–	Same fabric as handle 12002.24 (AM380). Deep-cut grooves.
AM383	12002.27	Pal	1	18	Sh	LRA 5	1	–	–	–	–	–
AM384	12002.29	Pal	3	85	W	LRA 5	3	–	–	–	–	–

Context 12011 (mostly A.D. mid-sixth to 600, with some seventh century: single FW joins with 12002 and 12012?)
(Plates 71–73)

Cat	Dbase	Fabric	NS	Wt	S	Form	No	%	Dia	De	Ill	Comments
AM385	12011.56	Fabric 13B	1	176	R/N/Hfr	Form 14A	1	15	11 in	–	PL. 71	Type piece. Here inner rim is convex. Wide handle, concave pinched rim top.
AM386	12011.63	Fabric 13B	1	14	R/N Fr	Form 14A	1	10	9 in	–	–	Concave top. Similar to 12011.56 (AM385).
AM387	12011.62	Fabric 13B	1	239	Rfr/N/H	Form 14A	1	15	–	–	PL. 71	Could be this variant. Rim obscured.
AM388	12011.79	Fabric 13B	1	104	R/N/Hfr	Medium/small Form 14A	1	15	10 in	–	PL. 71	Pinched rim top, ridge on inner face of rim.
AM389	12011.59	Fabric 13B ZG	1	238	R/N/Hfr	Form 15C	1	11	11 in	–	PL. 71	Type piece. Large amphora. Beveled rim top and inner face. Wide, large springing handle with 5 to 6 concave moldings. Fired almost white.
AM390	12011.55	Fabric 13B ZG	2	307	R/N/H	Form 16B	1	32	12 in	P	PL. 71	Unique. Plain rim face, with lid seat. Good profile. Wide handle. Almost white surface. Yellow-ochre fabric. Grooved rim top. Part of paint stroke below handle on neck. Good example of fabric, with some rectangular calcite(?).
AM391	12011.61	Fabric 13B	1	218	R/N/Hfr	Form 16B?	1	13	c.c.11	–	–	Thick handle. Rim obscured, but large version. Rim not grooved. Could be as 12011.55 (AM390).
AM392	12011.89	Fabric 13B	1	127	Hst/N	Form 16?	1	–	–	P	–	Painted band. Coat of mortar.
AM393	12011.57	Fabric 13B	1	89	R/N	Form 17A	1	21	10 in	P	PL. 71	A wide horizontal brown band of paint on neck. Pale red core, buff surfaces. Cf. 7065.3 (AM343), also classified under this variant.
AM394	12011.88	Fabric 13B	1	65	Rfr/N/Sh	Form 17A	1	–	–	P	–	Painted band across neck. Wide diameter.
AM395	12011.67	Fabric 13B	1	311	R/H/N/Sh	(Medium) Form 15A or 17A variant	1	15	10 in	P	PL. 71	Type piece. Unique. Small square projecting rim. Relatively short neck is not usual type. Band of horizontal paint on neck. No trace on shoulder, but due to this being handle area. Coat of mortar-stones and occasional charcoal stuck to vessel. The multiribbed handle is as that of Form 15A 7064.1 (AM338).

Cat	Dbase	Fabric	NS	Wt	S	Form	No	%	Dia	De	Ill	Comments
AM396	12011.58	Fabric 13B	1	106	R/N/Hfr	Form 17B	1	25	10 in	P	PL. 71	A wide diameter with a stepped rim face. Unique. Streak of paint on handle.
AM397	12011.64	Fabric 13B	3	454	Hfr/Sh	Handle 4/Forms 15–17	3	–	–	–	–	Handles for large modules. White-yellow-buff, usual fabric. Wide handles, as 12011.55 (AM390); 5 cm; 3.8 cm, 5 concave ribs; 4.8 cm.
AM398	12011.65	Fabric 13B	1	252	Hfr/N	Handle 4/Forms 15–17	1	–	–	–	–	Five concave ribs, wide handle as 12011.59 (AM389). Large module.
AM399	12011.66	Fabric 13B	2	304	Hfr/Sh	Handle 4/Forms 15–17	2	–	–	–	–	Pale red core, buff surface. Large variant.
AM400	12011.93	Fabric 13B	8	715	Bfr/Wfr	Base 8A	8	–	–	–	–	Fired pale green. One identical treatment to base of 7036.1 (AM296)
AM401	12011.106	Fabric 13B	1	51	Bfr/Wfr	Base 8A	1	–	–	–	–	Double groove, as 7036.2 (AM298).
AM402	12011.101	Fabric 13B	1	55	Sh	Cf. Forms 15–17	1	–	–	–	–	Large module. Painted border band motif.
AM403	12011.91	Fabric 13B	3	262	Hst/Sh	Cf. Forms 15–17	3	–	–	P	–	Large module.
AM404	12011.92	Fabric 13B	5	975	Sh/W	Cf. Forms 15–17	5	–	–	P	–	Large modules. One shoulder with painted "spiral" and body; one shoulder/wall with painted border band motif and plain band beneath; one wall with band; one shoulder with small painted schematic "spiral" and border band motif on shoulder/wall.
AM405	12011.98	Fabric 13B	1	124	Sh/Wfr	Cf. Forms 15–17	1	–	–	P	–	Large module. Band covers lower and upper carination. Narrow painted border band motif, then part of spiral.
AM406	12011.99	Fabric 13B	2	126	Sh	Cf. Forms 15–17	2	–	–	P	–	Large module.
AM407	12011.100	Fabric 13B	15	1119	W	Cf. Forms 15–17	15	–	–	–	–	Large module.
AM408	12011.76	Fabric 13B	1	65	R/N/Hfr	Small Form 14A	1	10	8 in	–	PL. 72	Small module of Form 14A.
AM409	12011.80	Fabric 13B	1	66	R/N/Hfr	Small Form 14A	1	18	8 in	–	PL. 72	Small diameter. Small module of Form 14A. Handle projection is short.
AM410	12011.82	Fabric 13B	12	82	R/N/Hfr	Small Form 14A	1	10	–	–	–	Same rim as 12011.76 (AM408).
AM411	12011.81	Fabric 13B	1	110	R/N/H	Small Form 16A	1	10	–	–	–	Fabric different? Light groove on rim top, as large amphora Form 16A. Otherwise is a jug (these have a grooved rim top, as this variant).
AM412	12011.75	Fabric 13B	1	20	R/N	Small Form 16B	1	13	9 in	P	PL. 72	As AM390 (12011.55) but smaller module. Painted horizontal band at base of neck (not illustrated).
AM413	12011.90	Fabric 13B	1	77	R/N/Hfr	Small Form 16C?	1	15	8 in	–	PL. 72	Good grooved-beveled rim top. Could also be a jug.
AM414	12011.72	Fabric 13B Melted	1	21	R/N	Small Form 17A variant	1	17	7 in	P	PL. 72	Unique. Fabric pale green, painted band across mid rim and neck top. Has a rather thin neck, rim bent inward. Thin mortar or lime-scale. "Melted" fabric.

Cat	Dbase	Fabric	NS	Wt	S	Form	No	%	Dia	De	Ill	Comments
AM415	12011.68	Fabric 13B Melted	1	39	R/N	Small Form 17A or Form 18	1	22	9 in	P	PL. 72	Same "melted" fabric as 7062.1 (**AM334**). Pale red core and buff surfaces. Horizontal painted band on neck. Light band rim, cf. larger module pieces 7065.3 (**AM343**) and 12011.57 (**AM393**).
AM416	12011.84	Fabric 13B	1	116	R/N/Hfr	Small Form 17A or Form 15A	1	8	c. 8 in	–	PL. 72	Lightly modeled band rim. Obscured.
AM417	12011.69	Fabric 13B	1	19	R/N fr	Small Form 17	1	22	9 in	–	–	–
AM418	12011.78	Fabric 13B	1	89	R/N/Hfr	Small Form 17	1	15	8 in	–	–	–
AM419	12011.70	Fabric 13B	1	93	R/N/Hfr	Small Form 18	1	25	8 in	P	PL. 72	Type piece. Rim top flattened, bent. Paint on side of handle.
AM420	12011.71	Fabric 13B	1	41	R/N/Hst	Small Form 18?	1	20	7.5 in	–	PL. 72	Handle is unusually narrow. Rim bent back. Fired pale green. Could also be a jug.
AM421	12011.74	Fabric 13B	1	73	R/N/Hfr	Small Form 19	1	20	10 in	–	PL. 72	Plain rim and rim face. Cf. 12012.31 (**AM528**).
AM422	12011.77	Fabric 13B ZG	1	144	R/N/H	Small Form 19	1	11	8 in	–	PL. 72	Rounded rim top, bent in. Light band. Unique.
AM423	12011.73	Fabric 13B	1	188	H/N/Sh	Small Form 17	1	–	–	P	–	Painted spiral. Classic fabric with red core.
AM424	12011.86	Fabric 13B	9	615	Hfr/Sh	Small Form 17	9	–	–	–	–	All short and probably small Form 17. Handle/neck and handle/shoulder fragments present.
AM425	12011.94	Fabric 13B	31	1,744	Sh/W	Small Form 17	31	–	–	–	–	Many with lime-scale and/or mortar.
AM426	12011.95	Fabric 13B	26	1,579	Sh/W	Small Form 17	26	–	–	–	–	–
AM427	12011.96	Fabric 13B	18	687	Sh/W	Small Form 17	18	–	–	–	–	–
AM428	12011.97	Fabric 13B	2	116	Bfr/W	Base 8B	2	–	–	–	–	–
AM429	12011.107	Fabric 13B	1	28	Bfr/Wfr	Base 8B	1	–	–	G	–	Double grooved band, small size.
AM430	12011.122	Fabric 13B	1	24	Bfr/Wfr	Base 8B	1	–	–	–	–	–
AM431	12011.102	Fabric 13B	41	1,961	W	Small Form 17	41	–	–	–	–	Not painted. Flagon size walls.
AM432	12011.87	Fabric 13B	6	783	Hfr/Sh	Small Form 17	6	–	–	–	–	Small handle, as 12011.76 (**AM408**).
AM433	12011.60	Fabric 13B	1	29	R/N Fr	Small Form 17 variant	1	15	8 in	–	PL. 72	Similar rim type to 12011.85 (**AM434**). Thick, rounded top. Pale red fabric and buff-cream surfaces.
AM434	12011.85	Fabric 13B?	1	25	R/N Fr	Unclassified	1	15	7 top in	G	PL. 72	Could be a jug. Double shallow grooved band on neck. This and the thick rim but small diameter suggests not in this series. Residual mid-third century, given burning?

Cat	Dbase	Fabric	NS	Wt	S	Form	No	%	Dia	De	Ill	Comments
AM435	12011.127	Fabric 13B?	2	200	W	–	1	–	–	–	–	Fired green. White calcite(?) more common, with black material.
AM436	12011.103	Fabric 1	1	56	Hst/Sh/Nfr	Forms 12–13	1	–	–	CB	–	Third-century residual piece. Classic Fabric 1 amphora.
AM437	12011.120	Local?	1	124	Sh	–	1	–	–	CB	–	Twelve-grooved fine combed band at base of neck.
AM438	12011.121	Local?	1	66	Sh	–	1	–	–	CB	–	Not Fabric 13B. Fine lime: similar fabric to 12011.120 (**AM437**).
AM439	12011.123	Regional	2	158	Sh	–	2	–	–	–	–	One with three wide grooved bands, smoothed and common .5 mm lime. Not Fabric 1; the other fine with occasional fine red inclusions. Not Fabric 13 group. Large amphorae or jars.
AM440	12011.1	Sinope argile claire	1	55	R/N/Hfr	Sinope	1	25	4.5 in	–	PL. 73	Narrow handle with central rib (3 cm).
AM441	12011.7	Sinope argile claire	1	85	Hfr/N	Sinope	1	50	–	–	PL. 73	Handle width 3 cm.
AM442	12011.2	Sinope argile claire	2	105	Sh	Sinope	1	–	–	Di	–	Dipinto on shoulder.
AM443	12011.3	Sinope argile claire	1	78	Hfr/Nfr	Sinope	1	–	–	–	–	Handle width 3 cm.
AM444	12011.4	Sinope argile claire	1	99	Hfr	Sinope	1	–	–	–	–	Pronounced central rib. Handle width 3 cm.
AM445	12011.5	Sinope argile claire	1	85	Hst/Sh	Sinope	1	–	–	–	–	–
AM446	12011.6	Sinope argile claire	1	137	Hfr	Sinope	1	–	–	–	–	Handle width 3 cm.
AM447	12011.8	Sinope argile claire	19	963	W	Sinope	19	–	–	–	–	–
AM448	12011.9	Sinope argile claire	2	203	Sh	Sinope	2	–	–	–	–	–
AM449	12011.10	Sinope argile claire	1	106	Bfr/W	Sinope	1	–	–	–	PL. 73	As usual, clay patted-flattened on the outside.
AM450	12011.11	Sinope argile claire	1	33	B	Sinope	1	100	–	–	–	–
AM451	12011.12	Sinope argile claire	1	12	Bfr	Sinope	1	15	–	–	–	–

Cat	Dbase	Fabric	NS	Wt	S	Form	No	%	Dia	De	Ill	Comments
AM452	12011.13	Sinope argile claire	1	60	Wfr/Bfr	Sinope	1	–	–	–	–	–
AM453	12011.14	Sinope var	1	82	Hfr	Sinope	1					Concave handle face (3 cm). Fired brown-orange, with a cream coat.
AM454	12011.15	Sinope var	1	79	Hfr	Sinope	1	–	–	–	–	Width 3 cm. Cream surfaces, rather smooth. Fine volcanics present. Presumably a Sinope variant. Orange fabric, not "argile claire."
AM455	12011.44	Chersonesos? ZG69	1	115	B	Base 10	1	100	–	–	PL. 73	Type piece. Unique. Pointed toe, with wide floor. Fabric is hackly, uneven with common fine to .5 mm lime, occasional rounded dark brown material, occasional gold mica flake, chert(?), moderate rounded fine quartz, occasional hard white lime(?). A coarse hackly fabric. Similar conical bases belonging to a narrow-neck Sinope-style amphora with two wide flat handles are common in mid-fifth-century deposits in Beirut. The latter are Chersonesian amphorae. The fabric analysis (ZG69) suggested similarities with Euphrates clay sources.
AM456	12011.47	As LRA 3/Ephesos region	1	98	B	Ung/Base 9A	1	100	–	–	PL. 73	Type piece. Ephesos unguentarium, here dense and fired dark brown. Toe twisted and pinched.
AM457	12011.48	As LRA 3	2	173	W	Ung/Base 9A	1	–	–	–	PL. 73	Same form and size. Another vessel. Too thick for LRA 3.
AM458	12011.49	As LRA 3	1	30	W	Ung/Base 9A	1	–	–	–	–	Same ware, dark orange-brown surfaces.
AM459	12011.50	As LRA 3 var	1	121	B/Wfr	Ung/Base 9B	1	–	–	–	PL. 73	Gray core. Large toe, more like an amphora.
AM460	12011.109	Fine Samos	1	49	Sh	Samos	1	–	–	–	PL. 73	Probably a fine-fabric Samos Cistern Amphora (see text). Concave ribbing.
AM461	12011.45	Related to Samos	1	182	Hfr	Handle 4	1	–	–	–	PL. 73	Type piece. Thick rounded handle. Pale orange-brown surface and pale orange fabric. Common-abundant fine mica and dust. Finely sandy. Even. Fine Samos fabric. For similar rounded square handles associated with amphorae typologically related to Samos amphorae, typical in mid- to late sixth-century contexts in Butrint, see Reynolds (2002).
AM462	12011.52	LRA 1 ZG80	1	148	R/N/Hfr	LRA 1	1	20	9 top	–	PL. 73	Wide handle. Bulbous neck and rolled everted rim. Yellowish-buff outer surface, pale red to buff inside.
AM463	12011.24	LRA 1E ZG76	1	170	R/N/Hfr	LRA 1	1	25	9 top in	–	PL. 73	Short R/N small handle with a shallow concave rim band likely. Regular rim. Pale red core and dark buff edges-surfaces. Common fine lime, occasional 2 mm lump. Smooth surfaces, not sandy. Fabric is compact, even, with inclusions set into matrix. Red stone present. Probably as 7006.13 (AM292).

Cat	Dbase	Fabric	NS	Wt	S	Form	No	%	Dia	De	Ill	Comments
AM464	12011.25	LRA 1F ZG77	1	80	R/N/Hfr	LRA 1	1	12	11 out	–	PL. 73	Distinctive cream coat all over. Pale red edges and dark yellow-ochre core. Common fine lime reactions are distinctive. Abundant pin holes on surface. Rim is everted and has a small diameter. Inner neck indented.
AM465	12011.26	LRA 1G ZG78	1	109	N/Shfr	LRA 1	1	20	–	–	PL. 73	Heavy. Pale orange-red edges and dark yellow-ochre core. Granular, but hard fired. Abundant hard white limestone(?), some black volcanic, rounded quartz. Common concave voids from quartz holes. Abundant lime dots on surface. No mica flakes. Found in Beirut contexts.
AM466	12011.27	LRA 1A	4	430	Sh/W	LRA 1	1	–	–	Di	–	Dipinto. Compact orange-brown fabric.
AM467	12011.28	LRA 1	2	140	Sh/Wfr	LRA 1	1	–	–	–	–	Pale yellow-cream surface. Orange-brown fabric. Well fired.
AM468	12011.29	LRA 1A	1	91	W	LRA 1	1	–	–	–	–	Lime, red stone, and semiclear inclusions, as 7060.8 (AM327). Orange-brown. Well fired.
AM469	12011.30	LRA 1A	1	52	W	LRA 1	1	–	–	–	–	–
AM470	12011.31	LRA 1A	1	50	W	LRA 1	1	–	–	–	–	–
AM471	12011.32	LRA 1	1	44	W	LRA 1	1	–	–	–	–	–
AM472	12011.33	LRA 1	1	43	W	LRA 1	1	–	–	–	–	–
AM473	12011.34	LRA 1	1	35	W	LRA 1	1	–	–	–	–	–
AM474	12011.35	LRA 1	1	61	W	LRA 1	1	–	–	–	–	–
AM475	12011.36	LRA 1	1	28	W	LRA 1	1	–	–	–	–	–
AM476	12011.37	LRA 1	1	28	W	LRA 1	1	–	–	–	–	Cream-yellow surface. Abundant gray inclusions.
AM477	12011.38	LRA 1	1	20	W	LRA 1	1	–	–	–	–	Fired yellow-white surfaces and pale orange-yellow fabric.
AM478	12011.39	LRA 1	1	20	W	LRA 1	1	–	–	–	–	Pale yellow fabric and surface.
AM479	12011.40	LRA 1	1	95	W	LRA 1	1	–	–	–	–	Pale yellow-white surface-greenish, pale salmon-orange fabric, sandy but compact.
AM480	12011.41	LRA 1A ZG79	1	93	W	LRA 1	1	–	–	–	–	Thick-walled sandy fabric with gold mica. Eastern Cyprus?
AM481	12011.42	LRA 1	1	26	W	LRA 1	1	–	–	–	–	Smooth, fired pale green surfaces.
AM482	12011.43	LRA 1	1	23	W	LRA 1	1	–	–	–	–	–
AM483	12011.53	LRA 1	1	41	W	LRA 1	1	–	–	–	–	Pale red-brown.
AM484	12011.54	LRA 1	1	15	W	LRA 1	1	–	–	–	–	Pale red-brown.
AM485	12011.117	LRA 1	1	43	W	LRA 1	1	–	–	–	–	–
AM486	12011.51	Import	1	42	W	–	1	–	–	–	–	Not Kapitän 2, though surface and ribbing close. Could be as **AM455**? (Chersonesian). Calcite? Lumps of oxide, quartz, sandwich fabric.
AM487	12011.108	Cilician	1	161	Hfr/N	Agora G 198	1	–	–	–	–	Vertical neck. Handle section damaged, could well be single rod (4 cm wide). And therefore in Agora G 198 class, not Dressel 2–4 (Empereur and Picon 1989; Robinson 1959). Residual. First- or second-century piece. Orange fine fabric with fine to .5mm dark brown oxide pellets.

Cat	Dbase	Fabric	NS	Wt	S	Form	No	%	Dia	De	Ill	Comments
AM488	12011.18	Pal 1	1	162	H/Sh	LRA 5 / Pieri 3	1	–	–	–	–	Probably the fabric connected to Gaza, cf. 5001.1 (**AM263**). Rather heavy-dense. Pale orange-brown fabric with pale red-brown surface. Scattered rounded fine quartz in a fine fabric. Not sandy.
AM489	12011.110	Pal 2	1	82	W	LRA 5	1	–	–	–	–	Deep-cut ribs. Unclear if Gazan variant fabric, with pimply sandy but compact surfaces. As 12011.20 (**AM493**).
AM490	12011.111	Pal 2	1	25	Shfr	LRA 5	1	–	–	–	–	Same ware as **AM489**.
AM491	12011.112	Pal 2	1	36	Bftr/Wfr	LRA 5	1	–	–	–	–	–
AM492	12011.19	Pal 1	5	114	W	LRA 5	5					One with plaster. One burnt. Probably same fabric as 12011.18 (**AM488**).
AM493	12011.20	Pal 2	2	80	W	LRA 5	2	–	–	–	–	Similar dense fabric with .5 mm lime.
AM494	12011.21	Pal 3	1	24	W	LRA 5	1	–	–	–	–	Larger rounded quartz and lime. Perhaps from Caesarea.
AM495	12011.22	Pal 4	1	32	Bfr	LRA 5	1	–	–	–	–	Rather layered break, fine. Cream surface and pale orange-brown fabric. Finer fabric than the others. Abu Mena fabric?
AM496	12011.23	(North) Pal 5	1	21	W	Late Agora M 334?	1	–	–	–	–	Carrot bodied likely. Thin walled with pronounced ribbing upper section, plain lower. Perhaps a small module late Agora M 334 (Reynolds, 2005a, for sixth- to seventh-century examples in Caesarea, Istanbul, and Rome). Fine fabric with moderate .5 mm rounded oxide pellets. Exports of this type occur in one large late sixth–early seventh-century context in Beirut (BEY 006.5503).
AM497	12011.113	Pal?	1	56	W	Aqaba amphora? Or late Agora M 334	1	–	–	–	–	Carrot-shaped lower body sherd. Fine rounded quartz, fired dark brown. Pimply surfaces inside. Not Beirut. Probably not Agora M 334. Could be Aqaba? (e.g., Whitcomb 2001, fig. 2b).
AM498	12011.17	Fine Gaza	1	41	W	LRA 4	1	–	–	–	–	Only sherd. So Gazan is rare.
AM499	12011.16	Fine Egyptian	1	247	B	Egyptian base	1	100	–	–	PL. 73	Long cone toe. Spiral.
AM500	12011.114	Fine Egyptian	1	115	W	–	1	–	–	–	–	
AM501	12011.116	Import	1	100	W	Unclassified	1	–	–	–	–	Surface fired dark red-brown, with an orange fabric. Dense. Fairly conical-carrot bodied. Not Palestinian.

Context 12012 (Plate 74) (A.D. 525–500 FW dominant; with early seventh century)

Cat	Dbase	Fabric	NS	Wt	S	Form	No	%	Dia	De	Ill	Comments
AM502	12012.25	Fabric 13B	1	124	R/N/Hfr	Form 14A	1	23	10 in	–	PL. 74	Type piece. Does show how close this is to Form 16A. Same size as 7061.1 (**AM332**). Beveled-grooved rim top. Rim thickened inside. Medium-size oval handle.
AM503	12012.20	Fabric 13B ZG	1	34	R/N	Form 15C	1	10	11 top in	–	PL. 74	Square rim. Beveled inner face, as 12012.24 (**AM505**).

Cat	Dbase	Fabric	NS	Wt	S	Form	No	%	Dia	De	Ill	Comments
AM504	12012.19	Fabric 13B	1	43	R/N	Form 15C (or Form 17A)	1	10	c. 10 in	–	PL. 74	Large thick square rim, flat top, inner face beveled. Probably this variant, or as Form 17A.
AM505	12012.24	Fabric 13B	1	165	R/N/Hfr	(?Medium) Form 15C	1	23	9 in	–	PL. 74	Too large for the smaller modules, though the handle is relatively small (in comparison to type piece 12011.59: **AM389**). Classic fabric.
AM506	12012.33	Fabric 13B	1	95	R/N/Hfr	Form 16C	1	10	c. 10 in	–	PL. 74	Type piece. Thickest rim variant for this shape. Shape close to 7004.1 (**AM270**).
AM507	12012.21	Fabric 13B	4	349	R/N/H/Sh	Medium Form 18	1	50	9 in	–	PL. 74	Type piece. Unique. Good profile. 12011.70–71 (**AM419-420**) may be smaller modules of this type. Fairly wide neck. Painted band on lower neck.
AM508	12012.29	Fabric 13B	1	125	R/N/Hfr	Form 19	1	20	9 in	–	PL. 74	Plain face and rim top. Inner neck well ribbed.
AM509	12012.30	Fabric 13B	1	142	R/N/Hfr	Form 19 likely	1	10	–	–	PL. 74	Flat top, rim obscured. Wide handle.
AM510	12012.45	Fabric 13B	1	276	Hst/Sh	Cf. Forms 15–17	1	–	–	P	–	Painted border band motif near handle. End of broad band above it.
AM511	12012.46	Fabric 13B	1	160	Sh	Cf. Forms 15–17	1	–	–	P	–	Painted border band motif and "small version" (of the same: i.e., loops?) on mid shoulder.
AM512	12012.47	Fabric 13B	1	56	Sh	Cf. Forms 15–17	1	–	–	P G	–	Painted border band motif below double groove band, not combed.
AM513	12012.39	Fabric 13B	1	165	Hfr/Nfr	Cf. Forms 15–17	1	–	–	–	–	Wider (5 cm).
AM514	12012.48	Fabric 13B	2	346	Hst/Sh	Cf. Forms 15–17	2	–	–	P	–	Just a few dashes of paint.
AM515	12012.49	Fabric 13B	1	35	Hfr/Sh	Cf. Forms 14–17	1	–	–	P	–	Painted.
AM516	12012.38	Fabric 13B	4	414	Hfr/N	Cf. Forms 14–17	4	–	–	–	–	Medium size, cf. 12012.25 (**AM502**).
AM517	12012.52	Fabric 13B	1	111	Bfr/W	Base 8A	1	–	–	–	–	Coat of plaster inside and over break.
AM518	12012.53	Fabric 13B	1	66	Bfr/W	Base 8A	1	–	–	–	–	–
AM519	12012.54	Fabric 13B	1	32	Sh	Cf. Forms 15–17	1	–	–	P	–	Painted filled circle, cf. "spiral."
AM520	12012.55	Fabric 13B	6	239	W	Cf. Forms 15–17	6	–	–	–	–	–
AM521	12012.23	Fabric 13B	1	25	R/N	Small Form 15B	1	20	9 in	–	PL. 74	Probably a small module of type as 7306.1 (**AM354**) and 7060.24 (**AM301**).
AM522	12012.27	Fabric 13B	1	41	R/N	Small Form 15C	1	25	8 in	P	PL. 74	Type piece. Wide painted band on neck. Rim face flat band. Small painted module of Form 15C (or of Form 14A).
AM523	12012.26	Fabric 13B	1	39	R/N/Hsm	Small Form 16A	1	10	c. 8 in	P	PL. 74	Thin rim, grooved top. As 7061.1 (**AM332**), but short neck. Painted band on neck. Small module of Form 16A?
AM524	12012.60	Fabric 13	1	54	R/N	Small Form 16C	1	20	13 out	P	PL. 74	Pronounced grooved-flanged rim top. Narrow painted band on lower neck.

Cat	Dbase	Fabric	NS	Wt	S	Form	No	%	Dia	De	Ill	Comments
AM525	12012.22	Fabric 13B	1	19	R/N fr	Small Form 17 variant	1	15	9 in		PL. 74	Type piece. Shallow band rim, cupped shape. Flat top. Unique.
AM526	12012.36	Fabric 13B	1	99	R/N/Hfr	Small Form 17	1	10	–		–	Maybe this.
AM527	12012.28	Fabric 13B	1	110	R/N/Hfr	Small Form 19	1	23	9 in	–	PL. 74	Thin rim, thickened on inside. Plain rim face. Wide handle.
AM528	12012.31	Fabric 13B	1	107	R/N/Hfr	Small Form 19	1	15	8 in	–	PL. 74	Plain vertical face. Convex top. Medium, oval handle
AM529	12012.32	Fabric 13B ZG	1	107	R/N/Hfr	Small Form 19 likely	1	10	c. 9in	–	PL. 74	Light horizontal concave top. Handle width 4 cm.
AM530	12012.37	Fabric 13B	2	131	Hfr	Cf. Small Form 17	2	–	–	–	–	–
AM531	12012.40	Fabric 13B	1	100	H	Cf. Small Form 17	1	–	–	–	–	Width 4 cm.
AM532	12012.42	Fabric 13B	3	348	Hst/Sh/Wfr	Cf. Small Form 17	4	–	–	P	–	Painted. Two with mortar-plaster.
AM533	12012.43	Fabric 13B	1	112	Hst/Sh	Cf. Small Form 17	1	–	–	P	–	Painted.
AM534	12012.50	Fabric 13B	1	11	Bfr	Base 8B	1	–	–	–	–	–
AM535	12012.51	Fabric 13B	1	47	Bfr/Wfr	Base 8B	1	–	–	–	–	–
AM536	12012.44	Fabric 13B	9	358	Sh	Cf. Small Form 17	9	–	–	P	–	Painted.
AM537	12012.56	Fabric 13B	1	22	Shfr/Nfr	Cf. Small Form 17	1	–	–	P	–	Painted.
AM538	12012.57	Fabric 13B	6	175	W	Cf. Small Form 17	6	–	–	–	–	–
AM539	12012.41	Fabric 13B	4	323	Hfr	Small Form 19?	4	–	–	–	–	Small, cf. 12012.32 (**AM529**) or 12012.29 (**AM508**).
AM540	12012.58	Regional	3	156	W	Unclassified	3	–	–	–	–	–
AM541	12012.1	Sinope argile claire	16	2,055	R/H/Hst/W/Bfr	Sinope	1	100	5 top	–	–	Rim uneven, as usual. Lime reaction rims on surface, cf. examples at Seleucia-on-the-Orontes.
AM542	12012.2	Sinope argile claire	1	43	R/N/Hfr	Sinope	1	20	–	–	–	Handle width 4 cm.
AM543	12012.3	Sinope argile claire	1	42	Hfr/N	Sinope	1	–	–	–	–	–
AM544	12012.4	Sinope argile claire	1	150	H	Sinope	1	–	–	–	–	Width 4 cm.
AM545	12012.5	Sinope argile claire	1	29	N	Sinope	1	–	–	–	–	–
AM546	12012.6	Sinope argile claire	5	288	Sh/W	Sinope	5	–	–	–	–	Five different vessels.

Cat	Dbase	Fabric	NS	Wt	S	Form	No	%	Dia	De	Ill	Comments
AM547	12012.7	Sinope red	1	22	Nfr/Shfr	Sinope	1	–	–	–	–	Fired pale orange-red.
AM548	12012.8	Sinope argile claire	4	99	W	Sinope	1	–	–	–	–	Fired pale pink inside with a greenish-buff surface. Same lime reactions.
AM549	12012.9	LRA 1 ZG81	1	70	Hfr/Shfr	LRA 1	1	–	–	–	PL. 74	Fired pale red-brown with abundant lime. Interesting fabric. Folded ridge down handle is distinctive.
AM550	12012.10	LRA 1 ZG82	1	57	Hst/N	LRA 1 Ceramic disc?	1	–	–	–	–	Cut down as small ceramic disc? Otherwise, is worn. 5.3 cm diameter. Abundant fine lime and common fine black volcanics.
AM551	12012.12	LRA 1 ZG83	1	100	Hfr/Sh	LRA 1	1	–	–	–	–	Handle width 4 cm. Handle sloping well inward, like a fifth-century type, with a central groove. Residual?
AM552	12012.11	LRA 1	1	17	Bfr	LRA 1	1	–	–	–	–	Could also be Fabric 13. Fired pale green, common .5 mm black inclusions.
AM553	12012.13	LRA 1	13	538	W	LRA 1	13	–	–	–	–	–
AM554	12012.15	Pal 1	1	152	H/Sh	LRA 5	1	–	–	–	–	Handle width 2 cm. Heavy, (reddish) brown fabric. Thin handle. Narrow angled shallow grooving.
AM555	12012.16	Pal 2	1	128	H/Sh	LRA 5	1	–	–	–	–	Pimply surfaces. Heavy. Pale orange fabric and very pale red-brown surfaces. Small ring with central rib (3 cm). Battered.
AM556	12012.17	Gaza	1	78	Hfr/Wfr	LRA 4	1	–	–	–	–	Small narrow strap like ring handle (3 cm). Should be contemporary.
AM557	12012.18	LRA 3	1	50	Bfr	Ung/Base 9A	1	–	–	–	–	Uneven. Worn. A little abrasive.
AM553	12012.13	LRA 1	13	538	W	LRA 1	13	–	–	–	–	–
AM554	12012.15	Pal 1	1	152	H/Sh	LRA 5	1	–	–	–	–	Handle width 2 cm. Heavy, (reddish) brown fabric. Thin handle. Narrow, angled, shallow grooving.
AM555	12012.16	Pal 2	1	128	H/Sh	LRA 5	1	–	–	–	–	Pimply surfaces. Heavy. Pale orange fabric and very pale red-brown surfaces. Small ring with central rib (3 cm). Battered.
AM556	12012.17	Gaza	1	78	Hfr/Wfr	LRA 4	1	–	–	–	–	Small narrow strap like ring handle (3 cm). Should be contemporary.
AM557	12012.18	LRA 3	1	50	Bfr	Ung/Base 9A	1	–	–	–	–	Uneven. Worn. A little abrasive.

NOTES

1. Finds and contexts published here come from trenches excavated by Oxford Archaeology for The Packard Humanities Institute rescue excavations at Zeugma in 2000: Trenches 1, 2, 4, 5, 7, 9, 10, 11, 12, 13, 15, 18, and 19. Finds recovered from other areas in 2000 will be published separately by their respective excavators: the Gaziantep Museum, the University of Nantes, and the Zeugma Initiative Group.
2. Reynolds 2005a.
3. Konrad 2001.
4. Miglus et al. 1999, 42–3, Tafel 42, paralleled at Samarra.
5. Konrad 2001b.
6. Orssaud 1992, 221.
7. I would also like to thank Catherine Abadie-Reynal for similarly sharing her knowledge and allowing me to examine the material from the excavations by the University of Nantes. Hans Curvers kindly provided me with a copy of Fokke Gerritsen's important unpublished work on the Balih Valley, as well as the Hammam-et-Turkman I report. I was assisted in every respect by employees of Oxford Archaeology during my stay at Birecik, for which I would like express my warm thanks to Adam Brossler and Jennifer Cooledge (who both saved me much valuable time by engaging in amphora sticking sessions), to Andy Millar and to Philippa Walton. My work was greatly aided by Sait Yilmaz, who facilitated my constant demands for pottery from the storerooms. I would very much like to thank all the Turkish staff in charge of the guest rooms, restaurant facilities and security at Birecik, who offered me friendship and hospitality during what was undoubtedly a most pleasant stay. Chris Doherty's work on the analysis of the amphora fabrics, together with his expertise and knowledge of region has been a considerable boon, for which I am indebted. Finally I must thank William Aylward for his understanding, regular stream of information and guidance during the preparation of this report, and for his editorial work on the manuscript.
8. Toll 1946, e.g., pl. 49a, one of two complete examples from Tomb 54 at Dura-Europos, pl. 43.
9. Reynolds 2005a. Tell Dor: Ariel et al. 1985, fig. 1. Tell Michal: Singer-Avitz 1989, 142, fig. 9.17 (Persian). Fischer 1989 (Hellenistic). For early Roman amphorae of this class in Galilee, see Diez Fernandez 1983, forms T 1.3–4.
10. Tell Kannâs: al-Radi and Seeden 1980: 107, figs. 33 and 52; Finet 1979, 83, fig. 6. Dibsi Faraj: Finet 1979, 61.
11. Coin of Domitian: Toll 1946, 132–9.
12. Finet 1979.
13. Finet 1970, fig. 6.
14. Abel and Barrois 1928. Attic and Hellenistic lamps and black glaze are present.
15. Abel and Barrois 1927, 128, fig. 1B–C, Tomb 1.
16. Abel and Barrois 1928, 195, pl. 54c, Tomb 22.
17. Abel and Barrois 1928, pl. 54d and 70, Tomb 49.
18. Gerritsen, unpublished.
19. Gerritsen, unpublished.
20. Isidore of Charax, writing in the Persian Gulf, probably in the late first century B.C. Raqqa / Nicephorium: Gerritsen, unpublished 13–14, with reference to Chaumont 1984.
21. Reynolds 2000.
22. Reynolds 2004b.
23. See the following chapter by Doherty: "Petrographic Analysis of Transport Amphorae."
24. Reynolds 2003a; Reynolds, 2005a, Section 1.2b.
25. Reynolds 2005a, Section 1.3; for Qasrawet 2530, see Arthur and Oren 1998.
26. Degeest 2000, figs. 186–92 and cover photograph.
27. Reynolds 1999; 2003a; Reynolds 2005a, Sections 1.4 and 1.7; Reynolds 2004a, fig. 35.
28. Robinson 1959, Agora M 334; Reynolds 2005a, Section 1.7.
29. **AM112**: Context 2010, the lower half of a vessel; Abadie-Reynal 2004.
30. Arthur and Williams 1992; see also Williams 2005.
31. South Shields on Hadrian's Wall: 109 sherds, representing at least five vessels, in a deposit of A.D. 250–350.
32. Arthur and Williams 1992, 253–4.
33. Reynolds 2002a.
34. E.g., contexts 2039, 2081; not in the Catalogue but observed by Philip Kenrick: sherds in 2183, 2197? and 11047. Similar finds have been noted in excavations at Zeugma by the University of Nantes: Abadie-Reynal, 2004.
35. Oren-Pascal and Bernal Casasola 2000; Bernal Casasola 2000; Reynolds 2005b.
36. In the Imperial Baths, BEY 045; Reynolds 1999; 2000; 2005b.
37. Spanish oil: Berni Millet 1998.
38. **AM223**: 2278.1; Keay 1984, 95–9.
39. E.g., Meylan Krause 2002, figs. 619–24; Reynolds 1995, 40–2.
40. **AM175**: 2039.2; **AM176**: 2039.5; Keay 1984, 172–8.
41. Oates 1959, 233, pl. 50.60.
42. Robinson 1959, Agora P 65–6; see Lemaître 1997.
43. Reynolds 1999, fig. 199, for an example of an early third-century Gazan amphora; for a discussion of early Palestinian exports, see Reynolds, 2005a and b and c.
44. Abadie-Reynal 2004.
45. As the early Roman "argile claire" Sinope small-module amphorae: Šelov 1986.
46. For excavations of kiln sites: Kassab Tezgör 1998; Erten et al. 2004; Kassab Tezgör and Tatlican 1998; Garlan and Kassab Tezgör 1996.
47. E.g., Reynolds 2003b, fig. 4.2.
48. E.g., Reynolds 2003b, 541, fig. 4.3.
49. Uscatescu 2003, 549, Figs. 1–2.
50. Empereur and Picon 1989: location maps of "production sites" on figs. 18–9.
51. Reynolds 2005a.
52. Curtis 1991, 118–9.
53. For early imperial small modules, see Šelov 1986.
54. Curtis 199, 91–6, 167–8, Plate 7a.
55. Reynolds 2005b.
56. Empereur and Picon 1989; Demesticha and Michaelides 2001; Demesticha 2003.
57. Reynolds 1995; 2005a and b.
58. Personal observation; Reynolds 2005b, n. 214.
59. E.g., Van Alfen 1996; Pieri 2005; Decker 2000.
60. Reynolds 2005a; personal observation.
61. For the form, see Reynolds 1995, 71–2; Peacock and Williams 1986, Class 56; Pieri 2005.
62. Marseille: Bonifay, Carre, and Rigoir 1998; Bien 2005. Carthage: Fulford and Peacock 1984. For the relatively rare supply of LRA 5 in the West, with the exception of Carthage, see Reynolds 1995 and forthcoming.
63. Reynolds 2005b; Fulford and Peacock 1984; Bonifay, Carre, and Rigoir 1998.
64. Examples in the Cripta Balbi: Saguì, Ricci, and Romei 1997, 36, fig. 2.7, "Crypta Balbi 1"; Reynolds 2005a.
65. Whitcomb 2001, fig. 2b.
66. It is probably this example that is on display in the Bodrum Museum gardens. My thanks to George Bass for showing me the unpublished report on this important wreck.
67. I am grateful to John Mitchell for suggesting that sanctified oil, rather than some other product, was the most likely content for these unguentaria.

68. Tocra: Hayes 1971. Western Mediterranean sites, e.g., Cartagena and Alicante: Reynolds 1993, Misc 7; Berrocal Caparrós 1996.
69. Hayes (1971) had long stated that the stamps on this type, that included a reference to a bishop, were for the cult of saints. The numerous finds in Palestine, however, led him to believe that the source might lie in that region. I would like to thank Jean-Pierre Sodini for suggesting a Lycian source for this unguentarium. Joanita Vroom in turn suggested that the Limyra finds might indicate a connection with the cult of St. Nicolas.
70. Cottica 2000.
71. Reynolds 2002b.
72. For the type, see Isler (1969) and Arthur (1985; 1990). For finds in the West, see Bonifay, Carre, and Rigoir (1998), Remolà i Vallverdú (2000), Reynolds (1995, 76), and Reynolds (2005b, Tables 14 and 16).
73. Reynolds 2002b.
74. Reynolds 1999.
75. Reynolds 1999; 2003b.
76. Cox 1949, 14–5: ARS 45, 49, and 50.
77. Bost et al. 1992.
78. Reynolds 1995, 40–2.
79. For a discussion of these issues, see Reynolds 2005a and b.
80. Mackensen 1984, 45–8, for tables summarizing the fine wares; Konrad 2001a.
81. For guidance see Keay 1984; Peacock and Williams 1986; Reynolds 2005a. For Levantine types, see Robinson 1959.
82. See the following chapter by Doherty: "Petrographic Analysis of Transport Amphorae."
83. See the following chapter by Doherty: "Petrographic Analysis of Transport Amphorae."
84. See the following chapter by Doherty: "Petrographic Analysis of Transport Amphorae."
85. Toll 1946, 132–139, these tombs falling into chronological Groups III and V: one burial in Tomb 6 occurred with a coin of Domitian. Four coins of Orodes II, 51–38 b.c., in Tomb 23 and one in Tomb 36 give some clue as to the late first-century date of some of the burials.
86. See the following chapter by Doherty for the geographical relationship between the two main groups of inclusions: igneous and metamorphic minerals washed downriver from Turkey, and calcareous inclusions derived from the Tertiary limestone formations that are characteristic of northern Syria; note that the fabrics resemble those of Islamic pottery at Raqqa: color photographs of fabrics, for example, in Miglus et al. 1999, Taf. 101.
87. See the following chapter by Doherty: "Petrographic Analysis of Transport Amphorae."
88. See the following chapter by Doherty: "Petrographic Analysis of Transport Amphorae."
89. See the following chapter by Doherty: "Petrographic Analysis of Transport Amphorae."

BIBLIOGRAPHY

Abadie-Reynal, C. 2004. "Les amphores d'importation trouvées à Zeugma: Présentation préliminaire." In *Transport Amphorae and Trade in the Eastern Mediterranean: International Colloquium at the Danish Institute at Athens, 26–29 September 2002*, edited by J. Eiring and J. Lund, 15–21. Aarhus: Aarhus University Press.

Abel, A., and A. Barrois. 1927. "Fouilles de l'École Archéologique Française de Jérusalem effectuées à Neirab du 24 septembre au 5 novembre 1926." *Syria* 8:126–42.

———. 1928. "Fouilles de l'École Archéologique Française de Jérusalem effectuées à Neirab du 12 septembre au 6 novembre 1927." *Syria* 9:186–206, 303–19.

Alfen, P.G. 1996. "New Light on the 7th Century Yassi Ada Shipwreck: Capacities and Standard Sizes of LRA 1 Amphoras." *JRA* 9:189–213.

Ariel, D.T., et al. 1985. "A Group of Stamped Hellenistic Storage Jar Handles from Dor." *IEJ* 35:135–52.

Arthur, P. 1986. "Apunti sulla circulazione delle ceramica medievale a Napoli." In *III Congreso Internazionale sulla ceramica Medievale nel Mediterraneo Occidentale*, 545–54. Firenze: All'Insegna del Giglio.

———. 1990. "Anfore dall'alto Adriatico e il problema del Samos cistern type." *AquilNost* 61:282–95.

Arthur, P., and E.R. Oren. 1998 "The North Sinai Survey and the Evidence of Transport Amphorae for Roman and Byzantine Trading Patterns." *JRA* 11:193–212.

Arthur, P., and D. Williams. 1992. "Campanian Wine, Roman Britain, and the 3rd Century A.D." *JRA* 5:250–60.

Bavant, B., and D. Orssaud. 2001. "Stratigraphie et typologie: Problèmes posés par l'utilisation de la céramique comme critère de datation: L'exemple de la fouille de Déhès." In *La céramique Byzantine et proto-islamique en Syrie-Jordanie (IVe–VIIIe siècles apr. J.-C.). Actes du colloque tenu à Amman les 3, 4 et 5 décembre 1994*, edited by E. Villeneuve and P.M. Watson, 33–48. BAHBeyrouth 159. Beirut: Institut français d'archéologie du Proche-Orient.

Bernal Casasola, D. 2000. "Las ánforas béticas en los confines del imperio: Primera aproximación a las exportaciones a la *Pars Orientalis*." In *Congreso Internacional 'Ex Baetica Amphorae,' Universidad de Sevilla, 17–20 December 1998*, edited by G. Chic Garcia, 935–88. Écija: Editorial Gráficas.

Berni Millet, P. 1998. *Las ánforas de aceite de la bética y su presencia en la Cataluña romanaa*. Collecció Instrumenta 4. Barcelona: Universitat de Barcelona.

Berrocal Caparrós, M.C. 1996. "Late Roman Unguentarium en Carthago-Nova." *Congreso Arqueológico Nacional* 23:119–28.

Bien, S. 2005. "Des niveaux du VIIe siècle sous le Music-hall de l'Alcazar à Marseille," In *LRCWI: Late Roman Coarse Wares, Cooking Wares and Amphorae in the Mediterranean: Archaeology and Archaeometry (Conference Papers, Held at Barcelona, 14–16 March 2002)*, edited by J.M. Gurt, J. Buxeda, and M.A. Cau. BAR-IS 1340. Oxford: Archaeopress.

Bonifay, M., M.B. Carre, and Y. Rigoir. eds. 1998. *Fouilles à Marseille: Les mobiliers (Ier-VIIe siècles ap. J.-C.)*. Études Massiliètes 5. Paris: Errance.

Bost, J.-P., et al. 1992. *L'epave Cabrera III (Majorque): Échanges commerciaux et circuits monétaires au milieu du IIIe siècle après Jésus-Christ*. Publications du Centre Pierre Paris 23. Paris: Diffusion de Boccard.

Chaumont, M.L. 1984. "Études d'histoire Parthe V: La route royale des Parthes de Zeugma à Séleucie du Tigre d'après l'itinéraire d'Isidore de Charax." *Syria* 61:63–107.

Cottica, D. 2000. "Unguentari tardo antichi dal *Martyion* di Hierapolis, Turchia." *MÉFRA* 112:999–1021.

Cox, D.H. 1949. *The Excavations at Dura-Europos, Final Report*. Vol.

4.1, pt. 2, *The Greek and Roman Pottery*. New Haven: Yale University Press.

Curtis, R.I. 1991. *Garum and Salsamenta: Production and Commerce in Materia Medica*. Studies in Ancient Medicine 3. Leiden: Brill.

Decker, M. 2000. "Food for an Empire: Wine and Oil Production in North Syria." In *Economy and Exchange in the East Mediterranean During Late Antiquity. Proceedings of a Conference at Somerville College, Oxford, 29 May 1999*, edited by S. Kingsley and M. Decker, 69–86. Oxford: Oxbow.

Degeest, R. 2000. *The Common Wares of Sagalassos: Typology and Chronology*. Studies in Eastern Mediterranean Archaeology III. Turnhout: Brepols.

Demesticha, S. 2003. "Amphora Production on Cyprus during the Late Roman Period." *VIIeme Congrès International sur la Céramique Médiévale en Méditerranée Thessaloniki, 11–16 October 1999*, edited by C. Bakirtzes, 469–76. Athens: Caisse des Recettes Archéologiques.

Demesticha, S., and D. Michaelides. 2001. "The Excavation of a Late Roman 1 Amphora Kiln in Paphos." In *La céramique Byzantine et proto-islamique en Syrie-Jordanie (IVe–VIIIe siècles apr. J.-C.). Actes du colloque tenu à Amman les 3, 4 et 5 décembre 1994*, edited by E. Villeneuve and P.M. Watson, 289–96. BAHBeyrouth 159. Beirut: Institut français d'archéologie du Proche-Orient.

Diederichs, C. 1980. *Salamine de Chypre, IX: Céramiques Hellenistiques, Romaines et Byzantines*. Paris: Diffusion de Boccard.

Diez Fernandez, F. 1983. *Ceramica comun romana de la Galilea: Aproximaciones y diferencias con la ceramica del resto de Palestina y regiones circundantes*. Madrid: Escuela Biblica.

Empereur, J.Y., and M. Picon. 1989. "Les régions de production d' amphores impériales en Méditerranée orientale." In *Amphores romaines et histoire économique: Dix ans de recherches. Actes du colloque de Sienne (22–24 mai 1986)*, 223–48. CÉFR 114. Rome: École Française de Rome.

Erten, H.N., D. Kassab Tezgör, I.R. Türkmen, and A. Zararsız. 2004. "The Typology and Trade of the Amphorae of Sinope: Archaeological Study and Scientific Analyses." In *Transport Amphorae and Trade in the Eastern Mediterranean: International Colloquium at the Danish Institute at Athens, 26–29th September 2002*, edited by J. Eiring and J. Lund, 103–15. Aarhus: Aarhus University Press.

Finet, A. 1979. "Bilan provisoire des fouilles belges du Tell Kannâs." In *Archaeological Reports from the Tabqa Dam Project, Euphrates Valley, Syria*, edited by D.N. Freedman, 79–95. AASOR 44. Cambridge: American Schools of Oriental Research.

Fischer, M. 1987. "Hellenistic pottery (Strata V–III)." In *Excavations at Tel Michal, Israel*, edited by Z. Herzog, G. Rapp, and O. Negbi, 177–87. Tel Aviv: Publications of the (Sonia and Marco Nadler) Institute of Archaeology, Tel Aviv University.

Freedman, D.N. 1979. *Archaeological Reports from the Tabqa Dam Project-Euphrates Valley, Syria*. AASOR 44. Cambridge: American Schools of Oriental Research.

Fulford, M.G., and D.P.S. Peacock. 1984. *Excavations at Carthage: The British Mission*. Vol. 1, pt. 2, *The Avenue du President Habib Bourguiba, Salammbo: The Pottery and Other Ceramic Objects from the Site*. Sheffield: British Academy from the University of Sheffield.

Garlan, Y., and D. Kassab Tezgör. 1996. "Prospection d'ateliers d'amphores et de ceramiques de Sinope." *Anatolia Antiqua* 4:325–34.

Gerritsen, F.A. "The Balikh Valley, Syria, in the Hellensitic and Roman-Parthian Age: An Archaeological Study of Settlement and Land Use Patterns." Ph.D. diss., University of Amsterdam.

Hayes, J.W. 1971. "A New Type of Early Christian Ampulla." *BSA* 66:243–8.

Isler, H.P. 1969. "Heraion von Samos: Eine frühbyzantinische Zisterne." *Athenische Mitteilungen* 84:203–30.

Kassab Tezgör, D. 1998. "Prospection sous-marine près de la côte Sinopéene: Transport d'amphores depuis l'atelier et navigation en Mer Noire." *Anatolia Antiqua* 6:443–9.

Kassab Tezgör, D., and I. Tatlican. 1998. "Fouilles des ateliers d'amphores à Demirçi, près de Sinope en 1996 et 1997." *Anatolia Antiqua* 6:423–42.

Keay, S.J. 1984. *Late Roman Amphorae in the Western Mediterranean: A Typology and Economic Study: The Catalan Evidence*. BAR-IS 196. Oxford: British Archaeological Reports.

Konrad, M. 2001a. *Resafa*. Vol. 5, *Der spätrömische Limes in Syrien: Archäologische Untersuchungen an den Grenzkastellen von Sura, Tetrapyrgium, Cholle und in Resafa*. Mainz am Rhein: Philipp von Zabern.

———. 2001b. "Ummayad Pottery from Tetrapyrgium (Qseir as-Seileh), North Syria: Traditions and Innovations." In *La céramique Byzantine et proto-islamique en Syrie-Jordanie (IVe–VIIIe siècles apr. J.-C.). Actes du colloque tenu à Amman les 3, 4 et 5 décembre 1994*, edited by E. Villeneuve and P.M. Watson, 163–91. BAHBeyrouth 159. Beirut: Institut français d'archéologie du Proche-Orient.

Lapp, P.W. 1961. *Palestinian Ceramic Chronology, 200 B.C.–A.D. 70*. New Haven: American Schools of Oriental Research.

Lázaro, A.I. 1988. "The Period X Pottery." In *Hammam et-Turkman I: Report on the University of Amsterdam's 1981–84 Excavations in Syria, II*, edited by M.N. Van Loon, 499–599. Istanbul: Nederlands Historisch-Archeologisch Instituut te Istanbul.

Lemaître S. 1997. "L'amphore de type Agora F65/66, dite 'monoansée': Essai de synthèse à partir d'exemplaires lyonnais." In *Actes du Congrès du Mans, 8-11 mai 1997*, edited by L. Rivet, 311–20. Marseille: Société Française d'Étude de la Céramique Antique en Gaule.

Lyonnet, B. 2001. "Prospection archéologique du Haut-Khabour (Syrie du Nord-East): Problématique, méthodologie et application à la période byzantino-sassinade." In *La céramique Byzantine et proto-islamique en Syrie-Jordanie (IVe–VIIIe siècles apr. J.-C.). Actes du colloque tenu à Amman les 3, 4 et 5 décembre 1994*, edited by E. Villeneuve and P.M. Watson, 23–32. BAHBeyrouth 159. Beirut: Institut français d'archéologie du Proche-Orient.

Mackensen, M. 1984. *Resafa I: Eine befestigte spätantike Anlage vor den Stadtmauern von Resafa*. Mainz am Rhein: Philipp von Zabern.

Meylan Krause, M.F. 2002. *Domus Tiberiana: Analyses stratigraphiques et céramologiques*. BAR-IS 1058. Oxford: Archaeopress.

Miglus, P.A., et al. 1999. *Ar-Raqqa, I: Die frühislamische Keramik von Tall Aswad*. Mainz am Rhein: Philipp von Zabern.

Oates, D., and J. Oates. 1959. "Ain Sinu: A Roman Frontier Post in Northern Iraq." *Iraq* 21:207–42.

Oren-Pascal, M., and D. Bernal Casasola. 2000. "Ánforas sudhispánicas en *Caesarea Maritima*: Un ejemplo de importación de vino, aceite y conservas de pescado béticas en *Iudaea*." In *Congreso Internacional "Ex Baetica Amphorae." Universidad de Sevilla, 17–20 December 1998*, edited by G. Chic Garcia, 989–1033. Écija: Editorial Gráficas.

Orssaud, D. 1991. "La céramique." In *Halabiyya-Zenobia, place forte du limes oriental et la Haute-Mésopotamie au VI siècle, II: L'architecture publique, religieuse, privée et funéraire*, edited by J. Lauffray, 260–75. Paris: Institut Français d'Archéologie du Proche-Orient.

———. 1992. "Le passage de la céramique byzantine à la céramique islamique: Quelques hypothèses à partir du mobilier trouvé à Déhès." In *La Syrie de Byzance à l'Islam, VII-VIII siècles. Actes du Colloque International, Lyon/Paris 11–15th September 1990*, edited by P. Canivet and J.P. Rey-Coquais. Damascus: Institut Français de Damas.

Peacock, D.P.S., and D.F. Williams. 1986. *Amphorae and the Roman Economy: An Introductory Guide*. London: Longman.

Pieri, D. 2005. *Le commerce du vin oriental à l'époque byzantine (Ve–*

VIIe siècles): Le témoinage des amphores en Gaule. BAHBeyrouth 174. Beirut: Institut français d'archéologie du Proche-Orient.

al-Radi, S., and H. Seeden. 1980. "The AUB Rescue Excavations at Shams ed-Din Tannira." *Berytus* 28:88–126.

Remolà i Vallverdú, J.A. 2000. *Las ánforas tardo-antiguas en Tarraco (Hispania Tarraconensis)*. Colleció Instrumenta 7. Barcelona: Universitat de Barcelona Publicacions.

Reynolds, P. 1995. *Trade in the Western Mediterranean, A.D. 400–700: The Ceramic Evidence*. BAR-IS 604. Oxford: Tempus Reparatum.

———. 1999. "Pottery Production and Economic Exchange in 2nd Century Berytus: Some Preliminary Observations of Ceramic Trends from Quantified Ceramic Deposits from the Anglo-Lebanese Excavations in Beirut." *Berytus* 43:35–110.

———. 2000a. "The Beirut Amphora Type, First Century B.C.–Seventh Century A.D.: An Outline of Its Formal Development and Some Preliminary Observations of Regional Economic Trends." *Rei Cretariae Romanae Fautorum Acta*: 387–95.

———. 2000b. "Baetican, Lusitanian and Tarraconensian Amphorae in Classical Beirut: Some Preliminary Observations of Trends in Amphora Imports from the Western Mediterranean in the Anglo-Lebanese Excavations in Beirut (BEY 006, 007 and 045)." In *Congreso Internacional "Ex Baetica Amphorae," Universidad de Sevilla, 17–20 December 1998*, edited by G. Chic Garcia, 1035–60. Écija: Editorial Gráficas.

———. 2002. "The Pottery." In "Roman and Late-Antique Butrint: Excavations and Survey 2000–2001," edited by W. Bowden, R. Hodges, and K. Lako. *JRA* 15:221–9.

———. 2003a. "Amphorae in Roman Lebanon: 50 B.C. to A.D. 250." *Archaeology and History in Lebanon* 17:120–30.

———. 2003b. "Lebanon." In "De Rome à Byzance; de Fostat à Cordoue: Evolution des faciès céramiques en Mediterranée, Ve–IXe siècles." *VIIeme Congrès International sur la céramique Médiévale en Méditerranée Thessaloniki, 11–16 October 1999*, edited by C. Bakirtzes, 536–46. Athens: Caisse des Recettes Archéologiques.

———. 2004a. "The Pottery." In "Two Rock-cut Roman Tombs in Chhîm," edited by R. Ortali and B. Stuart. *Bulletin d'Archéologie et d'Architecture Libanaises* 6:107–34.

———. 2004b. "Italian Fine Wares in First Century AD Beirut: The Assemblage from the Cistern Deposit BEY 006 12300/12237." In *Early Italian Sigillata: The Chronological Framework and Trade Patterns, Proceedings of the First International ROCT Conference, Leuven May 7–8, 1999*, edited by J. Poblome, P. Talloen, R. Brulet, and M. Waelkens, 117–32. BABesch Suppl. 10. Leuven: Peeters.

———. 2005a. "Levantine Amphorae from Cilicia to Gaza: A Typology and Analysis of Regional Production Trends from the 2nd to 6th Centuries." In *LRCWI: Late Roman Coarse Wares, Cooking Wares and Amphorae in the Mediterranean: Archaeology and Archaeometry (Conference papers, held at Barcelona, 14-16th March 2002)*, edited by J.M. Gurt, J. Buxeda, and M.A. Cau. BAR-IS 1340. Oxford: Archaeopress.

———. 2005b. "Hispania in the Late Roman Mediterranean: Ceramics and Trade." In *Hispania in Late Antiquity: Twenty-first Century Approaches*, edited by K. Bowes and M. Kulikowski, 369–486. Leiden: Brill.

———. Forthcoming. "A Late Fatimid, Early Zirid Pottery Assemblage." In "Excavations at Bir Ftouha, Carthage," edited by Rossiter, J., et al. *Karthago*.

Robinson, H.S. 1959. *The Athenian Agora, V: Pottery of the Roman Period*. Princeton: American School of Classical Studies at Athens.

Saguì, L., R. Ricci, and D. Romei. 1997. "Nuovi dati ceramologici per la storia economica di Roma tra VII e VIII secolo." In *La céramique médiévale en Méditerranée: Actes du 6e congrès de l'AIECM2, Aix-en-Provence (13–18 novembre 1995)*, edited by G. Démians d'Archimbaud, 35–48. Aix-en-Provence: Narration.

Šelov, D.B. 1986. "Les amphores d'argile claire des premiers siecles de notre ere en mer Noire." In *Recherches sur les amphores Grecques*, edited by J.Y. Empereur and Y. Garlan, 395–400. *BCH* Suppl. 13. Paris: Diffusion de Boccard.

Singer-Avitz, L. 1987. "Local Pottery of the Persian Period (Strata XI–VI)." In *Excavations at Tel Michal, Israel*, edited by Z. Herzog, G. Rapp, and O. Negbi, 115–44. Tel Aviv: Publications of the (Sonia and Marco Nadler) Institute of Archaeology.

Toll, N.P. 1946. *The Excavations at Dura-Europos*. Pt. 2, *The Necropolis*. New Haven: Yale University Press.

Uscatescu, A. 2003. "Report on the Levant Pottery (5th–9th Century A.D.)." In "De Rome à Byzance; de Fostat à Cordoue: Evolution des faciès céramiques en Mediterranée, Ve–IXe siècles." *VIIeme Congrès International sur la céramique Médiévale en Méditerranée Thessaloniki, 11–16th October 1999*, edited by C. Bakirtzes, 546–58. Athens: Caisse des Recettes Archéologiques.

Whitcomb, D. 2001. "Ceramic Production at Aqaba in the Early Islamic Period." In *La céramique Byzantine et proto-islamique en Syrie-Jordanie (IVe–VIIIe siècles apr. J.-C.). Actes du colloque tenu à Amman les 3, 4 et 5 décembre 1994*, edited by E. Villeneuve and P.M. Watson, 297–303. BAHBeyrouth 159. Beirut: Institut français d'archéologie du Proche-Orient.

Williams, D.F. 2005. "Fabric Characterisation of Late Roman Amphorae from the Eastern Mediterranean." In *LRCWI: Late Roman Coarse Wares, Cooking Wares and Amphorae in the Mediterranean: Archaeology and Archaeometry (Conference papers, held at Barcelona, 14–16 March 2002)*, edited by J.M. Gurt, J. Buxeda, and M.A. Cau. BAR-IS 1340. Oxford: Archaeopress.

· CHAPTER FOUR ·

Petrographic Analysis of Transport Amphorae

Chris Doherty

INTRODUCTION

Reported here are the findings of a thin-section study of 56 coarse wares from the rescue excavations at Zeugma.[1] The main aim of this petrographic study is to characterize the sherds and determine the consistency of fabric groups based on field observations made by the Paul Reynolds, and to respond to specific questions asked of the samples by Paul Reynolds. In addition, this analysis will show whether single or multiple clay sources were used, as well as the degree to which raw materials were modified by the potters. Anomalous fabrics (those that appear at odds with the nature of locally available clay) are further considered to attempt to determine their possible provenance. Table 1 lists the sample details. For background information on the samples discussed, the reader is advised to see the chapter "Petrographic Analysis of Table and Kitchen Wares" in this volume, following the chapter by Philip Kenrick, "Pottery Other Than Transport Amphorae."

Lab ref.	Sample ref.	Amphora catalogue	Fabric group	Form
ZG28	2010.7	AM93	Fabric 1	Form 12E
ZG29	2012.2	AM125	Fabric 1	Form 12B
ZG30	2012.2	AM125	Fabric 1	Form 12B
ZG31	2012.3	AM126	Fabric 1	Form 12B
ZG32	2039.8	–	Fabric 1	Jar as PT387
ZG33	2039.16	AM155	Fabric 1-related	Form 3D
ZG34	2011.2	AM115	Fabric 1-related	Handle
ZG35	2012.11	AM123	Fabric 1-related	Form 9
ZG36	2012.13	AM118	Fabric 1-related	Form 3F
ZG37	2012.14	AM120	Fabric 1-related	Form 3G
ZG38	2012.20	AM133	Coarse Fabric 1	Base 1G
ZG39	2039.11	AM164	Coarse Fabric 1	Form 13A variant
ZG40	7003.4	–	Coarse Fabric 1	Combed wavy band on shoulder of jug / flagon
ZG41	2039.25	AM171	Fabric 2	Base 1G variant
ZG42	2260.1	AM219	Fabric 2	Form 3F
ZG43	2080.16	AM183	Fabric 2	Form 3F
ZG44	2086.1	AM202	Fabric 2	Form 13D
ZG45	2039.20	AM158	PR Fabric 8	Form 10
ZG46	2039.21	AM161	PR Fabric 8	Form 11A
ZG47	2080.12	AM186	PR Fabric 8	Form 11B
ZG48	2080.13	AM187	PR Fabric 8	Form 11
ZG49	2080.14	AM185	PR Fabric 8	Form 11A
ZG50	7062.4	–	PR Fabric 8	Painted jug wall
ZG51	2010.6	AM110	Fabric 13	Form 14A
ZG52	2080.4	AM194	Fabric 13	Form 14B
ZG53	2154.1	–	Fabric 13	Mortarium
ZG54	5034.1	AM264	Fabric 13	Form 17A?
ZG55	7026.1	AM295	Fabric 13	Small 17A variant
ZG56	7036.1	AM296 / 303	Fabric 13	Base 8A / AM17?
ZG57	12012.59	–	Fabric 13	Impressed decoration jug
ZG58	7006.14	AM287	Local / regional	Base 3
ZG59	7007.2	AM77	Coarse Fabric 1	Form 2A
ZG60	15095.4	AM25	Fabric 1?	Form 1A

Table 1. Zeugma amphorae and related coarse-ware sherds submitted for fabric analysis (continued on following page).

Lab ref.	Sample ref.	Amphora catalogue	Fabric group	Form
ZG61	15095.9	AM29	Fabric 1?	Form 3B
ZG62	15095.11	AM46	Fabric 1?	Form 7A
ZG63	2278.1	AM223	Gallic?	Gallic amphora?
ZG64	2158.1	AM217	Koan	Dressel 2-4
ZG65	2011.1	AM116	Guadalquivir?	Dressel 2-4
ZG66	7007.1	AM88	South Spanish?	Base 5
ZG68	Tile fragments	AM455	–	Base 10 / spatheion
ZG69	12011.44	–	–	–
ZG70	2012.17	AM143	LRA 1D	LRA 1
ZG71	7006.13	AM292	LRA 1A	Ceramic disc cut from LRA 1
ZG72	7060.8	AM327	LRA 1A (sample 1)	LRA 1
ZG73	7060.8	AM327	LRA 1A (sample 2)	LRA 1
ZG74	7060.9	AM328	LRA 1B	LRA 1
ZG75	12002.13	AM374	LRA 1	LRA 1
ZG76	12011.24	AM463	LRA 1E	LRA 1
ZG77	12011.25	AM464	LRA 1F	LRA 1
ZG78	12011.26	AM465	LRA 1G	LRA 1
ZG79	12011.41	AM480	LRA 1	LRA 1
ZG80	12011.52	AM462	LRA 1	LRA 1
ZG81	12012.9	AM549	LRA 1	LRA 1
ZG82	12012.10	AM550	LRA 1	Ceramic disc cut from LRA 1
ZG83	12012.12	AM551	LRA 1	LRA 1
ZG27	Euphrates sand	–	Reference only	–

Table 1. Zeugma amphorae and related coarse-ware sherds submitted for fabric analysis (continued).

RESULTS

This program of petrographic analysis addresses several queries relating to fabric groups for Zeugma amphorae, these groups having been established in the field by the pottery specialist. Accordingly, the findings of this analysis are presented here as replies to those specific questions.

Fabric 1

This is a red-brown firing fabric that is sand-rich and has a large number of inclusion types. This indicates a derivation from a relatively complex geology and is entirely consistent with Zeugma.[2] Inclusions are moderately well sorted and angular to subangular (though softer lithologies are better rounded). These inclusions represent natural sand; none of the members of this fabric group is tempered. However, the two 2012.2 sherds (ZG29 and ZG30: **AM125**), although related to Fabric 1, should be considered a different fabric or subfabric. These have a relatively low inclusion concentration (<10%), which is also finer-grained.

Question: How consistent is Fabric 1? **Response:** A significant amount of variation exists in Fabric 1. Some of this may be explained by the use of clays at increasing distance from the main alluvial channel, where it would be expected that differing contents of sand, carbonate, organic matter, etc., would give rise to clays of subtly differing forming, drying, and firing properties. Two separate fabrics are proposed here:

- Type Fabric 1: comprising 2010.7 (**AM93**) and 2039.8 (jar, **PT387**)
- Fine Fabric 1: comprising 2012.2 (ZG29 and ZG30: **AM125**)

Sherd 2012.3 (**AM126**) is intermediate between these two, showing similarities with both although with closer affinities to the type Fabric 1.

Lab ref.	I.D.	Catalogue	Initial fabric group	Revised fabric group
ZG28	2010.7	AM93	Fabric 1	Fabric 1
ZG29	2012.2	AM125	Fabric 1	Fine Fabric 1
ZG30	2012.2	AM125	Fabric 1	Fine Fabric 1
ZG31	2012.3	AM126	Fabric 1	Fabric 1
ZG32	2039.8	As PT387	Fabric 1	Fabric 1

Table 2. Fabric 1 members.

Fabric 1–Related

These are similar to Fabric 1 in terms of their inclusion types, morphologies, frequencies, and the clay properties, minor differences being mainly gradational. The one exception here is 2012.11 (**AM123**).

Question: Is 2039.16 (**AM155**: Form 3D) a compact version of this fabric or something different? **Response:** This is very similar to the type Fabric 1, from which it differs only by having fewer inclusions (though of the same type) and a very fine clay matrix (with no conspicuous silt content or mica). This is a Fabric 1 variant or subfabric.

Question: Where do 2011.2 (**AM115**), 2012.11 (**AM123**), 2012.13 (**AM118**), and 2012.14 (**AM120**) fit in? **Response:** 2011.2 (ZG34: **AM115**) is the same as Fine Fabric 1. 2012.13 (ZG36: **AM118**) is a high-fired fabric as indicated by the complete composition of primary carbonate grains, but otherwise it remains essentially Fabric 1. Sherd 2012.14 (ZG37: **AM120**) is also Fabric 1 (coarse) but shows a relatively narrow range of inclusion sizes and a paucity of very fine-grained material (silt). In the latter respect it is very similar to 2039.16 (ZG33, **AM155**: Form 3D).

Question: Is 2012.11 (ZG35: **AM123**) (Form 9) a separate fabric? **Response:** Yes, this is a new fabric and is characterized by a very calcareous matrix, very few siliclastics (i.e., "quartz sand"), being dominated by carbonate inclusions and a significant proportion of highly weathered basic/ultrabasic material (i.e., gabbro and basalt, including serpentine). The carbonate grains typically show a very irregular morphology and are fine-grained (micritic) but occasionally with coarser calcite (polyphase microsparite) developed in cavities. These features identify this material as a mixture of mainly soil carbonate (caliche) and lesser inclusions derived from outcrops of micritic limestone. Significantly the calcareous matrix does not contain microfossils (foraminifera). This fabric is made of clay that is clearly distant from a major river channel (i.e., the Euphrates) as it lacks a quartz-dominated sand. It is unlikely that this is simply edge-of-Euphrates-floodplain material as this would account for the calcareous matrix but not the inclusions, which are significantly different from those represented by the Birecik sand.[3] It is more likely that this clay is from a wadi eroding a limestone formation with basic and (lesser) intermediate igneous intrusions in the immediate catchment.

Question: Is 2012.2 (**AM125**) close to the Syrian group (i.e., Fabrics 13 and amphora Fabric 8)? **Response:** This is different from Syrian amphora Fabric 8 but shows a few similarities with Syrian Fabric 13, notably the very carbonate-rich matrix. For example, there are general matrix similarities with 2080.4 (**AM194**) and 5034.1 (**AM264**), although the inclusion types are different. Despite this, it is concluded that 2012.11 (**AM123**) is not of the Syrian group because it differs in one fundamental way. In addition to being highly calcareous (particularly Fabric 13) the Syrian fabrics also contain abundant microfossils (Foraminifera). Their presence indicates the use of a marine or brackish water clay and not a freshwater clay associated with a large river system such as the Euphrates. Although Fabric 1 and other local fabrics do contain very occasional Foraminifera, these can be shown to have been derived from the reworking or Quaternary or Tertiary marls and limestones, as evidenced by the typical recrystalization the microfossil cavities.

A much better match is seen between 2012.11 (**AM123**) and Coarse Fabric 1, 7003.4 (not catalogued: shoulder with combed wavy lines, probably a flagon, not amphora).

Lab ref.	I.D.	Catalogue	Initial fabric group	Revised fabric group
ZG33	2039.16	**AM155**	Fabric 1-related	Coarse Fabric 1
ZG34	2011.2	**AM115**	Fabric 1-related	Fine Fabric 1
ZG35	2012.11	**AM123**	Fabric 1-related	New fabric
ZG36	2012.13	**AM118**	Fabric 1-related	Coarse Fabric 1
ZG37	2012.14	**AM120**	Fabric 1-related	Coarse Fabric 1

Table 3. Fabric 1–Related members.

Coarse Fabric

This fabric comprises three members, although even to the naked eye these three immediately show some obvious differences:

- 2012.20, **AM133**, the finest member; essentially the same as Fabric 1.
- 2039.11, **AM164**, coarser than 2012.20 (**AM133**), but again essentially type 1; contains garnet (single observation).
- 7003.4, not catalogued (combed wavy band); With a relatively high content of serpentinite/altered basalt this sherd is more similar to 2012.11 (**AM123**) and should be considered a different fabric.

It is suggested that this coarse fabric be discontinued, as 2012.20 (**AM133**) is no more coarse than Fabric 1, and 7003.4 is compositionally distinct, leaving 2039.11 (**AM164**) as the only member.

Lab ref.	I.D.	Catalogue	Initial fabric group	Revised fabric group
ZG38	2012.20	**AM133**	Coarse Fabric	Fine Fabric 1
ZG39	2039.11	**AM164**	Coarse Fabric	Coarse Fabric 1
ZG40	7003.4	Not catalogued: combed wavy band	Coarse Fabric	New Fabric: same as ZG35

Table 4. Coarse fabric members.

Fabric 2

Question: How uniform is Fabric 2? **Response:** The visual (textural) similarity evident to the naked eye is not maintained at thin-section level. Instead this fabric group exhibits a fair amount of compositional variation.

Question: Fabric 2 is considered to be the same as Fabric 1 but with more lime. Is this correct? **Response:** This presumably refers to lime inclusions rather than fine-grained lime in the clay body. An increase of the latter would result in a paler fired color whereas Fabric 2 members fire to the same reddish-orange color as Fabric 1.

In fact only two members of this fabric (2039.25 / **AM171** and 2080.16 / **AM183**) have more lime inclusions, the other two (2260.1 / **AM219** and 2086.1 / **AM202**) being essentially the same as Fabric 1.

However, there is a significant difference between these two lime-rich fabrics. Sherd 2039.25 (**AM171**) could be taken as the type Fabric 2 example, although there still is not a great difference from Fabric 1. Sherd 2080.16 (**AM183**) is significantly different, being both much more carbonate rich, and having dacite, psammite, and schistose material as the main inclusion types.

Question: Does local amphora 2086.1 (**AM202**: Form 13D) belong, or is it Fabric 1? **Response:** AM202 is Fabric 1.

Lab ref.	I.D.	Catalogue	Initial fabric group	Revised fabric group
ZG41	2039.25	AM171	Fabric 2	Fabric 2: abundant carbonate
ZG42	2260.1	AM219	Fabric 2	Fabric 1
ZG43	2080.16	AM183	Fabric 2	Separate fabric: dacite and schist with abundant carbonate
ZG44	2086.1	AM202	Fabric 2	Fabric 1

Table 5. Fabric 2 members.

Amphora Fabric 8

This is considered to be a separate, very coarse painted group, differing from the Fabric 13 Syrian group, although similarly based on a Foraminera-bearing calcareous clay. The clay matrix of Fabric 8 is more iron-rich than Fabric 13, typically developing a pale orange color on firing in contrast to the greenish hue of the latter. The inclusions also differ from Fabric 13, notably having more iron-rich material (weathered basalt), and minor amounts of arkose and tuff.

Question: Is it very coarse? **Response:** No, unless coarse is used to describe the ferruginous inclusions (above). 2039.21 (**AM161**) and 2080.13 (**AM187**) have conspicuous ferruginous material, seen to a lesser extent in 7062.4 (painted-jug fragment). 2080.14 (**AM185**) is a reduced piece with a lower overall siliclastic component and correspondingly a noticeable development of subparallel shrinkage voids.

Question: 2039.20 / **AM158** is the type piece — how similar are the other proposed members? **Response:** The others are essentially the same except for 2039.21 (**AM161**) and 7062.4 (painted-jug fragment). 2039.21 (**AM161**) should be considered as a subfabric, being similar to the type Fabric 8 except in having rounded lateritic grains. 7062.4 also has rounded lateritic grains, but here the calcareous matrix lacks foraminifera and has abundant schistose / tectonized inclusions. Fabric 8 members and 7062.4 (painted jug) are sufficiently different to be considered different fabrics, but are related through subfabric 2039.21 (**AM161**):

- 2039.20, **AM158**, standard Fabric 8 — limestone-rich matrix with chert / quartzite / basalt sand.
- 2039.21, **AM161**, different fabric: has rounded ferruginous / lateritic clast (absent from 2039.20 / **AM158**).
- 2080.12, **AM186**, standard Fabric 8 — same as 2039.20 (**AM158**).
- 2080.13, **AM187**, similar to 2039.21 / **AM161** but has less fines in matrix.
- 2080.14, **AM185**, Fabric 8, as 2039 and 2080.12.
- 7062.4, painted-jug fragment, distinct fabric, characterized by rounded ferruginous / lateritic grains, a high proportion of tectonized material, and a very calcareous matrix.

Lab ref.	I.D.	Catalogue	Initial fabric group	Revised fabric group
ZG45	2039.20	AM158	PR Fabric 8	Fabric 8
ZG46	2039.21	AM161	PR Fabric 8	Fabric 8: lateritic subfabric
ZG47	2080.12	AM186	PR Fabric 8	Fabric 8
ZG48	2080.13	AM187	PR Fabric 8	Fabric 8
ZG49	2080.14	AM185	PR Fabric 8	Fabric 8
ZG50	7062.4	Painted jug fragment	PR Fabric 8	Separate fabric: tectonized

Table 6. Amphora Fabric 8 members.

Fabric 13: Syrian Painted

The immediate visual impression is that these members do belong to the same fabric group. There is a general consistency of color (allowing for differences expected from different firings), the grain size is reasonably uniform, and all members are flecked through with reddish inclusions that represent the iron-rich alteration products of basic igneous rocks.

This fabric group is easily distinguished from local Zeugma fabrics by having a highly calcareous matrix, rich in foraminifera. There are also significant differences in inclusion types. Fabric 13 has a notable paucity or absence of granite, trachytic basalt, and serpentine compared with the local Zeugma fabrics.

Question: How consistent is the group? **Response:** The table shows that that all but two are considered to be of the same Fabric (13). Of the outsiders, 7026.1 (**AM295**) has a very high carbonate content (matrix) and a low siliclastic content. The latter includes schistose / tectonized material. 7036.1 (**AM296 / 303**) has abundant granodiorite and a very high concentration of carbonates.

Question: Is 2080.4 (**AM194**) a coarse version of this fabric? **Response:** No, although lateritic material (derived from basalt weathering) is more conspicuous in this fabric. The impressed-decoration jug 12012.59 (as **PT491**) is confirmed as belonging to Fabric 13.

Lab ref.	I.D.	Catalogue	Initial fabric group	Revised Fabric group	Form
ZG51	2010.6	AM110	Fabric 13	Fabric 13	Form 14
ZG52	2080.4	AM194	Fabric 13	Fabric 13	–
ZG53	2154.1	–	Fabric 13	Fabric 13: coarser variety	Mortarium
ZG54	5034.1	AM264	Fabric 13	Fabric 13	–
ZG55	7026.1	AM295	Fabric 13	Separate fabric: schistose	–
ZG56	7036.1	AM296/AM303	Fabric 13	Separate fabric: granodioritic	–
ZG57	12012.59	–	Fabric 13	Fabric 13	Small jug with impressed decoration, as PT491

Table 7. Fabric 13 members (amphorae and other forms).

Following the initial study of all amphora fabrics presented in this report, I made a reassessment of Fabric 13 amphorae and plain wares (e.g., mortars) based on a larger number of samples. These included a greater cross section of the range of Syrian painted-amphora variants. The aim was to establish whether it was possible to distinguish fabric subgroups and associated typological variants within the data set and hence identify distinct production centers or workshops within the Syrian plain and amphora series.

The sample chosen for analysis comprised the following:

Sample	Context	Catalogue	Form
Amphorae			
ZG51	2010.6	AM110	Large Form 14A
–	7060.2	AM300	Large Form 14A
ZG52	2080.4	AM194	Large Form 14B
–	7003.2	AM266	Large Form 14B
–	7026.2	AM294	Small Form 15A
–	7064.1	AM338	Large Form 15A
–	7306.1	AM254	Large/Medium Form 15B
–	12011.59	AM389	Large Form 15C
–	12012.20	AM503	Large Form 15C
–	12012.19	AM504	Large Form 15C (or Form 17A)
–	7006.7	AM282	Large Form 16A
–	7004.1	AM270	Large Form 16A
–	12011.55	AM390	Large Form 16B
–	7003.1/7004.2	AM271	Small Form 17D
–	7065.4	AM346	Small Form 17F
ZG55	7026.1	AM295	Small Form 17A variant

Sample	Context	Catalogue	Form
Amphorae			
ZG54	5034.1	AM264	Large Form 17A?/Base 8A
ZG56	7036.1/7065.15	AM296/303	Large Form 17A/Base 8A
–	7060.3	AM304	Large Form 17A? (shoulder)
–	12012.32	AM529	Small Form 19
–	12011.77	AM422	Small Form 19
–	7005.1	AM278	Small Form 19 or small Form 17A
Plain forms			
–	7060.38	–	Jug
ZG53	–	–	Mortarium
ZG57	12012.59	–	Jug with impressed decoration as PT491

Table 8. Samples used for reassessment of Fabric 13 amphorae and plain wares.

Fabric 13 is a relatively uniform fabric group in which apparent differences are mainly due to slight variations in inclusion proportions, with textures also modified in some cases by high firing (e.g., color development, loss of carbonate inclusions, "granularity," etc.) There is no systematic correlation between fabric elements and amphora subgroups.

Main Points

1) Overall this fabric group does exhibit some variation, but with one or two exceptions, there are few fundamental differences in composition. What we see are varying proportions of a relatively consistent suite of rock and mineral inclusions, combined with gradations in mean inclusion size.

2) Given the above, there are no criteria that can be used to further subdivide Fabric 13 into subfabrics, again with a few exceptions. Most fabrics share a large proportion of a common set of inclusion types, i.e.: chert, monocrystalline quartz, polycrystalline quartz (mosaic), polycrystalline quartz (preferred orientation), vein quartz, quartz-epidote, orthoclase, plagioclase, granite, granodiorite, myrmekite, rhyolite, dacite, andesite, acid igneous groundmass, trachyte: (undifferentiated) basalt, (undifferentiated) basaltic glass, olivine basalt, weathered basalt, ferruginous alteration (basalt-derived laterite), volcanic ash, clinopyroxene, serpentine, hornblende, colorless magnesian amphibole, fibrous brown amphibole, muscovite biotite, biotite/muscovite schist sandstone, and chlorite (phyllite).

It is possible to indicate those fabrics in which, say, basalt or acid igneous inclusions predominate but in practice it is very unreliable to further subdivide in this way. Overall the similarity in inclusion types indicate that most of the Fabric 13 members are made from clay from the same alluvial system, and are entirely consistent with a Euphrates provenance or from neighboring drainage.

Variations in grain size and inclusion: Clay ratios are again conspicuous but do not provide a workable basis on which to construct subfabrics. It must be remembered that such differences, although conspicuous, can merely reflect natural variation occurring within the clay deposit over short stratigraphic and lateral distances. This is particularly the case in an alluvial system such as the Euphrates, which floods seasonally, and whose successive terraces will vary compositionally and texturally. Different production centers are not suggested by the variation of inclusion sizes and proportions seen in the majority of Fabric 13 members.

3) The second defining characteristic of this fabric is the calcareous nature. This has two components, the calcareous clay matrix and discrete inclusions. Both components have the same source, namely the Tertiary limestone formations which outcrop extensively in northern Syria and locally in southern Turkey (including in the immediate hinterland of Zeugma).

Fabric 13 sherds therefore have a suite of noncalcareous inclusions derived from the erosion of mainly igneous and metamorphic rocks by Turkey headwaters, and a calcareous matrix and inclusion set derived from erosion on the limestone formations in the middle course of the Euphrates and tributaries. As expected, the limestone component increases south of Zeugma where Tertiary limestones outcrop extensively. By contrast, the local Zeugma fabrics have a much lower carbonate content (both as inclusions and fine-grained matrix) as indicated by their overall more reddish color when fully oxidized.

The proportion and grain size of the calcareous inclusion in Fabric 13 are seen to vary significantly, but again differences are gradational. These inclusions are mainly of fine-grained limestone (micrite) and microfossils (foraminifera) but there is also some soil carbonate (caliche). Where inclusions are very abundant the fabric has what has been described as a granular appearance. Where these carbonate inclusions are smaller, less abundant, or, importantly, have been largely lost through firing, the matrix appears to be made from a more plastic clay.

4) Despite this relative uniformity of the Fabric 13 sherds, there a small number that show sufficient differences to perhaps warrant subfabric status. These are:

- 7003.2 / **AM266** (Large Form 14B) and 7060.3 / **AM304** (Large Form 17A?): These both lack the typical high concentration of limestone inclusion and/or calcareous matrix of typical Fabric 13 sherds. Of the two, 7003.2 / **AM266** is more calcareous, but here limestone inclusions are sparse and there are very few foraminifera. 7060.3 / **AM304** has a much lower carbonate content, as indicated by the reddish fired color. Both sherds are further distinguished by having a high concentration of very fine silt and by containing volcanic ash (and having a correspondingly high frequency of acid/intermediate igneous inclusions). Overall these features suggest a more northerly origin than for typical Fabric 13 sherds.

- 7060.38 (not Fabric 13?): Again lacking the distinctive carbonate signature of Fabric 13. This could be related to the above subfabric but lacks conspicuous volcanic ash. Again a source north of Syria is suggested.

5) Given the continuous variation in Fabric 13, it is not possible to uniquely match either Fabric 6 or the Fabric 8 fine-ware example with any specific Fabric 13 amphora subgroup. The best matches appear to be Fabric 6 with 12012.19 / **AM504** (Form 15C or Form 17A) and Fabric 8 with 7065.4 / **AM346** (Small Form 17F).

Early Roman

Question: How consistent is this group? **Response:** All members reflect the local Euphrates sediment characteristics, i.e., moderately lime-rich clays that lack foraminifera (except derived material). The inclusions show good agreement with those in the reference sand sampled at Birecik. Differences exist but are gradational, being mainly variations in the proportions and sizes of a consistent set of inclusions.

Petrographic analysis suggests three separate fabrics/subfabrics.

7006.14	**AM287**	Characterized by very abundant fine sand: micaceous
7007.2	**AM77**	A different fabric from 7006.14 (**AM287**). Fine sand is absent, clasts are few and typically much larger. Grain types are essentially the same as for 7006.14 (**AM287**) but mica is rare
15095.4	**AM25**	Same fabric as 7007.2 (**AM77**), slightly more chert
15095.9	**AM29**	Similar to 7007.2 (**AM77**) and 15095.4 (**AM25**) but with lower total inclusion content
15095.11	**AM46**	Similar to 15095.4 (**AM25**), 15095.9 (**AM29**), and 15095.11 (**AM46**) but higher fired: slightly more fine sand

Question: Are any related to Fabric 1? **Response:** Yes (see table 9).

Question: Are any related to Syrian fabrics? **Response:** No, these are all local fabrics.

Lab ref.	I.D.	Catalogue	Initial fabric group	Revised fabric group
ZG58	7006.14	**AM287**	Early Roman: local/regional	Micaceous
ZG59	7007.2	**AM77**	Early Roman: Coarse Fabric 1	As Fabric 1
ZG60	15095.4	**AM25**	Early Roman: local/regional	As Fabric 1
ZG61	15095.9	**AM29**	Early Roman: local/regional	As Fine Fabric 1
ZG62	15095.11	**AM46**	Early Roman: local/regional	As Fine Fabric 1

Table 9. Early Roman fabrics.

Long-Distance Imports

These represent a range of proposed long-distance imports at Zeugma that have been tentatively identified by the pottery specialist. A comparison is made here with the corresponding published descriptions (Peacock and Williams 1986) in order to verify provenance by direct fabric analysis.

Lab ref.	I.D.	Catalogue	Initial fabric group	Revised fabric group
ZG63	2278.1	AM223	Gallic amphora?	Yes: similar to Class 27 fabric
ZG64	2158.1	AM217	Dressel 2-4	Possible: similar to Class 3/10 Campanian fabric
ZG65	2011.1	AM116	Dressel 2-4 Guadalquivir?	Yes: good match with Class25/Dressel 20
ZG66	7007.1	AM88	Spanish amphora base?	Matches local Euphrates clay
ZG68	–	–	Tile fragments	Matches local Euphrates clay
ZG69	12011.44	AM455	Hollow spatheion base	Not matched: some similarities to Euphrates clay

Table 10. Long-distance imports.

Question: 2278.1 (ZG63: AM223) Is this a Gallic amphora? **Response:** A very micaceous silty fabric with a low lime content. Inclusions are natural and fine grained (mean 0.1 mm) and include clinopyroxene, monocrystalline quartz, sheared quartz-mica composite grains ("schist"), micrite, muscovite, psammite, soil carbonate (abundant), and vein quartz (often iron-stained). Basic igneous material is absent. Micas commonly show micro-kinking, confirming their metamorphic origin. This is similar to the micaceous fabric described for Class 27 (inc. Pelichet 47, Gauloise 4) although it is not clear from the published description how much metamorphic material this type fabric permits.

2158.1 (ZG64: AM217)
Dressel 2-4 handle

A red-firing fabric with a low lime content. Inclusions are natural (i.e., not temper), and have a mean grain size of 0.3 mm. These include aegerine-augite (single), chert, augite, plagioclase, polycrystalline quartz, potassium feldspar, and soil/secondary carbonate. This fabric is clearly derived from a basic igneous rock (basalt-trachyte) and appears similar to the published Class 3/10 Campanian fabric or equivalent.

2011.1 (ZG65: AM116)
Dressel 2-4 coarse fabric: Guadalquivir?

A noncalcareous fabric derived from an acid to intermediate igneous parent. Inclusions are coarse (mean 1 mm), are well rounded, and represent added temper. These are mainly quartz, orthoclase, rhyolitic groundmass, microgranite, and quartz-hornblende composites (granodiorite). Limestone and basic igneous lithologies are absent (rare augite), and metamorphics are represented by rare psammites and quartz-mica selvages. This fabric does show much similarity with the Guadalquivir fabric published for Class 25/Dressel 20, although the latter is very general.

7007.1 (ZG66: AM88)
Spanish amphora base?

A red-buff firing fabric with a wide range of abundant inclusions. These are natural, have a mean grain size of 0.5 mm, and include basalt, biosparite, clinopyroxene (augite), epidote, ferruginous alteration (basalt-derived), monocrystalline quartz, muscovite, plagioclase, polycrystalline quartz, serpentine, sheared quartz-mica selvages, surface/soil carbonate, trachytic basalt, and vein quartz. It is not possible to match this with a published Spanish fabric, but this mineral assemblage is essentially that shown by the local Fabric 1.

ZG68 Tile fragments

A calcareous fabric tempered with medium sand (mean 0.5 mm) comprising basalt, chert, clinopyroxene, dacite, foraminera, granite, granodiorite, micrite, monocrystalline quartz, plagioclase, rhyolite, serpentine (trace), trachytic basalt, and vein quartz. These inclusions are those found in the Euphrates sediment at Zeugma.

12011.44/AM455 (ZG69)
Hollow spatheion base

A buff-red firing fabric with a relatively high concentration of ferromagnesian minerals and carbonates. This is a high-fired fabric in which primary carbonate grains have undergone thermal decomposition. Inclusions have a mean grain size of 0.4 mm and include basalt, chert, colorless amphibole, clinopyroxene, foraminera, granite, granodiorite, hornblende, micrite, orthoclase, polycrystalline quartz, serpentine, sheared quartz, and vein quartz. Again there is much overlap here with the Euphrates inclusions, although the amount of basic igneous material is low.

LRA 1 Fabrics

Fourteen undifferentiated LRA 1 fabrics were analyzed. These are described in the following section and suggestions of possible groupings are made.

Lab ref.	I.D.	Catalogue	Fabric group
ZG70	2012.17	AM143	LRA 1
ZG71	7006.13	AM292	LRA 1
ZG72	7060.8	AM327	LRA 1
ZG73	7060.8	AM327	LRA 1
ZG74	7060.9	AM328	LRA 1
ZG75	12002.13	AM374	LRA 1
ZG76	12011.24	AM463	LRA 1
ZG77	12011.25	AM464	LRA 1
ZG78	12011.26	AM465	LRA 1
ZG79	12011.41	AM480	LRA 1
ZG80	12011.52	AM462	LRA 1
ZG81	12012.9	AM549	LRA 1
ZG82	12012.10	AM550	LRA 1
ZG83	12012.12	AM551	LRA 1

Table 11. LRA 1 fabrics.

2012.17 / AM143: A calcareous pale-green (high-fired) fabric that has lost much of its primary carbonate. Inclusions (mean grain size = 0.3 mm) are abundant and are predominantly limestone but also include chert, clinopyroxene, hornblende, limestone, monocrystalline quartz, plagioclase, sheared quartz +/ selvages, vein quartz.

7006.13 / AM292: Buff-red fired fabric characterized by a very high silt content. Inclusions (mean grain size = 0.4 mm) comprise biosparite, chert, colorless (Mg) amphibole, clinopyroxene, ferruginous alteration, micrite, plagioclase, serpentine, sheared quartz +/ selvages, and soil / secondary carbonate. All carbonate appears micritic due to thermal decomposition.

7060.8 / AM327: Buff-firing calcareous fabric with a relatively high fine sand content. Inclusions (mean grain size = 0.4 mm) are predominantly limestone (thermally decomposed) including foraminifera, basalt, chert, colorless amphibole, clinopyroxene, ferruginous alteration, hornblende (rare), monocrystalline quartz, and orthoclase.

7060.8 / AM327: Buff-firing calcareous fabric with biosparite limestone fragments, basalt (rare), chert, chromite (rare), colorless amphibole, clinopyroxene (rare), granodiorite, hornblende, monocrystalline quartz, orthoclase, and soil carbonate. The mean grain size is 0.3 mm.

7060.9 / AM328: Buff-orange fabric with a low inclusion content without conspicuous carbonate. Basalt-derived grains dominate, the full assemblage comprising basalt (>90%), chert (rare), clinopyroxene, ferruginous alteration, monocrystalline quartz (rare), plagioclase, serpentine (rare). The mean grain size is 0.5 mm.

12002.13 / AM374: A high-fired greenish calcareous fabric. Inclusions (mean 0.3 mm) are dominated by carbonate (now thermally decomposed) with basalt, chert (rare), colorless amphibole, clinopyroxene, ferruginous alteration, hornblende, monocrystalline quartz, orthoclase, plagioclase, polycrystalline quartz, serpentine (after clinopyroxene), surface carbonate, vein quartz.

12011.24 / AM463: An orange-red noncalcareous fabric dominated by basalt-derived inclusions (mean 0.5 mm). These comprise basalt (>95%), clinopyroxene, epidote, ferruginous alteration, granite (rare), monocrystalline quartz (rare), orthoclase (rare), plagioclase, serpentine (after clinopyroxene), and weathered basalt.

12011.25 / AM464: A red-orange fabric characterized by a high proportion of carbonate grains (mean 0.2 mm), most of which are thermally decomposed. Other inclusions are chert, colorless amphibole, clinopyroxene, monocrystalline quartz, plagioclase, and secondary / soil carbonate.

12011.26 / AM465: An orange fabric in which the apparent color density is diluted by a very high fine sand content. Inclusions (mean 0.5 mm) comprise andesite, chert, clinopyroxene, ferruginous alteration, granite, granodiorite, hornblende, micrite, monocrystalline quartz, orthoclase, plagioclase, soil carbonate, and weathered basalt.

12011.41 / AM480: Very similar to 12011.26 / AM465 but slightly coarser (mean 0.6m) and having a lower total inclusion content. Irregular pores are common, suggesting shrinkage of an overwet paste. These are now lined with secondary carbonate. Inclusions are biotite, chert, clinopyroxene, dacite, epidote, foraminifera, hornblende, micrite, plagioclase, polycrystalline quartz mosaic, rhyolite, sheared quartz +/ selvages, and weathered basalt.

12011.52 / AM462: A light orange high-fired fabric, again with color dilution due to a very high inclusion content. Inclusions (0.5 mm) comprise chert, chlorite, colorless amphibole, clinopyroxene, hornblende, micrite, monocrystalline quartz, orthoclase, serpentine, surface carbonate, vein quartz (iron-stained), and weathered basalt.

12012.9 / AM549: An orange-red fabric with a very high inclusion content and characterized by abundant biosparite limestone (with minimal thermal decomposition). Inclusions comprise clinopyroxene, epidote, ferruginous alteration, garnet, micrite, monocrystalline quartz, muscovite, orthoclase, plagioclase (zoned euhedra), and sheared quartz +/ selvages.

12012.10 / **AM550**: A pale green high-fired calcareous fabric showing extensive loss of primary carbonate due to firing. Inclusions (mean 0.5 mm) are not abundant and include basalt (rare), clinopyroxene (rare), dacite, granite (graphic variety, single observation), hornblende, micrite, orthoclase, plagioclase, polycrystalline quartz mosaic, and serpentine (rare).

12012.12 / **AM551**: A greenish-brown high-fired calcareous fabric with a high concentration of natural fine sand. Inclusions (mean 0.5 mm) include basalt (rare), chert, clinopyroxene, granite (graphic type, single observation), micrite, monocrystalline quartz, and sheared quartz +/ selvages.

Possible Groups

Ten of the fourteen LRA samples make up four fabric groups. These are:

1. 2012.17 (**AM143**) and 12002.13 (**AM374**)
2. 7060.9 (**AM328**) and 12011.24 (**AM463**)
3. 7006.13 (**AM292**) and 7060.8 (**AM327**, both samples)
4. 12011.25 (**AM464**), 12011.41 (**AM480**), and 12012.9 (**AM549**)

Fabric Summaries

2010.7 (ZG28: **AM93**)

Carbonates = 40% wt. Siliclastics = 60% wt. Calcareous matrix (Y/N) Y. Mean grain size = 0.25 mm. Inclusions matrix (high/medium/low) = H. Temper: no. Inclusions: basalt, biosparite, biotite, chert, clinopyroxene, diorite, epidote, ferruginous alteration, foraminifera, garnet, granite, hornblende, micrite, monocrystalline quartz, muscovite, orthoclase, plagioclase, serpentine, sheared quartz ± selvages, weathered basalt.

2012.2 (ZG29: **AM125**)

Carbonates = 20% wt. Siliclastics = 80% wt. Calcareous matrix (Y/N) N. Mean grain size = 0.2 mm. Inclusions matrix (high/medium/low) = L. Temper: no. Inclusions: basalt, chert, colorless amphibole, clinopyroxene, ferruginous alteration, foraminifera hornblende, micrite, monocrystalline quartz, orthoclase, plagioclase, serpentine (rare), trachyte (undifferentiated), weathered basalt.

2012.2 (ZG30: **AM125**)

Carbonates = 30% wt. Siliclastics = 70% wt. Calcareous matrix (Y/N) N. Mean grain size = 0.15 mm. Inclusions matrix (high/medium/low) = M. Temper" no. Inclusions chert, clinopyroxene, ferruginous alteration, hornblende, micrite, muscovite, plagioclase, serpentine (rare), trachyte (undifferentiated), weathered basalt.

2012.3 (ZG31: **AM126**)

Carbonates = 30% wt. Siliclastics = 70% wt. Calcareous matrix (Y/N) N. Mean grain size = 0.25 mm. Inclusions matrix (high/medium/low) = M. Temper: no. Inclusions: acid igneous groundmass, basalt, chert, clinopyroxene, epidote, granite, hornblende, micrite, monocrystalline quartz, muscovite, orthoclase, plagioclase, polycrystalline quartz, sheared quartz +/ selvages, trachyte (undifferentiated), serpentine (rare).

2039.9 (ZG32: jar, as **PT387**)

Carbonates = 40% wt. Siliclastics = 60% wt. Calcareous matrix (Y/N) N. Mean grain size = 0.25 mm. Inclusions matrix (high/medium/low) = H. Temper: no. Inclusions: acid igneous groundmass, basalt, biotite, chert, clinopyroxene, diorite, epidote, granite, hornblende, monocrystalline quartz, muscovite, plagioclase, sheared quartz +/-selvages, trachyte (undifferentiated).

2039.16 (ZG33: **AM155**)

Carbonates = 30% wt. Siliclastics = 70% wt. Calcareous matrix (Y/N) N. Mean grain size = 0.3 mm. Inclusions matrix (high/medium/low) = M. Temper: possible (bimodal). Inclusions: basalt, colorless amphibole, clinopyroxene, crystal tuff (single, rhyolitic), dacite, micrite, polycrystalline, serpentine (rare), sheared quartz ± selvages, trachyte (undifferentiated).

2011.2 (ZG34: **AM115**)

Carbonates = 40% wt. Siliclastics = 60% wt. Calcareous matrix (Y/N) N. Mean grain size = 0.15 mm. Inclusions matrix (high/medium/low) = M. Temper: no. Inclusions: andesite, chert, clinopyroxene, hornblende, monocrystalline quartz, muscovite, plagioclase, sandstone, serpentine (rare), volcanic ash.

2012.11 (ZG35: **AM123**)

Carbonates = 70% wt. Siliclastics = 30% wt. Calcareous matrix (Y/N) Y. Inclusions matrix (high/medium/low) = M. Temper: no. Inclusions: chert, clinopyroxene, epidote, ferruginous alteration, micrite, olivine basalt, plagioclase, serpentine (rare), soil carbonate.

2012.13 (ZG36: **AM118**)

Carbonates = 20% wt. Siliclastics = 80% wt. Calcareous matrix (Y/N) Y. Mean grain size = 0.25 mm: Inclusions matrix (high/medium/low) = H. Temper: no. Inclusions: acid igneous groundmass, chert, clinopyroxene, epidote, ferruginous alteration, granite, hornblende, micrite, monocrystalline quartz, polycrystalline quartz (equant), polycrystalline quartz (orientated), serpentine (rare), trachyte (undifferentiated), weathered basalt.

2012.14 (ZG37: **AM120**)

Carbonates = 60% wt. Siliclastics = 40% wt. Calcareous matrix (Y/N) Y. Mean grain size = 0.4 mm. Inclusions matrix (high/medium/low) = M–H. Temper = sand tempered. Inclusions: basalt, chert, chlorite (fired), clinopyroxene, ferruginous alteration, granite, hornblende, micrite, monocrystalline quartz, myrmekite, orthoclase, polycrystalline quartz, trachyte (undifferentiated).

2012.20 (ZG38: **AM133**)

Carbonates = 10% wt. Siliclastics = 90% wt. Calcareous matrix (Y/N) N. Mean grain size = 0.4 mm. Inclusions matrix (high/medium/low) = M. Temper: no. Inclusions: biosparite, chert, chlorite (fired), clinopyroxene, foraminifera granite, micrite, polycrystalline quartz, sheared quartz ± selvages, trachyte (undifferentiated), weathered basalt.

2039.11 (ZG39: **AM164**)

Carbonates = 10% wt: Siliclastics = 90% wt: Calcareous matrix (Y/N) N, silty. Mean grain size =0.5 mm. Inclusions matrix (high/medium/low) = M. Temper: no. Inclusions: andesite, chert, chlorite, clinopyroxene, dacite, ferruginous alteration, granite, micrite, monocrystalline quartz, orthoclase, plagioclase, polycrystalline quartz mosaic, serpentine, trachyte (undifferentiated), weathered basalt.

7003.4 (ZG40: not catalogued, combed wavy band)

Carbonates = 30% wt. Siliclastics = 70% wt. Calcareous matrix (Y/N). Mean grain size = 0.7 mm. Inclusions matrix (high/medium/low) = M. Temper: possible temper. Inclusions: basalt, chert, clinopyroxene, ferruginous alteration, foraminifera, serpentine (common), trachyte (undifferentiated), weathered basalt.

2039.25 (ZG41: **AM171**)

Carbonates = 20% wt. Siliclastics = 80% wt. Calcareous matrix (Y/N) N. Mean grain size = 0.25 mm. Inclusions matrix (high/medium/low) = M: Temper: no. Inclusions: biosparite, chert, clinopyroxene, dacite, epidote, foraminifera, granite, granodiorite, gypsum, hornblende, plagioclase, serpentine (single), sheared quartz ± selvages.

2260.1 (ZG42: **AM219**)

Carbonates = 15% wt. Siliclastics = 85% wt. Calcareous matrix (Y/N) Y, silty. Mean grain size =0.5 mm. Inclusions matrix (high/medium/low) = M. Temper: no. Inclusions: acid igneous groundmass, colorless amphibole, clinopyroxene, foraminifera, hornblende, orthoclase, plagioclase, sheared quartz +/ selvages, trachyte (undifferentiated).

2080.16 (ZG43: **AM183**)

Carbonates = 20% wt. Siliclastics = 80% wt. Calcareous matrix (Y/N) Y. very high silt content. Mean grain size = 0.25 mm. Inclusions matrix (high/medium/low) = M. Temper: no. Inclusions: chert, clinopyroxene, epidote, granodiorite, hornblende, micrite, muscovite, orthoclase, plagioclase.

2086.1 (ZG44: **AM202**)

Carbonates = 20% wt. Siliclastics = 80% wt. Calcareous matrix (Y/N) Y. Mean grain size = 0.3 mm. Inclusions matrix (high/medium/low) = M. Temper: no. Inclusions: chert, colorless amphibole, clinopyroxene, epidote, fibrous brown amphibole, foraminifera, plagioclase, micrite, polycrystalline quartz, trachyte (undifferentiated).

2039 (ZG45: **AM158**)

Carbonates = 10% wt. Siliclastics = 90% wt. Calcareous matrix (Y/N) Y. Mean grain size = 0.5 mm. Inclusions matrix (high/medium/low) = M. Temper: no. Inclusions: biotite, chert, clinopyroxene, epidote, ferruginous alteration, foraminifera, hornblende, micrite, monocrystalline quartz, plagioclase (distinctive euhedral), polycrystalline quartz, serpentine (rare), sheared quartz ± selvages.

2039.21 (ZG46: **AM161**)

Carbonates = 40% wt. Siliclastics = 60% wt. Calcareous matrix (Y/N) Y. Mean grain size = 0.4 mm. Inclusions matrix (high/medium/low) = M. Temper: no. Inclusions: chert, clinopyroxene, epidote, garnet, foraminifera, hornblende, monocrystalline quartz, polycrystalline quartz, serpentine, sheared quartz ± selvages, weathered basalt.

2080.12 (ZG47: **AM186**)

Carbonates = 30% wt. Siliclastics = 70% wt. Calcareous matrix (Y/N) Y. Mean grain size = 0.75 mm. Inclusions matrix (high/medium/low) = M. Temper: yes. Inclusions: biosparite, basalt, chert, clinopyroxene, epidote, foraminifera, monocrystalline quartz, olivine (rare), orthoclase, plagioclase, serpentine, sheared quartz +/ selvages, trachyte (undifferentiated).

2080.13 (ZG48: **AM187**)

Carbonates = 30% wt. Siliclastics = 70% wt. Calcareous matrix (Y/N) Y. Mean grain size = 0.5 mm. Inclusions matrix (high/medium/low) = M. Temper: yes. Inclusions: andesite, arkose, basalt, chert, clinopyroxene, epidote, foraminifera, granite, monocrystalline quartz, orthoclase, plagioclase, polycrystalline quartz (equant), polycrystalline quartz (orientated), tuff, weathered basalt.

2080.14 (ZG49: **AM185**)

Carbonates = 60% wt. Siliclastics = 40% wt. Calcareous matrix (Y/N) Y. Mean grain size = 0.4 mm. Inclusions matrix (high/medium/low) = M. Temper: yes. Inclusions: biotite, clinopyroxene, epidote, monocrystalline quartz, olivine (rare, altered), plagioclase, serpentine, tuff.

7062.4 (ZG50: painted jug fragment)

Carbonates = 50% wt. Siliclastics = 50% wt. Calcareous matrix (Y/N) Y. Mean grain size = 0.7 mm. Inclusions matrix (high/medium/low) = H. Temper: yes. Inclusions: arkose, chert, clinopyroxene, diorite, epidote, granite, monocrystalline quartz, plagioclase, polycrystalline quartz, serpentine, trachyte (undifferentiated), tuff (single grain).

2010.6 (ZG51)

Carbonates = 70% wt. Siliclastics = 30% wt. Calcareous matrix (Y/N) Y. Mean grain size = 0.5 mm. Inclusions matrix (high/medium/low) = M. Temper: no. Inclusions: basalt, clinopyroxene, epidote, foraminifera, garnet, granite, micrite, sheared quartz ± selvages.

2080.4 (ZG52: **AM194**)

Carbonates = 80% wt. Siliclastics = 20% wt. Calcareous matrix (Y/N) Y. Mean grain size = 0.8 mm. Inclusions matrix (high/medium/low) = L–M. Temper: possible? Inclusions: basalt, basaltic glass, chert, clinopyroxene, foraminifera, monocrystalline quartz, micrite, muscovite, orthoclase, sheared quartz ± selvages, vein quartz.

2154.1 (ZG53: mortarium)

Carbonates = 30% wt. Siliclastics = 70% wt. Calcareous matrix (Y/N) Y. Mean grain size = 0.6 mm. Inclusions matrix (high/medium/low) = M. Temper: yes. Inclusions: chert, clay pellets, clinopyroxene, ferruginous alteration, garnet, hornblende, monocrystalline quartz, orthoclase, plagioclase, sheared quartz ± selvages.

5034.1 (ZG54: **AM264**)

Carbonates = 70% wt. Siliclastics = 30% wt. Calcareous matrix (Y/N) Y. Mean grain size = 0.2 mm. Inclusions matrix (high/medium/low) = M. Temper: possible?: Inclusions: andesite, basalt, clinopyroxene, hornblende, monocrystalline quartz, orthoclase, plagioclase, rhyolite.

7026.1 (ZG55: **AM295**)

Carbonates = 80% wt. Siliclastics = 20% wt. Calcareous matrix (Y/N) Y. Mean grain size = 0.2 mm. Inclusions matrix (high/medium/low) = M (silty). Temper: no. Inclusions: basalt, biotite, chert, colorless amphibole, clinopyroxene, ferruginous alteration, foraminifera, monocrystalline quartz, psammite, quartz-mica schist, serpentine, sheared quartz ± selvages.

7036.1 (ZG56: **AM296/303**)

Carbonates = 80% wt. Siliclastics = 20% wt. Calcareous matrix (Y/N). Mean grain size = 0.2 mm. Inclusions matrix (high/medium/low) = H. Temper: no. Inclusions andesite, basalt (rare), chert, colorless amphibole, clinopyroxene, epidote, ferruginous alteration, foraminifera, granodiorite, granodiorite, hornblende, micrite, plagioclase, polycrystalline quartz, psammite, rhyolite, serpentine, sheared quartz ± selvages.

12012.59 (ZG57: impressed-decoration jug)

Carbonates = 60% wt. Siliclastics = 40% wt. Calcareous matrix (Y/N) Y. Mean grain size = 0.3 mm. Inclusions matrix (high/medium/low) = M. Temper: possible. Inclusions: basalt, chert, clinopyroxene, foraminifera, orthoclase, micrite, plagioclase (zoned euhedra), rhyolite, trachyte (undifferentiated).

7006.14 (ZG58: **AM287**)

Carbonates = 20% wt. Siliclastics = 80% wt. Calcareous matrix (Y/N) Y. Mean grain size = 0.1 mm. Inclusions matrix (high/medium/low) = H. Temper: no. Inclusions: basalt, biosparite, chert, clinopyroxene, epidote, foraminifera, ferruginous alteration, hornblende, monocrystalline quartz, muscovite, plagioclase, trachyte (undifferentiated).

7007.2 (ZG59: **AM77**)

Carbonates = 40% wt. Siliclastics = 60% wt. Calcareous matrix (Y/N) Y. Mean grain size = 0.4 mm. Inclusions matrix (high/medium/low) = M. Temper: no. Inclusions: andesite, chert, clinopyroxene, hornblende, micrite, plagioclase, vein quartz, weathered basalt.

15095.4 (ZG60: **AM25**)

Carbonates = 5% wt. Siliclastics = 95% wt. Calcareous matrix (Y/N) Y. Mean grain size = 0.25 mm. Inclusions matrix (high/medium/low) = L. Temper: no. Inclusions: chert, colorless amphibole, clinopyroxene, hornblende, monocrystalline quartz, orthoclase, plagioclase.

15095.9 (ZG61: **AM29**)

Carbonates = 30% wt. Siliclastics = 70% wt. Calcareous matrix (Y/N) Y. Mean grain size = 0.2 mm. Inclusions matrix (high/medium/low) = L. Temper: no. Inclusions clinopyroxene, ferruginous alteration, granodiorite, foraminifera, hornblende, micrite, monocrystalline quartz, orthoclase, polycrystalline quartz, weathered basalt.

15095.11 (ZG62: **AM46**)

Carbonates = 20% wt. Siliclastics = 80% wt. Calcareous matrix (Y/N) Y. Mean grain size = 0.15 mm. Inclusions matrix (high/medium/low) = L. Temper: no. Inclusions: chert, plagioclase, foraminifera, granite, micrite, rhyolite, weathered basalt, clinopyroxene, muscovite, olivine (single observation).

2278.1 (ZG63: **AM223**)

Carbonates = 15% wt. Siliclastics = 85% wt. Calcareous matrix (Y/N) N, very silty. Mean grain size = <0.1 mm. Inclusions matrix (high/medium/low) = VH. Temper: no. Inclusions: clinopyroxene, monocrystalline quartz, micrite, muscovite, sheared quartz +/selvages, surface/soil carbonate (abundant), vein quartz.

2158.1 (ZG64: **AM217**)

Carbonates = 20% wt. Siliclastics = 80% wt. Calcareous matrix (Y/N) Y. Mean grain size = 0.3 mm. Inclusions matrix (high/medium/low) = M. Temper: no. Inclusions: aegerine-augite (single), chert, clinopyroxene, plagioclase, polycrystalline quartz, potassium feldspar, soil carbonate.

2011.1 (ZG65: **AM116**)

Carbonates = 0% wt. Siliclastics = 100% wt. Calcareous matrix (Y/N) N. Mean grain size = 1 mm. Inclusions matrix (high/medium/low) = L (silty). Temper: yes. Inclusions: clinopyroxene, epidote, granodiorite, hornblende, orthoclase, psammite, rhyolite, sheared quartz ± selvages.

7007.1 (ZG66: **AM88**)

Carbonates = 15% wt. Siliclastics = 85% wt. Calcareous matrix (Y/N) N. Mean grain size = 0.5 mm. Inclusions matrix (high/medium/low) = M-H. Temper: no. Inclusions: basalt, biosparite, clinopyroxene, epidote, ferruginous alteration, monocrystalline quartz, muscovite, plagioclase, polycrystalline quartz, serpentine, sheared quartz +/-selvages, surface/soil carbonate, trachyte (undifferentiated), vein quartz.

(ZG67 omitted)

Tile fragments (ZG68)

Carbonates = 30% wt. Siliclastics = 70% wt. Calcareous matrix (Y/N) Y. Mean grain size = 0.5 mm. Inclusions matrix (high/medium/low) = M. Temper: yes. Inclusions: basalt, chert, clinopyroxene, dacite, foraminifera, granite, granodiorite, micrite, monocrystalline quartz, plagioclase, rhyolite, serpentine (trace), trachyte undifferentiated, vein quartz.

12011.44 (ZG69: **AM455**)

Carbonates = 40% wt. Siliclastics = 60% wt. Calcareous matrix (Y/N) Y. Mean grain size = 0.4 mm. Inclusions matrix (high/medium/low) = M. Temper: yes. Inclusions: basalt, chert, colorless amphibole, clinopyroxene, foraminifera, granite, granodiorite, hornblende, micrite, orthoclase, polycrystalline quartz, serpentine, sheared quartz ± selvages, vein quartz.

2012.17 (ZG70: **AM143**)

Carbonates = 50% wt. Siliclastics = 50% wt. Calcareous matrix (Y/N) Y. Mean grain size = 0.3 mm. Inclusions matrix (high/medium/low) = H. Temper: no. Inclusions: chert, clinopyroxene, hornblende, monocrystalline quartz, plagioclase, sheared quartz ± selvages, vein quartz.

7006.13 (ZG71: **AM292**)

Carbonates = 50% wt. Siliclastics = 50% wt. Calcareous matrix (Y/N) N, silty/fine sand. Mean grain size = 0.4 mm. Inclusions matrix (high/medium/low) = M. Temper: no. Inclusions: biosparite, chert, colorless amphibole, clinopyroxene, ferruginous alteration, micrite, plagioclase, serpentine, sheared quartz ± selvages, surface carbonate.

7060.8 (ZG72: **AM327**)

Carbonates = 65% wt. Siliclastics = 35% wt. Calcareous matrix (Y/N) Y. Mean grain size = 0.4 mm. Inclusions matrix (high/medium/low) = M. Temper: no. Inclusions: basalt, chert, colorless amphibole, clinopyroxene, ferruginous alteration, foraminifera, micrite, monocrystalline quartz, orthoclase.

7060.8 (ZG73: **AM327**)

Carbonates = 50% wt. Siliclastics = 50% wt. Calcareous matrix (Y/N) Y. Mean grain size = 0.3 mm. Inclusions matrix (high/medium/low) = M. Inclusions: basalt (rare), biosparite, chert, chromite (rare), colorless amphibole, clinopyroxene (rare), granodiorite, hornblende, monocrystalline quartz, orthoclase, surface carbonate.

7060.9 (ZG74: **AM328**)

Carbonates = 30% wt. Siliclastics = 70% wt. Calcareous matrix (Y/N) N. Mean grain size = 0.5 mm. Inclusions matrix (high/medium/low) = L. Temper: no. Inclusions: basalt (>90% all inclusions), chert (rare), clinopyroxene, ferruginous alteration, monocrystalline quartz, plagioclase, serpentine (rare).

12002.13 (ZG75: **AM374**)

Carbonates = 50% wt. Siliclastics = 50% wt. Calcareous matrix (Y/N) Y. Mean grain size = 0.3 mm. Inclusions matrix (high/medium/low) = M-H. Temper: no. Inclusions: basalt, chert (rare), colorless amphibole, clinopyroxene, ferruginous alteration, hornblende, monocrystalline quartz, orthoclase, plagioclase, polycrystalline quartz, serpentine (after clinopyroxene), surface carbonate, vein quartz.

12011.24 (ZG76: **AM463**)

Carbonates = 5% wt. Siliclastics = 95% wt. Calcareous matrix (Y/N) N. Mean grain size = 0.5 mm. Inclusions matrix (high/medium/low) = H. Temper: no. Inclusions: basalt (>95%), clinopyroxene, epidote, ferruginous alteration, granite, monocrystalline quartz, orthoclase, plagioclase, serpentine (after clinopyroxene), weathered basalt.

12011.24 (ZG77: **AM463**)

Carbonates = 70% wt. Siliclastics = 30% wt. Calcareous matrix (Y/N) Y. Mean grain size = 0.2 mm. Inclusions matrix (high/medium/low) = H. Temper: no. Inclusions: biosparite, chert, colorless amphibole, clinopyroxene, foraminifera (rare, derived), micrite, monocrystalline quartz, plagioclase, surface carbonate.

12011.26 (ZG78: **AM465**)

Carbonates = 60% wt. Siliclastics = 40% wt. Calcareous matrix (Y/N) Y. Mean grain size = 0.6 mm. Inclusions matrix (high/medium/low) = H. Temper: no. Inclusions: andesite, chert, clinopyroxene, ferruginous alteration, granite, granodiorite, hornblende, micrite, monocrystalline quartz, orthoclase, plagioclase, soil carbonate, weathered basalt.

12011.41 (ZG79: **AM480**)

Carbonates = 30% wt. Siliclastics = 70% wt. Calcareous matrix (Y/N) Y. Mean grain size = 0.5 mm. Inclusions matrix (high/medium/low) = M. Temper: no. Inclusions: biotite, chert, clinopyroxene, dacite, epidote, foraminifera, hornblende, micrite, plagioclase, polycrystalline quartz, rhyolite, sheared quartz ± selvages, weathered basalt.

12011.52 (ZG80: **AM462**)

Carbonates = 70% wt. Siliclastics = 30% wt. Calcareous matrix (Y/N) Y. Mean grain size = 0.5 mm. Inclusions matrix (high/medium/low) = M. Temper: no. Inclusions: chert, chlorite, colorless amphibole, clinopyroxene, hornblende, micrite, monocrystalline quartz, orthoclase, serpentine, surface carbonate, vein quartz, weathered basalt.

12012.9 (ZG81: **AM549**)

Carbonates = 60% wt. Siliclastics = 40% wt. Calcareous matrix (Y/N) Y. Mean grain size = 0.5 mm. Inclusions matrix (high/medium/low) = H. Temper: no. Inclusions: clinopyroxene, epidote, ferruginous alteration, garnet, micrite, monocrystalline quartz, muscovite, orthoclase, plagioclase (zoned euhedra), sheared quartz +/ selvages.

12012.10 (ZG82: **AM550**)

Carbonates = 80% wt. Siliclastics = 20% wt. Calcareous matrix (Y/N) Y, overfired pale green. Mean grain size = 0.5 mm. Inclusions matrix (high/medium/low) = M. Temper no. Inclusions: basalt (rare), clinopyroxene (rare), dacite, granite (graphic, single observation), hornblende, micrite, orthoclase, plagioclase, polycrystalline quartz mosaic, serpentine (rare).

12012.12 (ZG83: **AM551**)

Carbonates = 70% wt. Siliclastics = 30% wt. Calcareous matrix (Y/N) Y. Mean grain size = 0.5 mm. Inclusions matrix (high/medium/low) = M-H. Temper: no. Inclusions: basalt (rare), chert, clinopyroxene, granite (graphic type, single observation), micrite, monocrystalline quartz, sheared quartz ± selvages.

NOTES

1. In addition to the 56 ceramic samples, a reference sample of sand taken from the Euphrates at Birecik was also submitted for analysis. Thin-section analysis of the sand sample was supplemented by scanning electron microscopy (SEM).
2. See table 3 in chapter 2, this volume.
3. See table 3 in chapter 2, this volume.

· CHAPTER FIVE ·

Ceramic Oil Lamps

Mahmoud Hawari

INTRODUCTION

This chapter publishes ceramic oil lamps discovered during the rescue excavations at Zeugma in 2000.[1] The lamps presented here were found by archaeologists in Trenches 1, 2, 4, 5, 7, 9, 10, 11, 12, 13, 15, 18, and 19.[2] The assemblage comprises 213 specimens (L1–213), of which 31 are complete and almost complete, and 182 are fragments, and it provides valuable evidence for the chronology of the site.[3] The range of lamps in the assemblage indicates numerous fabrics and types, corresponding with the known history of the site, dating from the Hellenistic period to the Islamic period. While the majority of these lamps are common finds on contemporary sites in Anatolia and in the Levant, a minority of lamps in the assemblage are only known at Zeugma. The lamps are classified into nine types, which are described with a discussion on their dating based on the contexts in which they were found and on parallels from other sites and collections. The Catalogue is arranged by date and type. Table 2 presents the data by archaeological context in order to shed light on distribution of the finds and period of use at Zeugma.

Scope and Methods

Preliminary quantification of the lamps was carried out by the excavators in 2000 and 2001, when four- or five-digit context numbers were assigned to all finds at Zeugma. A fair number of lamps and lamp fragments were also inventoried and assigned small find (SF) numbers at this time. During my firsthand study of the lamps at Zeugma in 2002, I identified additional lamp fragments among the finds, sometimes more than one for the same context, and I assigned numerical extensions to the context number in order to distinguish each specimen (e.g., 9183.1, 9183.2). I also recorded the following data for all specimens: provenience, dimensions, physical appearance, state of preservation, notes on manufacture, fabric, form, and other distinguishing features such as slip and decoration. All of this information provides the basis for the typology and dates in this chapter.

This study encompasses both wheel-made and mold-made lamps. Technical details of manufacturing lamps have already been discussed by numerous scholars elsewhere, so only brief comments are called for in the discussion and catalogue that follow. Numerous fabrics are present. The vast majority of specimens were generally made from variable local clays, particularly a variety of buff ware. Only a small minority of lamps were imported.

Throughout my study, chronology and dating were established on the basis of two factors: 1) the archaeological contexts in which the lamps were found, particularly contexts with dated pottery groups published by Philip Kenrick in this volume; 2) comparable material from published excavations in Anatolia and the Levant, as well as material in museum collections. Cross references to coins and other datable objects from the lamp contexts published here can be found in "Context Descriptions" in volume 1. The overall date-range for the lamps published here is from the second half of the second century B.C. to the eleventh century A.D. This corresponds quite well to the range of dates given by the other ceramic material found in the excavations.

COMPARATIVE MATERIAL

The location of Zeugma on the Euphrates in southeast Anatolia, far away from the Mediterranean, has implications for the sources of comparative material. In terms of the pottery wares, particularly the oil lamps, Zeugma has naturally more in common with those sites in its vicinity and downstream along the river's lines of communication, and less in common with central and western Anatolia or the southern Levant.

Greek/Hellenistic and Roman lamps are well recorded, and their typology and chronology have been analyzed meticulously by scholars such as H. B. Walters, O. Broneer, R. H. Howland, and Bailey. This is the typology utilized by subsequent publications of lamp collections or excavated assemblages. However, it is a typology based on finds in Corinth, the Athenian Agora, and western Anatolia, a long way from Zeugma, both culturally and geographically. Even the large collection of Hellenistic and Roman lamps in the British Museum contains few lamps from southern Anatolia and Syria.

The relatively close coastal cities of Antioch and Tarsus are helpful sources for parallels, although both sites were excavated more than half a century ago.[4] The most useful comparative sources can be found at sites along the Euphrates in Syria, where Dura-Europos offers more comparative material than Rusafa for the Hellenistic and early to mid-Roman periods. The stratigraphy of the Hellenistic levels at Dura-Europos was largely incidental to the excavation of the Parthian and Roman levels; few Hellenistic lamps from there have been published. For the late Roman and early Islamic periods some parallels are found at Déhès, even though the numerous excavations and surveys carried out in the river valleys of Syria in the last two decades have shown remarkably disappointing evidence for lamps. Other sites in Syria and Palestine with parallels to the Zeugma material are Bet Shean and Hamat Gader. Additional comparative material is found in museums and private collections, such as the Cyprus Museum, the Schloessinger Collection, the Royal Ontario Museum, and the Anawati Collection (Toronto). Published sources for the sites and museums mentioned above are cited below in the pertinent catalogue entries.

TYPOLOGY

The lamps are classified into nine distinctive types, and these are arranged in chronological order and typological progression. However, this arrangement should not be regarded as a strict indication of chronological progression. Types and variants sometimes overlap within a given period. The dates proposed for some types can be narrowed down since some of the lamps listed come from closely datable archaeological contexts. Others are relatively dated on the basis of typological consideration of shape, decorative details, and fabric, with examples found at other sites.

Type 1 (L1–4): Wheel-Made Lamps, Hellenistic (Second to Early First Century B.C.), PL. 75

There are only four fragments of this type, which are the earliest found at Zeugma. This is a wheel-made lamp that has a rounded, closed body with a raised base, hollowed out conically underneath, and a narrow convex rim band surrounding a medium-size sunken filling-hole. The nozzle is deep, narrow, and flat-topped with a small wick-hole and steep sloping underside. This lamp is generally made from reddish-brown clay with fine slip on the exterior.

This type is well known from Corinth and the British Museum collections. The earliest lamps date from the seventh century B.C., but none of the Zeugma specimens antedates the second century B.C. The early types are generally shallow and open in form, with a short nozzle.[5] Later ones tend to be deeper, more closed, with longer nozzles.[6] The lamps of this type are similar to Antioch Types 2 and 3, which are dated from the third to early second century B.C.[7] Similar lamps can be identified with Type 2 at Dura-Europos dated to the first century B.C.[8]

Two fragments of this type (L2 and L3) recovered from the backfilling behind a major terrace wall in Trench 15 (context 15009), along with Hellenistic fine ware dated to the early first century A.D., are probably residual.[9] The two other fragments of this type (L1 and L4) did not come from well-dated contexts, and thus their dating is based on the identification of their fabric and shape. Although no contexts were found that could clearly correspond to the earliest occupation of the site, the earliest stratified deposits with Hellenistic pottery were dated to the second half of the second century B.C., a date that is more plausible for this lamp.[10]

Type 2 (L5–42): Early Roman to Flavian/Trajanic (First Century A.D.), PLS. 75–80

One almost complete lamp (L36) and 37 fragments of this type of lamp belong to the corpus of lamps published here. The type is closely related to Broneer's Type 18 at Corinth, Type 50C at the Athenian Agora, dated to the second or third quarters of the first century A.D., and to Ephesos lamps in the British Museum.[11] But it is a generic relation rather than a specific one. It imitated the so-called Ephesos lamps and it enjoyed great popularity in the eastern Mediterranean and the Levant. At the Museum of Cyprus these lamps are termed Ephesos lamps.[12] In the Schloessinger Collection, lamps of this type are classified as Roman lamps with Hellenistic features.[13]

Ephesos lamps and their imitations are mold-made gray-ware lamps covered with black or gray glaze. Their body is more or less circular, double convex in profile, and they usually have a small filling-hole with a narrow discus surrounded by an upstanding collar. The nozzle, made in the mold with the rest of the lamp, is long and slightly spatulated in shape. The vertical strap-like or loop-handle, separately made, is relatively large and attached to the collar and shoulder. The base ring is circular in shape. The shoulder is either plain or decorated with low relief of radial or floral and vegetal schematic designs of leaves and fruit, sometimes carelessly executed. The ring base is sometimes decorated with a rosette within a circle in relief. The handle is often decorated with incised plain bands or herringbone designs.

The type has three variants, which differ in the shape of the connection between the disc and nozzle. Variant A (L5–35) has a large filling-hole marked off by a ridge and an encircling rosette or ovolo. Some of the lamps appear to have separately made handles and some handles were mold-made. This type or variant seems to be similar to Group 9 at Tarsus, dated from the late first century B.C. to the first half of the first century A.D., to Type 25 at Antioch, dated to the late first century A.D., and to Type 3 at Dura-Europos, dated to the first century A.D.[14] According to Baur, these lamps were probably imported to Dura-Europos from Antioch. It is plausible to assume this also could be true at Zeugma. Three fragments of this type (L16, 28, 29) were recovered from the same backfilling behind a major terrace wall in Trench 15 (context 15095), along with Hellenistic fine ware dated to the early first century A.D.[15] Similar lamps were found as far away as the Parthian site of Seleucia-on-the-Tigris.[16]

Variant B (L36–38), which developed from Variant A, has a ridge encircling the flat disk and extending up to the nozzle and around the wick-hole, forming a trough or a channel. The latter feature indicates the general tendency for the progression of lamps over the following centuries:

a more pronounced channel between the filling-hole and the wick-hole. **L36** and five fragments of lamps were found in two other contexts (7002, 7023) that are dated to the late first century A.D.[17] A further 24 fragments of lamps were identified as belonging to this type. It seems possible that **L37** and **L38** are imported examples of the Ephesos-type lamps.

Variant C (**L39–42**) has a more pear-shaped body than Variant B, with a large filling-hole surrounded by a rosette design and a rounded short nozzle with a volute on each side.

Lamps of this type with Hellenistic features continued for a time into the Roman period. However, this type of lamp is dated by Hayes from the late second century B.C. to the early first century A.D.[18] Parallels to this type are also found at Corinth, at the Athenian Agora, where they are dated from the late second century to the early first century B.C., and at Antioch and Tarsus.[19]

Type 3 (L43–62): Roman Discus Lamps, Early First to Early Third Century A.D., PL. 81

This mold-made type with decorated discus is the most typical lamp of the Roman period, of which only 23 fragments were recovered from the excavations at Zeugma. The occurrence of similar lamps from Antioch and Dura-Europos shows that the type has a wide area of distribution.[20]

The lamp of this type is characterized by a round body, a discus and a small, round nozzle, a small filling-hole, and a flat base. It has seven variants, which differ in the shape of the nozzle and the decoration on the rim. The discus is generally plain with simple incised concentric circles, but some are decorated with floral or geometric designs. Some lamps lack handles, but others have small pierced ones. They also differ in size and in the clay from which they are made. Most of these lamps lack the fancy figural decoration of their Italian and Hellenistic counterparts and seem to be locally made, mainly with thick orange-brown and dark-brown clay. However the thinness of the walls of some lamps (such as **L44** and **L46**), made from fine gray and light-brown clay slipped with reddish-brown, suggests they might be imports.

Variant A (L43–48): Plain Discus Lamps with Short Rounded Nozzles, Late First to Early Second Century A.D., PL. 81

This type of lamp was made locally from thick orange-brown and dark-brown clay. The rim is generally plain with no decorations except circular grooves.

Variant B (L49–57): Miscellaneous Discus Lamps with Decorated Rims, PL. 81

The excavators found various fragments of discus lamps, which differ in the clay used. The rim is decorated with floral or geometric designs. Some of these seem to be imported lamps made from fine gray, light brown and pinkish-brown clay, slipped with brown-black and reddish-brown.

Variant C (L58): Discus Lamp with Knife-Pared Nozzle

The nozzle, probably formed by hand and attached to the body, has knife-paring on the sides.

Variant D (L59): Discus Lamp with Bow-Shaped Nozzle

The concave disk is set off from the shoulder by three circular grooves. A line and a dot on either side mark the border between the nozzle and the body. The nozzle is small and rounded. Perlzweig, who calls this a "U-shaped" nozzle, dates these lamps to the late third century in Athens.[21]

Variant E (L60–61): Discus Lamps with Vertical Handle-Shields, PL. 81

This discus lamp has a vertical handle-shield designed as a leaf with its segments emerging from volutes in outline relief. It is made of orange, red-slipped clay and well fired. It is decorated with triangles filled with dots.

Variant F (L62): Local Imitation of an Attic Lamp, Third Century A.D., PL. 81

The handle is small, upright, and pierced. The discus is decorated with a rosette design consisting of small petals. Parallels can be found at Bet Shean, dated to the second century A.D., and in the Schloessinger Collection, dated to the mid-Roman period: second to fourth century A.D.[22]

Type 4 (L63–113): Dura-Europos Lamps, First Half of Third Century A.D., PLS. 82–86

Five complete lamps, four almost complete, and 41 fragments of lamps of this type, which constitute 23 percent of the total assemblage, were found at the excavations. This type of lamp is conveniently named after Dura-Europos, where a large quantity of lamps (155 in total) was found and thought to have been locally manufactured.[23]

The lamps of this type are made of buff, light brown, or black clay. The body is relatively small and round, and is molded in two parts. The top is flat or slightly convex and the base is flat. The nozzle is short and round-tipped. There are six variants of this type that differ in the shape of the upper part of the lamp and in the designs decorating the rim around the filling-hole. The designs include a rosette radiating from the ring of the filling-hole, rows of dots, clusters of leaves, and rope-shaped patterns. There are also plain lamps without designs. At Dura-Europos, Baur divided Type 5 into eight groups according to the decoration on their rims.[24] Likewise, based on the designs on their upper part, the lamps of this type are divided into six variants.

Variant A (L63–73), PLS. 82–83

The lamps of this variant have a rosette radiating from the filling-hole. This variant is the same as Dura-Europos Type 5, Group 1.[25]

Variant B (L74–89), PLS. 83–84

Flat-top lamps decorated with three concentric rows of dots or globules. This variant equals Dura-Europos Type 5, Group 3.[26]

Variant C (L90–103), PL. 85

These are plain-top lamps without any decoration.

Variant D (L104–105), PL. 85

These are flat-top lamps decorated with floral motifs, such as clusters of leaves and tendrils.

Variant E (L106–109), PL. 86

These are flat-top lamps decorated with a curious rope pattern and a crescent or sun at the nozzle. This variant equals Dura-Europos Type 5, Group 7.[27]

Variant F (L110–113), PL. 86

A sunken filling-hole and high shoulder, sometimes decorated with an ovate pattern. Variants C, D, and F may all resemble Dura-Europos Type 6, dating to the middle of the third century A.D., and Antioch Type 46.[28]

Six lamps of this type (**L66, L70, L80, L88, L107, L112**) come from contexts with evidence of destruction (2080, 2160, 18108), probably associated with the Sasanian sack, dated by historical sources and coins to A.D. 252/253.[29] This date corresponds well with Baur's dating of the Dura-Europos lamps—the first half or middle of the third century A.D.[30] There is no indication that these lamps were manufactured at Zeugma, where molds have not been found. The striking resemblance of some of these lamps, particularly with regard to their decoration, with those at Dura-Europos suggests that they were imports from the latter. The distribution of this type of lamp seems to be quite limited to the Euphrates region and was hardly found at other sites further south into the Levant or to the west of Anatolia.

Type 5 (L114–131): Two-Nozzle Lamps, First Half of Third Century A.D., PLS. 87–90

One almost complete lamp (**L119**) and 18 fragments of this type were found. This lamp is clearly mold-made and has an oblong body formed by two parts joined together. The two nozzles are incorporated into the body. The transverse ledge or knob handle on the upper part is separately made and pierced by a small hole from front to back. The filling-hole is usually small. The base is flat. The upper part is often plain, and sometimes there are traces of burnishing and an incised ladder pattern. The clay varies among buff, light brown, and gray.

The near-complete lamp (**L119**) and two other fragments of this type were found in contexts (2010, 2039) associated with the Sasanian sack of A.D. 252/253.[31] It is therefore plausible to date this type of lamp to the first half of the third century A.D. This type seems to be of a local production and exclusive to Zeugma. However, parallels to this type are found in Type 47a at Antioch, dated to the third century A.D.[32]

Type 6 (L132–134): Ovoid Lamps with Linear Patterns, First Half of Third Century A.D., PLS. 90–91

This lamp has an ovoid body formed by two molded parts. The clay is buff, light brown, or gray. The body is slightly convex, the filling-hole is relatively large and surrounded with a ridge, the nozzle is round and short, and the base is flat. The handle is upright, solid, and mold-made. The shoulder is usually decorated with linear patterns or semicircles.

One almost complete lamp and two fragments were found at the excavations. Another lamp (**L133**) has been found in a dated context (18108) associated with the Sasanian sack of A.D. 252/253.[33] This type of lamp is similar in shape to Type 51 at Antioch, where it is dated from the third into the fifth century A.D.[34] It is similar in decoration to three lamps at Dura-Europos, dated from fourth to fifth century.[35] Nonetheless, this lamp with linear patterns on the rim seems to have had limited production at Zeugma and was produced there in the first half of the third century.

Type 7 (L135–141): Oblong Lamps, Late Fifth Century–Early Sixth Century A.D., PLS. 92–93

Two almost complete lamps and five fragments of this type were discovered at Zeugma. This lamp has a small oblong or boat-shaped body formed by two molded parts joined together. The nozzle is incorporated into the body of the lamp. The tongue-shaped handle projects horizontally, but not higher than the lamp. The filling-hole is relatively large and surrounded by a ridge. The base is slightly convex. The decoration on the rim consists of various relief patterns, such as rows of dots and lines around the filling-hole. The lamps are made of a variety of clay, such as buff or light brown, with a brownish slip.

Most examples of this type were not found in securely dated deposits, except one almost complete lamp (**L135**) that was recovered from a relatively well-dated context (5048) associated with the layer of renewed building activity on the site, dated from the late fifth to early sixth century.[36] This type of lamp resembles in general form and decoration Type 53 at Antioch.[37] Lamps from this type are also widespread in the Levant. Thirty-seven complete lamps, 16 almost complete and 538 fragments, were found at Bet Shean, where they are dated to the fourth and fifth centuries.[38] At Hamat Gader, similar lamps were discovered and dated from the late fourth to early fifth century A.D.[39]

Type 8 (L142–212): Syro-Palestinian Lamps, Seventh to Eighth Century A.D., PLS. 94–108

Lamps of this type are the largest group found in the excavation at Zeugma. Seven complete lamps, 12 almost complete, and 54 fragments, equalling 33.5 percent of the entire corpus, constitute Type 8. It is a common type at sites throughout Syria and Palestine, where it is dated to the seventh and eighth centuries.[40] While this lamp has been found at Antioch and Tarsus, it is surprisingly almost absent at Dura-Europos, where only one complete such lamp is recorded.[41]

The fabric of the lamps is variable; generally it is buff but some are made from light brown clay that acquired a buff tone after firing. A few are made from light to dark brown, reddish-brown, orange-brown, and light to dark gray clay. These have a pear-shaped pointed body, which is formed of two molded parts joined together. The large filling-hole is surrounded by high ridge and by a second one that extends onto the nozzle and around the wick-hole, forming a straight shallow channel. In some cases, the outer ridge does not continue onto the nozzle. The handle on the outer ridge at the back of the lamp is conical. The base ring is circular and in some cases it follows the outline of the lamp.

The decoration in relief on the rim is rich and varied. There are usually one or two tiers of radial patterns on the rim of the lamp, bordered with lines ending in volutes and a chevron pattern along the nozzle. Curious designs or symbols are often found on the channel. Within the base ring there is occasionally a design, perhaps a potter's mark. There are three variants of this type depending on the shape of their upper body and the ornamentation on their rim, but there is no evidence that there are chronological differences.

Variant A (L142–191), PLS. 94–105

The large filling-hole is surrounded by a high ridge and by a second one that extend onto the nozzle and around the wick-hole, forming a straight shallow channel. There are several variations of the lamp, depending on their decorations. L142–152, L166–170, L180, and L187 seem to be related to the Schloessinger Collection's Islamic group I variant A with geometric decoration,[42] which is dated to the seventh and eighth centuries rather than the sixth century.

Variant B (L192–197), PLS. 106–108

This type of lamp is generally similar in form to Variant A but has a more pointed pear-shaped body, slightly lower in height with a smaller filling-hole and a flatter top. The rim around the filling-hole bears a simple decoration in the form of dots.

Variant C (L198–212)

Although this type of lamp has the same pear-shaped body, it differs from Variants A and B by the position of the knob handle on the juncture between the two halves, and by the decoration on the rim.

This type of lamp is widespread throughout the Levant and appears in different variation in terms of shape and decorations, including inscribed examples. Day, in her study of early Islamic and Christian lamps, suggests that these lamps appeared in the Umayyad period and continued to the Abbasid period, i.e., from the second half of the seventh century until the eighth century.[43] This lamp is equated to Type 23 by Kennedy, who dates it to the seventh and eighth centuries.[44] At Antioch, similar lamps were found and dated to the sixth century, though they continued in use later.[45] At Bet Shean, 37 complete lamps, 16 almost complete, and 227 fragments of lamps of this type were found and dated to the eighth century.[46] At Khirbet al-Mefjar near Jericho, lamps of this type were found in sealed deposits dated before the earthquake in A.D. 749.[47] Other parallels can be found at Hamat Gader,[48] in the Cyprus Museum,[49] in the Schloessinger Collection,[50] and in the Whiting Collections of Palestinian Pottery at Yale University.[51]

One complete lamp (L194), one almost complete lamp (L195), and 16 other fragments of this type were found in Trenches 7 and 12 in occupation and destruction contexts (7036, 7062, 7065, 12002, 12011, 12012) that are well dated to the first half of the seventh century A.D.[52] However, three fragments (L180, L182, L201) come from contexts (4008, 5078) that include Cypriot Red Slip Ware dated to the early sixth century A.D.[53] It is therefore possible on the basis of the stratigraphic evidence and parallels from other sites to suggest that this type of lamp appeared at Zeugma in the early sixth century and continued until the eighth century.

Type 9 (L213): Wheel-Made Lamp, Islamic, Ninth to Eleventh Century A.D., PL. 109

This type is wheel-made from two separately made parts joined together. It has a relatively high rim, sometimes with a loop-handle drawn from the rim to the middle of the body. It has a small rounded nozzle and the base is flat. It is made from black or grayish-brown clay.

Only one fragment of this type (L213) was discovered in Trench 1, which is distinguished from other trenches by the abundance of Islamic ceramic material. The fragment comes from context (1024), which is dated to the ninth century A.D.,[54] a date that marks the last stage in the history of ceramic oil lamps at Zeugma.

Parallels to this type of lamp are found in Déhès in northern Syria, dated to the ninth and tenth centuries, and at Qal'at Sem'an in northern Syria, dated to the eighth and ninth centuries.[55] At Bet Shean, three similar lamps are dated from the ninth to eleventh centuries A.D.[56] Also similar is Kennedy's Type 25.[57]

CONCLUSIONS

To conclude, we should attempt to provide answers to the following questions. What is the picture that emerges from the body of material presented above? What is the significance of the distribution of the various lamp types found at Zeugma in the different periods? Which are the common types at Zeugma that are typical of the region and which ones are exclusive to Zeugma? What is the significance of the quantity of each lamp? Can the distribution of types shed some light on relations between Zeugma and neighboring regions?

Table 1 summarizes the numbers and percentages of lamps of each type found at Zeugma, in comparison to those found in both Dura-Europos and Antioch. The broad outline of the development of the lamps at Zeugma can be briefly sketched. It appears there are two major lamp forms in this corpus. The first type, with a large filling-hole surrounded by a ridge, derives essentially from Hellenistic types and is popular in the Levant. The second type derives from the Roman discus lamp, with a small filling-hole and large discus, and it is more popular in Greece, Cyprus, and at Tarsus than in the Levant, although it was also made there.

The Hellenistic period marks a great change in the method of lamp-making. Lamps had been hand-made open saucers, but with Hellenization came the two-part molded lamp. Molded parts mean mass production, and by the Roman period saucer lamps were completely replaced, not reappearing until the twelfth century. Although the fabrication technique was virtually unchanged from the third century B.C. to the 12th century, the general shape of the lamp was modified. The circular reservoir with protruding nozzle became assimilated to an ovoid from that has been variously labeled pear-, shoe- or slipper-shaped. The reservoir capacity was increased by enlarging the side of the lamp, and the groove was placed between the wick-hole and the fill-hole, perhaps to serve originally as a channel to catch any oil that might miss the filling-hole and funnel it into the reservoir.

At Zeugma, the vast majority of lamps were locally manufactured and generally made from variable local clay, particularly a variety of buff ware. Only a small minority were imported. The earliest lamp from the rescue excavatoins is the Hellenistic wheel-made type (Type 1) found in an early first-century A.D. context. It is easily recognized by its convex top and flat-topped nozzle. This is a derivative of the so-called Broneer Type 7 / Howland Type 25 A, which had a wide distribution throughout the Hellenistic world. It is interesting to note the absence of the so-called delphiniform lamps, or birds' head lamps, from the Zeugma ceramic repertoire.[48] These were common in western Anatolia and Greece, but rare in the eastern Mediterranean in the second half of the second century and the beginning of the first century B.C.

By Roman times, mass production of lamps in two-part molds became the norm. This technique persisted until the seventh and eighth centuries A.D. in various Mediterranean lands. The introduction of molds paved the way for the development of relief ornament. The exchange of molds between production centers or the copying of impressions from existing lamps resulted in the occurrence of identical or similar lamps from different regions.

From an analysis of the whole corpus (table 1), we may deduce that four lamp types (Types 2–6), dating from the early to mid-Roman period, i.e., from the first century to mid-third century A.D., were found at Zeugma. In terms of quantity, these types constitute about 60 percent of the entire corpus. Type 4, which is the second most common at Zeugma, is represented by 51 examples and constitutes 23 percent, of the assemblage, compared with 155 lamps and 38.5 percent, respectively, at Dura-Europos. It seems that Type 2 has overlapped in the first century A.D. with Type 3, the common Roman discus lamp, of which variations continued until the third century. Type 4 seems to have evolved from Type 3 and coexisted with it at least during the first half of the third century, along with both Types 5 and 6. Types 4, 5, and 6 are associated with ceramic Group D, dated to the Sasanian destruction of A.D. 252/253.[59] No oil lamps dated between the mid-third century and the second half of the fifth have been found at Zeugma. This fact seems to correspond well with the lack of other ceramic material from the excavation during the same period, which suggests that the recovery of the city from the Sasanian sack may have taken a long time.[60]

Types 7 and 8 date to the late Roman period (mid-fifth to eighth century) and constitute 35.5 percent of the corpus published here. Type 7 was represented only by a small number of lamps, which were replaced by Type 8. The latter is the most common and plentiful lamp type from Zeugma, containing 17 complete and partially complete lamps and 54 lamp fragments, constituting 33.5 percent of the corpus. Type 9 dates from the ninth to the eleventh century and is only represented by one fragment that can be considered a chance find.

The lamps inscribed with simple designs and religious symbols, which primarily belong to Type 8, show the influence of Byzantine lamps in the Levant. Motifs at Zeugma include petaled rosettes (e.g., L142–143, L157, L197, but compare L5–6, L10, L19, L21–22) and geometric designs (L143–144, L149, L195). Other Christian symbols include a cross (L182, L186), a combination of an omega and a cross (L155), Greek letters (L187–189), and a palm branch (L132). Christian symbols are not a criterion for date and religious ethnicity in the Levant. They appear on Byzantine lamps from the fifth century and continued to the Early Islamic period (seventh to eighth centuries), at a time when a mixed Christian and Muslim population lived side by side.

The absence of figural representations in the Roman disc lamps (Type 3) is rather intriguing, but there is no evidence to suggest any religious prohibition and it could be a matter of local preference. Their counterparts from the first century A.D., corresponding to Broneer's Type 22, depict scenes with human and animal figures, as well as floral designs.[61] Likewise, a group of Syro-Palestinian round lamps decorated with a variety of geometric, floral, and figural designs, dating from the second to early third century A.D., has no parallels at Zeugma. Examples of this group of lamps are found at Tarsus, Antioch, Dura-Europos, and Palmyra.[62] The absence of such lamps could be a matter of their limited distribution along the trade routes at the time.

The problem of localization of certain types of lamps can only be properly discussed when hundreds of examples are found. No conclusions as to geographical distribution can be drawn from the very few lamps presented here. Examination of the present corpus from Zeugma indicates that most of the lamp types are characteristic to the region or to the whole of the eastern Mediterranean. The most striking examples are Types 2, 3, and 8, for which parallels come from numerous sites. Type 4 can be considered a regional type, being found in large quantities at Dura-Europos. Types 5 and 7 can be defined as local types that were probably manufactured at the site. Unfortunately, evidence to support this assumption, such as molds or production workshops, has not been recovered at Zeugma. Given the close ties with Dura-Europos, most intriguing is the absence from Zeugma of two types that were found in large quantity at Dura-Europos. These are the flat-topped lamps (101 in total) and wheel-made lamps with a deep bowl-shaped reservoir and broad mouth, normally called "Mesopotamian" (24 in total).[63] This can probably be explained as a preference by the inhabitants of Zeugma for Dura-Europos Type 5.

A significant and complex issue pertinent to the study of the present corpus is the extent to which we can use the lamps as absolute evidence for dating contexts or deposits, and for confirming chronological sequences. Even though lamps are used to date deposits if no coins or fine wares exist, it should be remembered that, unless we need to know whether we are in the Roman or Islamic periods, the known dates of most lamp types are not particularly promising. Few types, as we have seen in the current corpus, have firmly proven date ranges. Even when we have good evidence for dating, the date ranges of entire types seem to be at least 50–100 years. The Syro-Palestinian lamps (Type 8), one of the best dated in the Levant, have a range from the early seventh century through at least the mid-eighth century. Attempts have been made to identify variants of the type to narrow its date. It is hoped that further publication of well-stratified examples of this type will improve our knowledge of dates for the different subgroups.

A separate and interesting issue is the significance of marks on lamps—curious symbols or designs, letters and names, occasionally referred to as potters' marks. These can be found on lamp bases in the form of simple rays, stars, rosettes, circles, etc. Usually these marks are incised or stamped on the mold to indicate ownership of the lamp. Sometimes the marks were applied to the base after the lamp had been taken out of the mold, and this makes them hardly a reliable means to identify individual potters or production workshops.

The lamps published here represent only a fraction of the known types from the region. Only by combining the published material from many excavations and collections may we achieve a reasonably complete picture of lamp production. The present study should be viewed as another contribution to the growing corpus of known material to be considered in any future synthesis. It is also hoped that the assemblage presented here has the potential to refine the site's chronology and contribute to the overall archaeological understanding of Zeugma.

Type	Complete	Near complete	Fragment	Total	Percent	Total at Dura	Percent at Dura	Total at Antioch	Percent at Antioch
1	–	–	4	4	1.8	3 (Types 1 and 2)	0.7	31	16
2	–	1	37	38	16.6	15 (Type 3)	3.5	21 (Types 17–25)	10.8
3	–	–	20	20	9	58 (Type 6)	13.7	34 (Types 35–45)	17.5
4	5	4	41	51	23	155 (Type 5)	36.8	11 (Type 46)	2.5
5	–	1	18	19	8.5	None	–	2 (Type 47)	1
6	–	1	2	3	1.3	None	–	3 (Type 51)	1.5
7	–	2	5	7	3.2	None	–	3 (Type 53)	1.5
8	5	12	54	71	33.5	1	0.2	5 (Type 56)	2.5
9	–	–	1	1	0.5	None	–	13 (Types 57–60)	6.7
TOTALS	10	21	158	213	100	421	–	187	–

Table 1. Zeugma lamps by type, preservation status, and percentages per type compared to Dura-Europos and Antioch.

CERAMIC OIL LAMPS · 183

Context	Catalogue (preservation*)	Type and variant	Ceramic Group
1024.1	L198 (f)	8C	–
2000	L13 (f)	2A	–
2000	L69 (f)	4A	–
2000	L110 (c), L111 (f)	4F	–
2001	L20 (f)	2A	–
2002	L76 (f)	4B	–
2002	L98 (f)	4C	–
2006	L77 (f)	4B	–
2006	L93 (f), L94 (f)	4C	–
2010	L10 (f)	2A	D (A.D. 253)
	L120 (f)	5	
2011	L75 (f)	4B	–
2014	L71 (f)	4A	–
2019	L78 (f)	4B	–
2019	L121 (f)	5	–
2031	L163 (f)	8A	–
2039	L119 (h), L124 (f)	5	D (A.D. 253)
2046	L118 (f)	5	–
	L122 (f)	5	–
	L123 (f)	5	–
	L99 (f)	4C	–
2080	L66 (f)	4A	D (A.D. 253)
	L199 (f) intrusive	8C	
2081	L68 (f)	4A	
2105	L125 (f)	5	
2160	L112 (f)	4F	D (A.D. 253)
2162	L100 (f)	4C	–
2189	L11 (f)	2A	–
2191	L79 (f)	4B	D (A.D. 253)
2195	L45 (f)	3A	–
2261	L67 (f)	4A	–
2277	L82 (f)	4B	–
2283	L12 (f)	2A	C (Flavian/Trajanic)
2291	L200 (f)	8C	–
2294	L101 (f)	4C	–
2383	L1 (f)	1	–
2494	L185 (f)	8A	–

Context	Catalogue (preservation*)	Type and variant	Ceramic Group
4008	L182 (f)	8A	E (early sixth century A.D.)
5000	L142 (h), L143 (h),	8A	–
	L144 (h)	8A	
5048	L135 (h)	7	–
5078	L180 (f)	8A	E (early sixth century A.D.)
	L201 (f)	8C	
5123	L181 (f)	8A	–
5150	L59 (f)	3D	–
7000	L116 (f)	5	–
7002	L117 (f)	5	–
7006	L152 (h)	8A	–
7006	L8 (f)	2A	–
7007	L9 (f)	2A	C (Flavian/Trajanic)
7023	L5 (f), L7 (f),	2A	C (Flavian/Trajanic)
	L21 (f), L22 (f)	2A	
	L36 (h)	2B	–
7024	L156 (f)	8A	–
7026	L178 (f)	8A	F (early seventh century A.D.)
7036	L145 (h)	8A	F (early seventh century A.D.)
7060	L60 (f)	3F	–
	L147 (c), L158 (f),	8A	–
	L159 (f)	8A	
7062	L149 (h)	8A	F (early seventh century A.D.)
	L194 (c)	8B	
7064	L202 (f)	8C	–
7065	L150 (h), L151 (f)	8A	F (early seventh century A.D.)
7077	L137 (f)	7	–
7077	L161 (f), L186 (f)	8A	–
7106	L193 (c)	8B	–
7110	L6 (f)	2A	–
7150	L132 (h)	6	–

* c = complete; h = half; f = fragment

Table 2. *Quantification of the ceramic lamps, sorted by context. Ceramic groups refer to the chapter by Kenrick in this volume. (Continued on next page.)*

Context	Catalogue (preservation*)	Type and variant	Ceramic Group	Context	Catalogue (preservation*)	Type and variant	Ceramic Group
7180	L140 (f)	7	–	11106	L128 (f)	5	
7201	L203 (f)	8C	–	11112	L97 (f), L102 (f)	4C	
7202	L148 (f), L160 (f)	8A	–	12001	L164 (f), L165 (f),	8A	
7210	L204 (f)	8C	–		L169 (f), L170 (h)	8A	
7212	L155 (f)	8A	–	12001	L205 (f)	8C	
7214	L154 (f)	8A	F	12002	L206 (f)	8C	
	L195 (h)	8B	(early seventh century A.D.)	12004	L129 (f)	5	
				12007	L168 (c)	8A	
				12011	L187 (f), L188 (f),	8A	
7326	L157 (f)	8A			L189 (f), L190 (f),	8A	
7329	L46 (f)	3A		12011	L207 (f), L208 (f),	8C	
7964	L162 (f)	8A			L209 (f)	8C	
9000	L18 (f), L19 (f)	2A		12012	L210 (f), L211 (f),	8C	
9000	L91 (f)	4C			L212 (f)	8C	
9000	L136 (h)	7		13000	L39 (f)	2C	
9000	L177 (f)	8A		13000	L179 (f)	8A	
9001	L43 (f), L44 (f)	3A		13036	L73 (f)	4A	
9001	L62 (f)	3G		15000	L171 (f), L172 (f), L173	8A	
9001	L95 (f), L96 (f)	4C			(f), L174 (f), L175 (f)	8A	
9001	L108 (f)	4E		15001	L146 (h)	8A	
9001	L63 (f)	4A		15001	L196 (f)	8B	
9013	L65 (f)	4A		15002	L26 (f)	2A	
9013	L81 (f)	4B		15002	L58 (f)	3C	
9073	L64 (f)	4A		15002	L105 (f)	4D	
9073	L115 (f)	5		15002	L138 (f)	7	
9076	L17 (f)	2A		15002	L184 (f)	8A	
9082	L49 (f)	3B		15009	L2 (f), L3 (f) residual	1	B (late Augustan or Tiberian)
9144	L40 (f)	2C					
9156	L23 (f)	2A					
9183	L192 (h)	8B		15073	L139 (f)	7	
9183	L141 (f)	7		15095	L16 (f), L27 (f),	2A	B (late Augustan or Tiberian)
9183	L83 (f)	4B			L28 (f),		
9245	L92 (h)	4C					
9245	L153 (f)	8A			L54 (f)	3B	
10004	L126 (f)	5		15103	L166 (h)	8A	
10038	L50 (f)	3B		15114	L37 (f)	2B	
10038	L84 (f)	4B		15114	L29 (f)	2A	
10041	L72 (f)	4A		15150	L14 (f)	2A	
10064	L41 (f)	2C		15179	L61 (f)	3F	
10242	L213 (f)	9		15201	L30 (f), L31 (f), L32 (f)	2A	
11004	L114 (f)	5		15201	L47 (f)	3A	
11004	L191 (c)	8B		15207	L33 (f)	2A	
11028	L127 (f)	5		15211	L34 (f)	2A	
11040	L55	3B		15211	L35 (f)	5	
11046	L90 (c)	4C		15232	L197 (f)	8C	
11072	L51 (f), L52 (f), L53 (f)	3B		15237	L4 (f)	1	
11072	L24 (f), L25 (f)	2A					

* c = complete; h = half; f = fragment

Table 2 (continued). Quantification of the ceramic lamps, sorted by context. Ceramic groups refer to the chapter by Kenrick in this volume. (Continued on next page.)

Context	Catalogue (preservation*)	Type and variant	Ceramic Group
15237	L103 (f)	4C	
15286	L15 (f)	2A	
15286	L167 (f)	8A	
15292	L176 (f)	8A	
15321	L134 (f)	6	
18000	L130 (f)	5	
18001	L74 (h), L85 (f)	4B	
18001	L113 (f)	4F	
18054	L86 (f)	4B	
18061	L87 (f)	4B	
18061	L109 (f)	4E	
18061	L42 (f)	2C	
18070	L104 (h)	4D	
18070	L106 (h)	4E	
18083	L56 (f)	3E	
18085	L131 (f)	5	
18108	L107 (c)	4E	D (A.D. 253)
	L70 (c)	4A	
	L80 (c), L88 (f)	4B	
	L133 (f)	6	
18110	L48 (f)	3A	
18153	L89 (f)	4B	
19001	L38 (f)	2B	
19938	L57 (f)	3B	
unstratified	L183 (f)	8A	

* c = complete; h = half; f = fragment

Table 2 (continued). Quantification of the ceramic lamps, sorted by context. Ceramic groups refer to the chapter by Kenrick in this volume.

CATALOGUE

Type 1: Wheel-Made Lamp, Hellenistic, Second Half of Second to Early First Century B.C.

L1 (context 2383)

This is a part of a circular profile of a lamp with a sunken top. It is made from orange-brown clay with inclusions of black sand, and probably of local manufacture.

L2 (context 15009.1)   PL. 75
H. 3.8 cm

This is a fragment of a profile of a lamp made from light brown clay with trace of brown slip.

L3 (context 15009.2)
H. 3.7 cm

This is a fragment of a profile of a lamp made from light brown clay with brown slip on the exterior as well as on the interior of filling-hole.

L4 (context 15237.1)

This is a fragment of a lamp, of which part of the rounded body and filling-hole and the nozzle survived. The nozzle is round-tipped; its bridge is flat on top with angular sides. Similar: Agora in Athens (Howland 1958, Type 25).

Type 2: Early Roman-Flavian / Trajanic, First Century A.D.

Variant A

L5 (SF 515, context 7023)   PL. 75

This lamp, of which only part of the body and the nozzle were preserved, is made with buff-pinkish clay with red slip. The filling-hole is relatively small. The rich decorations consist of a radial pattern around the filling-hole, a branch of ivy leaves, a bunch of grapes and a palm leaf on the rim, two lines ending in volutes along the nozzle, and a floral motif within a circle on the base.
Similar: British Museum (Bailey 1975, Q511. WAA, PL. 102 [the Levant]); Schloessinger Collection (Rosenthal and Sivan 1978, 18, no. 38).

L6 (SF 609, context 7110)   PL. 76
H. 3.3 cm

This lamp, of which only half has survived, is made of pinkish-brown clay with red slip. The small filling-hole is surrounded by two ridges. The decorations on the lamp are varied: semicircles and dots on the rim, incisions and lines on the handle, and a flower motif within the base.

Similar: Dura-Europos (Baur 1947, 10–11, Type 3, nos. 18–19, PL. 1); British Museum (Bailey 1975, Q584. EA, PL. 112 [Egypt]).

L7 (SF 618, context 7023)   PL. 77

This lamp, of which the handle, a small part of the body, and the nozzle survived, is made from buff clay with red-brown slip. The handle is decorated with a ladder pattern. A volute can be seen on the nozzle.
Similar: Dura-Europos (Baur 1947, 8–9, Type 3, nos. 7, 8, 12, pl. 1).

L8 (SF 896, context 7006)   PL. 77

This lamp, of which only the handle and a small part of the body survived, is made of light brown clay with reddish-brown slip. The rim is decorated with a bunch of grapes motif. The handle is decorated with a herringbone pattern and the rim with leaves issuing out of the handle.
Similar: Dura-Europos (Baur 1947, 8–9, Type 3, nos. 7, 8, 12, pl. 1); Seleucia-on-the-Tigris (Débevoise 1934, 122, no. 387, pl. 12, fig. 2); Tarsus (Goldman and Jones 1950, no. 61, Group 6, fig. 95).

L9 (SF 900, context 7007)

This fragment of a lower part of a lamp with a circular ring base is made from orange-gray clay.

L10 (SF 2180, context 2010)   PL. 77

This is part of the lower half of a lamp and a handle made from buff clay. On the handle is a ladder design. The base has a multipetaled rosette motif.

L11 (SF 2250, context 2189)   PL. 78
H. 2.1 cm

This lamp, only half-preserved, resembles L7 and is made of pinkish-brown clay with reddish-brown slip. The decorations on the lamp include semicircles and a ladder pattern on the rim, incisions and lines on the handle, and a six-petaled rosette motif within the base.

L12 (context 2283)   PL. 78

Pinkish-gray clay with brown slip splashed not covering all the surface of lamp. The fragment is part of a double convex body and a long nozzle. The relief decoration on the rim consists of radial and ladder patterns and palmette design on the nozzle.

L13 (SF 2375, context 2000)   PL. 78
H. 2.2 cm

This lamp, of which only a part of the body and nozzle survived, is made of light brown clay with reddish-brown slip. The decorations on the rim consist of four leaves. On the lower part of the lamp there is a Greek inscription in relief that reads: ΛΑΡΔ (lambda, alpha, rho, delta). This is perhaps a potter's name or the name of the production place.

L14 (SF 3681, context 15150)

This lamp, of which only a part of the body and nozzle survived, is made from buff-pinkish clay with traces of red slip.

L15 (SF 3682, context 15286)

Only part of the handle survived of this lamp, which is made from yellowish clay with red-brown slip. Lines can be seen on the handle.

L16 (SF 4178, context 15095)

This lamp, of which the lower part of its nozzle is preserved, is made from pinkish clay with reddish-brown slip. Within the base is a multipetaled rosette.

L17 (SF 4187, context 9076)

Only the handle survived of this lamp which is made from yellowish clay. Lines can be seen on the handle.

L18 (SF 4190, context 9000)   PL. 78

This lamp, of which only the handle and part of the body survived, is made of light gray clay with traces of reddish-brown slip. The decorations on the rim are in the form of a branch of ivy leaves and dots, with a herringbone pattern on the handle.
Similar: Dura-Europos (Baur 1947, 8–9, Type 3, nos. 7, 8, 9, 12, fig. 5, pl. 1); Tarsus (Goldman and Jones 1950, no. 61, Group 6, fig. 95); Royal Ontario Museum (Hays 1980, 15–16, no. 57, pl. 7).

L19 (SF 4191, context 9000)   PL. 79

This lamp, of which only half is preserved and resembles lamp nos. 7 and 11, is made of buff clay with sand inclusions and covered with reddish-brown slip. The decorations on the lamp include semicircles on the rim, incisions and lines on the handle, and an eight-petaled rosette motif within the base.
Similar: Dura-Europos (Baur 1947, 9–10, Type 3, nos. 11, 13, pl. 1); Tarsus (Goldman and Jones 1950, no. 121, Group 10, fig. 97).

L20 (context 2001)

Only the handle survived of this lamp, which is made from gray clay. Two strips of herringbone design decorate the handle.

L21 (context 7023.1) PL. 79

This is the lower half of a lamp made from buff clay with brown slip. The handle is decorated with lines. The base has a six-petaled rosette motif.
Similar: Dura-Europos—rosette design on base (Baur 1947, 8–9, Type 3, nos. 11, 12, pl. 1).

L22 (context 7023.2) PL. 79

This is part of the lower half of a lamp made from yellowish-buff clay with reddish-brown slip. On the lower part of the nozzle is a ribbon of triangles motif. The base has a six-petaled rosette motif.
Similar: Tarsus (Goldman and Jones 1950, no. 119, Group 9, fig. 97).

L23 (context 9156)

Only a broken handle and part of the body survived of this lamp, which is made from pinkish-gray clay with traces of brown slip. Three lines design decorate the handle.

L24 (context 11072.3)

A small part of a handle of a lamp made from pink clay with reddish slip.

L25 (context 11072.4)

A part of a handle of a lamp made from pinkish-gray clay with a herringbone design on the handle.

L26 (context 15002)

Only the handle survived of this lamp, which is made from yellowish-brown clay with red slip. Herringbone design on the handle.

L27 (context 15095.1)

A handle of a lamp made from gray clay with black slip. Pattern of lines on the handle.

L28 (context 15095.2)

A handle of a lamp made from yellowish-brown clay with reddish-brown slip. Pattern of lines on the handle.

L29 (context 15114.2)

A handle survived of this lamp, which is made from buff clay. Herringbone design on the handle.

L30 (context 15201.1)

This lamp, of which only the handle and small part of the body survived, is made of light brown clay with red slip. Herringbone design on the handle.

L31 (context 15201.2)

This lamp, of which a small part of the body and handle survived, is made from light brown clay. The decoration on the rim and around the filling-hole consists of a schematic ribbon of leaves issuing from the handle.

L32 (context 15201.3) PL. 79

This lamp, of which only part of the body survived, is made of light brown clay with red slip. The decorations on the rim are in the form of branch of ivy leaves and a volute.

L33 (context 15207)

A fragment of a loop handle made of a pinkish-buff clay. It is decorated with a herring-bone pattern.

L34 (context 15211.1) PL. 79

This lamp, of which a small part of the rim survived, is made from light brown clay with traces of brown slip. The decoration on the rim consists of a four-petaled rosette.

L35 (context 15211.2)

This is a fragment of a profile and a handle of a lamp made from gray clay.

Variant B

L36 (SF 511, context 7023) PL. 79

This lamp, which is preserved almost complete, is made from fine orange-red clay with reddish-brown slip. The body is circular. The filling-hole is large and is surrounded by a grooved ridge. It was formed either after firing by breaking the discus irregularly, or during manufacture while the clay was still pliable. The nozzle is long, slightly splayed, and is outlined by a narrow ridge. The wick-hole is large. Only part of the loop handle survived.
Similar: Antioch (Waagé 1941, 61, Type 21:64, fig. 77); Tarsus (Goldman and Jones 1950, no. 79, Group 6, fig. 96); Samaria-Sebaste III (Crowfoot et al. 1957, 370, no. 5, fig. 87); Schloessinger Collection (Rosenthal and Sivan 1978, 12, no. 19); British Museum (Bailey 1975, Q161 [pl. 31], Q163

[pl. 32]); Museum of Cyprus (Oziol 1977, 62, nos. 138–9, Pl 8); Istanbul Archaeological Museum — lamps from the Levant (Antioch) — dated to first century B.C. (1995, 158–9, nos. 420–3); Louvre Museum (Lyon-Caen 1986, 56, nos. 125, 126); Royal Ontario Museum, dated from late second century B.C. to early first century A.D. (Hayes 1980, 15, 165, no. 55).

L37 (context 15114.1) PL. 80

A fragment of a broken spatulated nozzle of this type survived. It is made of gray clay and black slip.

L38 (context 19001) PL. 80

This is a fragment of a profile and a handle of a lamp that is made from light gray clay with black slip. The rim is decorated with a radiating pattern.

Variant C: Lamp with Volute Nozzle

L39 (SF 853, context 13000) PL. 80

This is a fragment of an upper part of a lamp, of which part of nozzle survived. The rim is decorated with a series of ovules around the discus, including a circle with dot in the center and a volute on the nozzle.
Similar: Anawati Collection, Toronto (Djuric 1995, 68, C206); Moscow Museum (Chrzanovski 1998, 49–50, no. 14).

L40 (SF 4182, context 9144) PL. 80

This is a fragment of a lamp, of which only part of the rim and the nozzle survived. It is made of gray clay. The rim is decorated with a rosette and volutes. The nozzle is flanked by a volute on either side.

L41 (context 10064)

This is part of a profile and a nozzle of a lamp made from light gray clay with traces of black-brown slip. The rim is decorated with circular grooves and a knob or a volute on the nozzle.
Similar: Bet Shean (Hadad 2002, Type 10, no. 19).

L42 (context 18061.3)

This is part of a rim and nozzle of a lamp made from gray clay fired to orange-brown on the surface. A tongue motif and volute designs are found on the rim.
Similar: Bet Shean (Hadad 2002, Type 28, no. 290).

Type 3: Roman Discus Lamp, Early First to Early Third Century A.D.

Variant A: Plain Discus Lamp with a Short Rounded Nozzle, Late First to Early Second Century A.D.

L43 (SF 4183, context 9001) PL. 81

This is part of a rim and small rounded nozzle. The discus is plain with no decoration.
Similar: Corinth (Broneer 1930, Type 25); Loeschcke 1919, Type 8; Bet Shean (Hadad 2002, Type 7).

L44 (SF 4192, context 9001) PL. 81

This is part of a profile of a lamp with a small nozzle and a low disc base indicated by a circle. It is made from light brown clay with light brown slip.

L45 (context 2195)

This is part of a profile of a lamp, which is made from light brown clay with reddish-brown slip.

L46 (context 7329) PL. 81

This is part of a profile and base of a lamp made from pinkish clay with dark brown slip. The discus is plain with no decoration.

L47 (context 15201.4)

Fragment of a rim and a nozzle of a lamp made of light brown clay with red slip.

L48 (context 18110) PL. 81

This is a fragment of a profile of a lamp made from yellowish-brown clay. Circular grooves are found on the rim.
Similar: Corinth (Broneer 1930, Type 25); Bet Shean (Hadad 2002, Type 7).

Variant B: Miscellaneous Discus Lamps with Decorated Rims

L49 (context 9082)

This is part of a rim of a lamp made from light gray clay with black-brown slip. The edge of the rim is decorated with circles design.
Similar: Bet Shean (Hadad 2002, Type 10).

L50 (context 10038.1) PL. 81

This is part of a profile of a lamp made from light clay with black-brown slip. The rim is decorated with a strip-of-circles design and circular grooves. In the discus there is a radiating design.

Similar: Bet Shean (Hadad 2002, Type 10, no. 19); Szentléleky 1969, no. 169a.

L51 (context 11072.1) PL. 81

This is part of a rim of a lamp made from orange-brown clay with reddish-brown slip. The edge of the rim is decorated with circles motif and volute design.
Similar: Bet Shean (Hadad 2002, Type 10, 11); Schloessinger Collection (Rosenthal and Sivan 1978, 90, nos. 387–8).

L52 (context 11072.2)

This is the lower part and rim of a lamp made from pinkish-gray clay with traces of yellowish-brown slip. The edge of the rim is decorated with a zigzag motif.
Similar: Bet Shean (Hadad 2002, Type 10, 11).

L53 (context 11072.5) PL. 81

A small fragment of an upper part of a lamp made from pinkish-gray clay. The shoulder is decorated with a relief design of volutes.

L54 (context 15095.3) PL. 81

This is part of a profile of a lamp made from buff clay with black slip. It is decorated with circular lines on the rim and a radial pattern on the discus.

L55 (context 11040)

A small fragment of a lower part of a lamp made from pinkish-gray clay.

L56 (context 18083)

This is a small fragment of a lamp made from yellowish-brown clay with traces of brown slip.

L57 (context 19938)

A fragment of the body and handle are made from pinkish-gray clay with reddish-brown slip outside. The rim is decorated with a strip of three rows of dots around the filling-hole. A ridge is found on top and below the handle.

Variant C: Discus Lamp with Knife-Pared Nozzle, Late First Century to Mid-Second Century A.D.

L58 (SF 3678, context 15002) PL. 81

Only part of the rim and nozzle of this lamp survived. It is made from gray clay with dark brown slip. The nozzle, probably formed by hand and attached to the body, has knife paring on the sides. The rim is decorated with three circular grooves around the discus.

Variant D: Discus Lamp with Bow-Shaped Nozzle

L59 (context 5150) PL. 81

Only part of the rim and nozzle of this lamp, which is made from buff clay, survived. The concave disc is set off from the shoulder by three circular grooves. A line and a dot on either side mark the border between the nozzle and the body. The nozzle is small and rounded. This lamp can be dated from the late first to the first half of the second century A.D.
Similar: British Museum (Bailey 1975, Type O); Bibliothèque Nationale (Hellmann 1987, pl. 32, 252–64).

Variant E: Discus Lamp with Horizontal Handle-Shield

L60 (SF 639, context 7060) PL. 81

Only the handle, with a triangular shape, has survived of this discus lamp. It is made of orange-red–slipped clay and well fired. It is decorated with triangles filled with dots.

L61 (context 15179) PL. 81

This handle-shield, which was part of a discus lamp, is made from light brown clay with black slip. It is designed as a leaf with its segments emerging from volutes in outline relief.
Similar: Corinth (Broneer 1930, Type 21).

Variant F: Athenian Lamp, Third Century A.D.

L62 (SF 4181, context 9001) PL. 81

This fragment of a profile and a handle of a discus lamp is made from light gray clay with black brown slip. The handle is small, upright and pierced. The discus is decorated with a rosette design consisting of small petals.
Similar: Bet Shean, dated to second century A.D. (Hadad 2002, 20, Type 10, nos. 32–3).

Type 4: Dura-Europos Lamp, First Half of Third Century A.D.

Variant A: Lamp with a Rosette Radiating from the Filling-Hole

L63 (SF 53, context 9001) PL. 82
L. 7.5 cm; W. 6.4 cm; H. 2.2 cm

This is the upper half of a lamp made from light brown clay. The decoration on the rim consists of a sixteen-petaled rosette design radiating from the ring of the filling-hole.

Similar: Dura-Europos (Baur 1947, 27, Type 5, Group 1, no. 124, fig. 9).

L64 (SF 844, context 9073)

This fragment of an upper part of a lamp is made from pinkish clay. The decoration on the rim consists of a sixteen-petaled rosette design radiating from the ring of the filling-hole.

L65 (SF 846, context 9013) PL. 82

This a fragment of an upper part of a lamp made from pinkish-gray clay. The decoration on the rim consists of a sixteen-petaled rosette design radiating from the ring of the filling-hole.
Parallel: Dura-Europos (Baur 1947, 30, Type 5, Group 1, no. 149, pl. 5).

L66 (SF 2152, context 2080) PL. 82
L. 6.5 cm; H. 2 cm

This lamp, of which almost half survived, is made from fine light brown clay and well fired. The decoration on the rim consists of a sixteen-petaled rosette design radiating from the ring of the filling-hole.
Parallel: Dura-Europos (Baur 1947, 27, Type 5, Group 1, no. 124, fig. 9, pl. 5).

L67 (SF 2269, context 2261) PL. 82
H. 2.1 cm

This lamp, of which part of the upper half survived, is made from light brown clay. The decoration on the rim consists of a multipetaled rosette design radiating from the ring of the filling-hole.
Parallel: Dura-Europos (Baur 1947, 39, Type 5, Group 1, no. 149, pl. 5).

L68 (SF 2374, context 2081) PL. 82

Only a fragment of a rim of a lamp is preserved, made from gray clay. The decoration on the rim consists of a multi-petaled rosette design radiating from the ring of the filling-hole.
Parallel: Dura-Europos (Baur 1947, 39, Type 5, Group 1, no. 149, pl. 5).

L69 (SF 2378, context 2000) PL. 82
W. 6.5 cm

This lamp, of which part of its upper half survived, is made from gray clay. The decoration on the rim consists of a multipetaled rosette design radiating from the ring of the filling-hole.

Parallel: Dura-Europos (Baur 1947, 39, Type 5, Group 1, no. 149, pl. 5).

L70 (SF 3466, context 18108) PL. 83
L. 7.6 cm; W. 6.4 cm

This is a complete lamp made from orange clay. The decoration around the filling-hole consists of a schematic multipetaled rosette design radiating from the ring of the filling-hole. A Greek inscription within the base reads ΒΑΓ ΓΟ, as in **L104**.

L71 (context 2014)

This is a fragment of an upper part of a lamp made from gray clay. The decoration around the filling-hole consists of a rosette design.

L72 (context 10041)

This is a fragment of an upper part of a lamp made from light orange clay. The decoration around the filling-hole consists of a schematic multipetaled rosette design radiating from the ring of the filling-hole.

L73 (context 13036)

This is a fragment of an upper part of a lamp made from gray clay. The decoration around the filling-hole consists of a rosette design.

Variant B: Lamps with a Flat Top Decorated with Three Concentric Rows of Dots or Globules

L74 (SF 923, context 18001) PL. 83
L. 7.4 cm; W. 6.4 cm; H. 2 cm

This is complete lamp made from fine buff clay. The decoration around the filling-hole consists of three rows of globule dots.
Parallel: Dura-Europos (Baur 1947, 32–3, Type 5, Group 3, no. 168, fig. 11, pl. 5).

L75 (SF 2087, context 2011) PL. 84
L. 7.7 cm; W. 6.6 cm; H. 2.3 cm

This lamp, which almost half of it survived, is made from fine light brown clay. The decoration around the filling-hole consists of three rows of globule dots.
Parallel: Dura-Europos (Baur 1947, 32–3, Type 5, Group 3, no. 168, fig. 11, pl. 5).

L76 (SF 2157, context 2002)   PL. 84
W. 6.2 cm; H. 2.2 cm

This lamp, of which part has survived, is made from fine light brown clay. The upper part of the lamp is decorated with dots.

L77 (SF 2183, context 2006)

Only a fragment of the nozzle and upper part of a small lamp is preserved; made from light gray clay.

L78 (SF 2185, context 2019)

Only a fragment of the rim of the lamp is preserved; made from gray clay. Three rows of dots decorate the rim.

L79 (SF 2238, context 2191)

Only a fragment of the nozzle and upper part of a small lamp is preserved; made from light gray clay. Three rows of dots decorate the rim.

L80 (SF 3462, context 18108)   PL. 84
L. 7.8 cm; W. 6.5 cm; H. 2.1 cm

This is complete lamp made from fine buff clay. The decoration around the filling-hole consists of three rows of globular dots.

L81 (SF 3513, context 9013)

Only a fragment of the nozzle and upper part of a small lamp is preserved; made from light gray clay. Three rows of dots decorate the rim.

L82 (context 2277)

This is a fragment of an upper part of a lamp made from light gray clay. The rim is decorated by rows of dots.

L83 (context 9183.2)

This is a fragment of a profile of a lamp made from gray clay fired to light orange. A dot design decorates the rim.

L84 (context 10038.2)

This is a fragment of a profile of a lamp made from light gray clay. There is a dot pattern on the rim.

L85 (context 18001)

These are two fragments of the upper rim and filling-hole of the same small lamp made from buff clay. A dot design decorates the rim.

L86 (context 18054)

This is a fragment of a profile of a lamp made from gray clay fired to light orange. A dot design decorates the rim.

L87 (context 18061.1)

This is a fragment of a profile of a lamp made from gray clay. A dot pattern decorates the rim.

L88 (context 18108)

This is a fragment of an upper part of a lamp made from buff clay. A dot pattern appears on the rim.

L89 (context 18153)

This is a fragment of a profile of a lamp made from buff clay. A dot design decorates the rim.

Variant C: Lamps with a Plain Top with No Decoration

L90 (SF 243, context 11046)   PL. 85
L. 6.8 cm; W. 6.4 cm; H. 2.1 cm

This complete lamp, which has a round body and very small nozzle, is made from buff-pinkish clay. Its rim has no decorations.
Parallel: Dura-Europos (Baur 1947, 36, Type 5, Group 4, no. 210, fig. 12, pl. 5).

L91 (SF 375, context 9000)   PL. 85
L. 7.6 cm; W. 6.9 cm; H. 2.2 cm

This lamp, of which almost half survived, has a slightly convex top with a tiny filling-hole and nozzle. It is made from fine light gray clay.

L92 (SF 750, context 9245)   PL. 85
L. 7 cm; W. 6.9 cm; H. 2.2 cm

This almost complete lamp is made from gray clay. Both the nozzle and filling-hole are broken. The rim is plain.

L93 (SF 2182, context 2006)

This lamp, of which part of its upper half survived, is made from light brown clay.

L94 (SF 2184, context 2006)

This is a fragment of a lower part of a lamp made from buff clay.

L95 (SF 4184, context 9001)

This is a fragment of a lower part of a lamp made from pinkish-orange clay.

L96 (SF 4185, context 9001)

This is a fragment of a lower part of a lamp made from light gray clay.

L97 (SF 4210, context 11112)

This is a fragment of a lower part of a lamp made from light gray clay.

L98 (context 2002)

This is a fragment of a lower part of a lamp made from gray clay fired to buff.

L99 (context 2046)

This is a fragment of a lower part of a lamp made from light gray clay with inclusions of black sand.

L100 (context 2162)

This is a fragment of a lower part of a lamp made from light gray clay.

L101 (context 2294)

Only a fragment of the nozzle and upper part of a small lamp is preserved; made from pinkish-gray clay.

L102 (context 11112)

This is a fragment of a lower part of a lamp made from gray clay.

L103 (context 15237.3)

This is a fragment of a profile of a lamp made from gray clay fired to black.

Variant D: Lamps with a Flat Top Decorated with Floral Motifs, Such as Clusters of Leaves and Tendrils

L104 (SF 930, context 18070) PL. 85
L. 7.7 cm; W. 6.4 cm; H. 2.3 cm

This is complete lamp made from pink clay. The decoration on the shoulder around the filling-hole consists of a garland with leaves bound up in sections, or a laurel wreath. A Greek inscription within the circular base reads: ΒΑΓ ΓΟ, as in L70.

Similar: For decoration, see Szentléleky 1969, nos. 147a, 148a, pp. 96–7.
Parallel: Dura-Europos (Baur 1947, 40–1, Type 5, Group 6, nos. 251, 252, fig. 15, pl. 6).

L105 (SF 3679, context 15002)

This is a fragment of an upper part of a lamp made from fine yellowish-gray clay. The decoration around the filling-hole consists of a repetitive pattern of clusters of leaves.

Variant E: Lamps with a Flat Top Decorated with a Curious Rope Pattern

L106 (SF 860, context 18070) PL. 86
L. 7 cm; W. 6.1 cm; H. 2.3 cm

This is complete lamp made from fine buff clay and well fired. The decoration on the rim consists of rope pattern with leaves around the filling-hole.
Parallel: Dura-Europos (Baur 1947, 41–2, Type 5, Group 7, nos. 256, 263, pl. 6).

L107 (SF 3454, context 18108) PL. 86
L. 8.5 cm; W. 7.8 cm; H. 2.3 cm

This complete lamp, with a small knob handle on either side, is made from black clay. The decoration on the rim consists of a rope pattern with leaves around the filling-hole and a crescent motif with a dot inside it, found on the nozzle. The base has a circle with branch motif.

L108 (SF 4186, context 9001)

This is a fragment of a profile of a lamp made from buff clay.

L109 (context 18061.2)

This is a fragment of an upper part of a lamp made from gray clay fired to light brown. A rope pattern appears on the rim.

Variant F: Lamps with a Sunken Filling-Hole and High Shoulder, Sometimes Decorated with an Ovate Pattern

L110 (SF 2038, context 2000) PL. 86
L. 8.6 cm; W. 7.8 cm; H. 2.3 cm

This complete lamp, with some partial damage on the rear, is made from buff clay. The decoration on the rim consists of a chevron pattern and a ridge around the discus.

L111 (context 2000)   PL. 86

H. 3 cm

This is a fragment of a profile of a lamp made from gray clay. A chevron pattern and a circular ridge decorate the rim.

L112 (context 2160)

This is a fragment of an upper part of a lamp made from light gray clay with inclusions of black sand.

L113 (context 18001)

This is a fragment of a profile of a lamp made from buff well-fired clay. A chevron pattern and three circular lines decorate the rim.

Type 5: Two-Nozzle Lamp, First Half of Third Century A.D.

L114 (SF 406, context 11004)   PL. 87

This is a fragment of a profile of a lamp made from brown clay.

L115 (SF 845, context 9073)

This is a fragment of a body and handle of a lamp made from gray clay.

L116 (SF 895, context 7000)   PL. 87

L. 9.3 cm; W. 8.8 cm; H. 4.6 cm

This lamp, of which almost half survived, is made from buff pinkish clay. The decoration on the rim consists of three strips of ladder design.

L117 (SF 898, context 7002)

This fragment of a body and small nozzle of a lamp is made from pinkish-gray clay.

L118 (SF 2188, context 2046)

This is a fragment of a base of a lamp made from pinkish-gray clay.

L119 (SF 2147, context 2039)   PL. 88

This almost complete lamp is made from light brown clay. The rim is incised with a ladder design.

L120 (SF 2181, context 2010)

A fragment of a nozzle of a lamp made from gray clay.

L121 (SF 2186, context 2019)

This fragment of a body and handle of a lamp is made from light gray clay fired to buff.

L122 (SF 2187, context 2046)   PL. 89

A fragment of a body, including nozzle and handle, of a lamp made from gray clay.

L123 (SF 2377, context 2046)   PL. 89

A fragment of a lamp body including a nozzle and handle, made from light brown clay fired to gray on surface.

L124 (context 2039)

Two fragments of a profile of a lamp made from grayish-brown clay burnished on the surface.

L125 (context 2105)

A fragment of a nozzle of a lamp made from dark gray clay with remains of iron oxide.

L126 (context 10004)

A fragment of the lower part of a lamp made from orange-gray clay.

L127 (context 11028)   PL. 90

This lamp, of which part of the upper half and handle survived, is made from pinkish-gray clay. The decoration on the rim consists of two strips of ladder design.

L128 (context 11106)

A fragment of the lower part of a lamp made from gray clay.

L129 (context 12004)

This lamp, of which part of the upper half and handle survived, is made from pinkish-gray clay.

L130 (context 18000)

A fragment of the upper part of a lamp made from gray clay.

L131 (context 18085)

A fragment of the upper half of a lamp made from light gray clay fired to light brown on the surface. The decoration on the rim consists of one strip of ladder design.

Type 6: Ovoid Lamps with Linear Patterns, First Half of Third Century A.D.

L132 (SF 887, context 7150)   PL. 90
W. 6.2 cm; H. 3 cm

This almost compete lamp, with a broken nozzle, is made from buff-yellow clay. The rim is decorated with four patterns, each made out of a dot within three concentric semicircles. Dots are also found around the wick-hole. The base is decorated with a potter's mark in the form of a schematized palm branch within a circle, as in the example at the Moscow Museum.
Parallel: Moscow Museum (Chrzanovski and Zhuravlev 1998, 155, no. 104, p. 164).

L133 (SF 3403, context 18108)   PL. 91
W. 6 cm; H. 3.6 cm

This is a fragment of the lower part of a lamp made from pink clay.

L134 (SF 3680, context 15321)   PL. 91

This fragment of the upper part of a lamp with a handle is made from light orange clay. The rim is decorated with closely set linear wavy lines and volutes.
Similar: Dura-Europos, dated to "Late Syrian (?) fourth–fifth centuries" (Baur 1947, 71, Type 10, nos. 408–10, pl. 13); Antioch (Waagé 1941, Type 4?).

Type 7: Oblong Lamps, Late Fifth to Early Sixth Century A.D.

L135 (SF 89, context 5048)   PL. 92
L. 8.6 cm; W. 5.7 cm; H. 3 cm

This almost compete lamp is made from yellowish-brown clay with reddish-brown slip. The raised disc around the filling-hole is edged by a groove and decorated with three rows of dots. A deep groove at tongue handle cuts the disc at rear. The nozzle (now broken) has a trapezoidal shape. The base is emphasized by a circular ridge and a dot in the center. There are two other dots under the nozzle.
Parallel: British Museum, from Dèhès in North Syria, dated fifth to sixth century (Bailey 1988, 289, Q2343 WAA, pl. 61, fig. 146); Anawati Collection, "Boat-shaped" Syro-Palestinian (Djurik 1995, 78–9, nos. C264, C266).
Similar: Antioch (Waagé 1941, 67, no. 159, fig. 80).

L136 (SF 747, context 9000)   PL. 93
L. 7.1; W. 5.8 cm; H. 4.5 cm

This lamp, of which only half survived, is made from light yellowish clay with red slip outside. It has a flat rim with three ridges around the filling-hole. The tongue handle is raised and decorated by three grooves. There are two dots on the nozzle and two others below the handle.
Similar: Cyprus Museum, dated as Byzantine (Oziol 1977, 271, nos. 820, 822, PL. 45).

L137 (SF 905, context 7077)

A fragment of handle and the base of this lamp are made from yellowish-brown clay with red slip. The rim is decorated with three rows of dots around the filling-hole. A ridge is found on top of the handle.

L138 (SF 4176, context 15002)

A fragment of the handle and base of this lamp are made from orange-brown clay with reddish-brown slip. The handle is decorated with a groove on either side. A radiating pattern and dots can be seen on the base.

L139 (SF 4177, context 15073)

A fragment of the handle and base of this lamp are made from orange-brown clay with brown slip. The handle is decorated with a groove on either side. A radiating pattern and dots can be seen on the base.

L140 (SF 4208, context 7180)   PL. 93

This lamp, of which only the upper half survived, is made from light brown clay with reddish-brown slip outside. The disc around the filling-hole is decorated with three rows of dots. A ridge around the rim extends to the nozzle, which now is broken. The tongue handle is flat and marked by a ridge.

L141 (context 9183.1)

This fragment of body and handle are made from pinkish-gray clay with reddish-brown slip outside. The rim is decorated with a strip of three rows of dots around the filling-hole. A ridge is found on top and below the handle.

Type 8: Syro-Palestinian Lamps, Late Sixth to Eighth Century A.D.

Variant A

L142 (SF 69, context 5000)   PL. 94
L. not preserved; W. 7 cm; H. 4.8 cm

This oval lamp, with three-quarters of it preserved, is made from buff-pinkish clay. It has a nozzle-channel and a large filling-hole with a low ridge around it. Two concentric bands of ladder pattern surround the filling-hole. Part of a sign, probably an alpha, in relief appears on the nozzle-channel. The base ring is decorated with a seven-branched radiating pattern in relief.

Parallel: The British Museum, from the Huran, Syria, dated seventh to eighth century (Bailey 1988, 287, Q2328 MLA, pl. 60, fig. 138).
Similar: Cyprus Museum (Oziol 1977, 262, no. 790, pl. 43); Schloessinger Collection (Rosenthal and Sivan 1978, 132, no. 538); Anawati Collection (Djuric 1995, 101, no. C330); Day 1942, 71, no. 2, pl. 11; Kennedy 1963, 111, Type 23, no. 775, pl. 28; Baramki 1944, no. 7, Group 1, pl. 17; Da Costa 2001, 246, Type 23, fig. 4:4.

L143 (SF 70, context 5000) PL. 95
L. not preserved; W. 6.4 cm; H. 4.1 cm

This lamp, which is almost complete, is made from buff clay. It has a large filling-hole with a high ridge surrounded by a channel and extends into the nozzle. A decoration is formed by a strip of radial pattern on the rim with two volutes on either side of the nozzle surround the filling-hole. The base ring is decorated with a seven-branched radiating pattern.
Similar: Apamea (Napoleone and Balty 1969, 128–9, no. 30, fig. 35).

L144 (SF 80, context 5000) PL. 96
L. not preserved; W. 6.4 cm; H. 4.3 cm

This lamp, which is almost complete, is made from buff-pinkish clay with patches of cement rendering on the exterior. The nozzle is damaged. A strip of radial pattern on the rim surrounds the filling-hole. Within the base ring there is a geometric design in the form of a parallelogram with a rectangle and a dot in the center. A ridge can be seen below the nozzle.
Similar: Apamea (Napoleone and Balty 1969, 128–9, no. 30, fig. 35); Anawati (Djuric 1995, 90, no. C288).

L145 (SF 501, context 7036) PL. 97
L. 8.2 cm; W. 6.5 cm; H. 4.2 cm

This lamp, which is almost complete, is made from buff clay. It has a large filling-hole with a high ridge surrounded by a channel that extends into the nozzle. A decoration is formed by a strip of radial pattern on the rim with two volutes on either side of the nozzle. The nozzle has a curious U-shape design with two lines across it and a dot. The base ring is decorated with a circle pattern.

L146 (SF 588, context 15001) PL. 97
L. 8.8 cm; W. 6.3 cm; H. 4.5 cm

This lamp, which is almost complete, is made from buff clay. The nozzle is partly damaged. A decoration is formed by a strip of radial pattern on the rim with two volutes on either side of the nozzle. The nozzle has a curious geometric design in the shape of U with a triangle and an X inside it. The base ring has another curious sign inside it that might be a potter's mark.
Similar: Anawati Collection (Djuric 1995, 94, no. C303).

L147 (SF 625, context 7060) PL. 97
L. 9.4 cm; W. 7.3 cm; H. 4.8 cm

This complete lamp is made from buff clay. It has a large filling-hole with a high ridge surrounded by a channel that extends into the nozzle. A decoration is formed by two strips of radial pattern on the rim with a volutes and a chevron design on either side of the nozzle. On the channel are a cross and chevron designs. A smaller cross is found on either side of the knob handle. Within the base ring is a design in the shape of the letter M.

L148 (SF 636, context 7202) PL. 97

This is a fragment of an upper part of a lamp made from buff-pink well-fired clay. A radial pattern on the rim can be found.

L149 (SF 638, context 7062) PL. 98
L. 9 cm; W. 8.2 cm; H. 5.2 cm

This lamp, of which three-quarters has survived, is made from buff pinkish clay. The nozzle is damaged. A decoration is formed by a strip of radial pattern on the rim with a volute on either side of the nozzle. The nozzle has a curious geometric design in the shape of parallelogram and a dot inside it.

L150 (SF 658, context 7065) PL. 98
L. 9.2 cm; W. 7.2 cm; H. 4.5 cm

This lamp, of which three-quarters has survived, is made from buff clay. The nozzle and part of the body are damaged. The decorations on the rim are in the form of a strip of radial pattern on the rim with a volute on either side of the nozzle. The channel has a chevron motif.

L151 (SF 665, context 7065)

This is a fragment consisting of a knob handle and part of the lower body of a lamp made from buff clay. Part of a radial design and a volute can be found.

L152 (SF 736, context 7006) PL. 99
L. not preserved; W. 7.2 cm; H. 4.5 cm

This lamp, of which three-quarters has survived, is made from buff well-fired clay. The nozzle is damaged. The decorations on the rim are in the form of a radial pattern bordered by a ridge ending in a volute on either side of the nozzle. The channel has a branch motif.

L153 (SF 751, context 9245)

This fragment of an upper part of a lamp is made from buff clay with a brown slip. Lines and semicircle patterns are found.

L154 (SF 882, context 7214) PL. 100

This is a fragment of an upper part of a lamp made from buff clay. A radial design is found.

L155 (SF 885, context 7212) PL. 100

This fragment of an upper part of a lamp is made from buff-pinkish and well-fired clay. A radial pattern can be seen, as well as a cross design on the channel.

L156 (SF 897, context 7024)

This fragment of an upper part of a lamp is made from yellowish-gray clay. A radial pattern and ladder design can be seen.

L157 (SF 899, context 7326) PL. 100

This is a fragment of a lower part of a lamp made from light gray clay. The base ring is decorated with a six-petaled rosette within a circle. Tow ridges are found under the nozzle.

L158 (SF 901, context 7060)

This is a fragment of an upper part of a lamp, including a tall knob handle, made from orange-gray clay. A radial pattern and ladder design can be seen.

L159 (SF 902, context 7060) PL. 100

This is a fragment of an upper part of a lamp, including part of a filling-hole, made from pinkish-gray clay. Three strips of a ladder, zigzag, and radial patterns can be seen.

L160 (SF 903, context 7202)

This fragment of an upper part of a lamp, including part of a filling-hole, is made from pinkish clay. A strip of a radial pattern can be seen.

L161 (SF 904, context 7077)

This fragment of an upper part of a lamp, including part of a filling-hole, is made from light gray clay. Two strips of a radial pattern can be seen.

L162 (SF 906, context 7964)

This is a fragment of an upper part of a lamp, including a tall knob handle, made from orange-gray clay. A radial pattern and ladder design can be seen.

L163 (SF 2286, context 2031) PL. 100

This fragment of an upper part of a lamp, including part of the filling-hole, is made from buff-pink clay. A strip of a palm leaf flanked by semicircle design can be seen.

L164 (SF 3167, context 12001)

This fragment of an upper part of a lamp, including part of a filling-hole and a wick-hole, is made from buff-brownish clay. One strip of a radial pattern bordered by a ridge ending in a volute can be seen.

L165 (SF 3175, context 12001)

This fragment of a lower part of a lamp is made from buff clay. The base ring is decorated with a six-petaled rosette.

L166 (SF 3656, context 15103) PL. 101
L. not preserved; W. 6.5 cm; H. 4.4 cm

This almost complete lamp is made from buff clay. The nozzle is damaged. A decoration is formed by one strip of radial pattern on the rim with a volute on either side of the nozzle. On the channel there is a triangular design. Within the base ring is a curious design, probably a potter's mark that happens to resemble the shape of the modern Euro currency sign.

L167 (SF 3683, context 15286)

A fragment of a profile, including a handle, of a lamp is made from gray clay.

L168 (SF 3688, context 12007) PL. 102
L. 9.6 cm; W. 7 cm; H. 3.9 cm

This complete lamp is made from buff clay. A decoration is formed by one strip of radial pattern on the rim with a volute on either side of the nozzle. On the channel there is a design of a circle with a dot in the middle as well as four other dots. Within the base ring is a cross design made with four dots.

L169 (SF 3689, context 12001)

This is the lower half of a lamp made from buff well-fired clay. Three ridges mark the lower part of the nozzle.

L170 (SF 3690, context 12001) PL. 103

This is part of a profile of a lamp made from buff-pink clay. The rim is decorated by a strip of radial pattern bordered by a ridge ending with a volute on either side of the nozzle. A volute can also be seen near the knob handle. On the channel there is a design of a star.

L171 (SF 4171, context 15000)

This is a fragment of a base of a lamp, made from buff clay.

L172 (SF 4172, context 15000)

This is a fragment of lamp, including a tall knob handle, made from pinkish clay. Traces of radial design can be seen.

L173 (SF 4173, context 15000)

This is a fragment of an upper part of a lamp, including part of the filling-hole and a knob handle, made from pinkish buff clay. A strip of a radial design can be seen.

L174 (SF 4174, context 15000)

This is a fragment of a base of a lamp, made from gray-buff clay.

L175 (SF 4175, context 15000)

This is a fragment of an upper part of a lamp, including part of the filling-hole and a knob handle, made from pinkish-buff clay. A geometric pattern can be seen adjacent to the handle.

L176 (SF 4179, context 15292)

This is a fragment of an upper part of a lamp, including part of the filling-hole, made from gray-buff clay. A radial pattern can be seen.

L177 (SF 4189, context 9000) PL. 103

This is a fragment of a base of a lamp, made from buff clay. The base is decorated with a four-pointed pattern set with a circular ladder design.

L178 (SF 4207, context 7026)

This is a fragment of an upper part of a lamp, including part of the filling-hole and a knob handle, made from yellowish-buff clay. A strip of a radial design and a volute can be seen.

L179 (SF 4209, context 13000) PL. 103

This is a fragment of an upper part of a lamp, including part of the filling-hole, made from yellowish-brown clay. A ladder design and a U-shape design are present.

L180 (SF 4211, context 5078) PL. 104

This is a fragment of an upper part of a lamp, including part of the filling-hole, made from buff well-fired clay. A strip of a radial design can be seen.

L181 (SF 4212, context 5123) PL. 104

This a fragment of an upper part of a lamp, including part of the filling-hole, made from buff clay. A strip of a radial design and a volute can be seen.

L182 (SF 4214, context 4008) PL. 104

This is a fragment of a lamp, including a nozzle and filling-hole, made from buff clay. The rim is decorated by a strip of radial pattern bordered by a ridge ending with a volute on either side of the nozzle. On the channel there is a design in the shape of the male sign.
Similar: Cyprus Museum (Oziol 1977, 262, Type 19, no. 789, pl. 43).

L183 (SF 4215, unstratified) PL. 104

This is a fragment of a lower part of a lamp with a circular ring base, made from yellowish-brown clay.

L184 (SF 4233, context 15002)

This is a fragment of an upper part of a lamp, including part of the filling-hole, made from light brown clay. A strip of a radial and a chevron design on either side of the rim can be seen.

L185 (context 2494)

This is a fragment of a lower part of a lamp with a circular ring base, made from buff clay.

L186 (context 7077) PL. 105

This is a fragment of a base of a lamp, made from orange clay. An eight-pointed cross design is set in the base ring.

L187 (context 12011.1) PL. 105

This is a fragment of an upper part of a lamp, including part of the filling-hole and knob handle, made from orange clay. A strip of a radial and a chevron design on either side of the rim can be seen and a volute on the side of the nozzle.

A design in the shape of the Greek letter alpha appears on the channel.

L188 (context 12011.2)   PL. 105

This is a fragment of a base of a lamp, made from buff clay. A design in the shape of the Greek letter alpha appears within the base ring.

L189 (context 12011.3)   PL. 105

This is a fragment of a nozzle of a lamp, made from dark grey clay. A design in the shape of the Greek letter alpha appears on the channel. A volute appears on the side of the nozzle.

L190 (context 12011.4)   PL. 105

This a fragment of an upper part of a lamp, including part of the filling-hole, made from dark-gray clay. A rosette within a circle motif and a dot decorate the rim.

Variant B

L191 (SF 216, context 11004)   PL. 105
L. 9.2 cm; W. 6.4 cm; H. 3.5 cm

This complete lamp is made from buff and well-fired clay. The base follows the outline of the lamp. A pattern of large dots decorates the rim.
Similar: Cyprus Museum (Oziol 1977, 260–261, Type 19, nos. 279–81).

L192 (SF 485, context 9183)   PL. 106
L. not preserved; W. 6 cm; H. 3.8 cm

This almost complete lamp is made from buff clay. The nozzle is damaged. No ridge can be found surrounding the filling-hole. The rim is decorated with dot pattern. The base has a pronounced spiral.

L193 (SF 507, context 7106)   PL. 107
L. 9.2 cm; W. 6.2 cm; H. 3.9 cm

This complete lamp is made from buff-brown clay. A shallow ridge around the filling-hole does not extend to the nozzle. There is a radial pattern on the rim and branch-with-two-leaves motif between the filling-hole and the wick-hole.

L194 (SF 642, context 7062)   PL. 107
L. 10.8 cm; W. 6.9 cm; H. 4.1 cm

This complete lamp is made from buff-orange clay. The rim is decorated with dot motif. On the channel there is an X design with large dots.
Similar: Apamea (Napoleone and Balty 1969, 114–5, no. 4, fig. 28).

L195 (SF 880, context 7214)   PL. 107
L. not preserved; W. 7.1 cm; H. 3.3 cm

This almost complete lamp is made from buff-pinkish well-fired clay. The nozzle is damaged. The rim is decorated with a radial design and the channel has a parallelogram and a dot in the middle. Along the lower part of the nozzle are two parallel ridges.
Parallel: Apamea (Napoleone and Balty 1969, 114–5, no. 1, fig. 28).

L196 (context 15001)   PL. 108
L. 9.8 cm; W. 8 cm; H. 5 cm

This is a fragment of an upper part of a lamp, including part of the filling-hole and knob handle, made from light orange clay with inclusions of fine black sand. A strip of ladder design surrounds the filling-hole.

Variant C

L197 (SF 3667, context 15232)   PL. 108
L. 5.8 cm; W. not preserved; H. 2.5 cm

This is part of a pear-shaped molded lamp made from light gray clay and is well fired. A radial pattern decorates the rim around the filling-hole. A rosette design is found within the base ring.

L198 (context 1024.1)

This is a fragment of a base of a lamp, made from buff clay.

L199 (context 2080)

This is a fragment of an upper part of a lamp, including part of the filling-hole, made from pinkish-gray clay with inclusions of fine black sand. A strip of a ladder design on the rim can be seen.

L200 (context 2291)

This is a small fragment of a profile of a lamp, including the handle. A semicircular design is found on the rim.

L201 (context 5078)

This is a fragment of an upper part of a lamp, including part of the filling-hole, made from pinkish-gray clay with inclusions of fine black sand. A strip of a ladder design on the rim can be seen.

L202 (context 7064)

This fragment of an upper part of a lamp, including part of the filling-hole and a knob handle, is made from buff clay. A strip of a radial design adjacent to the handle can be seen.

L203 (context 7201)

This is a fragment of an upper part of a lamp, including part of the filling-hole, made from yellowish-gray clay. A strip of ladder design and a strip of zigzag design decorate the rim.

L204 (context 7210)

This is a fragment of an upper part of a lamp, including a knob handle, made from buff clay. A strip of a radial design adjacent to the handle can be seen.

L205 (context 12001)

This is a fragment of an upper part of a lamp, including the filling-hole and knob handle, made from buff clay. A strip of radial design is found around the filling-hole.

L206 (context 12002)

This is a fragment of an upper part of a lamp, including part of the filling-hole and knob handle, made from light gray clay. A radial design is found on either side of the handle.

L207 (context 12011.5)

This is a fragment of an upper part of a lamp, including part of the filling-hole and knob handle, made from orange clay. A strip of a radial design on the side of the handle can be seen.

L208 (context 12011.6)

This is a fragment of an upper part of a lamp, including part of the filling-hole, made from light gray clay.

L209 (context 12011.7)

This is a fragment of an upper part of a lamp, including part of the filling-hole, made from orange-pinkish clay.

L210 (context 12011.8)

This is a fragment of an upper part of a lamp made from buff clay. A zigzag and dots design can be found.

L211 (context 12012.1)

This is a fragment of an upper part of a lamp, including part of the filling-hole and knob handle, made from buff clay. A radial design is found on the side of the handle.

L212 (context 12012.2)

This is a fragment of a lower part of a lamp, including part of a ring base, made from buff clay.

Type 9: Wheel-Made Lamps, Islamic, Ninth to Eleventh Century A.D.

L213 (context 1024.2) PL. 109

This is a fragment of a profile of lamp, including a base and nozzle, made from black clay. It is poorly fired.

Similar: Qal'at Sem'an, dated to the eighth and ninth centuries (Orssaud and Sodini 1997, 63–7, Group 1, fig. 1:1–6); Bet Shean (Hadad 2002, 106, Type 38, no. 468, Type 40, no. 470); Kennedy 1963, 91, Type 25, no. 797, pl. 29.

NOTES

1. My study of the ceramic oil lamp assemblage in Turkey, stored mainly at Birecik and partly at the Gaziantep Museum, was carried out during my two visits in June and August 2002. Throughout the study period I stayed at the Birecik compound, where the administrative staff from the Gaziantep Museum and Oxford Archaeology (OA) provided invaluable help. Amongst the former, I would like to thank Said Yilmaz, representative of the Gaziantep Museum, for his kind assistance and support. Amongst the latter, I am grateful to Adam Brossler, Andy Millar, and Philippa Walton for their cooperation and help. Thanks also go to Luke Adams, from OA, who made the pencil drawings of the lamps and prepared them for publication, and to Bruce Sampson for producing the photographs of the required specimens. I have benefited from discussions and exchange of views with Philip Kenrick, who carried out the study of the pottery (other than amphorae) from the Zeugma 2000 excavations. He kindly provided me with his pottery report, which included reasonably well-dated contexts upon which I enhanced the dating of some lamps types. And finally, I am also grateful to William Aylward for providing advice and support.
2. Lamps from areas excavated by other teams in 2000, namely the Gaziantep Museum, the University of Nantes, and the Zeugma Initiative Group, are not published here.
3. Nine undiagnostic lamp fragments are not included in the catalogue, one fragment each from the following nine contexts: 2089, 2154, 2189, 5090, 7044, 11040, 15211.3, 15237.2, 18083.
4. Antioch: Waagé 1931; 1941 (the latter is more of a comprehensive study of all lamps from the site. Tarsus: Goldman and Jones 1950.
5. Bailey 1975, nos. Q21–Q52, pls. 8–11; Hayes 1980, nos. 10–1.
6. Bailey 1975, nos. Q53–Q103, pls. 12–9; Hayes 1980, nos. 22–3; Rosenthal and Sivan 1978, 10, no. 11.
7. Waagé 1941, 56, nos. 6–12, fig. 75.
8. Baur 1947, 6–7, nos. 4–6, figs. 1–4.
9. Kenrick, this volume, Ceramic Group B.
10. Kenrick, this volume, Ceramic Group A.
11. Corinth: 1930, 61–6, nos. 301–311, pl. 6. Athens: Howland 1958, 173, Type 50C, pl. 50. British Museum: Bailey 1975, 99–105, nos. 159–80.
12. Oziol 1977, 60–63, nos. 134–42.
13. Rosenthal and Sivan 1978, 18, no. 38.
14. Tarsus: Goldman and Jones 1950, 91–2, Group 9, nos. 117–23, figs. 96–7. Antioch: Waagé 1934, 59–61, no. 1834. Dura-Europos: Baur 1947, 8–11, Type 3, nos. 7–8, fig 5.
15. Kenrick, this volume, Ceramic Group B.
16. Débevoise 1934, 120–2, figs. 373–87.
17. Kenrick, this volume, Ceramic Group C.
18. Hayes 1980, 15.
19. Corinth: Broneer 1930, Type 19. Athens: Howland 1958, Type 49. Antioch: Waagé 1934, Type 19. Tarsus: Goldman and Jones 1950, 79, Group 6, pl. 96.
20. Antioch: Waagé 1941, 63–5, Types 35–46, nos. 85–130, figs. 81–2. Dura-Europos: Baur 1947, 44–56, Type 6, pl. 7.
21. Perlzweig 1961, 87–8.
22. Bet Shean: Hadad 2002, 20, Type 10, nos. 32–33. Schloessinger Collection: Rosenthal and Sivan 1978, 90, 328.
23. Baur 1947, 26–44, Type 5, nos. 124–279.
24. Baur 1947, 26–44, Type 5, nos. 124–279.
25. Baur 1947, nos. 168 ff.
26. Baur 1947, nos. 168–209.
27. Baur 1947, nos. 256–72.
28. Dura-Europos: Baur 1947, nos. 280 ff. Antioch: Waagé 1941, nos. 120–30, fig. 79.
29. Kenrick, this volume, Ceramic Group D.
30. Baur 1947, 26.
31. Kenrick, this volume, Ceramic Group D.
32. Waagé 1941, 65, nos. 131–2.
33. Kenrick, this volume, Ceramic Group D.
34. Antioch: Waagé 1941, 66–7, nos. 152–4, fig. 80).
35. Baur 1947, nos. 341–3.
36. Kenrick, this volume, Ceramic Group E.
37. Waagé 1941, 67, nos. 158–60, fig. 80.
38. Hadad 2002, 26, Type 16, nos. 53–73.
39. Coen Uzzielli 1997, 320–2, fig. 1, pls. 1:5–6, 2.
40. Day 1942, 71.
41. Baur 1947, 71, no. 411, pl. 13.
42. Rosenthal and Sivan 1978, 132, nos. 538–41.
43. Day 1942, 66–71.
44. Kennedy 1963, 89–90.
45. Waagé 1941, 67–8, Type 56, fig. 81.
46. Hadad 2002, 82–94, Type 36, nos. 356–419.
47. Baramki 1944, 73, pls. 17–8.
48. Coen Uzzielli 1997, 326–8, fig. 13, pls. 7:5–6; 8.
49. Oziol 1977, pl. 43:771–807.
50. Rosenthal and Sivan 1978, nos. 533–62.
51. Kennedy 1963, 83, Type 23, Group A, nos. 761–75.
52. Kenrick, this volume, Ceramic Group F.
53. Kenrick, this volume, Ceramic Group F.
54. Kenrick, this volume, Ceramic Group G.
55. Déhès: Orssaud 1980, 258. Qal'at Sem'an: Orssaud and Sodini 1997, 63–7, Group 1.
56. Hadad 2002, 106, Type 40, no. 470.
57. Kennedy 1963, 91.
58. Cf. Walters 1914, 42–4.
59. Kenrick, this volume, Ceramic Group D.
60. Kenrick, this volume.
61. Broneer 1930, 73–6.
62. Tarsus: Goldman and Jones 1950, 95, Group 16. Antioch (Type 460), Dura-Europos (Type 6) and Palmyra: Amy and Seyrig 1936, Syria 17, 264, pl. 50–1; Michalowski 1964, 132–6, Group 4.
63. Flat-topped: Baur 1947, 11–26, Type 4, nos. 22–123. Wheel-made "Mesopotamian": Baur 1947, 58–69, Type 8, nos. 348–71.

BIBLIOGRAPHY

Amy, R., and H. Seyrig. 1936. "Recherches dans la nécropole de Palmyre, Lampes." *Syria* 17:262–4.

Baily, D.M. 1975. *Catalogue of Lamps in the British Museum, London*. Vol. 1, *Greek, Hellenistic and Early Roman Pottery Lamps*. London: British Museum Press.

———. 1988. *Catalogue of Lamps in the British Museum, London*. Vol. 3, *Roman Provincial Lamps*. London: British Museum Press.

Baramki, D.C. 1942. "The Pottery from Khirbet al-Mefjar." *QDAP* 10:65–104.

Baur, P.V.C. 1947. *The Excavations at Dura-Europos*. Pt. 3, *The Lamps*. New Haven: Yale University Press.

Broneer, O. 1930. *Corinth IV*. Vol. 2, *Terracotta Lamps*. Cambridge, MA: Harvard University Press.

Bruneau, P. 1965. *Exploration archéologique de Délos. 26: Les lampes*. Paris: Éditions de Boccard.

Chrzanovski, L., and D. Zhuravlev. 1998. *Lamps from Chersonesos in the State Historical Museum—Moscow*. Rome: "L'ERMA" di Bretschneider.

Clarke, G.W., et al. 2002. *Jebel Khalid on the Euphrates, Report on the Excavations 1986–1996*, vol. 1. *MeditArch* Suppl. 5. Sydney: Mediterranean Archaeology.

Coen Uzzielli, T. 1997. "The Oil Lamps." In *The Roman Baths of Hammat Gader: Final Report*, edited by Y. Hirschfeld, 319–46. Jerusalem: Israel Exploration Society.

Crowfoot, G.W., J.W. Crowfoot, and K.M. Kenyon. 1957. *The Objects from Samaria: Samaria-Sebaste*, vol. 3. London: Palestine Exploration Society.

Da Costa, K. 1988. "Byzantine and Early Islamic Lamps: Typology and Distribution." In *La céramique Byzantine et proto-islamique en Syrie-Jordanie (IVe-VIIIe siècles apr. J.-C.). Actes du colloque tenu à Amman les 3, 4 et 5 décembre 1994*, edited by E. Villeneuve and P.M. Watson, 241–57. BAHBeyrouth 159. Beirut: Institut français d'archéologie du Proche-Orient.

Day, F.E. 1942. "Early Islamic and Christian Lamps." *Berytus* 7:65–79.

Débevoise, N.C. 1934. *Parthian Pottery from Selucia-on-the-Tigris*. Ann Arbor: University of Michigan Press.

Djuric, S. 1995. *Ancient Lamps from the Mediterranean: The Anawati Collection Catalogue I*. Toronto: Elka.

Goldman, H., and F.F. Jones. 1950. "The Lamps." In *Excavations at Gozlu Kule, Tarsus, I: The Hellenistic and Roman Periods*, edited by H. Goldman, 84–134. Princeton: Princeton University Press.

Hadad, S. 2002. *The Oil Lamps from the Hebrew University Excavations at Bet Shean*. Jerusalem: Institute of Archaeology, Hebrew University of Jerusalem.

Hayes, J.W. 1980. *Ancient Lamps in the Royal Ontario Museum I: Greek, Roman Clay Lamps*. Toronto: Royal Ontario Museum.

Hellmann, M.-C. 1987. *Lampes Antique de la Bibliothéque Nationale II, Fonds general: Lampes pré-Romaines et Romaines*. Paris: La Bibliotheque.

Howland, R.H. 1958. *The Athenian Agora IV: Greek Lamps and Their Survivals*. Princeton: Princeton University Press.

Kassab Tezgör, D., and T. Sezer. 1995. *Catalogue des lampes terre cuite muse archéologique d'Istanbul*. Vol. 1, *Epoque protohistorique, archaïque, classique et hellénistique*. Paris: Diffusion de Boccard.

Kennedy, C.A. 1963. "The Development of the Lamps in Palestine." *Berytus* 14:67–115.

Loeschck, S. 1919. *Lampen aus Vindonissa: Ein Beitrag zur Geschichte von Vindonissa und des Antiken Beleuchtungswesens*. Zürich: Beer.

Lyon-Caen, C. 1986. *Catalogue des lampes en terre cuite grecques et chretiennes*. Paris: Musée du Louvre.

Michalowski, K. 1964. *Palmyre, Fouilles Polonaises 1962*. Warszawa: Panstwowe Wydawnictwo Naukowe.

Modrzewska, I. 1988 *Studio Iconologico delle Lucerne Siro-Palestinesi de IV–VII Sec. D.C., RdA* Suppl. 4. Roma: G. Bretschneider.

Napoleone-Lemaire, J., and J. Balty. 1969. *Fouilles d'Apamée de Syrie, I*. Vol. 1, *L'église a atrrium de la grande colonnade*. Brussels: Centre belge de recherches archéologiques à Apamée de Syrie.

Orssaud, D. 1980. "La céramique." In "Dehès (Syrie du Nord), Campagnes I–III (1976–1978). Recherrches sur l'habitat rural," edited by J.-P. Sodini, et al., 234–66. *Syria* 57:1–304.

Orssaud, D., and J.-P. Sodini. 1997. "Les Lampes tournées de Qal'at Sem'an et leurs parallèles dans le basin méditerranéen." In *La céramique medieval en Méditerranée. Actes du VI congrès de l'AIECM2 Aix-en-Provence (13–18 Novembre 1995)*, edited by G.D. d'Archimbaud, 63–72. Aix-en-Provence: Narration.

Oziol, T. 1977. *Salamine de Chypre VII: Les lampes du musée de chypre*. Paris: Diffusion de Boccard.

Perlzweig, J. 1961. *The Athenian Agora VII: Lamps of the Roman Period*. Princeton: Princeton University Press.

Rosenthal, R., and R. Sivan. 1978. *Ancient Lamps in the Schlossinger-Heginbottom Collection Qedem 8*. Jerusalem: Institute of Archaeology, Hebrew University of Jerusalem.

Szentléleky, T. 1969. *Ancient Lamps*. Budapest: Akademiai Kiado.

Waagé, F.O. 1934. "Lamps, Pottery, Metal and Glass Ware." In *Antioch-on-the-Orontes*. Vol. 1, *The Excavations of 1932*, edited by G. Elderkin, 58–75. Princeton: Princeton University Press.

———. 1941. "Lamps." In *Antioch-on-the-Orontes*. Vol. 3, *The Excavations 1937–1939*, edited by R. Stillwell, 55–82. Princeton: Princeton University Press.

Walters, H.B. 1914. *Catalogue of the Greek and Roman Lamps in the British Museum*. London: Printed by Order of the Trustees.

· CHAPTER SIX ·

Terracotta Figurines

Jeffrey Gingras and William Aylward

DISCUSSION

The terracotta objects discussed in this chapter were found in Trenches 1, 2, 4, 5, 7, 9, 10, 11, 12, 13, 15, 18 and 19 during the rescue excavations at Zeugma in 2000.[1] Trenches 2 and 18 had the greatest concentrations of terracotta objects, with six and five items, respectively. Only one archaeological context had more than a single terracotta represented. This was context 9301, which yielded part of a draped figurine (**TC7**) and a fragment with vegetal ornament (**TC20**).

In addition to these two artifacts, five other terracottas belong to contexts dated to the Sasanian sack of A.D. 252/253 (**TC1, TC2, TC4, TC13, TC16**).[2] Among these are part of a half-draped Aphrodite statuette (**TC1**) from context 18108, a fragment of a draped figurine (**TC2**) from context 18083, a Papposilenus figurine (**TC4**) from context 2158, and a fragment of a miniature theatrical mask (**TC16**) from context 9073. Other terracotta figurines datable by their contexts are **TC18** (late Augustan or Tiberian) and **TC9** (seventh century A.D.).[3] The latter is probably residual. Thus, the terracottas from the dated contexts suggest the Roman period up to the sack of A.D. 252/253 as the principal phase of use of terracotta figurines at Zeugma. None of the terracottas need be Hellenistic.

Over half the terracottas are fragments of anthropomorphic figurines (**TC1–TC14, TC17, TC19**). Five are whole or partial female heads (**TC10–TC14**), and two are fragments of miniature theatrical masks (**TC15, TC16**). A bird, probably a dove, is the only example of an animal (**TC18**). Architectural ornament may have been the function of **TC20**. The two fragments of theatrical masks (**TC15, TC16**) and the Papposilenos figurine (**TC4**) are welcome evidence in support of a theater, a building that is suspected but not yet proven for Zeugma by archaeological excavation.[4]

The Zeugma terracottas are worthy of comparison with terracottas from Dura-Europos, more for their differences than for their similarities.[5] Plaques are well represented at Dura-Europos, but are absent at Zeugma. Theatrical masks of the type found at Zeugma were not found at Dura-Europos. The predominant animal among the terracottas at Dura-Europos is the horse, which does not appear in the Zeugma corpus. Most terracottas at Dura-Europos were handmade, but mold-made figurines at Zeugma are in the majority.[6] Reasons for these rather stark differences undoubtedly lie in the Parthian culture of Dura-Europos and the dominant Roman influence at Zeugma. Still, it seems that neither site had a particular proclivity for terracotta figurines.[7] It would be rash to conjure up the absence of local clay sources to explain the cause of such disinterest at Zeugma, especially since the ceramics at Zeugma attest to the mining of local clay.[8] Local stone may have been the preferred medium for sculpture at Dura-Europos, but at Zeugma stone sculpture has not been found in amounts sufficient to support a similar conclusion. Most of the figurines at Zeugma are mold-made, and the mass production implied by these finds suggests that more terracottas are probably to be found elsewhere at the site. Indeed, the dearth of terracottas found in the rescue excavations of 2000 reflects the focus of excavation in a residential district of the city. Terracotta figurines are by no means foreign to private domestic contexts, but, in their primary function as votives, they are likely to be present in greater numbers at sanctuaries. Yet excavations in the sanctuary identified in Trench 15 at Zeugma yielded only three terracottas, and these add little to the epigraphic and sculptural evidence for the ruler cult of the Commagenian kings found there. Among these figurines, only the bird belongs to a context securely dated to the lifetime, albeit the very end, of the Commagenian ruler-cult sanctuary.[9] The other two terracottas from Trench 15 (**TC6, TC19**) may be intrusive.

More evocative for religion at Zeugma are the five fragments that preserve female heads. Regrettably, these are all rather worn, and without clues for specific attribution. Regional goddesses of great popularity — Dea Syria, Tyche, Cybele, Atargatis — seem to be ruled out by the absence of their distinctive headgear.[10] Only the dove, like the one preserved in **TC18**, is an occasional component of their iconography.[11] For the female heads, Aphrodite seems a possibility, particularly because of the Aphrodite Anadyomene terracotta figurine from Trench 18 (**TC1**). She must have been of some importance at Zeugma if one considers that the excavators found three other representations of her in the rescue excavations of 2000: two in bronze (**BR153, BR154**) and one in animal bone (**B29**).[12] **TC14** may represent Hermes, but only on the basis of the striking comparison of the youthful facial features and star-shaped wreath to a well-preserved Hermes from Tomb 24 at Dura-Europos, where he appears as psychopompos with caduceus. **TC14** was a surface find from near the heart of the city, and so an original funerary context is unlikely. If the figurine does depict Hermes, then he perhaps appeared as patron of the marketplace at Zeugma.

CATALOGUE

All dimensions are in cm; the following abbreviations are used:
- M.P.H. = maximum preserved height
- M.P.W. = maximum preserved width

Figure 1. **TC1.**

TC1 (SF 3455, context 18108)
Fragment of draped figurine
M.P.H. 8.7 cm; M.P.W. 4.6 cm; wall thickness .4–1 cm   FIG. 1

Three fragments that join. Preserves torso, arms, and legs above the knees. Head, lower legs, and part of back missing. S-shaped pose with left hand obscuring pudenda. Drapery tied in a knot just below the hips. Nipples and naval rendered by small dimples. Fingers articulated on hands. Fingerprints visible on interior. The pose and drapery are consistent with statuettes of half-draped Aphrodite. For the type in other media at Zeugma, see **BR153–154, B29**.
Similar: Lang-Auinger 2003, TK1; Downey 1977, 158–9, nos. 11–14; Delivorrias et al. 1984, no. 689; Burn and Higgins 2001, nos. 2305, 2306; Muller 1996, 878; Grandjouan 1961, nos. 3, 6, 20; Rostovtzeff 1944–, pl. XVII fig. 2; Mollard-Besques 1963, nos. a-LY 1546, b-MYRINA 1033, c-LY 1588, d-B° 127, e-B° 80, f-MYRINA 965, a-MYR 19, a-LY 1553, b-MYRINA 1026, c-B° 95, d-MYR 20, e-M 10, f-B° 53, e-MYRINA 961, d-MYRINA 24.

Figure 2. **TC2.**

TC2 (SF 3384, context 18083)
Fragment of draped figurine
M.P.H. 3.7 cm; M.P.W. 3.65 cm;
wall thickness .2-.7 cm   FIG. 2

Fragment of draped figurine with belt and traces of headgear (Phrygian cap?) preserved on shoulders. Well-preserved details. Mold-made. Fingerprints visible on interior. Pose and accoutrements are somewhat similar to figurines of Attis.
Similar: Burn and Higgins 2001, no. 2183.

Figure 3. **TC3.**

TC3 (SF 2150, context 2038)
Head and upper torso of draped figurine
M.P.H. 8.9 cm; M.P.W. 7 cm; wall thickness .8 cm   FIG. 3

Two fragments that join. Preserves head, part of upper body, and one arm. Trace of drapery preserved at neck. Object held in arm is not identifiable. Very worn. Preserves

only traces of mouth, nose, eyes, and hairline. Mold-made. Preserves trace of seam for connection between front and back. Fingerprints visible on interior and exterior.
Parallel: Higgins 1954, nos. 121–4, 288, 290, 336, 337, 655, 657–9, 811, 940, 1208; Török 1995, no. 114.

Figure 4. TC4.

TC4 (SF 2227, context 2158)
Fragment of draped figurine
M.P.H. 10 cm; M.P.W. 4.4 cm; wall thickness 3.5 cm   FIG. 4

Papposilenus figurine. Preserves torso, legs, and part of both arms; broken at neck and feet. Left arm holds a cane and a sack, or perhaps a tambourine. Proper right arm was raised at least to shoulder height. Chest covered by long beard.
Parallel: Burn and Higgins 2001, nos. 2257, 2379, 2656, 2658, 2787, 2788; Davidson and Thompson 1943, no. 68; Grandjouan 1961, nos. 505, 507; Merker 2000, no. I42; Mollard-Besques 1963, no. C-MYR 670; Muller 1996, no. 1091; Robinson 1952, nos. 380 A–C; Vafopoulou-Richardson 1991, nos. 42, 43.

Figure 5. TC5.

TC5 (SF 4126, context 7002)
Fragment of draped reclining figurine
M.P.H. 3.4 cm; M.P.W. 5.3 cm; wall thickness .4 cm   FIG. 5

Preserves draped right arm and shoulder of a reclining figurine, perhaps a banqueter. Arm draped by a himation; hand holds a decorated two-handled cup, probably a kantharos. Fingerprints preserved on back.
Similar: Grandjouan 1961, no. 237l; Fjeldhagen 1995, no. 95.

Figure 6. TC6.

TC6 (SF 4319, context 15103)
Fragment of draped figurine
M.P.H. 6.45 cm; M.P.W. 4.35 cm;
wall thickness .4–.9 cm   FIG. 6

Preserves front and small part of back (left) of draped figurine on a base. Drapery (himation?) obscures the feet. Mold-made. Fingerprints visible on interior.
Similar: Thompson 1963, nos. 94, 152.

Figure 7. TC7.

Figure 9. TC10. *Photo (left) and drawing (right).*

TC7 (SF 3081, context 9301)
Fragment of draped figurine
M.P.H. 4.85 cm; M.P.W. 4.2 cm;
wall thickness .2–.5 cm   FIG. 7

Preserves lower part of draped figurine on a base. Feet protrude from below the drapery. Back is slightly convex and without detail. Mold-made.

TC8 (SF 4317, context 19006)
Fragment of draped figurine
M.P.H. 4.25 cm; M.P.W. 3.6 cm; wall thickness .7 cm

Fragment of drapery, perhaps part of a kolpos. Very worn.
Similar: Merker 2000, nos. C24; Muller 1996, no. 31.

TC10 (SF 921, context 18014)
Head of female figurine
M.P.H. 6 cm; M.P.W. 4.5 cm; wall thickness .4 cm   FIG. 9

Preserves head of female figurine with possible Knidian coiffure. Broken at neck; very worn. Over-sized eyes and mouth, robust cheeks. Venus rings on neck. Earlobes (or earrings?) rendered by small protuberances. Hair falls to shoulders and is articulated by small indentations. Mold-made.
Similar: Bonanno 1979, no. 18; Burn and Higgins 2001, no. 2253; Fjeldhagen 1995, no. 143.

Figure 10. TC12.

TC9 (SF 4321, context 12011)
Fragment of draped figurine
M.P.H. 4.5 cm; M.P.W. 4.9 cm;
wall thickness .1–.2 cm   FIG. 8

Preserves part of drapery, perhaps from the upper torso. Mold-made.
Similar: Thompson 1963, no. 4; Muller 1996, no. 1.

Figure 8. TC9.

TC11 (SF 504, context 7003)
Head with petasos
M.P.H. 5.35 cm; M.P.W. 3.4 cm;
wall thickness .15–.5 cm   FIG. 10

Preserves head of figurine with petasos, broken at neck. Mold-made. Preserves trace of seam for connection between front and back. Fingerprints visible on interior.
Similar: Török 1995, nos. 216, 217; Lang-Auinger 2003, TK65.

Figure 11. TC12.

TC12 (SF 876, context 18110)
Head of female figurine
M.P.H. 3.35 cm; M.P.W. 3.15 cm;
wall thickness .2 cm   FIG. 11

Preserves front half of head with vestiges of red paint; hair crowned by a stephane. Broken at neck. Preserves fingerprints on back. Similar in fabric, scale, and workmanship to TC1.
Parallel: Mollard-Besques 1963, nos. f-MYRINA 979, c-B° 165, e-IHA 6; Grandjouan 1961, nos. 372, 337, 353; Thompson 1963, nos. 253–71; Török 1995, nos. 216, 217; Higgins 1954, no. 123; Downey 2003, no. 51.

Figure 13. TC14.

TC14 (SF 3412, context 19000)
Fragment of head of figurine
M.P.H. 4.85 cm; M.P.W. 4.2 cm;
wall thickness .5–1 cm   FIG. 13

Preserves proper right side of head. Broken at back. Somewhat abstract facial features. The head is framed by a star-shaped wreath, with rays perhaps meant to depict broad triangular leaves. Wreath has incised lines and impressed dots. Mold-made.
Similar: Fjeldhagen 1995, no. 127; Downey 2003, no. 57.

Figure 12. TC13.

TC13 (SF 2131, context 2014)
Head of female figurine
M.P.H. 5.6 cm; M.P.W. 4.6 cm; wall thickness .2 cm   FIG. 12

Head of a female figurine, broken at neck. Very worn. Mold-made. Preserves trace of seam for connection between front and back.

Figure 14. TC15.

TC15 (SF 1015, context 1056)
Fragment of miniature theatrical mask
M.P.H. 5.5 cm; M.P.W. 4.7 cm; wall thickness .4 cm   FIG. 14

Preserves nose and mouth; broken on all sides. Stylized mouth and wide nostrils. Spalling below mouth.
Parallel: Mollard-Besques 1963, nos. a-MYR 347, b-MYR 349; Török 1995, no. 232; Grandjouan 1961, no. 528.

Figure 15. TC16.

TC16 (SF 134, context 9073)
Fragment of miniature mask
M.P.H. 10.5 cm; M.P.W. 7.5 cm;
wall thickness .4–.8 cm   FIG. 15

Two fragments that join. Preserves parts of forehead, nose, and chin with a trace of what may be a beard. Two protrusions from the forehead are consistent with representations of Pan and Silenus. Pierced in middle of forehead. Burnt interior. Mold-made. Small fragment of iron attached to nose, probably postdepositional.
Similar: Burn and Higgins 2001, nos. 2267, 2462, 2833; Davidson and Thompson 1943, no. 78; Török 1995, nos. 234, 235, 237; Thompson 1963, no. 132.

Figure 16. TC17.

TC17 (SF 919, context 18015)
Fragment of anthropomorphic leg
M.P.H. 4 cm: M.P.W. 3 cm; wall thickness 1.6 cm   FIG. 16

Preserves foot and part of calf. Worn; break difficult to distinguish.
Similar: Burn and Higgins 2001, nos. 2451, 2820, 2821; Thompson 1963, no. 141; Török 1995, no. 321.

Figure 17. TC18.

TC18 (SF 591, context 15009)
Bird
M.P.H. 4 cm; M.P.W. 7.5 cm; thickness .9 cm   FIG. 17

Bird with folded wings, perhaps a dove, with details for wing, beak, and eye; broken at end of tail. Mold-made, solid construction. Bird figurines similar to this one in construction, but resembling a rooster in appearance, were discovered in Trenches 3 and 8.
Similar: Higgins 1954, nos. 183, 275, 569, 692; Burn and Higgins 2001, 2409, 2410, 2856; Grandjouan 1961, no. 846; Davidson and Thompson 1943, no. 95.

Figure 18. **TC19**.

TC19 (SF 599, context 15002)
Fragment of an anthropomorphic head
M.P.H. 6 cm; M.P.W. 3.6 cm   FIG. 18

Fragment of anthropomorphic head. Hand-made. Very worn.
Similar: Downey 2003, no. 78.

Figure 19. **TC20**.

TC20 (SF 841, context 9301)
Fragment of vegetal ornament
M.P.H. 7.4 cm; M.P.W. 6.7 cm   FIG. 19

Fragment of terracotta with vegetal ornament, perhaps architectural. Preserves one "leaf" with break at base of stem. Mold-made, solid construction.

TC21 (SF 633, context 7139)
Unidentifiable
mpl 6 cm; M.P.H. 5 cm

Fragment of a terracotta object — either the lower edge of a draped figurine or part of a stand for a figurine.

TC22 (SF 4127, context 2000)
Unidentifiable
mpl 8 cm; M.P.H. 9 cm

Fragment of a terracotta object. Perhaps a stand for a figurine.

TC23 (SF 2210, context 2043)
Unidentifiable
Dimensions not recorded

Fragment of a terracotta object. Perhaps a stand for a figurine.

TC24 (SF 2373, context 2081)
Unidentifiable
M.P.H. 8.9 cm; M.P.W. 7 cm; wall thickness .8 cm

Fragment of a terracotta object. One side smooth with no detail; opposite side has two bumps. Very worn. Mold-made. Preserves trace of seam for connection between front and back.

NOTES

1. Many thanks are due to Sarah Bauer, who examined the terracottas firsthand with William Aylward in 2002, and who compiled descriptive information for each specimen. Terracotta objects were also found in Trenches 3 and 8, managed by the Gaziantep Museum. The authors gratefully acknowledge the assistance of The Packard Humanities Institute and the Hilldale Undergraduate/Faculty Research Fellowship Committee at the University of Wisconsin.
2. See "Context Descriptions" in volume 1 and the chapter by Kenrick, this volume, for Ceramic Group D. For two terracottas from Zeugma dated to the early empire, see Gschwind 2003, 326–7, cat. 2–3.
3. **TC18**: context 15009 in Kenrick's Ceramic Group B. **TC9**: context 12011 in Kenrick's Ceramic Group F.
4. See further discussion in the section on public buildings in the chapter by Aylward, volume 1.
5. For the Dura-Europos terracottas, see Downey 2003, esp. 8–21.
6. For handmade figurines at Dura-Europos, see Downey 2003, 9.
7. At Dura-Europos, local stone was the primary medium for sculpture: Perkins 1973, 70.
8. See the chapter on pottery by Kenrick, this volume, especially the section on fabrics.
9. For the dating of the sanctuary, see the chapters by Crowther, Rose, and Aylward in volume 1.
10. For the iconography of Atargatis, see Bilde 1990, 168.
11. As in Bilde 1990, fig. 7 (from Jordan).
12. See further discussion in the section on religion in the chapter by Aylward in volume 1.

BIBLIOGRAPHY

Bilde, P. 1990. "Atargatis / Dea Syria: Hellenization of Her Cult in the Hellenistic-Roman Period?" in *Religion and Religious Practice in the Seleucid Kingdom*, edited by P. Bilde, 151–87. Aarhus: Aarhus University Press.

Bonanno, A. 1979. "Terracottas." In *Excavations at Sidi Khrebish Benghazi (Berenice)*. Vol. 2, edited by J.A. Lloyd, 65–90. Tripoli: Department of Antiquities.

Burn, L., and R. Higgins. 2001. *Catalogue of Greek Terracottas in the British Museum*. Vol. 3. London: British Museum.

Davidson, G.R., and D.B. Thompson. 1943. *Small Objects from the Pnyx*. Vol. 1. Hesperia Suppl. 7. Princeton: American School of Classical Studies at Athens.

Delivorrias, A., G. Berger-Doer, and A. Kossatz-Deissmann. 1984. "Aphrodite." *LIMC* 2.1:2–151.

Downey, S.B. 1977. *The Stone and Plaster Sculpture*. Los Angeles: Institute of Archaeology.

———. 2003. *Terracotta Figurines and Plaques from Dura-Europos*. Ann Arbor: University of Michigan Press.

Fjeldhagen, M. 1995. *Catalogue of Graeco-Roman Terracottas from Egypt: Ny Carlsberg Glyptotek*. Copenhagen: Ny Carlsberg Glyptotek.

Grandjouan, C. 1961. *Terracottas and Plastic Lamps of the Roman Period*. Athenian Agora 6. Princeton: American School of Classical Studies at Athens.

Gschwind, M. 2003. "Hellenistische Tradition contra italische Mode: Ein frühkaiserzeitlicher Keramikkomplex aus den türkischen Rettungsgrabungen in Zeugma am mittleren Euphrat." *Damaszener Mitteilungen* 13: 321–59.

Higgins, R. 1954. *Catalogue of the Terracottas in the Department of Greek and Roman Antiquities, British Museum*. London: British Museum.

Lang-Auinger, C., Hrsg., *Hanghaus 1 in Ephesos: Funde und Ausstattung*. Vienna 2003.

Merker, G.S. 2000. *Corinth: Results of Excavations Conducted by the American School of Classical Studies at Athens*. Vol. 18, pt. 4, *The Sanctuary of Demeter and Kore: Terracotta Figurines of the Classical, Hellenistic, and Roman Periods*. Princeton: The American School of Classical Studies at Athens.

Mollard-Besques, S. 1963. *Catalogue Raisonné des Figurines et Reliefs en Terre-cuite Grecs et Romains II Myrina*. Paris: Musée du Louvre.

Muller, A. 1996. *Les Terres Cuites Votives du Thesmophorion: De L'Atelier au Sanctuaire*. Etudes Thasiennes 17. Paris: École Française d'Athènes.

Perkins, A. 1973. *The Art of Dura-Europos*. Oxford: Clarendon Press.

Robinson, D.M. 1952. *Excavations at Olynthus Part XIV: Terracottas, Lamps, and Coins Found in 1934 and 1938*. Baltimore: Johns Hopkins Press.

Rostovtzeff, M., et al., eds. 1944–1952. *The Excavations at Dura-Europos, Preliminary Report on the Ninth Season, 1935–6*. 3 pts. New Haven: Yale University Press.

Thompson, D.B. 1963. *Troy: The Terracotta Figurines of the Hellenistic Period*. Suppl. Monograph 3. Princeton: Princeton University Press.

Thompson, H.A., and D.B. Thompson. 1987. *Hellenistic Pottery and Terracottas*. Princeton: American School of Classical Studies at Athens.

Török, L. 1995. *Hellenistic and Roman Terracottas from Egypt*. Rome: "L'ERMA" di Bretschneider.

Vafopoulou-Richardson, C.E. 1991. *Ancient Greek Terracottas*. Oxford: Ashmolean Museum.

· CHAPTER SEVEN ·

Bullae

Sharon Herbert

INTRODUCTION

This chapter[1] presents a group of 21 small clay sealings, of the type commonly known as bullae, found during the rescue project at Zeugma in 2000.[2] These are tiny clay pellets (average 15 mm dia.) that carried impressions of individuals' seal rings and were commonly used to close and notarize papyrus and parchment documents in the Hellenistic and Roman eras. Those under study here represent only a very small sample of the 140,000+ sealings unearthed at Zeugma from 1998 to 2000.[3] The overwhelming majority of the bullae from the site were found in the Gaziantep Museum excavations of Trench 3, where their presence in such vast and concentrated numbers suggests the existence of a public archive building.[4] In contrast, the sealings from the OA excavations were found in scattered and mostly surface contexts across the site. Twelve of the pieces under consideration here came to light in the spoil heap of Trench 4 (ZB9–21) and two (ZB7–8) were from Trench 13, the first a surface find and the second from Sasanian destruction debris of A.D. 252/253. There was a single item (ZB21) from Trench 2, also from Sasanian destruction debris. An intriguing group of six, the iconography of which suggest connections with Caesarea of Cappadocia (ZB1–6), came from various levels of the houses and shops of Trench 9.[5] In this chapter I will first locate the bullae from Zeugma in the context of known Hellenistic and Roman sealing practices and archives and then discuss the individual finds from the OA excavation areas of the PHI rescue project of 2000. I conclude with a catalogue.

HELLENISTIC AND ROMAN ARCHIVES AND SEALING PRACTICES

What we know of the sealing practices of the Hellenistic and Roman eras comes from a small number of excavated caches of clay sealings, commonly called archives, that range geographically from Carthage in the West to Seleucia-on-the-Tigris in the East and in date from the mid-fourth century B.C. to the early first century A.D. They vary in size from 38 sealings found at Elephantini in Upper Egypt to 30,000+ from the Italian excavations at Seleucia-on-the-Tigris.[6] Others include Artaxata in Armenia (8,000), Carthage (4,025), Cyrene (4,000), Delos (16,000+), Edfu (647), Gitana in Epirus (2,500), Kallipolis (600), Kedesh in the Upper Galilee (2,043), Nea Paphos (11,000), Pella (100+), Selinus (688), a small group found in the American excavations at Seleucia-on-the-Tigris (164), Uruk (897), and Wadi Daliyeh in the Judaean Desert (128+).[7] Further information comes from the plethora of papyrus documents from Egypt, which testify to the variety of transactions recorded — sales and leases, wills, marriage contracts, manumissions, and innumerable tax receipts and exemptions. These, though, come down to us, for the most part, recycled as cartonnage in animal mummies and have been stripped of their seals. It is rare to find both document and seals preserved together.[8] The unbaked clay pellets that seal the papyrus documents do not normally survive beyond a few decades without being subjected to fire — fire that inevitably destroys the records that the pellets sealed. The so-called archives that we have thus consist for the most part of clay sealings without their documents and present serious difficulties in interpretation.[9] The Zeugma finds are no exception. We have the baked sealings but no papyri. What is exceptional about the Zeugma material is the quantity — more than all the previous collections put together — and the date, which runs at least into the late second century A.D.

From the Hellenistic era there are three distinct types of clay sealings associated with papyri. These were recognized early on in the study of the bullae from Uruk and the American excavations at Seleucia-on-the-Tigris.[10] The first sealing type consists of a cylinder of clay or bitumen wrapped around the papyrus roll and impressed with multiple seals. String marks are sometimes visible on the interior of these. Rostovtzeff made the point that these "envelope" sealings are the only ones that should properly be called bullae.[11] The second type is a small clay pellet pierced by one or multiple string holes with a single seal impression on the obverse and papyrus or parchment impressions on the reverse. These are generally marked on the sides by fingerprints made in the process of impressing the seal into the pellet. Rostovtzeff called these medallions, and McDowell referred to them as convex appended sealings.[12] The third type is irregular in shape and exhibits no papyrus markings. These were attached to the loose end of the cords attached to papyri. Because most of this type found at Seleucia were large, McDowell concluded that they were used for the most part to fasten large containers, packages, or warehouses and called them "container appended sealings."[13] In fact, my own examination of more recently excavated collections of sealings shows that this type was in common use with papyri. I divide the two types of appended sealings on the basis of shape into "pinched" and "triangular." The pinched type (Rostovtzeff's "medallion" and McDowell's "convex appended sealing," type two above) has a convex obverse on which the seal is impressed and a slightly concave reverse that normally carries the marks of papyrus onto which the sealing was affixed. The triangular type has a flat obverse on which a single seal was impressed; it comes to a point at the reverse and bears no papyrus marks, but does carry fingerprints on the sides. These were not affixed to papyrus but rather folded around the cord that tied the roll. None of the sealings published here are of the envelope type; nine are pinched in shape, and four are triangular. The discovery of the vast majority of these types of sealings in Hellenistic contexts (only the Cyrene archive closes later than the first century B.C., and it runs just to A.D. 117) has led to the impression that these sealing practices are predominantly Hellenistic. The evidence from the papyri, however, shows that the medallion type continued in use until paper replaced papyrus and parchment in the medieval period.[14] Of particular interest for our study are a group of the so-called double documents from the Euphrates area dated to the mid-third century A.D.[15] There is as well a fourth type of sealing, which is solely Roman in date. These are generally known as "Untersiegelung."[16] They are flat and circular in shape and often carry the impression of papyrus on the back, but have no string holes or finger prints. None of this type has been reported from any of the published Hellenistic archives. Eight of the sealings published here are of this type.

Much has been written about the function of the Hellenistic seals and the archival practices they imply.[17] It is generally agreed that for the most part they served to protect the documents they sealed from illicit emendation. The envelope bulla, once it had dried around the rolled papyrus, would be difficult to remove without damage.[18] The convex appended sealings protected the sealed part of Greek "double documents" and bore the seals of contractors, witnesses, and officials, and they were also used on the exterior of rolled papyri.[19] The Roman Untersiegelung, on the other hand, seem to have served a different purpose. They did not seal the document, but rather were affixed to the bottom of an open sheet.[20] These were meant to be presented as official validation of what was written on the document, whether it be payment of import or export duties or road taxes.[21]

One significant class of Hellenistic sealed documents deals with taxes, payment of or exemption from. The largest group of these comes from Seleucia-on-the-Tigris, where over half of 30,000 sealings found in the Italian excavations deal with the salt tax. These seals bear the portrait of the Seleucid monarch and the year of the payment. The connection of large numbers of seals with imperial taxation has led to debate about the nature of the archives in which the seals were found. It has long been recognized that not all Hellenistic archives are "official" in the sense that they constitute royal or even municipal repositories of public records. Rather, many of the ancient archives are collections of personal records kept in individuals' houses, such as those from the American excavations at Seleucia-on-the-Tigris, or deposits in the care of private bankers, such as those from the house in the Skardana quarter on Delos.[22] The criteria that are generally applied to determine the official or nonofficial nature of any given archive center are the form of the building in which they were found and the nature of the representations on the bullae themselves. Buildings such as the archive found by the Italian excavators at Seleucia are clearly official. That structure is 140 m long and consists of two suites of seven long narrow interconnecting rooms with bays for shelves on both sides.[23] It is clearly a building designed and dedicated to storage of enormous numbers of records; the presence of such a building in one of the two major capitals of the Seleucid empire is hardly surprising. The subject matter of the bullae reinforces the public nature of the archive: over half record payment or exemption from the annual salt tax.[24] Other public archives were situated in temple complexes such as that at Hellenistic Uruk, where seals of Seleucid officials, such as the chreophylax and bibliophylax, came to light.[25] At the other end of the spectrum are the 16,000+ bullae from Delos, which were found in a private house of unexceptional form and from whose ca. 14,000 readable impressions only 30 (barely .02 percent) can be identified as official.[26] The finds from Seleucia-on-the-Tigris present a particularly interesting case for interaction between public and private archives in a single city. A number of the salt-tax sealings found in the large public archive excavated by the Italian team in the 1960s and 1970s have duplicates in the archives of the private houses excavated by the American team in 1930s. This implies that citizens took home and stored their own sealed copies of the tax documents deposited in the municipal archive. The Zeugma finds, as we will see below, also give evidence for both public and private archives in one town.

THE BULLAE

The discovery of 140,000+ bullae in Trench 3 at Zeugma presents compelling evidence for a large public archive in the vicinity of that trench. The 21 sealings published here, on the other hand, were found from one end of the site to the other, all in areas of houses or shops. Two came from Trench 13 at the western part of the site. The others were unearthed from the eastern sector of the site: one from Trench 2, twelve from Trench 4 and six from Trench 9. The majority were surface finds (ZB1–3, 7, 9–20) while three (ZB5–6, 21) came from Sasanian destruction debris layers and one from debris over a fourth-century A.D. floor (ZB6). Although none was found in anything approaching a primary context, they are most likely to have been in use in the areas in which they were found.

The most interesting group is the set of six (ZB1–6) found in Trench 9. These are all flat and circular in shape, the Roman Untersiegelung type. Four of these (ZB1, 3–5) bear impressions mimicking the imperial coins of Caesarea in Cappadocia, a city some 250 km northwest of Zeugma, and site of one of the two imperial mints in the East. The most common motif on the reverse of Caesarea's coins is Mt. Argaios, a local landmark and sacred spot. The mountain is sometimes represented as an image placed on an altar, but more often as itself, topped with an eagle, a crescent, or a star. In a number of cases it is shown with a naked man standing atop it and holding a scepter and a globe.[27]

This is the image on three of the Zeugma sealings. All three have Greek inscriptions. None can be deciphered, but it is clear they are not the same as those on the coins. This image does appear on a few published seals, most notably one of unknown provenance from the British Museum on which the mountain is actually named.[28] One of the Zeugma sealings (**ZB1**) bears the beginning of a year date below the mountain, but not the year itself. This is a popular image on the coins of Caesarea from the time of Tiberius through Macrinus, and nothing in the iconography points to a closer date. We are possibly helped by the fourth sealing (**ZB4**), which shows another more closely datable coin type of Caesarea. This is an unusually large piece, over twice the size of the other sealings. It shows a semidraped male figure seated to the left on a rock (Mt. Argaios again?). The head is frontal and radiate, and he holds a globe in his left hand. This is an image that to my knowledge appears only on the coins of Commodus and Septimius Severus minted at Caesarea.[29] **ZB4** carries a date in the exergue, year 11, if read from left to right, or year 13 if read from right to left. Both readings are present in the coins of Commodus.[30] If these can be connected with the coins of Commodus, we have a date of either A.D. 189 or 192. In any case, this sealing must date to the principate of Commodus or later. Why would we find these Caesarean images in a house or shop at Zeugma? Untersiegelung such as these were used to document payment of export tax or road duty in the Roman era.[31] In Egypt it was more common to charge the duty or road tax at the point of origin.[32] With these seals, then, we most likely have evidence for a merchant importing goods from Caesarea to Zeugma. These sealings happen to cluster in the same area where 150 coins of Caesarea dating from Commodus through Gordian III were found in a hoard, and this suggests that somebody in this quarter had particularly close connections with Caesarea.[33] The remaining two sealings (**ZB2, 5**) from the area bear male portraits, one with an inscription, most likely his name. It is tempting to see our merchant in these portraits, although given the official nature of Untersiegelung, it is more likely that the figure is a magistrate or other local administrator.

There are two other Untersiegelung types from the collection under discussion: **ZB9** from the spoil heap in Trench 4 and **ZB21** from a Sasanian debris layer in Trench 2. Both carry impressions that can be interpreted as official, and both find their closest parallels in Roman coin types. **ZB9** is impressed with a head of Apollo laureate, a common type on imperial coins.[34] Often these idealized laureate heads are meant to be the emperor himself, but, in the absence of an inscription, this is impossible to determine in this instance. **ZB21** shows busts of two draped figures facing one another.

The image is not very clear, but they appear to be wearing headdresses or crowns of some sort. Close parallels for this motif can be found in the coins of Samosata, which show the Tyche of Samosata facing the Tyche of another city.[35] The reverse of this piece is of some interest. It has a projecting knob, which would have been pressed through the papyrus document. This was an alternate method of attaching Untersiegelung to papyri.[36]

Of the remaining thirteen sealings in the group, nine (**ZB7, 10–12, 14, 19–20**) are the pinched shape of appended sealings and four (**ZB8, 13, 15, 20**) are triangular. In terms of sealing type, then, all could be either Hellenistic or Roman. All come from surface or topsoil layers. In terms of image they are an undistinguished lot. Only five have readable images of any sort. Three (**ZB10–12**) carry portrait busts of crude workmanship. One of these (**ZB11**) may be wearing a tiara similar to that favored by the late Hellenistic/early Roman kings of Commagene and Armenia.[37] The image on **ZB7** is that of a long-necked bird and **ZB17** carries a wreath or lotus bud.

The 21 bullae discovered in the OA excavation areas during the PHI rescue project at Zeugma in 2000 present a dramatically different profile than the other archives so far published. In a sense, what is most striking is what is missing from the collection. There are none of the "envelope" bullae common in the Hellenistic groups from Delos, Seleucia-on-the-Tigris, and Uruk. There are no royal Hellenistic portraits and no official inscriptions like those of the bibliophylax and chreophylax or salt-tax receipts from Uruk and Seleucia-on-the-Tigris. One would certainly expect to find all of these in a Hellenistic archive at large mercantile city such as Zeugma. In fact, all of the datable pieces in the group published here are Roman in date, and it seems probable that the archive or archives from which they came belonged to the Roman era of occupation. Another, in some ways more surprising, missing element is the representation of Greek gods so prevalent on both Hellenistic and Roman gems. Their absence from this collection may be just an accident of deposit and recovery patterns. On the other hand, the finds from Trench 9, at least, may be the remnant of some sort of specialized merchant's archive in which such sealings would not be relevant. This, though, is mere speculation. What is not speculation is that the larger corpus from Zeugma has the potential to extend our understanding of ancient archives and sealing practices well beyond the A.D. 117 closing date of the nomophoulakion at Cyrene, which until now has been the latest archive known. If the sealings from the larger archive building in Trench 3 share the lengthened time span of our group—and based on the relation between the public and private archives at Seleucia-on-the-Tigris, there is every expectation that they should—we should find a treasure trove of second- and possibly third-century A.D. sealings in that group.

CATALOGUE

With the exception of ZB13, each catalogue entry is preceded by illustratons of the objects described.

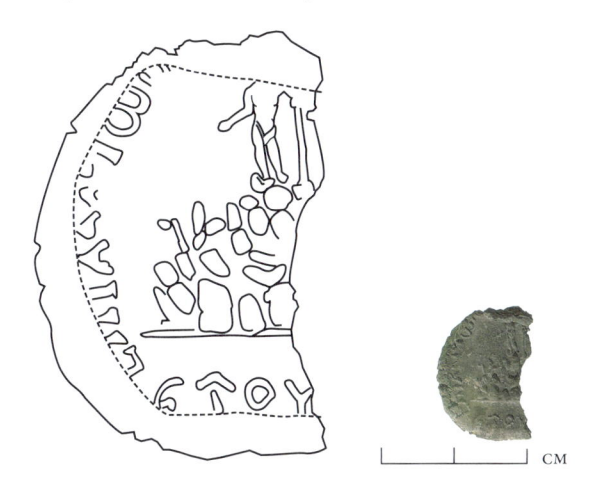

ZB1 (SF 367, context 9000)
Half preserved, M.P.D. 18 mm, grayish brown

Circular in shape with papyrus impressions on reverse and no string hole; no fingerprints on edges. On obverse, naked male, standing frontal on Mt. Argaios, staff or scepter in left hand, right arm extended to left. Misstamped with head missing. Two inscriptions in Greek, the first running from left to right around edge, most letters unclear with upper parts clipped in stamping. A definite omega visible at upper left. Below the mountain [ ] TOY (year ?). For parallels, see Sydenham 1933 no. 42, 87; 42 no. 92; 45 nos. 97 and 99; 52 no. 128; 57 no. 152; 76 no. 258; 80 no. 290a; 82 no. 303; 99 no. 408; Wroth 1964, 45 no. 2; 46 nos. 11–2; 47 no. 18; 50 nos. 37 and 45; 63 no. 150; 75 no. 233; Burnett et al. 1992 nos. 3620, 3649–51, 3655.

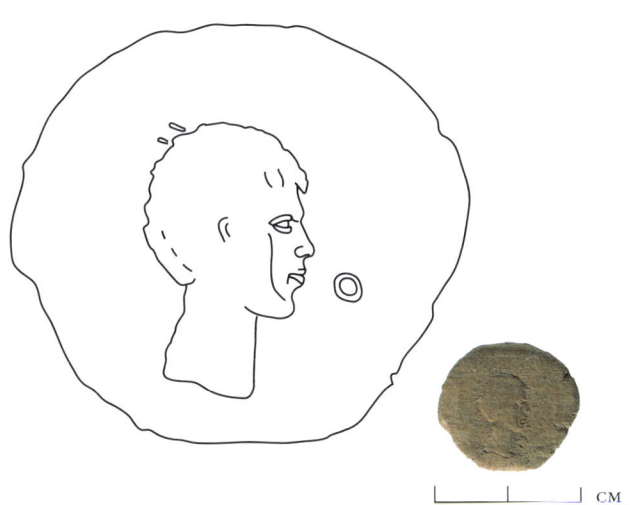

ZB2 (SF 368, context 9000)
Intact, M.P.D. 19 mm, reddish brown

Circular in shape, no clear string or papyrus markings on reverse; no fingerprints. On obverse, male portrait bust facing right; Roman veristic style with short hair, deep furrow from nose to chin. A single Greek (?) O in field to right.

ZB3 (SF 371, context 9000)
Intact, M.P.D. 18 mm, reddish brown

Circular in shape, no clear string hole or papyrus markings on reverse; no fingerprints. On obverse, naked male, standing frontal on Mt. Argaios, staff or scepter in left hand, right arm extended to left. Greek inscription running from lower left around edge, letters for the most part unclear but readable. Parallels as in **ZB1**.

ZB4 (SF 372, context 9120)
Intact, M.P.D. 44 mm, reddish brown

Circular in shape, no string hole, and no papyrus impressions on reverse; no fingerprints. On obverse, semidraped male figure seated to left on rock (Mt. Argaios?) with globe in left hand, right hand extended; frontal face, radiate. Date to lower left [ ] TI A. If this could be ascribed to Commodus, it would be year 11 of his principate (A.D. 188). For parallels, see Wroth 1964, 73 no. 217, and Sydenham 1933, 95 no. 384. A similar figure, however, appears on the coins of Septimius Severus minted at Caesarea (Sydenham 1933, 100 nos. 416, 417, A.D. 194).

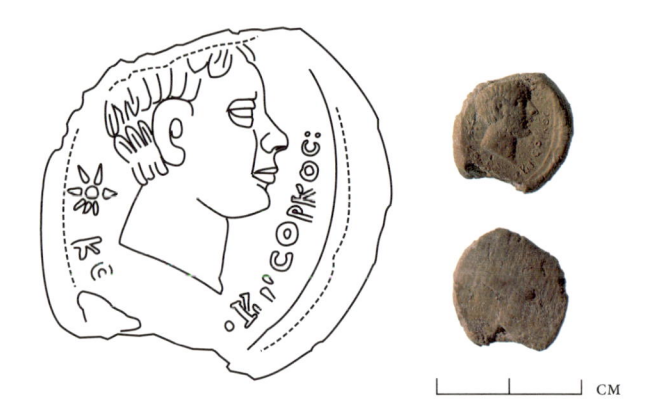

ZB5 (SF 390, context 9137)
Intact, M.P.D. 14 mm, reddish brown

Circular in shape, one string hole, and possible papyrus impression on reverse; no fingerprints. On obverse, male portrait bust facing right; private portrait in Julio-Claudian style. Star behind head, Greek inscription running upwards from lower right.

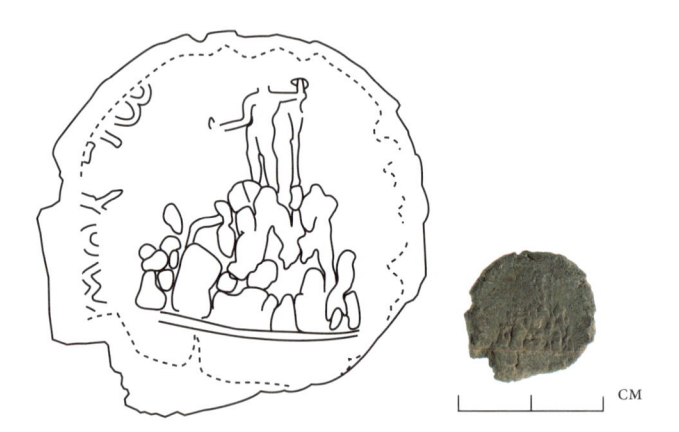

ZB6 (SF 447, context 9137)
Intact, M.P.D. 17 mm, grayish brown

Circular in shape, one string hole, and no papyrus impressions on reverse; no fingerprints. On obverse, naked male, standing frontal on Mt. Argaios, staff or scepter in left hand, right arm extended to left, head blurred to invisibility. Blurred Greek inscription running along left edge. Parallels as in **ZB1**.

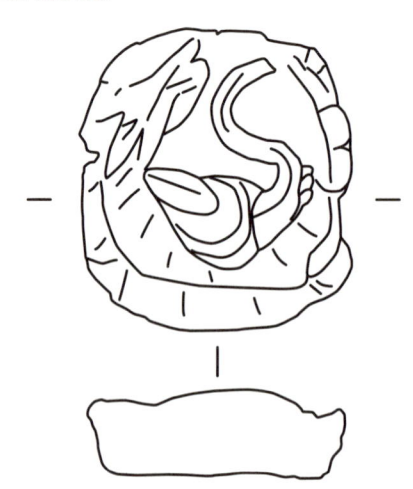

ZB7 (SF 852, context 13000)
Intact, M.P.D. 13 mm, very dark gray to black

Pinched shape with one string hole and papyrus impressions on reverse; fingerprints on sides. On obverse, long-necked bird, swan or goose to right.

ZB8 (SF 856, context 13036)
Intact, M.P.D. 13 mm, very dark gray to black

Triangular shape with one string hole and papyrus impressions on reverse; fingerprints on sides. On obverse, subject blurred.

ZB9 (SF 2167.01, context: Trench 4 spoil heap)
Three-quarters preserved, M.P.D. 18 mm, reddish brown

Circular in shape, no string hole or papyrus impressions on reverse; no fingerprints. On obverse, archaizing head of Apollo, facing right with laurel wreath in hair.

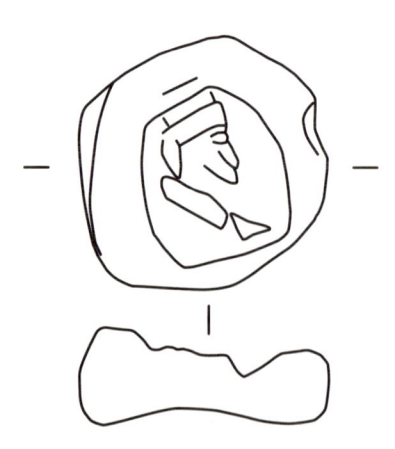

ZB10 (SF 2167.02, context: Trench 4 spoil heap)
Intact, M.P.D. 11 mm, grayish brown

Pinched shape with one string hole and papyrus impressions on reverse; fingerprints on sides. On obverse, male portrait bust facing right, may be wearing tiara. For parallels see Burnett et al. 1992, nos. 3841 and 3845.

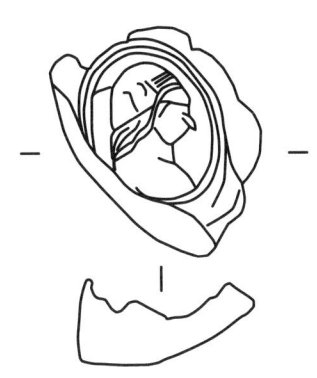

ZB11 (SF 2167.03, context: Trench 4 spoil heap)
Intact, M.P.D. 11 mm, grayish brown

Pinched shape with one string hole and papyrus impressions on reverse; fingerprints on sides. On obverse, portrait bust with high headdress. Possible parallel with coins of Antiochos of Commagene.

ZB12 (SF 2167.04, context: Trench 4 spoil heap)
Intact, M.P.D. 10 mm, red

Pinched shape with one string hole and possible papyrus impressions on reverse; fingerprints on sides. On obverse, male portrait bust, facing right.

ZB13 (SF 2167.05, context: Trench 4 spoil heap)
Half preserved, M.P.D. 11 mm, very dark gray to black

Triangular shape with one string hole, no papyrus impressions; fingerprints on sides. On obverse, too little preserved to identify subject.

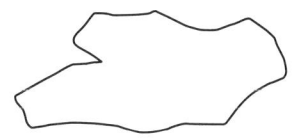

ZB14 (SF 2167.06, context: Trench 4 spoil heap)
Half preserved, M.P.D. 12 mm, very dark gray to black

Pinched shape with one string hole and papyrus impressions on reverse; fingerprints on sides. Face lost.

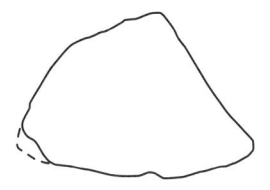

ZB15 (SF 2167.07, context: Trench 4 spoil heap)
Intact, M.P.D. 12 mm, very dark gray to black

Triangular shape with one string hole, no papyrus impressions; fingerprints on sides. Face lost.

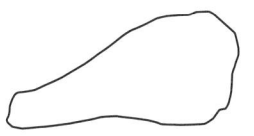

ZB16 (SF 2167.08, context: Trench 4 spoil heap)
Three-quarters preserved, M.P.D. 0.013, very dark gray to black

Pinched shape with one string hole and papyrus impressions on reverse; fingerprints on sides. Face lost.

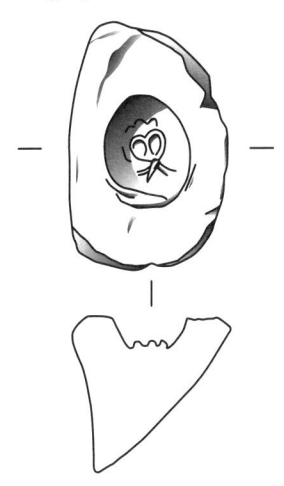

ZB17 (SF 2167.09, context: Trench 4 spoil heap)
Intact, M.P.D. 9 mm, very dark gray to black

Pinched shape with one string hole and papyrus impressions on reverse; fingerprints on sides. On obverse, unclear symbol, possibly a lotus bud or wreath.

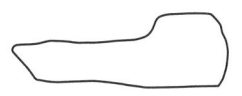

ZB18 (SF 2167.10, context: Trench 4 spoil heap)
Less than half preserved, M.P.D. 10 mm, very dark gray to black

Pinched shape with one string hole and papyrus impressions on reverse; fingerprints on sides. On obverse, subject unclear, perhaps visible with further cleaning.

ZB19 (SF 2167.11, context: Trench 4 spoil heap)
three-quarters preserved, M.P.D. 9 mm, reddish brown

Pinched shape with one string hole and papyrus impressions on reverse; fingerprints on sides. Face lost.

ZB20 (SF 2167.12, context: Trench 4 spoil heap)
Half preserved, M.P.D. 7 mm, reddish brown

Triangular shape with one string hole and possible papyrus impressions on reverse; fingerprints on sides. On obverse, subject unclear, perhaps visible with further cleaning.

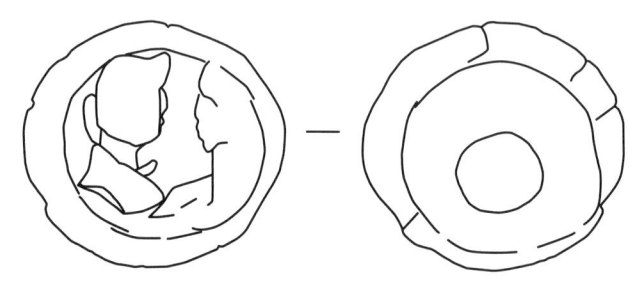

ZB21 (SF 2168, context 2019)
Intact, M.P.D. 14 mm, reddish brown

Circular in shape. No string hole or papyrus impressions on reverse; instead a knob projects for attachment to papyrus. On obverse, two busts facing, draped, possibly wearing crowns or turrets. See coin of Samosata, Wroth 1964, 119 no. 31.

NOTES

1. I spent five days in July of 2002 at the excavation camp in Birecik. During that time I examined the 16 bullae in the excavation store there and made one trip to view the five in the Gaziantep Museum briefly. I wish to thank William Aylward for the invitation to study the bullae from Zeugma and his efforts to locate the information and illustrations I have needed to complete this study. All the bullae were drawn by OA after my visit, but not all were photographed. Where photographs were available, I reworked the drawings using the digital enhancement equipment available for the study of the University of Michigan papyrus collection. This was especially useful for the Greek inscriptions, which were particularly difficult to decipher. I was immeasurably aided in this by Dr. Traianos Gagos, senior archivist of the Michigan papyrus collection. Lorene Sterner produced the final drawings of these pieces. My reading of the Roman portrait bullae was helped by the advice of Professor Brian Rose. My thanks to all. The responsibility for any errors is entirely mine.
2. There were initially 22 items identified as bullae by OA excavators. One of these, SF 2167.13, proved not to be a bulla. For an account of the excavation areas, see Tobin, volume 1.
3. Önal 2003, 9–10; Weitz 2000, 102.
4. Önal 2003, 9 10.
5. Tobin, volume 1, n. 112.
6. Elephantini: Rubensohn 1907. Seleucia-on-the-Tigris: Invernizzi 1996.
7. Artaxata: Khachatrian 1996. Carthage: Berges 1997. Cyrene: Maddoli 1965. Delos: Boussac 1988, 1992. Edfu: Milne 1916. Gitana: Preka-Alexandra 1996. Kallipolis: Pantos 1985. Kedesh: Herbert and Berlin 2003. Nea Paphos: Kyrieleis 1996. Pella: Boussac 1996, 513 n. 9. Selinus: Salinas 1883. Seleucia-on-the-Tigris: McDowell 1935. Uruk: Rostovtzeff 1932; Lindstrom 2003. Wadi Daliyeh: Leith 1997.
8. Vandorpe (1995, 1) cites only 180.
9. The rare exceptions to this rule are a few finds in Egypt, most notably the Elephantini cache and the Wadi Daliya find from the Judaean Desert. Invernizzi (2003) discusses this problem in some detail.
10. Uruk: Rostovtzeff 1932. Seleucia-on-the-Tigris: McDowell 1935.
11. The use of the term *bulla* is inconsistent. Taken from the Latin for "round item" or "button," it was not used for seals in antiquity. Rostovtzeff's distinction between the envelope sealings and others has not been maintained in English, where the term *bulla* is often used for all types of clay sealings. In recent years the practice has been to move away from its use altogether and substitute "sealing" or "seal impression."
12. Rostovtzeff 1932, 8; McDowell 1935, 3.
13. McDowell 1935, 10.
14. There are papyri with attached medallion sealings in the Michigan collection with Arab scripts dating to the eighth century A.D. (cf. MP1834). My thanks to Professors Arthur Verhoogt and Traianos Gagos for bringing these to my attention.
15. Bowersock 1991, 338.
16. Vandorpe 1995, 24.
17. See Vandorpe (1995) and Boussac and Invernizzi (1996) for overviews.
18. Invernizzi 2003, 304.
19. Vandorpe 1995, 3–8, 11–20.
20. Boak 1935, pl. 13.
21. Vondorpe 1995, 25–8; Sijpesteijn 1987, 46–9.
22. Seleucia-on-the-Tigris: McDowell 1935; Brown 1938. Delos: Boussac 1988, 1992.
23. Invernizzi 1976, 170.
24. Invernizzi 1968 and personal communication.
25. Rostovtzeff 1932; Bickerman 1938, 209.
26. Boussac 1992: 11–18.
27. Sydenham 1933, 42 nos. 87 and 92; 45 nos. 97 and 99; 52 no. 128; 57 no. 152; 76 no. 258; 80 no. 290a; 82 no. 303; 99 no. 408; Wroth 1964, 45 no. 2; 46 nos. 11–2; 47 no. 18; 50 nos. 37 and 45; 63 no. 150; 75 no. 233; Burnett et al. 1992, nos. 3620, 3649–51, 3655.
28. Walters 1926 no. 1662.
29. Wroth 1964, 73 no. 217; 75 no. 231; Sydenham 1933, 95 no. 384.
30. Wroth 1964, 72 no. 212; 73 no. 217.
31. Vondorpe 1995, 25.
32. Sijpesteijn 1987, 46–9.
33. See Butcher, volume 3, Hoard 1.
34. Burnett et al. 1992, 3611.
35. Wroth 1964, 119 no. 31 (dated to Septimius Severus).
36. Vandorpe 1995, 25.
37. Burnett et al. 1992, nos. 3841 and 3845.

BIBLIOGRAPHY

Auda, Y., and M.-F. Boussac. 1996. "Étude statistique d'un dépôt d'archive à Délos." In *Archives et Sceaux du Monde Hellénistique: Archivi e Sigilli nel Mondo Ellenistico; Torino, Villa Gualino, 13–16 Gennaio 1993*, edited by M.-F. Boussac and A. Invernizzi, 511–23. *BCH* Suppl. 29. Athens: Ecole Française d'Athènes.

Berges, D. 1997. "Die Tonsiegel aus dem Karthagischen Temple Archiv." In *Die Deutschen Ausgrabungen in Karthago*, edited by F. Rakob, 10–213. Mainz am Rhein: Philipp von Zabern.

Boak, A.E.R. 1935. "Custom Seals and Receipts." In *Soknopaiou Nesos: The University of Michigan Excavations at Dimê*, edited by A.E.R. Boak, 23–33. University of Michigan Studies, Humanistic Series 39. Ann Arbor: University of Michigan Press.

Boussac, M.-F. 1988. "Sceaux Déliens." *RA* 1988:307–40.

———. 1992. *Les Sceaux de Délos*. Vol. 1, *Recherches franco-helléniques* 2. Athens: École Française D'Athènes.

Boussac, M.-F., and A. Invernizzi, eds. 1996. *Archives et Sceaux du Monde Hellénistique: Archivi e Sigilli nel Mondo Ellenistico; Torino, Villa Gualino, 13–16 Gennaio 1993*. *BCH* Suppl. 29. Athens: Ecole Française d'Athènes.

Bowersock, G.W. 1991. "The Babatha Papyri, Masada and Rome." *JRA* 4:336–44.

Burnett, A., M. Amandry, and P.P. Ripolles. 1992. *Roman Provincial Coinage*. London: British Museum Press.

Herbert, S., and A. Berlin. 2003. "A New Administrative Center for Persian and Hellenistic Galilee." *BASOR* 329:13–59.

Invernizzi, A. 1968–1969. "Bullae from Seleucia." *Mesopotamia* 3–4:69–124.

———. 1971. "Bulles de Selucie-du-Tigre." *Annales Archeologiques Arabes Syriennes* 21:105–8.

———. 1995. "Seal Impressions of Achaemenid and Graeco-Persian Style from Seleucia on the Tigris." *Mesopotamia* 30:39–50.

———. 1996. "Gli archivi pubblici di Seleucia sul Tigri." In *Archives et Sceaux du Monde Hellénistique: Archivi e Sigilli nel Mondo Ellenistico; Torino, Villa Gualino, 13–16 Gennaio 1993*, edited by M.-F. Boussac and A. Invernizzi, 131–43. *BCH* Suppl. 29. Athens: Ecole Française d'Athènes.

———. 2003. "They Did Not Write on Clay: Non-Cuneiform Documents and Archives in Seleucid Mesopotamia." In *Ancient Archives and Archival Traditions: Concepts of Record-Keeping in the Ancient World*, edited by Maria Brosius, 302–22. Oxford: Oxford University Press.

Invernizzi, A., A. Bollati, and V. Messina. 2004. *Seleucia al Tigri: Le impronte di sigillo dagli Archivi*. 3 vols. Turin: Edizioni dell'Orso.

Khachatrian, Z. 1996. "The Archives of Sealings Found at Artashat (Artaxata)." In *Archives et Sceaux du Monde Hellénistique: Archivi e Sigilli nel Mondo Ellenistico; Torino, Villa Gualino, 13–16 Gennaio 1993*, edited by M.-F. Boussac and A. Invernizzi, 365–70. *BCH* Suppl. 29. Athens: Ecole Française d'Athènes.

Kyrieleis, H. 1996. "Ptolemäische porträts auf siegelabdrücken aus Nea Paphos (Zypern)." In *Archives et Sceaux du Monde Hellénistique: Archivi e Sigilli nel Mondo Ellenistico; Torino, Villa Gualino, 13–16 Gennaio 1993*, edited by M.-F. Boussac and A. Invernizzi, 315–20. *BCH* Suppl. 29. Athens: Ecole Française d'Athènes.

Leith, M.J.W. 1997. *Wadi Daliyeh: The Wadi Daliyeh Seal Impressions*. Oxford: Clarendon Press.

Lindström, G. 2003. *Uruk Siegelabdrücke auf Hellenistischen Tonbullen und Tontafeln*. Mainz am Rhein: Philipp von Zabern.

Maddoli, G. 1963–64. "Le cretule del Nomophylakion di Cirene." *Annuario Scuola Archeologica di Atene* 41–2:40–145.

McDowell, R.H. 1935. *Stamped and Inscribed Objects from Seleucia on the Tigris*. Ann Arbor: University of Michigan Press.

Milne, J.G. 1916. "Ptolemaic Seal Impressions." *JHS* 36:87–101.

Önal, M. 2003. *Mosaics of Zeugma*. Istanbul: A Turizm Yayinlari.

Pantos, P. 1985. *Τὰ σφραγίσματα τῆς αἰτωλικῆς Καλλιπόλεως*. Athens: University of Athens.

Preka-Alexandra, K. 1996. "A Group of Inscribed Impressions from Thesprotia, Greece." In *Archives et Sceaux du Monde Hellénistique: Archivi e Sigilli nel Mondo Ellenistico; Torino, Villa Gualino, 13–16 Gennaio 1993*, edited by M.-F. Boussac and A. Invernizzi, 195–8. *BCH* Suppl. 29. Athens: Ecole Française d'Athènes.

Rostovtzeff, M. 1932. "Seleucid Babylonia: Bullae and Seals of Clay with Greek Inscriptions." *YCS* 3:1–114.

Rubensohn, O. 1907. *Elephantine-Papyri*. Berlin: Weidmann.

Salinas, A. 1883. "Selinunte." *NSc* 8:287–314.

Sijpesteijn, P.J. 1987. *Customs Duties in Graeco-Roman Egypt*. Zutphen: Terra Publishing.

Vandorpe, K. 1995. *Breaking the Seal of Secrecy*. Leiden: Institute of Papyrology.

Walters, H.B. 1926. *Catalogue of the Engraved Gems and Cameos, Greek, Etruscan and Roman, in the British Museum*. London: British Museum Press.

Weitz, P. 2000. "Tonsiegel aus Kommagene (Doliche)." In *Gottkönige am Euphrat: Neue Ausgrabungen und Forschungen in Kommagene*, edited by J. Wagner, 101–4. Mainz am Rhein: Philipp von Zabern.

Wroth, W. 1964. Reprint. *Catalogue of the Greek Coins of Galatia, Cappadocia, and Syria*. Bologna: A. Forni. Original edition, London: The Trustees of the British Museum, 1899.

· CHAPTER EIGHT ·

Glass

R. A. Grossmann

INTRODUCTION

The present chapter provides an overview of glass finds recovered during rescue excavations at Zeugma in 2000. This survey covers the full chronological scheme of Zeugma as reflected in the archaeological record, from Seleucid through Early Islamic times, with emphasis on the Early, Middle, and Late Imperial periods.[1] The finds under consideration include glass vessels, window glass, and glass objects (mainly jewelry), as well as a small number of objects in other materials (e.g., faience) related to glass.[2] While it has been possible to publish only a small fraction of the glass recovered at Zeugma, the pieces chosen for publication are, for the most part, representative of larger classes of material; at the same time, an effort has also been made to treat atypical finds.

Methodology

This chapter was written with the assistance of notes compiled by Dr. Jennifer Price during a June 2002 visit to Zeugma, along with photos and drawings made by Oxford Archaeology. At the time of Dr. Price's visit, the majority of the glass finds excavated during the Zeugma 2000 excavations were kept at Birecik, while a smaller body of material was housed in the Gaziantep Museum; at present, the Zeugma glass has been transferred to Gaziantep. Dr. Price's notes, while thorough, were intended to be provisional. Her descriptions of individual pieces of glass are generally partial, consisting of only the most diagnostic features. Dimensions were rarely recorded. Regrettably, it has not been possible to supplement these notes through direct reexamination of the material. This study is, therefore, subject to certain limitations imposed by heavy reliance on photographs and drawings.

Quantitative Analysis

The glass finds from the Zeugma 2000 excavations total nearly 10,500 fragments.[3] Vessel glass accounts for a little less than half of that number (45.5 percent), window glass for a little more than half (54 percent); glass objects make up a minuscule fraction of the total (0.5 percent). The distribution of vessel glass fragments can be divided into three roughly equal groupings, with Trenches 2, 7, and 9 each accounting for around 20 percent, Trenches 1 and 18 each for 10 percent, Trenches 11, 12, and 15 each for 5 percent, and Trenches 4, 5, 10, 13, and 19 together for the final 5 percent. The distribution of window glass follows a contrasting pattern, with over 95 percent of the fragments found in Trench 2 in contexts datable to the mid-third century A.D. Due to the recording methods used, it has not been possible to calculate relative quantities of vessel glass by period, beyond offering that the bulk of finds in Trenches 2, 9, 11, and 18 come from mid-third century A.D. contexts and those in Trenches 1, 7, and 12 from contexts dating to the fifth century A.D. or later. It has also proven impossible to compute relative proportions of vessel types within the assemblage, beyond concluding that vessels used as tableware (e.g., bowls, cups, beakers, jars, flasks) far outnumber vessels devoted to other functions (e.g., bottles, unguent bottles, lamps).

Condition

The glass finds consist mainly of fragments, most of them quite small. Joining fragments are not uncommon, but in only a few instances have vessels been preserved nearly whole. This is, of course, to be expected of glass excavated in an urban setting, where much of what has been recovered is likely to be refuse of some sort. In addition to their fragmentary state, the glass finds all exhibit some degree of surface weathering, resulting from interaction with moisture in the burial environment. Typical weathering effects include cloudiness, iridescence, surface pitting, and/or flaking; in severe cases, these effects may obscure the color of the fabric and details of surface decoration. Besides normal weathering, a substantial portion of the Zeugma glass was also affected by exposure to extreme heat, principally from fires associated with the Sasanian attack on the city in A.D. 252/253, and, to a lesser extent, with a second wave of destruction inflicted by invading Arabs ca. A.D. 636.[4] The

Figure 1. **G42**. *Lump of fused glass.*

effects of exposure to heat include obscuring of surface color and detail, changes in fabric color, distortion of shape, and, in the most severe cases, fusion of multiple pieces into an aggregate mass of glass (fig. 1).[5] Variations in physical condition play a large role in determining the quantity of information that can be derived from a given piece of glass. At one extreme, many are simply unidentifiable; at the other, a single fragment may provide copious indications for technique, decoration, typology, and/or date.

Findspots

Glass was found in only a few closely datable construction contexts (e.g., foundation trenches, leveling layers) and occupation deposits; in both situations, the fragments are rarely diagnostic. Most of the glass finds come from one of two kinds of contexts: debris layers associated with destruction events (generally related either to the Sasanian attack of A.D. 253 or the Arab invasions of ca. A.D. 636) or postoccupation colluvium overlying settlement remains. The colluvium contexts tend to combine assorted material carried down from the slopes above, and a single context may contain glass spanning several hundred years. The destruction contexts also frequently include fragments of apparently mixed date, and in these instances it is necessary to question whether the particular amalgamation of fragments in a given context indicates simultaneous deposition, or if pieces of outlying date represent intrusions from other strata. Such matters are not always easily resolved and can confuse the chronology of certain types of glassware.

Dating

It is important to bear in mind that, while this chapter abides by a chronological scheme based on the history of Zeugma, these divisions of time do not correlate meaningfully with the history of glass. Many fragments are too small and/or generic to date closely. Furthermore, the date ranges for some techniques of manufacture and types of vessels and objects encountered at Zeugma remained standard over several centuries, extending outside the borders of a single period. For the sake of clarity, classes of material are discussed in the sections of the chapter dealing with the period to which they are customarily dated, with additional commentary offered where relevant.

GLASS VESSELS

I. Seleucid Period (300–64 B.C.)

Hellenistic glass is poorly represented, with only a single fragment plausibly dated to the Seleucid period.

Ia. Core-Formed Vessels

The complete absence of core-formed vessels in the assemblage is surprising.[6] The discovery of several fragments of core-formed glass at Dura-Europos demonstrates that the distribution of these vessels, produced on the Syro-Palestinian coast, extended inland to Seleucid cities along the Euphrates.[7]

Ib. Cast Vessels

Only one fragment of cast glass unearthed at Zeugma can be dated to the Seleucid period. A fragment preserving the rim and upper body of a conical bowl with a single horizontal wheel-cut groove on the interior wall just below the rim (G1) belongs to a class of cast drinking vessels produced on the Syro-Palestinian coast and traded extensively throughout the eastern Mediterranean beginning in the middle of the second century B.C.[8] A date between ca. 150 and 50 B.C. for this fragment is supported by its association with context 18090, an Early Imperial wall whose foundations cut into a late Seleucid (?) terrace.[9]

G1 context 18090
Conical bowl
Greenish FIG. 2

Fragment of rim and body. Upright rim with rounded edge. Straight side, sloping diagonally inward. On the interior, horizontal cut groove just below rim.
Similar: Grose 1979, group A.

II. Commagenian (64 B.C.–A.D. 18)

The Commagenian period at Zeugma encompasses a fertile era in the history of glass, during which technical advances allowed for increased production of cast glassware, while Roman expansion into Asia Minor fostered a major escalation of trade.[10] Cast bowls with linear-cut decoration in the Syro-Palestinian tradition continued to be produced

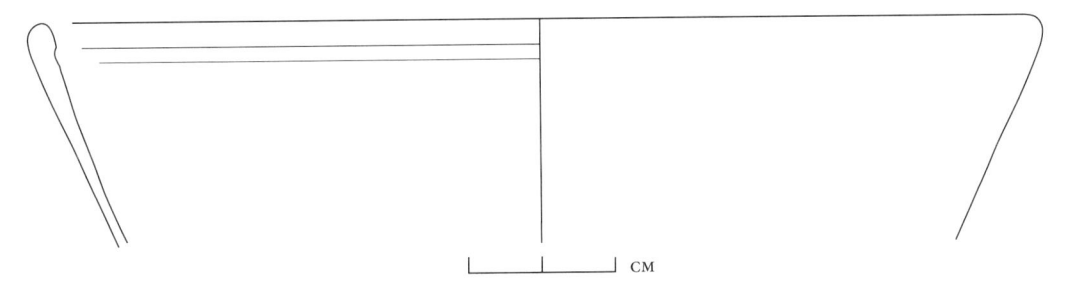

Figure 2. **G1.** *Conical bowl.*

into the middle decades of the first century A.D. but declined in popularity during the age of Augustus in favor of more elaborate products, including ribbed bowls and polychrome "mosaic" glass.

IIa. Cast Vessels (Linear-Cut)

A fragment preserving the rim and upper body of a cast bowl with a cut groove on the interior just below the rim (**G2**) was found in a late first-century B.C. to early first-century A.D. context (15232) in Trench 15 that also included fragments of Hellenistic fineware and Eastern Sigillata A.[11]

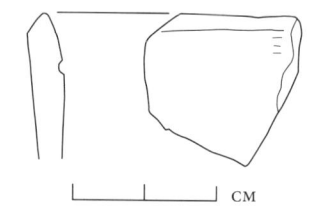

Figure 3. **G2**. *Broad, shallow bowl (?) (linear-cut).*

G2 context 15232
Broad, shallow bowl (?)
Greenish   FIG. 3

Fragment of rim and body. Upright rim with almost pointed edge. Short section of fairly straight side. On the interior, horizontal cut groove just below rim.
Similar: Grose 1979, group D.

IIb. Cast Bowls (Ribbed)

Cast ribbed bowls (sometimes called pillar-molded bowls) were the predominant class of glass tableware between the late first century B.C. and early first century A.D., though production continued at least into Flavian times.[12] The remnants of at least 10 ribbed bowls were excavated at Zeugma across a broad distribution of contexts. Naturally colored bluish-green glass appears to have been the standard fabric here, as it was throughout the eastern Mediterranean; one bowl may have been intentionally decolorized. The reconstructed profiles of these vessels illustrate two of the most common forms: the broad shallow bowl (**G3**) and the hemispherical bowl (**G4**), as well as a fairly widespread variant on the hemispherical bowl with an outsplayed rim (**G5**). It is noteworthy that the ribs differ in prominence and shape from one fragment to another. This heterogeneity makes it unlikely that the same workshop was responsible for all of the ribbed bowls found at Zeugma and argues against local manufacture for these vessels. The cast ribbed bowls, like the other vessels discussed thus far, were likely imported from the Syro-Palestinian coast, where they are known to have been made.[13]

G3 context 18002
Broad, shallow bowl
Bluish-green   FIG. 4

Fragment of rim and body. Upright rim with almost flat edge, sloping diagonally outward. Convex side, curving inward. On the interior, horizontal cut groove just below rim. On the exterior, upper part of one prominent vertical rib.
Similar: Isings 1957, form 3a; Grose 1979, group C.

Figure 4. **G3**. *Broad, shallow bowl (ribbed).*

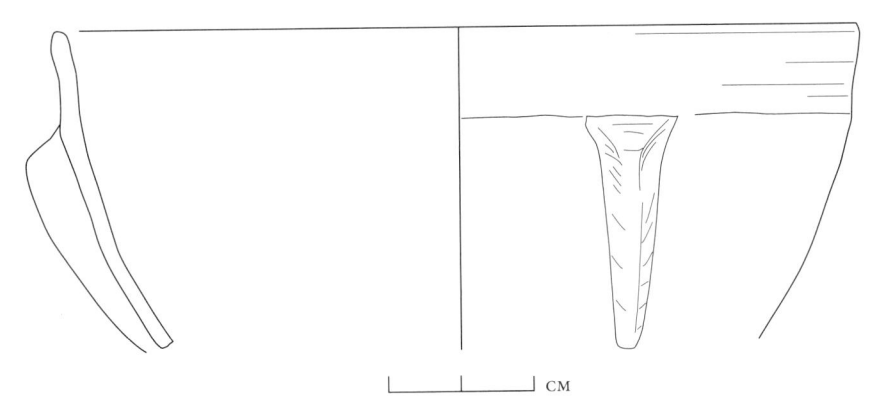

Figure 5. **G4.** *Hemispherical bowl (ribbed).*

G4 context 12000
Hemispherical bowl
Bluish-green   FIG. 5

Fragment of rim and body. Upright rim with rounded edge. Convex side, curving inward. On the exterior, most of one prominent vertical rib.
Similar: Isings 1957, form 3b; Grose 1979, group C.

G5 context 11028 (fragment joins with another found in context 11026)
Hemispherical bowl with outsplayed rim
Colorless (?)   FIG. 6

Fragment of rim and body. Outsplayed rim with flat edge. Convex side, curving inward. On the exterior, three (?) shallow vertical ribs.
Similar: Isings 1957, variant of form 3b; Grose 1979, group C.

IIc. Mosaic Vessels

Mosaic glass vessels of the late first century B.C. to early first century A.D., while still widespread, were less commonplace and surely more costly than those cast from monochrome glass.[14] A total of nine fragments of mosaic glass (**G6**) were found in two nearby contexts in Trench 2 (two fragments in context 2269 and seven in 2376). The fragments are all very similar in appearance and probably belong to a single vessel, reconstructed here as a broad, shallow bowl. The composite mosaic pattern is uncomplicated, consisting entirely of opaque yellow roundels with dark green centers, set in a dark green matrix (the blue areas on the fragments are iridescence). Although fairly simple in comparison with much contemporary mosaic glass, this single example of the technique preserved at Zeugma, certainly imported, was surely prized as a luxury item.

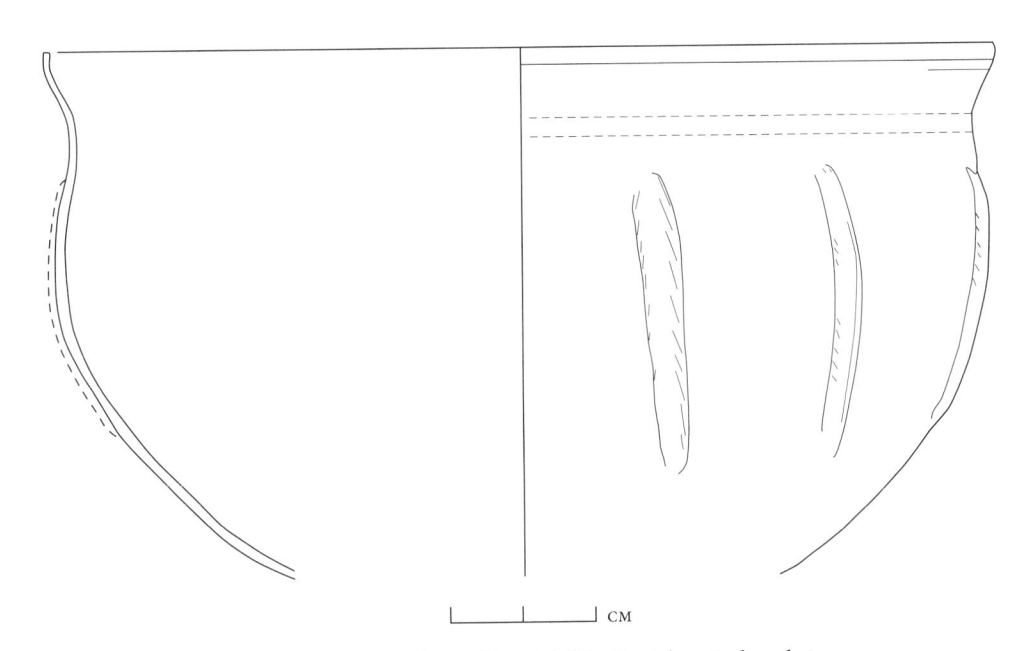

Figure 6. **G5.** *Hemispherical bowl (ribbed) with outsplayed rim.*

Figure 7. **G6**. *Broad, shallow bowl (composite mosaic).*

G6 contexts 2269 (two fragments) and 2376 (seven fragments)
Broad, shallow bowl
Dark green inlaid with opaque yellow roundels around green rods   FIG. 7 (context 2376 fragments only)

Nine fragments of rim and body (two pairs joining). Upright rim with rounded edge. Convex side, curving inward.
Similar: Grose 1989, family IV: noncarinated forms.

REMARKS

It is remarkable that nearly half of the ribbed bowl fragments and all of the mosaic glass published here were discovered in contexts associated with the Sasanian attack of the mid-third century A.D.[15] Although neither type of vessel ordinarily appears in assemblages later than the early second century A.D., their repeated incidence at Zeugma in third-century contexts, some of them deeply buried beneath layers of destruction and collapse, makes it unlikely that all of these fragments simply represent intrusions from overlying deposits of mixed material.[16] It is noteworthy that contexts containing fragments of three ribbed bowls and the mosaic glass vessel (**G6**) fall within a single house, the affluent House of the Bull.[17] It seems plausible that a small number of glass vessels manufactured between the late first century B.C. and the early first century A.D. survived into the third century A.D., safeguarded as heirlooms.

III. Early Imperial (A.D. 18–161)

The glass finds of the Early Imperial period are divided between vessels made using long-established casting techniques and those produced with more recently developed glassblowing technologies. Two new classes of cast tableware were introduced, differentiated by the presence or absence of color in the fabric. Finds of blown glass securely datable to the Early Imperial period are limited to a few small mold-blown vessels, along with a single fragment of a beaker with distinctive relief-cut decoration.

IIIa. Translucent Colored Cast Tableware

A very small portion of the cast glass finds from Zeugma are of translucent "peacock" blue glass, including four joining fragments of a hemispherical bowl (**G7**).[18] This distinctively colored fabric was used almost exclusively in the production of tableware in the second and third quarters of the first century A.D. Vessels made from translucent colored glass were much more popular in Italy and the northern provinces than in the eastern Mediterranean. It is likely, therefore, that only a few vessels of this sort were imported to Zeugma from the West.

G7 context 18001
Hemispherical bowl
"Peacock" blue

Four joining fragments of rim and body. Upright rim with rounded edge. Convex side, curving inward.
Similar: Grose 1989, family III: monochrome translucent colored fine wares.

IIIb. Colorless Cast Tableware (Plain)

By far more plentiful at Zeugma than colored glass are fragments of colorless cast bowls and plates.[19] The use of colorless fabrics for glass tableware became popular across the Roman Empire towards the end of the first century A.D. This class includes vessels made of both intentionally decolorized (i.e., clear) and naturally colorless (pale greenish and bluish-green) fabrics. Intentionally decolorized pieces appear to outnumber the naturally colorless at Zeugma substantially. Since both fabrics were cast in the same assortment of shapes, it is probable that vessels made of naturally colorless glass were simply less expensive. All three of the principal forms of colorless cast tableware are represented among the glass finds from Zeugma: the hemispherical bowl with high base-ring (**G8**); the broad, shallow bowl with base-ring (**G9**) and overhanging rim (**G10**); and the plate with wide sloping rim (**G11**) or overhanging rim.

GLASS · 223

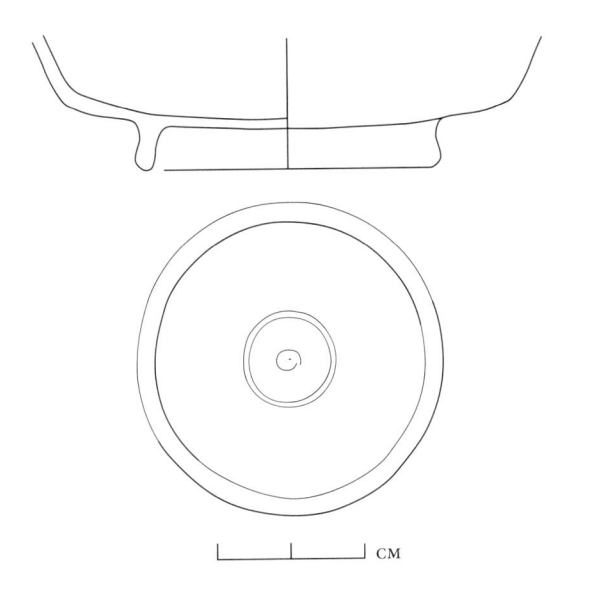

Figure 8. **G8.** *Hemispherical bowl.*

G8 context 2269
Hemispherical bowl
Colorless   FIG. 8

Two joining fragments of body and base. Fairly straight side, sloping diagonally inward. Angular transition from side to slightly convex bottom. Slightly outsplayed, high base-ring with rounded edge.

G9 context 18001
Broad, shallow bowl
Colorless   FIG. 9

Four joining fragments of body and base. Convex side, curving inward. Gradual transition from side to slightly convex bottom. Slightly outsplayed base-ring with rounded edge.

G10 context 2039
Broad, shallow bowl (?) with overhanging rim
Colorless   FIG. 10

Fragment of rim. Wide, nearly horizontal rim, with down-turned, overhanging edge.

G11 context 9082
Plate
Colorless   FIG. 11

Fragment of rim and body. Wide, nearly horizontal rim with rounded edge. Short section of slightly convex (?) side curving inward.

IIIc. Colorless Cast Tableware (Cut Decoration)

While most colorless cast vessels were left undecorated, about one-third of the fragments recovered at Zeugma have cut grooves on bases and/or rims; within this group, several have a pair of concentric circles cut into the interior surface of the bottom of the vessel (**G12**).[20] More ornately embellished are four fragments of a shallow cast dish with at least three irregular rows of oval and circular facets on the exterior (**G13**). While excavations at Zeugma have yielded an abundance of vessel fragments with facet-cut decoration (see below), this is the only cast example. A date of manufacture in the late first or early second century A.D. is suggested by the application of closely set facets over the whole surface of the vessel, rather than in zones, as was the norm on blown tableware with cut decoration datable to the Middle Imperial period. This dish, then, may mark the initial appearance at Zeugma of glassware with facet-cut decoration.

Figure 9. **G9.** *Broad, shallow bowl.*

Figure 10. **G10.** *Broad, shallow bowl with overhanging rim.*

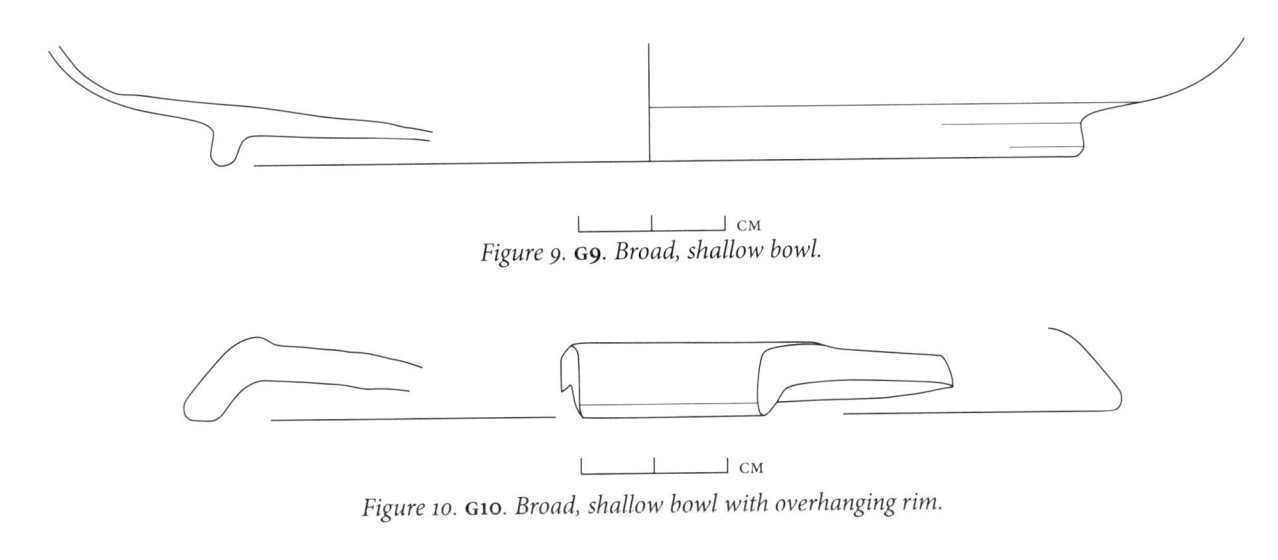

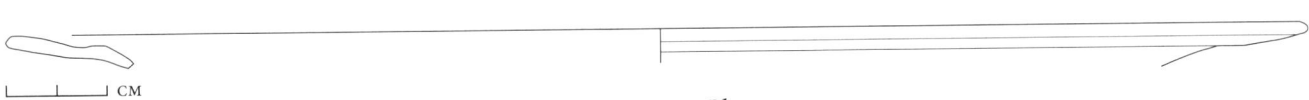

Figure 11. **G11.** *Plate.*

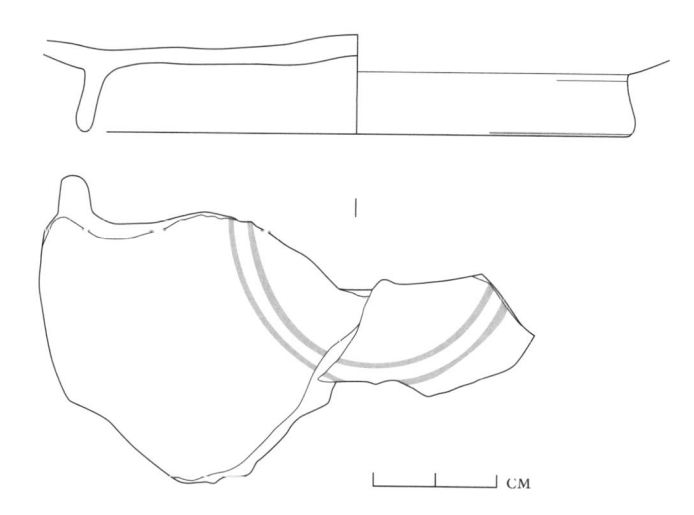

Figure 12. **G12.** *Broad, shallow bowl (?) (cut circles).*

G12 context 18001
Broad, shallow bowl (?)
Clear colorless   FIG. 12

Three joining fragments of body and base. Short section of convex side, curving inward. Gradual transition from side to nearly flat bottom. Slightly outsplayed, high base-ring with rounded edge. On the interior, two concentric cut circles near center of bottom.

G13 context 2046
Shallow dish (?)
Clear colorless   FIG. 13

Four joining fragments of rim and body. Upright rim with rounded edge. Short, convex side, curving inward. Gradual transition from side to flat bottom. On the exterior, three rows of irregularly shaped circular and oval cut facets.

REMARKS

The substantial numbers of colorless cast glass finds, combined with their distribution across contexts in Trenches 2, 9, and 18, demonstrate that this class of glass tableware was widespread at Zeugma. Relative quantities of extant fragments show that colorless cast bowls and plates were at least three times more common than cast ribbed bowls (see above), suggesting a more quotidian status, as well. The prevalence of colorless cast tableware may also relate to production nearer at hand, as similarities with material excavated at Dura-Europos raise the possibility that cities along the Euphrates were supplied by one or more regional workshops.[21] It is also worth remarking that fragments of colorless cast bowls and plates comprise a remarkably large share of the glass finds from both Zeugma and Dura-Europos. Moreover, it is probable that the inhabitants of both cities continued to use this type of tableware into the third century A.D., although it is rarely found elsewhere later than the mid-second century.[22] While residuality is a possibility in a few cases, another explanation is that conservative glass workshops in the region persisted in their adherence to familiar casting techniques for longer than has generally been recognized.[23] Consequently, it may be necessary to extend the accepted date range for colorless cast glass at Zeugma and other sites in the eastern Mediterranean by as much as a century.

IIId. Mold-Blown Vessels

Only a handful of mold-blown pieces recovered during the Zeugma 2000 excavations are datable with certainty to the Early Imperial period. One is a body fragment of a shallow bowl decorated with vertical ribs (**G14**), belonging to a class of mold-blown ribbed bowls produced during the second and third quarters of the first century A.D.[24] Fragments of a few mold-blown truncated conical beakers with protruding knobs (sometimes called "lotus-bud" beakers) (**G15**) are similarly dated.[25] Another fragment preserves the base and lower body of a small mold-blown bottle, jug, or flask (**G16**).[26] The pattern of upturned tongues in relief preserved on the sloping lower body of the fragment appears on a wide variety of small mold-blown perfume containers of the first century A.D., precluding precise identification of the vessel type; none of the decoration above the tongues is preserved.

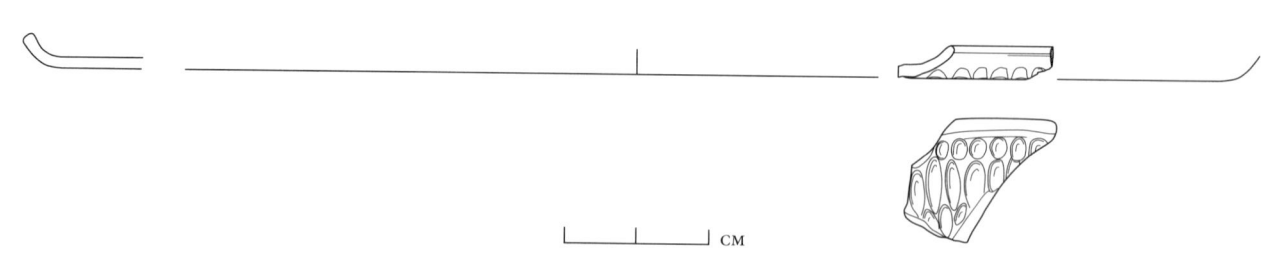

Figure 13. **G13.** *Shallow dish (facet-cut).*

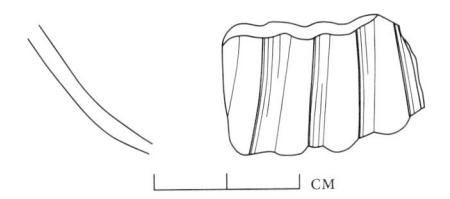

Figure 14. **G14.** *Shallow bowl (ribbed).*

G14 context 2269
Shallow bowl
Greenish (?) FIG. 14

Fragment of body. Convex side, curving inward. On the exterior, four shallow vertical ribs.

G15 context 2278
Conical beaker
Greenish-colorless

Fragment of body. Straight side, sloping diagonally inward. On the exterior, protruding knobs alternating with small circular bosses.
Similar: Isings 1957, form 31. Small circular bosses are a common decorative element on this type of beaker.

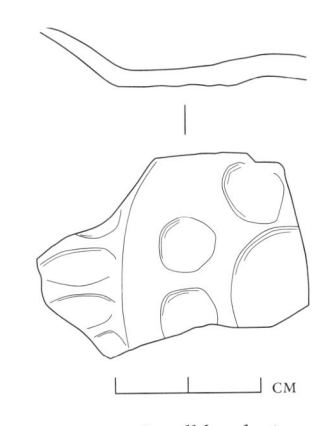

Figure 15. **G16.** *Small bottle, jug, or flask (mold-blown decoration).*

G16 context 9074
Small bottle, jug, or flask
Color not recorded FIG. 15

Fragment of body and base. Straight side, sloping diagonally inward. Angular transition from side to flat base. On the exterior, remains of four upturned tongues on lower body; on underside of base, design of roughly circular indentations around larger central depression, also roughly circular.
Similar: Clairmont 1963, nos. 28–32. The shape of the tongues is close to a small group of vessels from Dura-Europos, including two flasks (nos. 28–9) with a lattice design of conjoined lozenges on the body above the tongues. The design on the base of the Zeugma fragment, however, is without parallel at Dura-Europos and may be unique.

IIId. Blown Vessels (Relief-Cut)

A fragment of a conical beaker (**G17**) recovered at Zeugma illustrates a decorative technique known as relief-cutting, in which the cutting wheel was used to grind down parts of the exterior surface of a blown-glass blank, leaving other areas raised in relief. Beakers with relief-cut decoration date mainly to the later first and early second centuries A.D. The Zeugma example is unusual in the apparent absence of a zone of cut facets on the body.[27] It appears to belong to a relatively rare class decorated only with ground-out horizontal ribs.[28]

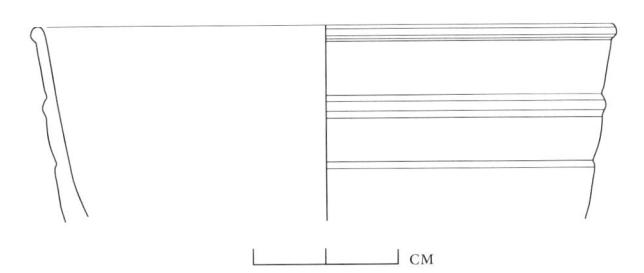

Figure 16. **G17.** *Conical beaker (ground-out ribs).*

G17 context 2189
Conical beaker
Yellowish-colorless FIG. 16

Fragment of rim and body. Upright rim with cracked-off edge, rounded by grinding. Nearly straight side, sloping diagonally inward. On the exterior, one convex horizontal molding in relief at rim and two more on upper body; broad recesses in between formed by grinding of surface.
Similar: Isings 1957, form 29 or 34. The vessel was blown thick, in order to leave the walls sufficiently sturdy after the recessed areas of the surface were ground away.

REMARKS

The scarcity of fragments securely datable to the Early Imperial period suggests that blown-glass vessels remained rare at Zeugma in the first and early second centuries A.D. The few mold-blown pieces were certainly imported—from the Syro-Palestinian coast, if not from the West.[29] The relief-cut beaker must also have been an import.[30] These vessels would have been highly valued as luxury items, and those found in third-century contexts were presumably kept as heirlooms.[31] It may not be coincidental that the fragment of the mold-blown ribbed bowl (**G14**) was found in the same context (2269) as finds of cast ribbed and mosaic glass (see above).

IV. Middle Imperial (A.D. 161–253)

The glass finds of the Middle Imperial period at Zeugma are characterized by both a major expansion in quantity and a diversification of form and function.[32] The finds include an extensive collection of tableware—bowls, dishes,

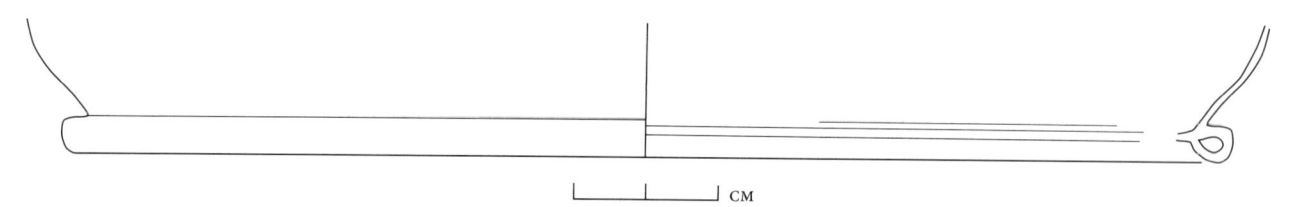

Figure 17. **G18**. *Dish or shallow bowl (pushed-in hollow base-ring).*

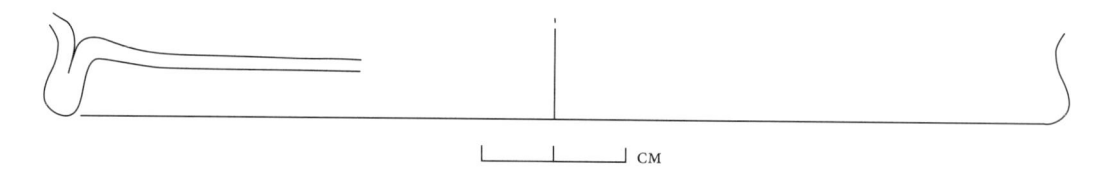

Figure 18. **G19**. *Dish or shallow bowl (pushed-in hollow base-ring).*

cups, and beakers for eating and drinking, as well as jars and flasks for serving; the majority of the tableware is plain, but a substantial portion is distinctively decorated with cut designs or applied ornament. In addition to tableware were found unguent bottles designed to hold scented oils, cosmetics, medicine, etc., as well as cylindrical and square bottles employed in large part for the storage and transport of goods.

IVa. Blown Tableware (Undecorated)

Fragments of undecorated blown-glass vessels are very numerous at Zeugma, appearing in many third-century deposits and colluvium layers. In spite of the prevalence of this material, these fragments are often difficult to type and to date closely. The greatest part consists of fragments preserving the convex, curving bodies of bowls and cups. More specifically, fragments of bases with pushed-in hollow base-rings (**G18–19**), belonging to dishes and shallow bowls, are quite common. Deeper bowls and cups with applied base-rings (**G20–21**) and pad bases (**G22**) also occur somewhat frequently. Rims are mostly simple, either fire-rounded (**G23**) or cracked off (**G24**); folded rims are rare. Particularly notable among the finds of plain blown glassware are a few fragments of goblets with solid, knobbed stems and separately blown feet (**G25–26**).[33]

G18 context 1010
Dish or shallow bowl
Yellowish-green   FIG. 17

Fragment of body and base. Convex side, curving inward. Angular transition from side to flat (?) bottom. Outsplayed base-ring with tubular edge, formed by folding.
Similar: Isings (1957), form 49; Vessberg 1956, shallow bowl type BIa.

G19 context 2332
Dish or shallow bowl
Pale bluish-green   FIG. 18

Fragment of base. Flat bottom. Slightly outsplayed base-ring, formed by folding.
Similar: possibly Isings 1957, form 97a; Vessberg 1956, shallow bowl type BIIa.

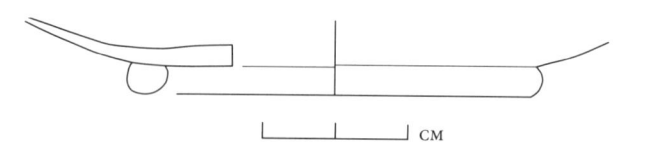

Figure 19. **G20**. *Hemispherical cup or bowl (applied base-ring).*

G20 context 9074
Cup or bowl
Bluish-green   FIG. 19

Fragment of body and base. Nearly straight side, sloping diagonally inward. Gradual transition from side to flat bottom. Applied base-ring with rounded edge.
Similar: possibly Isings 1957, form 85b. The shallow angle of the lower body suggests that the shape of this cup/bowl was roughly cylindrical.

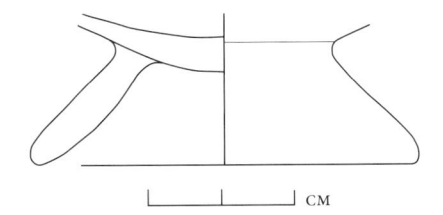

Figure 20. **G21**. *Deep bowl (applied base-ring).*

G21 SF 2128; context 2039
Deep bowl
Pale greenish   FIG. 20

Fragment of body and base. Convex, curving bottom. Applied diagonal base-ring with rounded edge.
Similar: Clairmont 1963, nos. 384–402. Many similar bases, associated with deep bowls, were found at Dura-Europos.

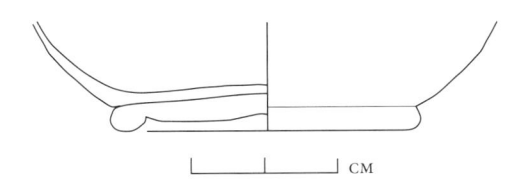

Figure 21. **G22**. *Hemipsherical cup or bowl (pad base).*

G22 context 2080
Hemispherical cup or bowl
Colorless   FIG. 21

Fragment of body and base. Convex side, curving inward; thicker towards bottom. Angular transition from side to slightly concave bottom. Pad base, tooled to form base-ring with rounded edge.
Similar: possibly Isings 1957, form 69. This type of vessel was popular in the later first and early second centuries A.D. and probably later. Examples with pad bases are relatively common.

G23 context 2002
Cylindrical cup or bowl
Colorless   FIG. 22

Fragment of rim and body. Vertical rim with thickened, fire-rounded edge. Straight, vertical side, beginning to curve towards bottom.

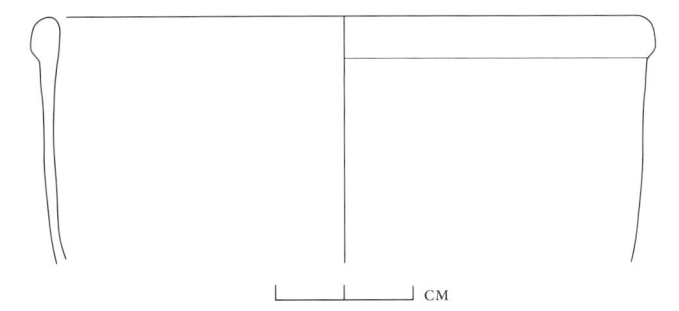

Figure 22. **G23**. *Cylindrical cup or bowl (fire-rounded rim).*

G24 context 2001
Convex bowl with outsplayed rim
Greenish-colorless   FIG. 23

Fragment of rim and body. Outsplayed rim with sloping, cracked-off edge, flattened by grinding. Convex side, curving inward.
Similar: Isings 1957, form 96a; Vessberg 1956, deep bowl type AI.

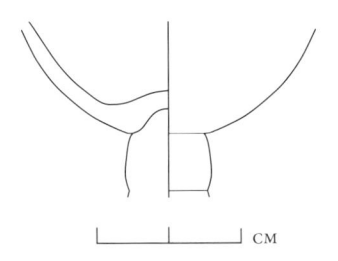

Figure 24. **G25**. *Goblet.*

G25 context 11047
Goblet
Greenish   FIG. 24

Fragment of body and stem. Convex side, curving inward. Angular transition from side to concave bottom. Solid, globular knobbed stem inserted into underside of concave bottom; very small section of a second knob (?) below first.
Similar: Clairmont 1963, nos. 460–7. Fragments of similar goblets, with either ovoid or bell-shaped bodies, were found at Dura-Europos.

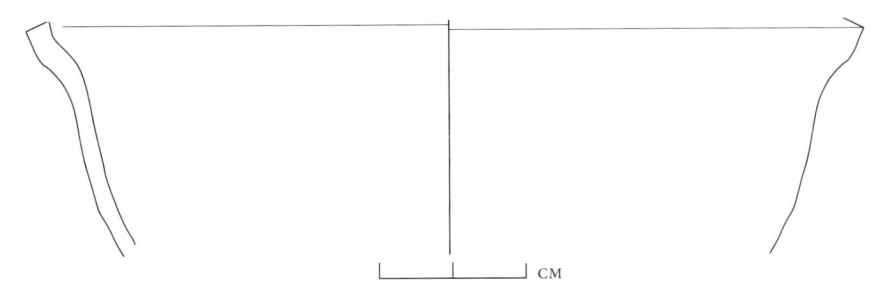

Figure 23. **G24**. *Convex bowl with outsplayed rim (cracked-off rim).*

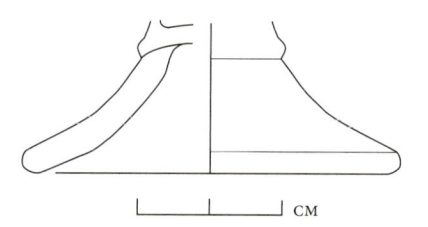

Figure 25. **G26**. *Goblet.*

G26 context 2080
Goblet
Colorless FIG. 25

Fragment of stem and foot. Lower section of knobbed stem. High, outsplayed foot, slightly concave, with rounded edge.

REMARKS

Fragments of jars and flasks occur much less frequently than bowls, dishes, and cups, indicating that glass vessels used for serving food and drink were not as widespread as those geared towards consumption. One of the best preserved vessels recovered at Zeugma is a small square jar (**G27**) with indented sides and outsplayed rim.[34] Another type of jar in use during this period was presumably globular, with a wide mouth and cylindrical neck (**G28**). Flasks with funnel-shaped mouths (**G29**) also came into use during the Middle Imperial period.

Figure 26. **G27**. *Square jar.*

G27 SF 452; context 9137
Square jar
Pale bluish-green FIG. 26

Intact except for small section of rim and neck. Outsplayed, nearly horizontal rim with edge folded out, up, and in. Short, funnel neck, tapering diagonally downward from rim to sloping shoulder. Slightly convex side, flattened manually; deep oval indent pressed into each of four sides. Concave base with central kick; pontil mark in center of base.

Similar: Whitehouse 1997, nos. 288–90, with additional bibliography. Small jars of this type are found with and without indentations in the body. The body may be left globular or, as in this case, made square by manually flattening the sides.

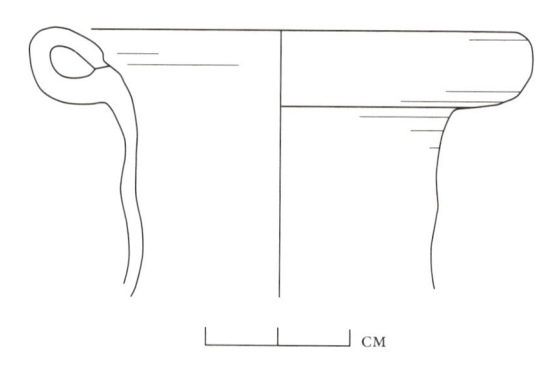

Figure 27. **G28**. *Jar (cylindrical neck).*

G28 SF 2328; context 2312
Jar
Greenish FIG. 27

Two fragments of rim and neck (distorted by heat). Outsplayed rim with rolled-in edge. Wide, cylindrical neck (slightly warped).

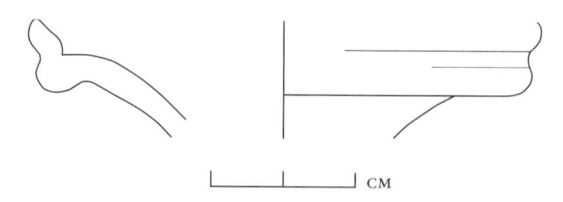

Figure 28. **G29**. *Flask (funnel-shaped mouth).*

G29 context 13036
Flask
Greenish-colorless (?) FIG. 28

Fragment of rim and mouth. Rim outsplayed and bent up into nearly vertical position; fire-rounded edge. Funnel-shaped mouth, tapering diagonally downward towards neck.

Similar: Clairmont 1963, no. 504. A flask with similar rim treatment was found at Dura-Europos.

REMARKS

Throughout the Roman world, glassblowing was responsible for the supplanting of pottery by glass as the preferred medium of tableware.[35] In archaeological terms, this is evident not only in an increase in the overall quantity of glass recovered, but also in a correlative decline in the proportional representation of tableware among the pottery finds. Blown-glass tableware seems to have arrived relatively late to Zeugma. If the cities around Vesuvius may be regarded as typical, the shift from pottery to glass was fully realized in Italy and the western provinces by the Flavian period.[36] At Zeugma, by contrast, demand for ceramic tableware seems to have diminished little between Augustan/Tiberian and Flavian (/Trajanic) times, whereas it had all but disappeared by the middle of the third century A.D.[37] The changeover from pottery to glass, therefore, must have come to pass at some point between the early second and mid-third centuries; unfortunately, the lack of pottery evidence for this intervening period does not allow the shift to be pinpointed more narrowly. The fact that a large proportion of the diagnostic glass fragments found in contexts associated with the Sasanian attack of A.D. 252/253 are characteristic of the later second and third centuries suggests that the major influx of blown glass to Zeugma took place in the Middle Imperial period. The belated introduction of blown glass on a large scale may be associated with the protracted popularity of cast glass (see above) as another manifestation of the conservatism of the region's glassmakers.

As the use of blown-glass tableware increased substantially at Zeugma in the Middle Imperial period, long-distance imports may no longer have sufficed to meet the demands of the city, which would have been better served by the establishment of local workshops. No direct evidence for glassmaking has been discovered at Zeugma, either in the form of provisions for production (i.e., furnaces, tools) or waste products (i.e., cullet, moils, misfires, etc.); this deficiency is hardly conclusive, however, since the Zeugma 2000 excavations focused on a primarily upscale, domestic area of the city, where a glass workshop was unlikely to have been located. It is worth considering that, while most of the ceramic tableware predominant through Flavian (/Trajanic) times is presumed to be local, no evidence for pottery production has come to light either.[38] It seems sensible that in the supplanting of ceramic tableware by glass, one local product would have been substituted for another.

IVb. Blown Tableware (Cut Decoration)

Various styles of wheel-cut decoration were employed on blown-glass tableware of the Middle Imperial period. Simple linear-cut decoration, consisting of series of horizontal abraded bands or deeper cut grooves, was the most common means employed to enliven the exterior surfaces of bowls (**G30**) and beakers (**G31**), as well as flasks (**G32–33**). In a more dramatic application of essentially the same linear-cutting technique, the body of a globular flask (**G34**) was embellished with a large number of parallel and intersecting grooves.

G30 context 11026
Convex bowl with outsplayed rim
Pale bluish-green   FIG. 29

Two fragments of rim and body. Outsplayed rim with nearly vertical, cracked-off edge, flattened by grinding. Convex side, bulging out from transition to rim before curving inward. On the exterior, four (?) horizontal abraded bands: one at transition from rim to body, one roughly in middle of body, and two on lower body.

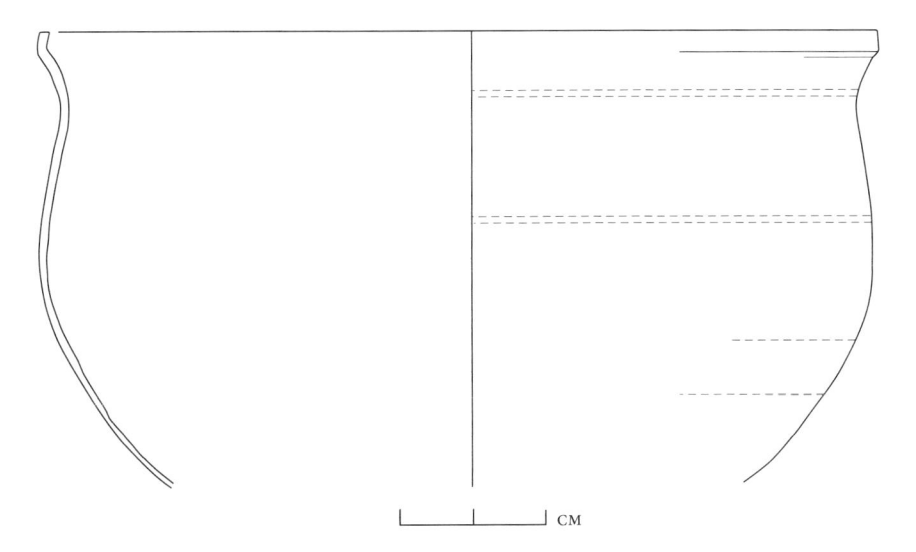

Figure 29. **G30**. *Convex bowl with outsplayed rim (linear-cut).*

Similar: shape as **G24**. Wheel-cut and abraded bands are common on bowls of this type at Cyprus and elsewhere.

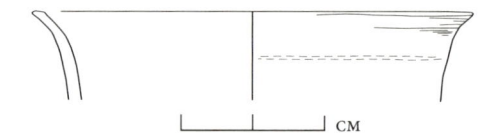

Figure 30. **G31**. *Conical or cylindrical beaker (linear-cut).*

G31 context 11026
Conical or cylindrical beaker
Greenish-colorless   FIG. 30

Two fragments of rim and body. Outsplayed rim with cracked-off edge, roughly ground. Straight side, sloping diagonally downward. On the exterior, at least one horizontal abraded band on upper body.

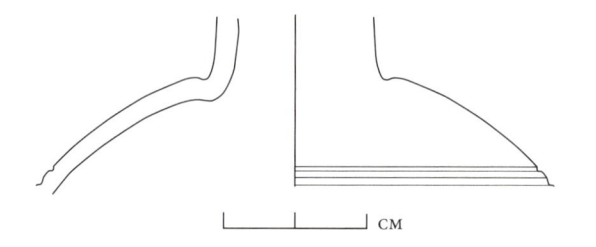

Figure 31. **G32**. *Globular flask (linear-cut).*

G32 context 9175
Globular flask
Colorless   FIG. 31

Two joining fragments of neck and body. Lower section of vertical, cylindrical (?) neck. Very short, slightly dipping shoulder. Convex side, expanding outward. On the exterior, two (?) horizontal wheel-cut grooves on upper body.
Similar: probably Isings 1957, form 103; form 104 is also a possibility, as the cylindrical lower neck may have opened out into a funnel mouth.

G33 SF 916; context 18001
Globular flask
Colorless (?)   FIG. 32

Fragment of rim and neck. Vertical rim with cracked-off edge, flattened by grinding. Cylindrical neck, expanding outward from rim before turning inward towards bottom; constriction at base of neck. On the exterior, five horizontal wheel-cut grooves on neck.
Similar: Isings 1957, form 103.

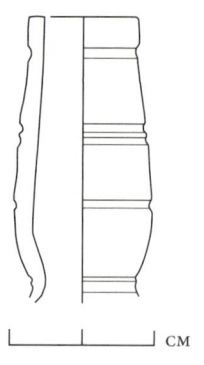

Figure 32. **G33**. *Globular flask.*

Figure 33. **G34**. *Globular flask (linear-cut).*

G34 context 9175
Globular flask
Colorless   FIG. 33

Nine (?) fragments of body. Convex side, expanding outward. On the exterior, numerous parallel and intersecting cut grooves.
Similar: shape as **G32–33**. Globular flasks decorated in this manner were also found at Dura-Europos (Clairmont 1963, nos. 540–1). For an intact parallel, with additional comparanda, see Whitehouse 1997, no. 433.

Also popular were blown-glass vessels, mostly bowls, with facet-cut decoration. In its most haphazard form, this consists of vertical rice-grain facets dispersed in irregular rows over part or all of the exterior surface of a vessel (**G35**). Most arrangements are more orderly, however, with facets occupying distinct zones. A common pattern features one or more rows of vertical rice-grain facets encircling the body of a bowl between sets of horizontal wheel-cut bands (**G36–37**). Alternatively, horizontally oriented rice-grain facets could be used instead of wheel-cut bands to divide the vessel into zones (**G38**).

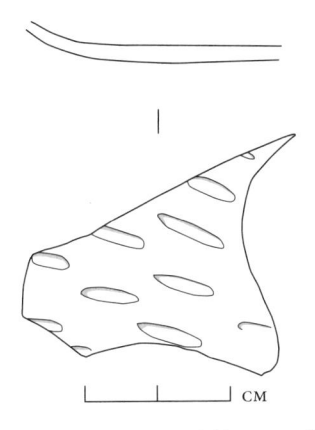

Figure 34. **G35**. *Bowl (facet-cut).*

G35 context 9175
Bowl
Colorless
FIG. 34

Fragment of body. Short section of convex side, curving inwards. Gradual transition from side to flat bottom. On the exterior, at least four horizontal rows of vertical rice-grain facets, irregularly sized and shaped.

G36 context 11034
Convex bowl with outsplayed rim
Colorless
FIG. 35

Fragment of rim and body. Outsplayed rim with cracked-off edge, roughly finished by grinding. Convex side, bulging out from transition to rim before curving inward. On the exterior, eight horizontal wheel-cut bands: one on upper body, six set closely together just below middle of body, and one on lower body; between the upper and middle bands, a horizontal row of vertical rice-grain facets, irregularly sized and shaped.

Similar: shape as **G24** and **G30**. Vessels with such simple combinations of linear- and facet-cut decoration are found at both eastern and western sites and were probably manufactured widely.

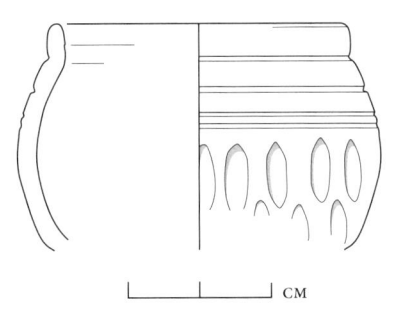

Figure 36. **G37**. *Cup (linear- and facet-cut).*

G37 context 18001
Hemispherical cup
Colorless
FIG. 36

Fragment of rim and body. Vertical rim with cracked-off edge, rounded by grinding. Convex side bulging out from below rim to middle of body before curving inward. On the exterior, four horizontal wheel-cut bands: one below rim and three on upper body; below the bands, two rows of rice-grain facets, irregularly sized and shaped.

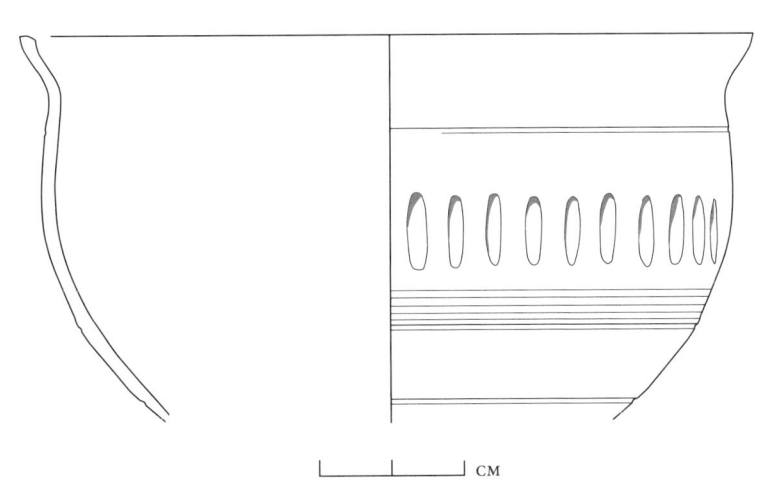

Figure 35. **G36**. *Convex bowl with outsplayed rim (linear- and facet-cut).*

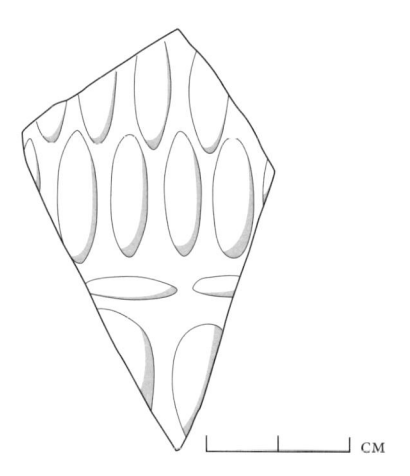

Figure 37. **G38.** *Bowl (facet-cut).*

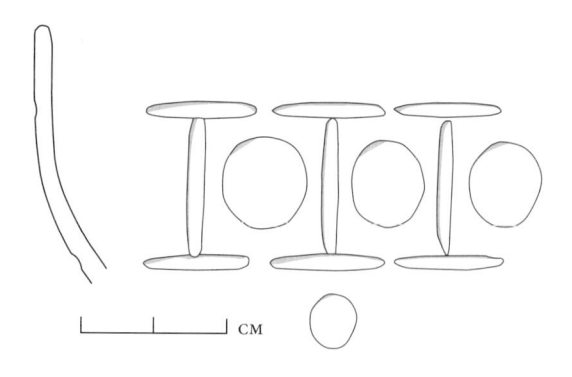

Figure 38. **G39.** *Deep bowl (geometric cut design).*

G38 context 18070
Bowl
Colorless   FIG. 37

Fragment of body. Convex side. On the exterior, two rows of vertical rice-grain facets; below, a band of horizontal rice-grain facets; below, a row of oval facets.
Similar: Clairmont 1963, 65–6, group C.

REMARKS

More complex geometric designs could also be made by facet-cutting. Multiple fragments (**G39-40**), belonging to one or more bowls (?), feature a pattern of circular facets alternating with I-shaped motifs, the latter formed by a vertical rice-grain facet sandwiched between two horizontal rice-grain facets.[39] Another fragment comes from a bowl decorated with wheel-cut circles separated by pairs of rice-grain facets (**G41**). Still visible on the outer layer of a fused lump of badly burned glass (see above) are slivers of what appear to be highly stylized floral motifs: leaves, flower petals, etc. (**G42**).

G39 context 9175
Deep bowl
Colorless   FIG. 38

Twelve fragments of rim and body (distorted by heat). Upright rim with cracked-off edge, rounded by grinding. Convex side, curving inward. On the exterior, a row of facet-cut I's alternating with roughly circular facets; below, another circular facet, probably belonging to second register of cut decoration.

G40 context 9175
Bowl (?)
Colorless   FIG. 39

Twelve fragments of body (distorted by heat). Body shape undetermined. On the exterior, a row of facet-cut I's alternating with roughly circular facets; below, a row of circular facets separated by pairs of diagonal lines, overlapping at ends; below, horizontal cut groove; below, another register of diagonal lines (?).

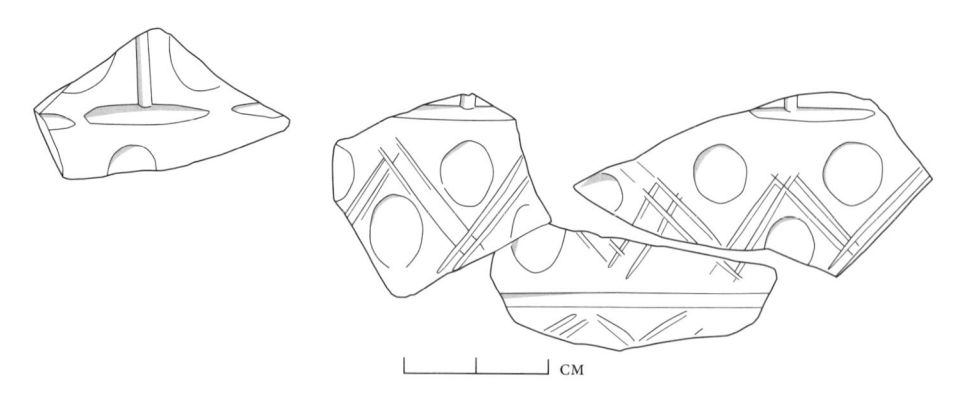

Figure 39. **G40.** *Bowl (?) (geometric cut design).*

G41 SF 4006; context 10000
Bowl
Colorless   FIG. 40

Fragment of body. Convex side, curving inward. Gradual transition to flat (?) bottom. On the exterior, wheel-cut circles separated by pairs of rice-grain facets.
Similar: Clairmont 1963, 70–2, group F.

G42 context 9175
Bowl
Colorless   FIG. 1, FIG. 41

Outer layer of fused lump of glass (distorted by heat). On the exterior, various cut patterns and cross-hatching.
Similar: Clairmont 1963, 77–9, group J.

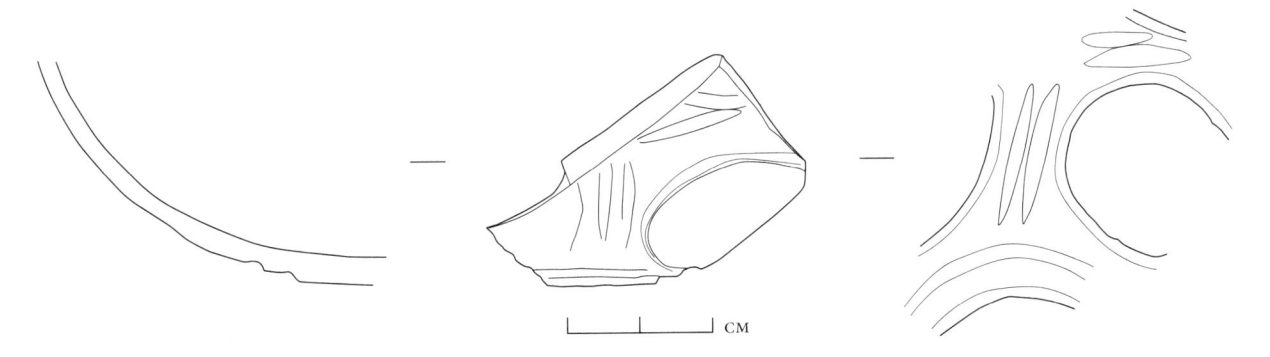

Figure 40. **G41**. *Bowl (geometric cut design).*

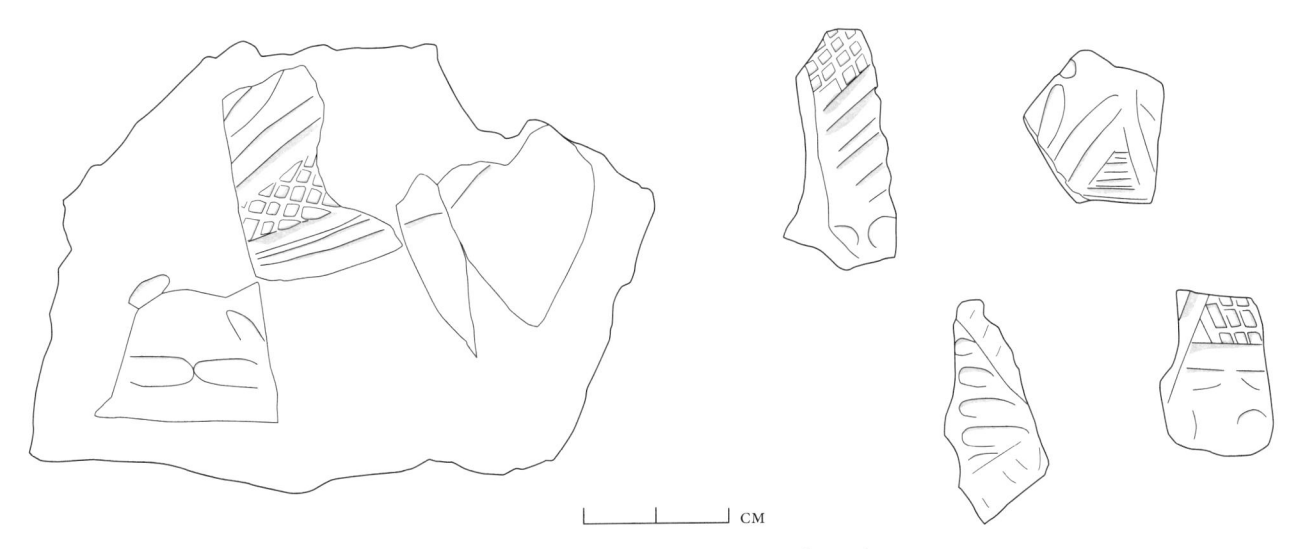

Figure 41. **G42**. *Bowl (geometric cut design).*

REMARKS

The popularity of blown tableware with cut decoration at Zeugma in the Middle Imperial period accords with the reigning fashion in glassware throughout the Roman Empire at that time. In general, glasscutters (*diatretarii*) are considered a professional group distinct from glassmakers (*vitrearii*). This distinction may have had little relevance for simple linear-cut decoration, whose application required little expertise. Even if a single craftsman did not serve as both glassmaker and glasscutter, there is no reason that both functions could not be contained within a single local workshop. Facet-cutting, on the other hand, was a more specialized skill and may have been practiced on a regional rather than a local level. Dura-Europos, where cut glass is known to have been made, has been proposed as a center of production in the East.[40] Parallels between cut designs favored at Dura-Europos and those seen on some of the finds from Zeugma seem to support that supposition. On the other hand, the decorative repertoire of the glasscutters at Dura-Europos evidently did not encompass all of the designs found at Zeugma, making it unlikely that the city's cut glass was supplied by a single source.

IVc. Blown Tableware (Applied Decoration)

A number of glass fragments found at Zeugma were decorated with applied glass threads of the same color as the fabric of the vessel. Applied decoration seems to have been used primarily, though not exclusively, on serving vessels (i.e., jars and flasks). One of the most distinctive examples is a funnel-mouthed flask with a thick coil applied to the rim (**G43**). A single fragment of a bowl (?) (**G44**) preserves part of a "spectacle" pattern formed by the intermittent pinching together of glass threads applied to the body of the vessel. Another fragment comprises the rim of a bowl with an applied corrugated band (**G44**).

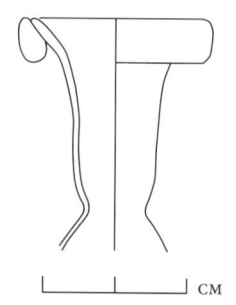

Figure 42. **G43**. *Flask (coil rim).*

G43 context 11047
Flask
Colorless   FIG. 42

Fragment of rim, mouth, and body. Slightly outsplayed rim with fire-rounded edge; thick coil applied to rim. Funnel-shaped mouth, tapering toward constriction at bottom. Below constriction, slightly convex side, expanding outward.
Similar: Clairmont, 1963, nos. 537–39.

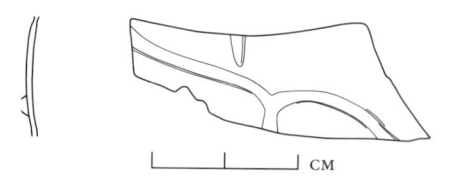

Figure 43. **G44**. *Bowl ("spectacle" pattern).*

G44 context 2039
Bowl (?)
Colorless   FIG. 43

Fragment of body. Convex side. On the exterior, "spectacle" pattern of applied threads, oriented horizontally; small section of single thread, oriented vertically.
Similar: Clairmont 1963, nos. 189–92. The small section of vertical thread on the Zeugma example must correspond to the vertical "rib" seen on several fragments of bowls with applied spectacle decoration found at Dura-Europos.

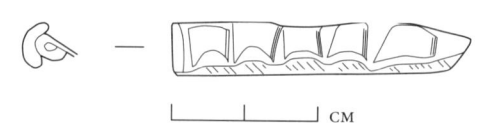

Figure 44. **G45**. *Bowl (corrugated band).*

G45 context 9003
Bowl
Greenish-colorless   FIG. 44

Fragment of rim. Outsplayed (?) rim with tubular edge, formed by folding down and in. Applied to the rim, section of corrugated band with five (?) ridges.
Similar: probably Isings 1957, form 43.

IVd. Blown Tableware (Pinched Decoration)

A few fragmentary glass vessels decorated with protruding points formed by pinching were recovered at Zeugma. One is a flask (**G46**), whose concave bottom is encircled by a ring of pinched "toes." Another is perhaps also a flask (**G47**), with five rows of pinched "warts" protruding from the body. Vessels with pinched "toes" and "warts" have been found mainly at Dura-Europos and other sites in Syria.

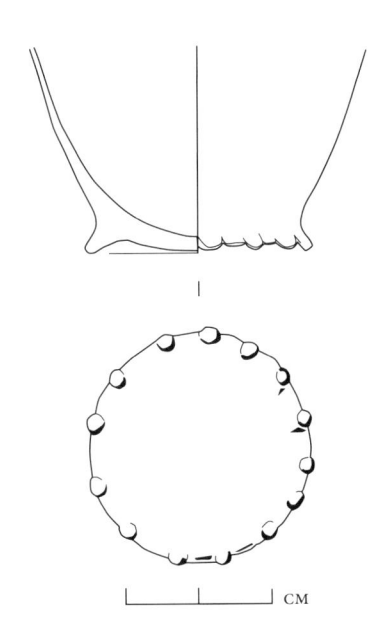

Figure 45. **G46**. *Flask (pinched "toes").*

G46 context 18070
Flask
Greenish-colorless   FIG. 45

Five joining fragments of body and base. Slightly convex side, curving inward. Gradual transition from side to concave bottom. Base-ring of fourteen pinched "toes."
Similar: Clairmont 1963, nos. 200–13. Most of the vessels from Dura-Europos with rings of pinched toes are identified as flasks.

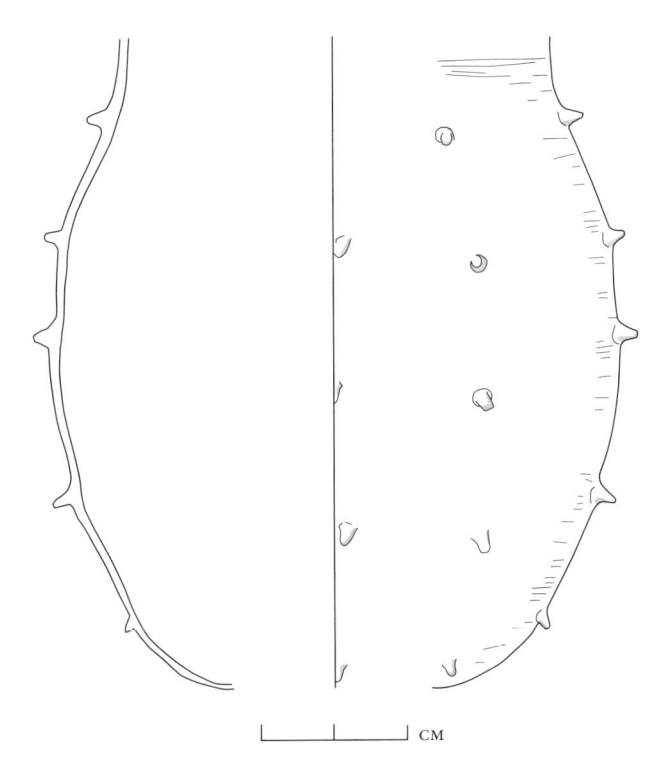

Figure 46. **G47**. *Flask (?) (pinched "warts").*

G47 context 11026
Flask (?)
Colorless   FIG. 46

Three fragments of body. Short section of cylindrical neck. Convex side, expanding outward from neck before curving inward toward slightly convex (?) bottom. On the exterior, five rows of pinched "warts."
Similar: Clairmont 1963, nos. 214–22. It should be noted, however, that the shape of this vessel finds no close parallel among the finds with pinched warts from Dura-Europos.

REMARKS

As with the blown tableware with cut decoration, glass vessels with applied and pinched decoration recovered at Zeugma bear considerable (though not perfect) resemblance to material from Dura-Europos, which may have supplied Zeugma with various classes of decorated glassware in the Middle Imperial period.

IVe. Unguent Bottles

Unguent bottles (sometimes called unguentaria or ampullae) are another category of blown-glass vessels found in quantity at Zeugma.[41] Among the simplest shapes to blow, unguent bottles tended to change little over time, making precise dating difficult. All of the pieces are undecorated and belong to common eastern Mediterranean types; local production seems probable. One nearly complete example of a squat unguent bottle (**G48**) can be dated to the late second or early third century A.D. Fragmentary examples include a club-shaped unguent bottle (**G49**) and two variants on a type with conical lower body (**G50–51**); all of these shapes were in use from the first through third centuries A.D. The lower half of a pipette-shaped unguent bottle (**G52**), found in a context (9137) associated with the Sasanian attack of A.D. 252/253, is a relatively early example of a type that became widespread in the fourth century.

Figure 47. **G48**. *Unguent bottle (squat).*

G48 context 2010
Unguent bottle
Bluish-green   FIG. 47

Intact except for minor surface damage. Outsplayed rim with rolled-in edge. Concave neck. Convex side. Concave base; pontil mark in center.
Similar: De Tommaso 1990, tipo 29.

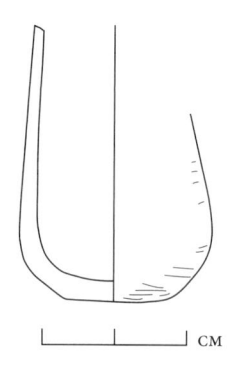

Figure 48. **G49**. *Unguent bottle (club-shaped).*

G49 context 15002
Unguent bottle
Bluish-green   FIG. 48

Fragment of body and base. Straight side, expanding outward. Convex bottom curving into flat base.
Similar: Isings 1957, form 82b1; De Tommaso 1990, tipo 70.

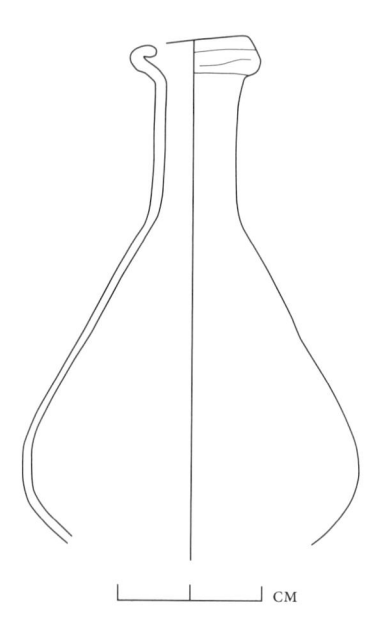

Figure 49. **G50**. *Unguent bottle (conical).*

G50 context 9001
Unguent bottle
Yellowish-brown   FIG. 49

Twenty fragments of rim, neck, and body. Outsplayed rim with edge folded in. Cylindrical neck. Straight side, expanding outward. Convex bottom.
Similar: Isings 1957, form 28a; De Tommaso 1990, tipo 42.

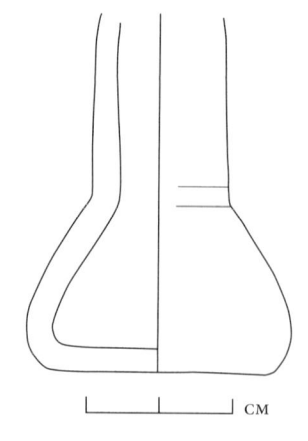

Figure 50. **G51**. *Unguent bottle (conical).*

G51 SF 3408; context 18070
Unguent bottle
Greenish   FIG. 50

Fragment of neck, body, and base. Vertical, cylindrical neck. Straight side, expanding outward. Convex bottom curving into flat base.
Similar: Isings 1957, form 28b. The types represented by **G50-51** differ only in the relative proportions of the neck and body.

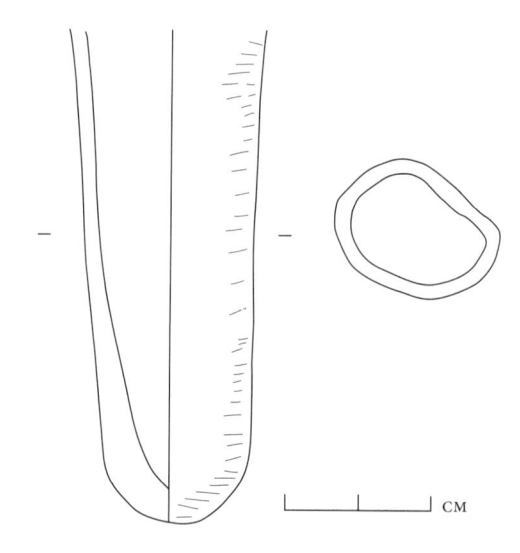

Figure 51. **G52**. *Unguent bottle (pipette-shaped).*

G52 SF 453; context 9137
Unguent bottle
Pale greenish-colorless   FIG. 51

Fragment of lower body and base. Straight side, sloping inward. Convex base.
Similar: Probably Isings 1957, form 105; De Tommaso 1990, tipo 57. Although the middle portion of the body is missing, the taper of the body suggests a central bulge. The pipette-shaped unguent bottle was most common in the fourth century A.D., but it is known from third-century contexts, as well; for examples from Dura-Europos, see Clairmont 1963, nos. 736–7.

IVf. Bottles

The use of blown-glass bottles for the storage and transport of goods, such as wine or oil, offered several advantages, including easy visibility and negligible effect on the taste or smell of the contents. Fragments of both cylindrical and square bottles were found at Zeugma, the latter in considerably larger number than the former. The best preserved cylindrical bottle (**G53**) was apparently free blown, squat rather than tall; the body is decorated with several series of horizontal abraded bands, rarely seen before the late second century A.D.[42] The square bottles are all mold blown, with designs in relief preserved on the undersides of several bases, variously interpreted as identifying the maker of the vessel or the vendor of the contents.[43] The designs in evidence at Zeugma include a flower with six petals (**G54**) and some sort of lattice pattern (**G55**). Mold-blown square bottles are conventionally dated to the later first and early second centuries A.D., but their use seems to have extended into the third century in the eastern Mediterranean.[44] The standard rim for both cylindrical and square bottles at Zeugma seems to have been folded in and flattened, forming a broad lip (**G56**). A "mushroom-shaped" variant (**G57**) was also used. Some, if not all, of about five detached fragments of broad strap-handles with fine vertical ribs (reeding) (**G58**) are probably to be associated with bottles.

G53 context 2046
Cylindrical bottle
Colorless   FIG. 52

Twenty-nine fragments of body and base. Convex shoulder, curving outward. Gradual transition from shoulder to

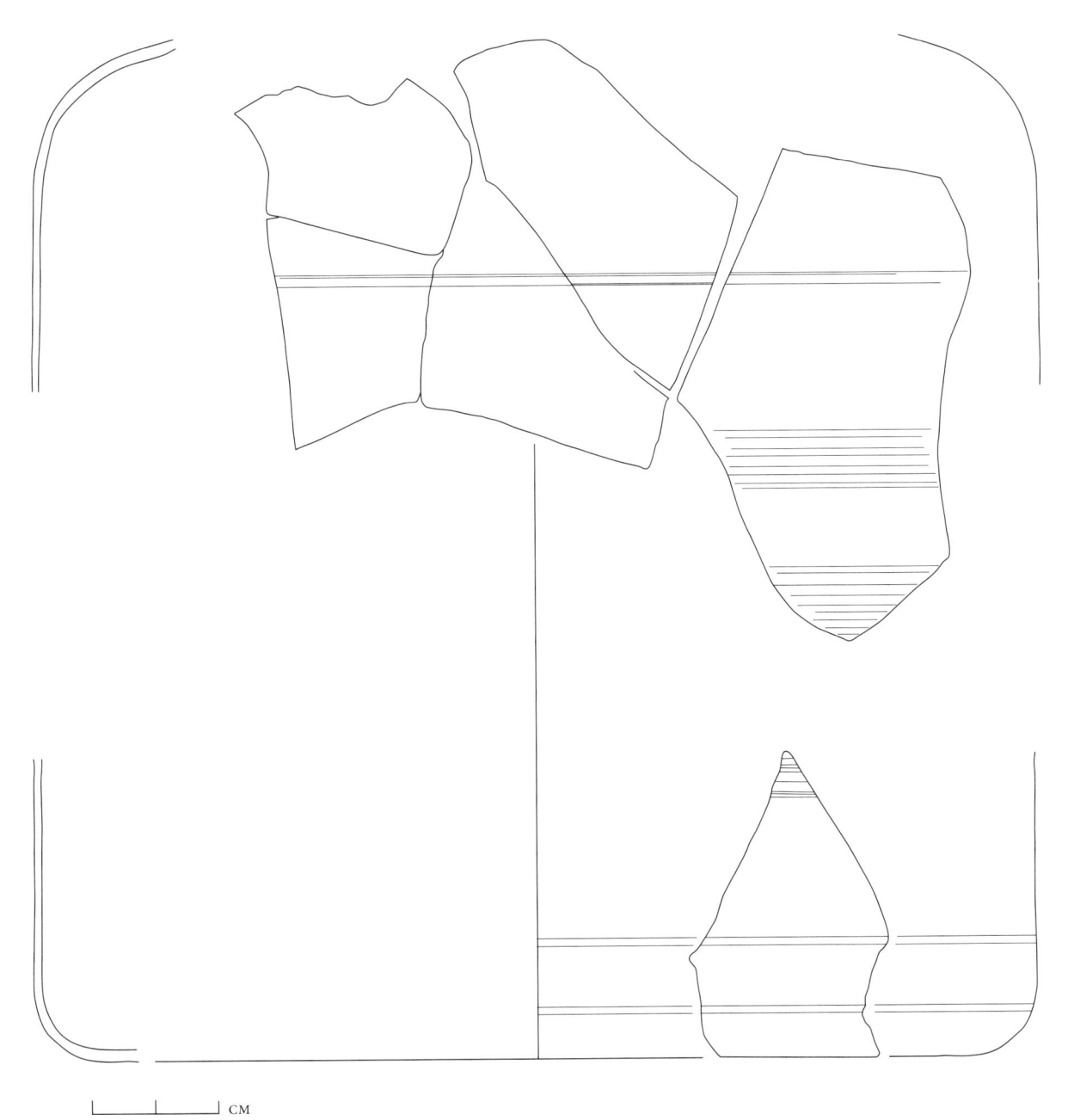

Figure 52. **G53**. *Cylindrical bottle (linear-cut).*

straight, vertical side, curving inward towards bottom. Flat (?) base. On the exterior; at least five (?) sets of horizontal abraded bands.

Similar: Isings 1957, form 51a. It is possible that these 29 fragments belong to two very similar cylindrical bottles.

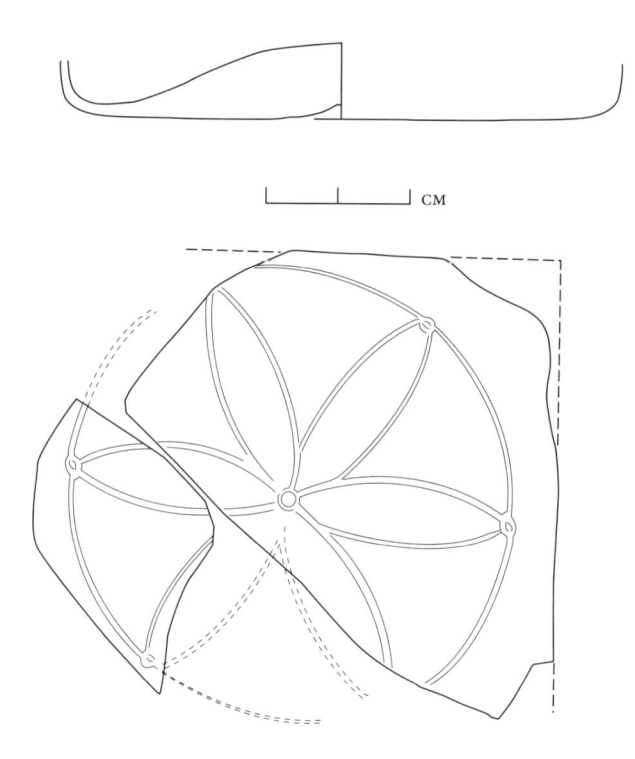

Figure 53. **G54**. *Square bottle (mold-blown design).*

Figure 54. **G55**. *Square bottle (mold-blown design).*

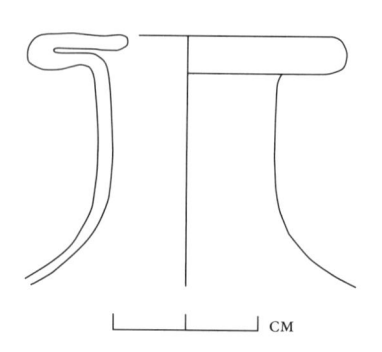

Figure 55. **G56**. *Bottle (flattened rim).*

G54 context 2312
Square bottle
Pale yellowish-green   FIG. 53

Three joining fragments of base. Flat base, thickening towards center; pontil mark in center. Mold-blown design on underside of base: flower with six petals within circular frame.

Similar: Isings 1957, form 50. A similar design appears on the base of a square bottle found in context 2269.

G55 SF 2328; context 2312
Square bottle
Greenish   FIG. 54

Four joining fragments of body and base. Straight, vertical side. Angular transition to slightly concave base. Mold-blown design on underside of base: lattice pattern within circular frame.

Similar: shape as **G54**. A similar lattice pattern, surrounded by four concentric circles, appears on the base of a square bottle found in context 9143.

G56 context 13036
Bottle
Greenish-colorless   FIG. 55

Four joining fragments of rim and neck. Horizontal rim, folded out, up, and in, then flattened. Cylindrical neck, curving outward towards bottom. Gradual transition from neck to slightly concave shoulder.

Similar: Charlesworth 1966, type 1a. It is not possible to determine whether **G56** belonged to a cylindrical or square bottle.

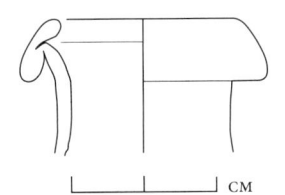

Figure 56. **G57**. *Bottle (mushroom-shaped rim).*

G57 context 1024
Bottle
Pale yellowish   FIG. 56

Fragment of rim and neck. Slightly outsplayed, sloping rim, folded out, up, and in. Cylindrical neck, curving slightly outward towards bottom.
Similar: Charlesworth 1966, type 1b.

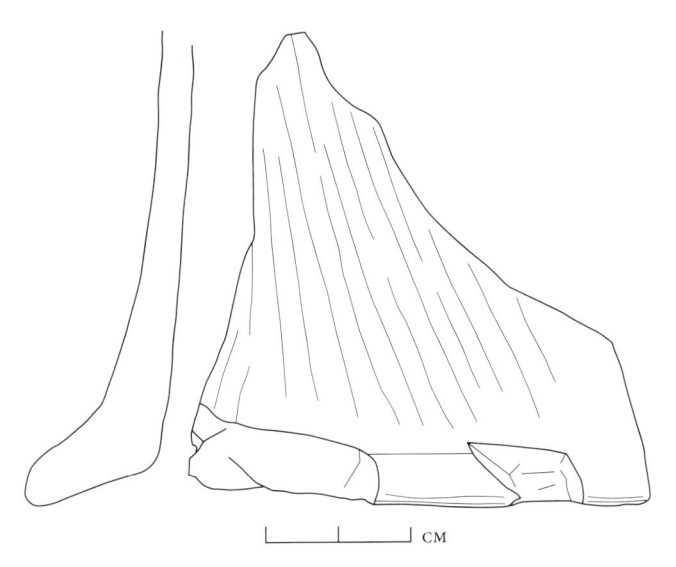

Figure 57. **G58**. *Bottle handle (reeded).*

G58 context 2046
Handle
Colorless   FIG. 57

Five joining fragments of handle. Section of broad strap-handle and lower terminal. On the exterior of handle, fine vertical ribs (reeding).

V. Late Imperial (A.D. 253–636)

Glass vessels of the Late Imperial period are well represented among the finds from Zeugma, regularly appearing in destruction contexts plausibly associated with an Arab invasion of ca. A.D. 636, as well as in colluvium deposits across the site. Based on style, most of this material appears to date between the later fourth and sixth centuries A.D., during which time Zeugma underwent something of a revival. The Late Imperial glass vessels encompass an assortment of tableware—both undecorated and decorated—along with a few pieces identifiable as lamps.[45]

Va. Blown Tableware (Undecorated)

In contrast to the preceding periods, the largest part of the blown-glass tableware of the Late Imperial period is comprised not of bowls and cups, but of goblets and beakers. Goblets were by far the most common class of glass vessel at Byzantine Zeugma, with fragments of as many as one hundred of these vessels recovered in the excavations. All belong to a standard type with a plain (rather than knobbed), hollow stem and a flaring foot with either a rounded (**G59**) or tubular (**G60**) edge. Also popular at this time were conical beakers with outsplayed, curving rims (**G61**).

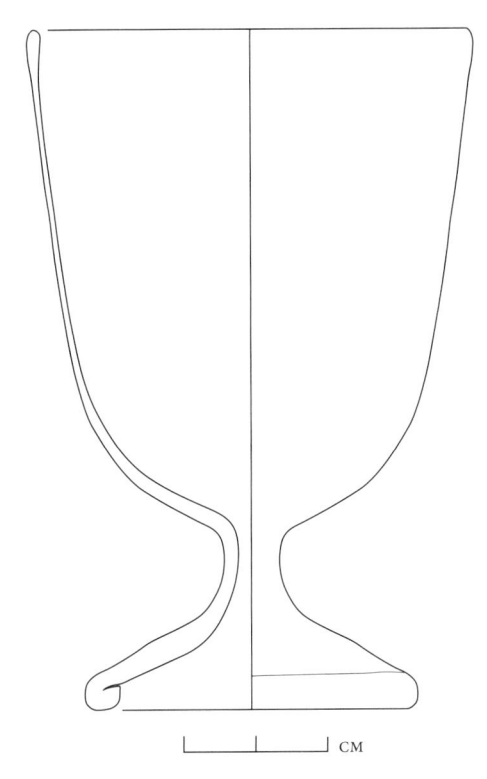

Figure 58. **G59**. *Goblet.*

G59 SF 496; context 7036
Goblet
Pale greenish   FIG. 58

Two fragments of rim, body, stem, and foot. Vertical rim with fire-rounded edge. Straight side, sloping inward towards convex, curving bottom. Short, hollow stem. Flaring foot with rounded edge, curving under.
Similar: Isings 1957, form 111. Goblets of this type came into use in the fourth century A.D. and continued to be produced for several centuries thereafter.

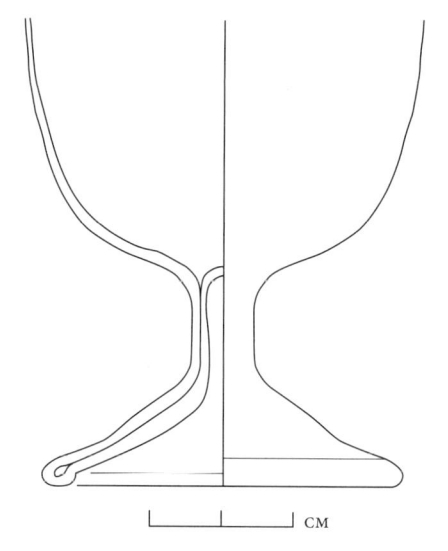

Figure 59. **G60**. *Goblet.*

G60 context 2000
Goblet
Greenish   FIG. 59

Fragment of body, stem, and foot. Convex side, curving inward. Cylindrical, hollow stem. Flaring foot with tubular edge, formed by folding.

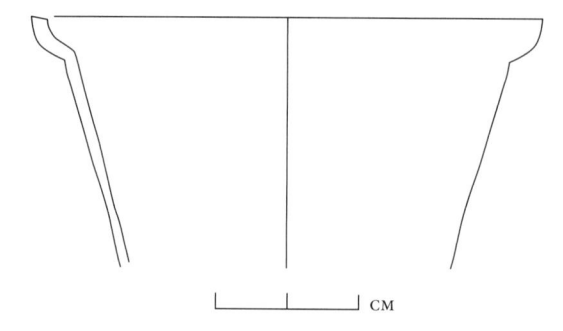

Figure 60. **G61**. *Conical beaker.*

G61 context 7000
Conical beaker
Greenish (?)   FIG. 60

Fragment of rim and body. Outsplayed, curving rim with cracked-off edge, flattened by grinding. Straight side, sloping inward.
Similar: Isings 1957, form 106c1 or 109c. As the base of this vessel was not found, it cannot be definitively assigned to one or the other of these types.

Bowls and cups, while less numerous than in the Middle Imperial period, were nonetheless still plentiful in the Late Imperial period at Zeugma. Small bowls with pushed-in hollow base-rings are fairly numerous (**G62–63**). Similarly shaped vessels with applied base-rings (**G64**) are also seen occasionally. A single example of a wound-coil base (**G65**) may belong to a bowl, as well. The standard rim seems to have been tubular, with the edge rolled inward (**G66**). More unusual is a fragment of a bowl with a double-folded rim (**G67**). Another noteworthy fragment belongs to a bowl with a fire-rounded rim and a projecting roll in the body (**G68**).

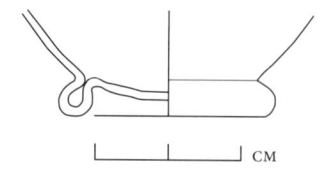

Figure 61. **G62**. *Hemispherical bowl (pushed-in hollow base-ring).*

G62 context 7077
Hemispherical bowl
Pale greenish   FIG. 61

Fragment of body and base. Convex side, curving inward. Gradual transition from side to convex bottom. Outsplayed base-ring with tubular edge, formed by folding.
Similar: Isings 1957, form 115. Bowls of this type were common in the Byzantine period throughout the eastern Mediterranean.

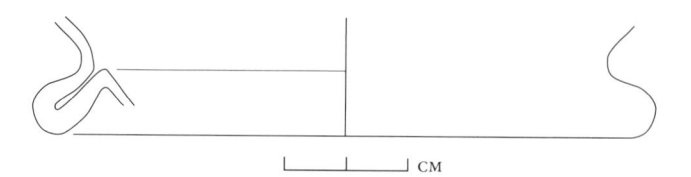

Figure 62. **G63**. *Bowl (pushed-in hollow base-ring).*

G63 context 1056
Bowl
Greenish-colorless   FIG. 62

Fragment of base. Short section of convex side, curving inward. Large, outsplayed base-ring with tubular edge, formed by folding.

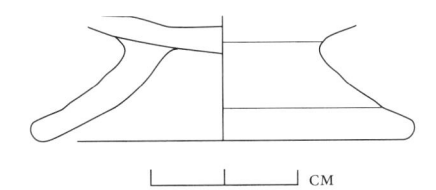

Figure 63. **G64**. *Bowl (applied base-ring).*

G64 context 5048
Bowl
Colorless   FIG. 63

Fragment of base. Slightly convex base. Large, outsplayed base ring, applied.
Similar: shape as **G21**. Despite its similarity to pieces of Middle Imperial date, this fragment can be dated to the Late Imperial period on the basis of its excavation context. Similar bases of comparable date have been found at Jalame (Weinberg and Goldstein 1988, nos. 145–51) and elsewhere.

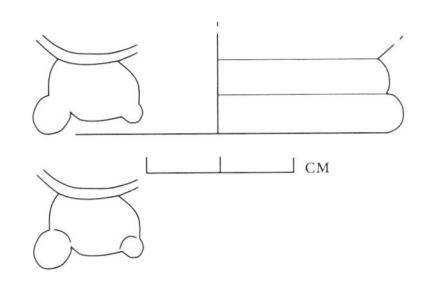

Figure 64. **G65**. *Bowl (?) (wound-coil base).*

G65 context 9000
Bowl (?)
Greenish   FIG. 64

Fragment of base. Concave bottom; pontil mark in center. Coil base-ring, twice wound.
Similar: von Saldern 1980, no. 196. A comparable fragment from Sardis, identified as a bowl, is not closely dated.

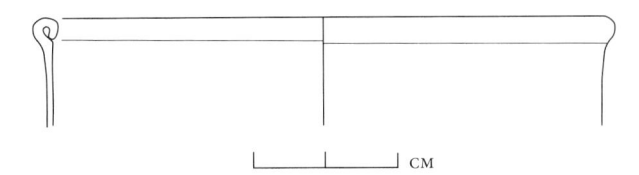

Figure 65. **G66**. *Cylindrical bowl (tubular rim).*

G66 context 1010
Cylindrical bowl
Bluish-green   FIG. 65

Fragment of rim and body. Slightly outsplayed, tubular rim, formed by rolling edge inward. Straight, vertical side.

G67 context 9000
Bowl
Greenish   FIG. 66

Fragment of rim and body. Rim folded out and down; edge rolled in. Short section of slightly convex side, curving inward.

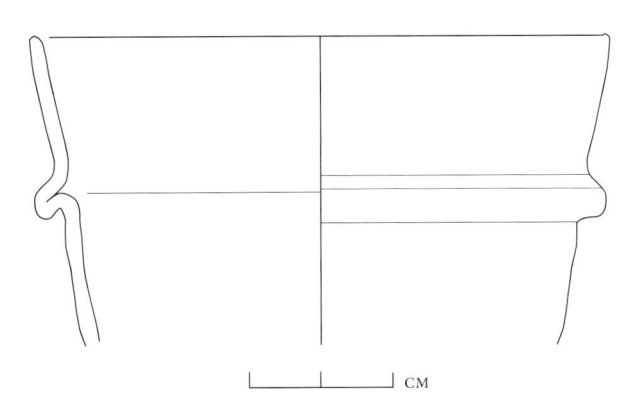

Figure 67. **G68**. *Bowl (projecting roll).*

G68 context 1024
Bowl
Bluish-green   FIG. 67

Fragment of rim and body. Vertical rim with fire-rounded edge. Straight side, sloping inward. Near middle of body, projecting roll, formed by tooling.
Similar: Weinberg and Goldstein 1988, no. 103.

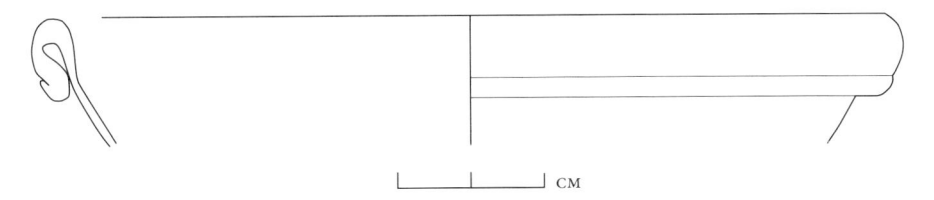

Figure 66. **G67**. *Bowl (double-folded rim).*

REMARKS

Serving vessels seem to have become more widespread at Zeugma in the Late Imperial period than they had been previously. A jar with bulbous body and short, tapering neck (**G69–70**) belongs to a type found throughout the eastern Mediterranean in the fourth and fifth centuries A.D.[46] Flasks with bulbous bodies and long necks opening into funnel-shaped mouths (**G71**) seem to have been especially popular at Zeugma; the rims of these vessels were generally fire-rounded, sometimes with a lip formed on one edge (**G72**) to aid in pouring. Other serving vessels with wide mouths and tubular rims (**G73**) are likely to have been jugs, since a number of jug handles (**G74–75**) were found in Late Imperial contexts.

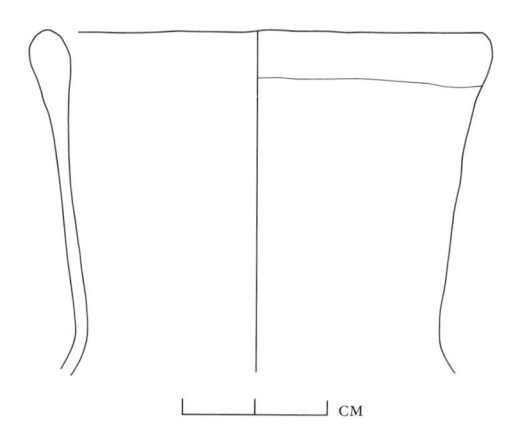

Figure 68. **G69**. *Bulbous jar.*

G69 context 7004
Jar
Bluish-green   FIG. 68

Fragment of rim, neck, and shoulder. Upright rim with thickened, fire-rounded edge. Neck tapering towards expanding shoulder.

G70 context 7004
Jar
Bluish-green   FIG. 69

Four joining fragments of body and base. Convex side, curving inward toward bottom. High, concave base; pontil mark in center.

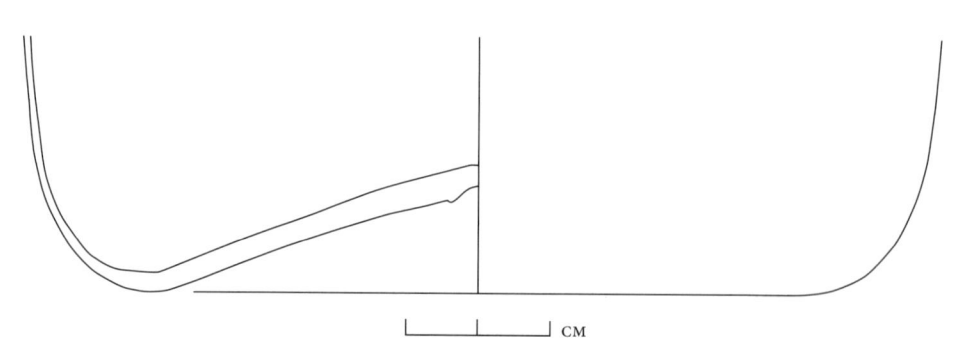

Figure 69. **G70**. *Bulbous jar.*

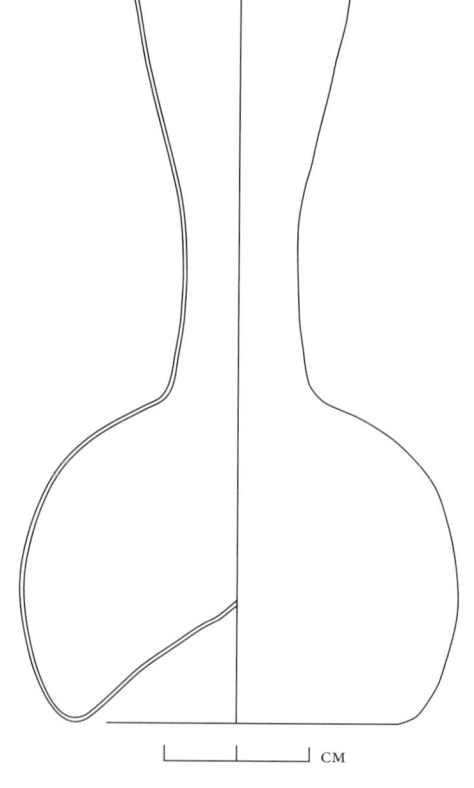

Figure 70. **G71**. *Flask (funnel-shaped mouth).*

G71 SF 496; context 7036
Flask
Pale greenish   FIG. 70

At least 20 fragments of mouth, neck, body, and base. Funnel-shaped mouth. Roughly cylindrical neck, expanding towards shoulder. Gradual transition from shoulder to convex side, expanding outward before curving inward towards bottom. High, concave base.
Similar: Isings 1957, form 104b.

GLASS · 243

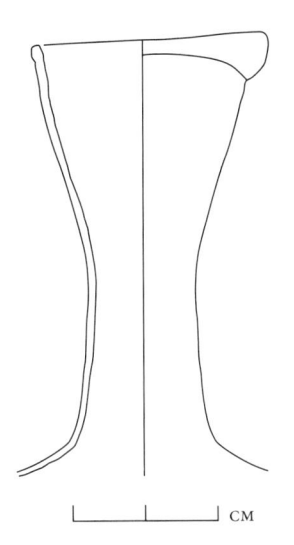

Figure 71. **G72**. *Flask (funnel-shaped mouth).*

G72 context 7003
Flask
Bluish-green   FIG. 71

Three joining fragments of rim, mouth, neck, and shoulder. Upright rim with fire-rounded edge; lip formed on one side. Funnel-shaped mouth. Roughly cylindrical neck, expanding slightly towards shoulder.
Similar: shape as **G71**.

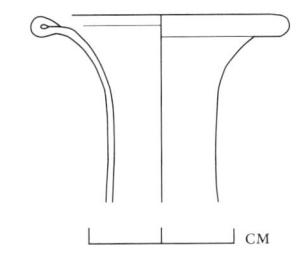

Figure 72. **G73**. *Jug (tubular-rim).*

G73 context 9000
Jug
Greenish   FIG. 72

Fragment of rim, mouth, and neck. Outsplayed, tubular rim, formed by rolling edge inward. Funnel-shaped mouth. Cylindrical neck.
Similar: probably Isings 1957, form 121.

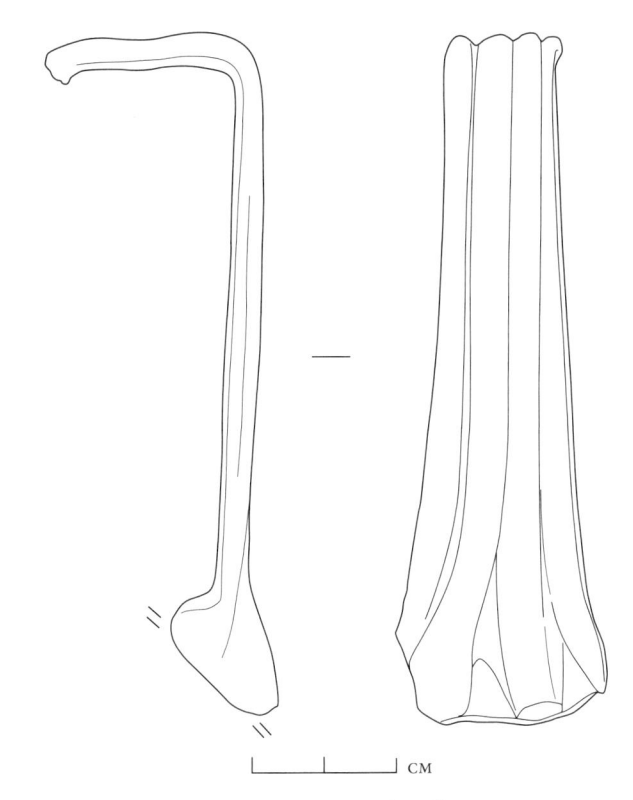

Figure 73. **G74**. *Jug handle.*

G74 SF 498; context 7023   FIG. 73
Jug handle
Bluish-green

Nearly intact handle. Strap-handle with nearly perpendicular bend; four vertical ribs.

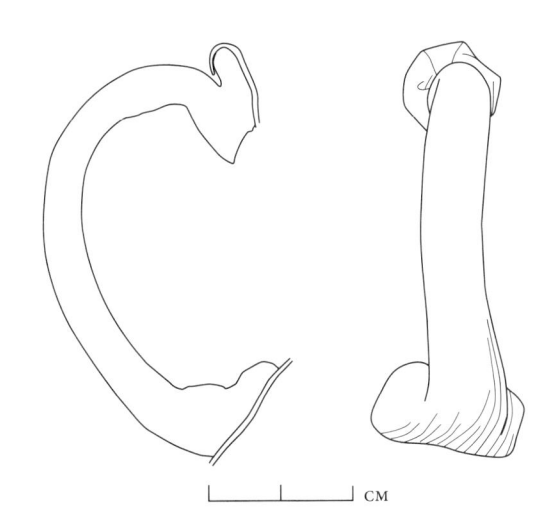

Figure 74. **G75**. *Jug handle.*

G75 context 7000
Jug handle   FIG. 74

Nearly intact handle. Curved coil handle; excess glass pinched into nearly vertical projection above upper terminal.

Vb. Blown Tableware (Cut Decoration)

Cut decoration continued to be used on blown-glass tableware in the Late Imperial period. The finds from Zeugma include a group of fragmentary beakers decorated with series of horizontal abraded lines (**G76**) or cut grooves (**G77–78**). A few fragments preserve more complex geometric cut designs (**G79**), including one whose intricacy suggests that it may have been part of a figural composition (**G80**), though the subject of the decoration is not clear.

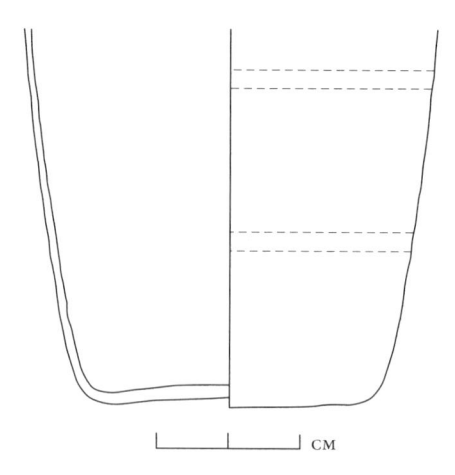

Figure 75. **G76**. *Conical beaker (linear-cut).*

G76 context 1036
Conical beaker
Colorless   FIG. 75

Two joining fragments of body. Straight side, sloping inward. Angular transition to slightly concave base. On the exterior, two sets of horizontal abraded lines.
Similar: Isings 1957, form 106b2.

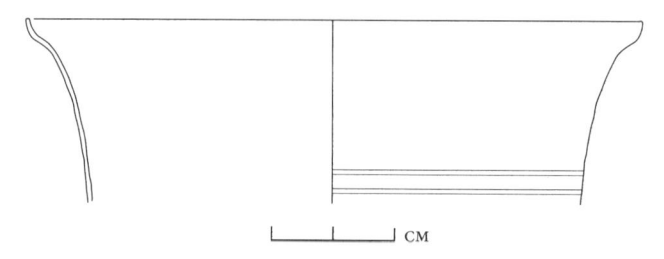

Figure 76. **G77**. *Conical beaker (linear-cut).*

G77 context 1024
Conical beaker
Colorless   FIG. 76

Fragment of rim and body. Outsplayed, curving rim with cracked-off edge, flattened by grinding. Straight side, sloping inward. On the exterior, two horizontal cut grooves towards middle of body.
Similar: shape as **G61**.

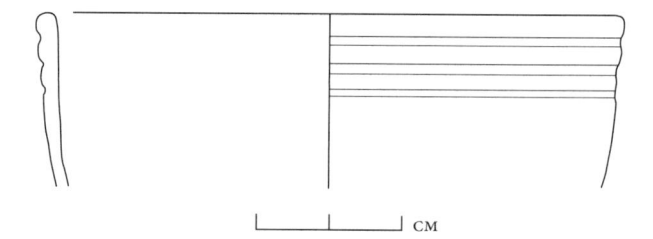

Figure 77. **G78**. *Conical beaker (linear-cut).*

G78 context 7060
Conical beaker
Greenish-colorless   FIG. 77

Fragment of rim and body. Vertical rim with cracked-off edge, rounded by grinding.
Nearly straight side, sloping inward. On the exterior, three horizontal cut grooves below rim.

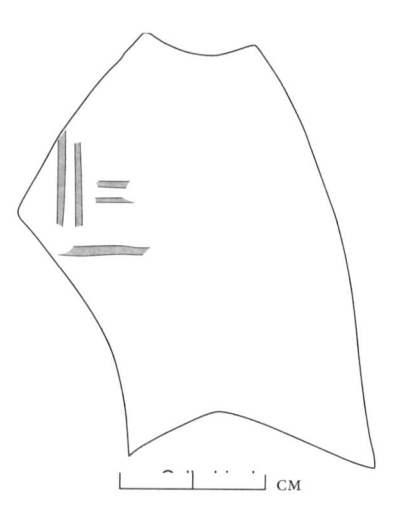

Figure 78. **G79**. *Cylindrical flask or jug (geometric cut design).*

G79 context 1010
Cylindrical flask or jug
Colorless   FIG. 78

Fragment of body. Straight, vertical side. On the exterior, incised design of vertical and horizontal lines.
Similar: possibly Isings 1957, form 126. Lightly incised geometric motifs, usually arranged in registers, are frequently seen on bottles, jugs, and flasks in the fourth and fifth centuries A.D. Too little survives of the vessel to reconstruct the precise shape or decorative scheme.

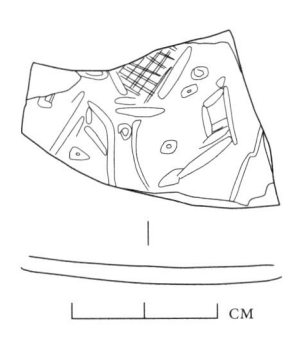

Figure 79. **G80**. *Shallow bowl (figured [?] cut design).*

G80 SF 4; context 11004
Shallow bowl (?)
Colorless   FIG. 79

Fragment of body. Nearly flat.
Similar: possibly Isings 1957, form 116b. The flatness of the fragment suggests that it comes from the bottom of the bowl.

Vc. Blown Tableware (Applied Decoration)

Glass vessels with applied decoration comprise a substantial portion of the decorated tableware of the Late Imperial period at Zeugma. In contrast with the fashion current in the Middle Imperial period (see above), the decoration applied to Late Imperial vessels tends be of differently colored glass from the main fabric. One such piece is a conical beaker of pale greenish glass with a ring of dark blue blobs encircling the body (**G81**). The rim of another beaker of bluish-green glass was decorated with a dark blue coil (**G82**). An unusual bowl features a horizontal trail of purple glass running around the body of the vessel just above a projecting roll (**G83**). The finds from Zeugma also include several examples of serving vessels (jugs and flasks) decorated with spirally wound trails of dark blue glass (**G84–85**).

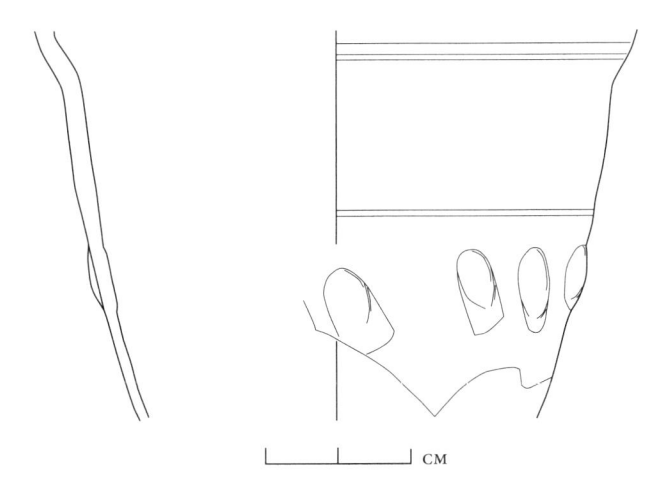

Figure 80. **G81**. *Conical beaker (blue blobs).*

G81 context 9000
Conical beaker
Pale greenish and dark blue   FIG. 80

Two joining fragments of rim and body. Slightly outsplayed rim with cracked-off edge, flattened by grinding. Straight side, sloping inward. On the exterior, remains of four blobs, forming ring around body; two (?) horizontal wheel-cut grooves: one below rim, the other above ring of dark blue blobs.
Similar: Isings 1957, form 106c2. Conical beakers decorated in this manner are dated to the fourth and fifth centuries A.D. For examples from Jalame, with an explanation of the manufacturing technique, see Weinberg and Goldstein 1988, nos. 404–12.

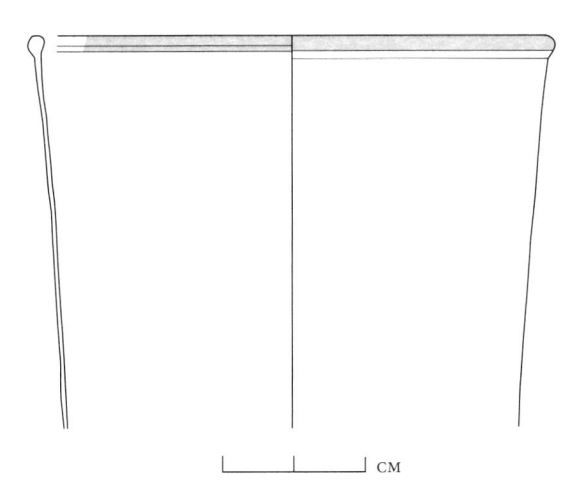

Figure 81. **G82**. *Cylindrical beaker (blue rim coil).*

G82 context 7036
Cylindrical beaker
Bluish-green and dark blue   FIG. 81

Five joining fragments of rim and body. Upright rim with fire-rounded edge. Straight side, sloping slightly inward. Dark blue coil encircling rim.
Similar: Gill 2003, nos. 88–9. Examples recovered at Amorium, dated to the fourth century A.D. or later, provide close parallels.

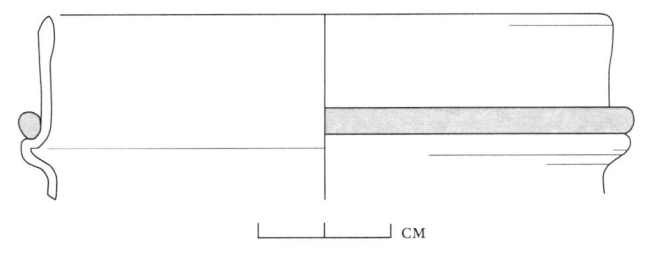

Figure 82. **G83**. *Bowl (projecting roll, coil).*

G83 context 12000
Bowl
Yellowish-green and purple   FIG. 82

Fragment of rim and body. Vertical rim with fire-rounded (?) edge. Straight, nearly vertical side. Partway down side, projecting roll, formed by tooling. Purple coil encircling body above projecting roll.

Similar: shape related to **G68**. The combination of a projecting roll and colored coil is unusual.

G84 context 12011
Jug
Bluish-green and dark blue   FIG. 83

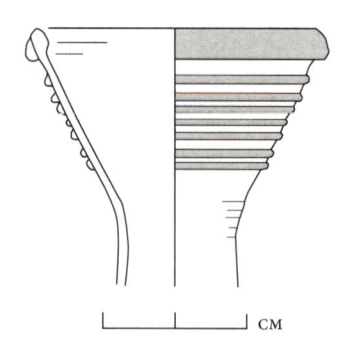

Figure 83. **G84**. *Jug (spirally wound trail).*

Fragment of rim, mouth, and neck. Upright rim with fire-rounded edge. Funnel-shaped mouth. Short section of cylindrical neck. On the exterior, thick, dark blue trail encircling rim; thinner trail wound seven times around mouth.

Similar: Weinberg and Goldstein 1988, nos. 207–16. Jugs decorated in this manner were common from the fourth century A.D. onward.

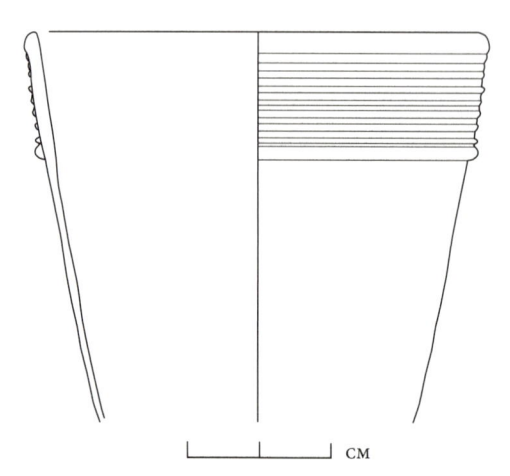

Figure 84. **G85**. *Flask (spirally wound trail).*

G85 context 7005
Flask
Greenish-colorless and dark blue   FIG. 84

Fragment of rim and neck. Upright rim with fire-rounded edge. Neck tapering from wide mouth. On the exterior, thin, dark blue trail wound eight times around neck below rim; below spirally wound trail, thicker trail encircling neck.

Similar: Weinberg and Goldstein 1988, nos. 272–81.

Vd. Blown Tableware (Gilded Decoration)

Glass vessels with gilded decoration are fairly rare and must have been among the most costly types of glassware. A single fragment of gilded glass (**G86**) was found in a Late Imperial destruction context (7203) at Zeugma. Oddly, the preserved section of gold leaf does not seem to have been worked into any sort of design, but was left as a solid band.

Figure 85. **G86**. *Beaker (?) (gilded).*

G86 context 7203
Beaker (?)
Greenish   FIG. 85

Fragment of rim and body (distorted by heat). Upright rim with cracked-off edge, rounded by grinding. Fairly straight side. On the exterior, horizontal cut groove below rim. Band of gold foil applied to body.

Ve. Mold-Blown Vessels

The small group of mold-blown vessels of the Late Imperial period found at Zeugma were all manufactured using a technique known as pattern-blowing, in which a gather of glass was blown into a mold, imparting a surface pattern, and then inflated further outside the mold. This technique was frequently used to create vessels with shallow ribs (**G87–88**). Various "honeycomb" patterns (**G89–90**), usually found on bowls and beakers, were also achieved in this way.

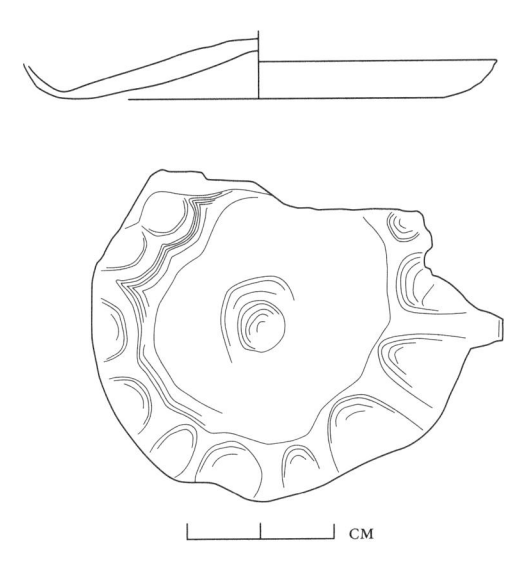

Figure 86. **G87**. *Flask (?) (ribs).*

G87 context 1010
Flask (?)
Bluish-green   FIG. 86

Fragment of body and base. Very short section of convex, curving (?) side, sloping inward. Concave base; pontil mark in center. On the exterior, irregularly shaped, rounded ribs, radiating from center of base.

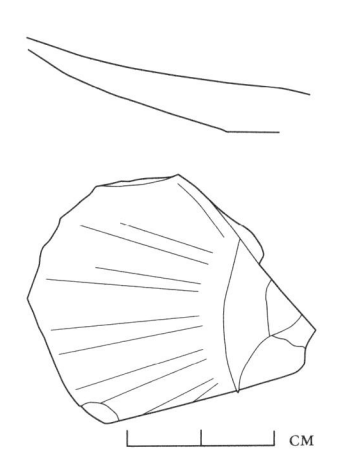

Figure 87. **G88**. *Broad, shallow bowl (?) (ribs).*

G88 context 7003
Broad, shallow bowl (?)
Bluish-green   FIG. 87

Fragment of body and base. Slightly convex side, curving inward. Flat base; pontil mark in center. On the exterior, straight, slender ribs radiating from center of base.

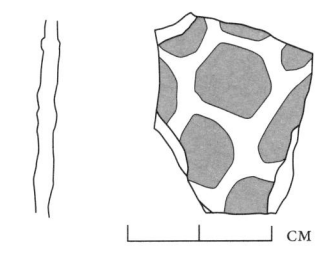

Figure 88. **G89**. *Beaker or bowl ("honeycomb" pattern).*

G89 context 1010
Beaker or bowl
Bluish-green   FIG. 88

Fragment of body. Nearly straight side. On the exterior, "honeycomb" pattern of irregularly shaped polygons.

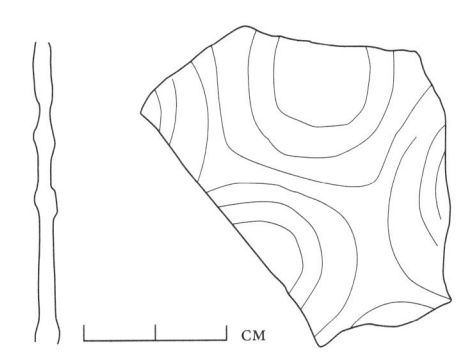

Figure 89. **G90**. *Beaker or bowl ("honeycomb" pattern).*

G90 context 1010
Beaker or bowl
Dark blue   FIG. 89

Fragment of body. Straight side. On the exterior, "honeycomb" pattern of irregularly shaped, concentric ovals.

Vf. Lamps

The Late Imperial period witnessed the application of glass vessels to yet another function—lighting. From the fourth century onwards, lamps became a major component of Byzantine glass production throughout the eastern Mediterranean.[47] A relatively small number of ceramic lamps datable to the fifth and sixth centuries was recovered at Zeugma, suggesting a decline in their use before a resurgence in the seventh and eighth centuries; glass lamps may have substantially filled this gap.[48] The finds from Zeugma include one mostly preserved example of a deep bowl-shaped hanging lamp with handles attached at the rim (**G91**), as well as numerous detached handles (**G92**) belonging to lamps of the same type. In addition to vessels securely identifiable as lamps, it is possible that some types treated here as tableware—goblets and conical beakers, in particular—may, in fact, have functioned as lamps.

Figure 90. **G91.** *Lamp with handles.*

G91 SF 652; context 7076
Hanging lamp
Pale bluish-green   FIG. 90

Twenty-seven joining fragments of rim, body, base, and handles. Upright rim folded out and down, forming tubular edge. Straight side, sloping inward, then curving toward bottom. Concave base. Three evenly spaced, vertical handles pulled out, in, and up from upper side, attached to outside of rim.
Similar: Isings 1957, form 134. This is the most common type of early Byzantine lamp found in the eastern Mediterranean.

G92 SF 4125; context 12024
Lamp handle
Pale greenish   FIG. 91

Fragment of rim, body, and handle. Upright rim folded out and down, forming tubular edge. Straight side. Vertical handle pulled out, in, and up from upper side, attached to outside of rim.

VI. Early Islamic (A.D. 636 and Later)

A small assortment of glass vessels found at Zeugma postdates the Arab invasion of ca. A.D. 636. All of this material comes from contexts in Trench 1, also the sole major source of Islamic pottery.[49]

VIa. Blown Tableware (Undecorated)

A number of fairly crude, thick-walled bowls, roughly hemispherical (**G93**) or cylindrical (**G94–95**) in shape, belong to a common class of Early Islamic blown-glass tableware. Probably datable to this period is a fragment preserving the funnel-shaped mouth of a flask or jug (**G96**), similar to those used in the Late Imperial period, but made of thicker glass. A squat, squarish bottle (**G97**) of an extremely widespread type may also have been used in table service.

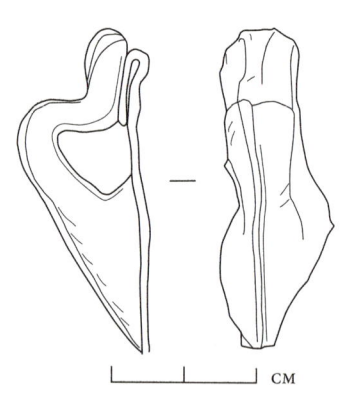

Figure 91. **G92.** *Lamp handle.*

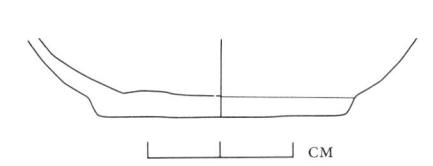

Figure 92. **G93**. *Hemispherical bowl.*

G93 context 1010
Hemispherical bowl
Colorless   FIG. 92

Fragment of body and base. Convex side, curving inward. Fairly gradual transition from side to roughly flat base.

G94 context 1010
Cylindrical bowl
Colorless   FIG. 93

Fragment of rim, body, and base. Upright rim with fire-rounded (?) edge; outer edge of rim slightly sheared. Slightly convex side, curving inward. Angular transition from side to roughly flat base

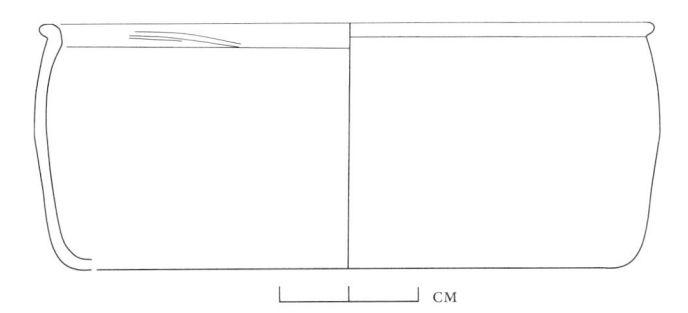

Figure 94. **G95**. *Cylindrical bowl.*

G95 context 1010
Cylindrical bowl
Bluish-green   FIG. 94

Fragment of rim, body, and base. Outsplayed rim with fire-rounded edge. Convex side, expanding outward before curving inward. Angular transition from side to roughly flat base.

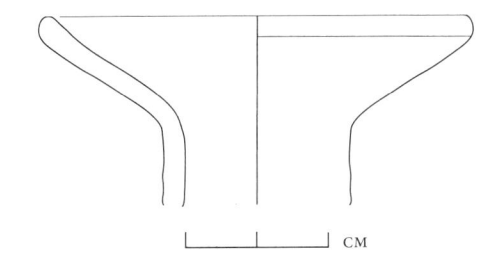

Figure 95. **G96**. *Flask or jug.*

G96 context 1010
Flask or jug
Yellowish-green   FIG. 95

Fragment of rim, mouth, and neck. Upright rim with fire-rounded edge. Funnel-shaped mouth. Cylindrical neck.

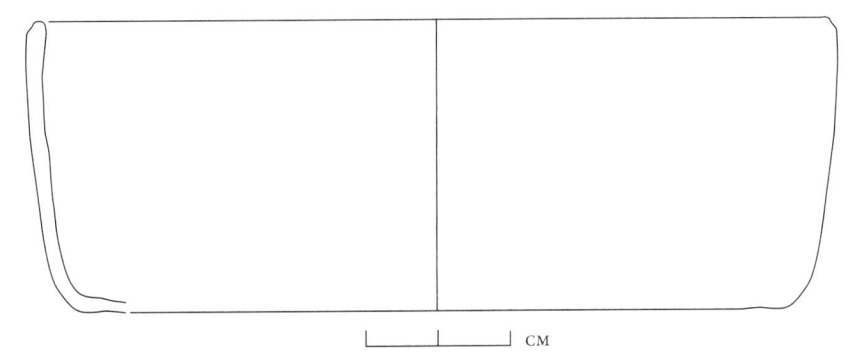

Figure 93. **G94**. *Cylindrical bowl.*

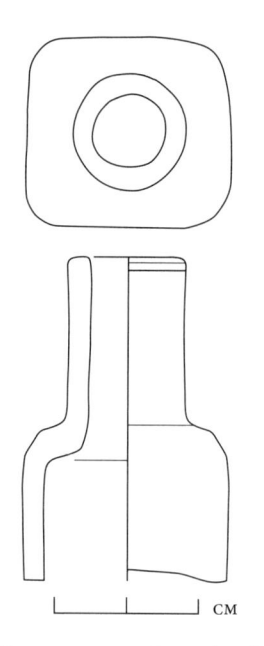

Figure 96. **G97**. *Squat bottle.*

G97 context 1024
Squat bottle
Colorless   FIG. 96

Fragment of rim, neck, and body. Vertical rim with fire-rounded edge. Cylindrical neck. Angular transition from neck to convex shoulder. Straight side, flattened manually.

VIb. Blown Tableware (Cut Decoration)

One glass vessel with cut decoration datable to the Early Islamic period was recovered. The fragment, perhaps belonging to a conical beaker, preserves part of a geometric design of horizontal grooves enclosed within a downturned triangle (**G98**).

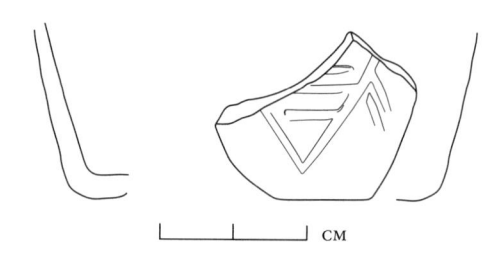

Figure 97. **G98**. *Conical beaker (?) (geometric cut design).*

G98 context 1024
Conical beaker (?)
Yellowish-colorless   FIG. 97

Fragment of body and base. Straight side, sloping inward. Angular transition from side to flat base. On the exterior, cut grooves forming downturned triangle, with additional horizontal grooves within.

VIc. Blown Tableware (Impressed Decoration)

In the Early Islamic period, glass vessels were sometimes decorated by impressing patterns into the exterior surface using a tong-like instrument. Impressed decoration may take many forms; a fragment from Zeugma features a variant on a common motif, consisting of a horizontal band of roughly circular medallions (**G99**).

G99 context 1024
Flask or jug (?)
Colorless   FIG. 98

Fragment of neck (?). Neck tapering towards body. Angular transition from neck to side. On the exterior, remains of two impressed concentric circles; above, scanty remains of additional impressed decoration (?).
Similar: Carboni 2001, cat. 3.56b. A nearly identical impressed pattern appears on the neck of a jug dated to the 10th or 11th century A.D.

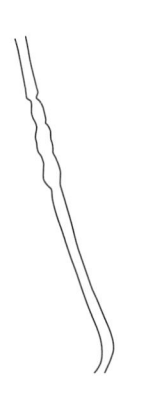

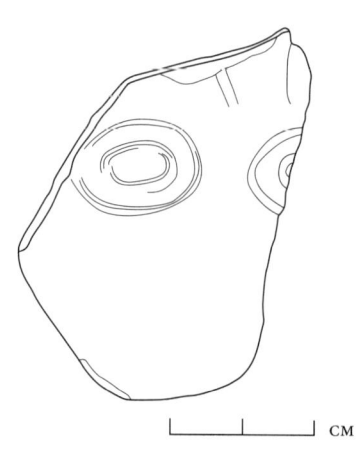

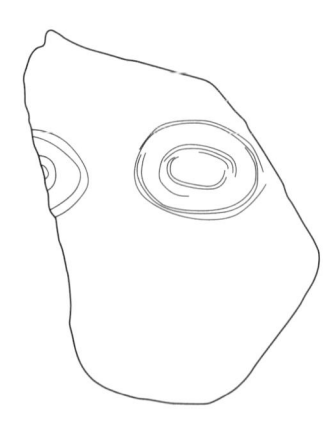

Figure 98. **G99**. *Flask or jug (?) (impressed decoration).*

VId. Mold-Blown Vessels

One mold-blown vessel datable to the Early Islamic period was recovered at Zeugma. A fragment preserving the lower body and base of a bottle was decorated with what appears to be a pattern of closely packed concentric circles (**G100**).

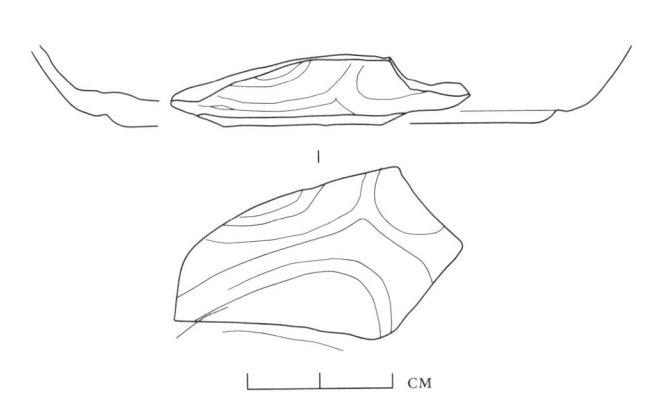

Figure 99. **G100**. *Bottle (mold-blown decoration).*

G100 context 1024
Bottle
Colorless
FIG. 99

Fragment of lower body and base. Slightly convex side, curving inward. Flat base. On the exterior, pattern of concentric circles in shallow relief.

WINDOW GLASS

The glazing of windows by setting rectangular panes of glass into metal frames was fairly common practice in Roman architecture.[50] Perhaps developed initially as a means to aid in the heating of bath buildings, the benefits of window glass—admitting light while regulating atmospheric conditions—were quickly seized upon for use in domestic settings. The tendency in scholarship on window glass to focus on the western provinces of the Roman Empire, especially Britain, enhances the importance of the Zeugma finds.[51]

More than 5,500 fragments of window glass account for over half of the total number of glass finds recovered from the Zeugma 2000 trenches published in this volume. With little variation, the fragments (**G101**) are flat, irregularly shaped, quite thin, and greenish in color.[52] Many have been affected by exposure to fire. The thinness of the glass, as well as the apparently double-glossy surface of the fragments, suggests that most, if not all, of the window glass from Zeugma was fabricated using the "muff" process.[53] In this method of manufacture, a blown cylinder of glass was cut longitudinally, then flattened to form a rectangular sheet, which could be cut into smaller panes. While small amounts of window glass were found in almost all of the trenches at Zeugma, over 95 percent of the material comes from contexts in Trench 2.[54] Within Trench 2, 10 individual contexts yielded substantial quantities of window glass, and a single context (2278) contained over half (53 percent) of the window glass fragments.[55]

G101 context 2095
Window glass
Pale greenish
FIG. 100

Twelve fragments of window glass.

Middle Imperial

Most of the contexts yielding substantial quantities of window glass fall within one of two neighboring houses—the House of the Bull and the House of the Helmets; the House of the Bull, in particular, was very rich in finds of window glass.[56] The earliest construction phases of both houses date to the Early Imperial period, though the installation of glazed windows is better considered an aspect of renovations undertaken in the Middle Imperial period.[57] The distribution of window glass fragments offers some indication of the probable locations of glazed windows within these two houses. The immense concentration of finds in a destruction layer (context 2278) covering the central courtyard of the House of the Bull can be explained by the placement of glazed windows in the walls of an upper story, which seem to have collapsed inward as a result of fire in the mid-third century A.D.; this hypothesis is further supported by the presence of several hundred additional fragments of window glass in a layer of mudbrick and rubble (2269) overlying context 2278. Significant amounts of window glass were also found in destruction contexts in rooms J, K, and M of the same house, which may mean that windows in the walls of these ground-floor rooms facing onto the courtyard were also glazed. The evidence for glazed windows in the House of the Helmets appears to follow a similar pattern. Although a rather modest quantity of window glass was recovered from destruction layers covering the peristyle court of the house, the discovery of an iron window frame (**IR269**) in one of these contexts (2251) bears out the likelihood that the windows of the upper story were glazed.

Late Imperial

The Zeugma 2000 excavations produced no finds of window glass datable to the Late Imperial period. The apparent absence of glazed windows in structures postdating the Sasanian siege is curious, as the use of window glass seems to have been more widespread in the Byzantine East than it had been earlier on.[58] The prosperous Late Imperial Peristyle House in Trench 7B—a Byzantine analogue to the House of the Bulls and the House of the Helmets—not

Figure 100. **G101**. *Window glass.*

only yielded no significant deposits of window glass, but the lack of cuttings on preserved limestone windowsills in rooms C and D of the house make it impossible for these windows, facing onto the courtyard, to have been glazed.[59]

GLASS OBJECTS

The glass finds from Zeugma include an assortment of small objects. Most of these are items of personal adornment—beads, bracelets, and rings. In addition to these, a few miscellaneous objects further attest to the wide variety of uses to which glass was put in antiquity.

I. Beads

Beads of glass and other related materials, strung together to make necklaces, were a common form of personal adornment in antiquity.[60] The approximately 20 beads recovered at Zeugma exhibit a considerable variety of shape and decoration. The dating of beads is often a problem, as the same styles and techniques of manufacture remained in use over long periods of time. The archaeological context in which a given bead was found may provide an indication of its date.

Ia. Monochrome Beads

All of the monochrome beads from Zeugma can probably be dated to the Early and Middle Imperial periods. The simplest type—the plain, globular bead (**G102–103**)—was found in greatest abundance. The use of brightly colored opaque glass, including yellow and green, is typical. Similarly shaped beads were also made from other materials, including faience (**G104**) and a yellowish-brown stone (**G105**), perhaps carnelian. Other types of monochrome beads recovered at Zeugma include an elongated, biconical bead of dark blue glass (**G106**) and a tripartite segmented bead of colorless glass (**G107**).[61]

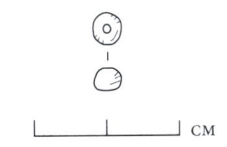

Figure 101. **G102.** *Globular bead.*

G102 SF 3176; context 18071
Globular bead
Opaque yellow   FIG. 101

Intact small, globular bead. Central perforation.

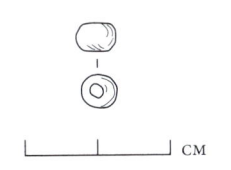

Figure 102. **G103.** *Globular bead.*

G103 SF 3671; context 15295
Globular bead
Opaque green   FIG. 102

Intact small, globular bead. Central perforation.

Figure 103. **G104.** *Globular bead (faience).*

G104 SF 859; context 18085
Globular bead
Faience (pale blue)   FIG. 103

Intact small, globular bead. Central perforation.

Figure 104. **G105.** *Globular bead (carnelian?).*

G105 SF 2207; context 2001
Globular bead
Carnelian (?)   FIG. 104

Intact small, globular bead. Central perforation.

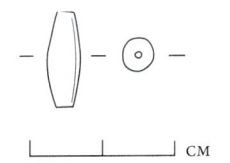

Figure 105. **G106.** *Biconical bead.*

G106 SF 506; context 7023
Biconical bead
Dark blue   FIG. 105

Intact long, biconical bead. Small, central perforation.

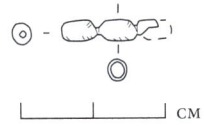

Figure 106. **G107.** *Segmented bead.*

G107 SF 441; context 9144
Segmented bead
Colorless   FIG. 106

Fragment of segmented bead. Two complete globular sections and part of a third.

Ib. Polychrome Beads

The finds include a few examples of more elaborate, polychrome glass beads. These are probably later in date than the monochrome beads, though none of them was found in a closely dated context. One is a roughly cylindrical bead, decorated with blobs of opaque yellow, blue, and white, set against a background fabric of undetermined color (**G108**); this type of decoration, sometimes called "crumb" decoration, was most popular between the third and fifth centuries A.D. Two more are elongated, roughly cylindrical beads of dark-colored glass, decorated with white and/or yellow threads (**G109–110**); beads decorated with colored threads were most popular between the third and fifth centuries A.D.

Figure 107. **G108.** *Cylindrical bead ("crumb" decoration).*

G108 SF 843; context 9133
Cylindrical bead
Ground color unknown   FIG. 107

Intact cylindrical bead. Blobs of opaque yellow, blue, and white.

Figure 108. **G109.** *Cylindrical bead (colored threads).*

G109 SF 2172; context 2107
Cylindrical bead
Black and white   FIG. 108

Nearly intact elongated cylindrical bead. White threads, some feathered, marvered into surface.

Figure 109. **G110.** *Cylindrical bead (colored threads).*

G110 SF 2083; context 2011
Cylindrical bead
Black, white, and yellow   FIG. 109

Nearly intact elongated cylindrical bead. Alternating white and yellow threads, mostly feathered, some marvered into surface.

II. Bracelets

Glass bracelets came into fashion in the eastern Mediterranean beginning in the third century A.D. and remained a standard costume accessory through the Islamic period.[62] As with beads, certain types of glass bracelets enjoyed great longevity. Consequently, the 12 fragmentary glass bracelets recovered at Zeugma must be dated largely on the basis of archaeological context.

IIa. Monochrome Bracelets

The most common type of glass bracelet at Zeugma, and one of the most widespread and long-lived of all, was the monochrome spirally twisted bracelet (**G111–G112**). Bracelets of this type are invariably circular in section and often black in color, though blue, purple, and green glass were also used; the twists may be clockwise or counterclockwise, arranged tightly or loosely. Spirally twisted bracelets seem to have reached Zeugma at an early date, since one fragmentary example, partially melted, was found in a destruction context (2012) associated with the Sasanian attack of A.D. 252/253. The majority of the finds, however, come from Late Imperial contexts, in line with the pinnacle of the type's popularity in the fourth and fifth centuries. A related type, the D-sectioned bracelet with prominent diagonal ribs (**G113**), is represented at Zeugma by a fragment found in a Late Imperial context (7321). Another type of bracelet, likely dating to the fourth or fifth century A.D., was decorated with circular protuberances (**G114**).

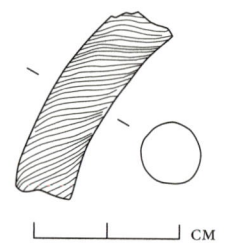

Figure 110. **G111.** *Bracelet (spirally twisted)*

G111 SF 3709; context 12011
Spirally twisted bracelet
Black   FIG. 110

Fragment of bracelet. Circular section. Counterclockwise twist.
Similar: Spaer 1988, type C1a.

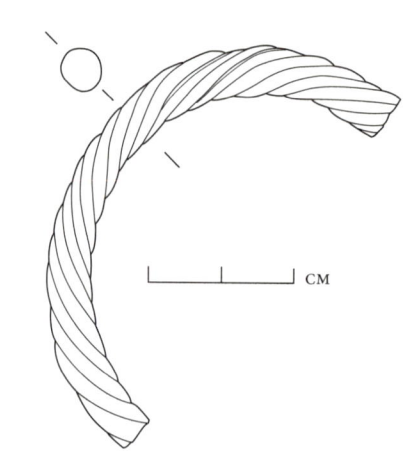

Figure 111. **G112.** *Bracelet (spirally twisted).*

G112 SF 629; context 7201
Spirally twisted bracelet
Black   FIG. 111

Fragment of bracelet. Circular section. Clockwise twist.
Similar: Spaer 1988, type C1b.

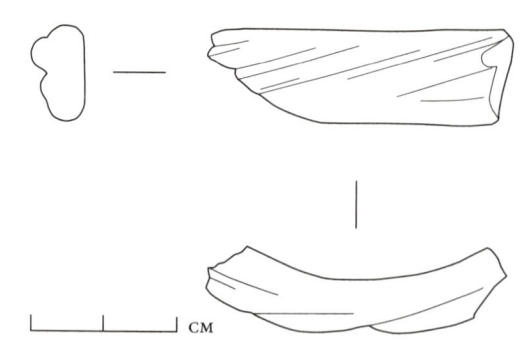

Figure 112. **G113.** *Bracelet (ribbed).*

G113 context 7321
Ribbed bracelet
Dark green   FIG. 112

Fragment of bracelet. D-shaped section. Prominent, diagonal ribs.
Similar: Spaer 1988, type B3b.

GLASS · 255

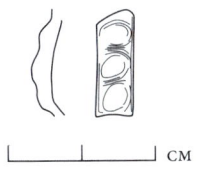

Figure 113. **G114.** *Bracelet (protuberances).*

G114 context 1024
Bracelet with circular protuberances
Color not known   FIG. 113

Fragment of bracelet. Row of circular protuberances on outside.
Similar: Spaer 1988, type B5b.

IIb. Polychrome Bracelets

Glass bracelets with polychrome decoration were produced mainly in the Islamic period.[63] A single example from Zeugma—decorated with intertwined red and white trails marvered into a black background (**G115**)—was found in a colluvium deposit (context 5150) along with pottery of Late Imperial date and may represent a Byzantine precursor of a future trend.

Figure 114. **G115.** *Bracelet (colored trails).*

G115 context 5150
Bracelet
Black, red, and white   FIG. 114

Fragment of bracelet. D-shaped section. Intertwined red and white trails, marvered into surface.

III. Rings

Fragments of finger rings comprise a small group within the glass finds from Zeugma. Two oval ring bezels of colored glass (**G116–117**) would have provided an inexpensive substitute for gems. Even more modest was a finger ring made entirely of faience, with a conical bezel (**G118**). All three of these objects evidently date to the Middle Imperial period.

Figure 115. **G116.** *Ring bezel.*

G116 SF 2246; context 2080
Ring bezel
Dark blue   FIG. 115

Intact ring bezel (broken and mended). Oval. Edges slightly beveled.

Figure 116. **G117.** *Ring bezel.*

G117 SF 2002; context 2000
Ring bezel
White and black   FIG. 116

Intact ring bezel. Oval. Edges beveled. Top surface opaque white; bottom surface black.

Figure 117. **G118.** *Finger ring (faience)*

G118 SF 3390; context 18070
Finger ring
Faience (greenish)   FIG. 117

Intact finger ring. Circular section. Spirally twisted, conical bezel.

IV. Miscellaneous Objects

This survey of glass objects recovered during the Zeugma 2000 excavations ends with discussion of a few miscellaneous pieces that further illustrate the broad functional range of ancient glass. One is a small, plano-convex disc of opaque black glass (**G119**) belonging to a class of objects generally datable to the Roman period and identified as gaming pieces. Another is a fragment of a spiral-twisted rod of pale bluish-green and blue glass (**G120**), which probably served as a stirring rod. Glass stirring rods are usually dated between the first and third centuries A.D., but a later date for this object is suggested by its findspot in a destruction deposit (context 7066) datable to the mid-seventh century A.D.[64]

Figure 118. **G119.** *Gaming piece*

G119 SF 2216; context 2001
Gaming piece
Black   FIG. 118

Intact gaming piece. Plano-convex disc.

Figure 119. **G120.** *Stirring rod.*

G120 context 7066
Stirring rod
Pale bluish-green and dark blue   FIG. 119

Fragment of stirring rod. Spirally twisted; alternating strands of bluish-green and dark blue.

NOTES

I wish to thank William Aylward (University of Wisconsin) for entrusting me with the publication of this material and for addressing numerous technical queries about the Zeugma 2000 excavations. Jennifer Price (University of Durham) was kind enough on several occasions to share insights based on her personal study of the Zeugma glass. I am grateful to Christopher S. Lightfoot (Metropolitan Museum of Art), who discussed a number of "tricky" objects with me. Finally, my gratitude is due Susan B. Matheson (Yale University Art Gallery), who got me hooked on ancient glass.

1. For the chronological scheme, see Aylward, volume 1.
2. Glass finds under consideration here come from the following trenches: 1, 2, 4, 5, 7, 9, 10, 11, 12, 13, 15, 18, and 19. Publication of the glass finds from Trenches 3 and 8 will appear elsewhere. This chapter does not treat glass tesserae, whether found loose or associated with specific mosaic pavements. For mosaics, see Dunbabin, volume 1.
3. All quantities and percentages are approximate. The total of 10,500 fragments excludes data from Trenches 3 and 8.
4. See Aylward, volume 1.
5. This lump of fused glass (**G42**) comes from context 9175, a badly burnt accumulation of collapse debris datable to the mid-third century A.D. The lump consists of at least eight distinct layers, each probably representing a separate vessel, which may have been stacked, one atop another, when affected by fire. Facet and linear-cut patterns remain visible in areas on the outermost layer.
6. For core-formed vessels of the Hellenistic period, see Grose (1989), 122–5; see also Stern and Schlick-Nolte 1994, 28–30 and 37–44; Jackson-Tal 2004, 13–5.
7. For core-formed vessels from Dura-Europos, see Clairmont 1963, 7.
8. For mid-Hellenistic cast vessels, see Grose 1979, 55–9; Grose 1989, 193–4; see also Jackson-Tal 2004, 17–9. For other finds of cast bowls with linear-cut decoration in Turkey, see Lightfoot 1993, 22–7.
9. See Tobin, volume 1.
10. On the conditions of the period and their relationship to the history of glass, see Grose 1983; Grose 1989, 241–4.
11. For early Roman cast vessels with linear-cut decoration, see Grose 1979, 63–5; Grose 1989, 247. For context 15232, see Aylward, volume 1.
12. For early Roman cast ribbed bowls, see Grose 1979, 60–3; Grose 1989, 244–247; see also Jackson-Tal, 21–2.
13. For other finds of cast ribbed bowls in Turkey, see Lightfoot 1993, 27–33.
14. For early Roman mosaic glass vessels, see Grose 1989, 31–5; see also Stern and Schlick-Nolte 1994, 53–72; Jackson-Tal 2004, 24.
15. The remainder of the ribbed bowl fragments were found in post-occupation/colluvium deposits.
16. An exception may be **G5**, found in third-century context 11028, but joining with a fragment found in the overlying colluvium layer 11026.
17. For the House of the Bull, see Tobin, volume 1.
18. For translucent colored cast tableware, see Grose 1989, 254–6; Grose 1991, 2–11. The fragments of peacock-blue glass reconstructed here as a hemispherical bowl were found in colluvium deposit 18001. Additional fragments of peacock-blue glass were recorded in context 9137, a burnt layer associated with the Sasanian attack of A.D. 253; very small and affected by heat, these fragments cannot be assigned to vessels of any particular shape.
19. For colorless cast tableware, see Grose 1991, 12–8.
20. The central portion of the bottom of **G12** is missing, but compar-

21. For colorless cast vessels from Dura-Europos, see Clairmont 1963, 18–25.
22. Most of the finds of colorless cast glass from Zeugma come from contexts associated with the Sasanian attack of A.D. 253. Although exact findspots were not recorded for many of the finds from Dura-Europos, it is likely that they come mainly from destruction deposits associated with a Sasanian siege of A.D. 255/6. At Karanis, too, much of the colorless cast glass seems to date to the second and third centuries A.D.; see Harden 1936, 49–51, 60–2, and 77–8.
23. For the suggestion that eastern Mediterranean workshops were slow to embrace glassblowing, see Stern 1999, 443.
24. For mold-blown ribbed bowls, see Stern 1995, 111–3. The fragment from Zeugma belongs to a bowl of the type represented by Stern's no. 14.
25. For truncated conical beakers with knot-shaped knobs, see Stern 1995, 103–8.
26. For small mold-blown bottles, jugs, and flasks, see Stern 1995, 74–86.
27. For the standard class of beakers with relief-cut moldings and facets, see Oliver 1984.
28. For brief discussion of vessels decorated with ground-out horizontal ribs, see Cool and Price 1995, 73–4.
29. Small mold-blown bottles, jugs, and flasks are thought to have been produced mainly by workshops on the Syro-Palestinain coast. Workshops producing mold-blown ribbed bowls and beakers with protruding knobs were evidently concentrated in the western and central Mediterranean provinces. Relatively few vessels of either type have been excavated at sites in Asia Minor.
30. Published vessels decorated with ground-out ribs come primarily from sites in Britain.
31. All fragments come from contexts associated with the Sasanian attack of A.D. 253, with the exceptions of **G15**, found in context 1024, a postoccupation accumulation of debris including material of mixed date, and possibly **G17**, found in context 2189, apparently a mixture of colluvium and wall collapse.
32. The functions of ancient glass vessels are often conjectural and sometimes ambiguous. Moreover, it is likely that many vessel types served multiple functions. For a glossary of vessel types and their presumed functions, see Stern 2001, 21–2.
33. The separately blown foot and solid, knobbed stem distinguishes goblets of the Middle Imperial period, which are rare, from their more typical counterparts of the Late Imperial period.
34. Some scholars classify vessels of this shape as unguent bottles; see, e.g., Hayes 1975, no. 272.
35. For the impact of the invention of glassblowing on Roman society, see Stern 1999.
36. Stern 1999, 469, n. 160.
37. Tableware accounts for 74.3 percent of the pottery finds of Augustan/Tiberian date (Kenrick Group B), 67.6 percent of the pottery finds of Flavian(/Trajanic) date (Kenrick Group C), and 6.7 percent of the pottery finds from the mid-third century A.D. (Kenrick Group D).
38. See Kenrick, this volume.
39. **G39–40** appear to be fragments of the same vessel, but even if they are not, the lower registers of decoration on **G39** probably resembled that preserved on **G40**.
40. Clairmont 1963, considers most of the cut glass found at Dura-Europos to have been made locally. Stern 2001, 137, suggests Dura-Europos as a regional center of production.
41. For the most common forms of unguent bottles, see De Tommaso 1990.
42. Cylindrical bottles with linear-cut decoration are sometimes assumed to have been used as tableware.
43. For square bottles, see Charlesworth 1966.
44. Charlesworth 1966, 31–2.
45. Assigning functions to particular forms of Late Imperial vessels is especially problematic. In particular, a number of vessel types discussed here as tableware (e.g., goblets, beakers, etc.) may also have been used as lamps.
46. It is probable that fragments **G69–70**, found in the same context, belong to a single vessel.
47. For a survey of glass lamps in use in Byzantine Anatolia, see Olcay 2001.
48. See Hawari, this volume. Table 1 shows the relative proportions of each lamp type within the assemblage. Type 7 (late fifth to sixth century A.D.) accounts for only 3.2 percent, whereas type 8 (seventh to eighth century A.D.) accounts for 33.5 percent of the total.
49. See Kenrick, this volume.
50. For Roman window glass generally, see Whitehouse 2001, 31–6.
51. Substantial quantities of window glass were recovered at Dura-Europos. This material receives occasional mention in the preliminary reports of the Yale-French Excavations but has not been systematically published. For a photograph of a fragment of window glass from Dura-Europos, see Grossmann 2002, 39, fig. 40.
52. Besides greenish glass, fragments of pale greenish and bluish-green window glass are fairly common; fragments of colorless (i.e., intentionally decolorized) window glass are rare.
53. On the use of the "muff" process to produce double-glossy window panes, see Allen 2002, esp. 109.
54. No window glass was found in Trenches 1 and 19. Fewer than five fragments were found in Trenches 4, 5, 10, and 15; fewer than 25 in Trenches 11, 12, 13, and 18; fewer than 100 in Trench 9; and fewer than 150 in Trench 7. Contexts in Trench 2 yielded over 5,000 fragments of window glass.
55. One hundred or more fragments of window glass were found in the following contexts in Trench 2: 2012, 2095, 2098, 2099, 2212, 2269, 2278, 2376, 2379, and 2383.
56. See Tobin, volume 1.
57. The "muff" process for the production of window glass seems to have come into general use in the later second or early third century A.D.
58. Large quantities of window glass found at Sardis are dated between the early fifth and early seventh centuries A.D.; see von Saldern 1980, 91–2. The evidence from Sardis is complemented by more recent finds from Amorium; see Gill 2002, esp. 101–3.
59. See Tobin, volume 1.
60. For a survey of ancient glass beads of the eastern Mediterranean, see Spaer 2001.
61. **G106** can be securely dated to the Early Imperial period on the basis of its context (7023), a leveling layer for a later floor.
62. For pre-Islamic glass bracelets, see Spaer 1988.
63. For glass bracelets of the Islamic period, see Spaer 1992.
64. A similar spirally twisted stirring rod of dark blue and opaque white glass (SF 488) was found in context 7007.

BIBLIOGRAPHY

Allen, D. 2002. "Roman Window Glass." In *Artefacts and Archaeology: Aspects of the Celtic and Roman World*, edited by M. Aldhouse-Green and P. Webster, 102–11. Cardiff: University of Wales Press.

Carboni, S. 2001. *Glass from Islamic Lands*. New York: Thames and Hudson.

Charlesworth, D. 1966. "Roman Square Bottles." *JGS* 8:26–40.

Clairmont, C.W. 1963. *The Excavations at Dura-Europos: Final Report IV, Part V, The Glass Vessels*. New Haven: Dura-Europos Publications.

Cool, H.E.M., and J. Price. 1995. *Roman Vessel Glass from Excavations in Colchester, 1971–85.* Colchester Archaeological Report 8. Colchester: Colchester Archaeological Trust Ltd. and English Heritage.

De Tommaso, G. 1990. *Ampullae Vitreae: Contenitori in vetro di unguenti e sostanze aromatiche dell'Italia Romana (I sec. a.C.–III sec. d.C.).* Rome: Giorgio Bretschneider.

Gill, M.A.V. 2002. *Amorium Reports, Finds I: The Glass (1987–1997).* BAR-IS 1070. Amorium Monograph Series 1. Oxford: Archaeopress.

Grose, D. 1979. "The Syro-Palestinian Glass Industry in the Later Hellenistic Period." *Muse* 13:54–67.

———. 1983. "The Formation of the Roman Glass Industry." *Archaeology* 36:38–45.

———. 1989. *The Toledo Museum of Art: Early Ancient Glass: Core-formed, Rod-formed, and Cast Vessels and Objects from the Late Bronze Age to the Early Roman Empire.* New York: Hudson Hills Press.

———. 1991. "Early Imperial Roman Cast Glass: The Translucent Coloured and Colourless Fine Wares." In *Roman Glass: Two Centuries of Art and Invention*, edited by M. Newby and K. Painter, 1–18. Occasional Papers of the Society of Antiquaries of London 13. London: The Society of Antiquaries of London.

Grossmann, R.A. 2002. *Ancient Glass: A Guide to the Yale Collection.* New Haven: Yale University Art Gallery.

Harden, D.B. 1936. *Roman Glass from Karanis.* University of Michigan Studies, Humanistic Series 41. Ann Arbor: University of Michigan Press.

Hayes, J.W. 1975. *Roman and Pre-Roman Glass in the Royal Ontario Museum: A Catalogue.* Toronto: Royal Ontario Museum.

Isings, C. 1957. *Roman Glass from Dated Finds.* Archaeologica Traiectina 2. Groningen: J.B. Wolters.

Jackson-Tal, R.E. 2004. "The Late Hellenistic Glass Industry in Syro-Palestine: A Reappraisal." *JGS* 46:11–32.

Lightfoot, C.S. 1993. "Some Examples of Ancient Cast and Ribbed Bowls in Turkey." *JGS* 35:22–38.

Olcay, B.Y. "Lighting Methods in the Byzantine Period and Findings of Glass Lamps in Anatolia." *JGS* 43:77–87.

Oliver, A., Jr. 1984. "Early Roman Faceted Glass." *JGS* 26:35–58.

von Saldern, A. 1980. *Ancient and Byzantine Glass from Sardis.* Archaeological Exploration of Sardis Monograph 6. Cambridge, MA: Harvard University Press.

Spaer, M. 1988. "The Pre-Islamic Glass Bracelets of Palestine." *JGS* 30:51–61.

———. 1992. "The Islamic Glass Bracelets of Palestine: Preliminary Findings." *JGS* 34:44–62.

———. 2001. *Ancient Glass in the Israel Museum: Beads and Other Small Objects.* Jerusalem: The Israel Museum.

Stern, E.M. 1995. *The Toledo Museum of Art: Roman Mold-blown Glass, the First Through the Sixth Centuries.* Rome: "L'ERMA" di Bretschneider in Association with the Toledo Museum of Art.

———. 1999. "Roman Glassblowing in a Cultural Context." *AJA* 103:441–84.

———. 2001. *Roman, Byzantine, and Early Medieval Glass, 10 BCE–700 CE: Ernesto Wolf Collection.* Ostfildern: Hatje Cantz Publishers.

Stern, E.M., and B. Schlick-Nolte. 1994. *Early Glass of the Ancient World, 1600 BC – AD 50: Ernesto Wolf Collection.* Ostfildern: Verlag Gerd Hatje.

Vessberg, O. 1956. "Glass: Typology, Chronology." In *The Swedish Cyprus Expedition*. Vol. 4, pt. 3, *The Hellenistic and Roman Periods in Cyprus*, edited by O. Vessberg and A. Westholm, 128–74 and 193–219. Stockholm: The Swedish Cyprus Expedition.

Weinberg, G., and S. Goldstein. 1988. "The Glass Vessels." In *Excavations at Jalame: Site of a Glass Factory in Late Roman Palestine*, edited by G. Weinberg, 38–102. Columbia: University of Missouri Press.

Whitehouse, D. 1997. *Roman Glass in the Corning Museum of Glass.* Vol. 1. New York: Hudson Hills Press.

———. 2001. "Window Glass between the First and Eighth Centuries." In *Il colore nel medioevo: Arte, simbolo, tecnica: La vetrata in occidente dal IV all'XI secolo. Atti delle Giornate di Studi Lucca 23-24-25 Settembre 1999*, edited by F. Dell'Acqua and R. Silva, 31–43. Lucca: Istituto Storico Lucchese.

PLATES

POTTERY

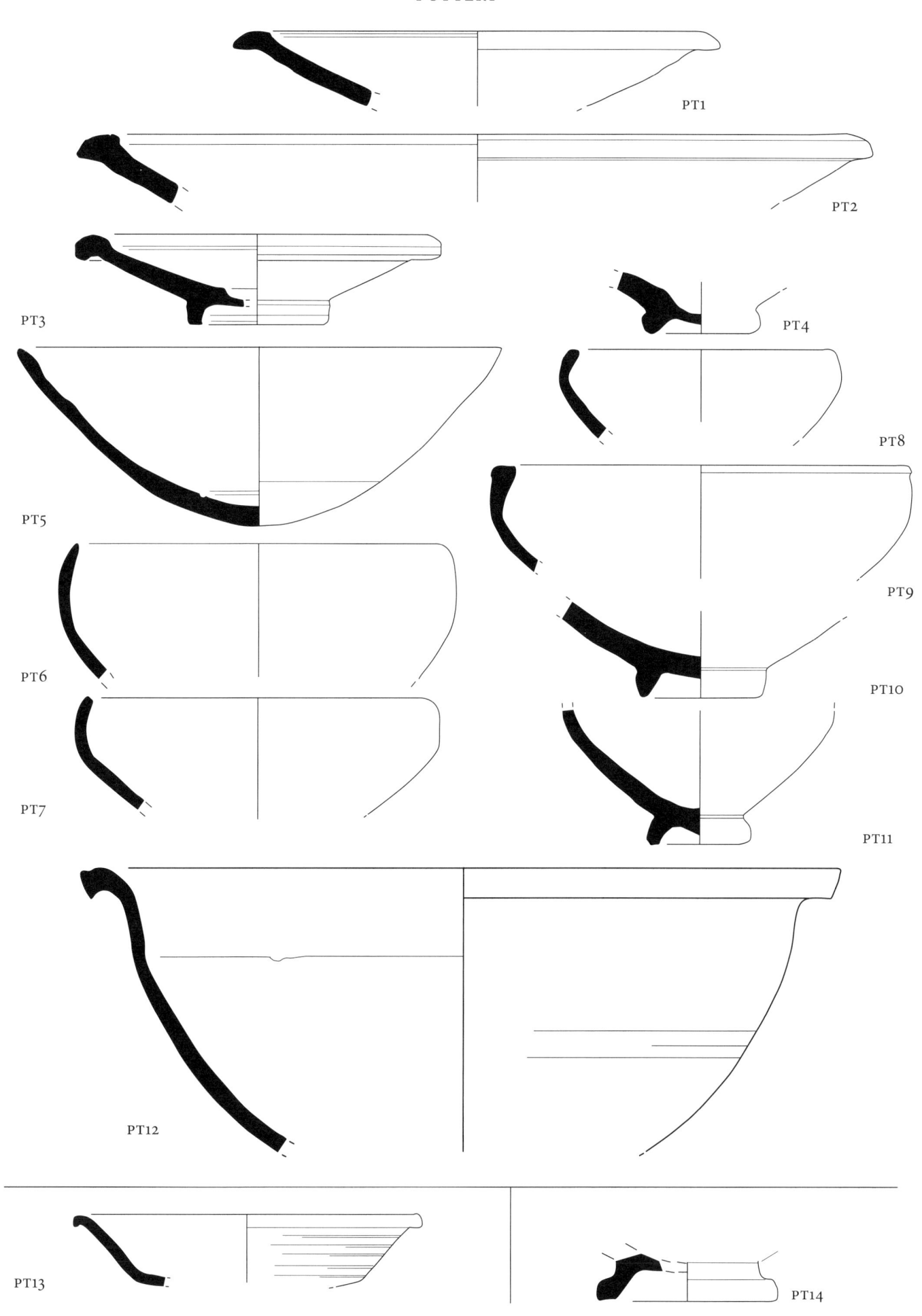

*Plate 1. Group A. Local Hellenistic fine ware (**PT1–12**); Hellenistic fine gray ware (**PT13**); Eastern Sigillata A (**PT14**). Scale 1:2.*

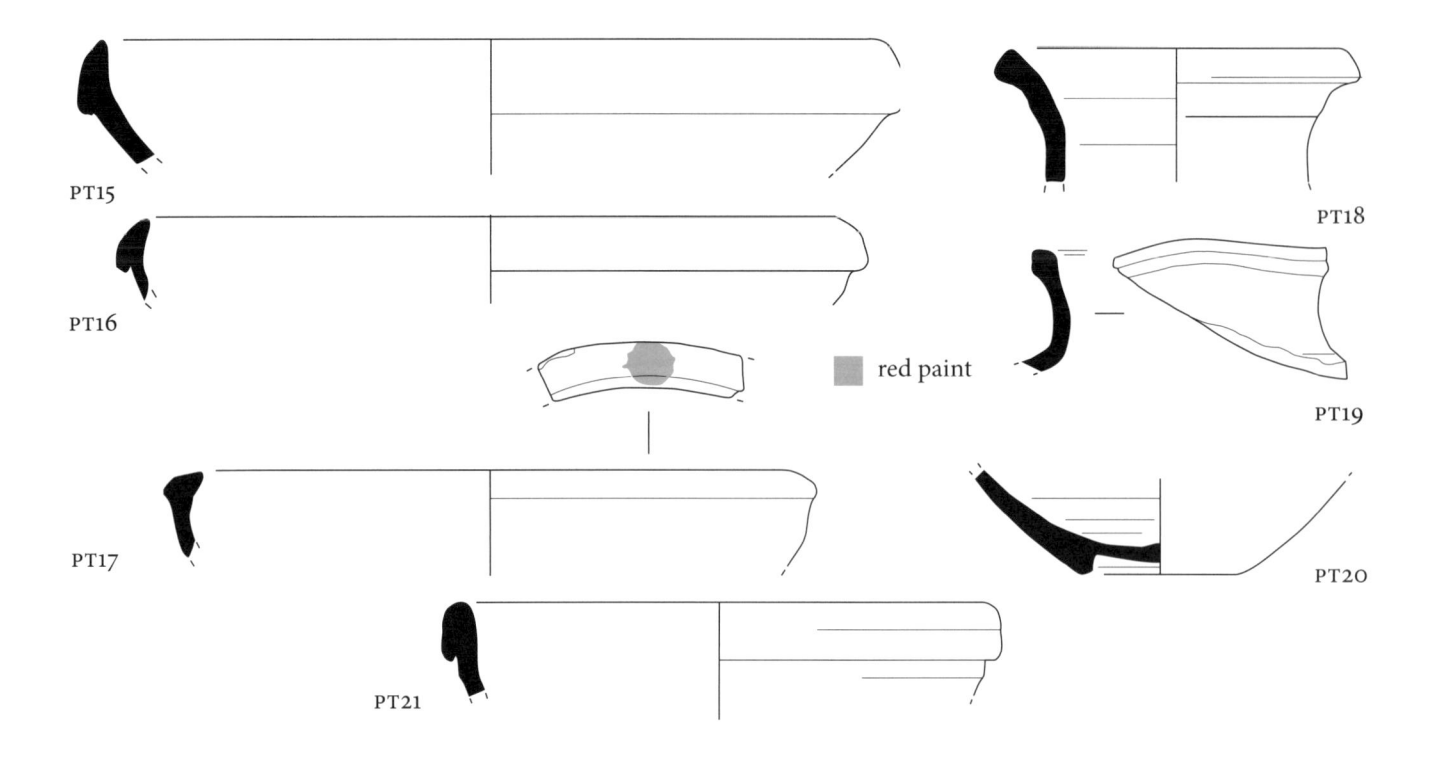

Plate 2. Group A. Buff ware 13 (PT15–18); Other buff wares (PT19, 20); Cooking ware 8 (PT21). Scale 1:3.

POTTERY

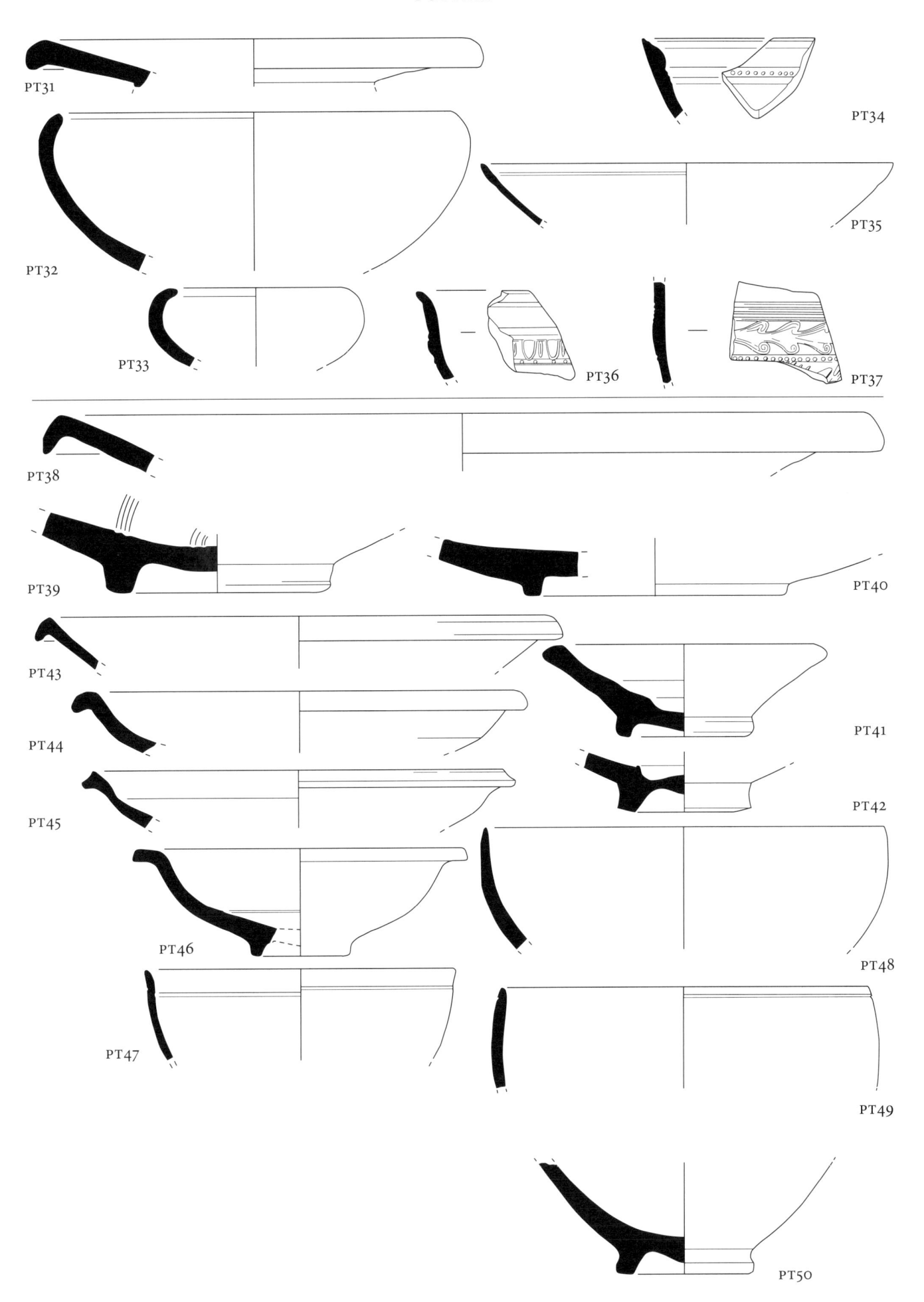

*Plate 3. Group B. BSP (**PT31–37**); Local Hellenistic fine ware (**PT38–50**). Scale 1:2.*

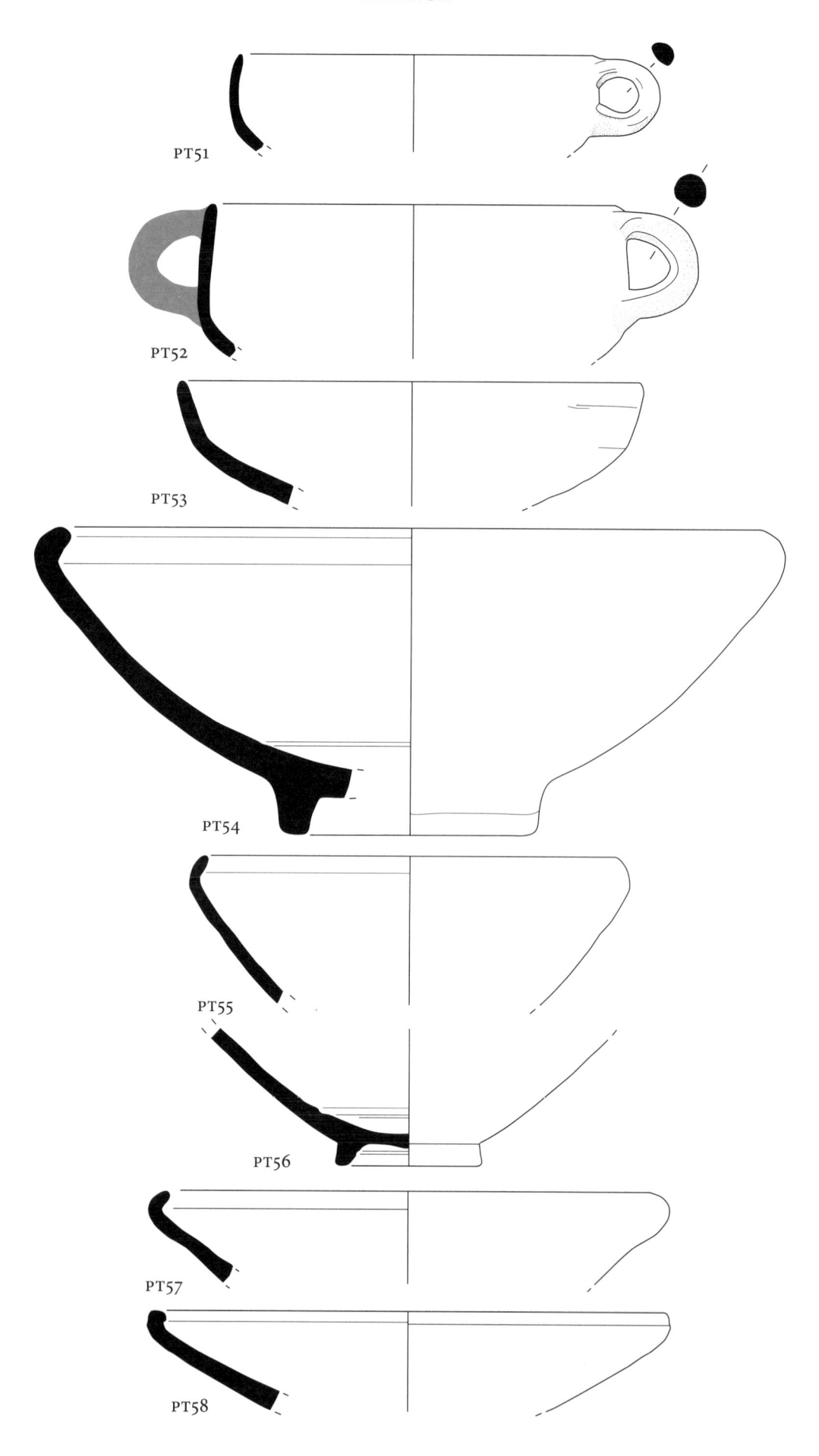

*Plate 4. Group B. Local Hellenistic fine ware (**PT51–58**). Scale 1:2.*

POTTERY

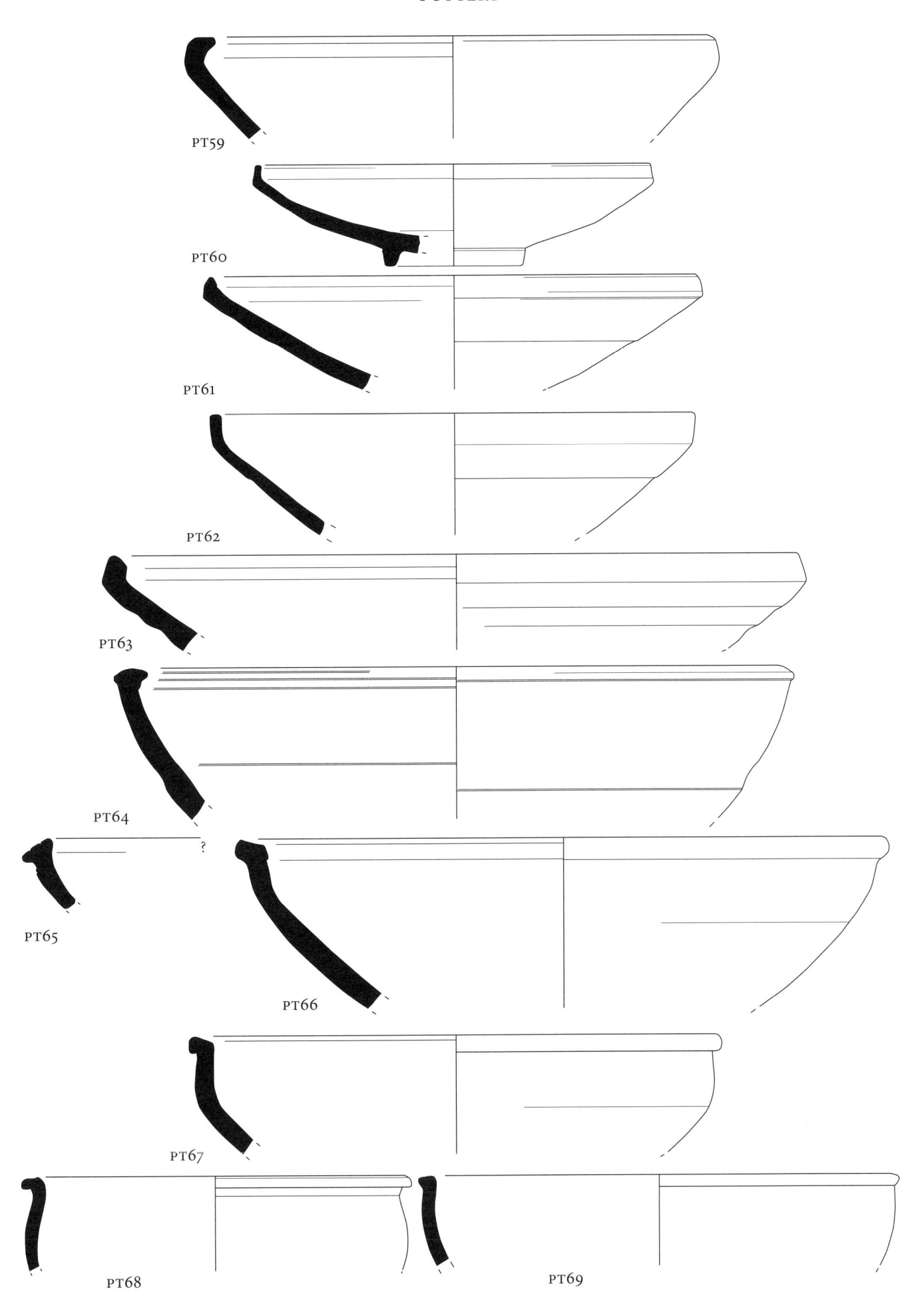

Plate 5. Group B. Local Hellenistic fine ware (PT59–69). Scale 1:2.

PT70

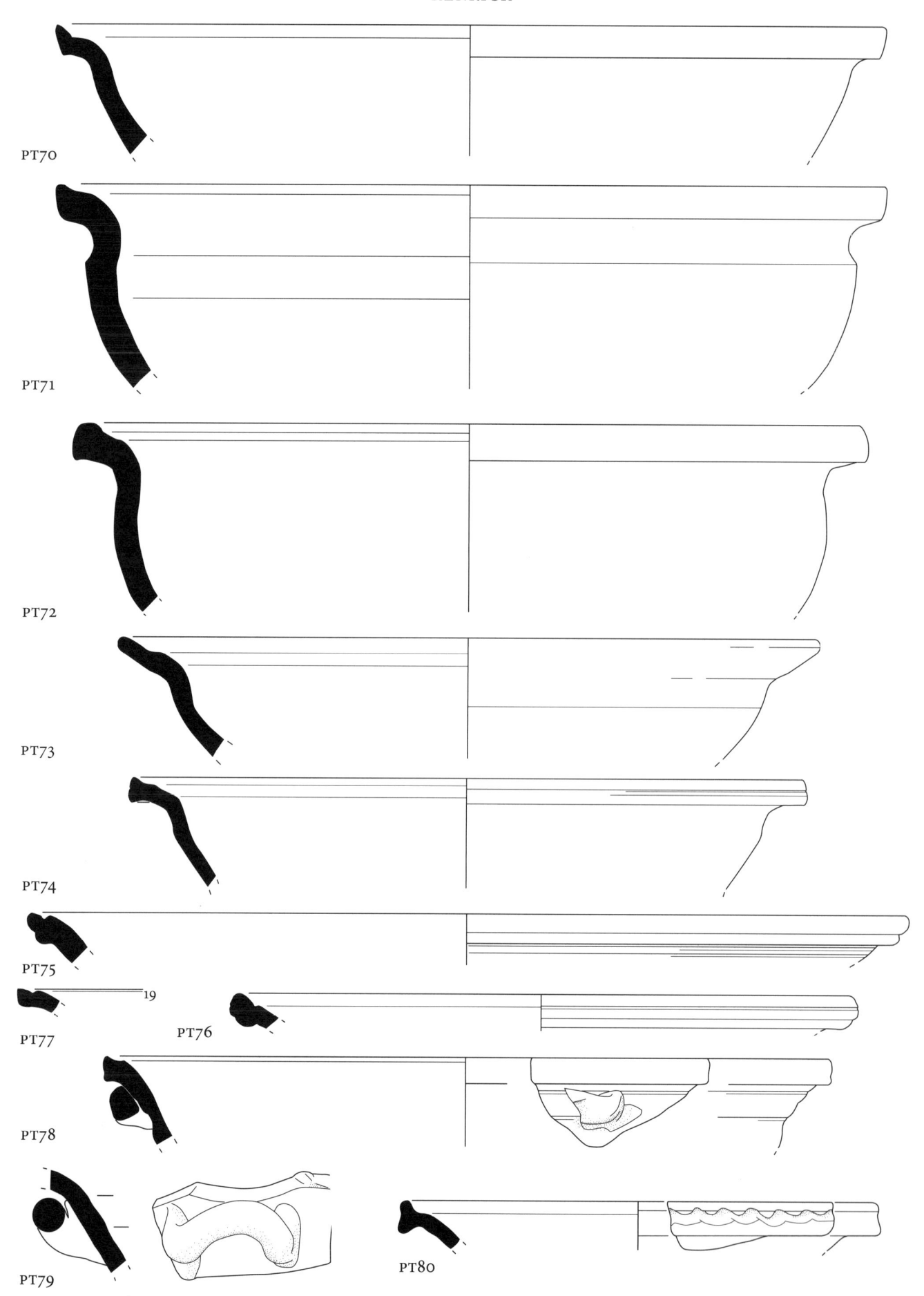

PT71

PT72

PT73

PT74

PT75

PT77 PT76

PT78

PT79 PT80

*Plate 6. Group B. Local Hellenistic fine ware (**PT70–80**). Scale 1:2.*

POTTERY

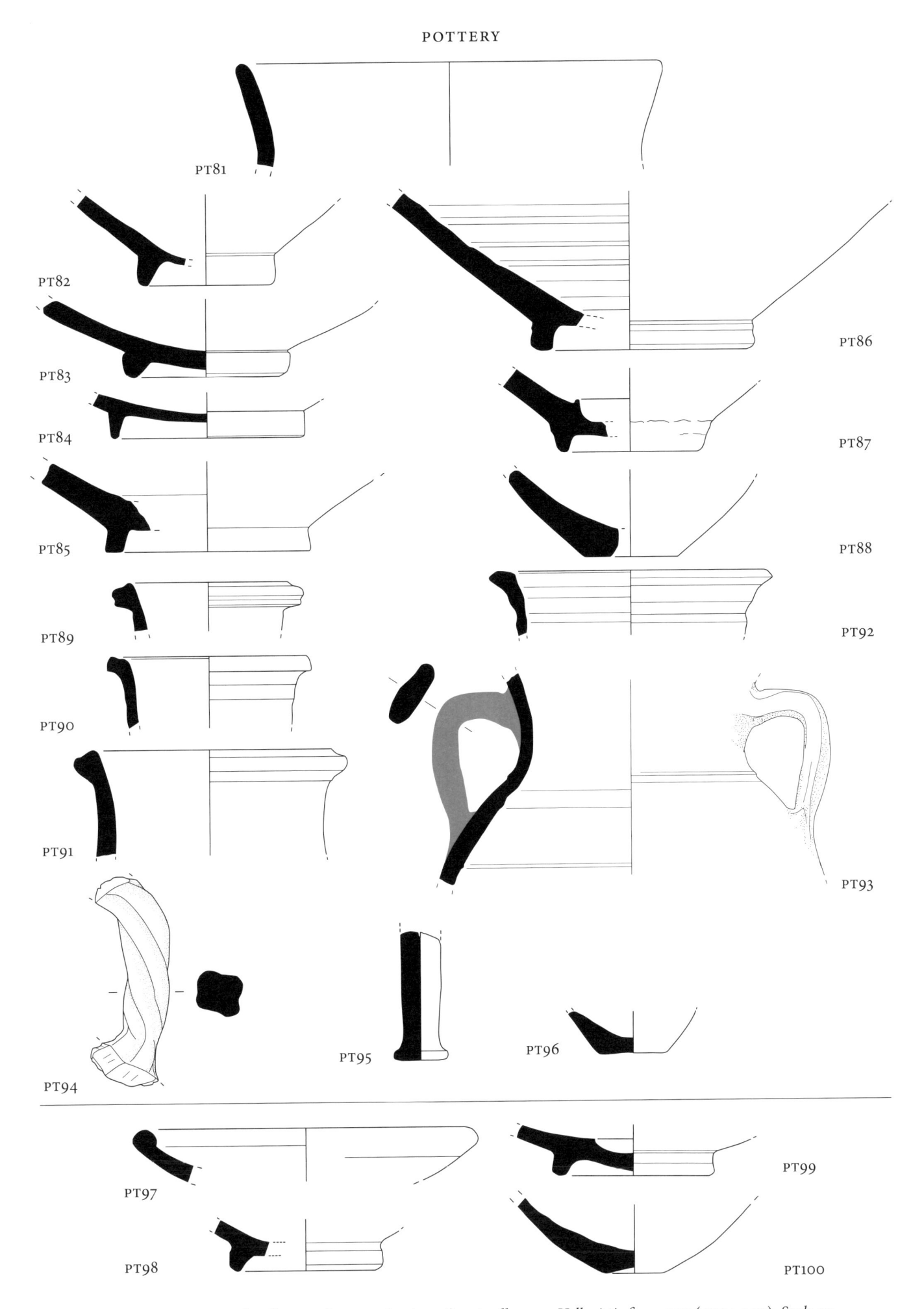

*Plate 7. Group B. Local Hellenistic fine ware (**PT81–96**); miscellaneous Hellenistic fine wares (**PT97–100**). Scale 1:2.*

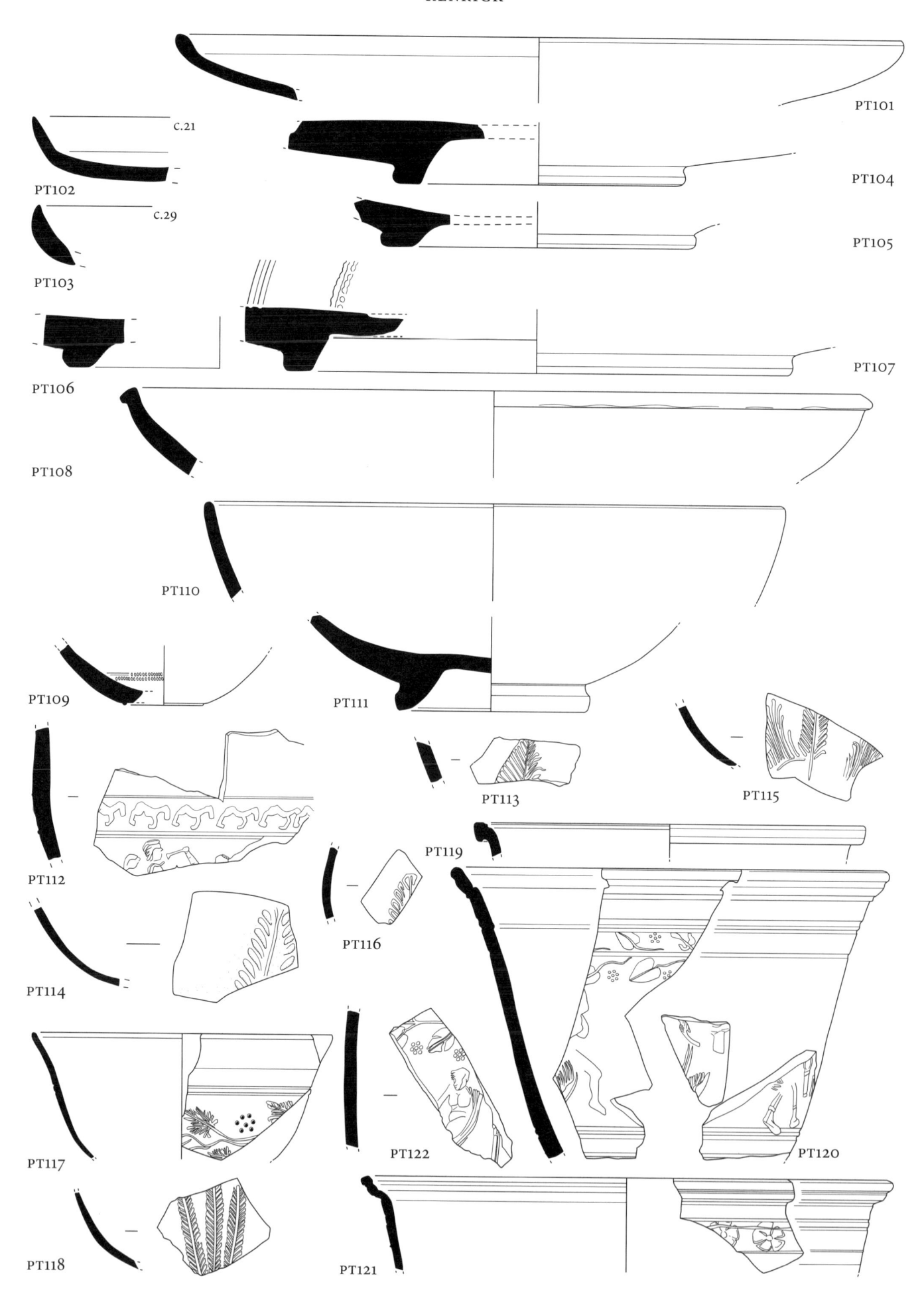

*Plate 8. Group B. Eastern Sigillata A (**PT101–122**). Scale 1:2.*

POTTERY

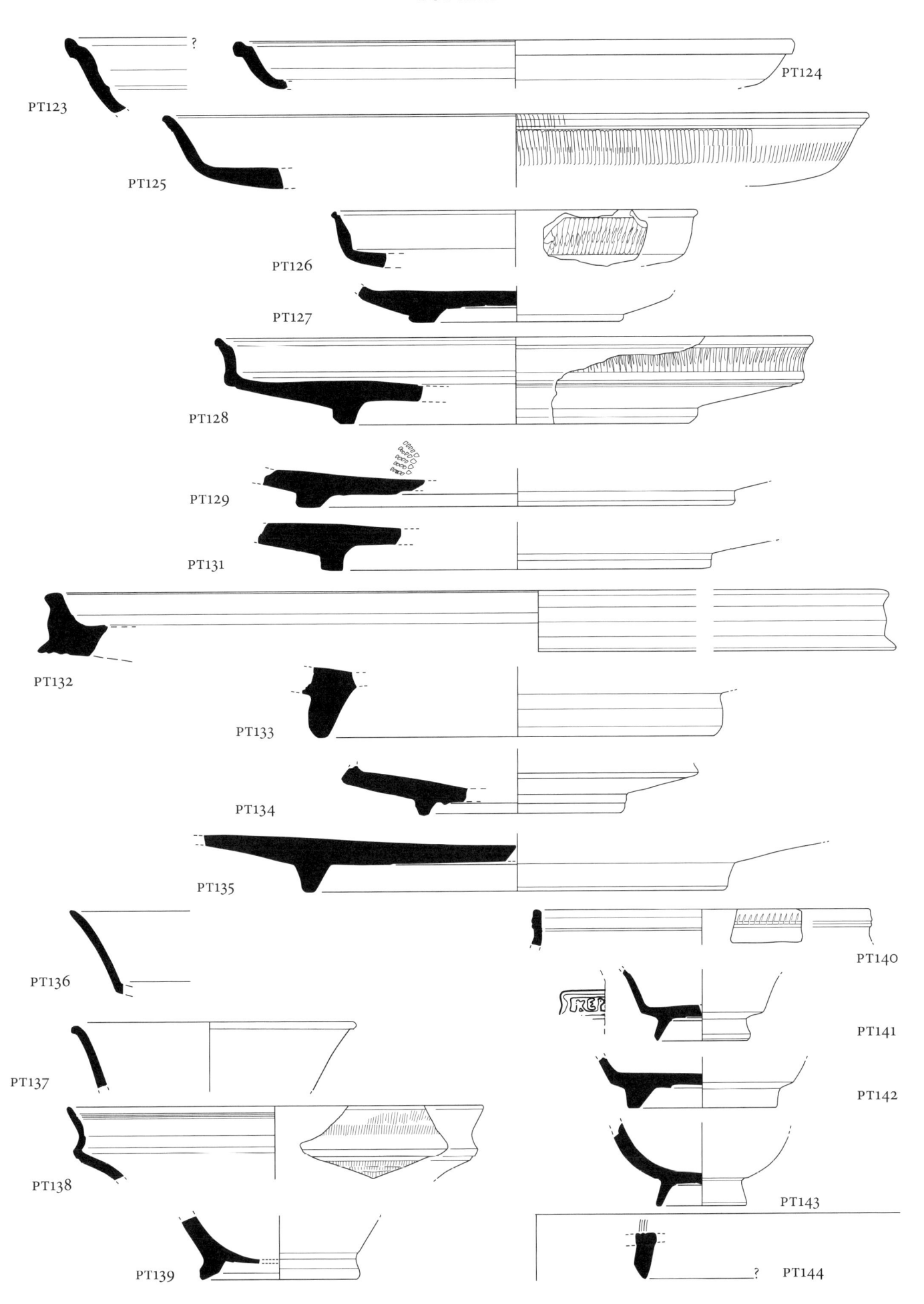

Plate 9. Group B. Eastern Sigillata A (PT123–143); Italian Sigillata (PT144). Scale 1:2 (stamp on PT141, 1:1).

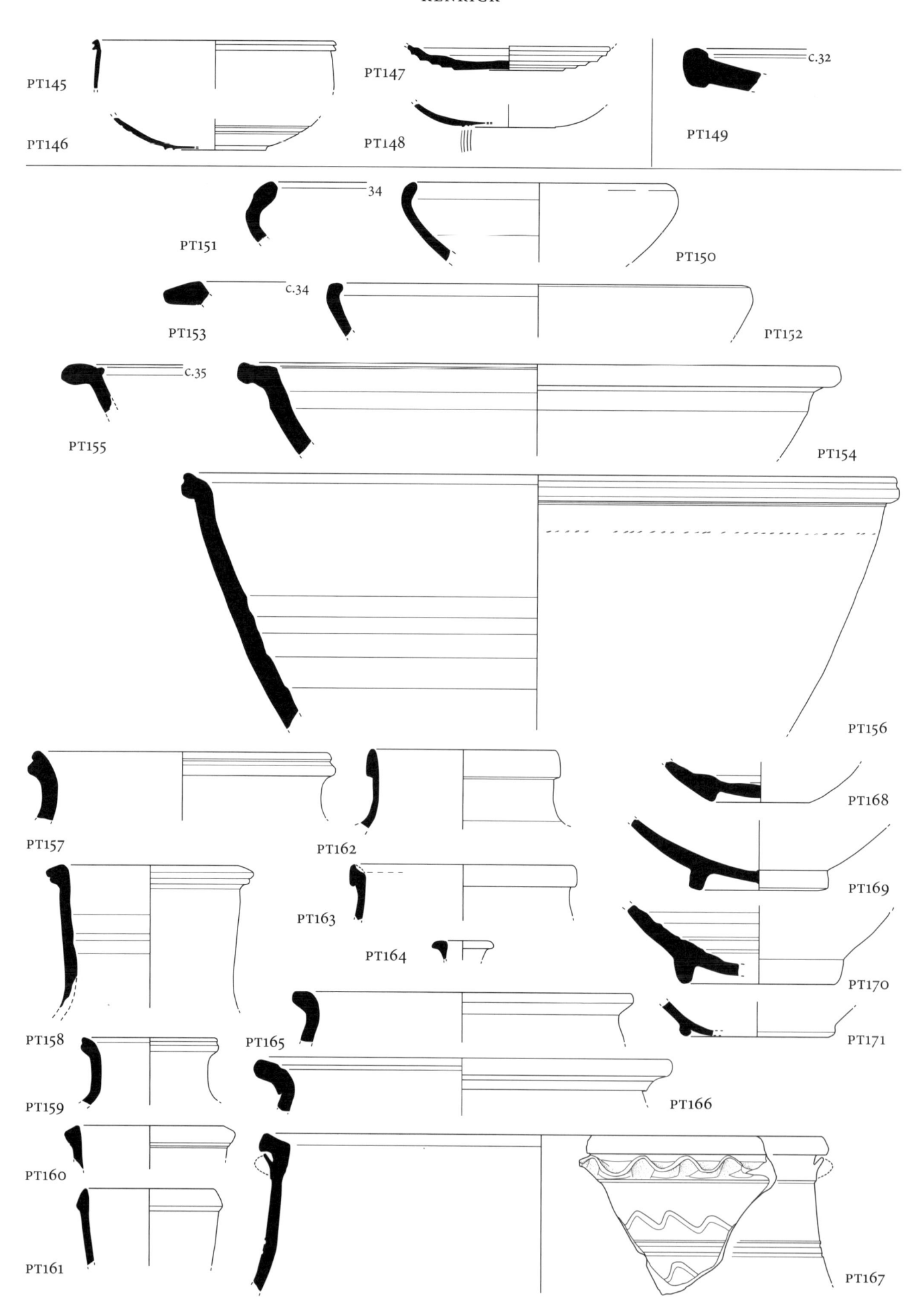

*Plate 10. Group B. Thin-walled wares (**PT145–148**); African Red Slip Ware (**PT149**). Scale 1:2.*
*Buff wares 1–4 (**PT150–171**). Scale 1:3.*

POTTERY

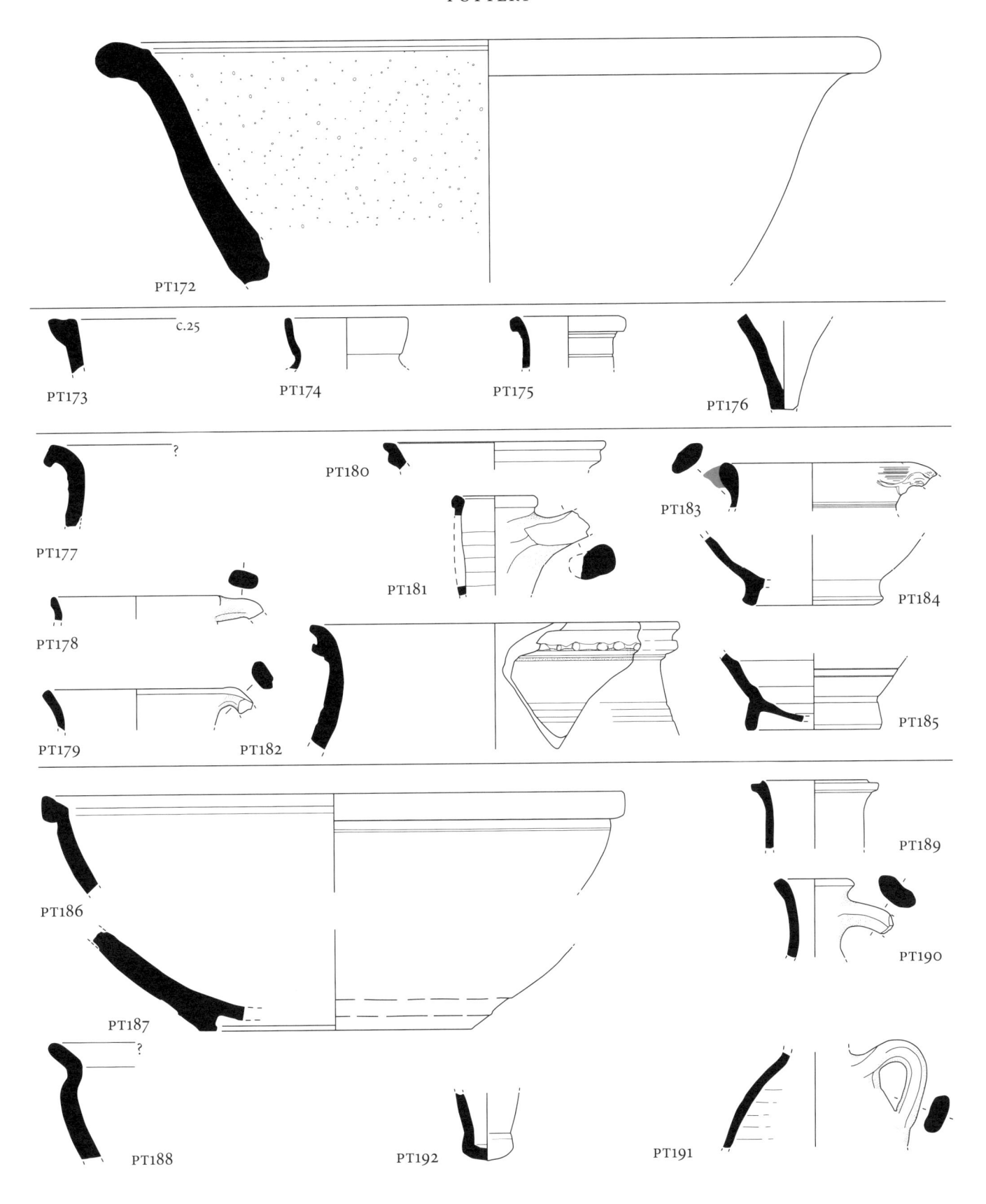

*Plate 11. Group B. Buff ware 6 (**PT172**); Buff ware 10 (**PT173–176**); Buff ware 13 (**PT177–185**); other buff wares (**PT186–192**). Scale 1:3.*

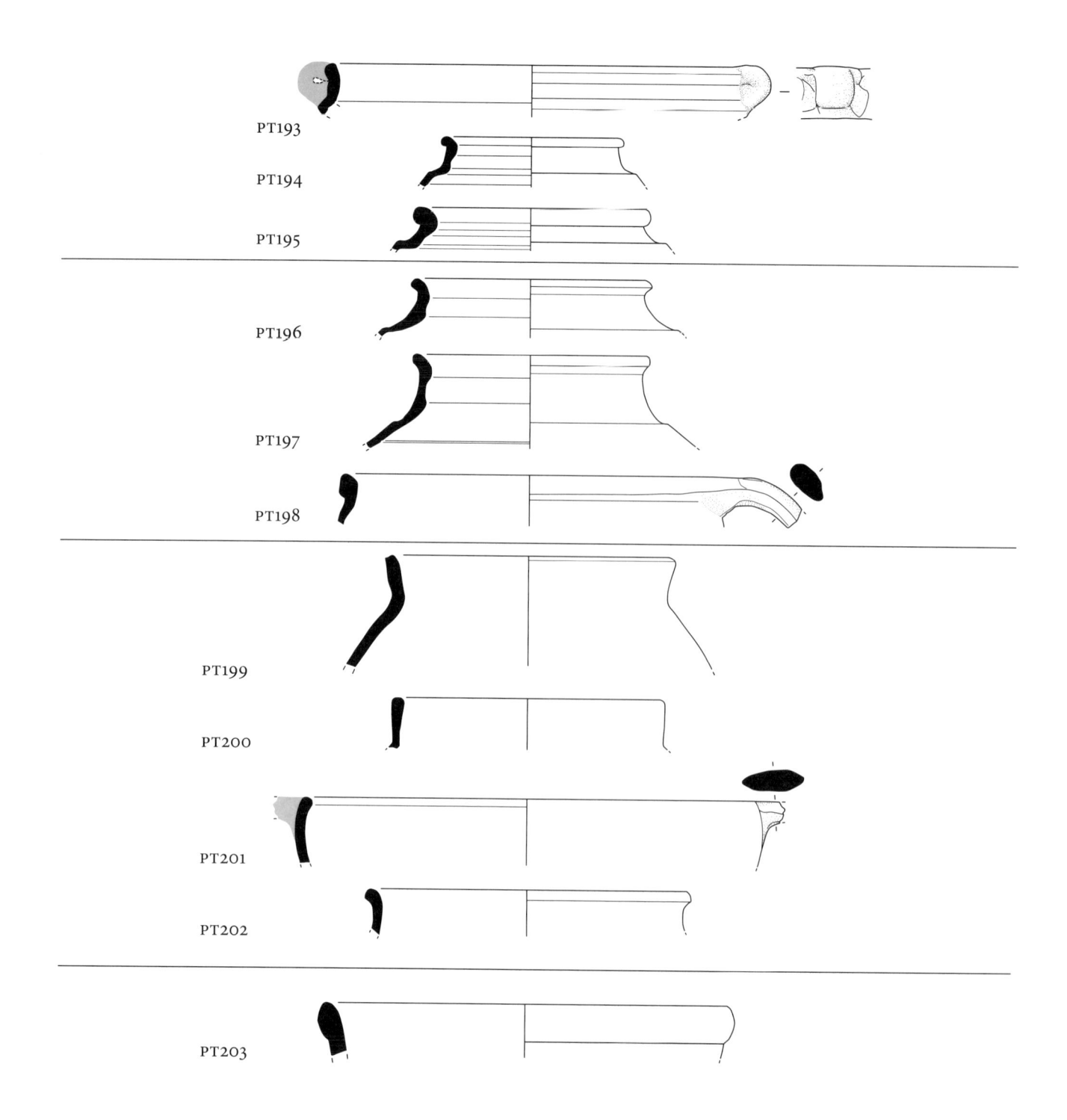

PT193
PT194
PT195
PT196
PT197
PT198
PT199
PT200
PT201
PT202
PT203

Plate 12. Group B. Cooking ware 1 (PT193–195); Cooking ware 2 (PT196–198); other cooking wares (PT199–202); Storage ware 5 (PT203). Scale 1:3.

POTTERY

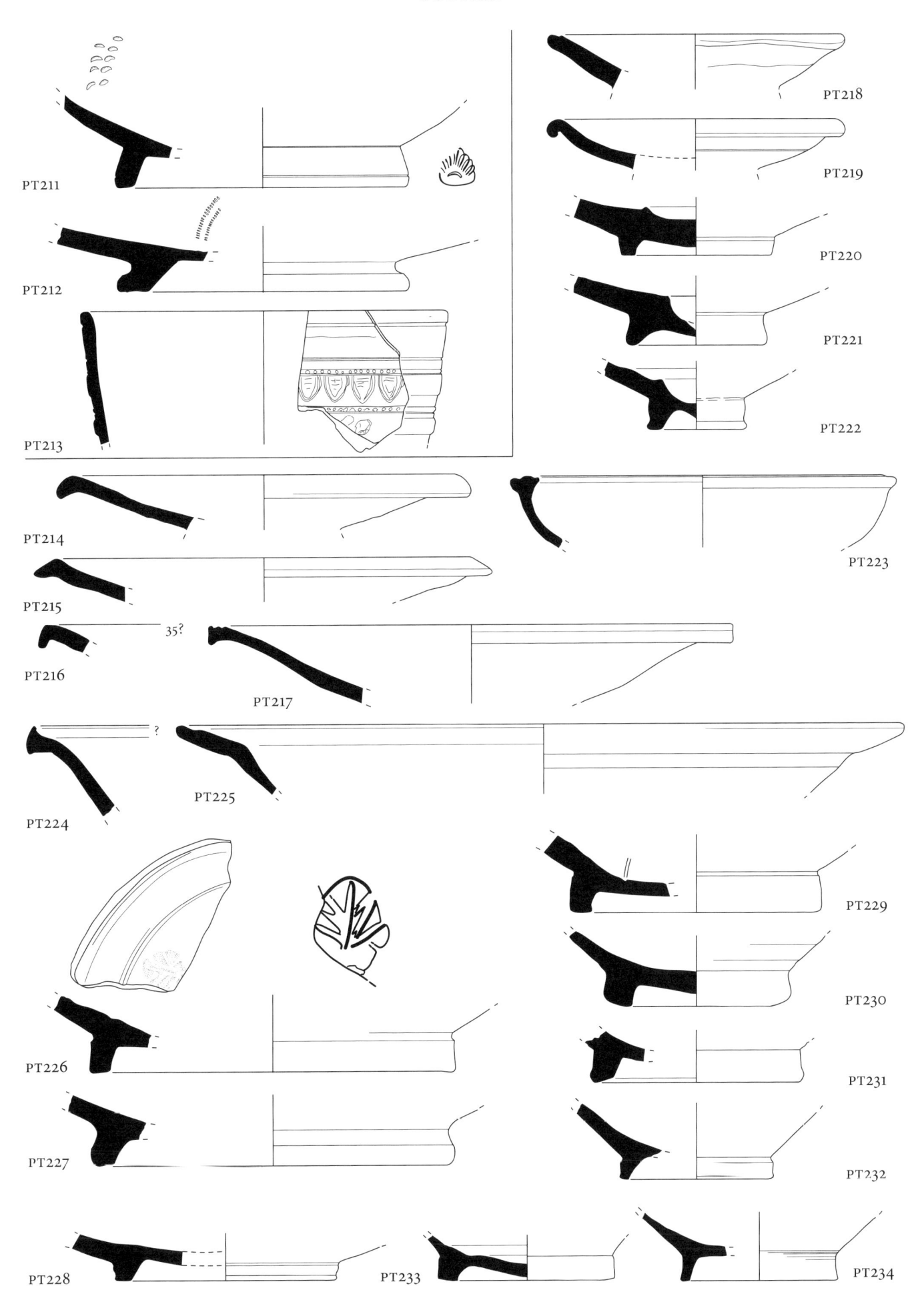

*Plate 13. Group C. BSP (**PT211–213**); local Hellenistic fine ware (**PT214–234**). Scale 1:2 (stamps on **PT211**, **PT226**, 1:1).*

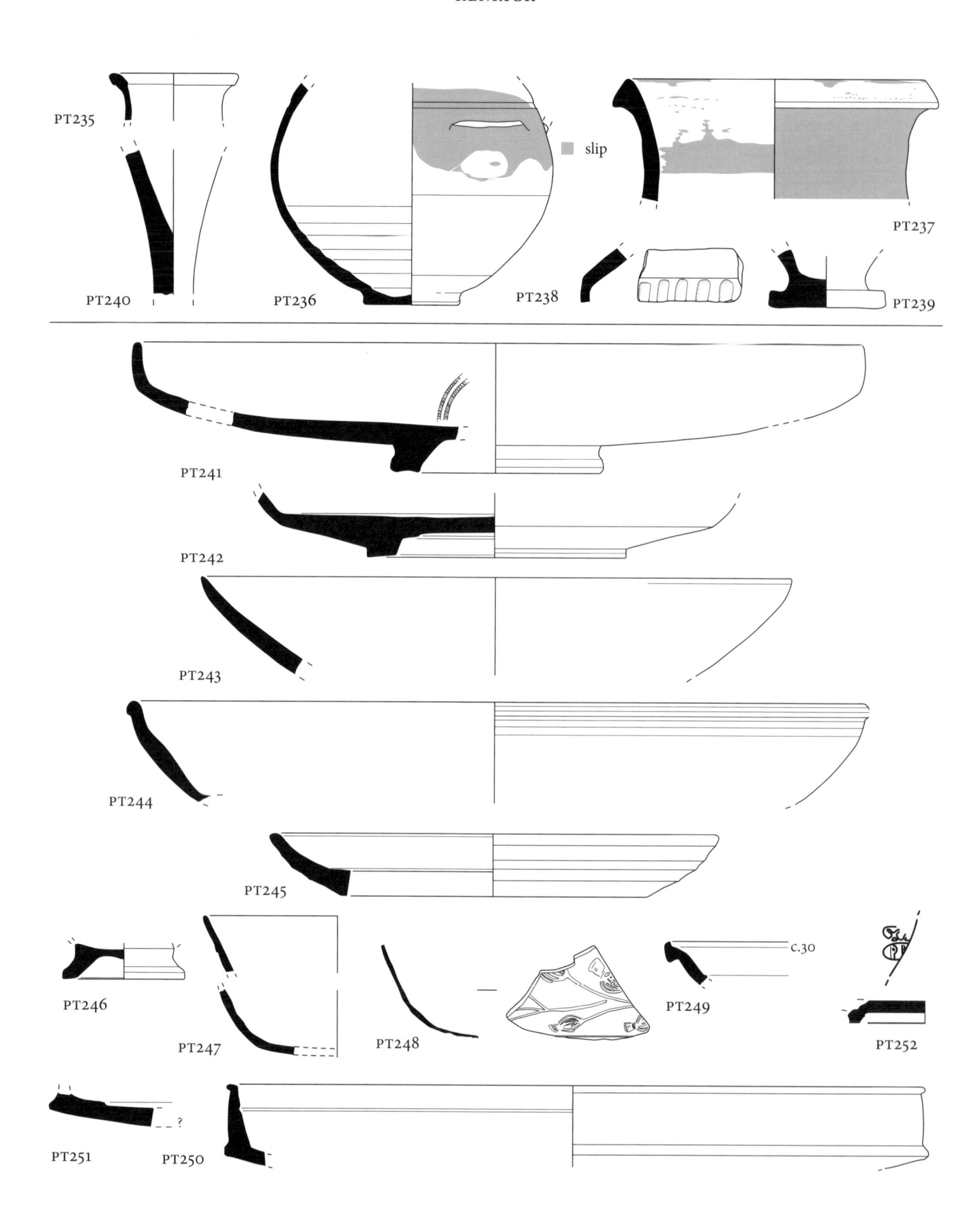

*Plate 14. Group C. Local Hellenistic fine ware (**PT235–240**); Eastern Sigillata A (**PT241–252**).
Scale 1:2 (stamp on **PT252**, 1:1).*

POTTERY

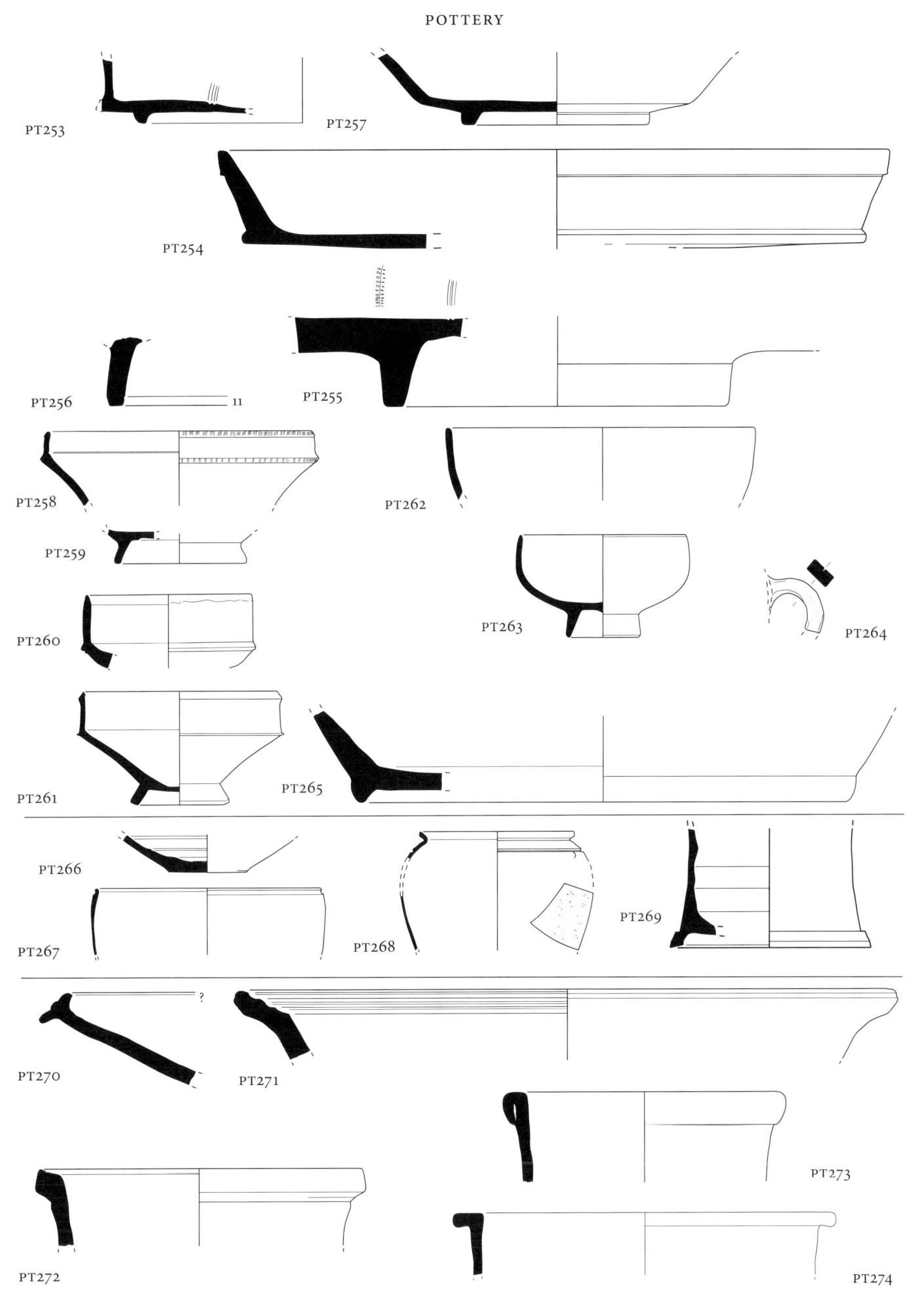

*Plate 15. Group C. Eastern Sigillata A (**PT253–265**); thin-walled wares (**PT266–268**);*
*miscellaneous fine ware (**PT269**). Scale 1:2. Buff wares 1–4 (**PT270–274**). Scale 1:3.*

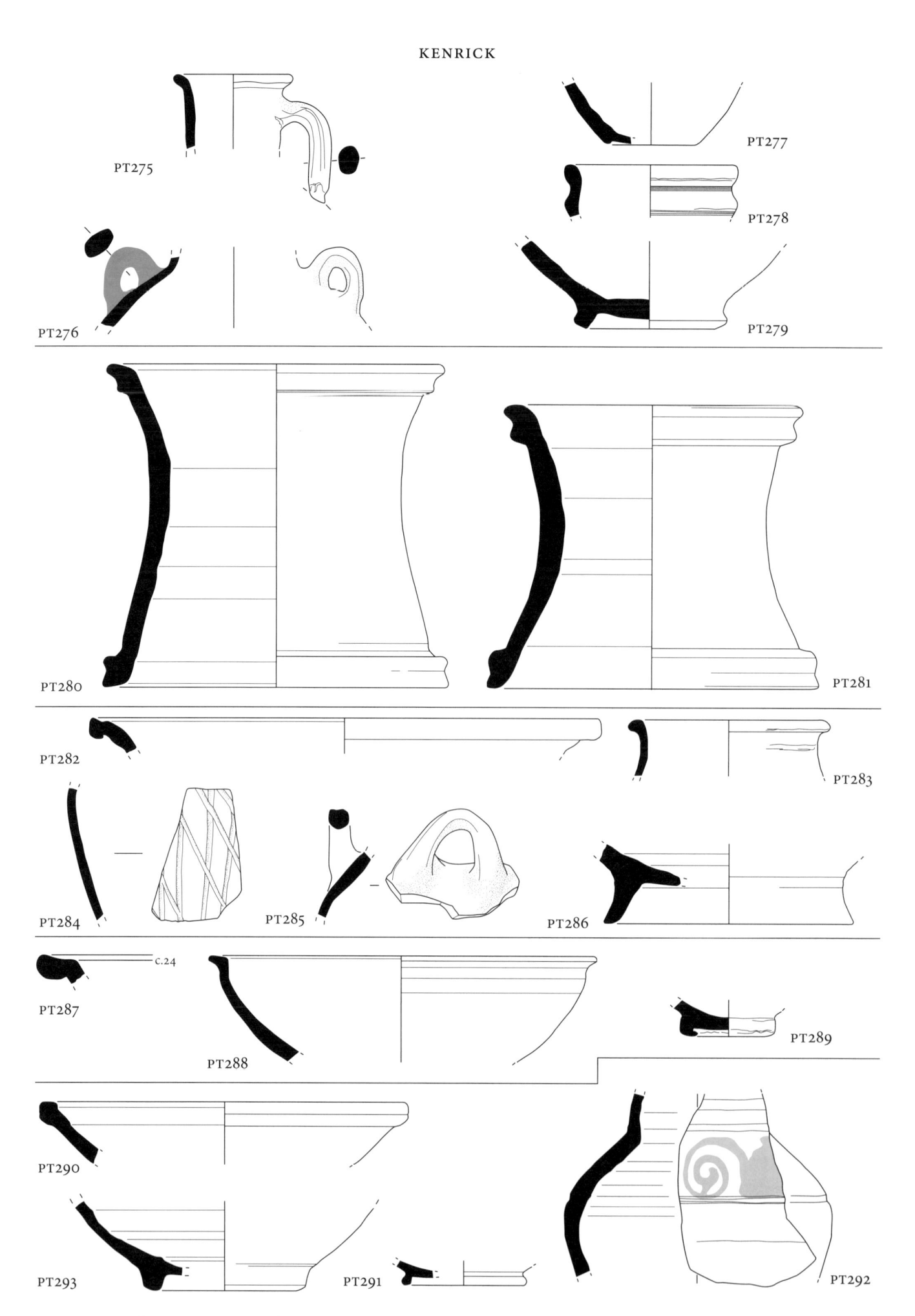

*Plate 16. Group C. Buff wares 1–4 (**PT275–279**); Buff ware 12 (**PT280, 281**); Buff ware 13 (**PT282–286**); Buff ware 14 (**PT287–289**); other buff wares (**PT290–293**). Scale 1:3.*

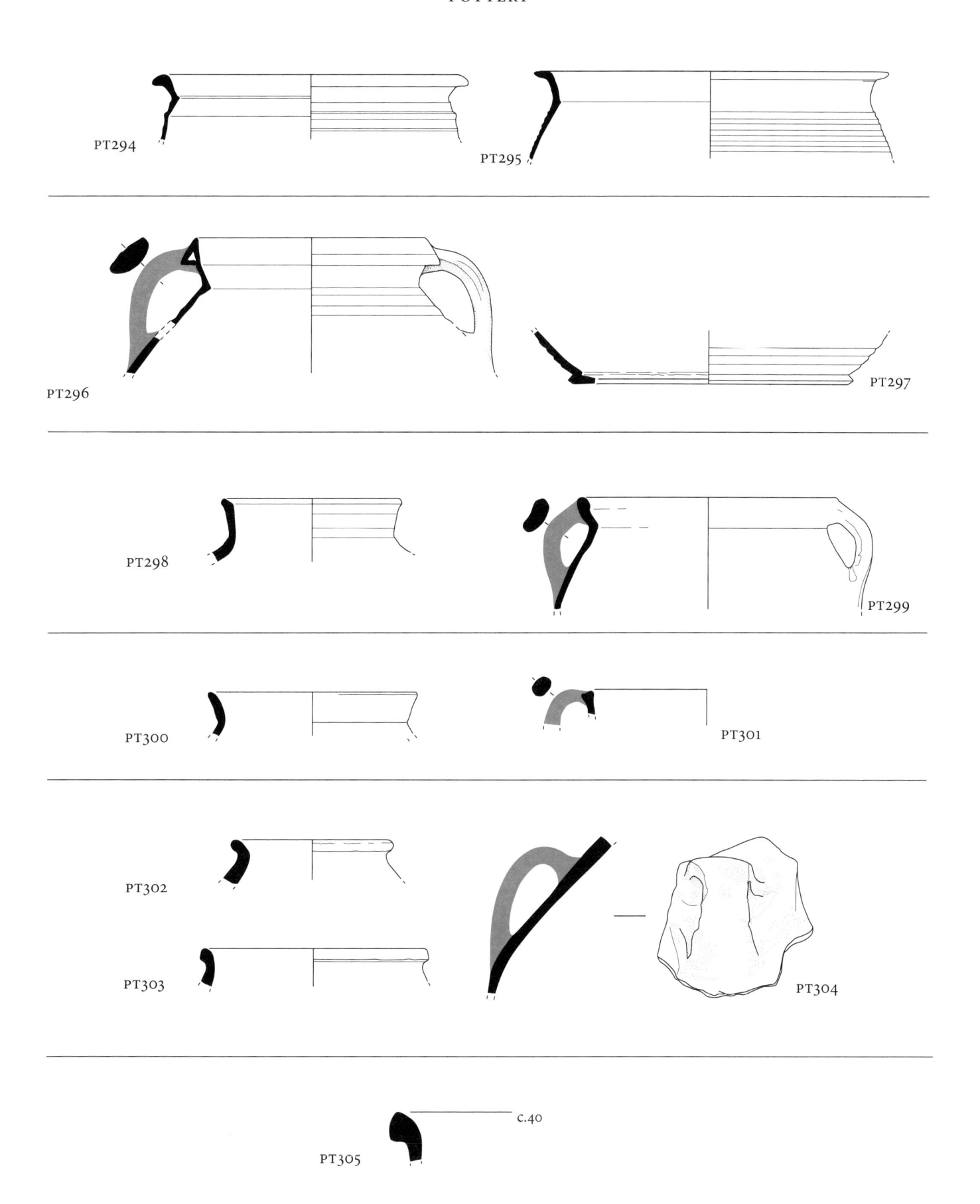

POTTERY

*Plate 17. Group C. Cooking ware 1 (**PT294, 295**); Cooking ware 2 (**PT296, 297**); Cooking ware 7 (**PT298, 299**); Cooking ware 8 (**PT300, 301**); Storage ware 2 (**PT302–304**). Scale 1:3. Storage ware 1 (**PT305**). Scale 1:6.*

KENRICK

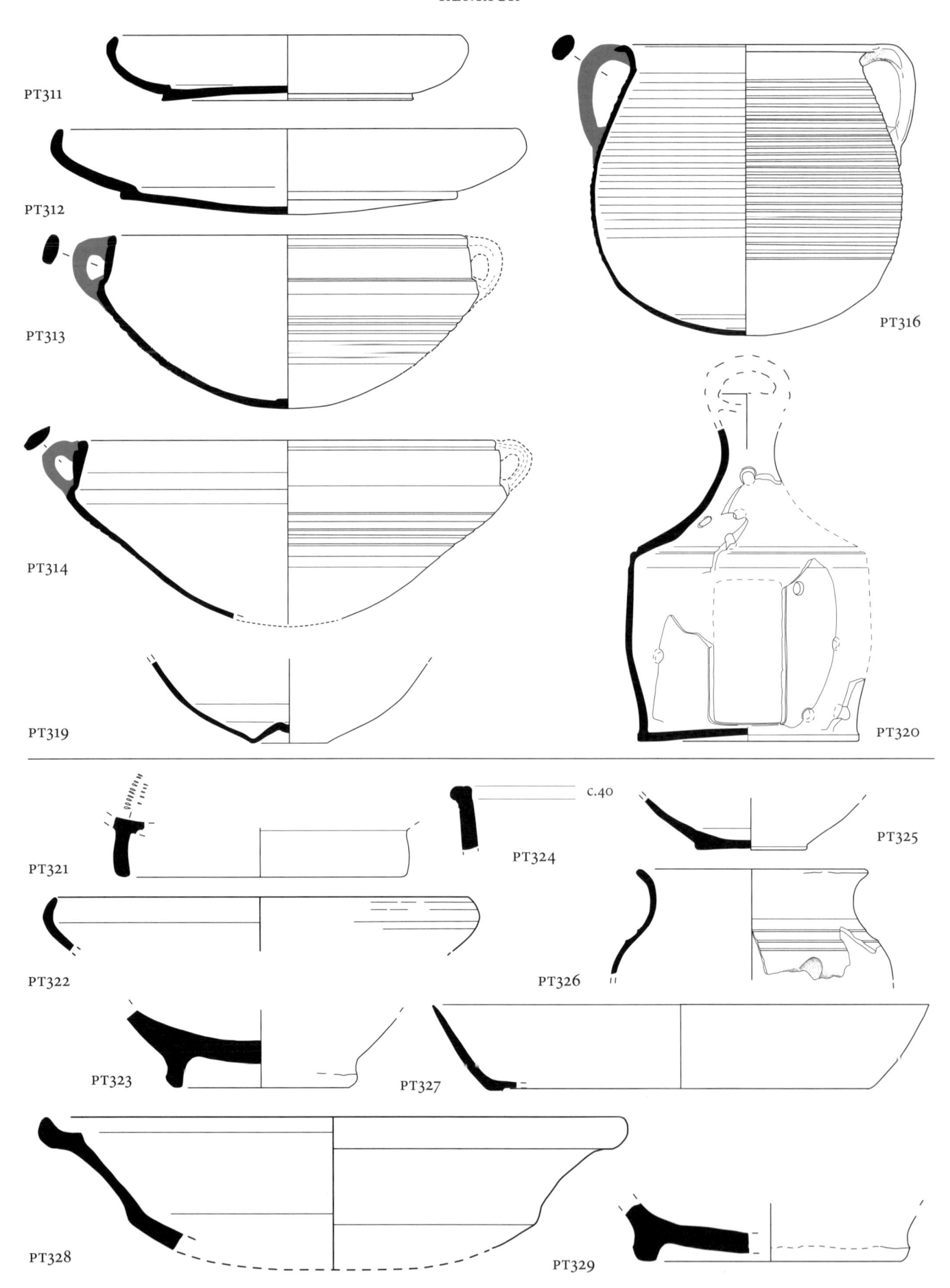

PT311

PT312

PT313

PT314

PT319

PT316

PT320

PT321

PT322

PT323

PT324

PT325

PT326

PT327

PT328

PT329

*Plate 18. Group D. Group of cooking-ware vessels from context 2176 (**PT311–320**). Scale 1:3. BSP (**PT321, 322**); local Hellenistic fine ware (**PT323**); Italian Sigillata (**PT324**); thin-walled wares (**PT325, 326**); African Red Slip Ware (**PT327**); "Parthian" glazed ware (**PT328, 329**). Scale 1:2.*

POTTERY

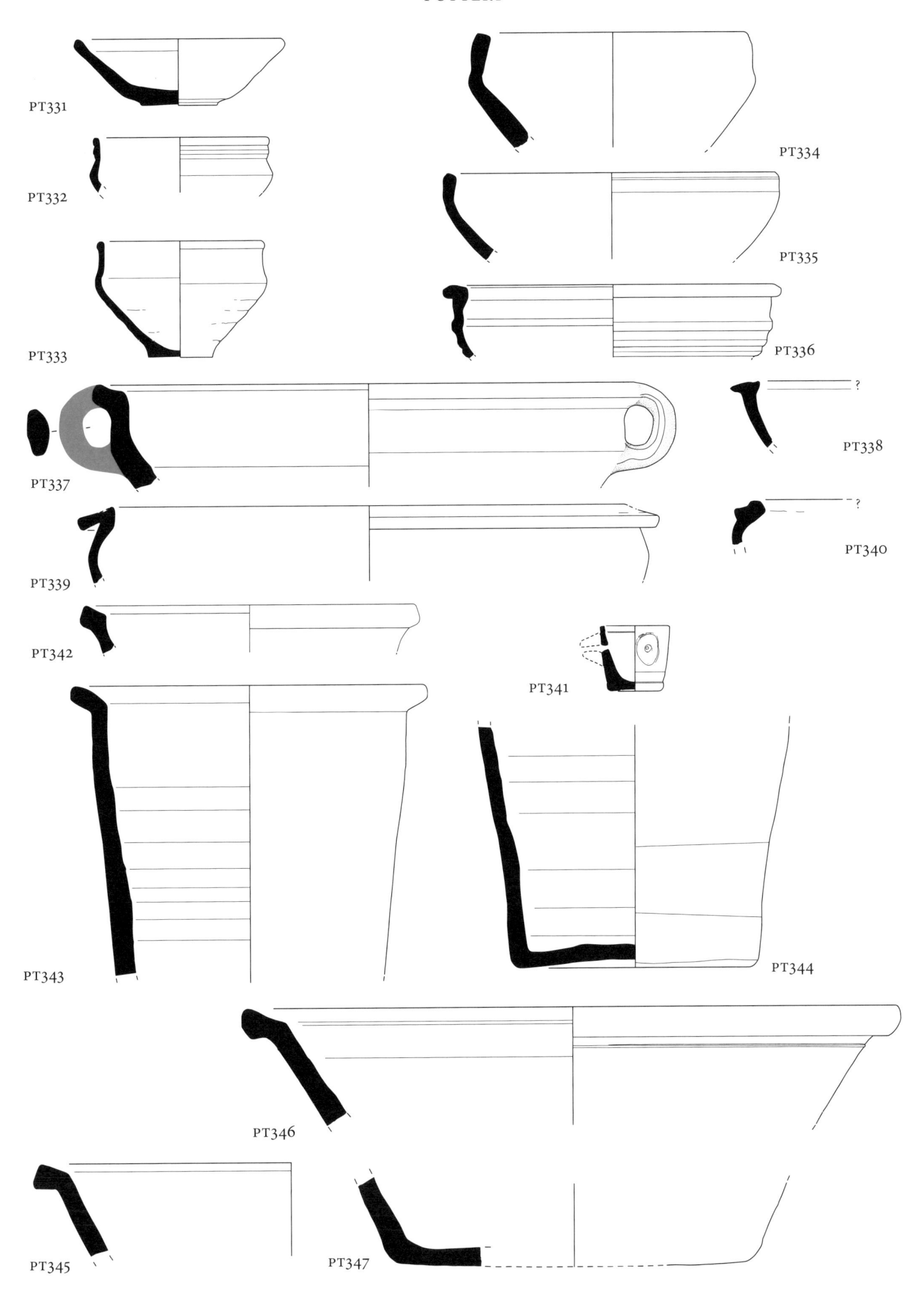

PT331
PT332
PT333
PT334
PT335
PT336
PT337
PT338
PT339
PT340
PT341
PT342
PT343
PT344
PT345
PT346
PT347

*Plate 19. Group D. Buff wares 1–3 (**PT331–347**). Scale 1:3.*

PT348 c.40

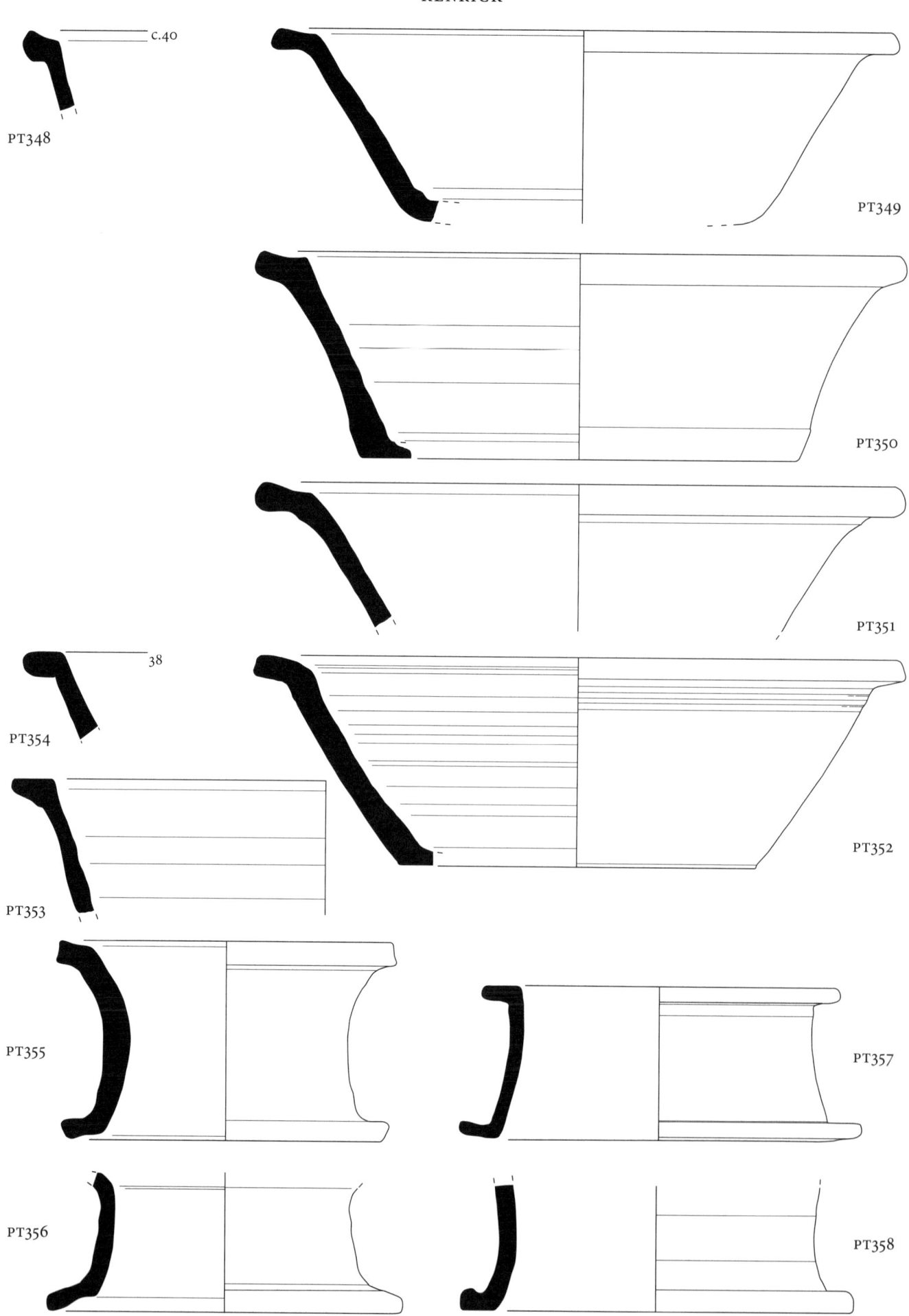

PT349

PT350

PT351

PT354 38

PT353

PT352

PT355

PT357

PT356

PT358

*Plate 20. Group D. Buff wares 1–3 (*PT348–358*). Scale 1:3.*

POTTERY

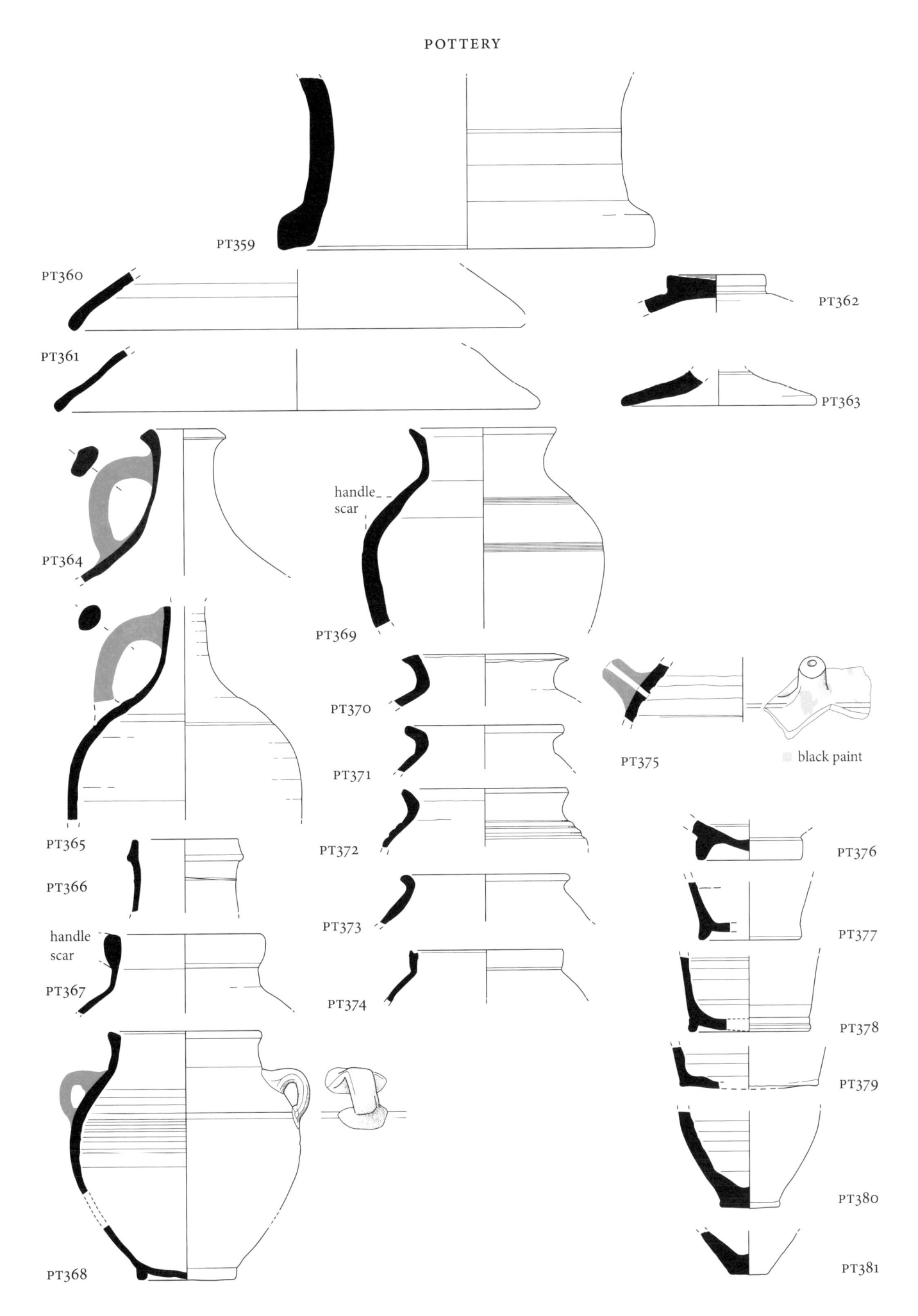

PT359
PT360
PT361
PT362
PT363
PT364
PT365
PT366
handle scar
PT367
PT368
PT369
handle scar
PT370
PT371
PT372
PT373
PT374
PT375
black paint
PT376
PT377
PT378
PT379
PT380
PT381

Plate 21. Group D. Buff wares 1–3 (PT359–381). Scale 1:3.

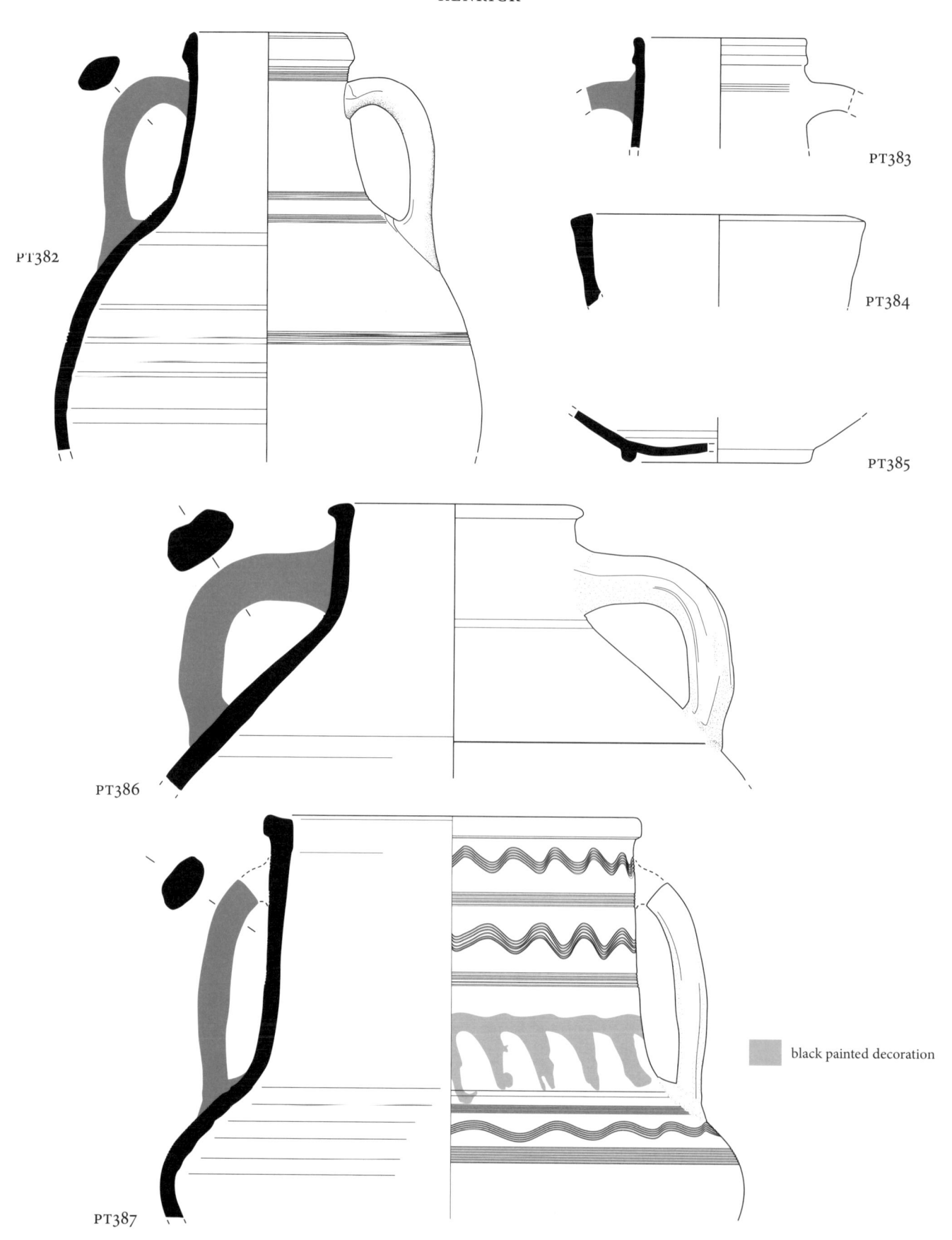

Plate 22. Group D. Buff wares 1–3 (PT382–387). Scale 1:3.

POTTERY

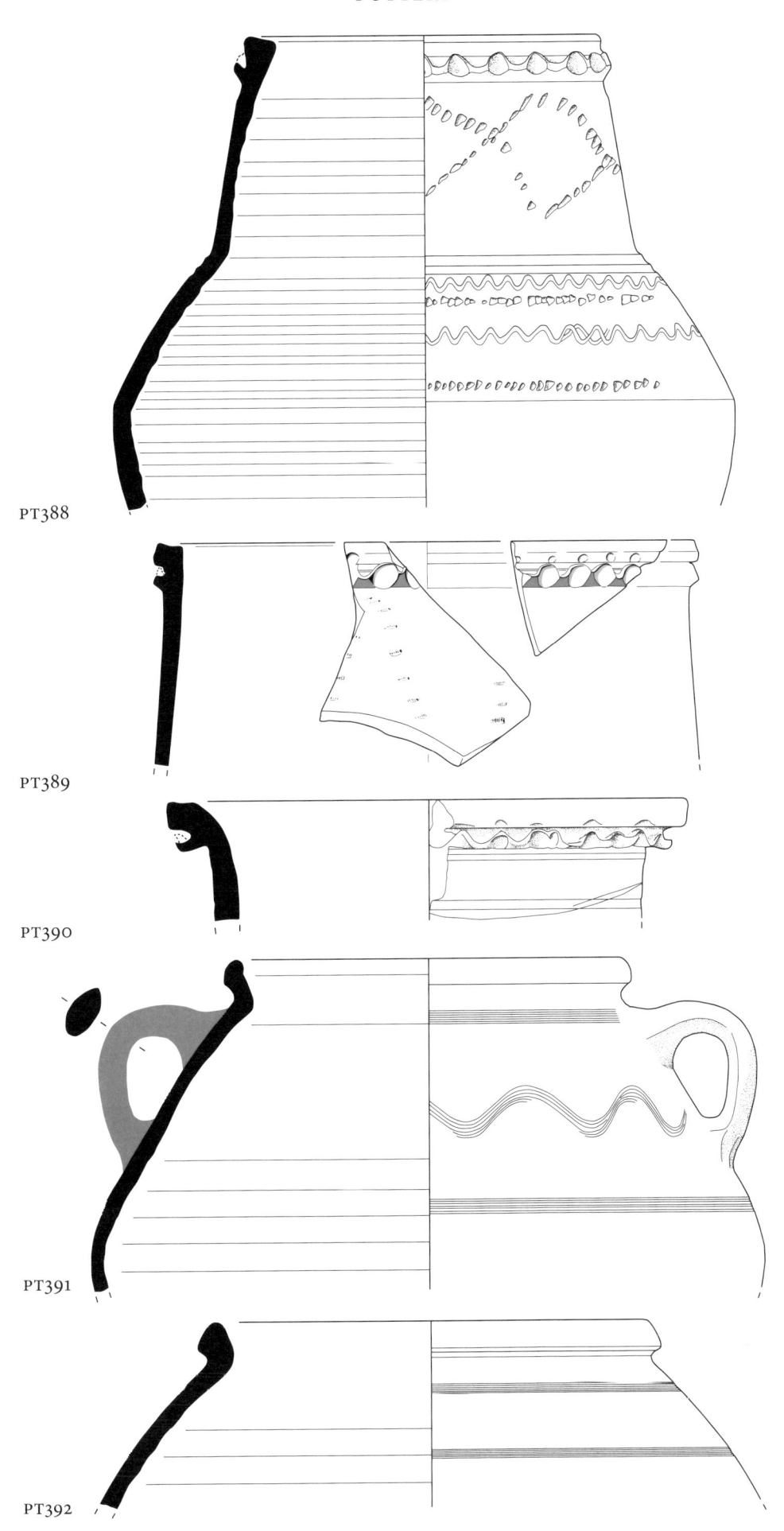

PT388

PT389

PT390

PT391

PT392

*Plate 23. Group D. Buff wares 1–3 (**PT388–392**). Scale 1:3.*

PT393

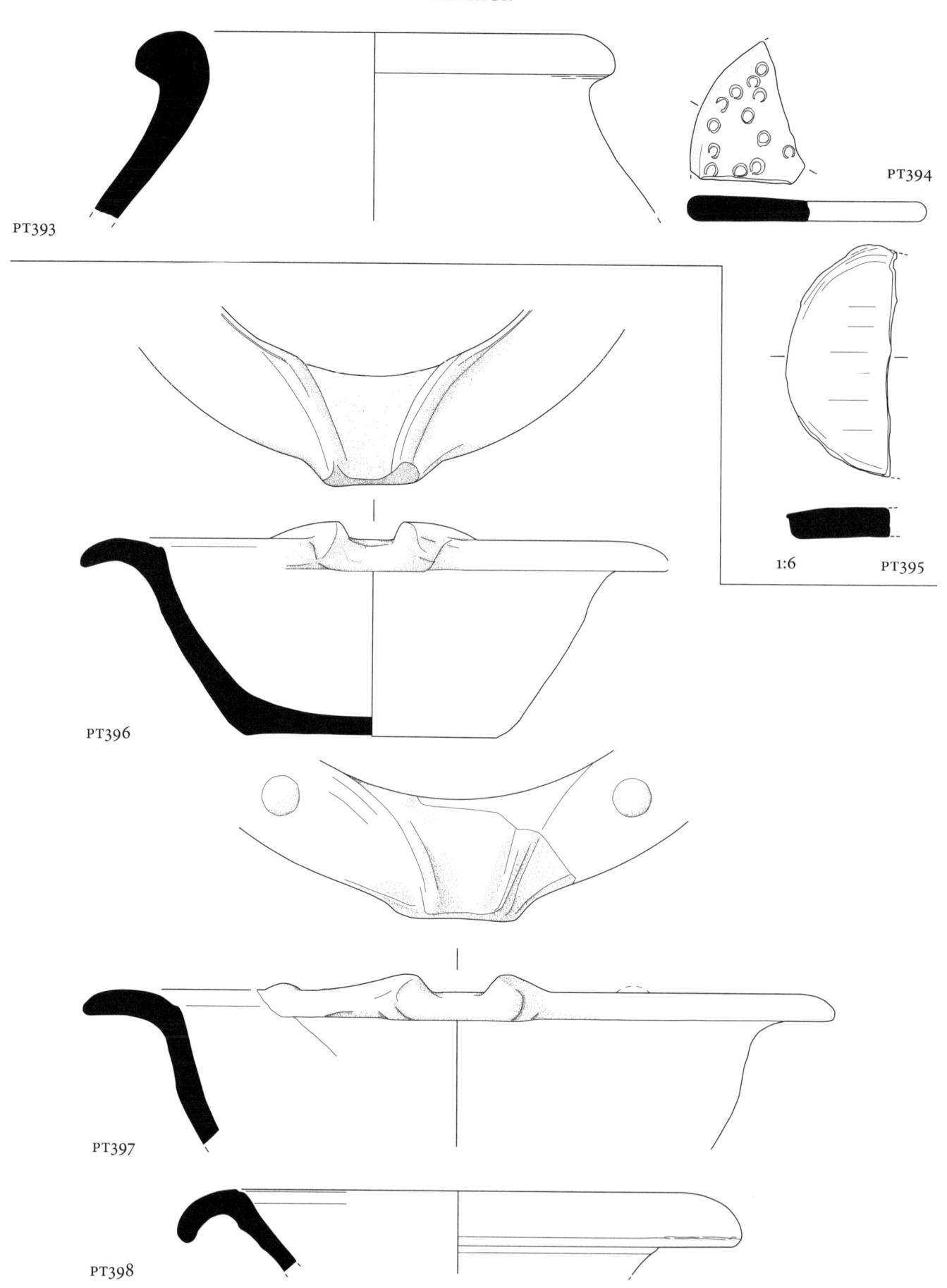

PT394

PT395   1:6

PT396

PT397

PT398

*Plate 24. Group D. Buff wares 1–3 (**PT393–395**); Buff ware 6 (**PT396–398**). Scale 1:3.*

POTTERY

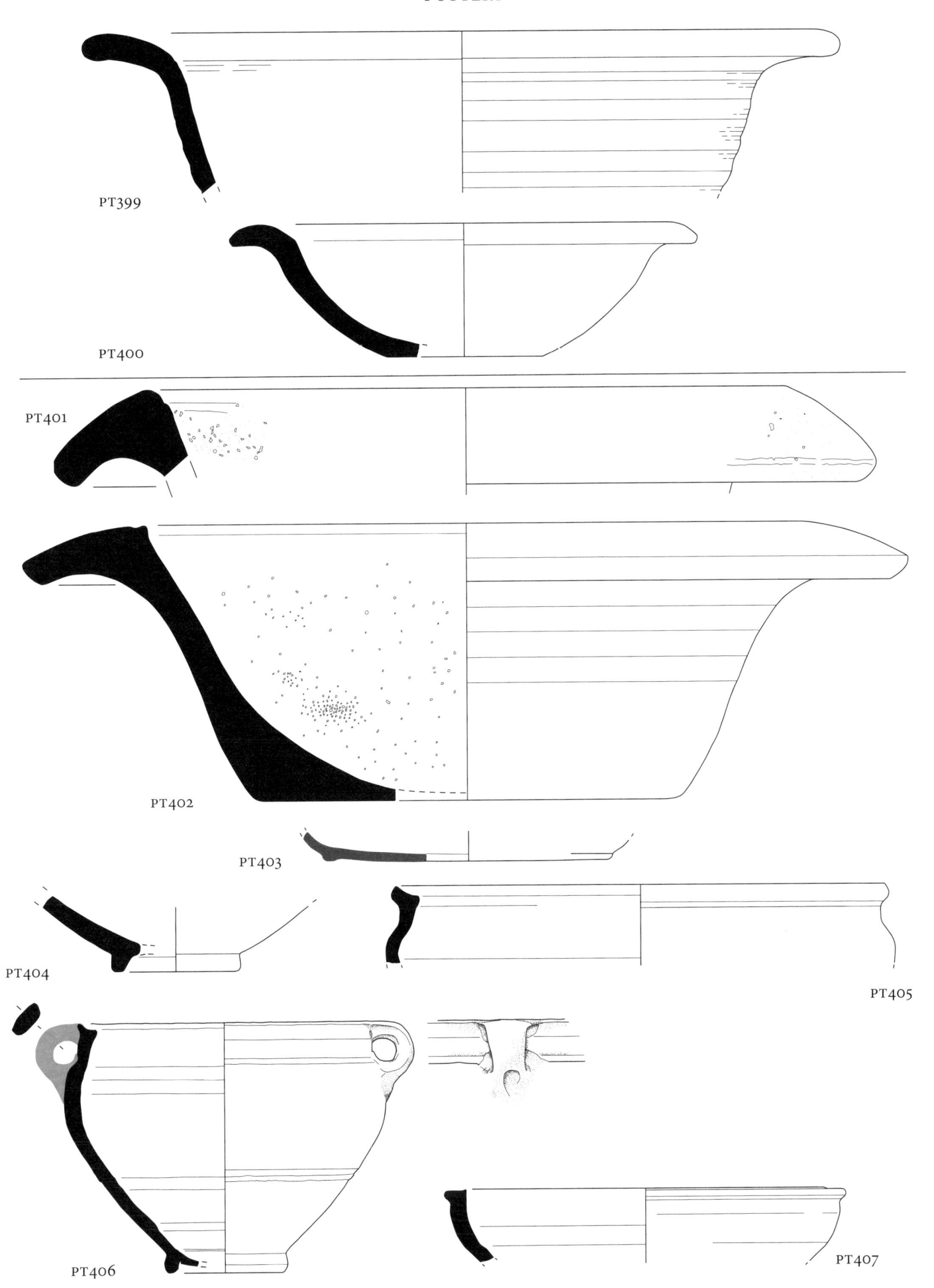

PT399
PT400
PT401
PT402
PT403
PT404
PT405
PT406
PT407

*Plate 25. Group D. Buff ware 6 (**PT399, 400**); other buff wares (**PT401–407**). Scale 1:3.*

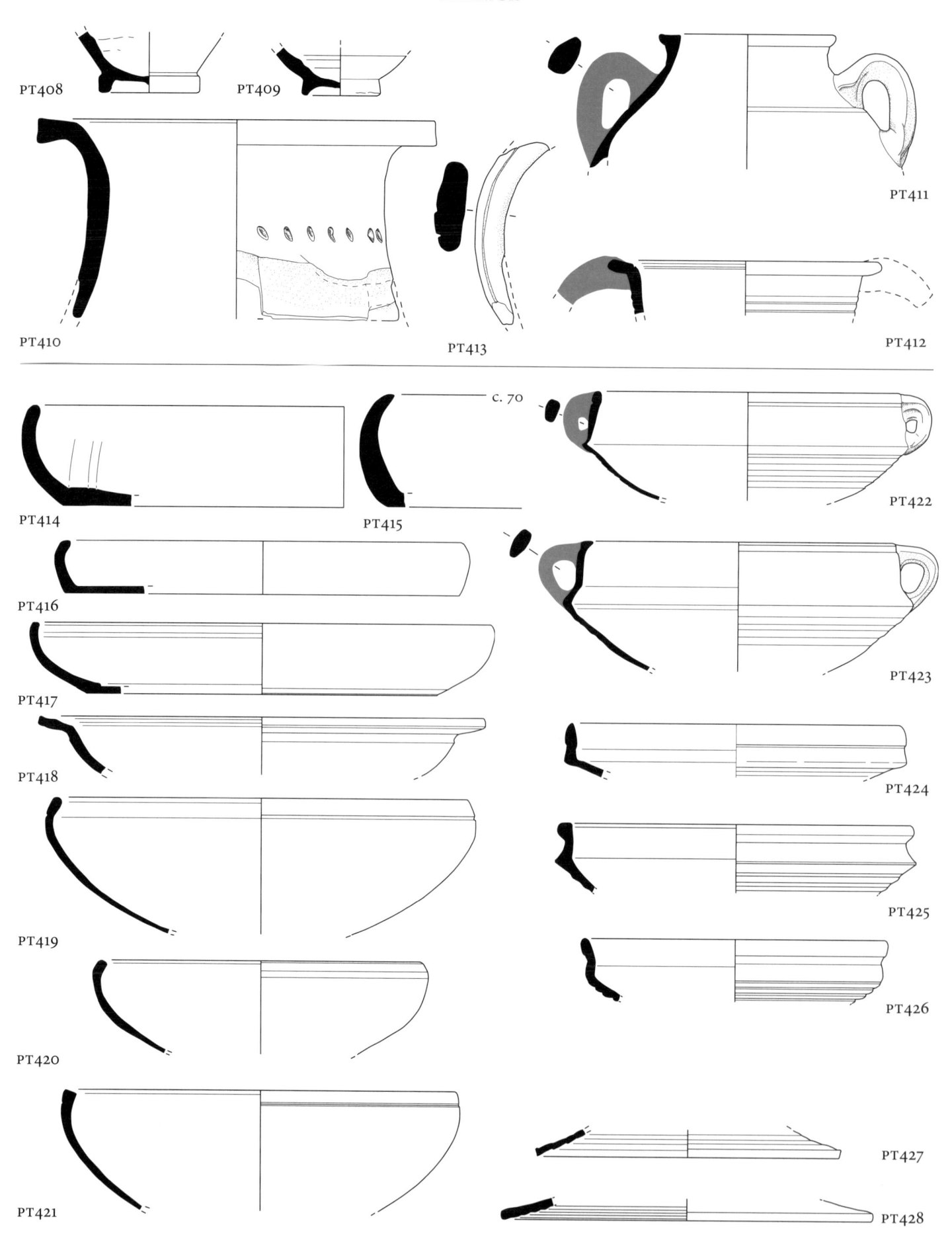

Plate 26. Group D. Other buff wares (PT408–413); Cooking ware 1 (PT414–428). Scale 1:3.

POTTERY

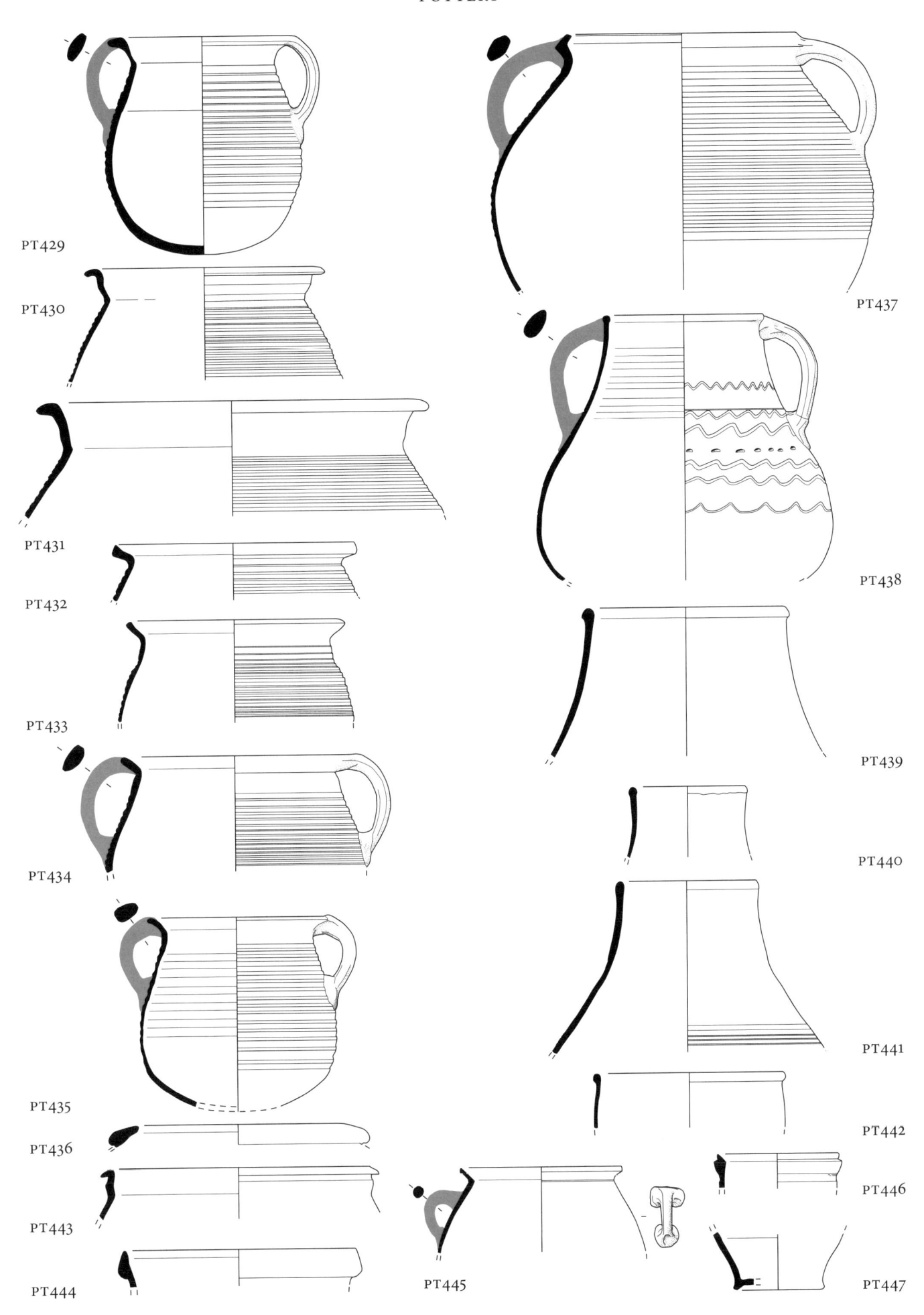

PT429
PT430
PT431
PT432
PT433
PT434
PT435
PT436
PT437
PT438
PT439
PT440
PT441
PT442
PT443
PT444
PT445
PT446
PT447

*Plate 27. Group D. Cooking ware 1 (**PT429–447**). Scale 1:3.*

KENRICK

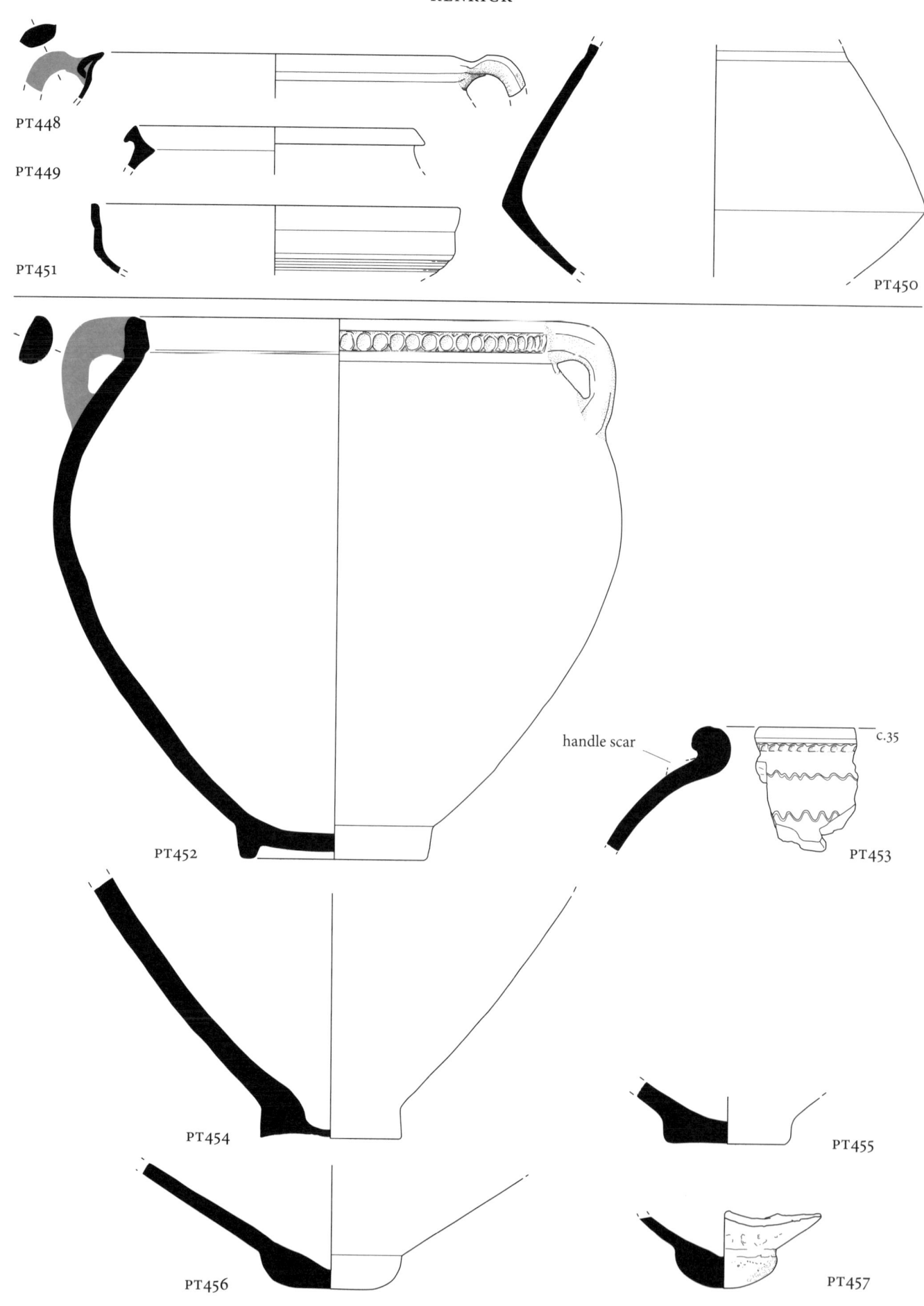

PT448
PT449
PT451
PT450
PT452
handle scar
PT453
PT454
PT455
PT456
PT457

Plate 28. Group D. Cooking ware 2 (PT448); other cooking wares (PT449–451). Scale 1:3.
Storage ware 1 (PT452–457). Scale 1:6.

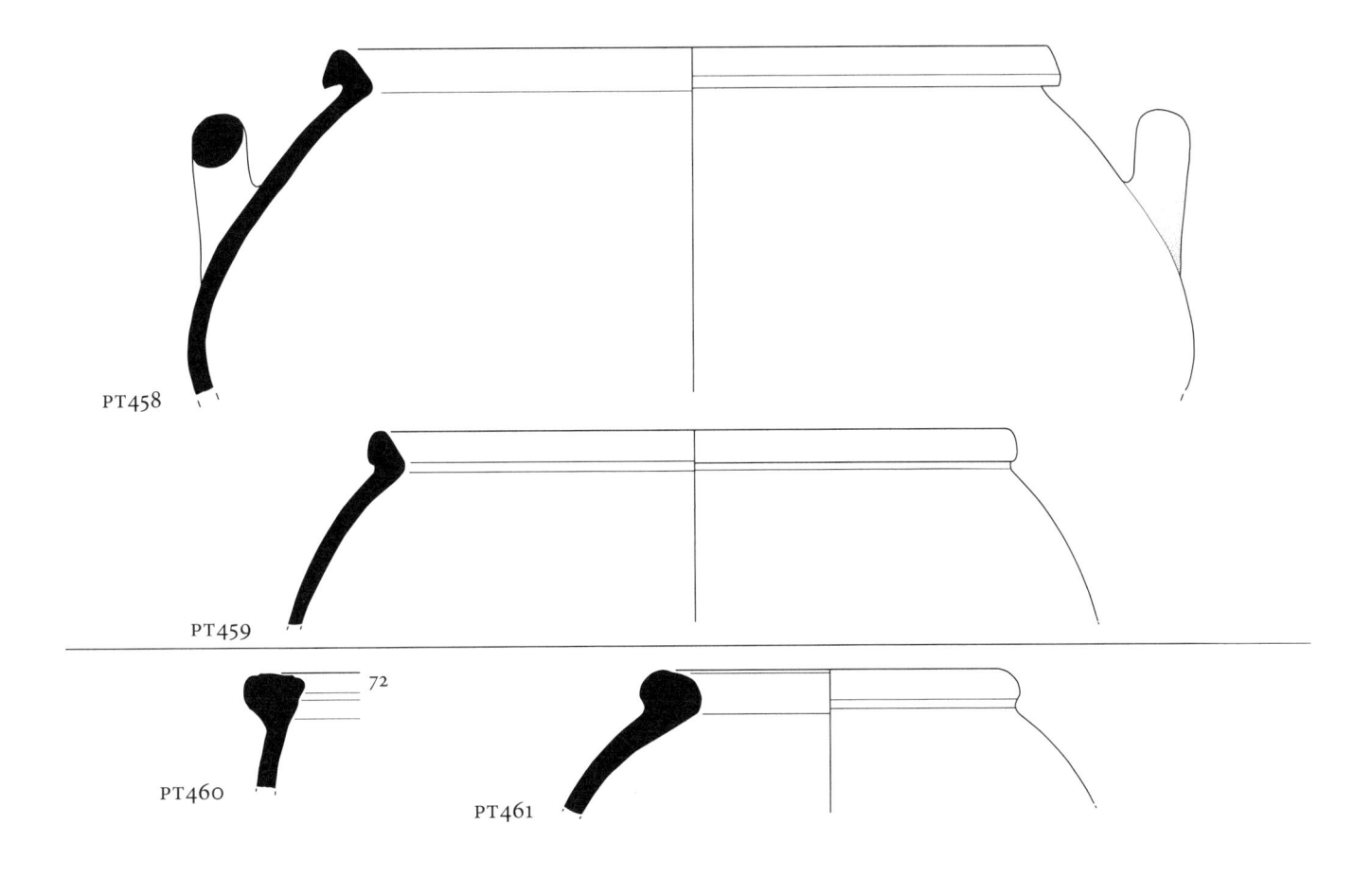

POTTERY

*Plate 29. Group D. Storage ware 2 (**PT458, 459**). Scale 1:3.*
*Storage ware 4 (**PT460, 461**). Scale 1:6.*

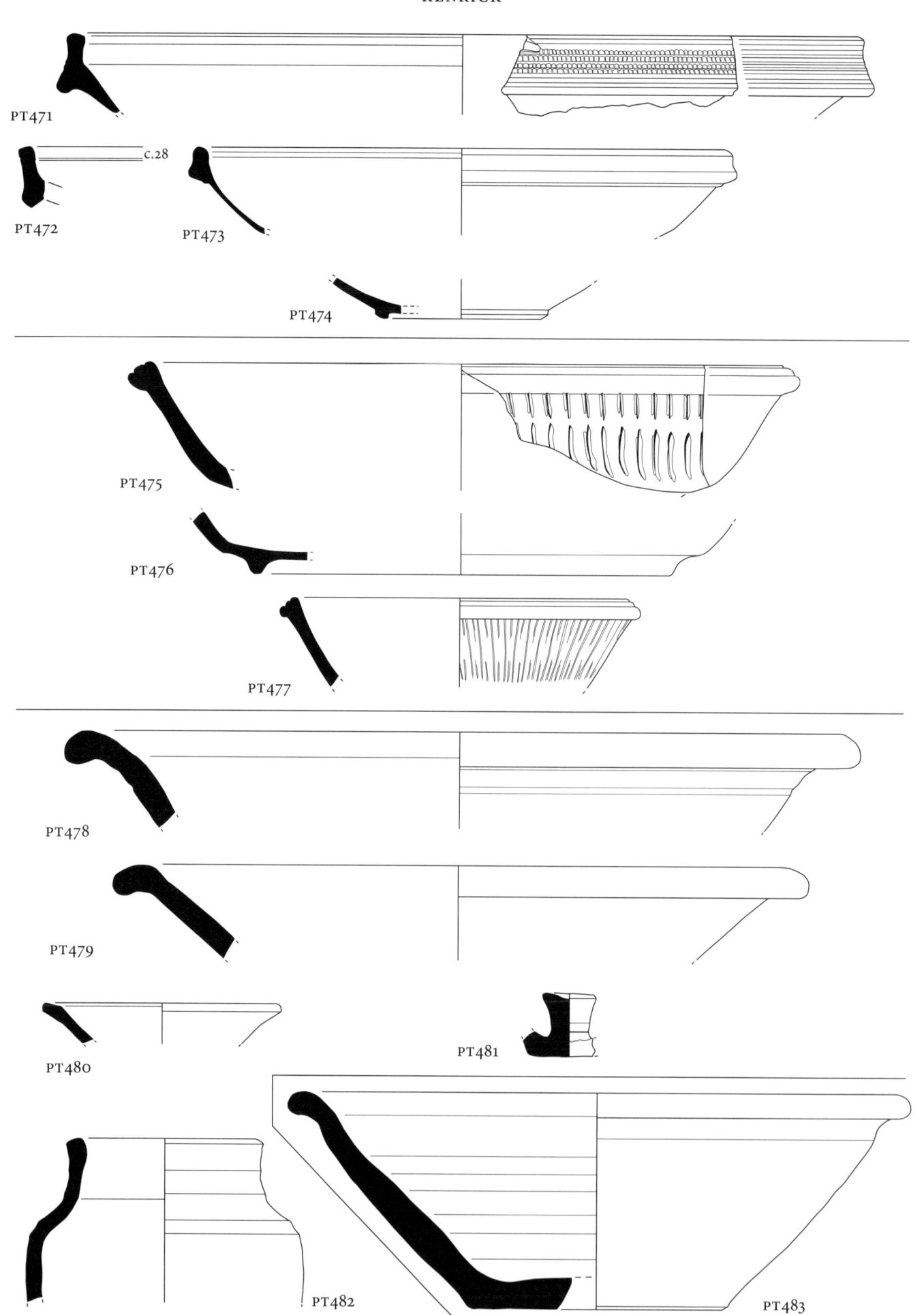

Plate 30. Group E. Phocaean Red Slip Ware (PT471–474); Cypriot Red Slip Ware (PT475–477). Scale 1:2. Buff wares 1–3 (PT478–482); Buff ware 6 (PT483). Scale 1:3.

POTTERY

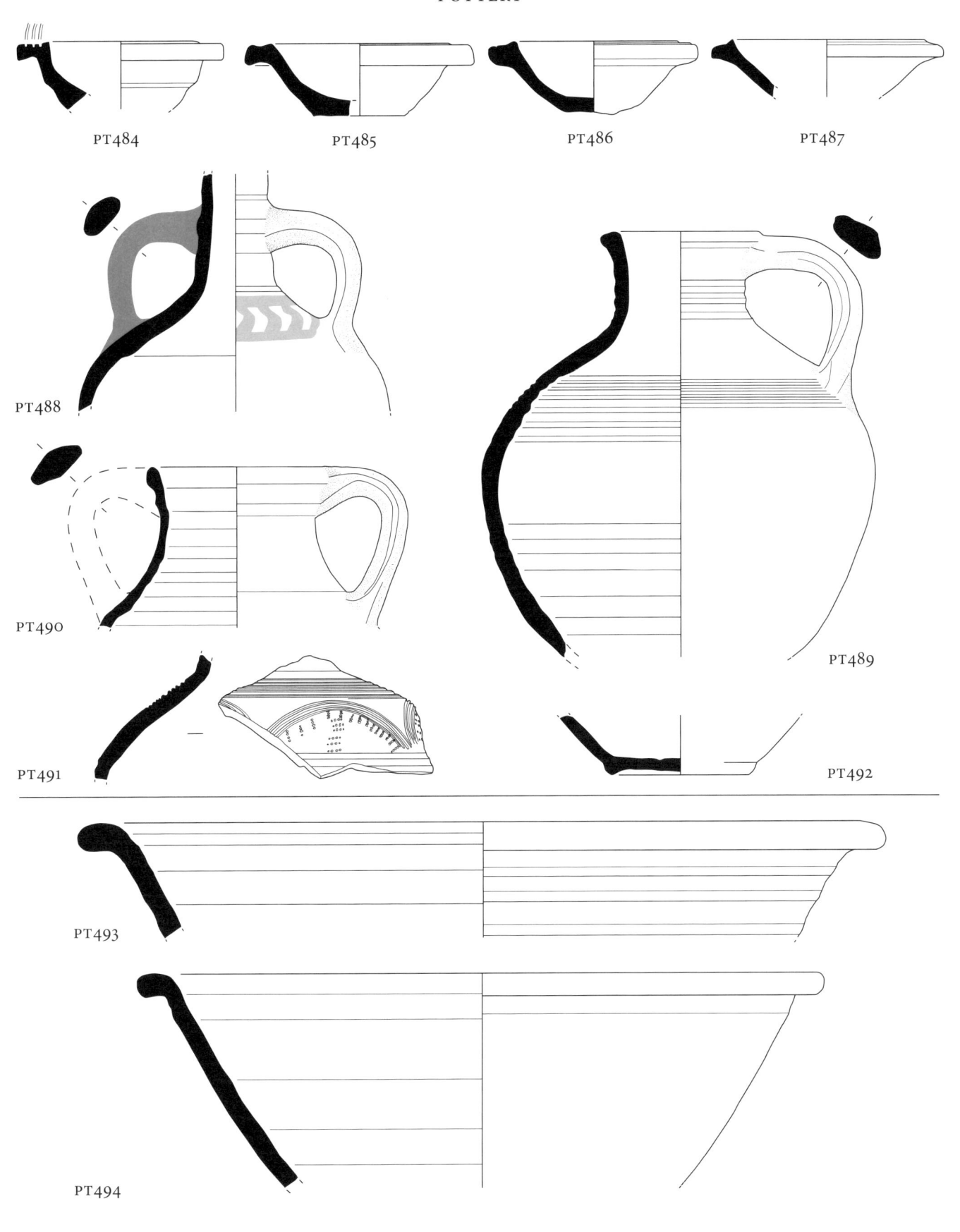

PT484   PT485   PT486   PT487

PT488

PT490

PT491   PT492   PT489

PT493

PT494

*Plate 31. Group E. Buff ware 8 (**PT484–492**); Buff ware 15 (**PT493, 494**). Scale 1:3.*

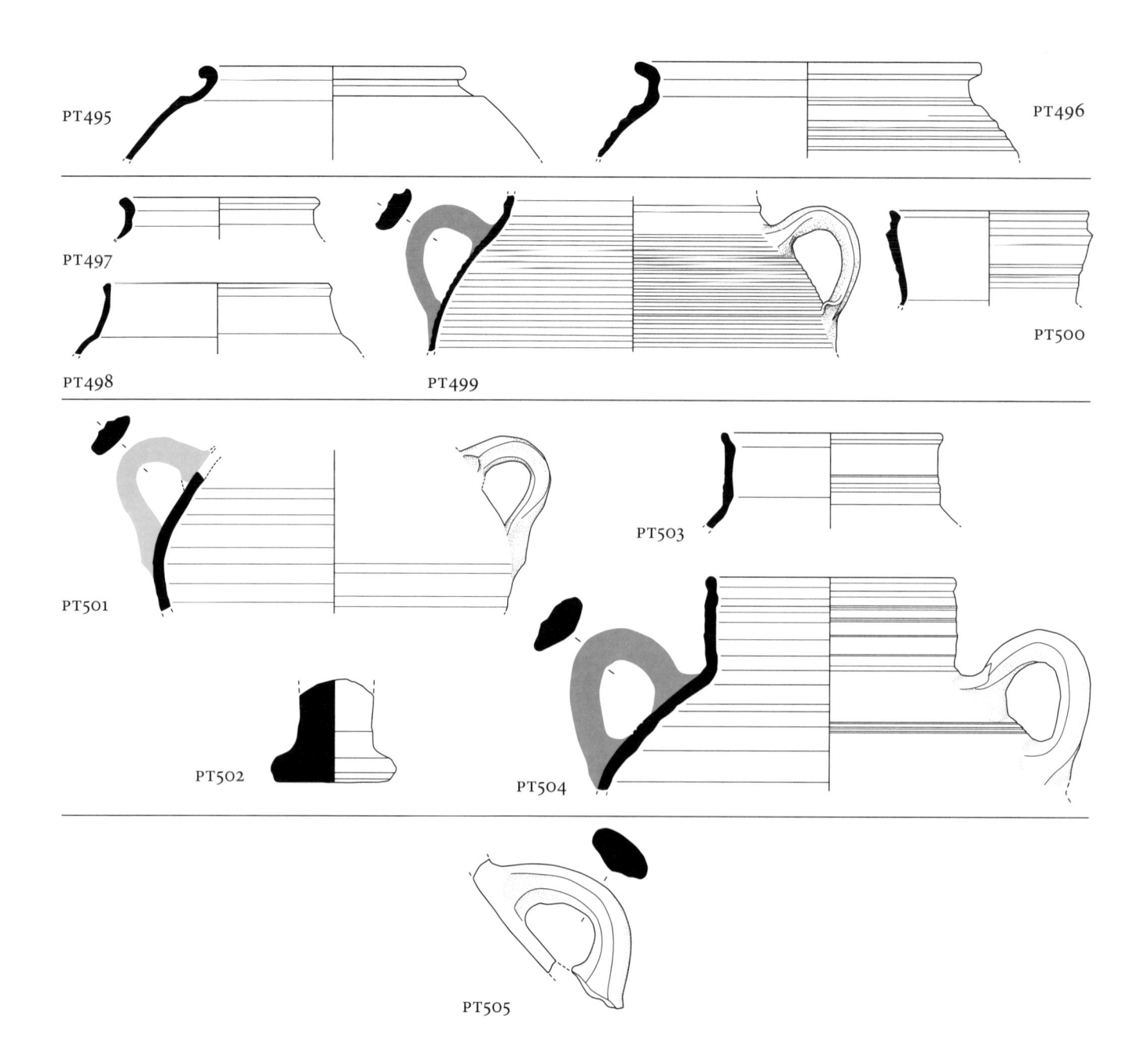

*Plate 32. Group E. Cooking ware 1 (**PT495, 496**); Cooking ware 2 (**PT497–500**); other cooking wares (**PT501–504**); Storage ware 5 (**PT505**). Scale 1:3.*

POTTERY

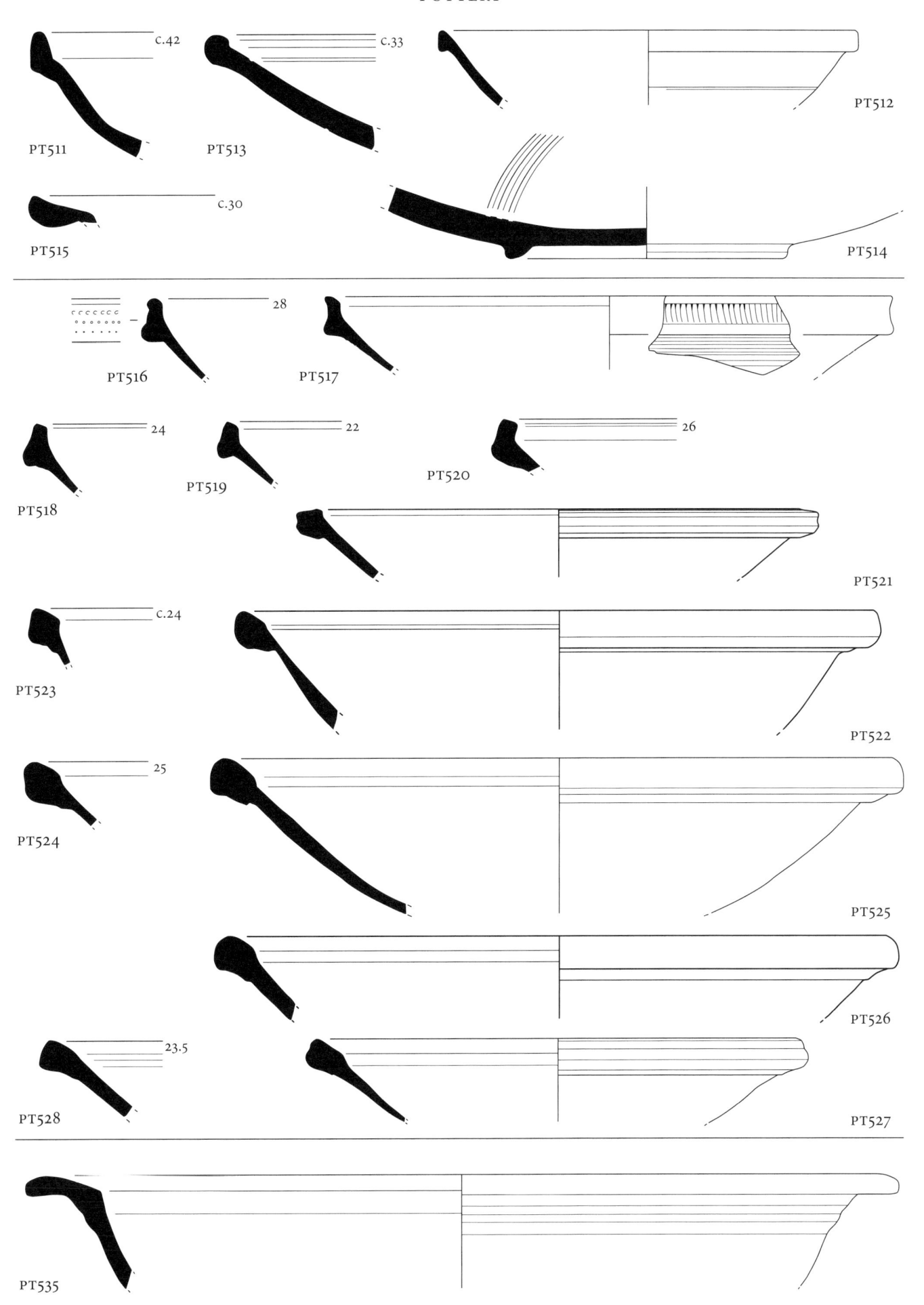

*Plate 33. Group F. African Red Slip Ware (**PT511–515**); Phocaean Red Slip Ware (**PT516–528**). Scale 1:2.*
*Buff ware 1 (**PT535**). Scale 1:3.*

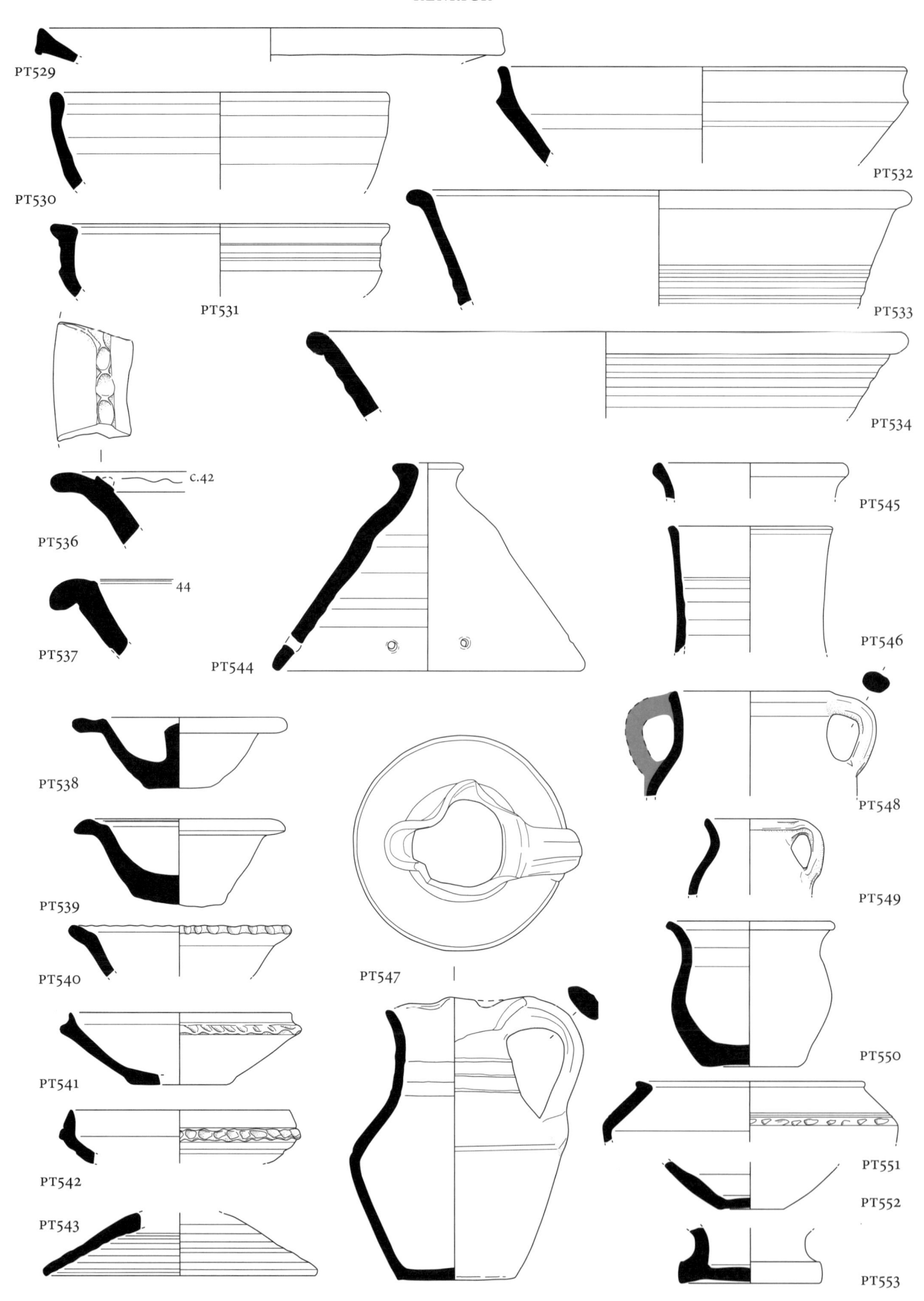

*Plate 34. Group F. Buff wares 1–4 (**PT529–534, 536–553**). Scale 1:3.*

POTTERY

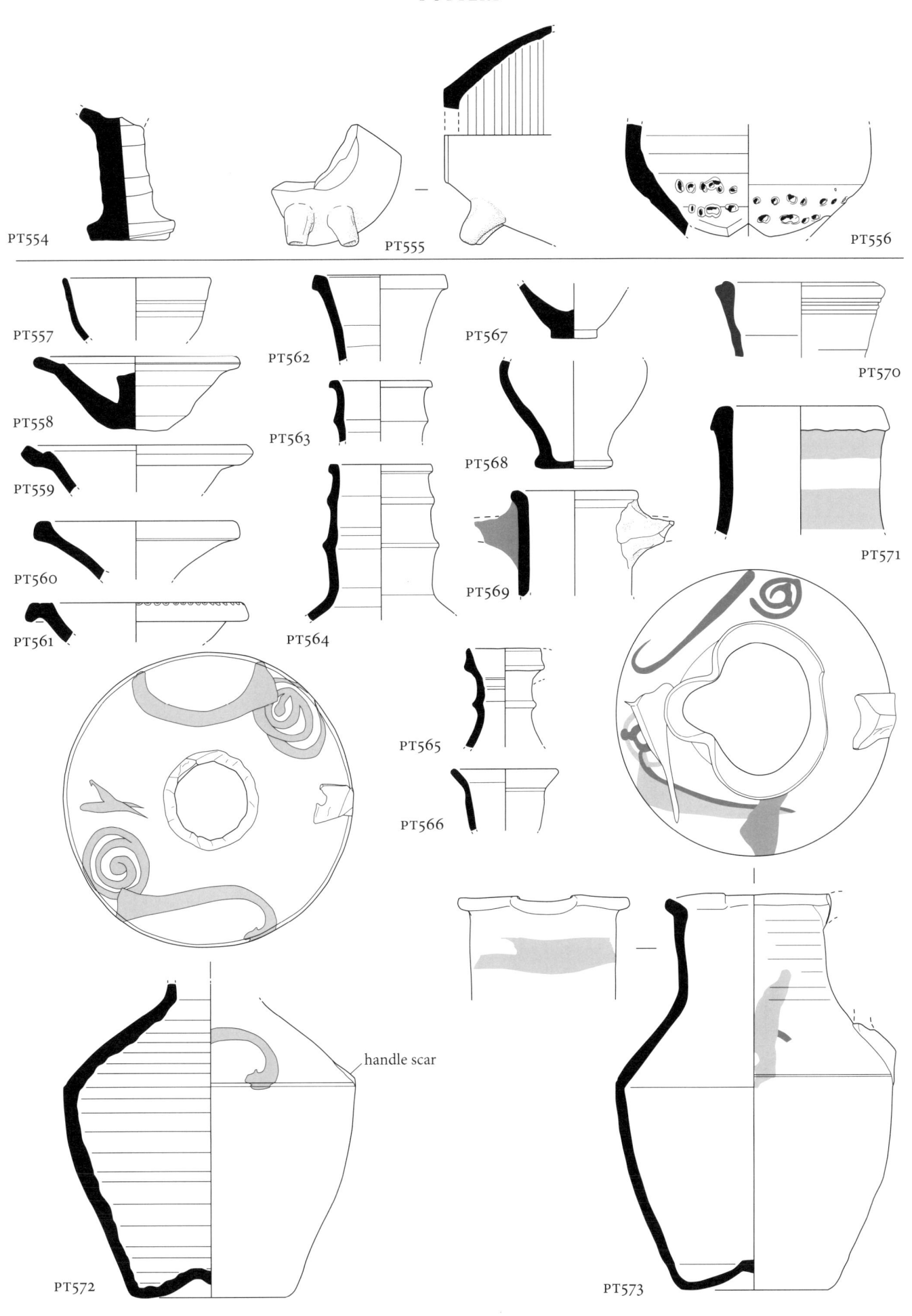

*Plate 35. Group F. Buff wares 1–4 (**PT554–556**); Buff ware 8 (**PT557–573**). Scale 1:3.*

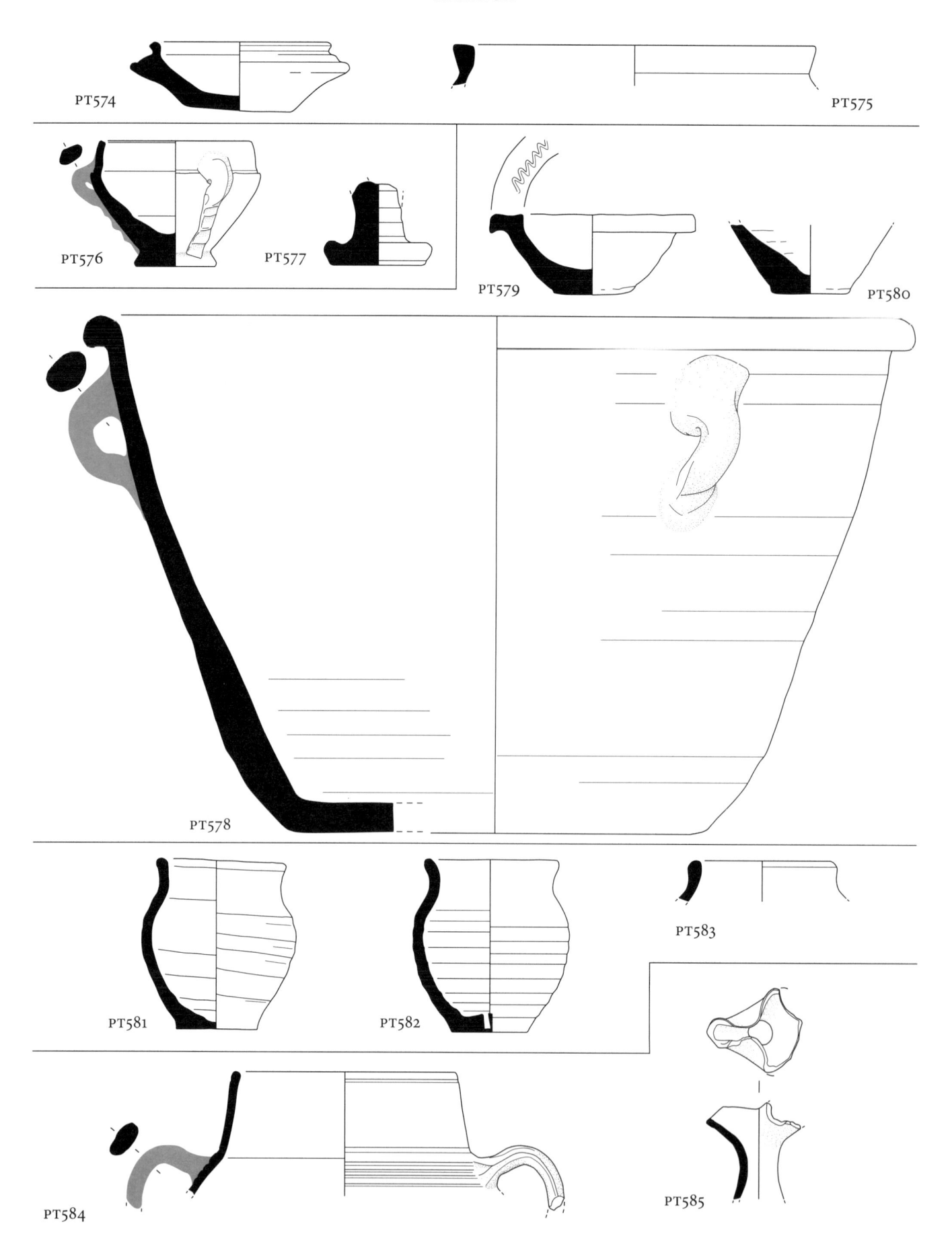

*Plate 36. Group F. Buff ware 10 (**PT574, 575**); Buff ware 13 (**PT576, 577**); Buff ware 15 (**PT578–580**); other buff wares (**PT581–583**); Cooking ware 1 (**PT584, 585**). Scale 1:3.*

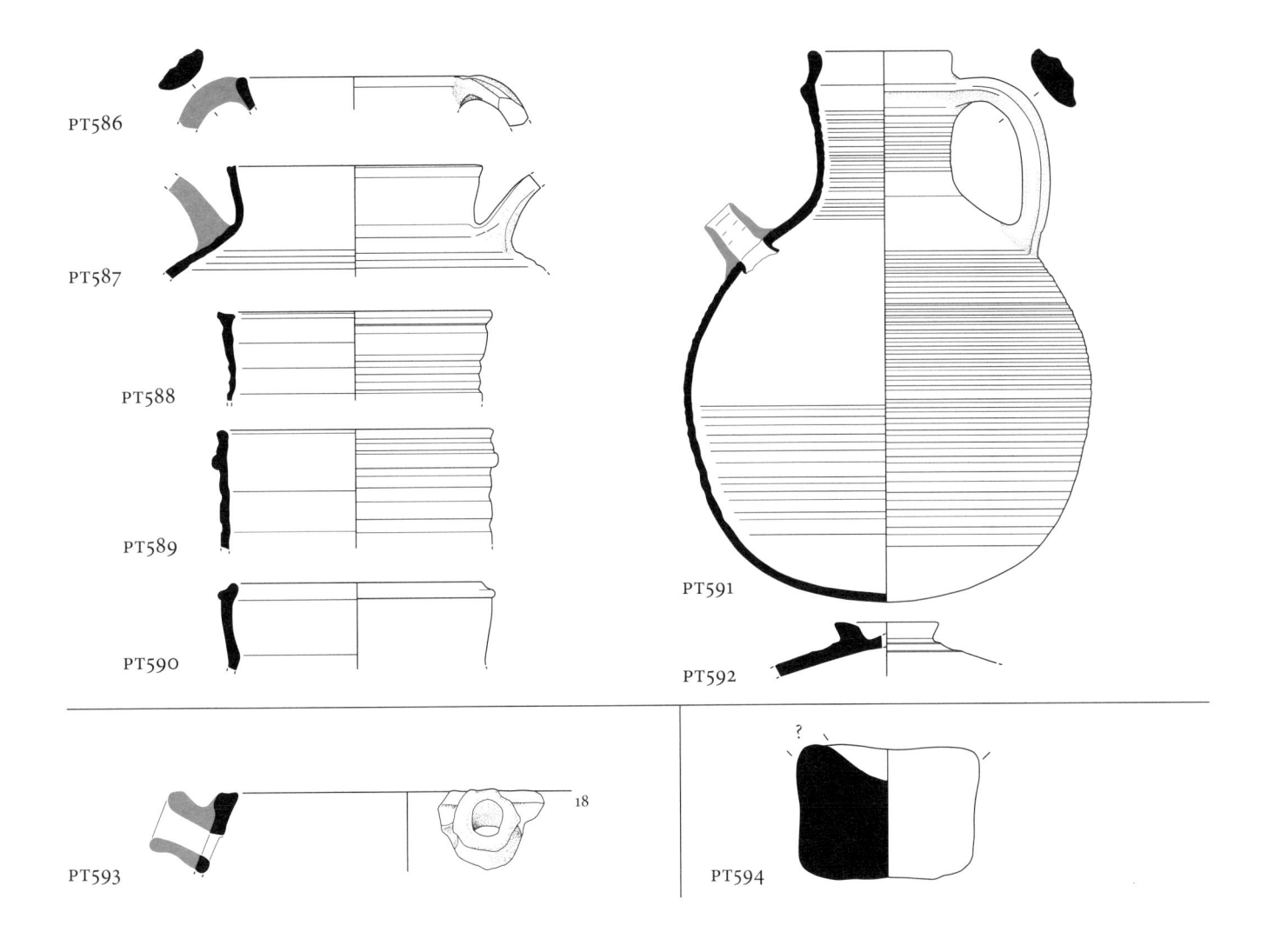

POTTERY

Plate 37. Group F. Cooking ware 2 (PT586–592); Cooking ware 6 (PT593); Storage ware (PT594). Scale 1:3.

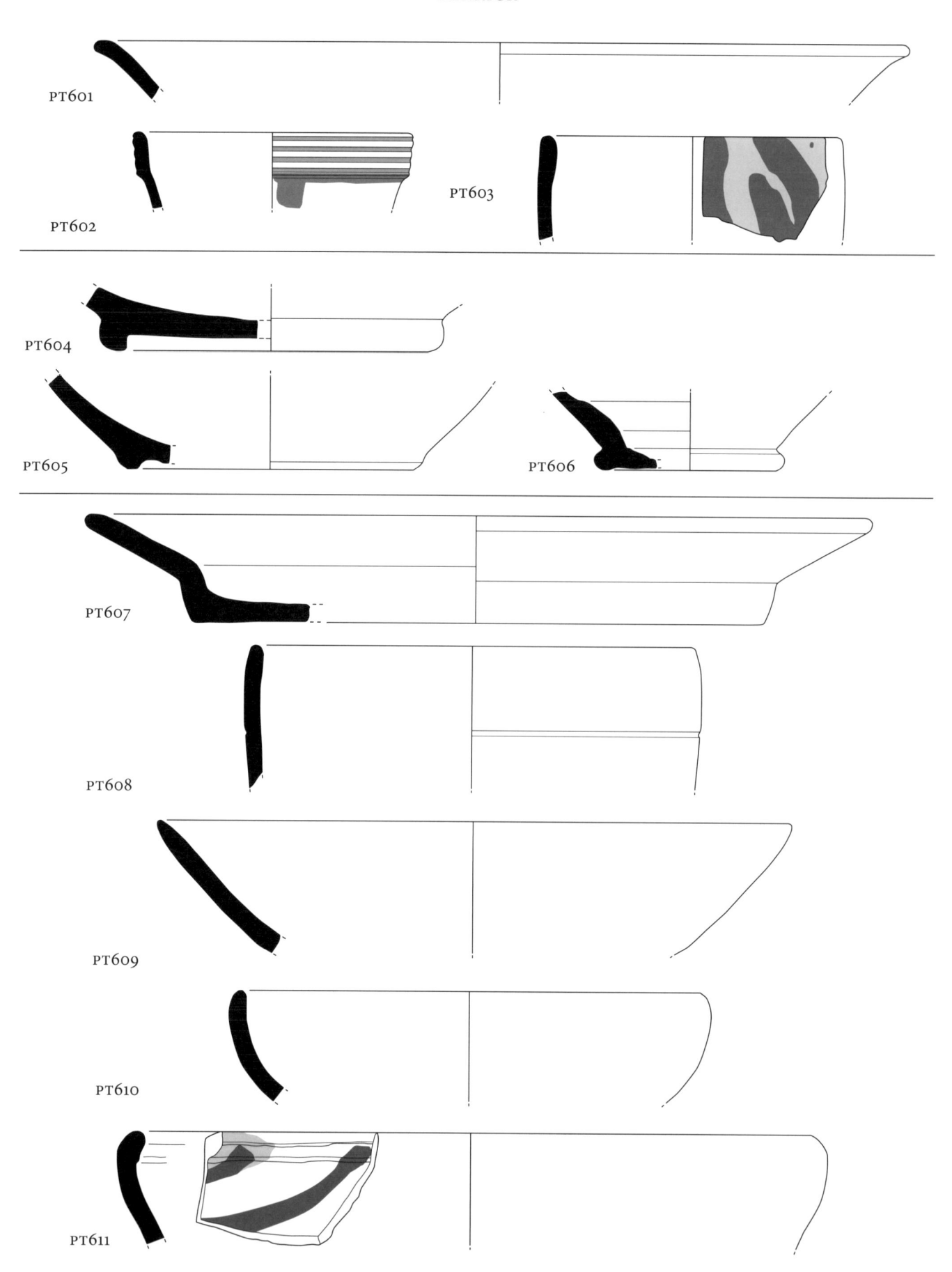

*Plate 38. Group G. Glazed ware 1 (**PT601–603**); Glazed ware 3 (**PT604–606**); Glazed ware 5 (**PT607–611**). Scale 1:2.*

POTTERY

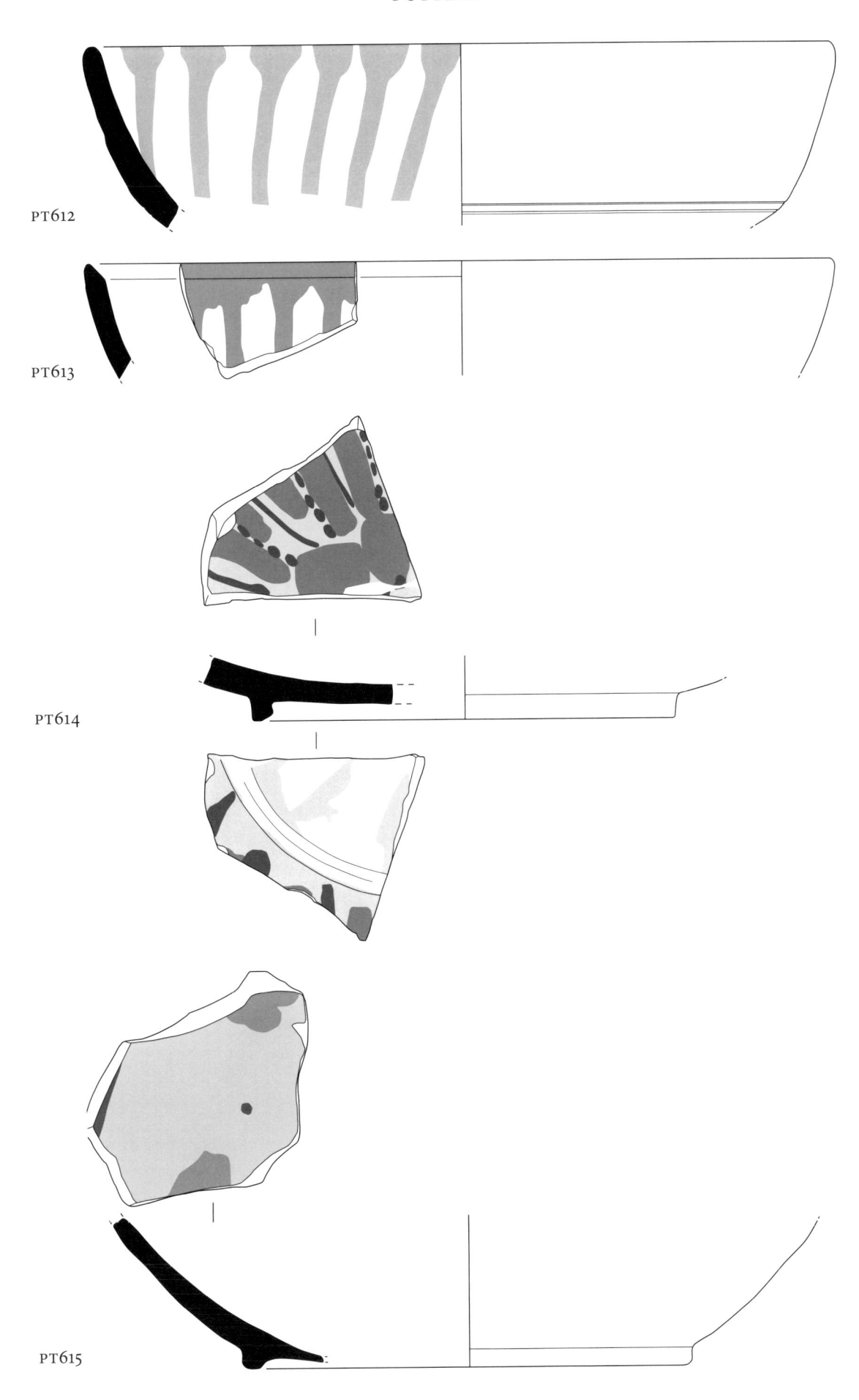

PT612

PT613

PT614

PT615

*Plate 39. Group G. Glazed ware 5 (**PT612–615**). Scale 1:2.*

PT617

PT616

PT618

PT619

PT620

PT621

PT622

*Plate 40. Group G. Glazed ware 5 (PT616, 617); other glazed ware (PT618). Scale 1:2.
Buff wares 1–3 (PT619–622). Scale 1:3.*

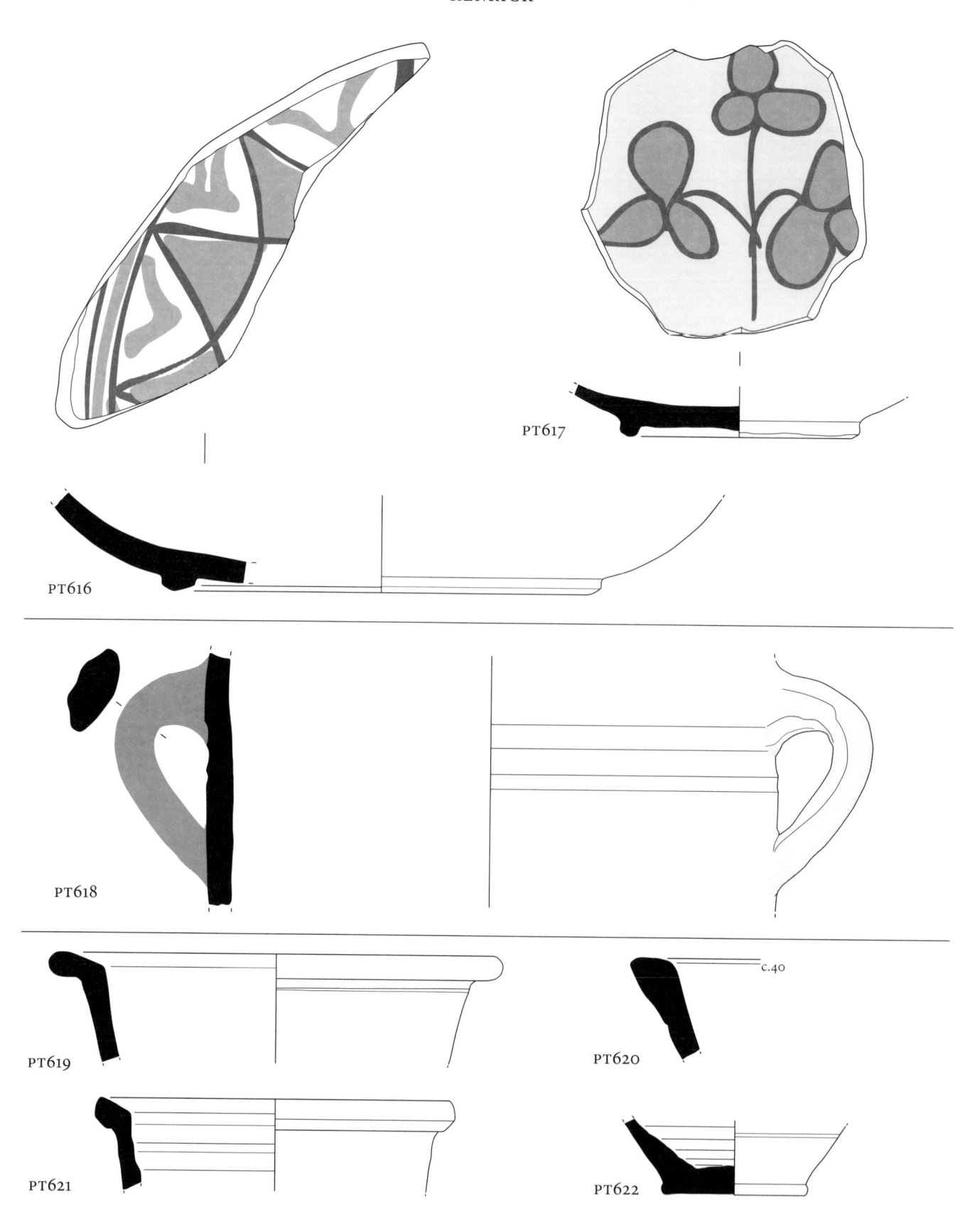

POTTERY

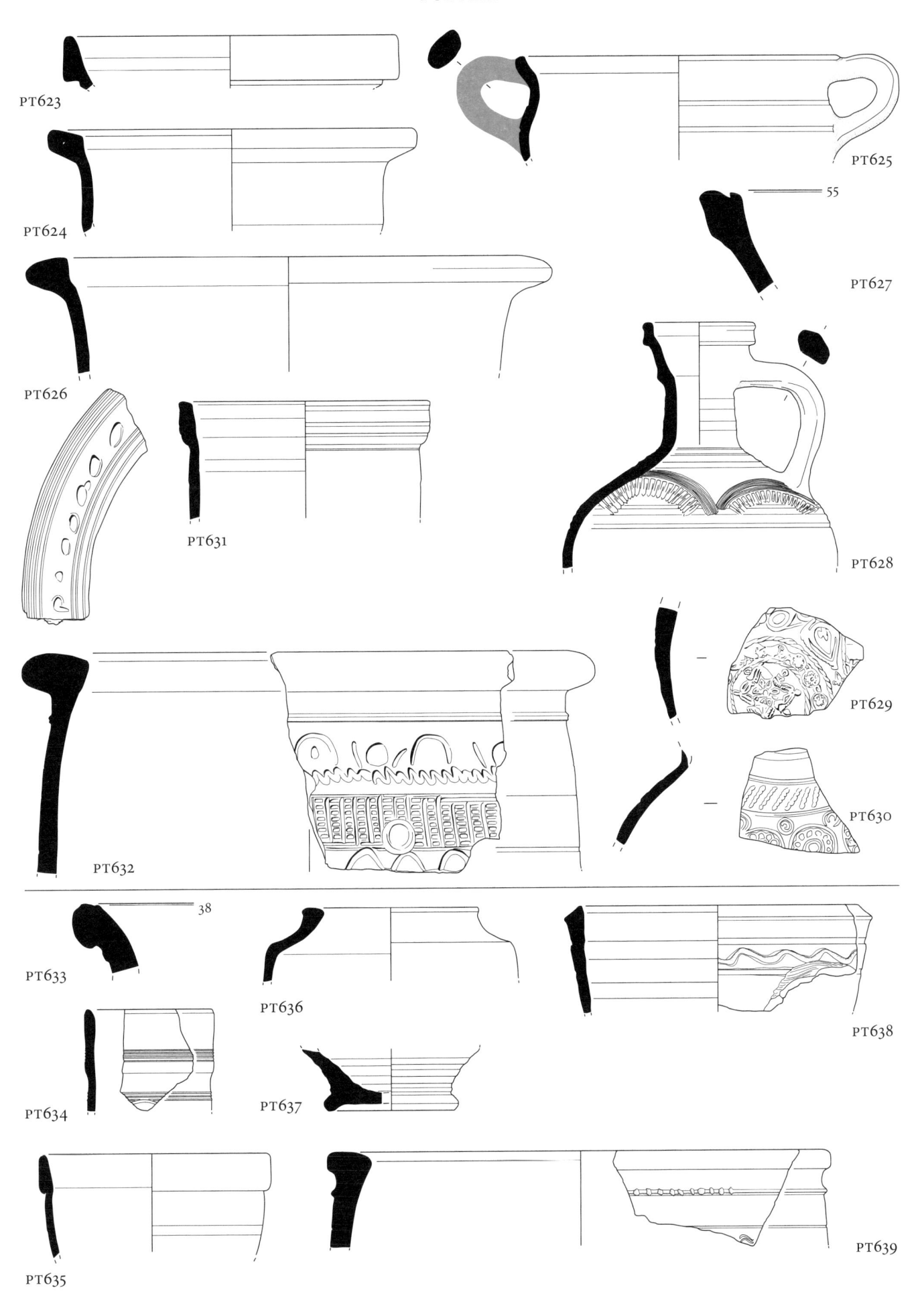

PT623
PT624
PT625
PT626
PT627
PT628
PT629
PT630
PT631
PT632
PT633
PT634
PT635
PT636
PT637
PT638
PT639

Plate 41. Group G. Buff ware 8 (PT623–632); Buff ware 10 (PT633–639). Scale 1:3 (PT629, 630, 1:2).

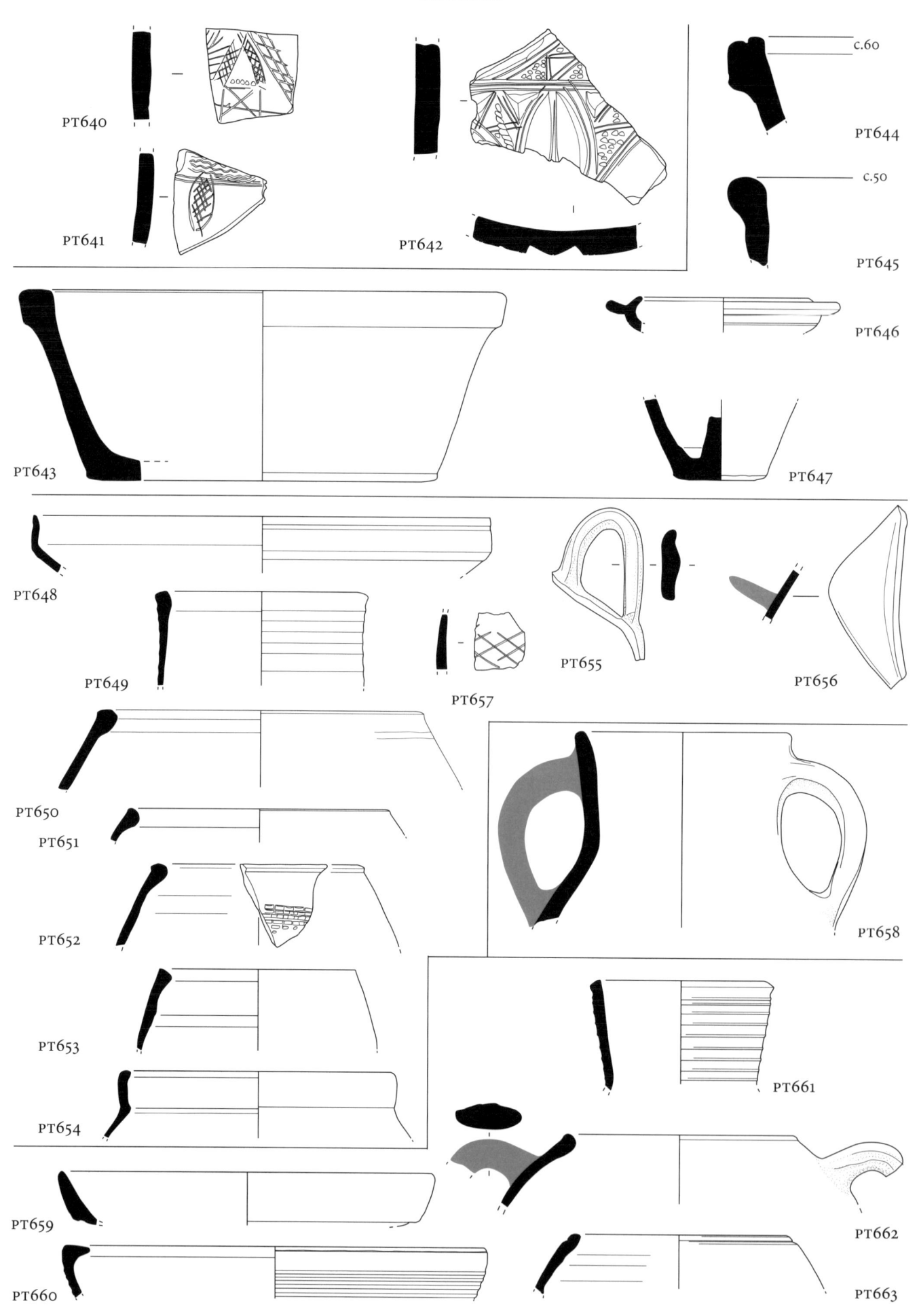

*Plate 42. Group G. Buff ware 10 (**PT640–642**); other buff wares (**PT643–647**); Cooking ware 2 (**PT648–657**); Cooking ware 9 (**PT658**); Cooking ware 10 (**PT659–663**). Scale 1:3.*

TRANSPORT AMPHORAE OF THE FIRST TO SEVENTH CENTURIES

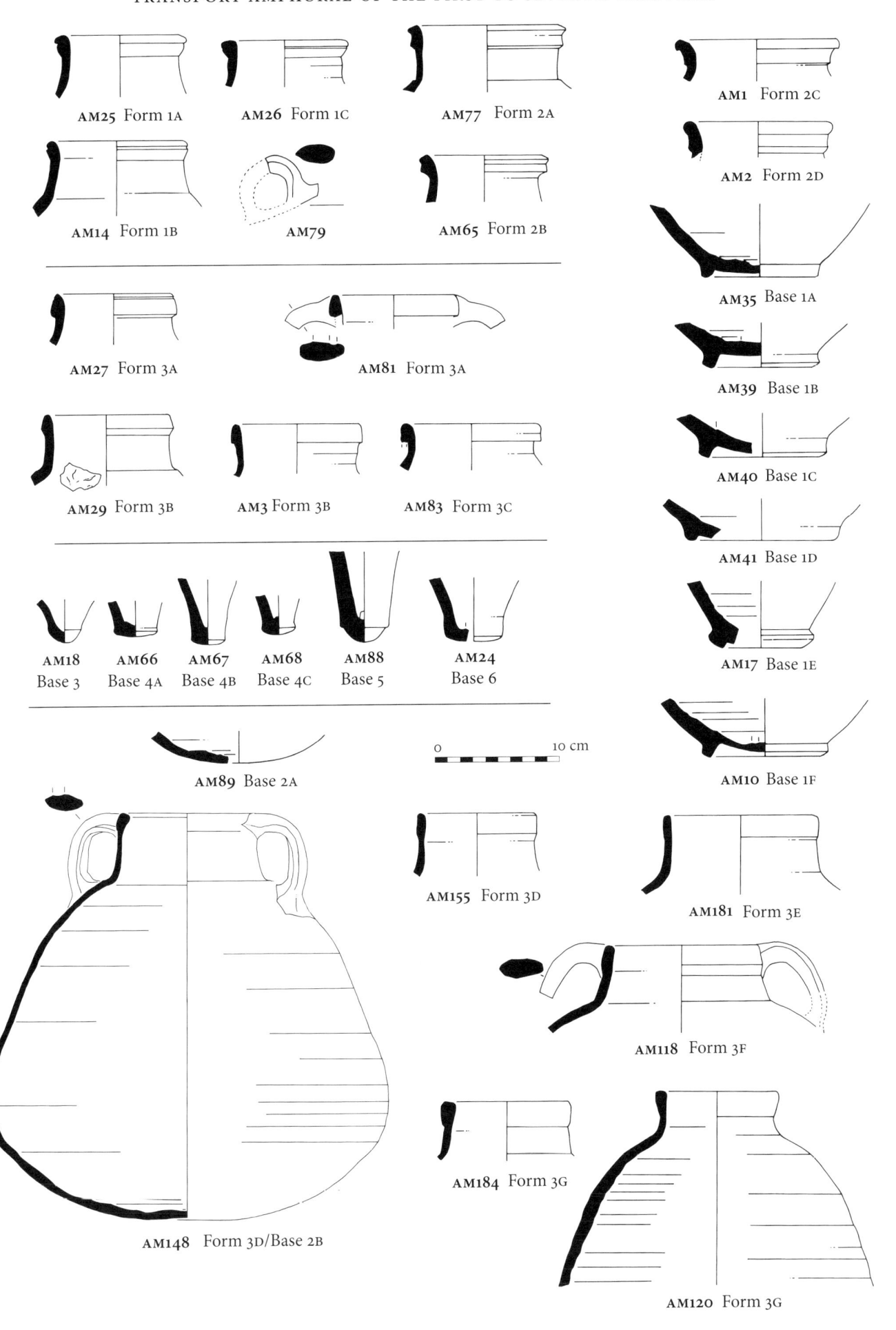

Plate 43. Typology. Form 1 to Form 3. Late Augustan/Tiberian to mid-third century A.D.

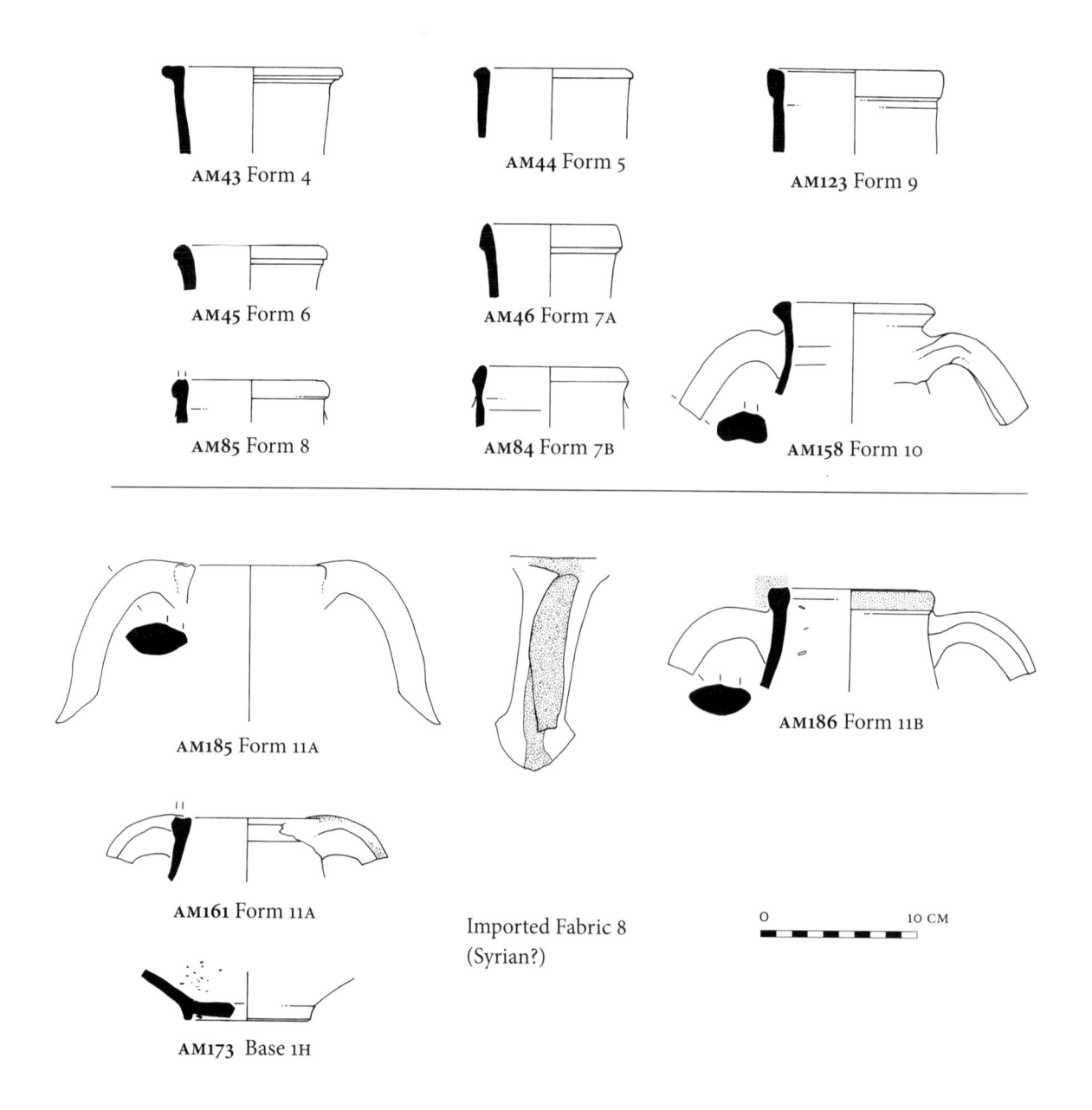

AM43 Form 4
AM44 Form 5
AM123 Form 9
AM45 Form 6
AM46 Form 7A
AM85 Form 8
AM84 Form 7B
AM158 Form 10
AM185 Form 11A
AM186 Form 11B
AM161 Form 11A
Imported Fabric 8 (Syrian?)
0   10 CM
AM173 Base 1H

Plate 44. Typology. Form 6 to Form 11. Late Augustan / Tiberian to mid-third century A.D.

TRANSPORT AMPHORAE OF THE FIRST TO SEVENTH CENTURIES

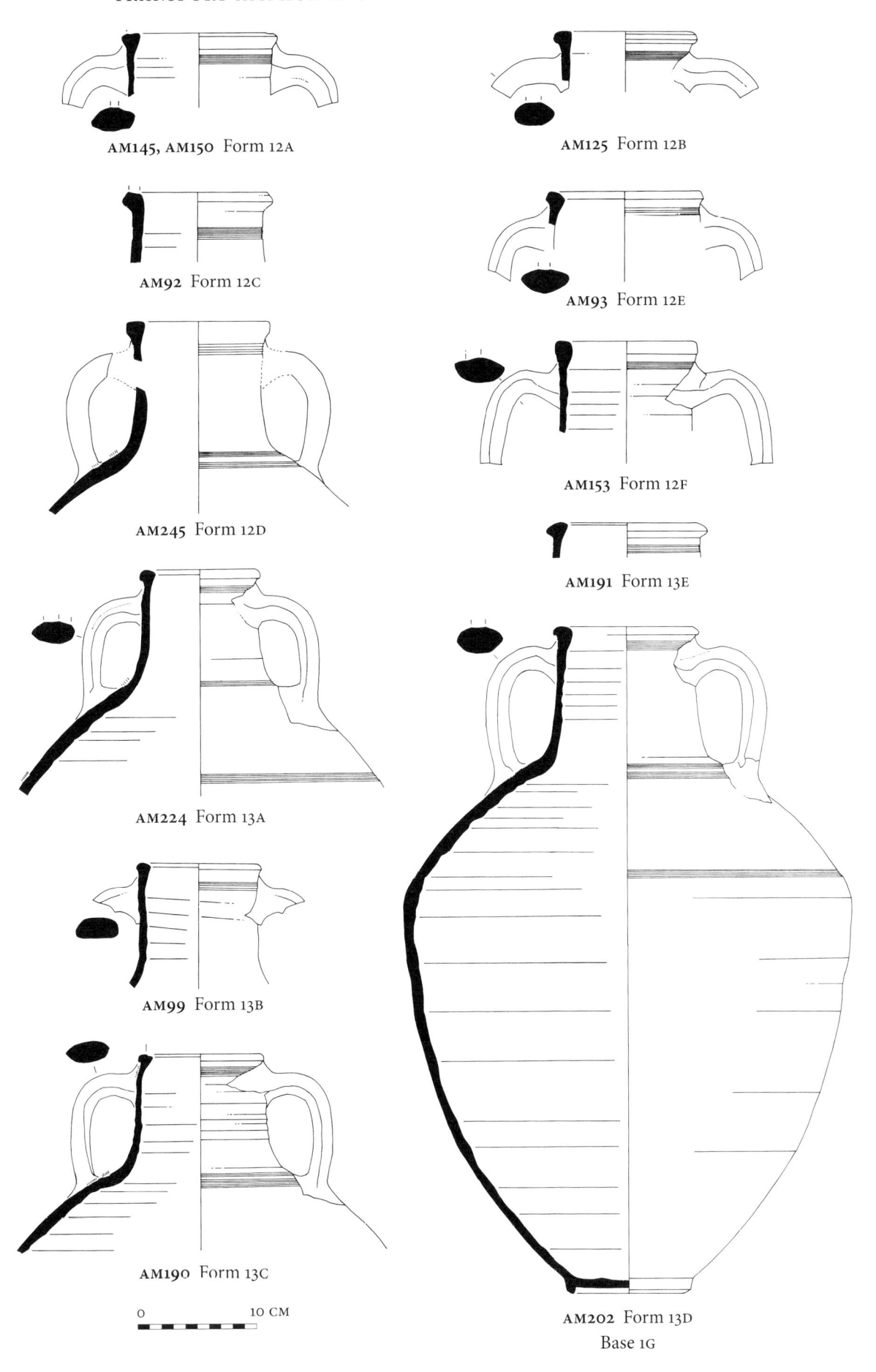

AM145, AM150 Form 12A

AM125 Form 12B

AM92 Form 12C

AM93 Form 12E

AM245 Form 12D

AM153 Form 12F

AM191 Form 13E

AM224 Form 13A

AM99 Form 13B

AM190 Form 13C

0　　　10 CM

AM202 Form 13D
Base 1G

Plate 45. Typology. Form 12 and Form 13 (Local Fabric 1). Mid-third century A.D.

REYNOLDS

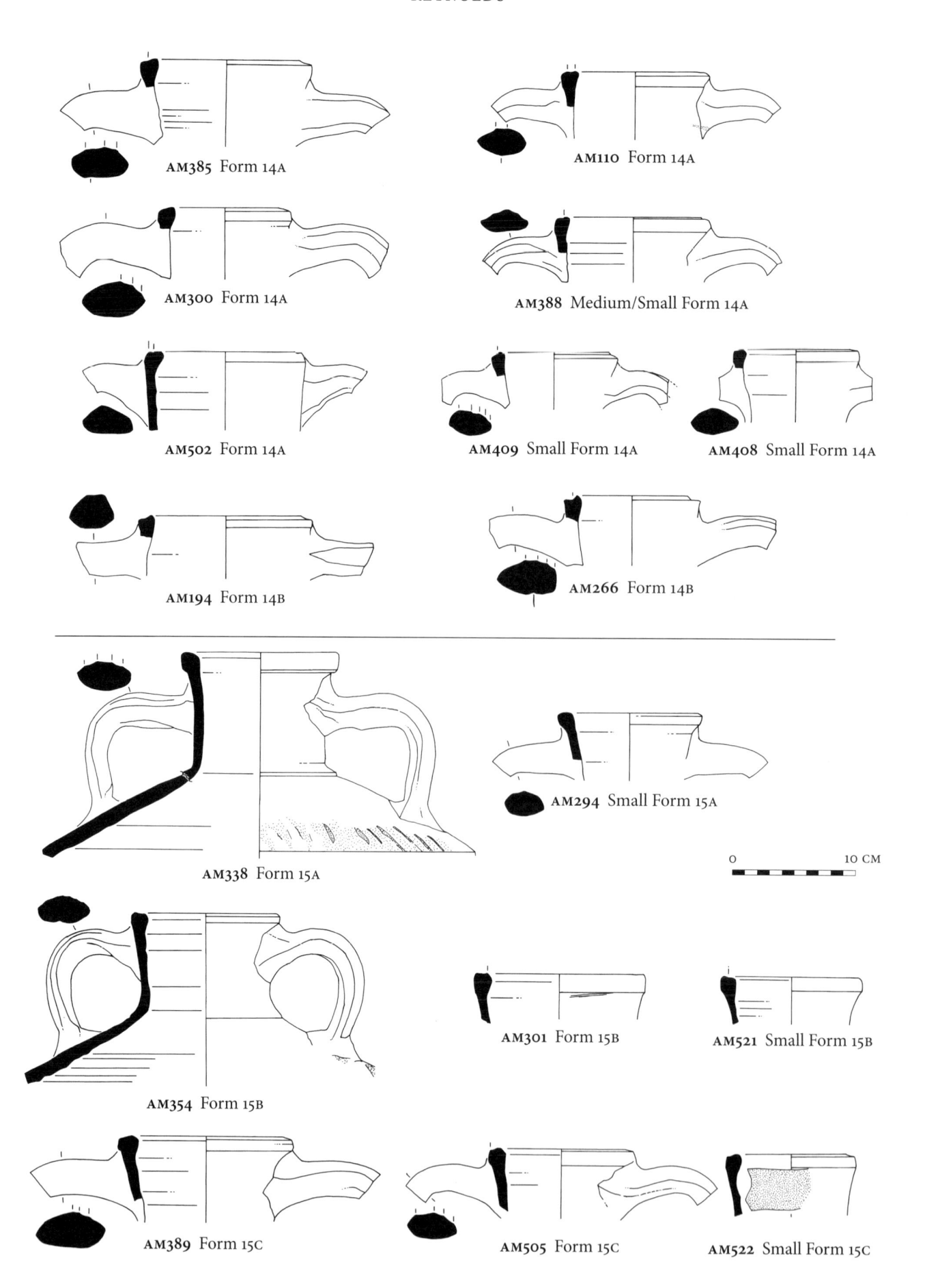

Plate 46. Typology. Form 14 and Form 15 (Syrian Fabric 13). Early seventh century A.D.

TRANSPORT AMPHORAE OF THE FIRST TO SEVENTH CENTURIES

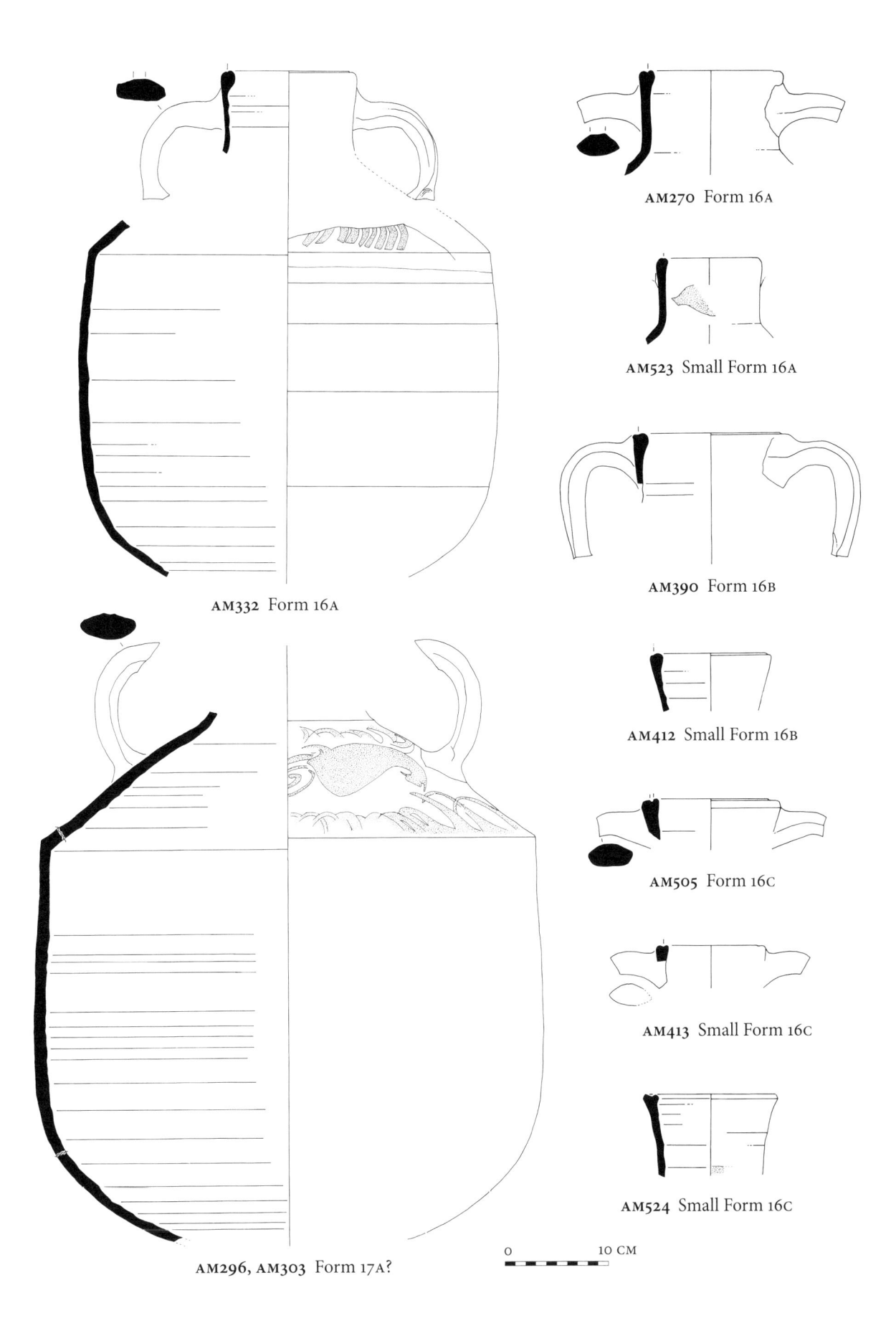

AM332 Form 16A

AM296, AM303 Form 17A?

AM270 Form 16A

AM523 Small Form 16A

AM390 Form 16B

AM412 Small Form 16B

AM505 Form 16C

AM413 Small Form 16C

AM524 Small Form 16C

0   10 CM

Plate 47. Typology. Form 16 (Syrian Fabric 13). Early seventh century A.D.

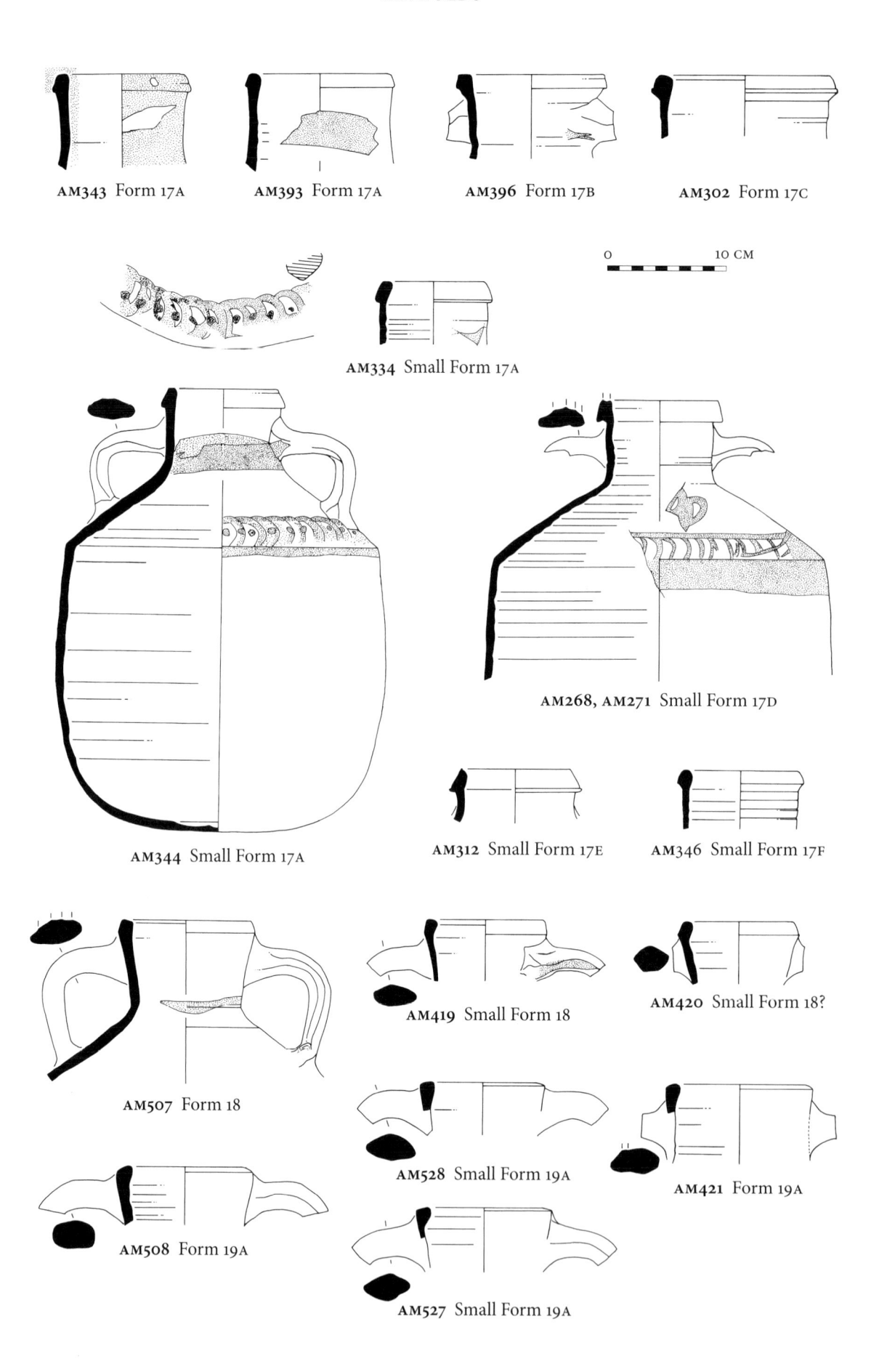

AM343 Form 17A   AM393 Form 17A   AM396 Form 17B   AM302 Form 17C

AM334 Small Form 17A

AM344 Small Form 17A

AM268, AM271 Small Form 17D

AM312 Small Form 17E   AM346 Small Form 17F

AM507 Form 18

AM419 Small Form 18   AM420 Small Form 18?

AM528 Small Form 19A   AM421 Form 19A

AM508 Form 19A

AM527 Small Form 19A

Plate 48. Typology. Form 17 to Form 19 (Syrian Fabric 13). Early seventh century A.D.

TRANSPORT AMPHORAE OF THE FIRST TO SEVENTH CENTURIES

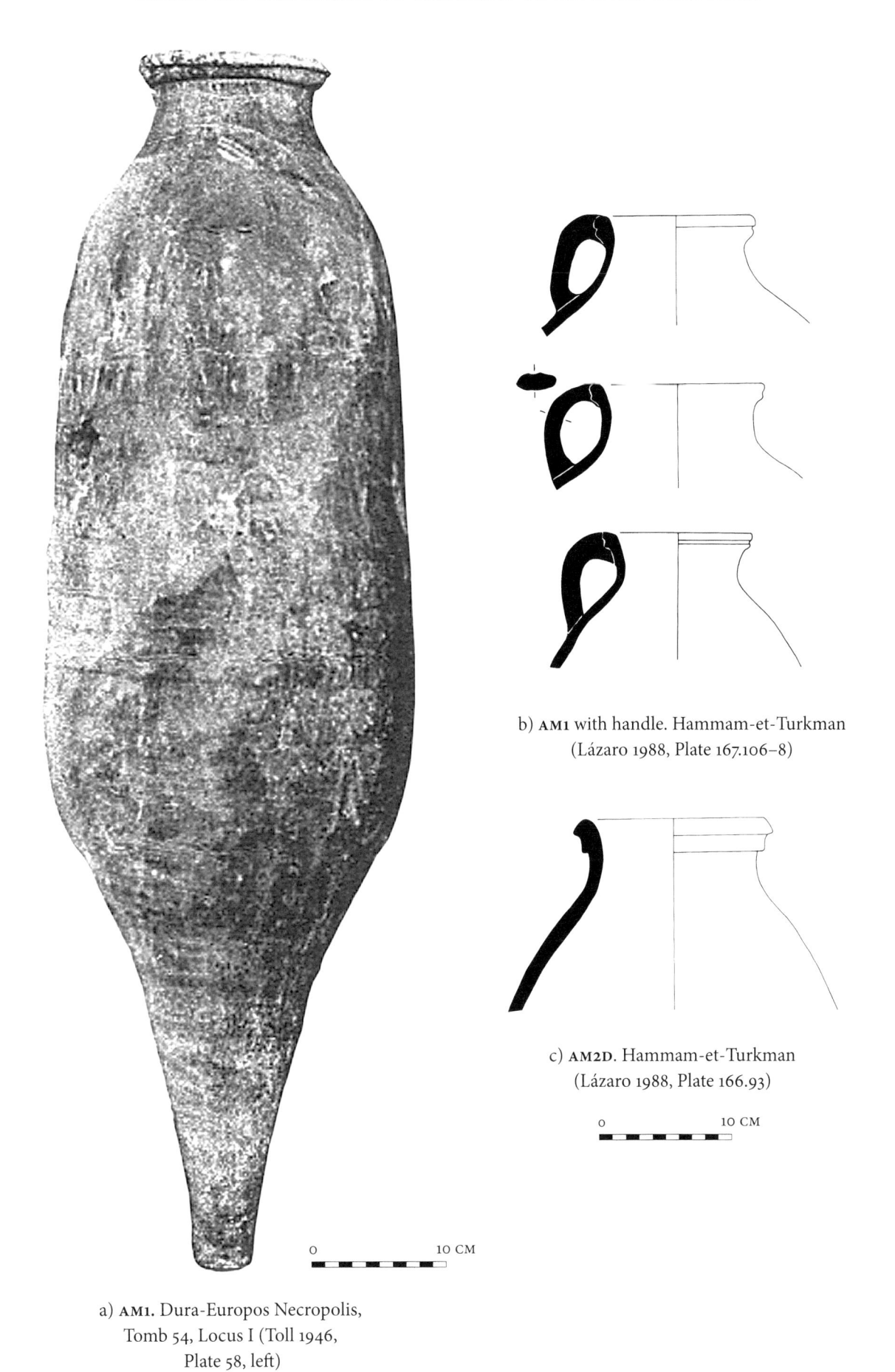

b) **AM1** with handle. Hammam-et-Turkman
(Lázaro 1988, Plate 167.106–8)

c) **AM2D**. Hammam-et-Turkman
(Lázaro 1988, Plate 166.93)

a) **AM1**. Dura-Europos Necropolis,
Tomb 54, Locus I (Toll 1946,
Plate 58, left)

Plate 49. Typology. Form 1 and Form 2 parallels from Dura-Europos and Hammam-et-Turkman.

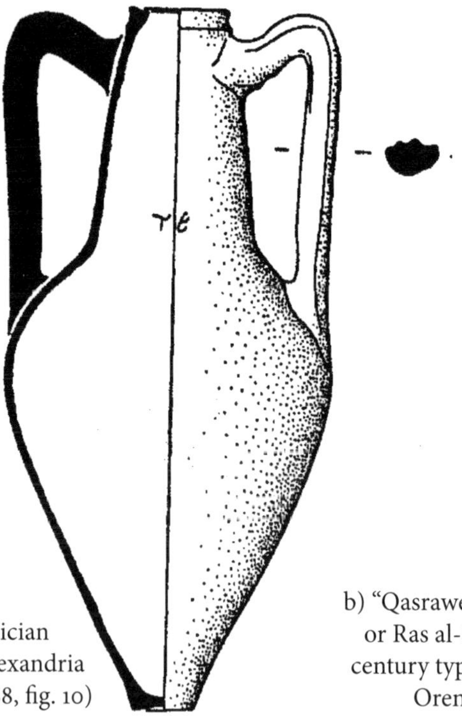

a) East Cilician Pompeii 5, Alexandria (Empereur 1988, fig. 10)

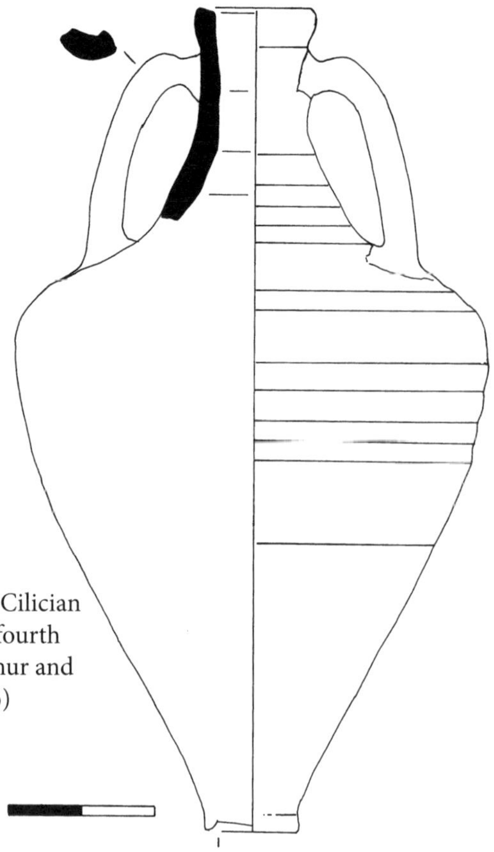

b) "Qasrawet 2530" East Cilician or Ras al-Basit, third–fourth century type (from Arthur and Oren 1998, fig. 5.9)

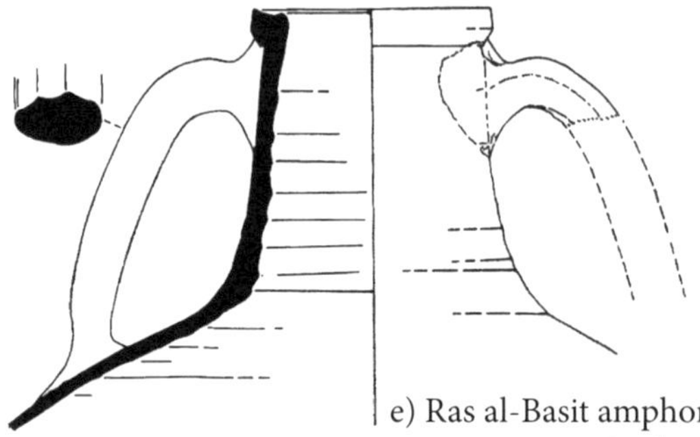

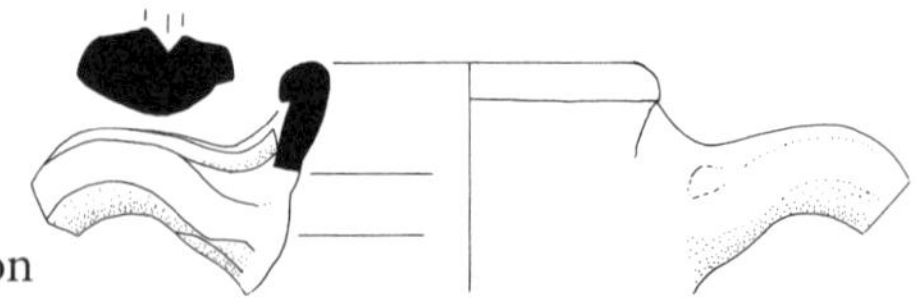

c) Ras al-Basit region 045.1242.34, early third century

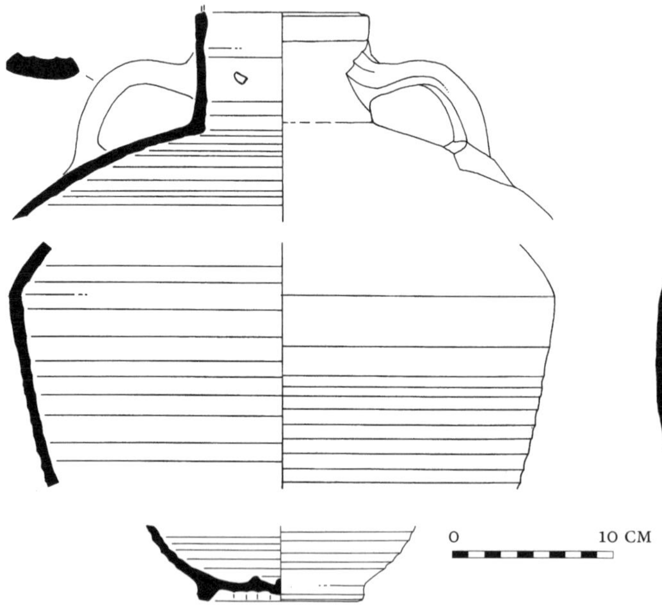

e) Ras al-Basit amphora, A.D. 100–150, Paphos (Hayes 1991, fig. 69.12)

f) Coastal Syrian "table amphora," Beirut 006.5256.13 and 27, A.D. 250–300?

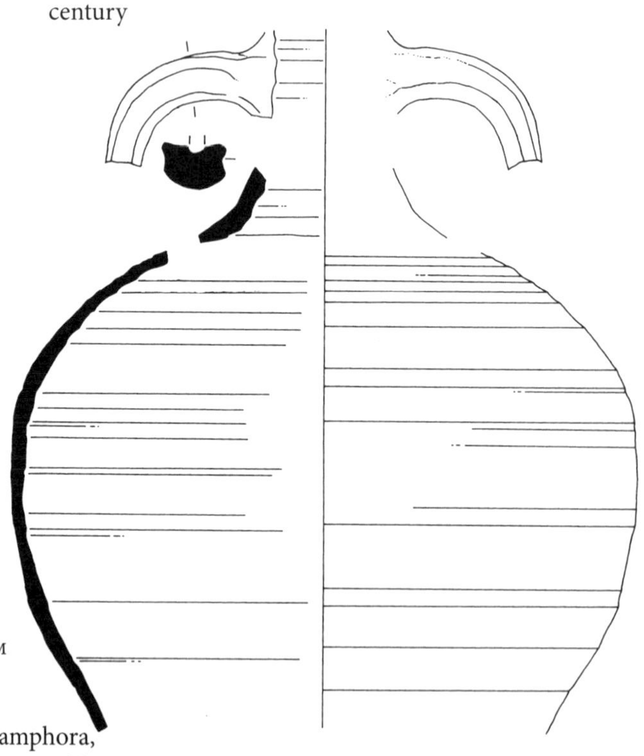

d) Ras al-Basit amphora, typical late, red-brown fabric 006.9429.68, c. A.D. 370–390

Plate 50. Typology. East Cilician and coastal Syrian (Ras al-Basit region) amphora types, mid-first to fourth centuries A.D.

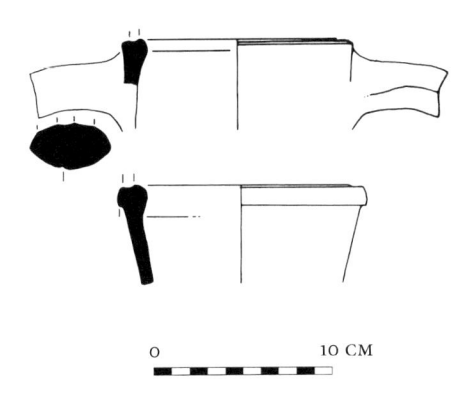

TRANSPORT AMPHORAE OF THE FIRST TO SEVENTH CENTURIES

a–b) Jabbul Plain Survey
(Aleppo): Site JP 99,
Form 16A (top) and Form 15C

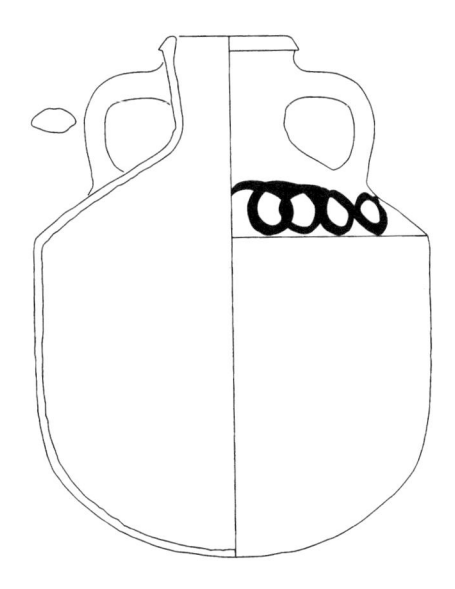

c) Déhès, Small Form 17A
(Bavant and Orssaud 2001,
fig. 5.25), early seventh century
(not to scale)

Plate 51. Typology. Form 15, 16, and 17 parallels from the Jabbul Plain and Déhès.

Context 7118

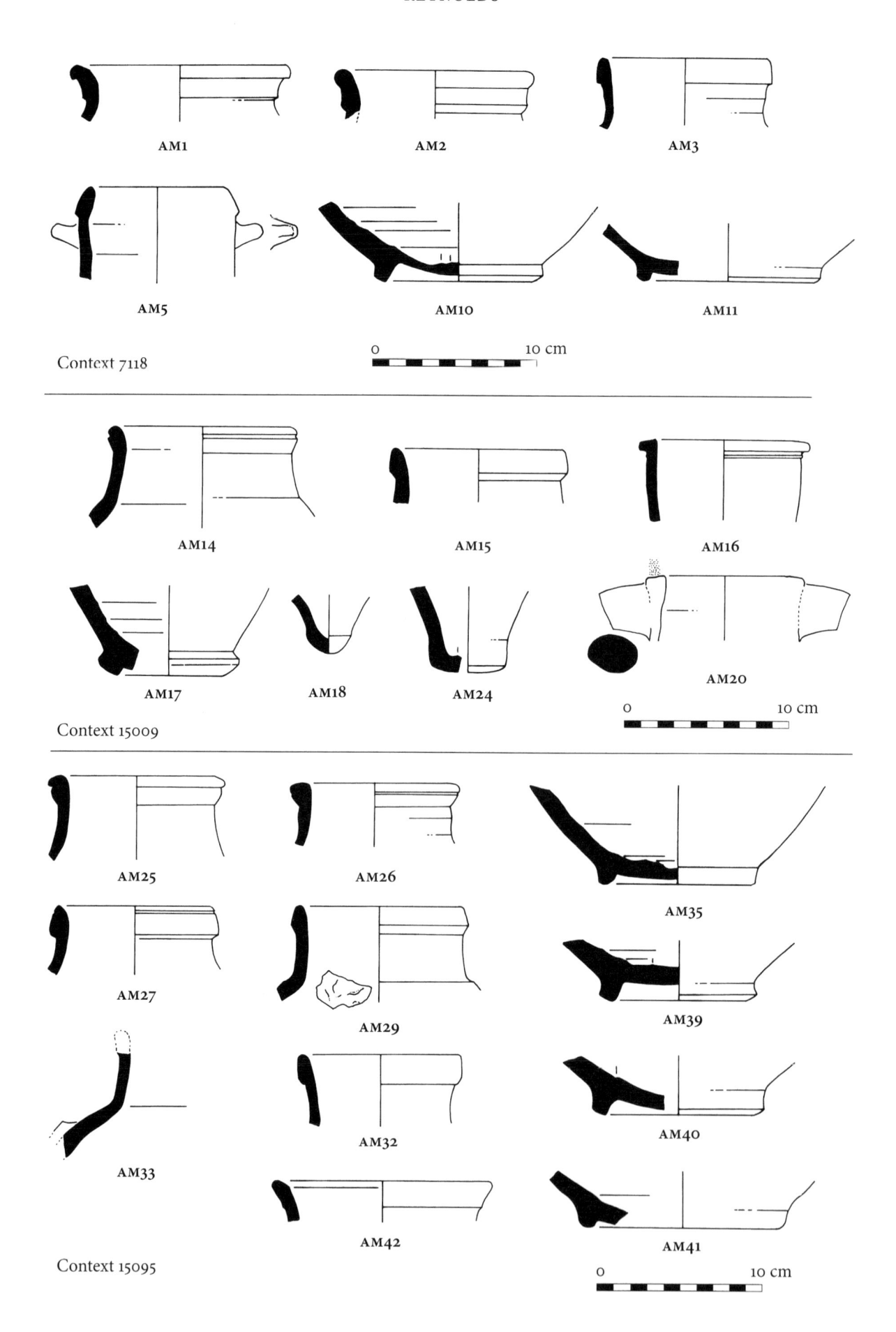

Context 15009

Context 15095

Plate 52. Contexts 7118, 15009, and 15095. Late Augustan/Tiberian.

TRANSPORT AMPHORAE OF THE FIRST TO SEVENTH CENTURIES

AM43
AM44
AM52
AM54
AM61
AM45
AM46
Late Augustan-Tiberian
Context 15095

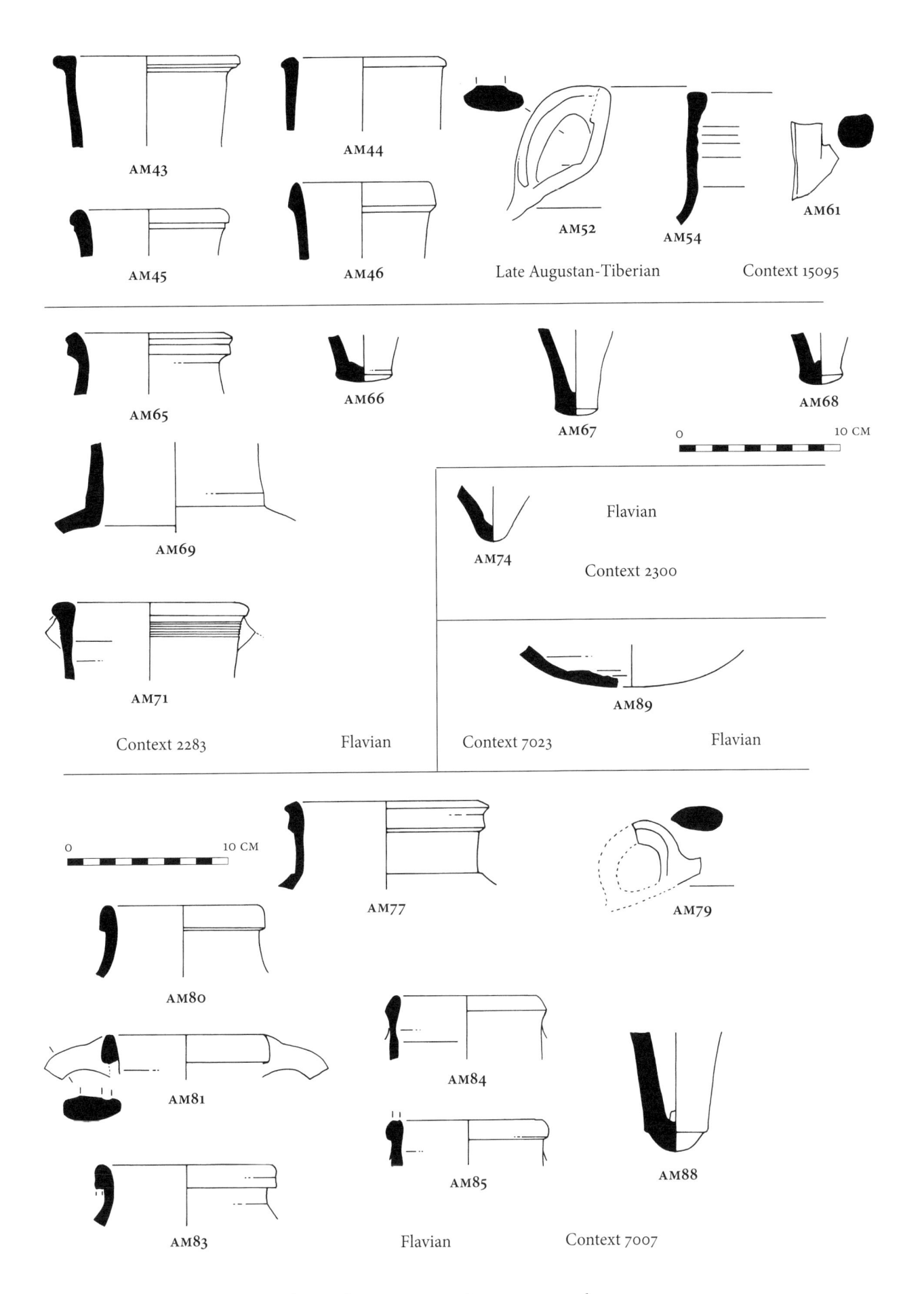

AM65
AM66
AM67
AM68
AM69
AM74
Flavian
Context 2300
AM71
AM89
Context 2283
Flavian
Context 7023
Flavian

AM77
AM79
AM80
AM81
AM84
AM85
AM88
AM83
Flavian
Context 7007

Plate 53. Contexts 15095, 2283, 2300, 7023, and 7007.

AM92 AM93

AM99

AM100

AM110

0   10 CM

Context 2010

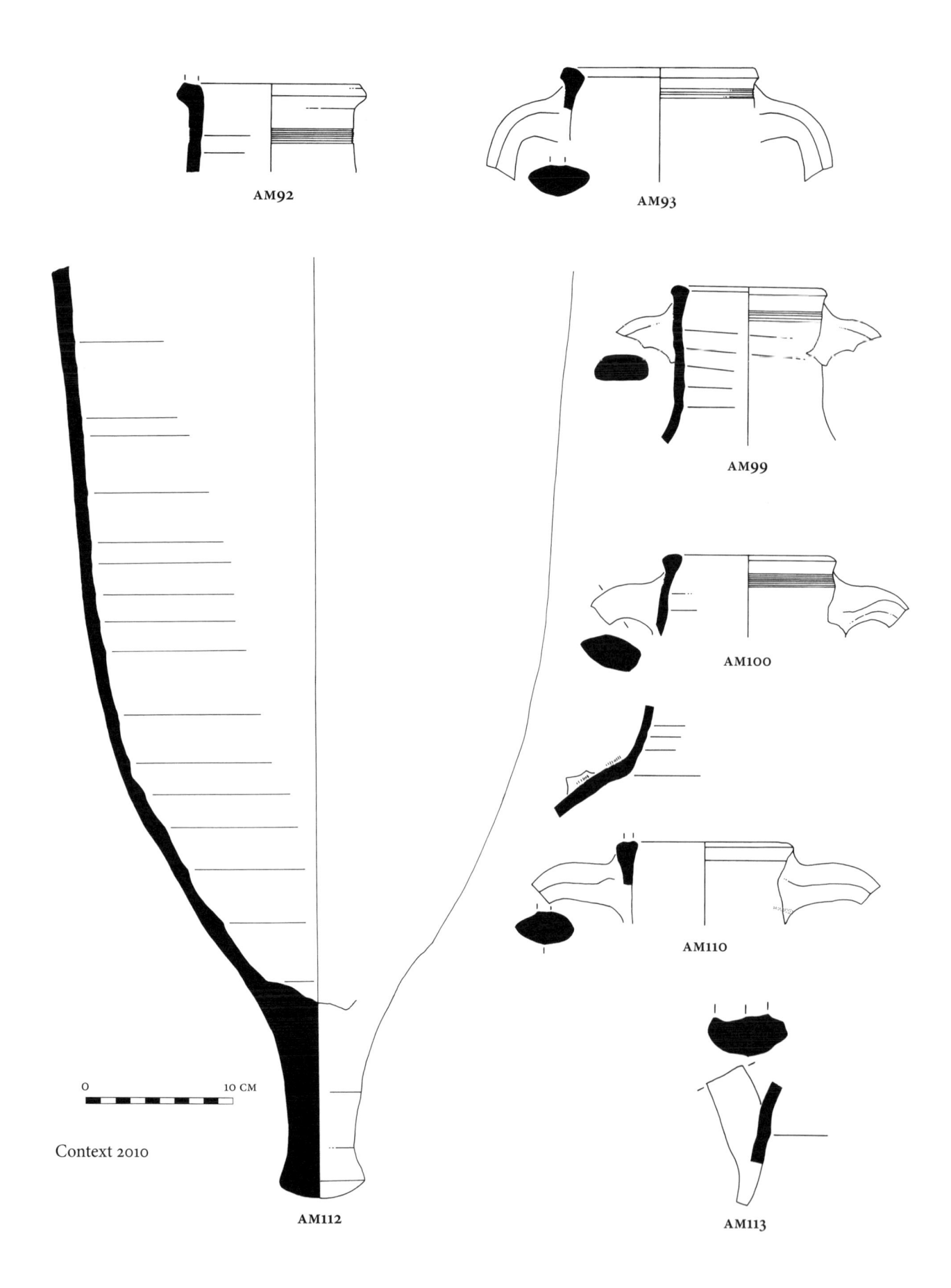

AM112 AM113

Plate 54. Context 2010. Mid-third century A.D.

TRANSPORT AMPHORAE OF THE FIRST TO SEVENTH CENTURIES

AM115

0 10 CM

AM116

Context 2011

Context 2012

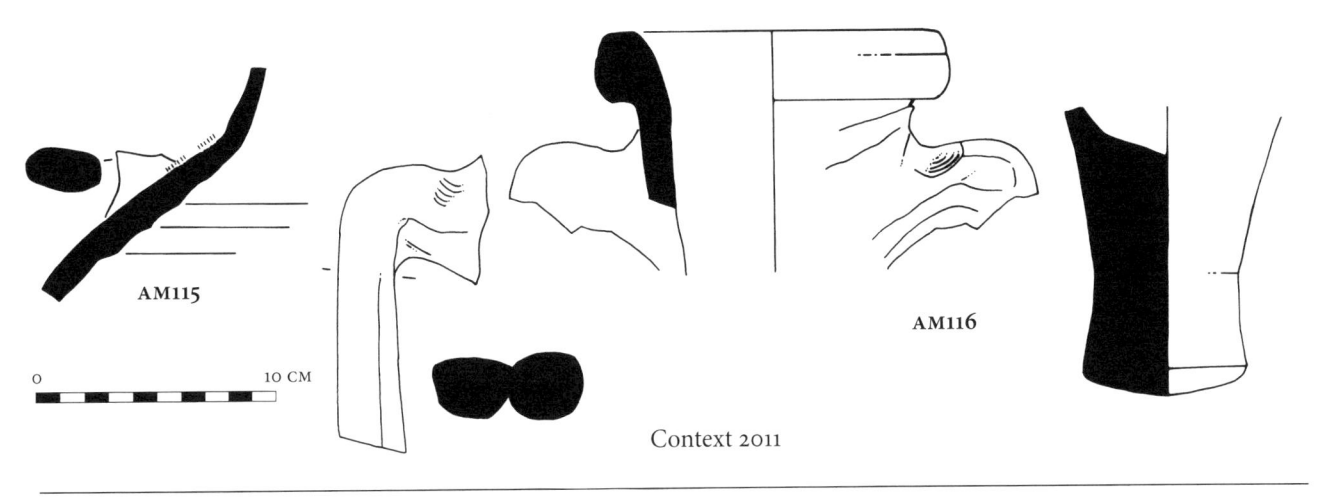

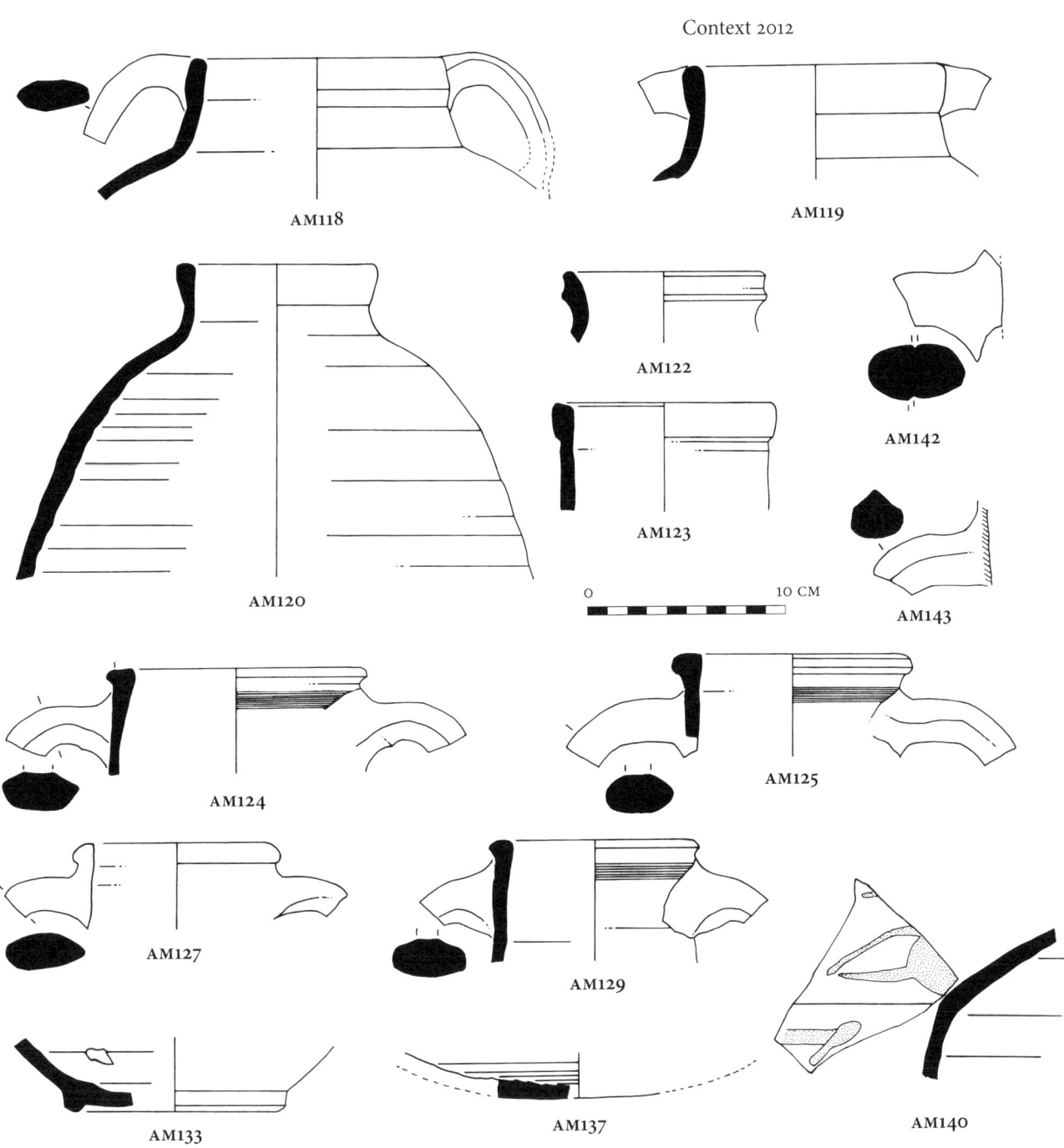

AM118

AM119

AM120

AM122

AM123

AM142

0 10 CM

AM143

AM124

AM125

AM127

AM129

AM133

AM137

AM140

Plate 55. Contexts 2011 and 2012. Mid-third century A.D.

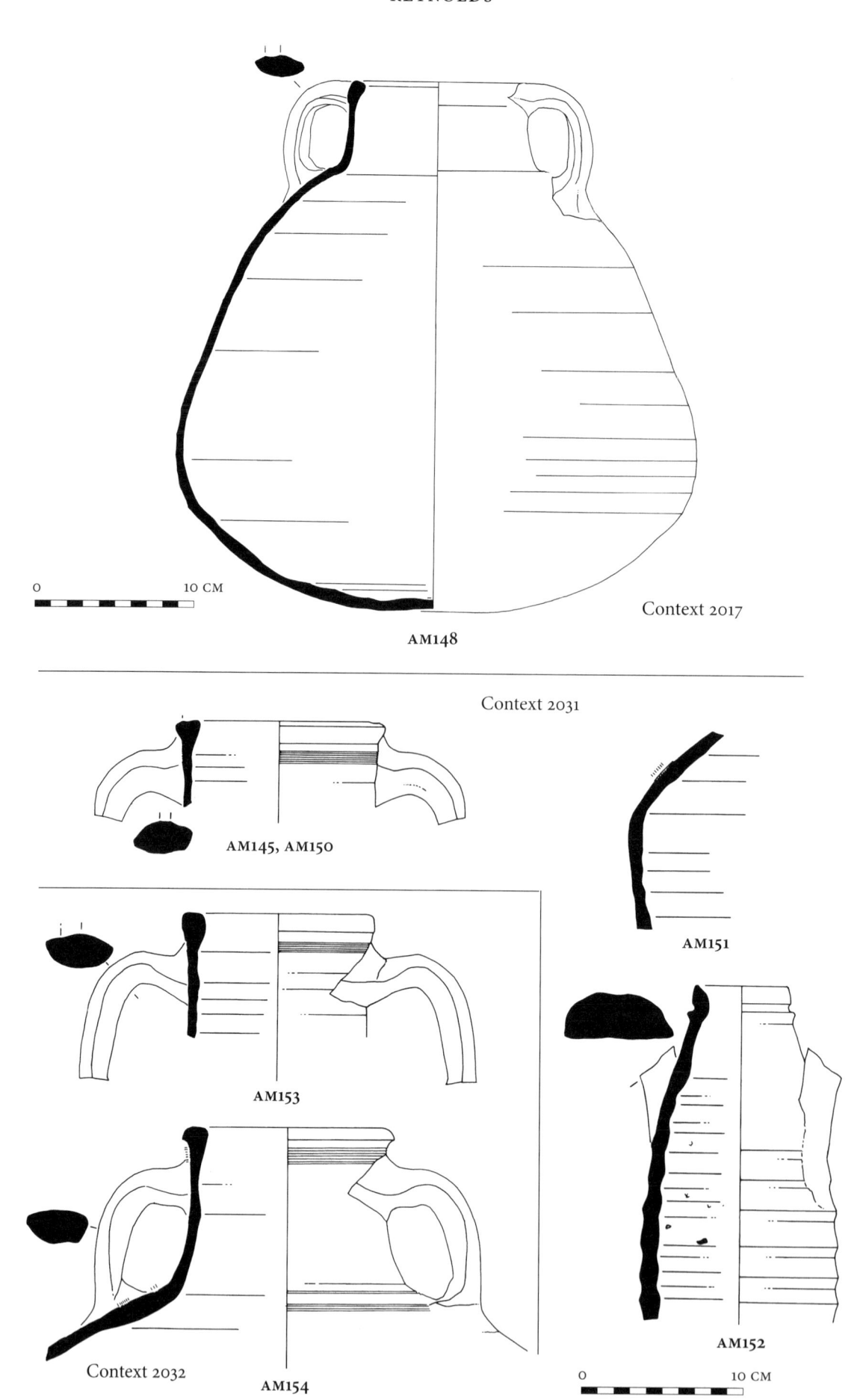

Plate 56. Contexts 2017, 2031, and 2032. Mid-third century A.D.

TRANSPORT AMPHORAE OF THE FIRST TO SEVENTH CENTURIES

AM155
AM156
AM158
AM157
AM160
AM161
AM162
AM164
AM165
AM170
AM168
AM169
AM171
AM173
AM174
AM175
AM178

Context 2039

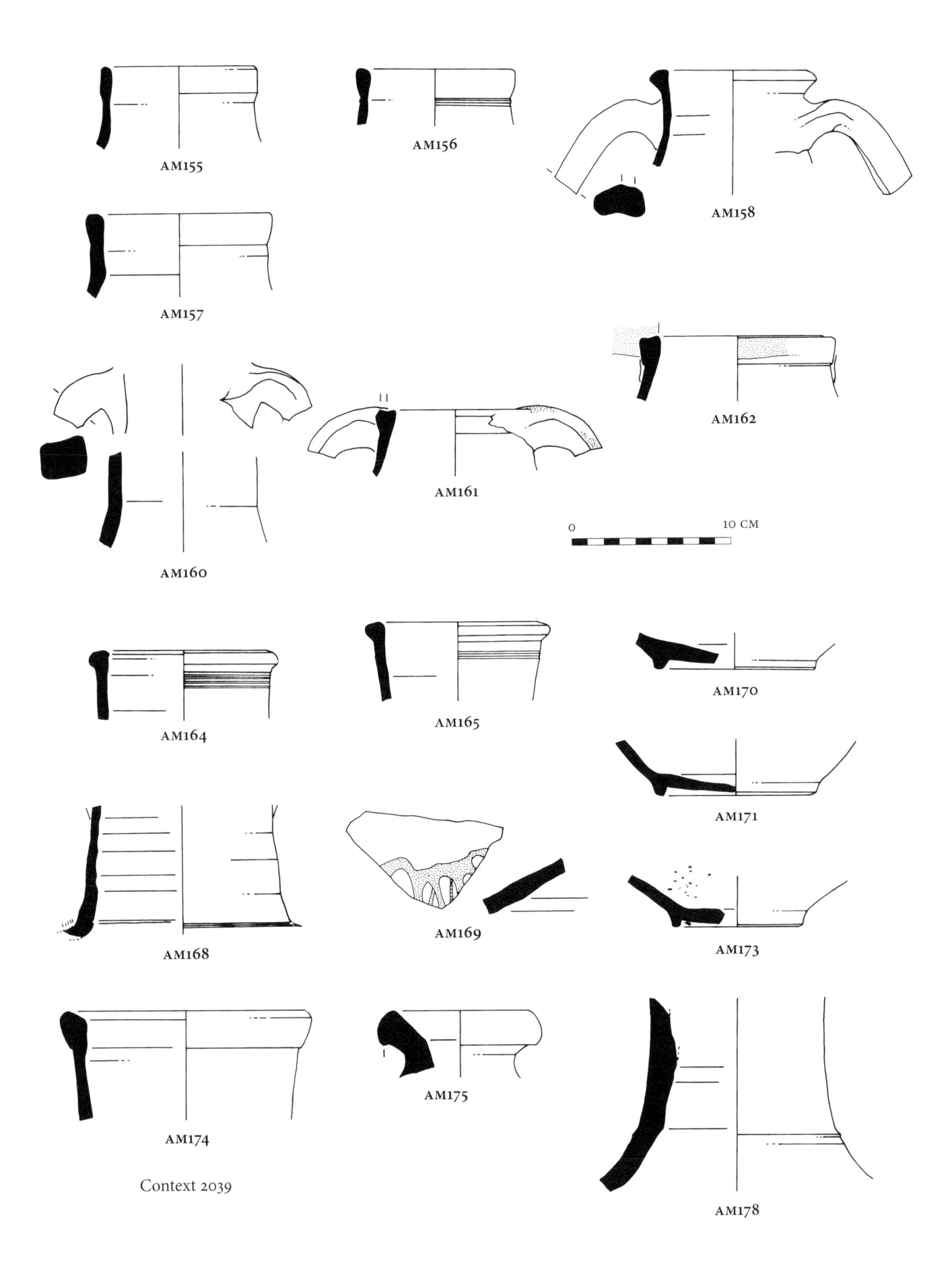

Plate 57. Context 2039. Mid-third century A.D.

AM181
AM182
AM184
AM183
AM185
AM186
AM189
AM191
AM190
AM194
AM195
AM196
AM197
AM198

Context 2080

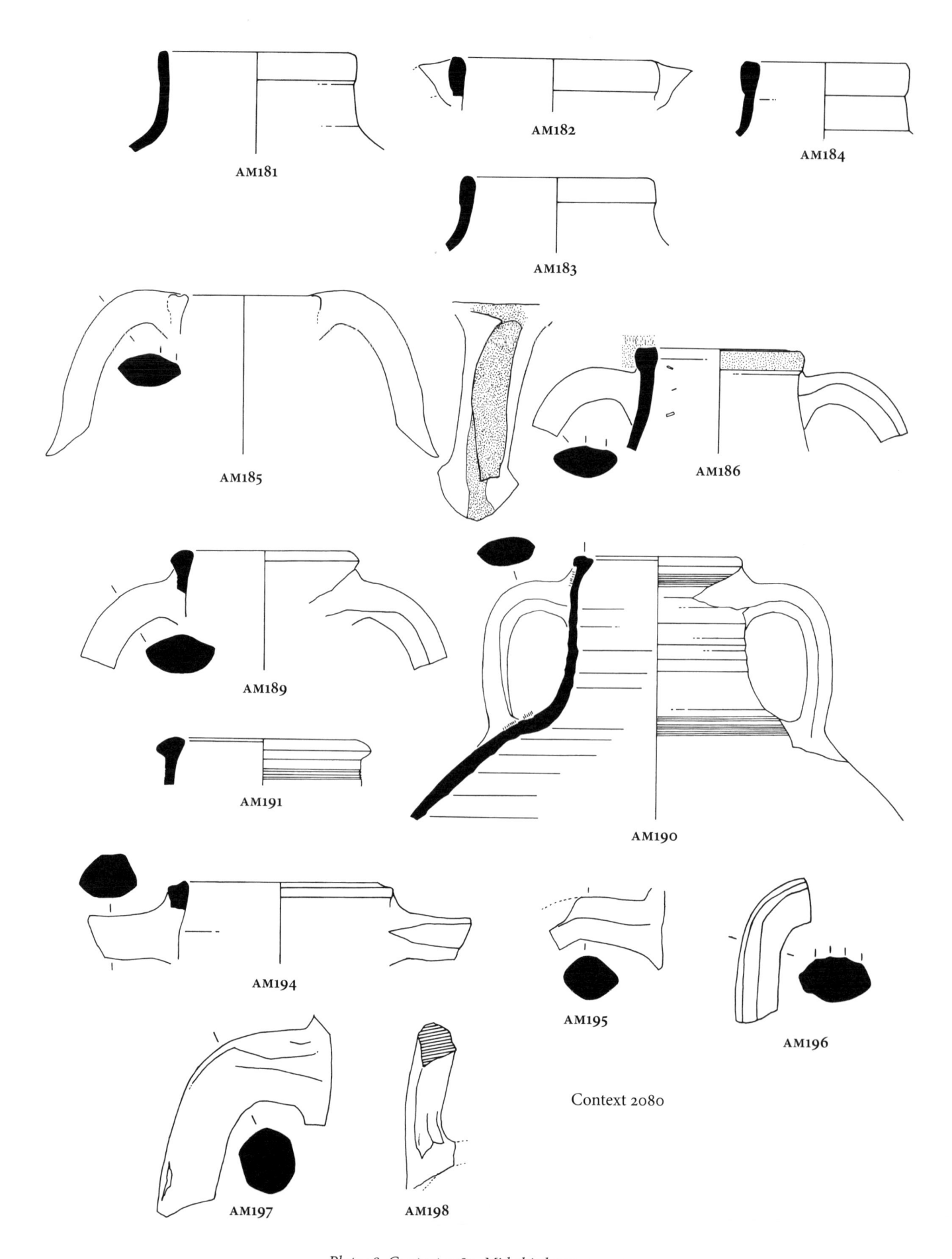

Plate 58. Context 2080. Mid-third century A.D.

TRANSPORT AMPHORAE OF THE FIRST TO SEVENTH CENTURIES

AM203

Context 2139

AM202

Context 2086

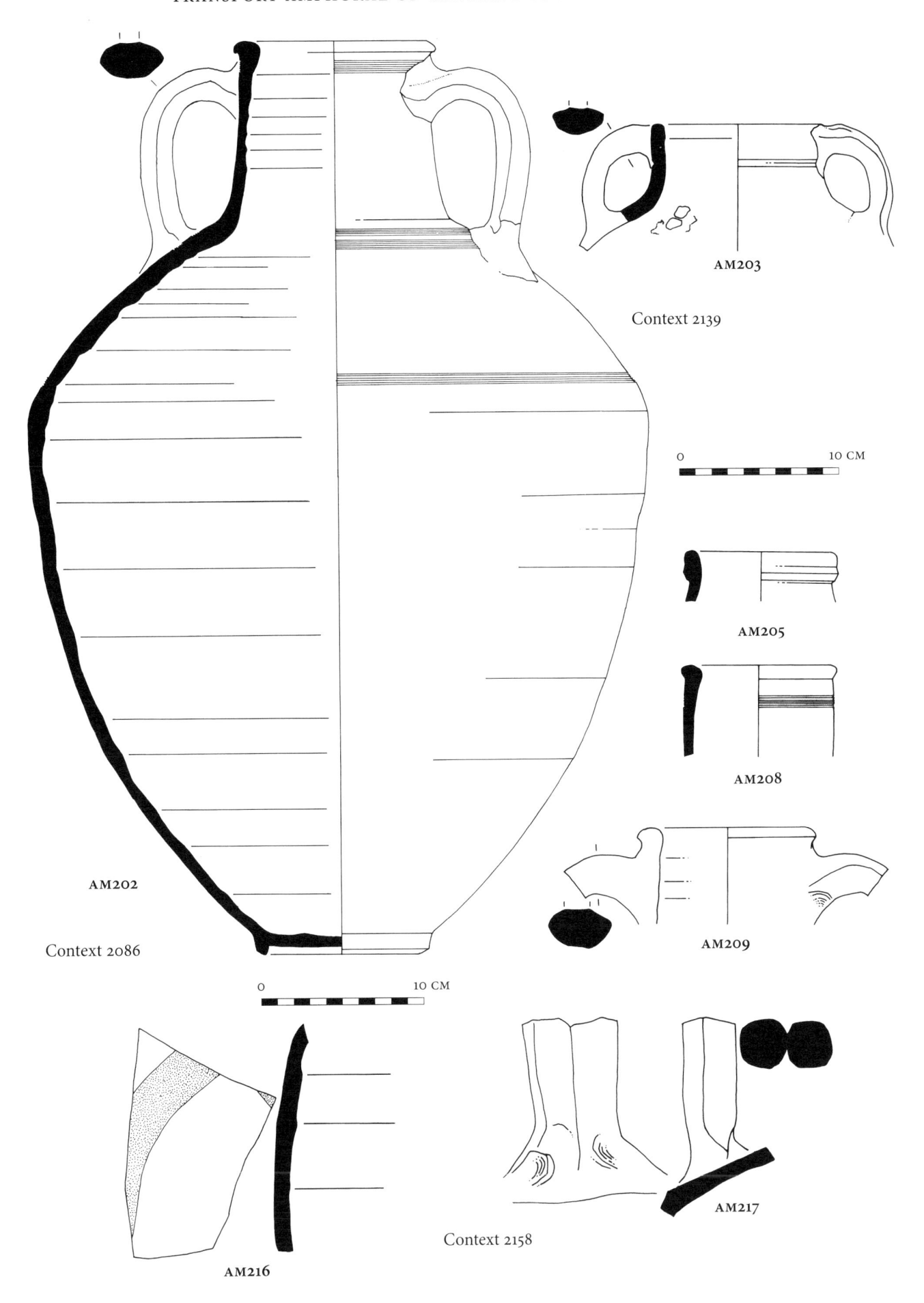

AM205

AM208

AM209

AM216

Context 2158

AM217

Plate 59. Context 2086, 2139, and 2158. Mid-third century A.D.

AM223

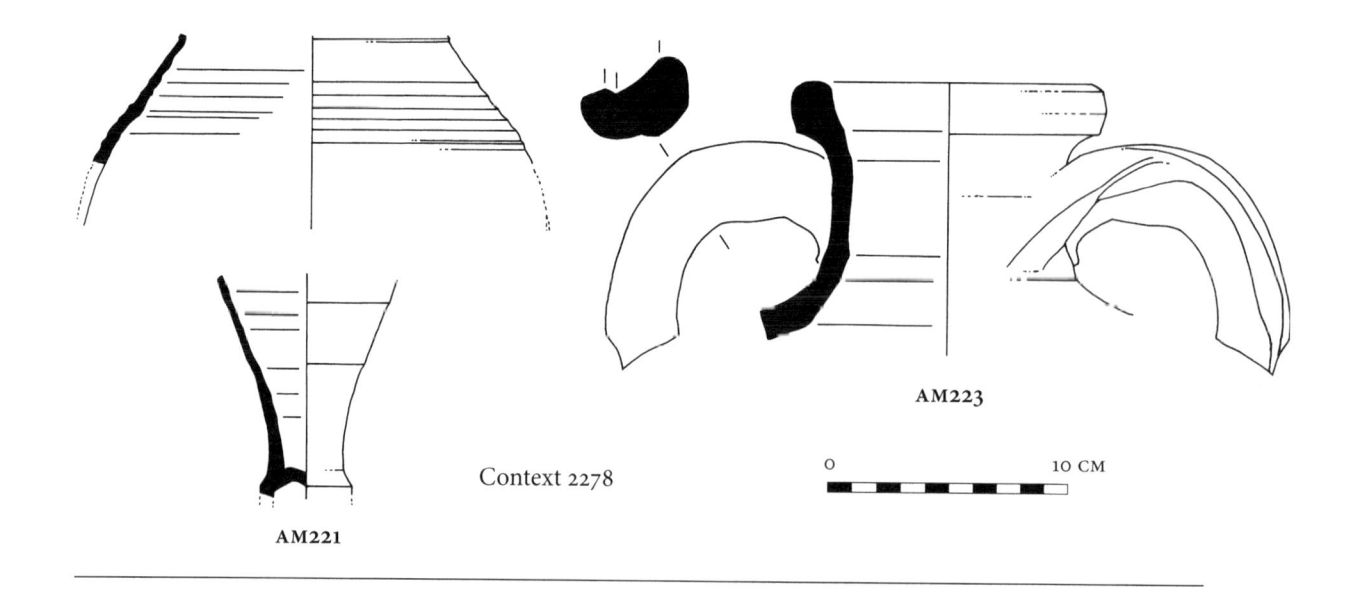

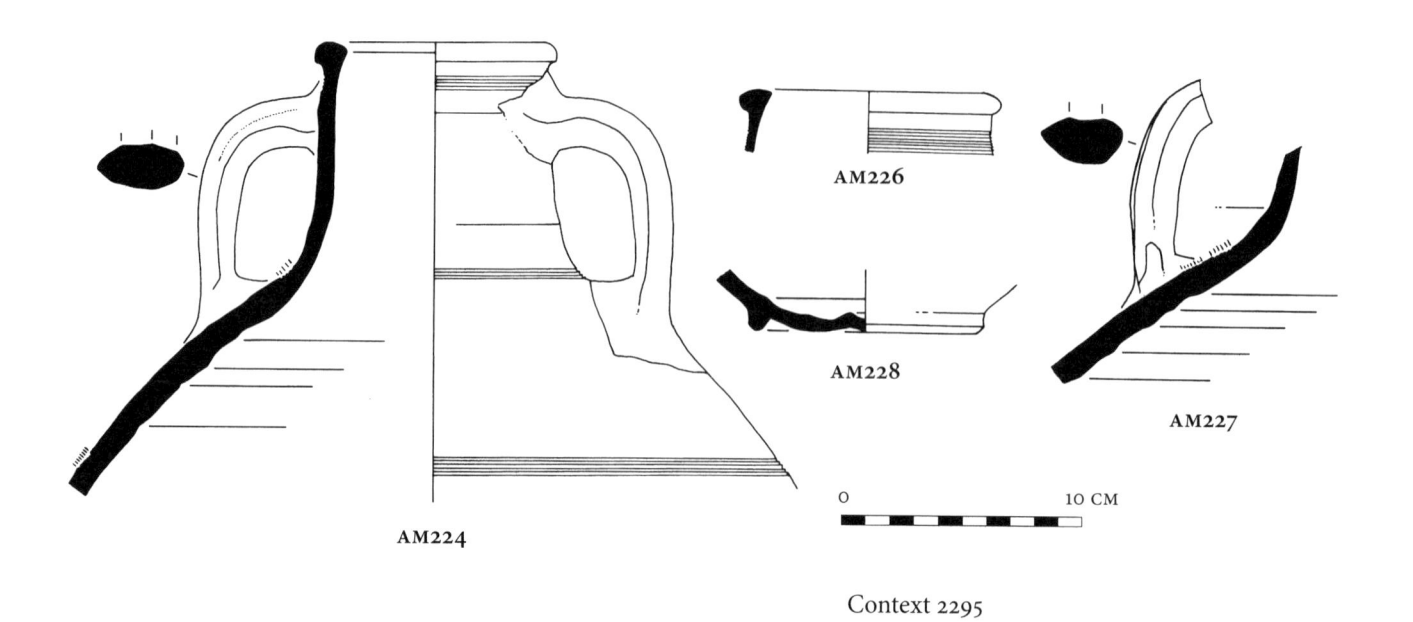

Context 2278

AM221

AM224

AM226

AM228

AM227

Context 2295

Plate 60. Contexts 2278 and 2295. Mid-third century A.D.

TRANSPORT AMPHORAE OF THE FIRST TO SEVENTH CENTURIES

AM238

AM239

AM242

AM245

AM246

AM244

Context 18108

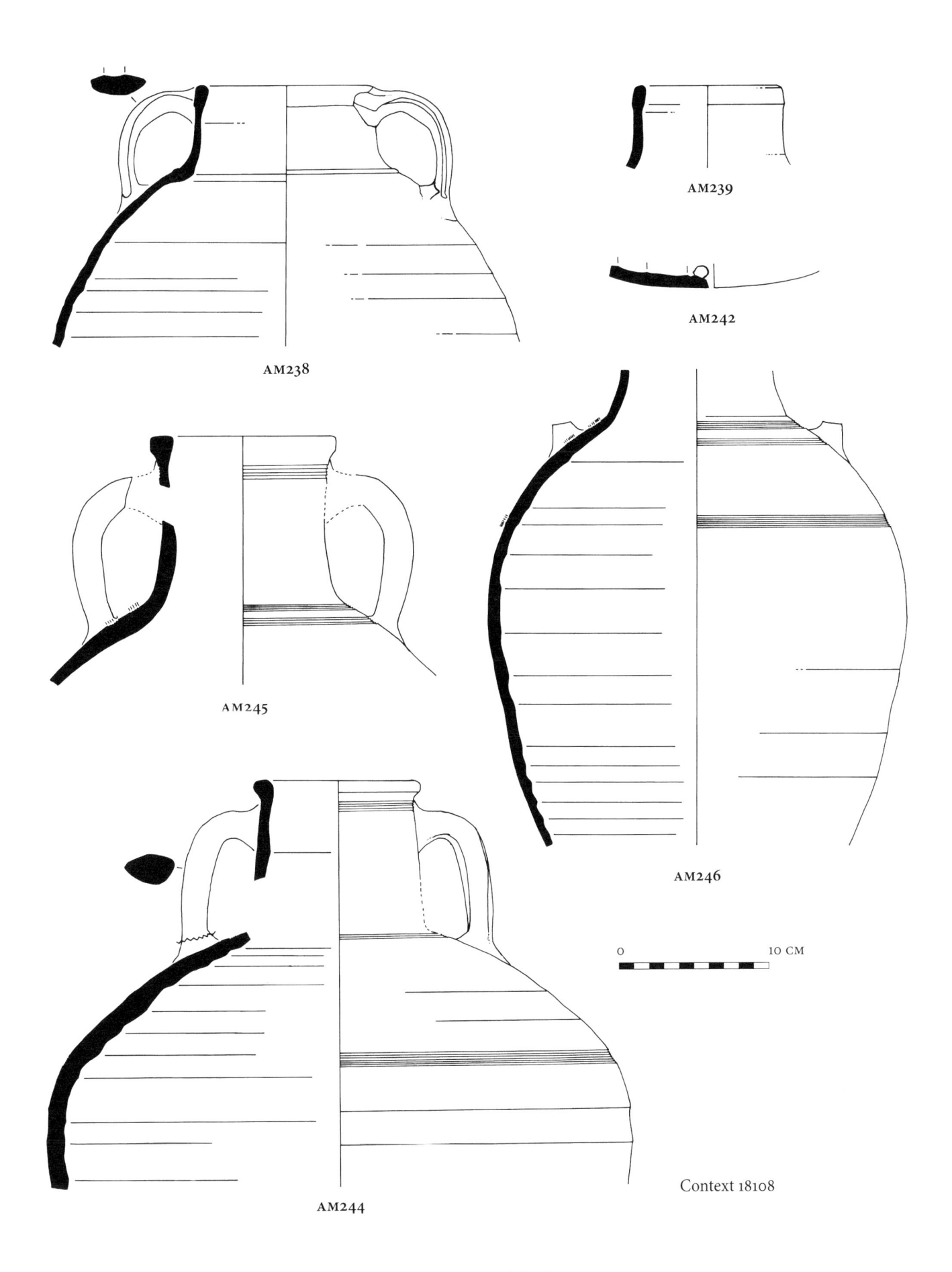

Plate 61. Context 18108. Mid-third century A.D.

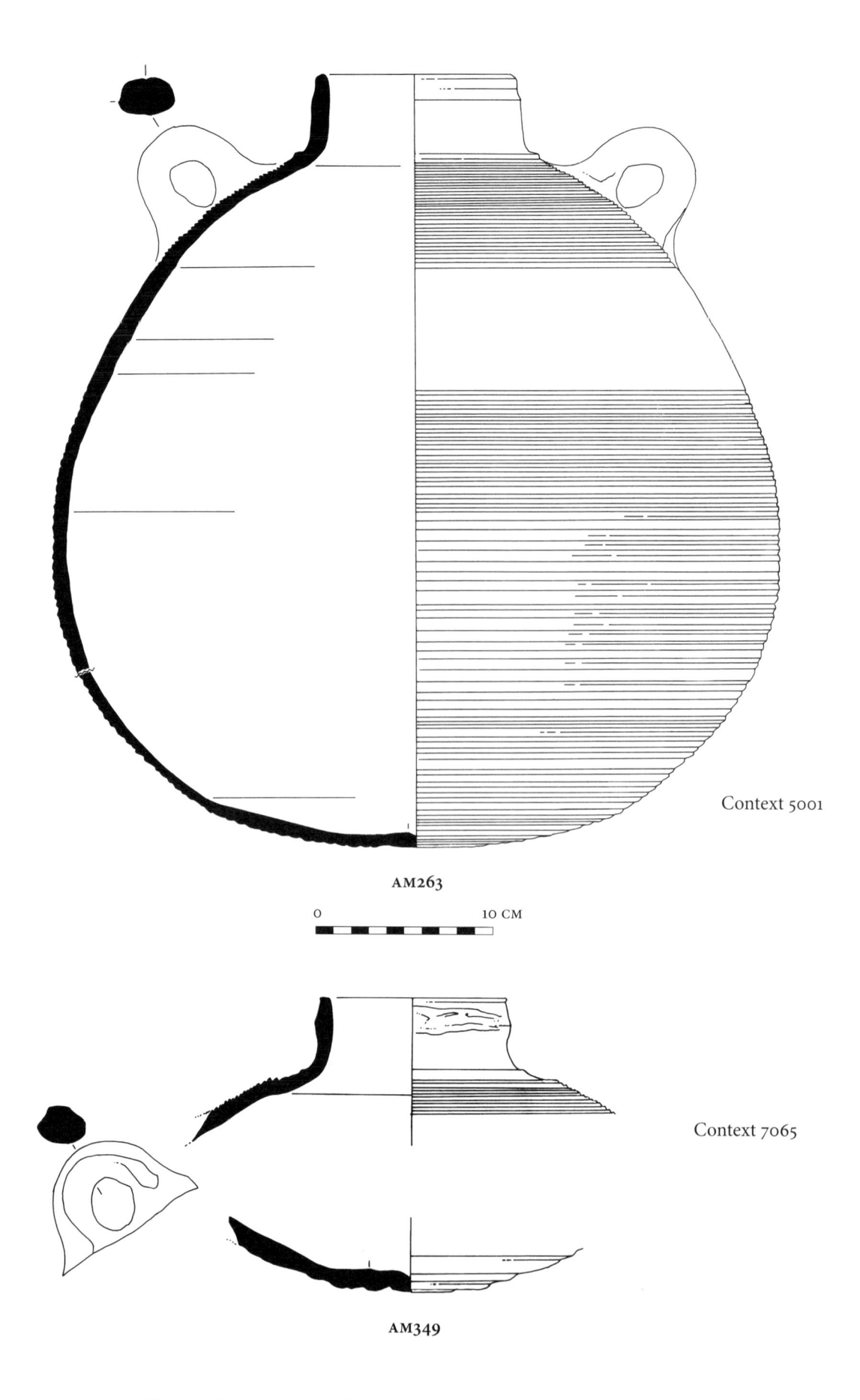

Plate 62. Contexts 5001 and 7065. Palestinian LRA 5. Early seventh century A.D.

TRANSPORT AMPHORAE OF THE FIRST TO SEVENTH CENTURIES

Context 5034

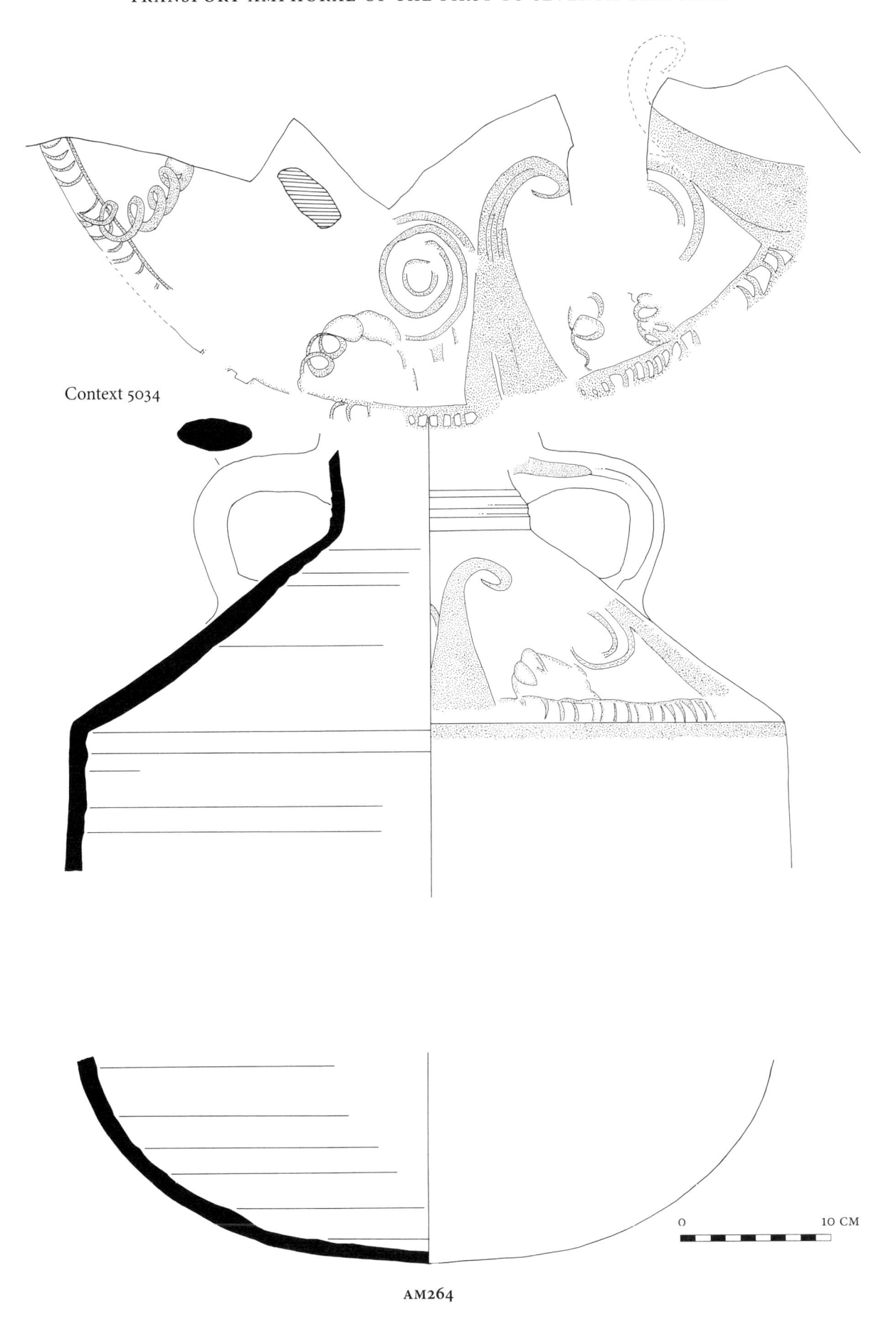

AM264

Plate 63. Context 5034.1. Large Form 17A. Early seventh century A.D.

REYNOLDS

Context 7003

AM265   AM266   AM267

0   10 CM

Context 7004

AM270   AM268, AM271

AM273

Context 7005

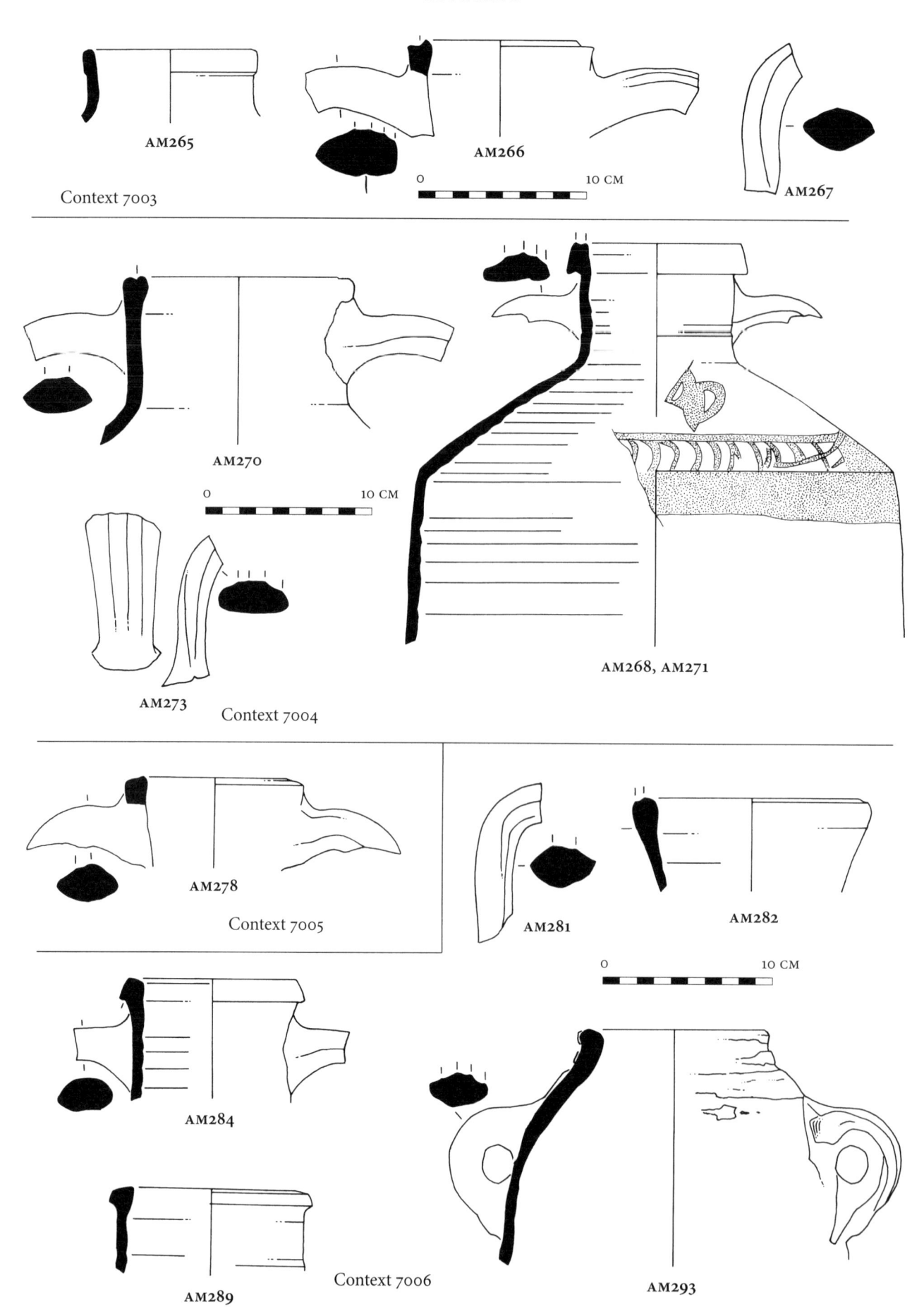

AM278   AM281   AM282

0   10 CM

AM284

AM289   Context 7006   AM293

Plate 64. Contexts 7003, 7004, 7005, and 7006. Early seventh century A.D.

AM294

AM295

Context 7026

Context 7060

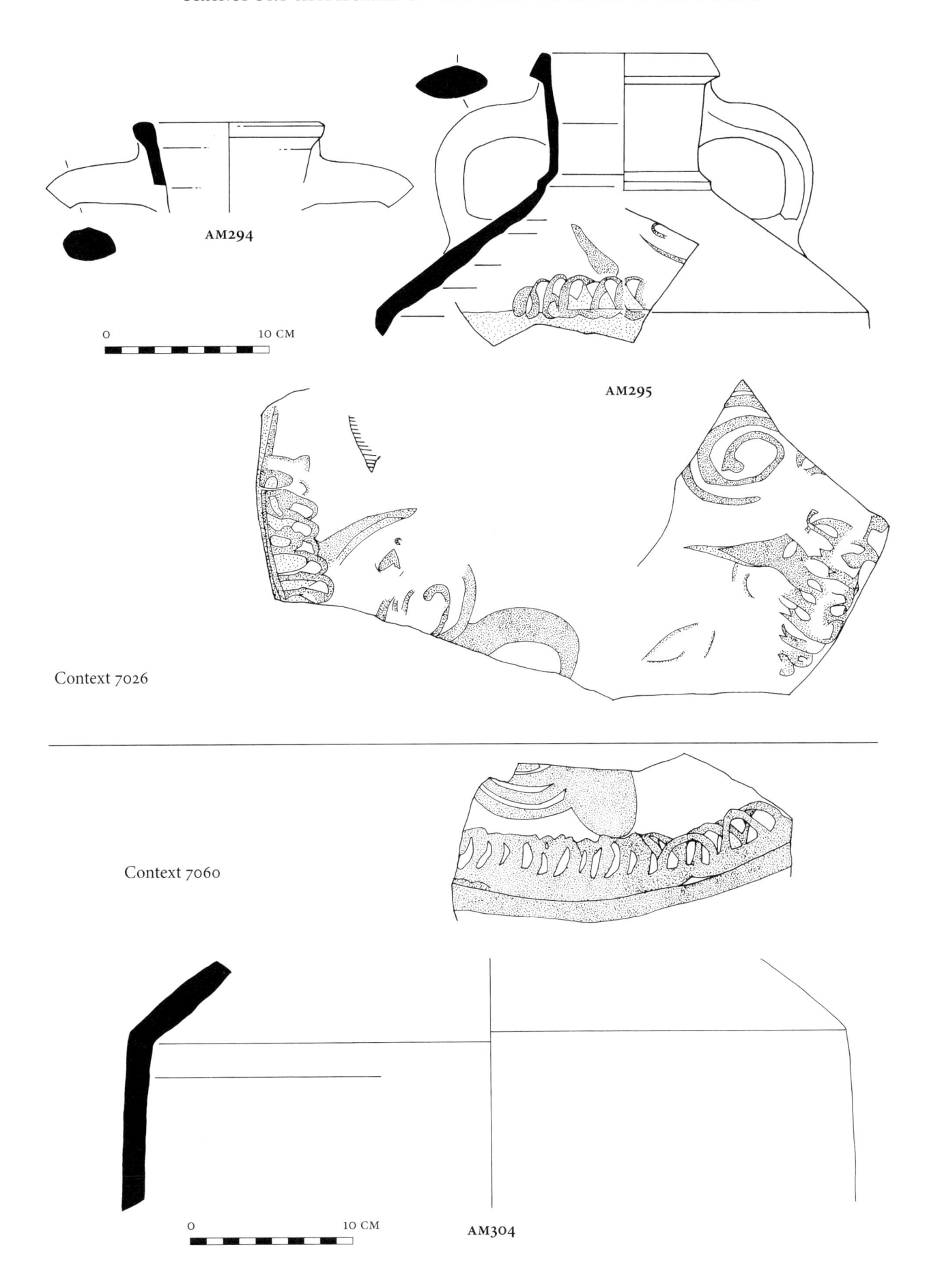

AM304

Plate 65. Contexts 7026 and 7060.3. Early seventh century A.D.

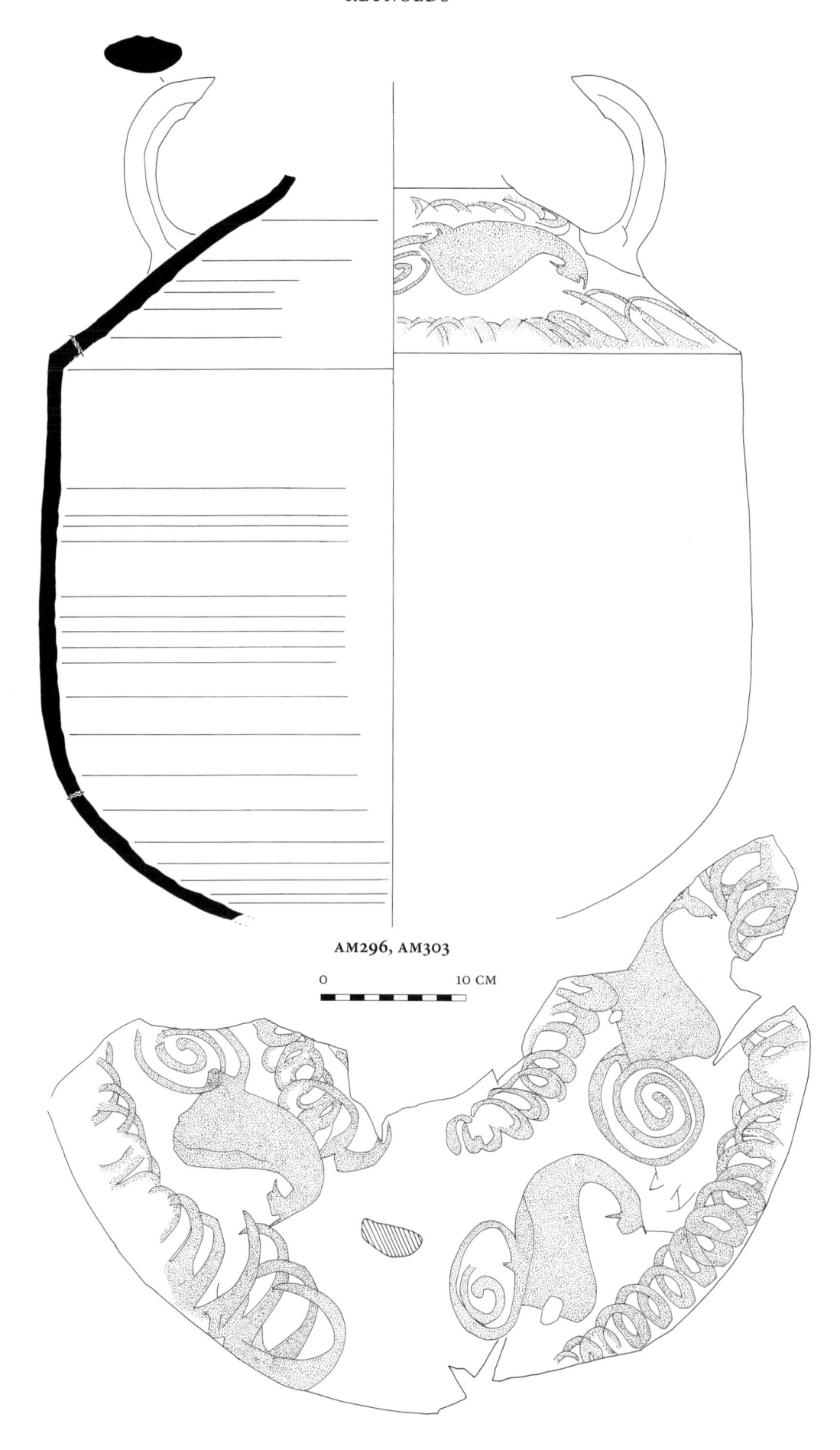

Plate 66. Contexts 7036.1/7060.15. Large Form 17A. Early seventh century A.D.

TRANSPORT AMPHORAE OF THE FIRST TO SEVENTH CENTURIES

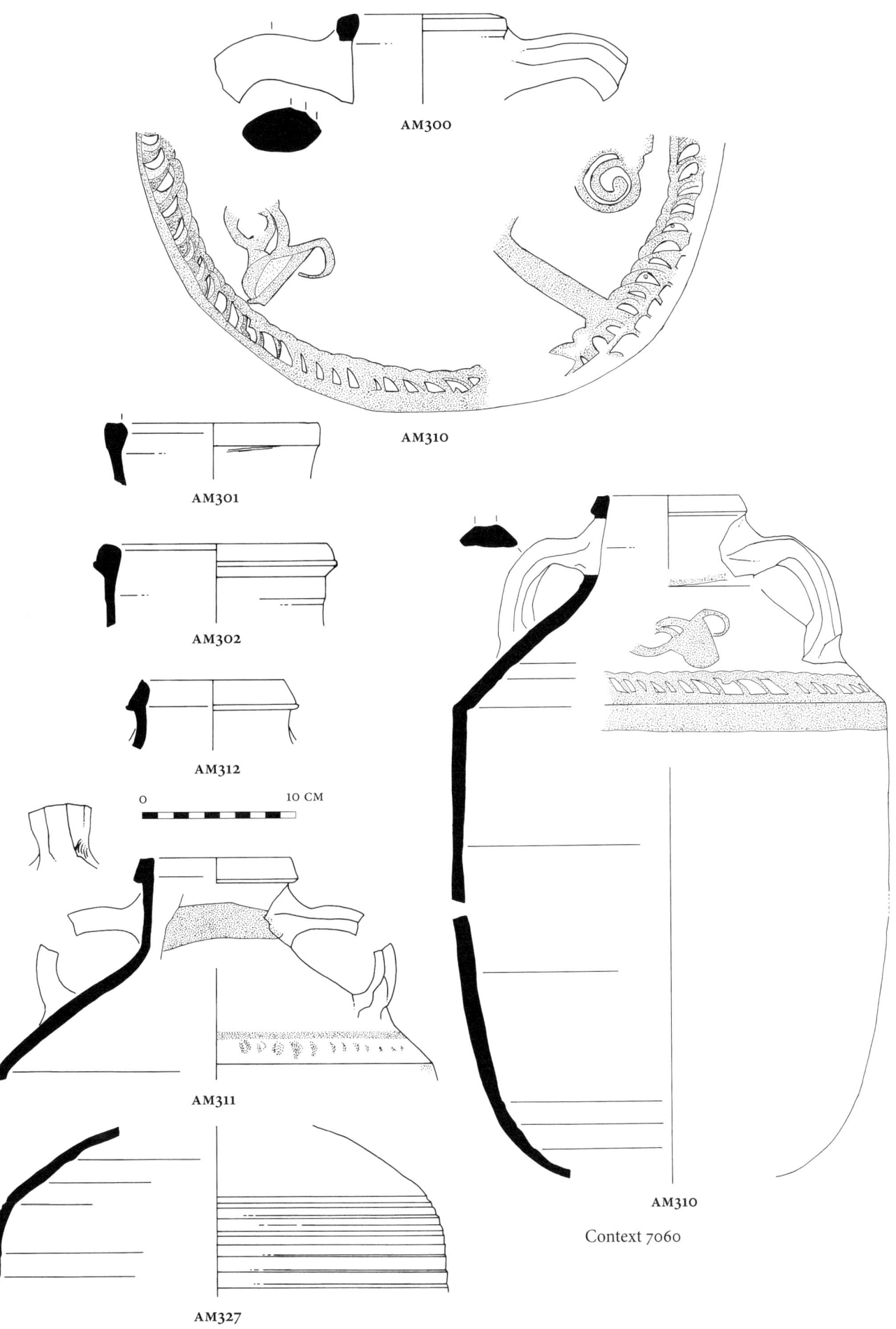

AM300

AM310

AM301

AM302

AM312

0   10 CM

AM311

AM310
Context 7060

AM327

Plate 67. Context 7060. Early seventh century A.D.

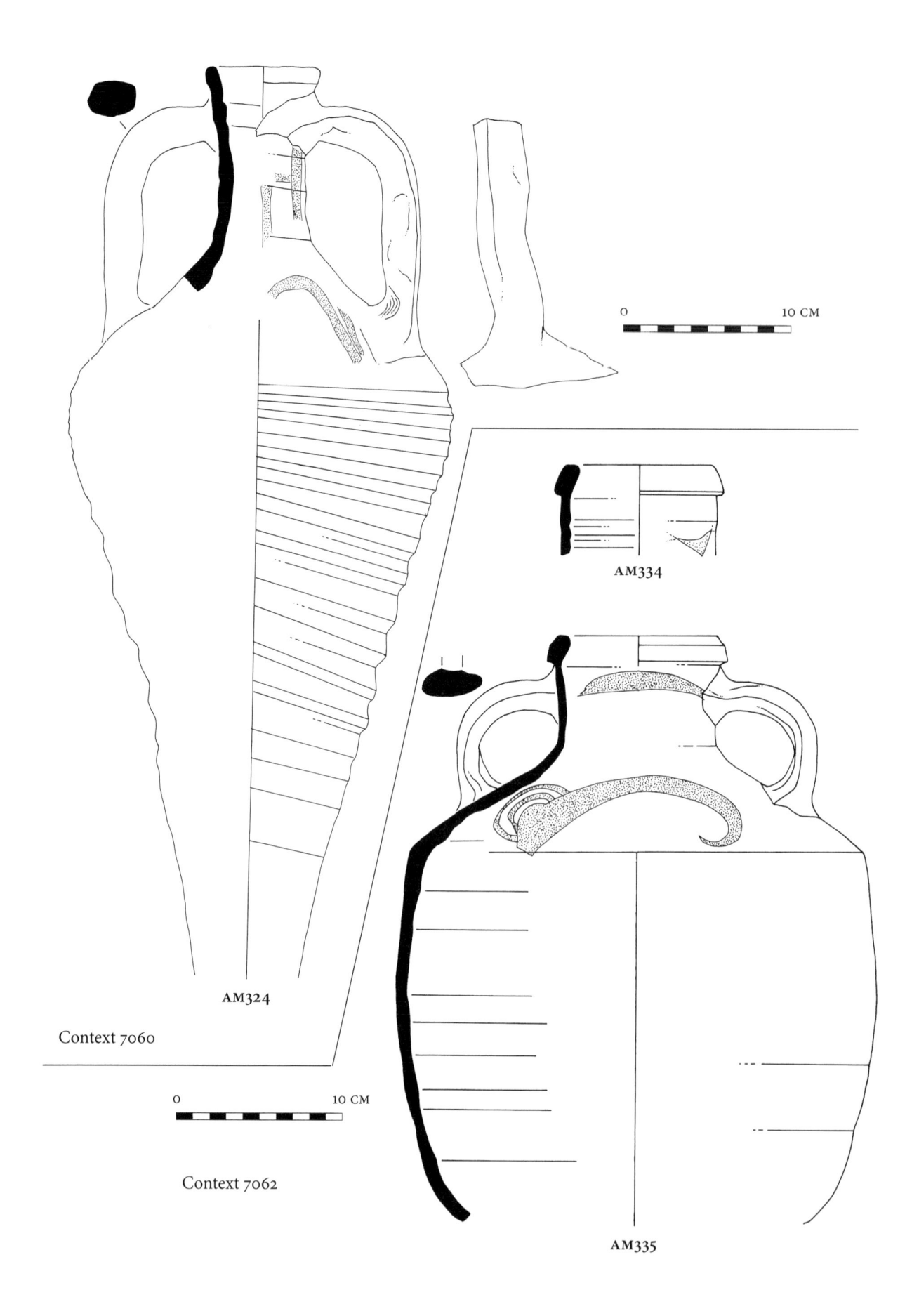

Plate 68. Contexts 7060.14 (Sinope amphora) and 7062 (Small Form 14A). Early seventh century A.D.

TRANSPORT AMPHORAE OF THE FIRST TO SEVENTH CENTURIES

AM332
Context 7061

AM337

AM338 AM339 AM342

Context 7064

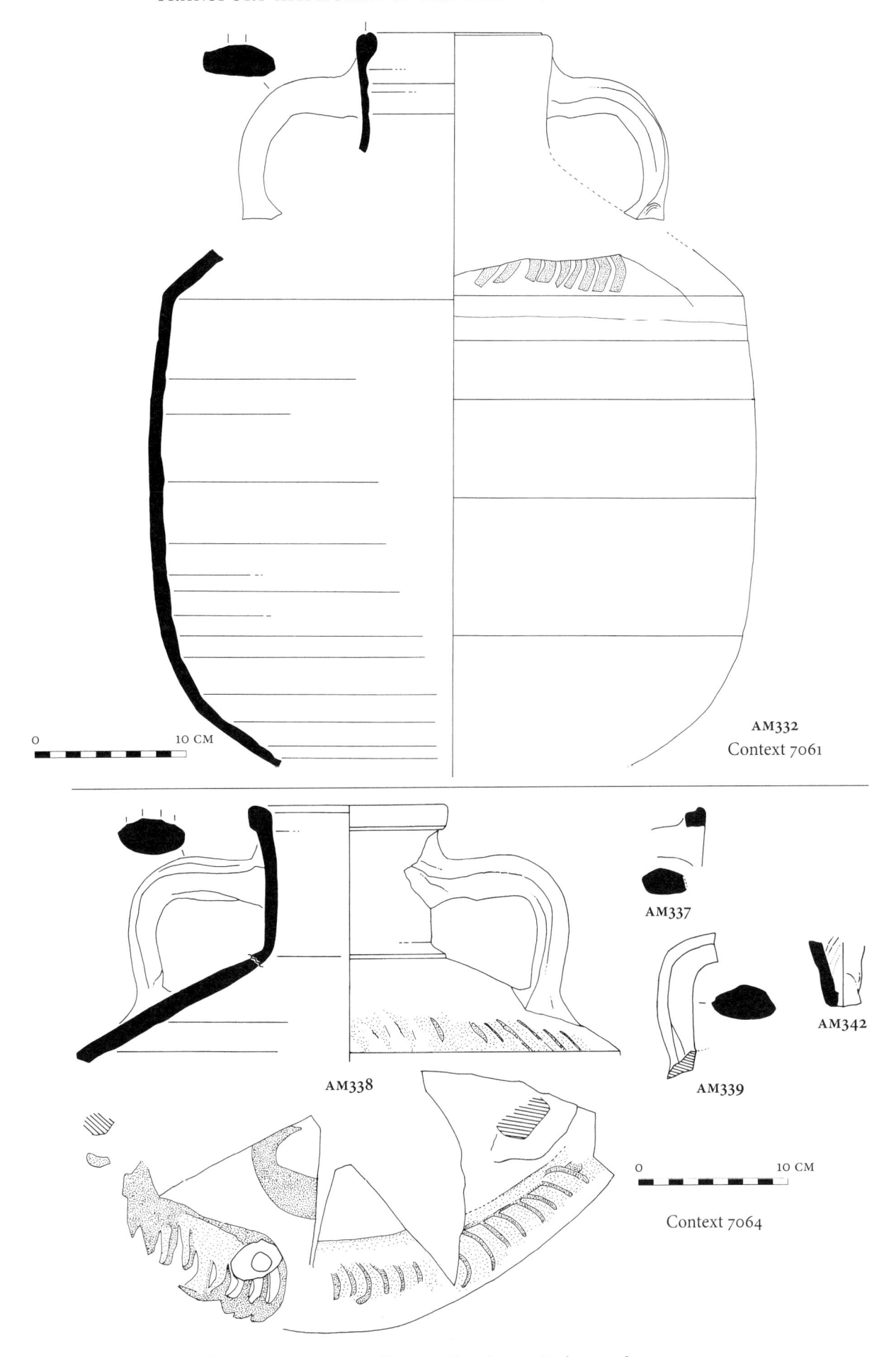

Plate 69. Contexts 7061.1 (Form 16A) and 7064. Early seventh century A.D.

AM343

AM345

AM346

Context 7065

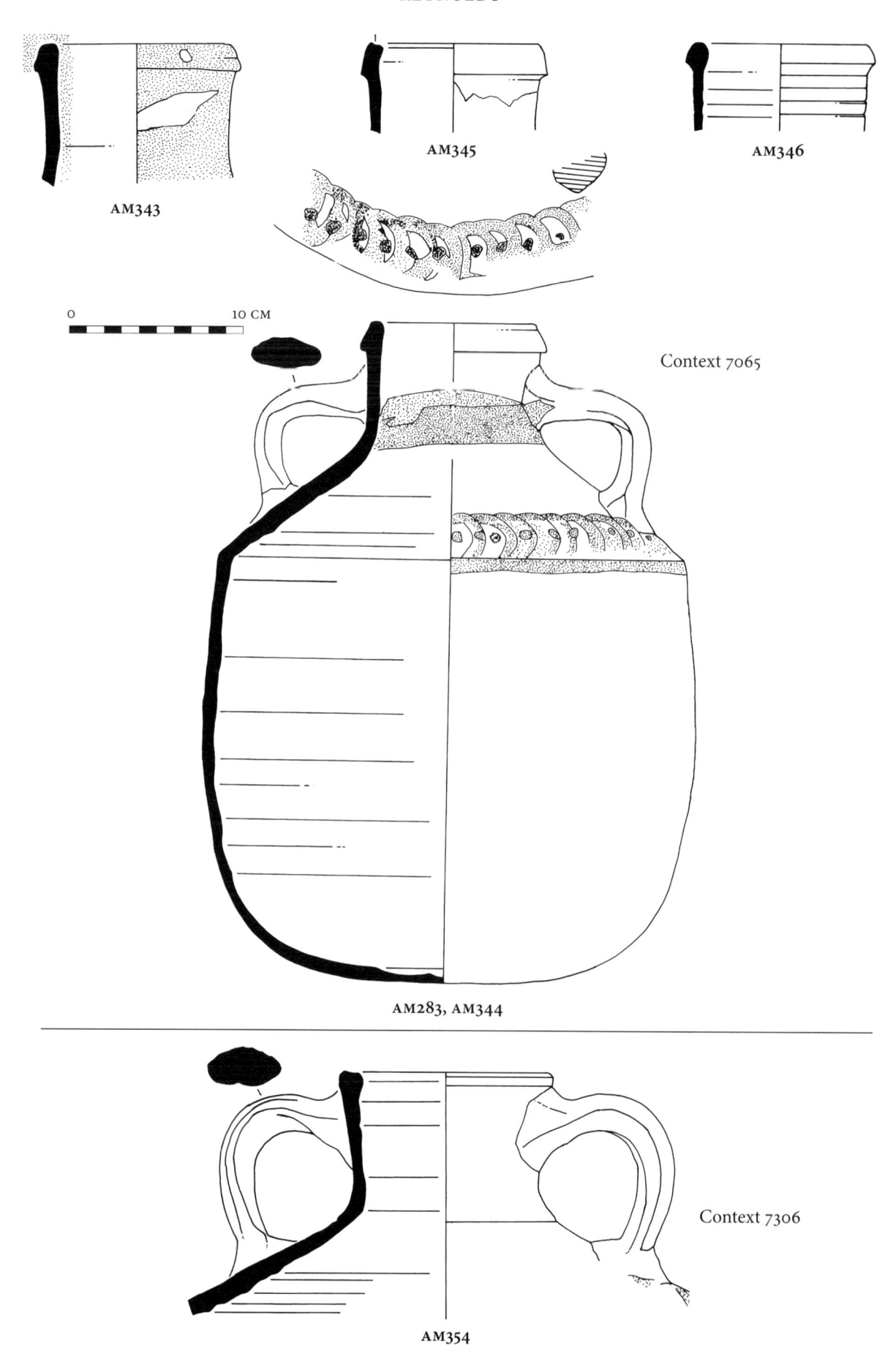

AM283, AM344

Context 7306

AM354

Plate 70. Contexts 7065 and 7306. Early seventh century A.D.

TRANSPORT AMPHORAE OF THE FIRST TO SEVENTH CENTURIES

AM356　　AM360　　AM361

Context 12002

0　　10 CM

AM385　　AM388

AM387　　AM389

AM393　　AM390

AM396　　AM395

Context 12011

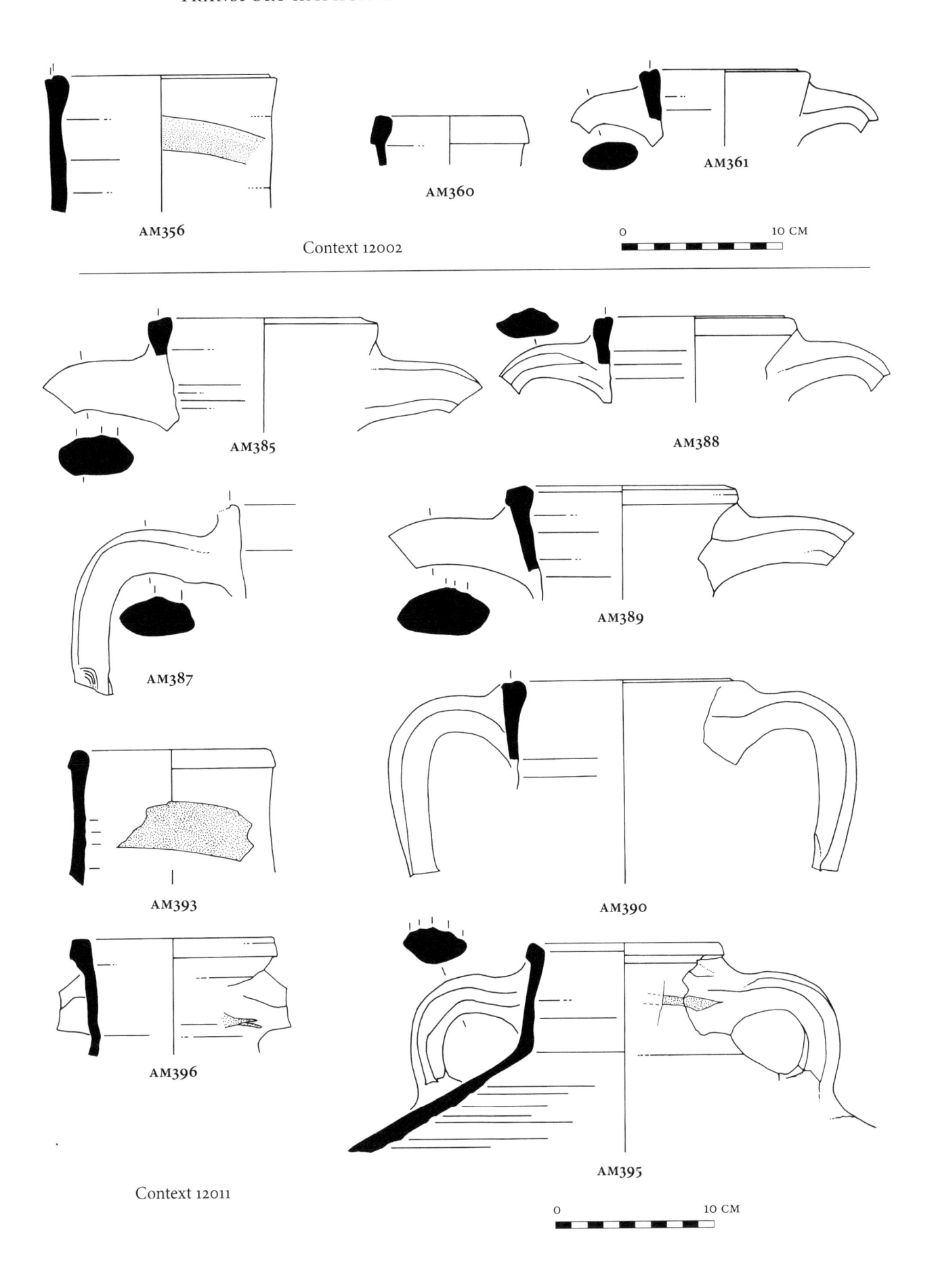

0　　10 CM

Plate 71. Contexts 12002 and 12011. Syrian painted amphorae. Early seventh century A.D.

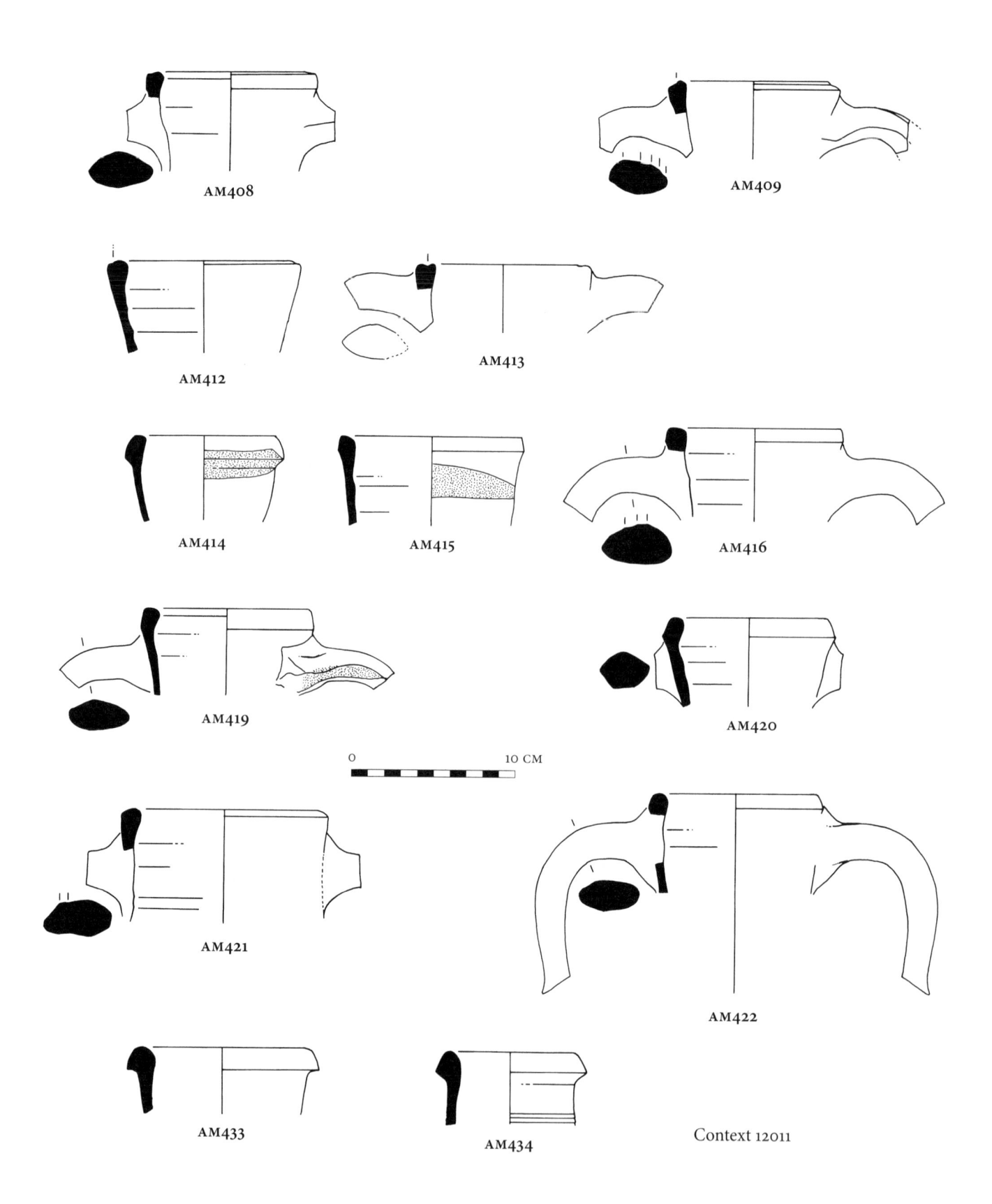

Plate 72. Context 12011. Syrian painted amphorae.

TRANSPORT AMPHORAE OF THE FIRST TO SEVENTH CENTURIES

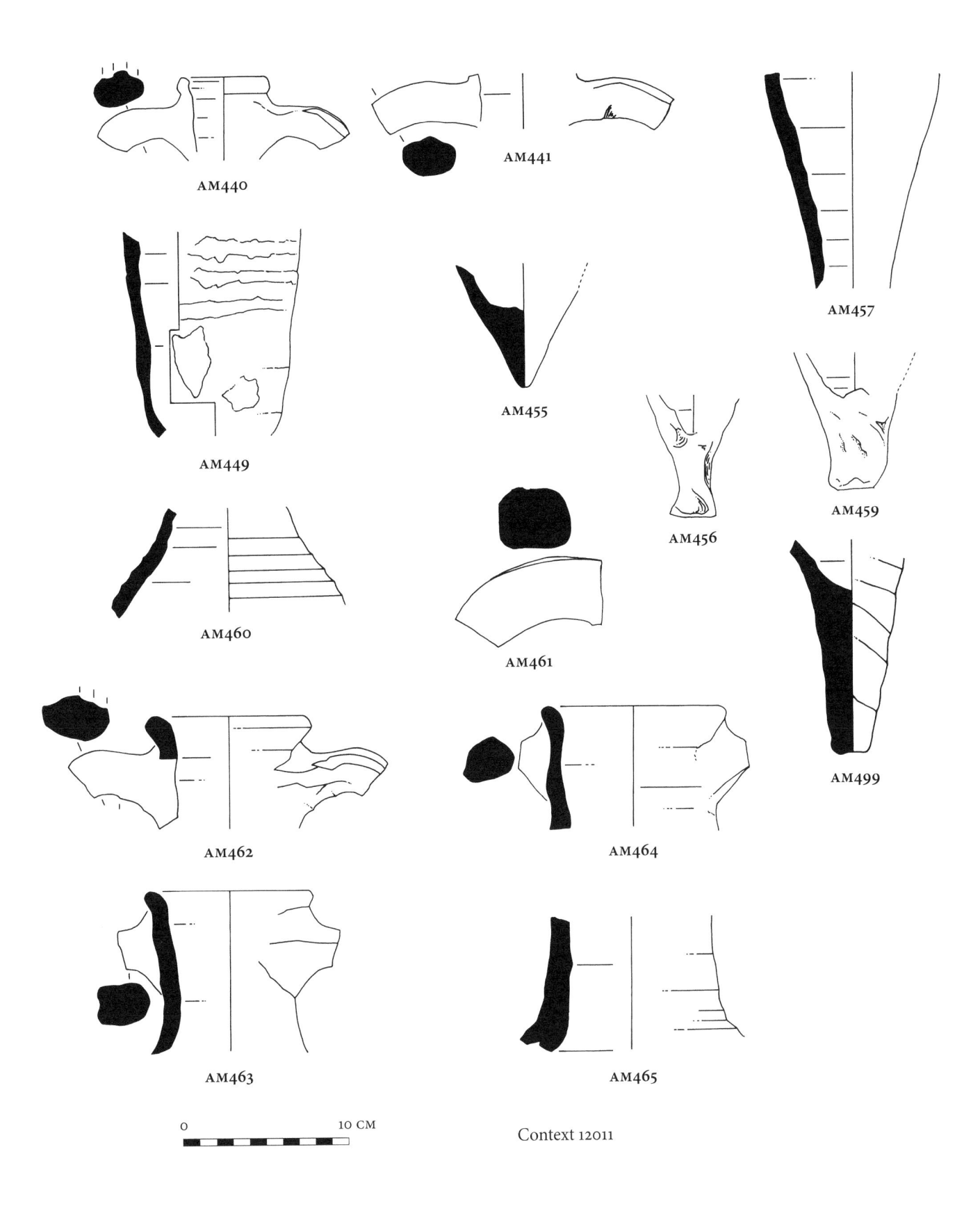

Plate 73. Context 12011. Non-Syrian imports.

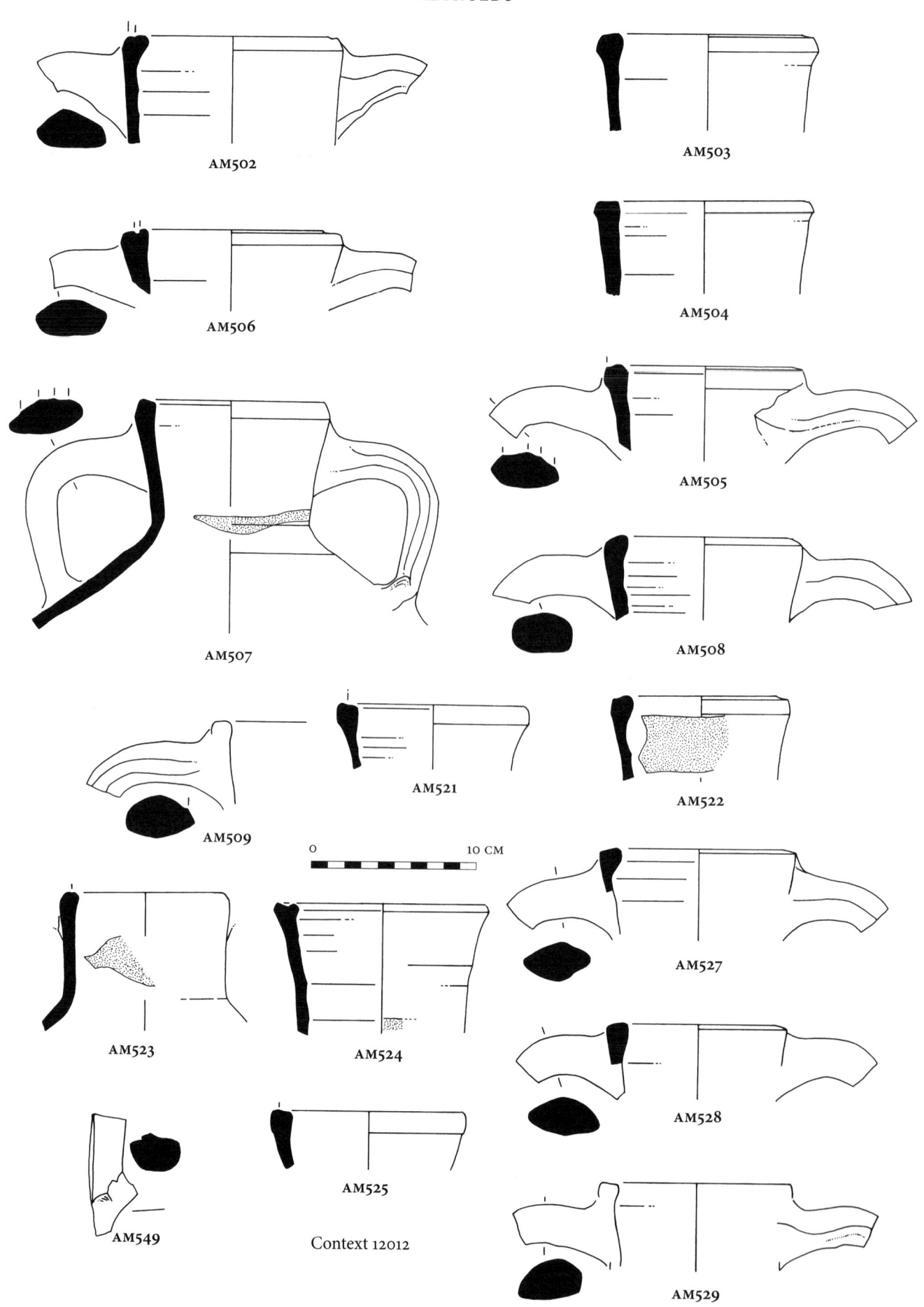

Plate 74. Context 12012. Early seventh century A.D.

CERAMIC OIL LAMPS

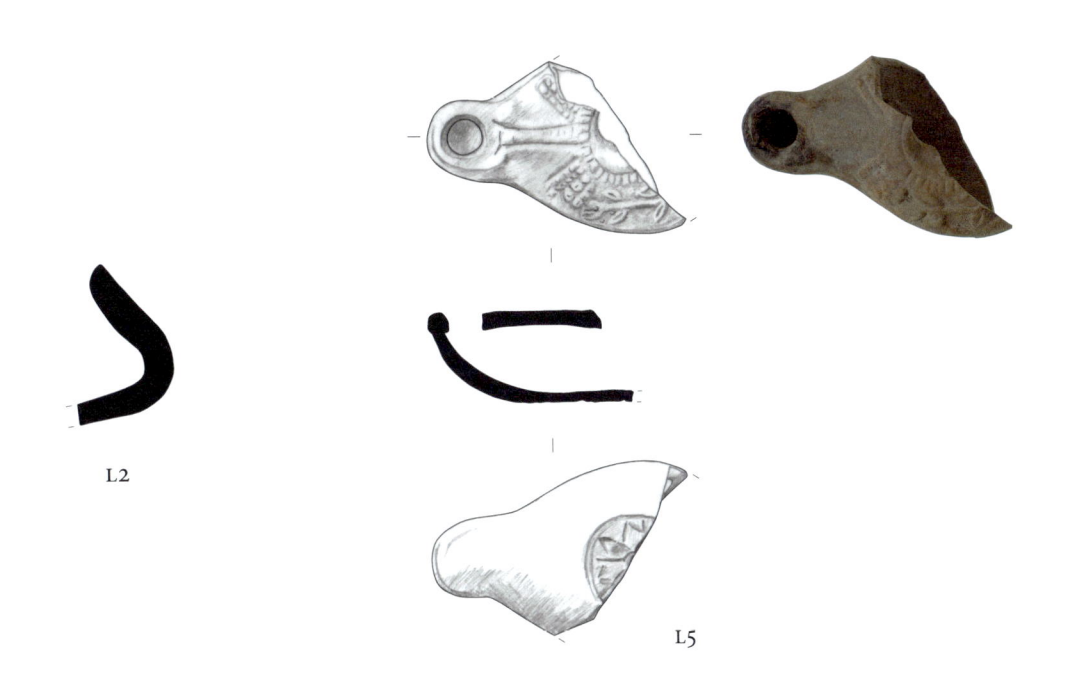

Plate 75. Type 1 (L2): Wheel-made lamps. Hellenistic: second half of the second to early first century B.C.
Type 2 (L5): Early Roman to Flavian / Trajanic (first century A.D.). Scale 1:2.

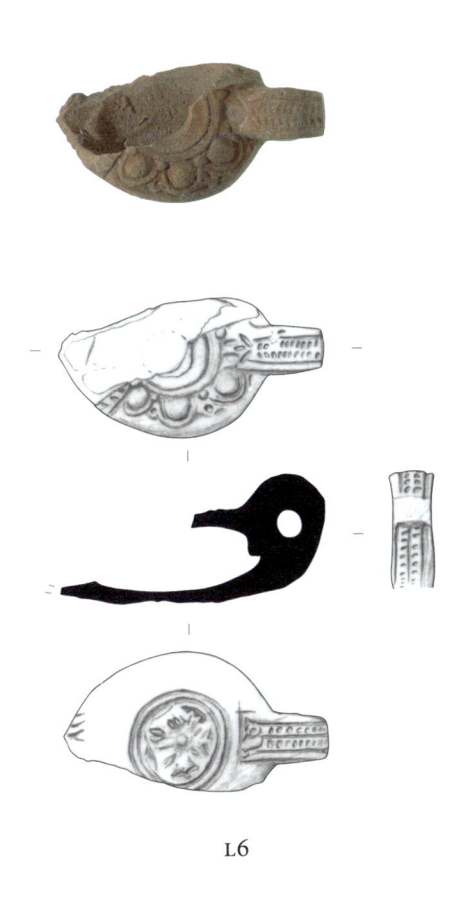

Plate 76. Type 2 (L6): Early Roman to Flavian / Trajanic (first century A.D.). Scale 1:2.

L7

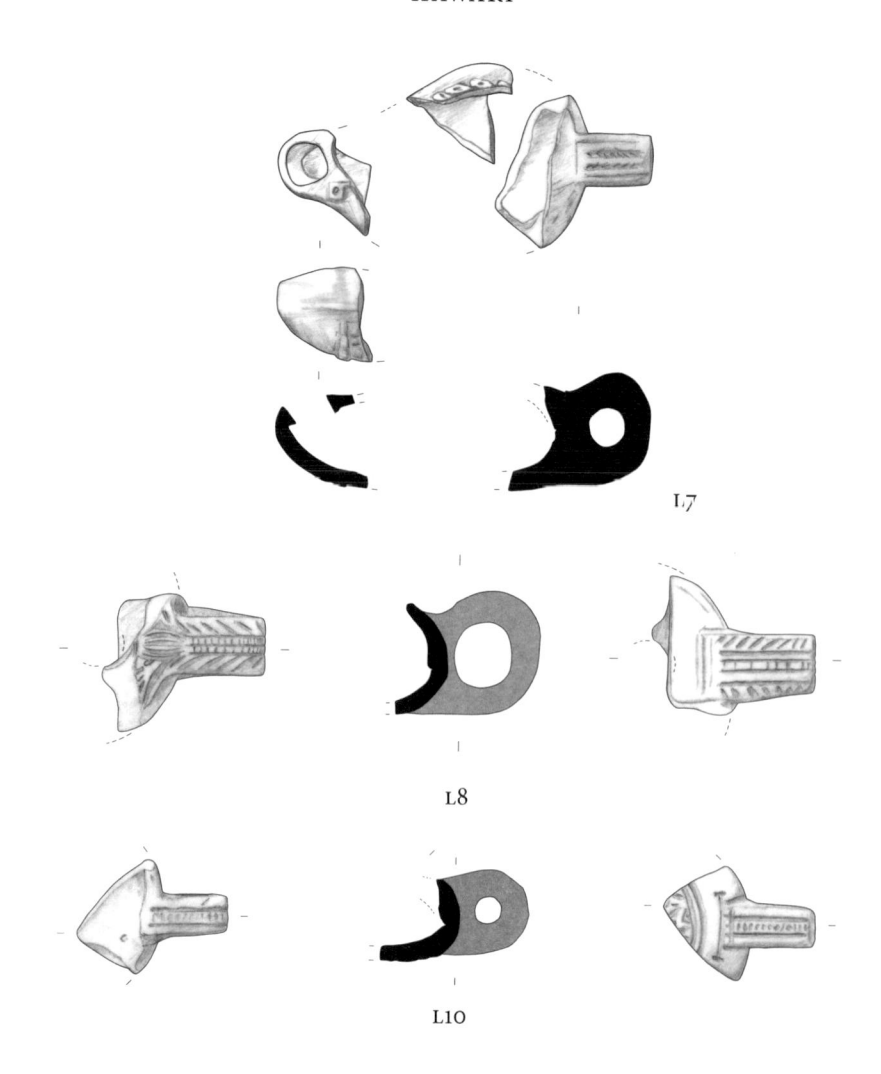

L8

L10

Plate 77. Type 2 (L7–10): Early Roman to Flavian/Trajanic (first century A.D.). Scale 1:2.

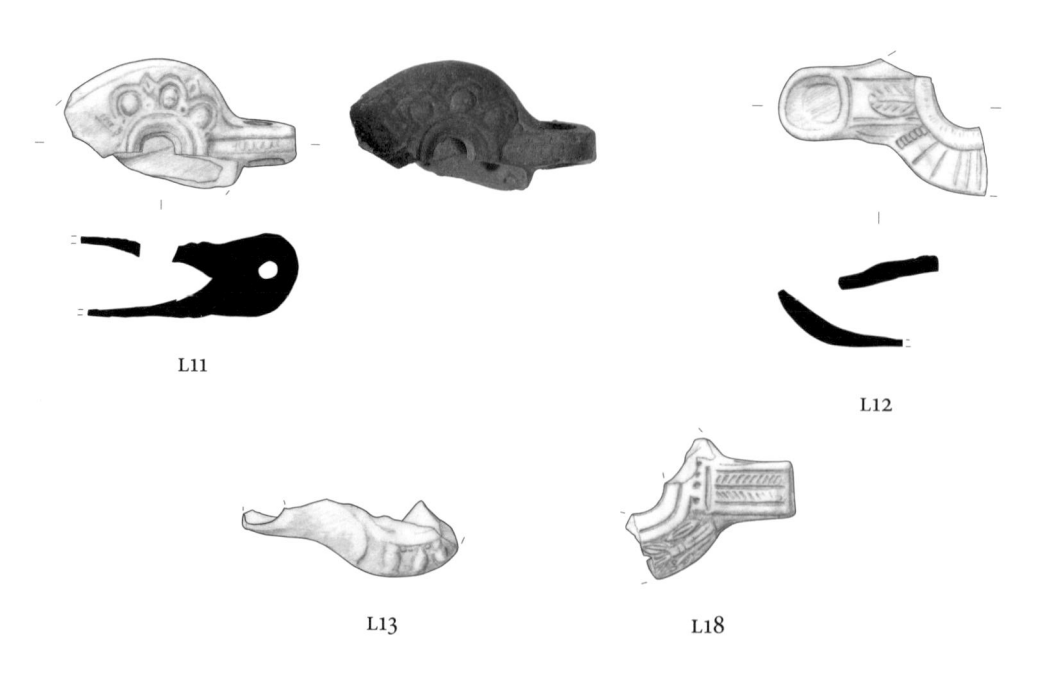

L11

L12

L13   L18

Plate 78. Type 2 (L11–18): Early Roman to Flavian/Trajanic (first century A.D.). Scale 1:2.

CERAMIC OIL LAMPS

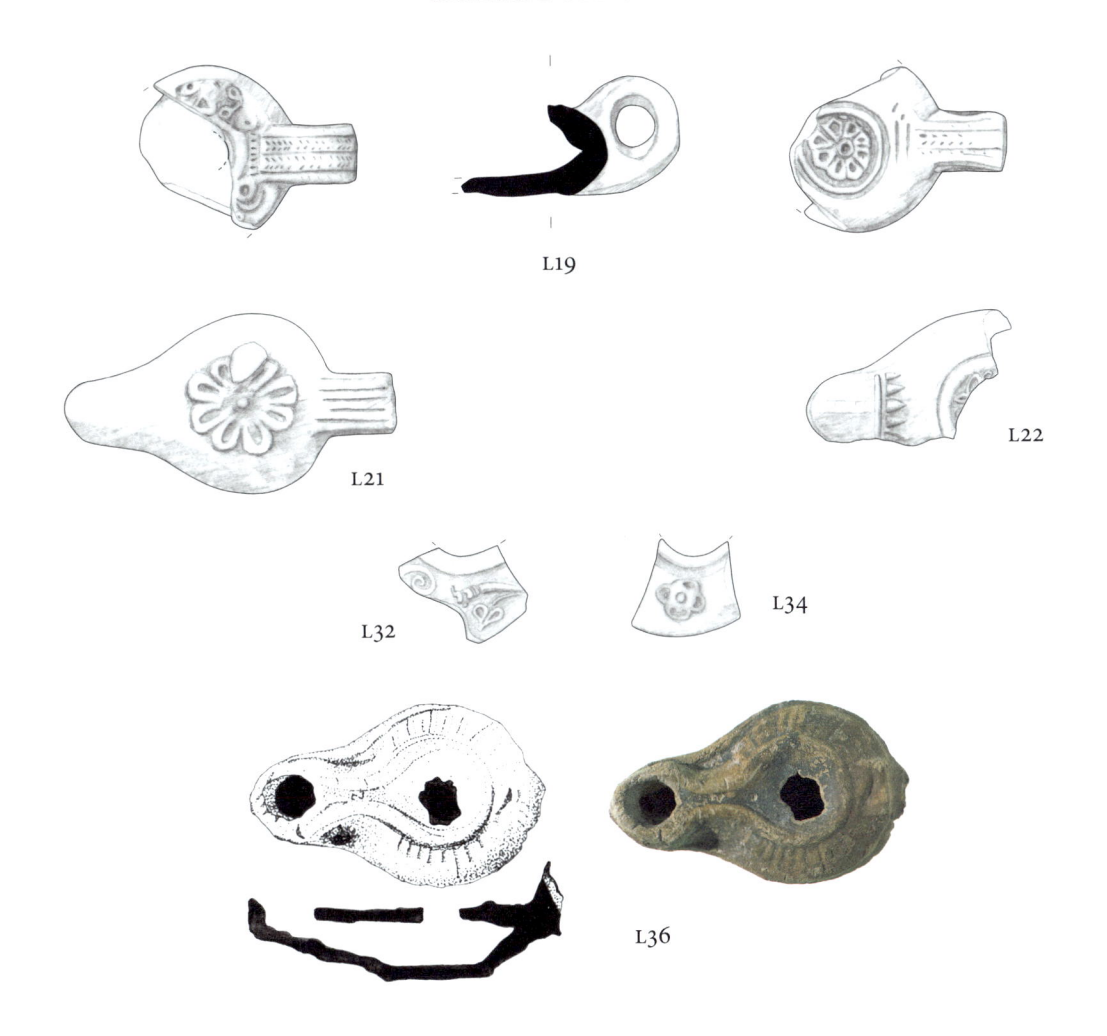

L19

L21 L22

L32 L34

L36

*Plate 79. Type 2 (**L19–36**): Early Roman to Flavian/Trajanic (first century A.D.). Scale 1:2.*

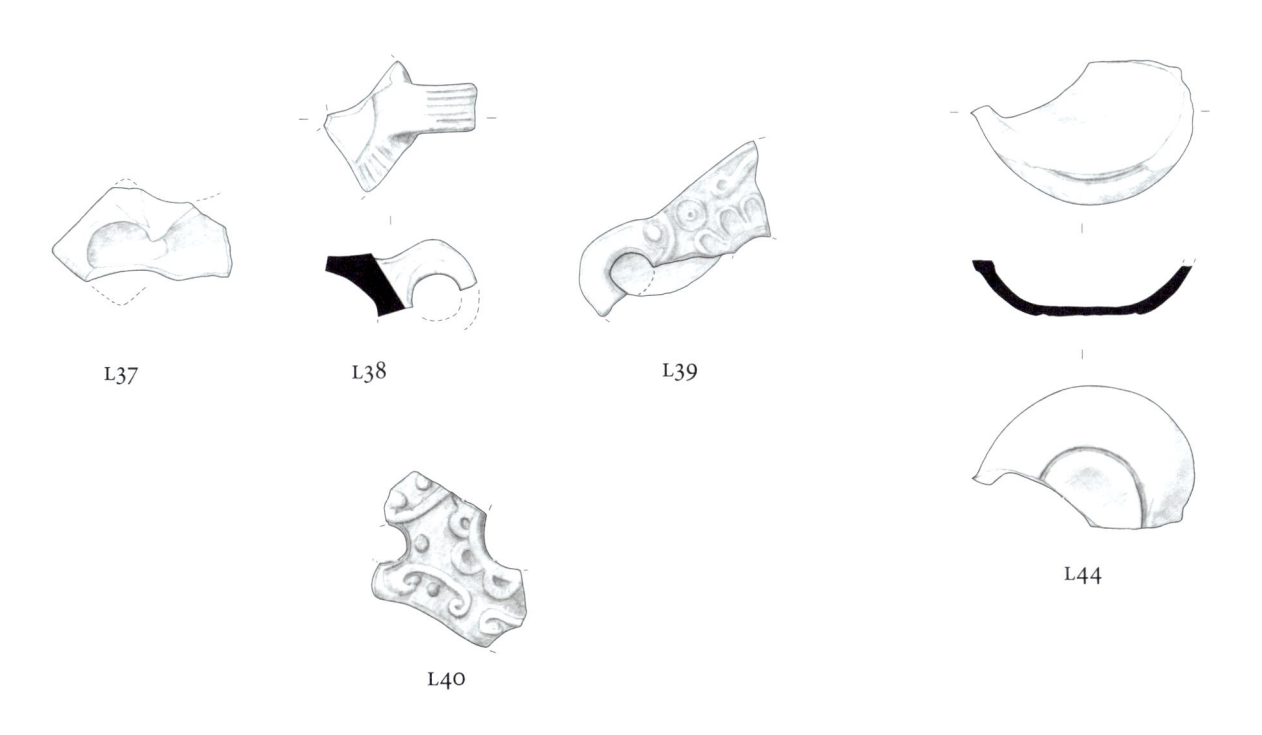

L37 L38 L39 L44

L40

*Plate 80. Type 2 (**L37–44**): Early Roman to Flavian/Trajanic (first century A.D.). Scale 1:2.*

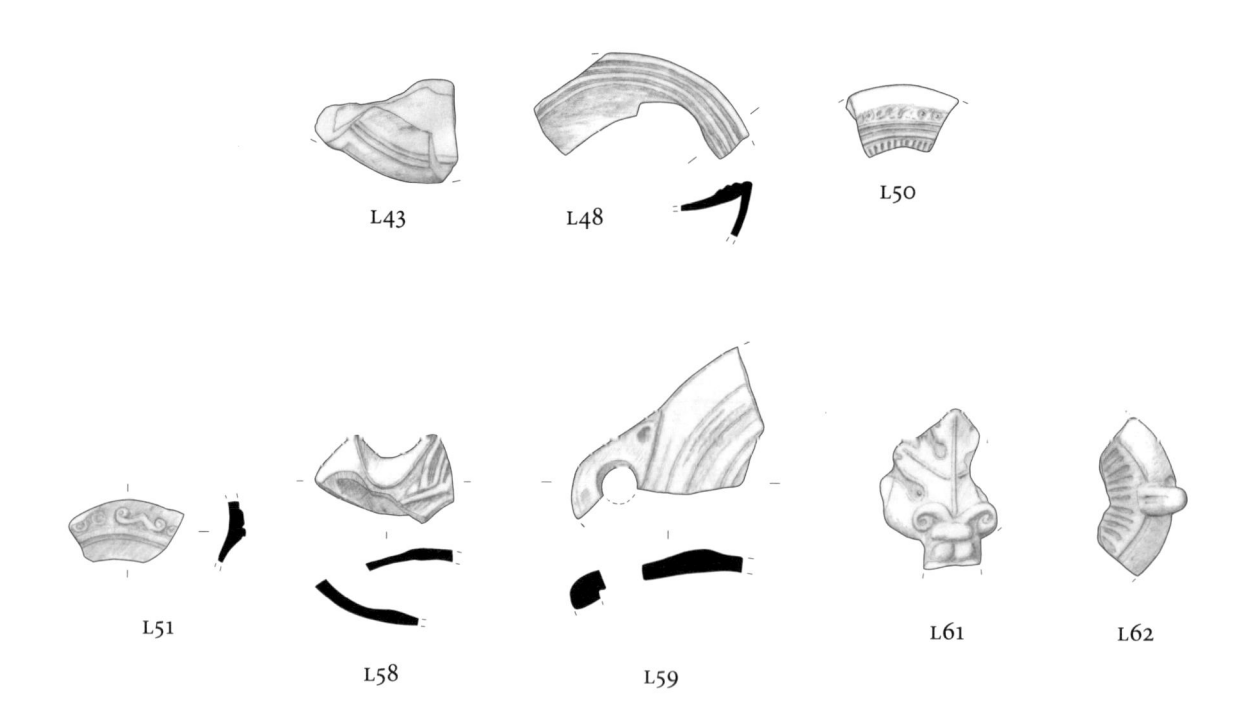

*Plate 81. Type 3 (**L43–62**): Roman discus lamps. Early first to early third century* A.D. *Scale 1:2.*

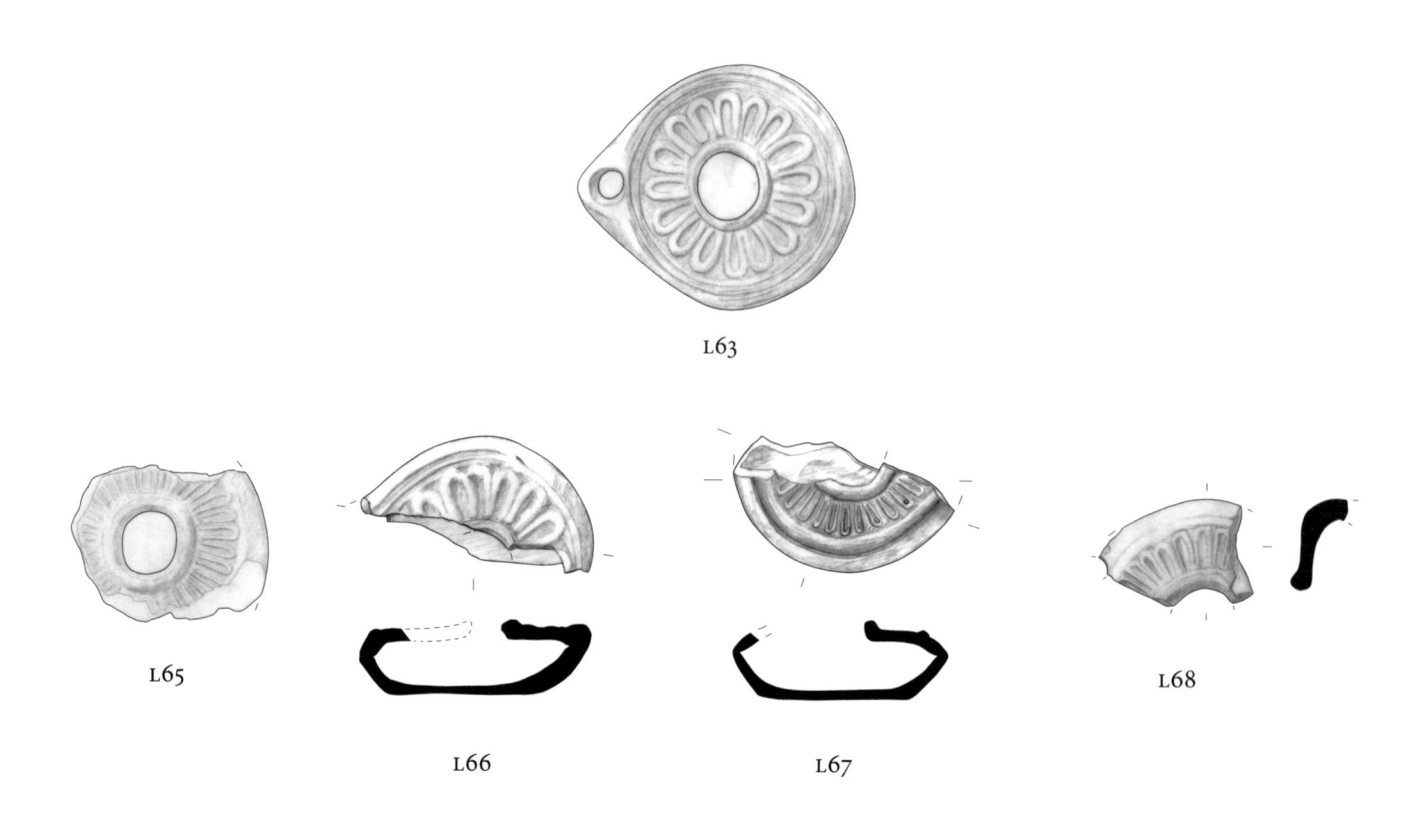

*Plate 82. Type 4 (**L63–68**): Dura-Europos lamps. First half of the third century* A.D. *Scale 1:2.*

CERAMIC OIL LAMPS

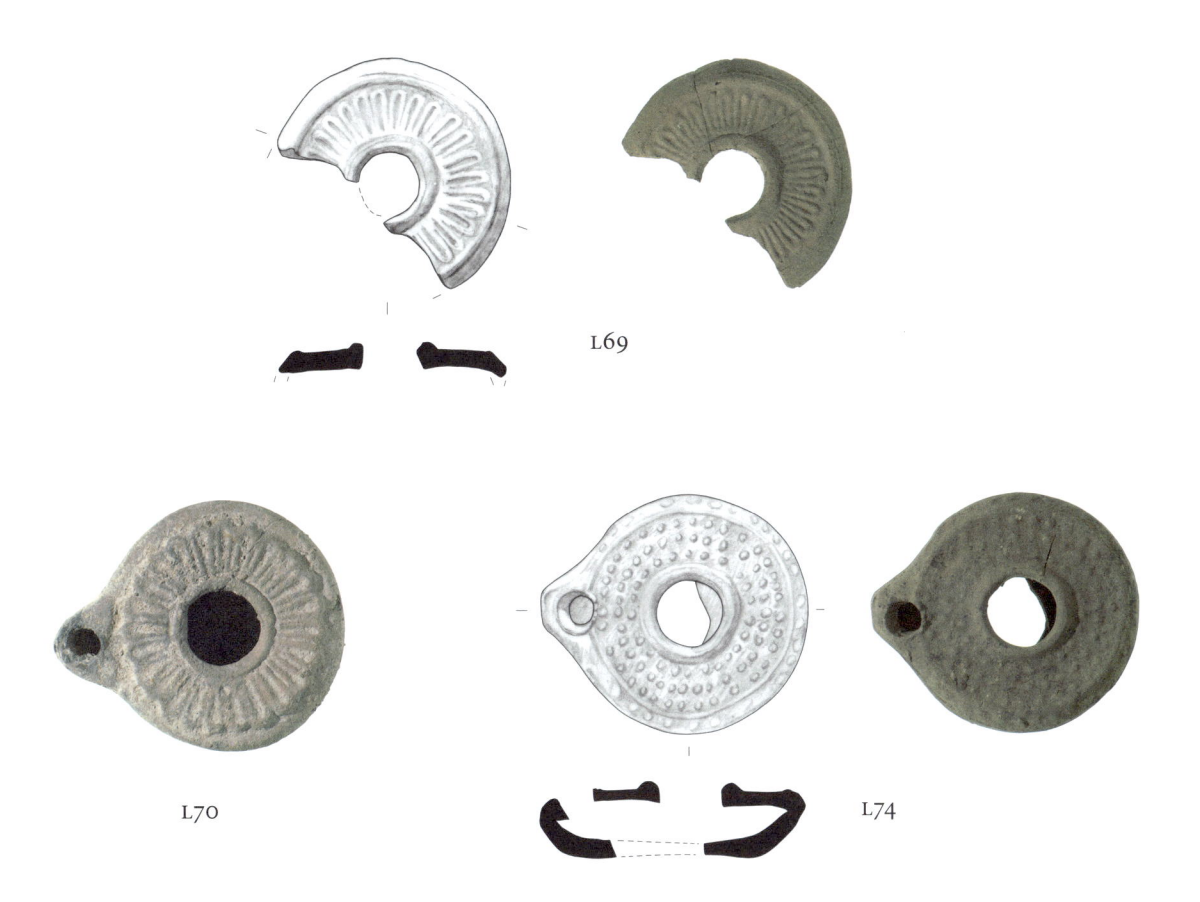

L69

L70   L74

*Plate 83. Type 4 (**L69–74**): Dura-Europos lamps. First half of the third century* A.D. *Scale 1:2.*

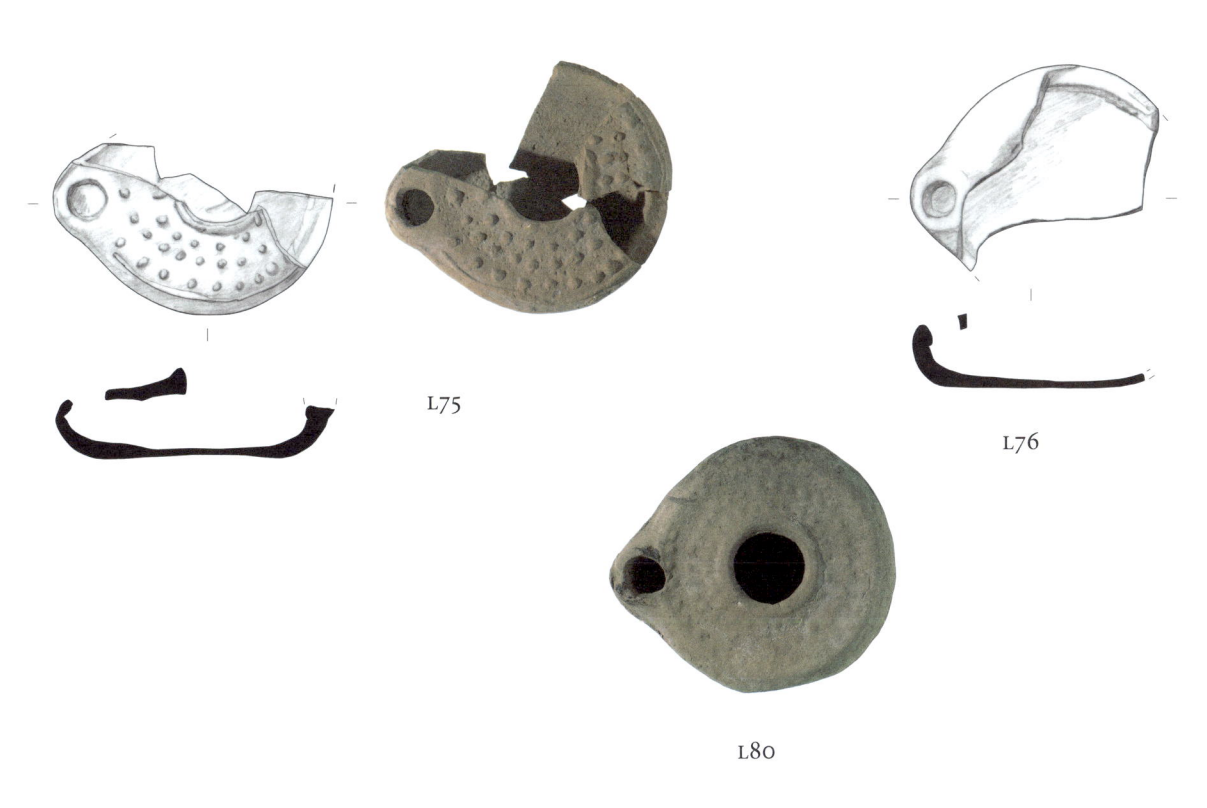

L75   L76

L80

*Plate 84. Type 4 (**L75–80**): Dura-Europos lamps. First half of the third century* A.D. *Scale 1:2.*

L90

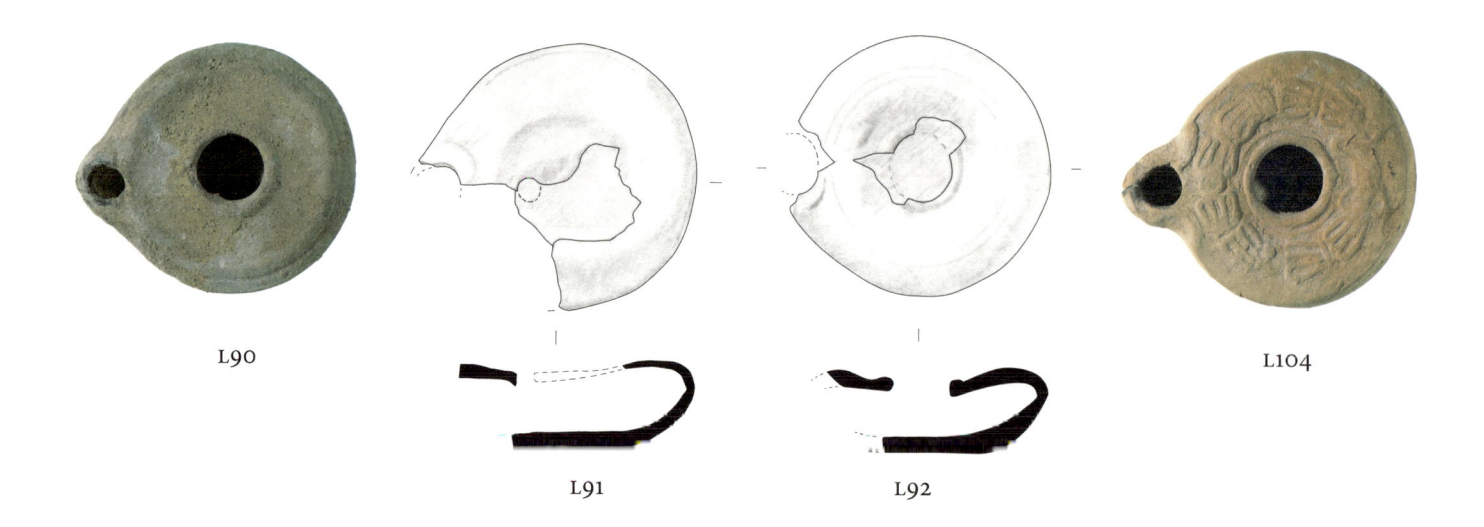

L91

L92

L104

Plate 85. Type 4 (L90–104): Dura-Europos lamps. First half of the third century A.D. Scale 1:2.

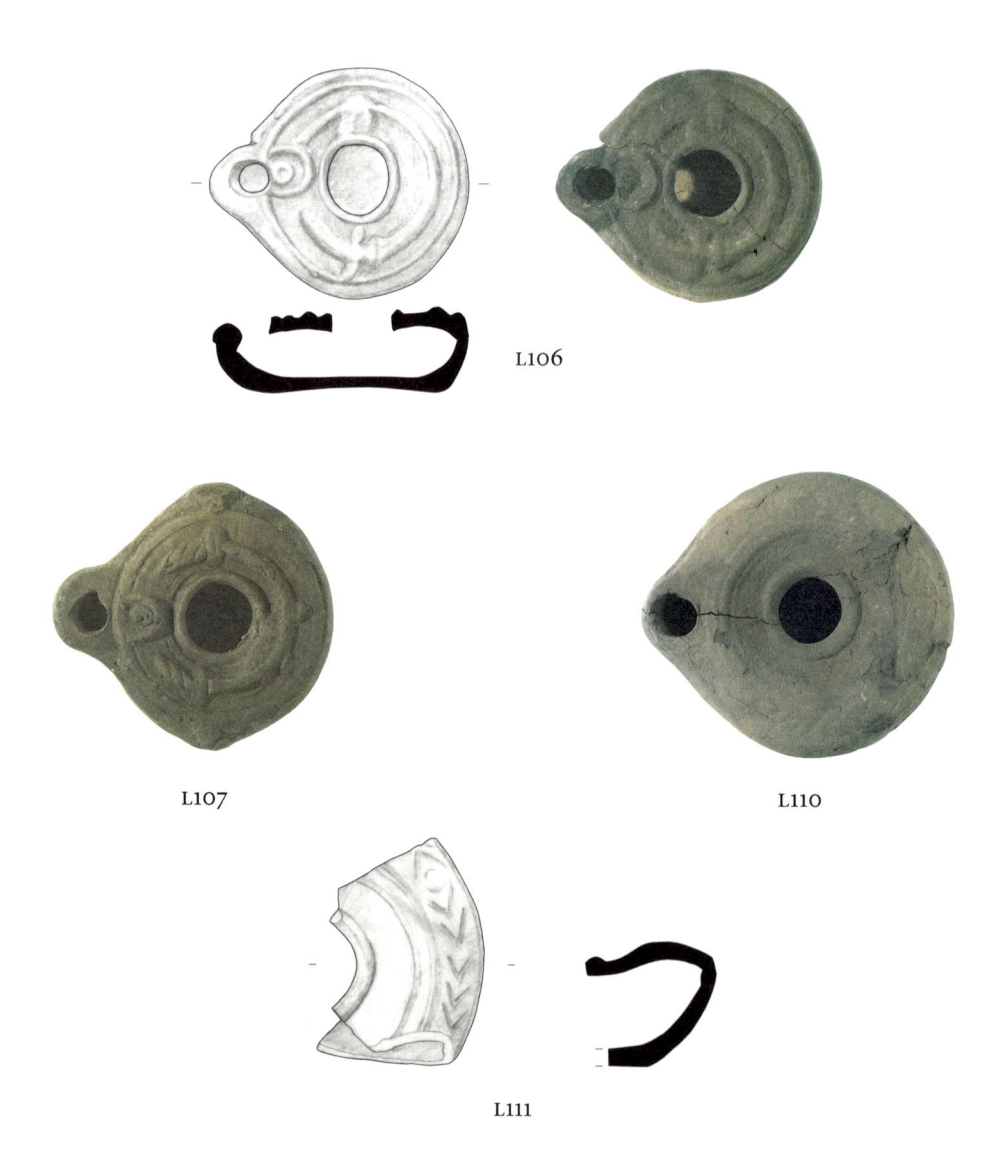

L106

L107

L110

L111

Plate 86. Type 4 (L106–111): Dura-Europos lamps. First half of the third century A.D. Scale 1:2.

CERAMIC OIL LAMPS

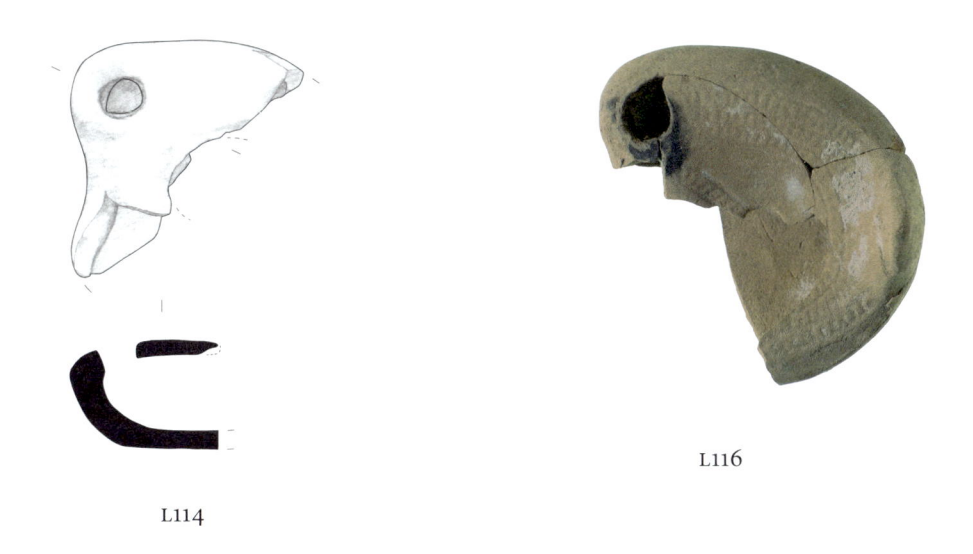

L114

L116

*Plate 87. Type 5 (**L114** and **L116**): Two-nozzle lamps. First half of the third century A.D. Scale 1:2.*

L119

*Plate 88. Type 5 (**L119**): Two-nozzle lamp. First half of the third century A.D. Scale 1:2.*

HAWARI

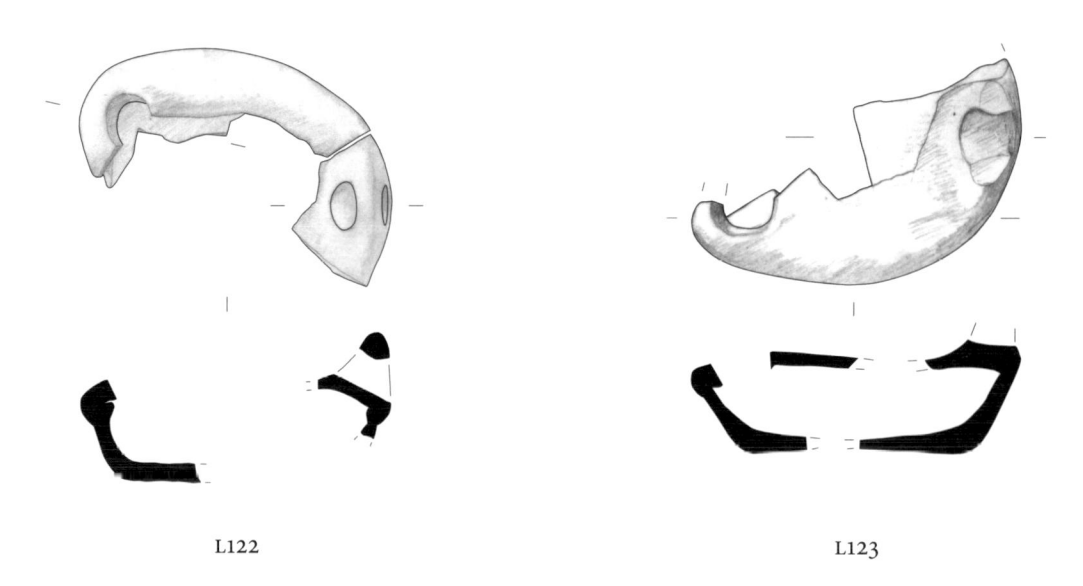

L122

L123

*Plate 89. Type 5 (**L122–123**): Two-nozzle lamps. First half of the third century A.D. Scale 1:2.*

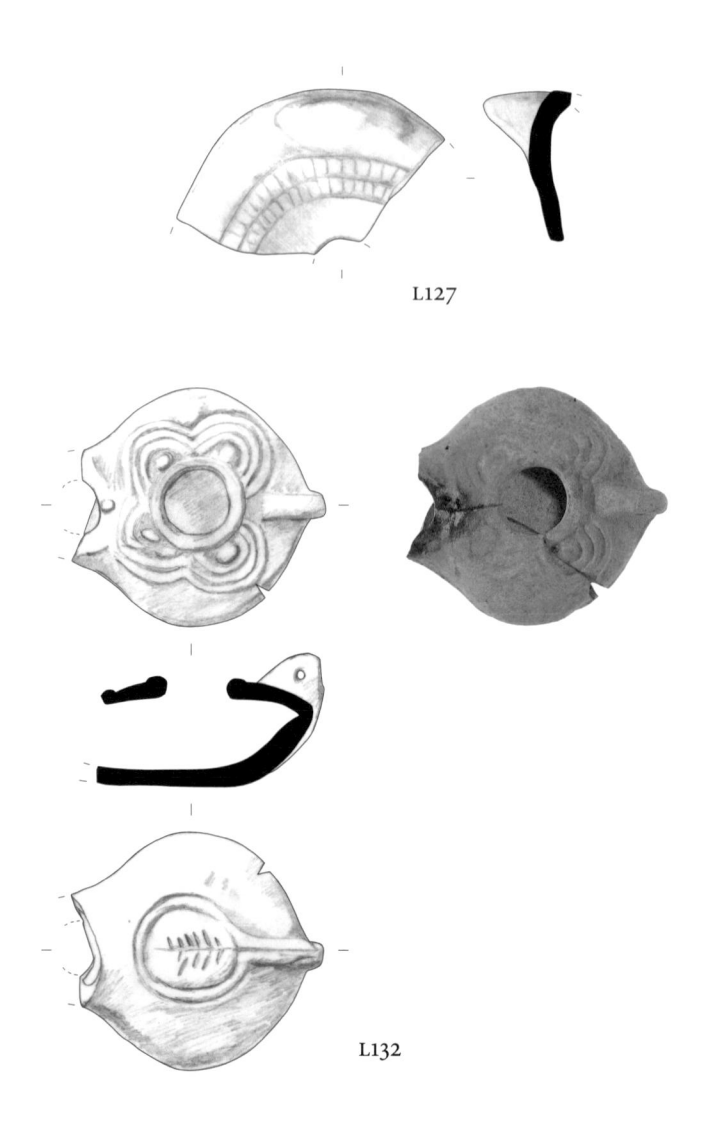

L127

L132

*Plate 90. Type 5 (**L127**): Two-nozzle lamp. First half of the third century A.D.*
*Type 6 (**L132**): Ovoid lamp with linear patterns. First half of the third century A.D. Scale 1:2.*

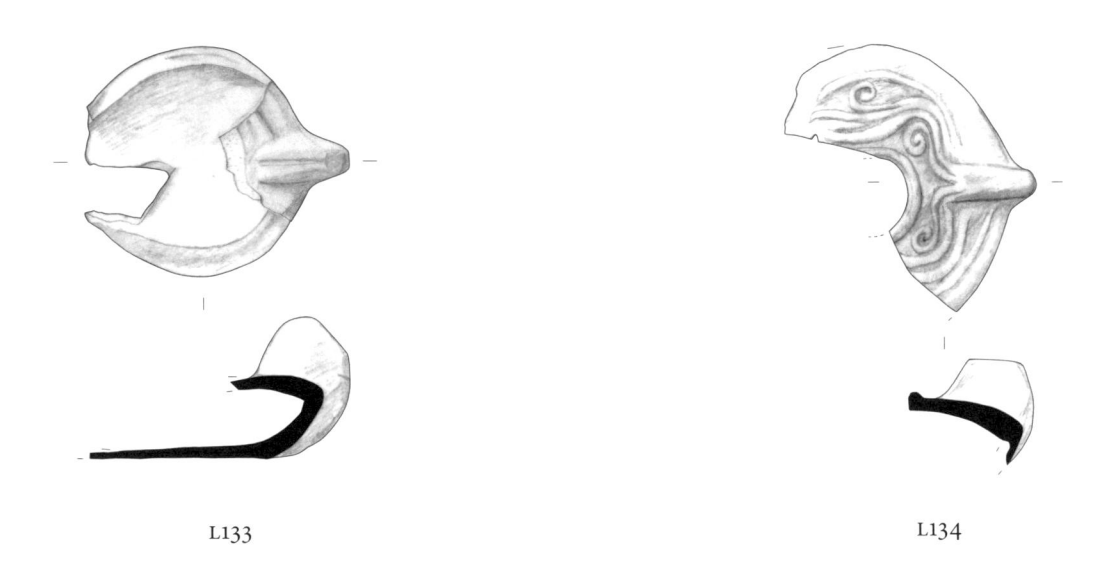

CERAMIC OIL LAMPS

L133

L134

*Plate 91. Type 6 (**L133–134**): Ovoid lamps with linear patterns. First half of the third century A.D. Scale 1:2.*

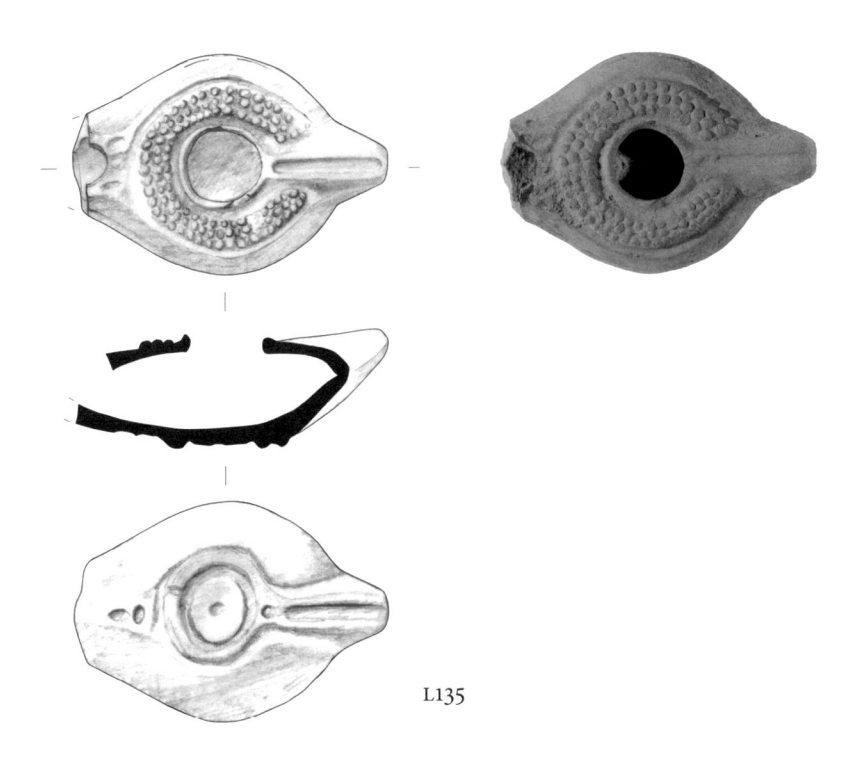

L135

*Plate 92. Type 7 (**L135**): Oblong lamp. Late fifth to early sixth century A.D. Scale 1:2.*

HAWARI

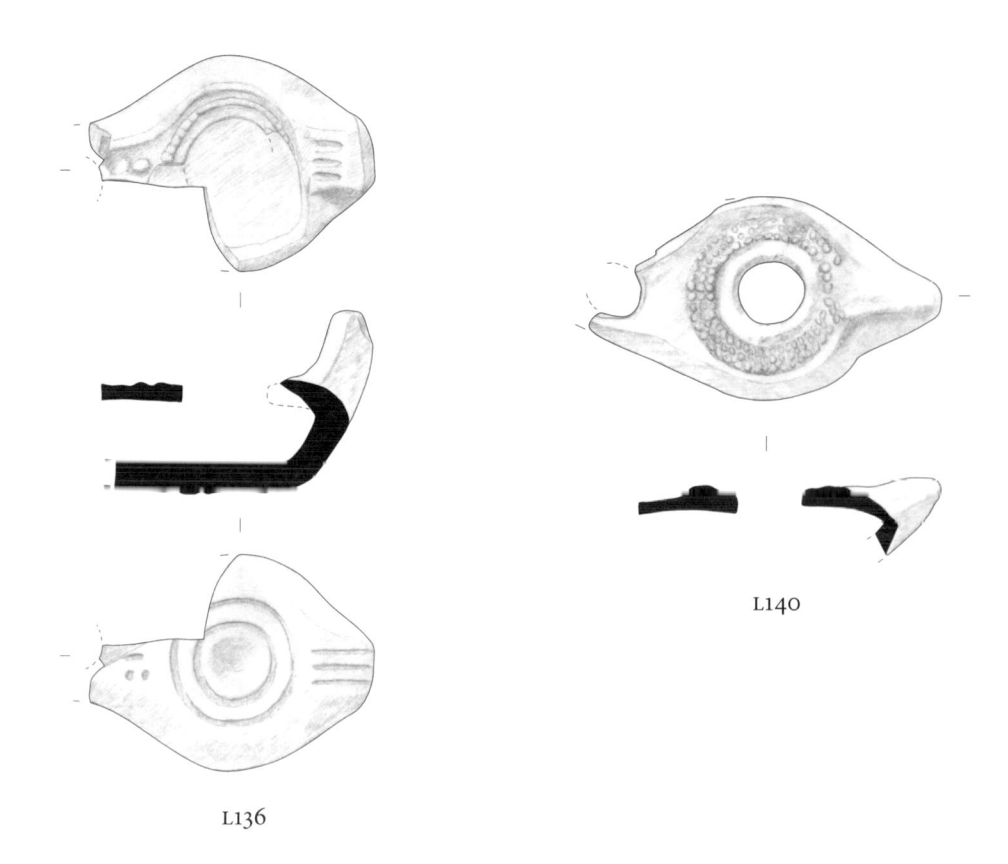

L140

L136

Plate 93. Type 7 (L136 and L140): Oblong lamps. Late fifth to early sixth century A.D. Scale 1:2.

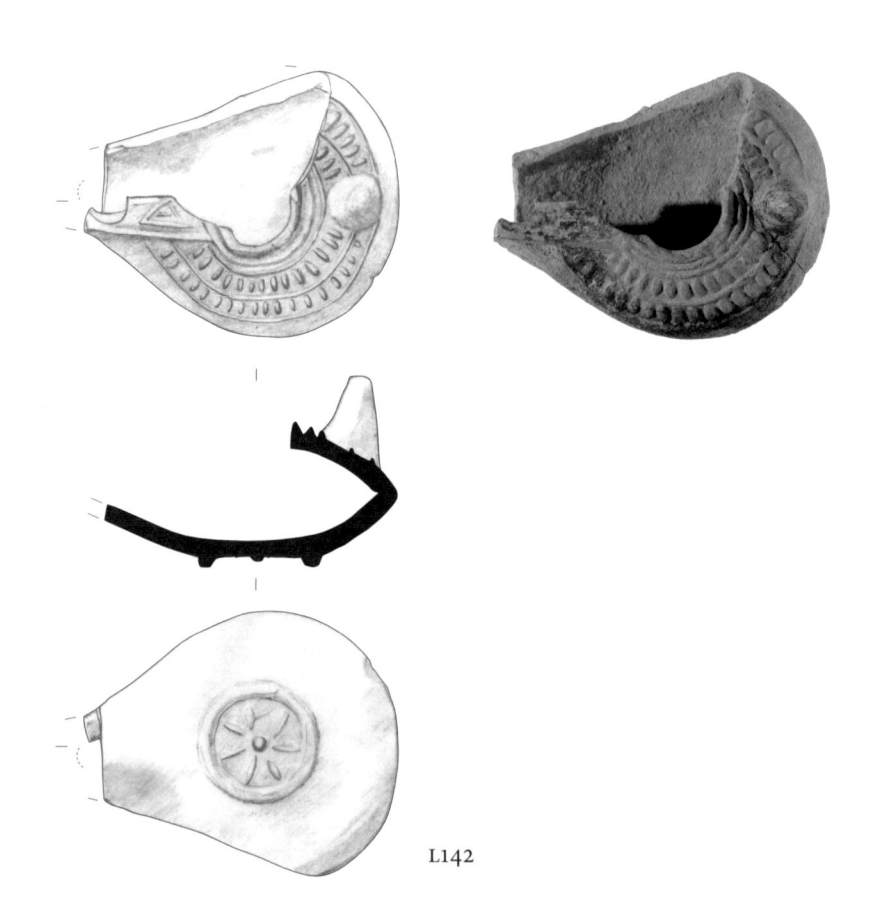

L142

Plate 94. Type 8 (L142): Syro-Palestinian lamp. Seventh to eighth century A.D. Scale 1:2.

CERAMIC OIL LAMPS

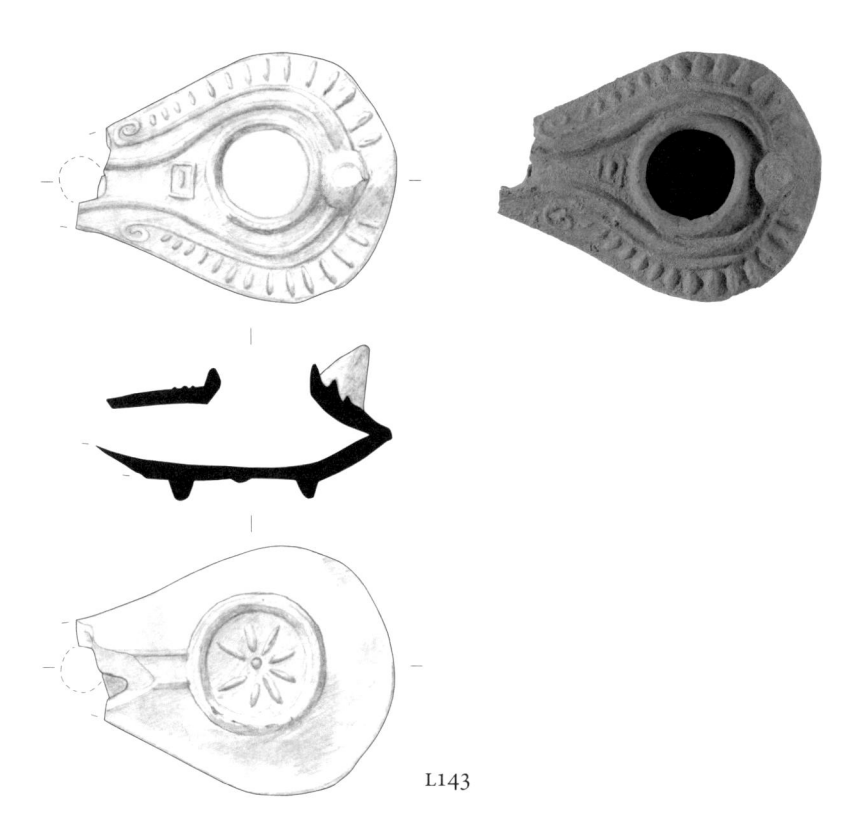

L143

*Plate 95. Type 8 (**L143**): Syro-Palestinian lamp. Seventh to eighth century A.D. Scale 1:2.*

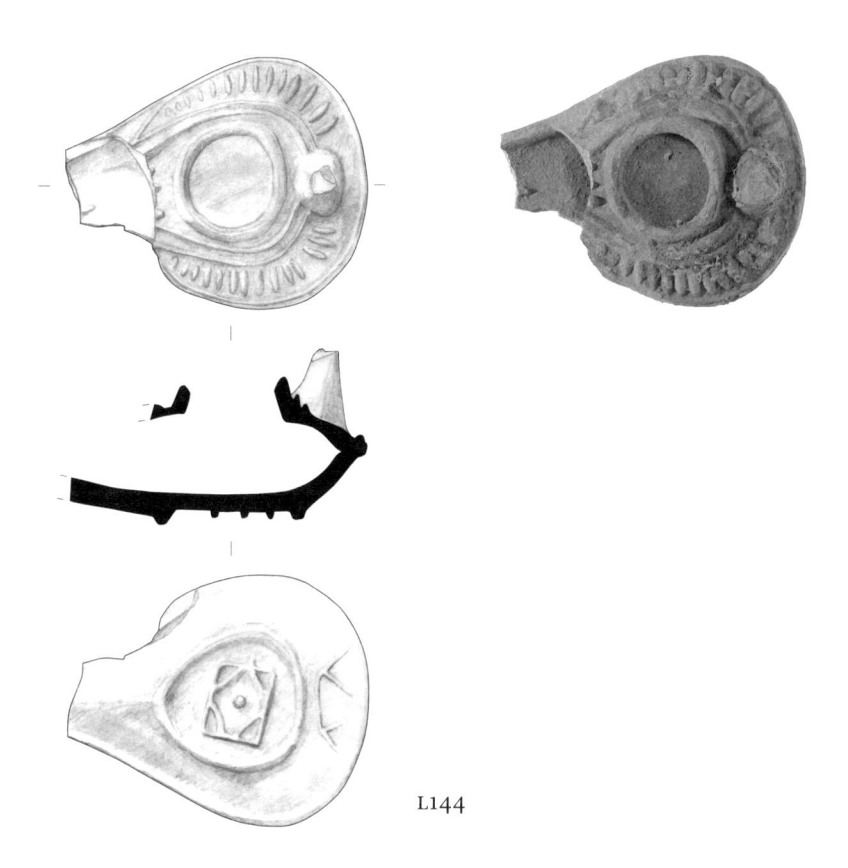

L144

*Plate 96. Type 8 (**L144**): Syro-Palestinian lamp. Seventh to eighth century A.D. Scale 1:2.*

L145   L146   L147

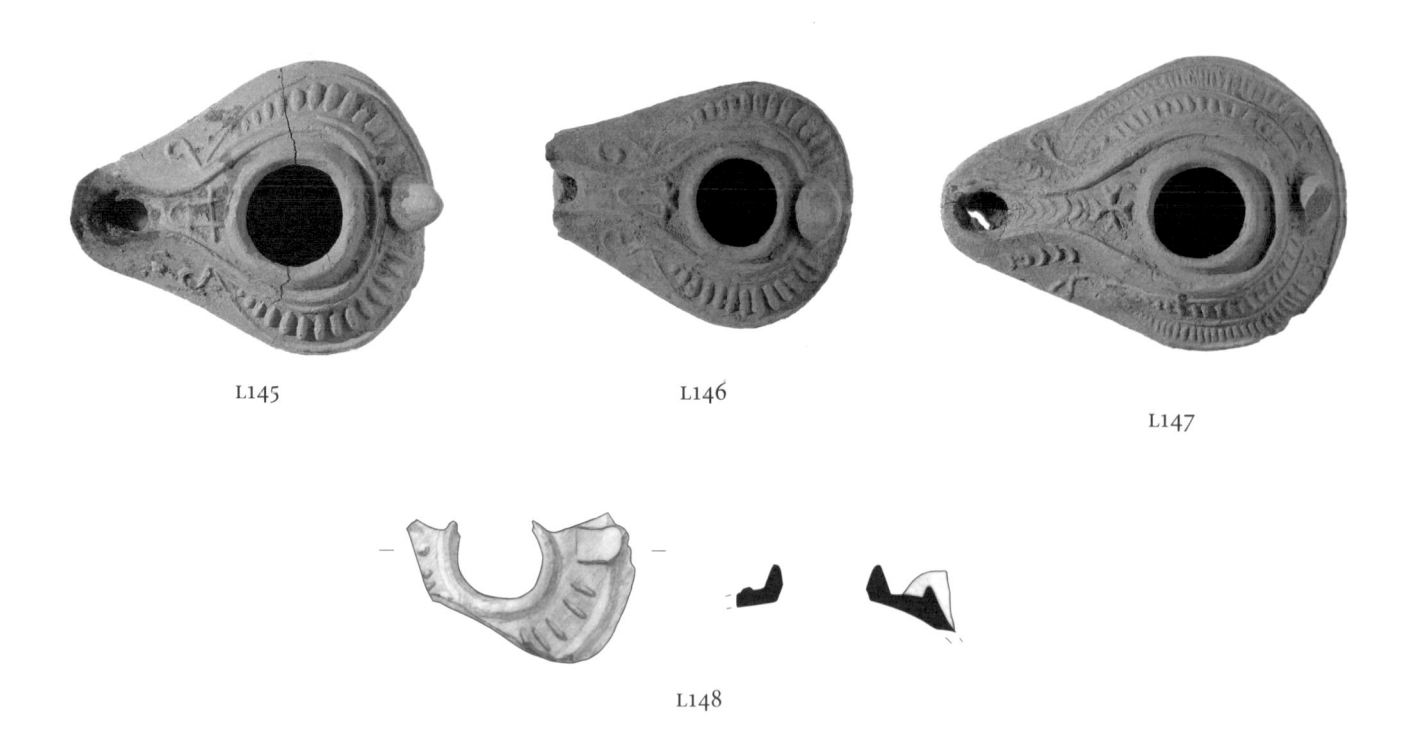

L148

Plate 97. Type 8 (L145–148): Syro-Palestinian lamps. Seventh to eighth century A.D. Scale 1:2.

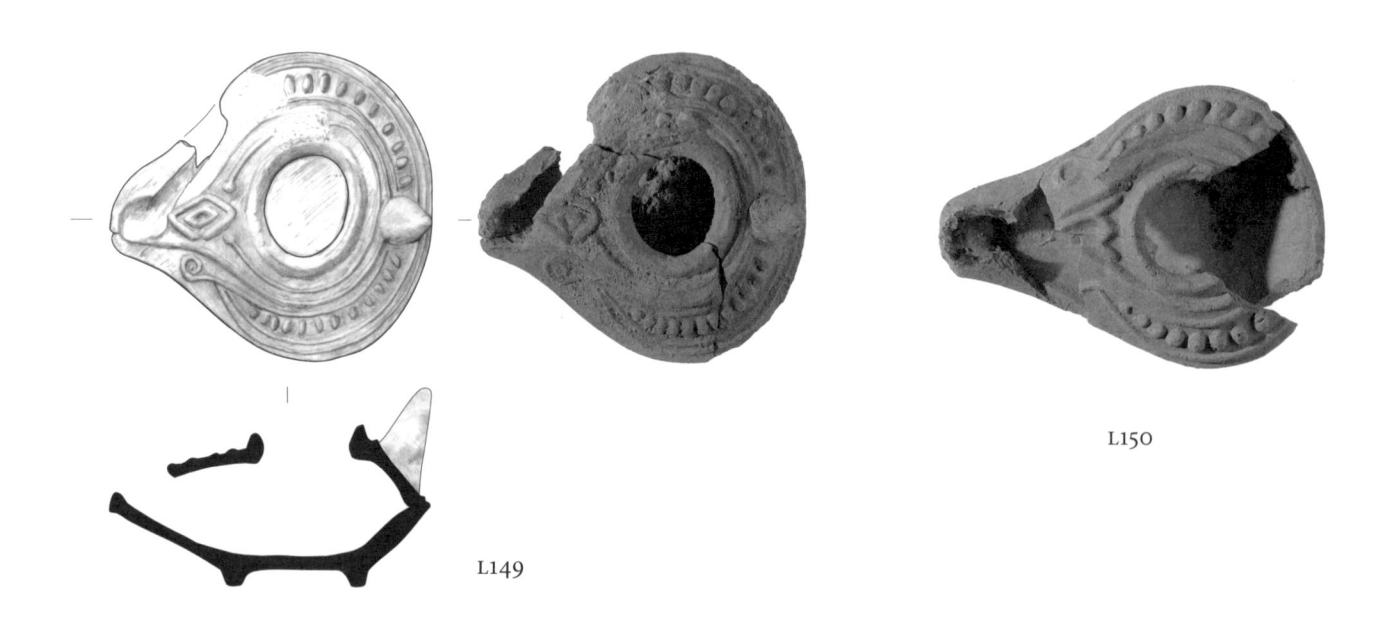

L150

L149

Plate 98. Type 8 (L149–150): Syro-Palestinian lamps. Seventh to eighth century A.D. Scale 1:2.

CERAMIC OIL LAMPS

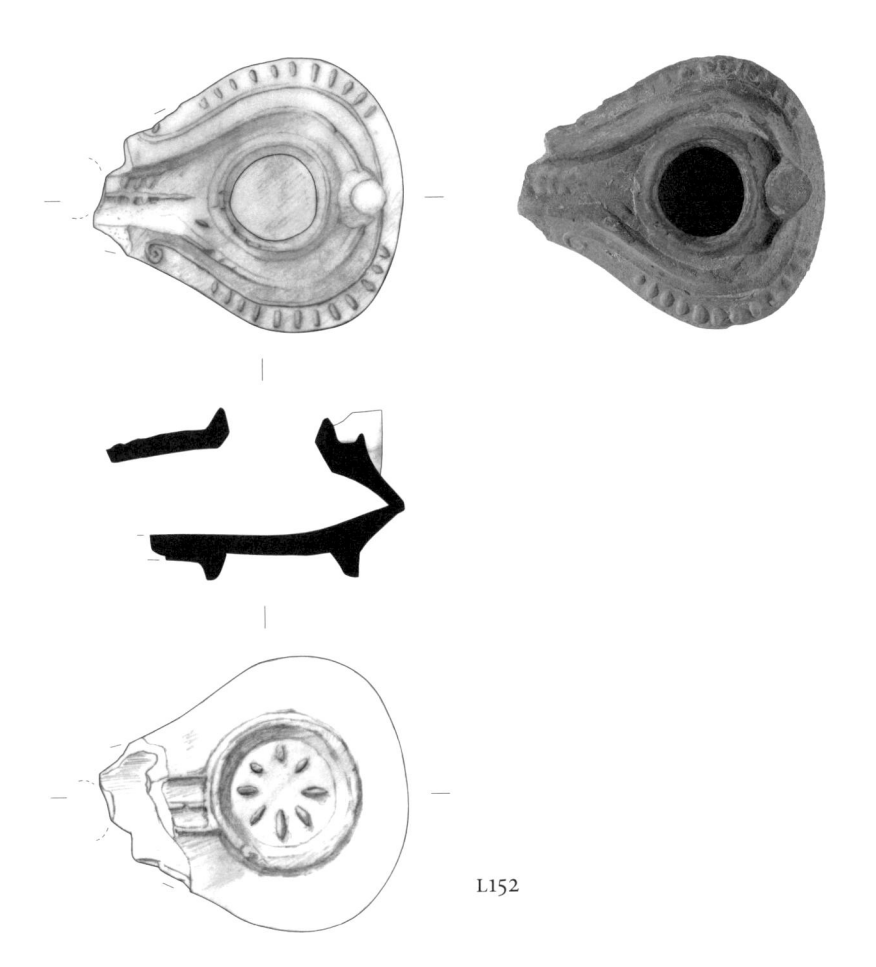

L152

Plate 99. Type 8 (L152): Syro-Palestinian lamp. Seventh to eighth century A.D. Scale 1:2.

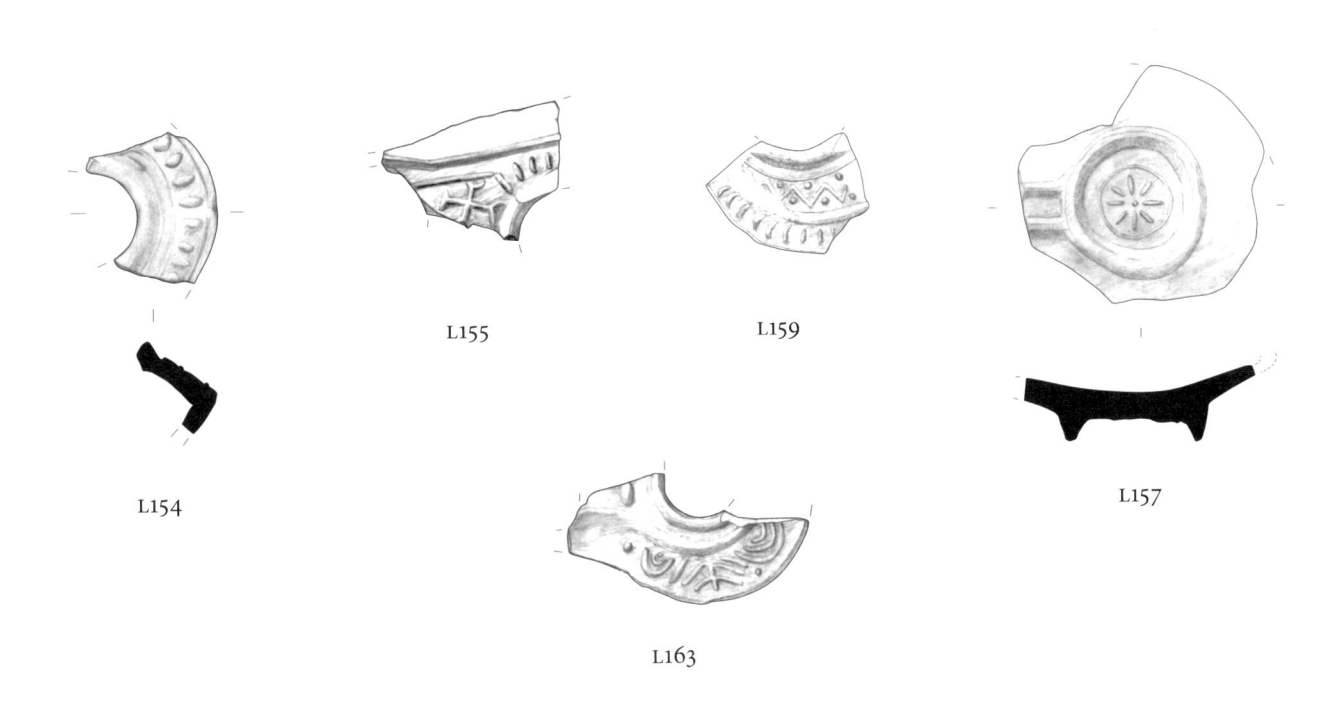

L155 L159

L154

L163

L157

Plate 100. Type 8 (L154–163): Syro-Palestinian lamps. Seventh to eighth century A.D. Scale 1:2.

L166

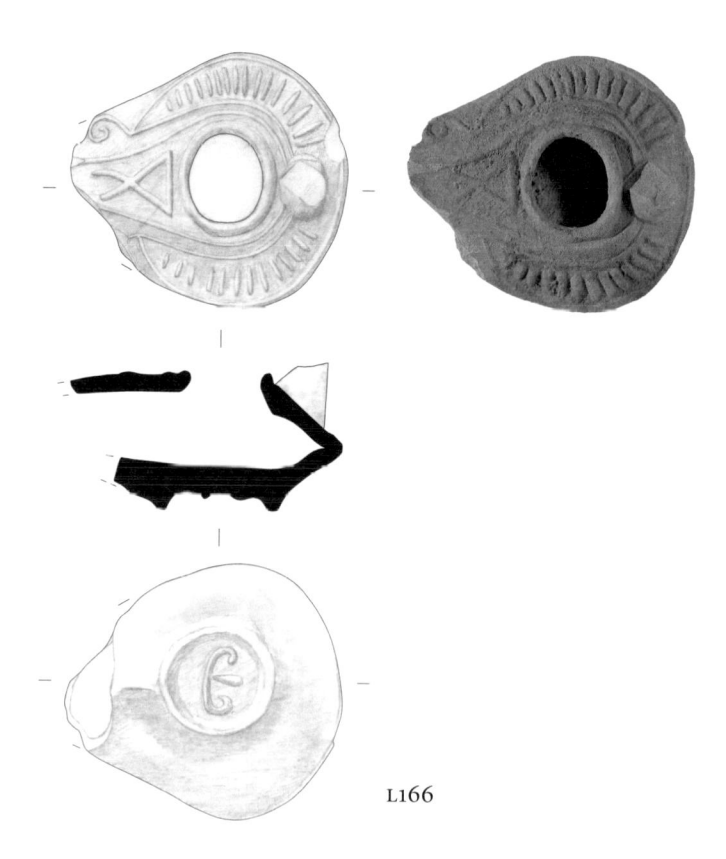

Plate 101. Type 8 (L166): Syro-Palestinian lamp. Seventh to eighth century A.D. *Scale 1:2.*

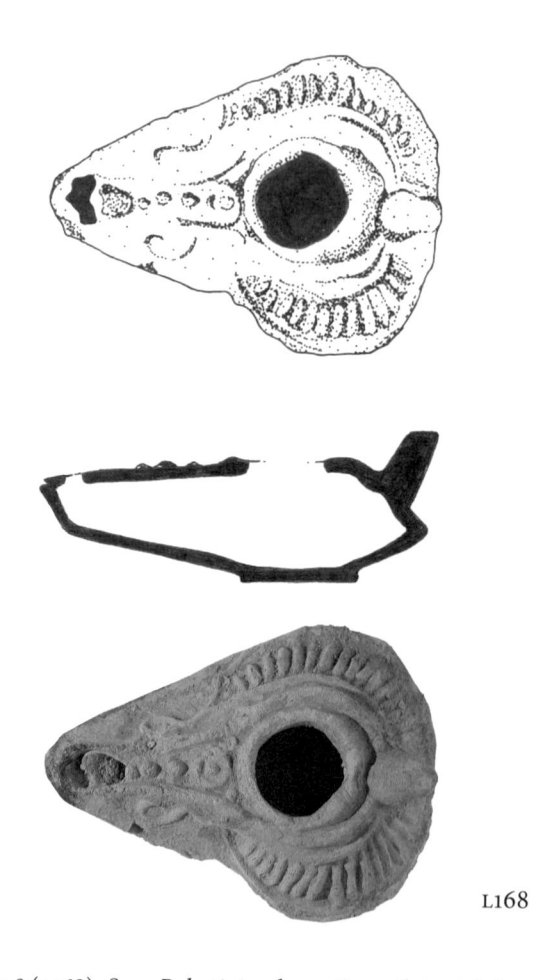

L168

Plate 102. Type 8 (L168): Syro-Palestinian lamp. Seventh to eighth century A.D. *Scale 1:2.*

CERAMIC OIL LAMPS

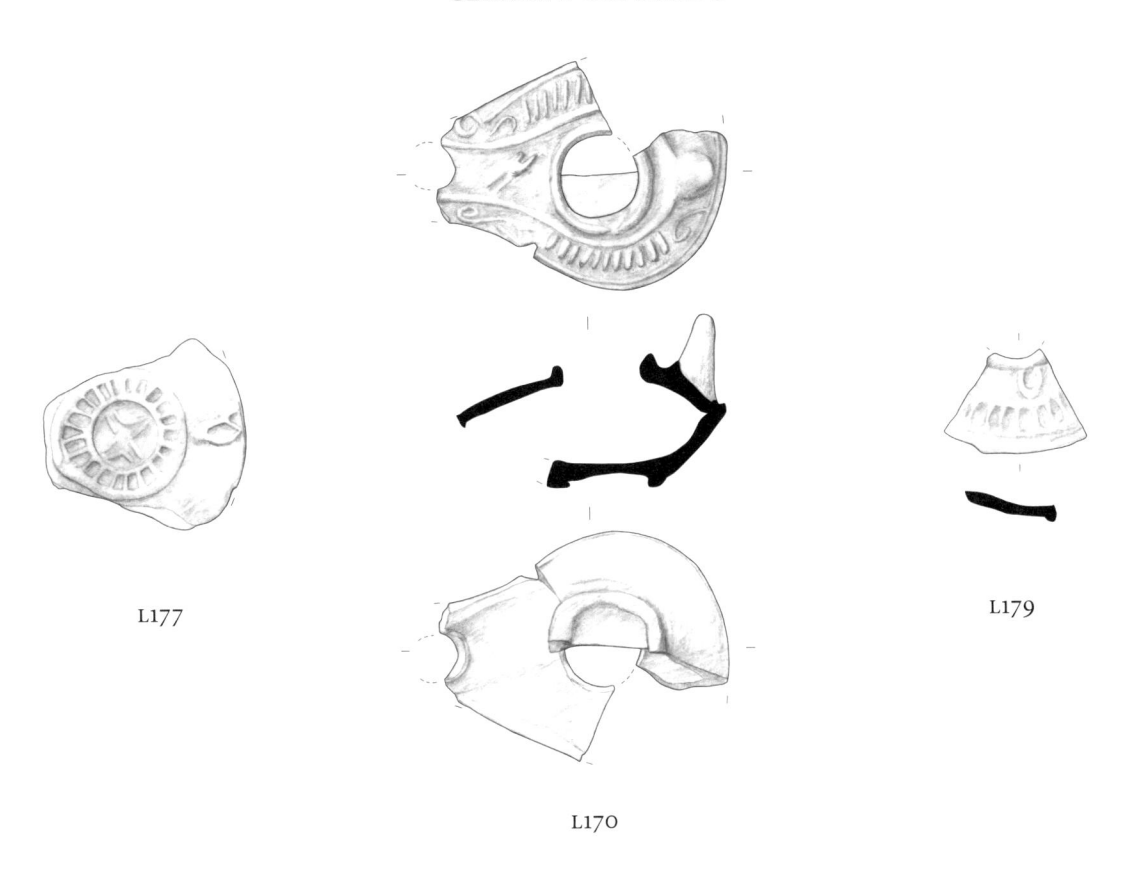

L177

L170

L179

Plate 103. Type 8 (L170–179): Syro-Palestinian lamps. Seventh to eighth century A.D. Scale 1:2.

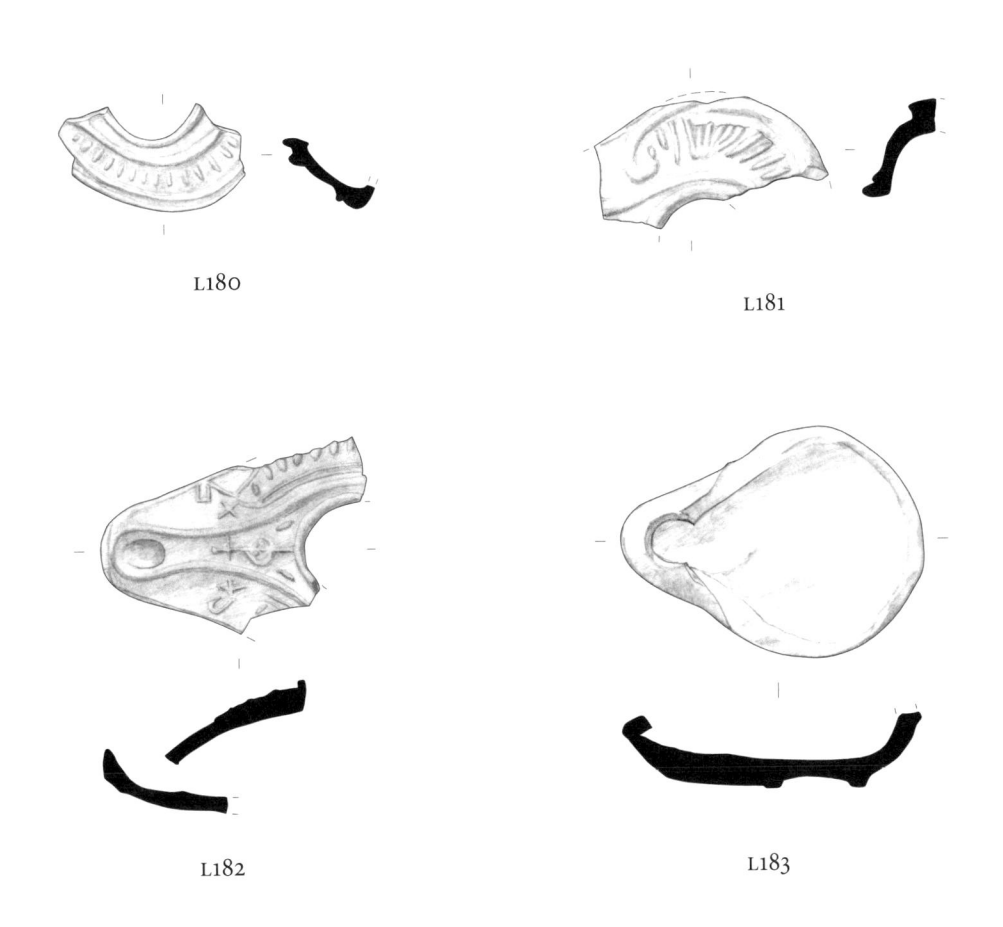

L180

L181

L182

L183

Plate 104. Type 8 (L180–183): Syro-Palestinian lamps. Seventh to eighth century A.D. Scale 1:2.

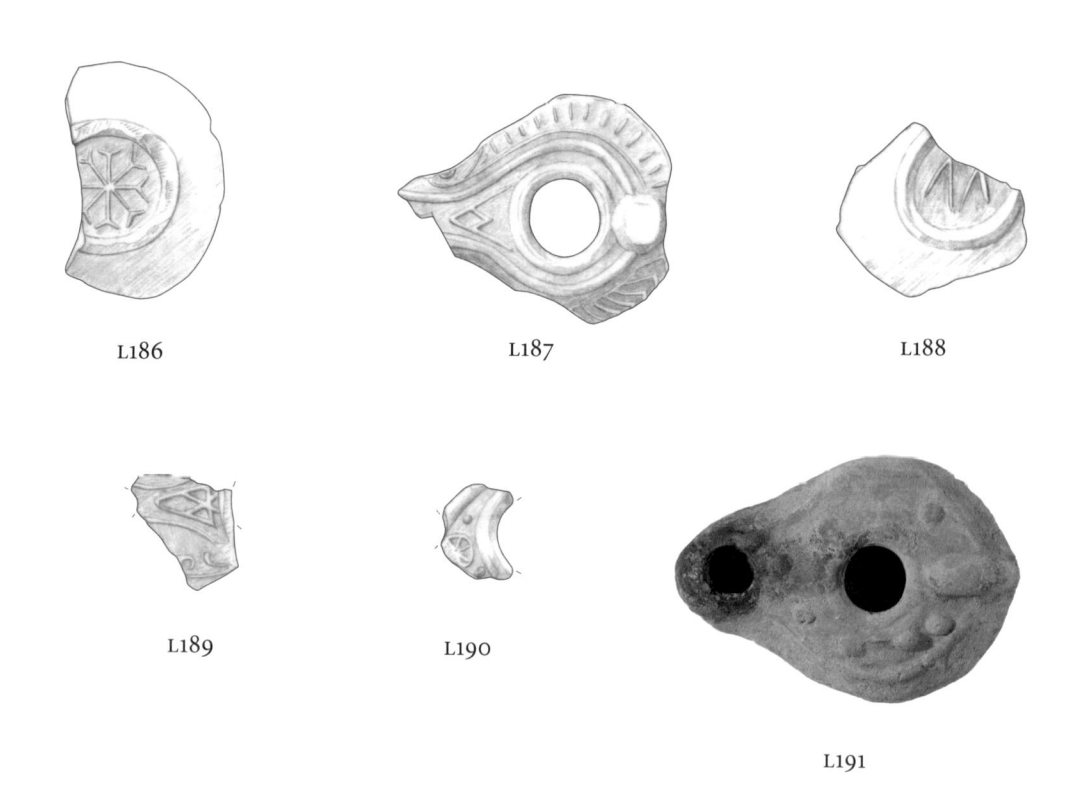

*Plate 105. Type 8 (**L186–191**): Syro-Palestinian lamps. Seventh to eighth century A.D. Scale 1:2.*

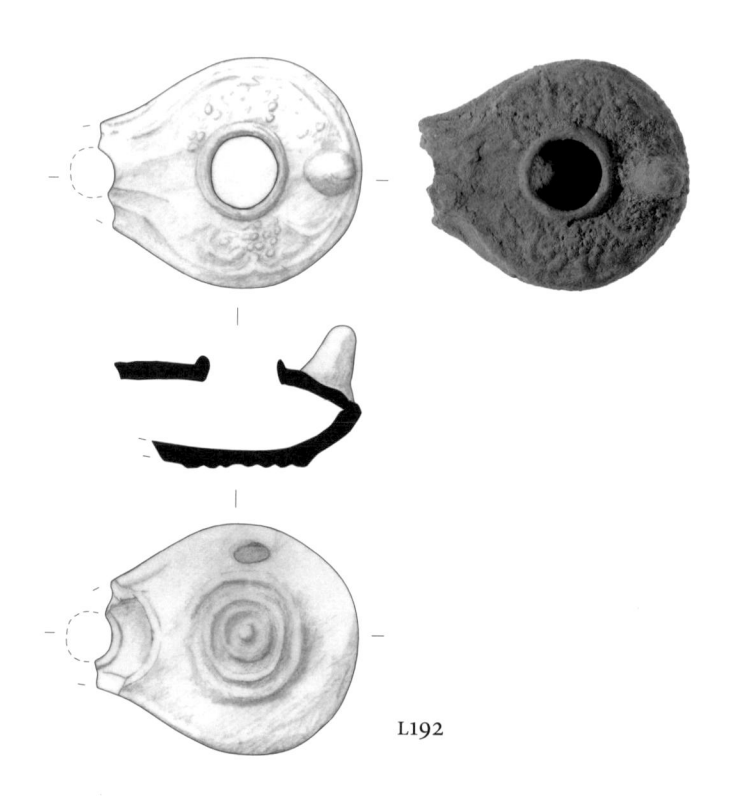

*Plate 106. Type 8 (**L192**): Syro-Palestinian lamp. Seventh to eighth century A.D. Scale 1:2.*

CERAMIC OIL LAMPS

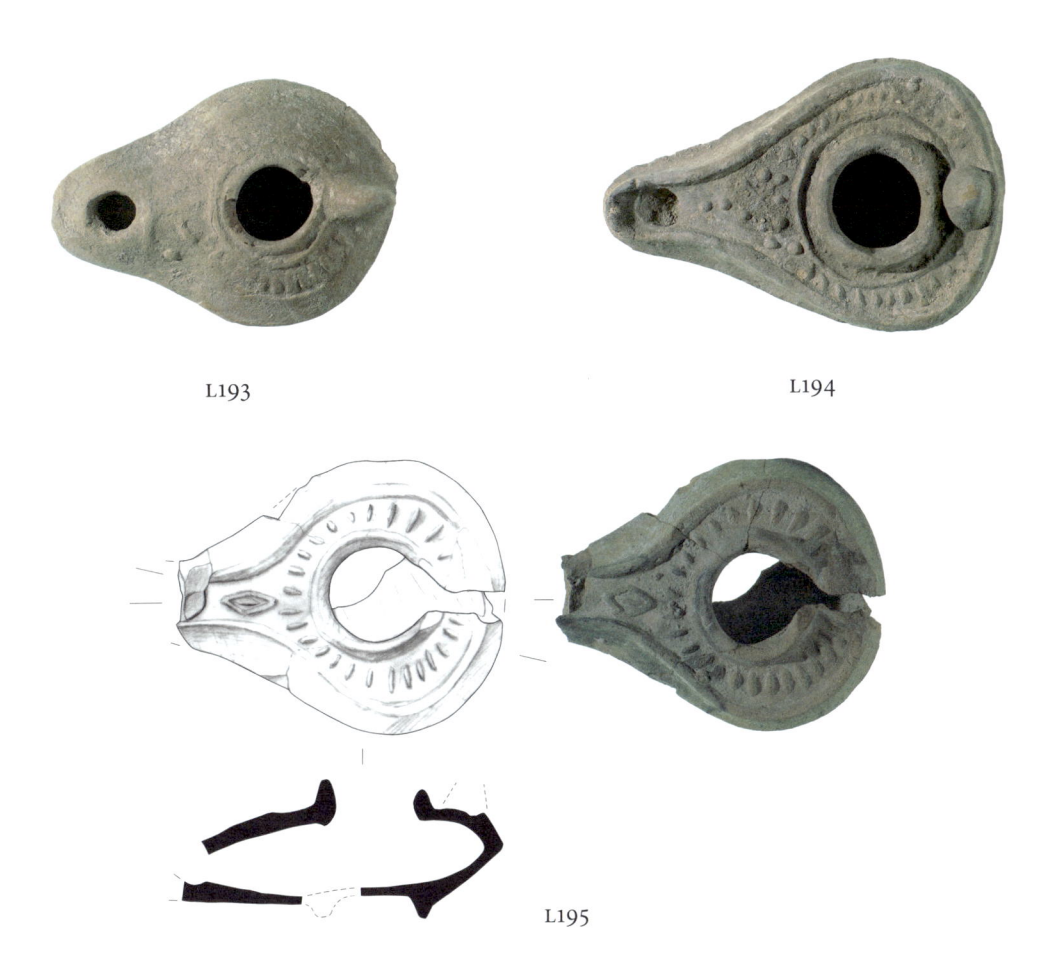

L193

L194

L195

*Plate 107. Type 8 (**L193–195**): Syro-Palestinian lamps. Seventh to eighth century A.D. Scale 1:2.*

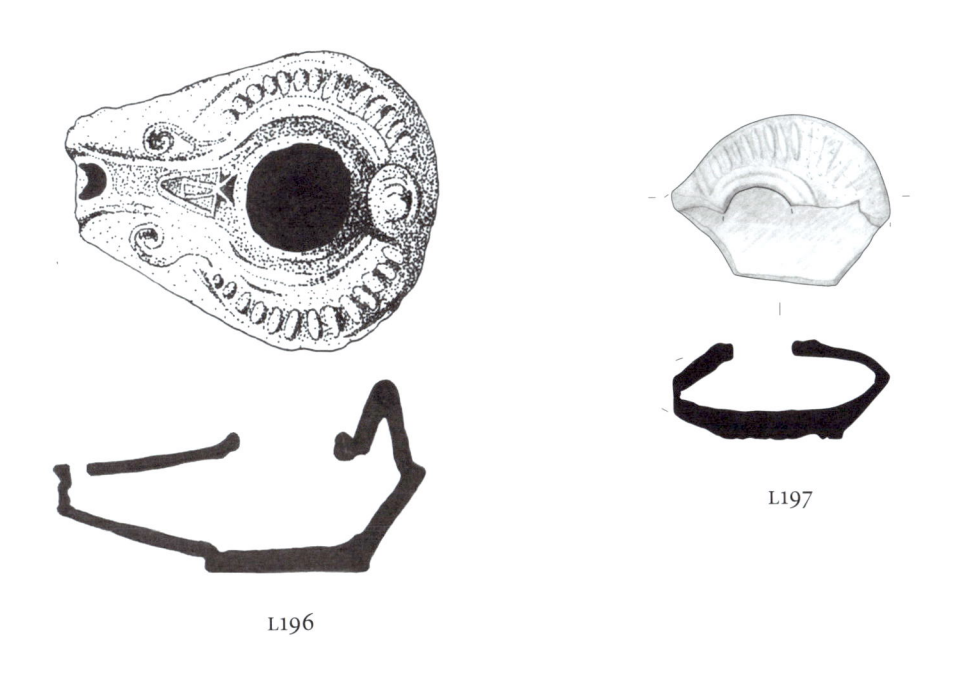

L197

L196

*Plate 108. Type 8 (**L196–197**): Syro-Palestinian lamps. Seventh to eighth century A.D. Scale 1:2.*

L213

Plate 109. Type 9 (L213): Wheel-made lamp. Islamic: ninth to eleventh century A.D. Scale 1:2.